IGNATIUS OF LOYOLA

Letters and Instructions

IGNATIUS OF LOYOLA

LETTERS AND INSTRUCTIONS

MARTIN E. PALMER, S.J.†

JOHN W. PADBERG, S.J.

JOHN L. MCCARTHY, S.J.

THE INSTITUTE OF JESUIT SOURCES
SAINT LOUIS

No. 23 in Series I: Jesuit Primary Sources in English Translations

© 2006 by the Institute of Jesuit Sources

The Institute of Jesuit Sources
3601 Lindell Blvd.
St. Louis, MO 63108
tel: [314] 633-4622
fax: [314] 633-4623
e-mail: ijs@jesuitsources.com

Library of Congress Control Number: 2006935927
ISBN: cloth-bound: 1-880810-67-0
        paper-bound: 1-880810-68-9

CONTENTS

The publication of this book has been made possible, in part, by the generous assistance of Ms. Mary Ann Wacker in gratitude for many years of spiritual guidance by Reverend George E. Ganss, S.J., founder of the Institute of Jesuit Sources, on the occasion of its forty-fifth anniversary.

INTRODUCTION

As I write these words on July 31, 2006, when we celebrate a feast day honoring the memory of St. Ignatius of Loyola and commemorate the 450th anniversary of his death, some seven hundred pages lie on the desk before me, an English translation of a selection of his letters and instructions. They range in time from his first extant letter, written in 1518 and only discovered a few decades ago, to his last letter, posted on the day before he died in 1556. Those two letters, both included in this present volume, could almost serve as bookends to the story of Ignatius's life and accomplishments. In that first letter of 1518, written three years before his conversion experience, he requested a favor from the King of Spain, personal permission to bear arms as a protection against a would-be assassin, angry at Ignatius for allegedly attempting to entice the man's mistress to himself. In the last letter, Ignatius, superior general of the Society of Jesus, then comprising almost one thousand members, also requested a favor. This time he asked the Jesuit superiors in Italy to extend the hospitality of their communities to a young man on his way to Germany to join the Carthusians. In between those two letters—the one exhibiting the self-centered concerns of a worldly courtier and the other demonstrating the personal attention that a dying man, one responsible for a religious order already spread abroad on several continents, could devote to an individual in need—is the corpus of almost seven thousand letters that help to portray the life and work of Ignatius.

The subjects to which Ignatius addressed himself in those letters range across a spectrum of personal, political, social, educational, financial, and religious concerns.[1] Even real-estate acquisitions claimed their share of his attention. The style and tone of his letters depended on the recipient, of course. While there was almost always a certain sobriety

---

[1] They are at least as varied as the ways in which he wrote his own name and signed his letters. In his later years he most often signed himself "Ignatius," an adaptation of his original Spanish name, Iñigo, made in the course of his stay in Paris. Even so, from that time on his name appears in the following additional forms: Inigo, Yñigo, Ynigo, Ygnigo, Ignatio, Inacio, and Ygnatio. Worth noting, moreover, is that the Christian names of those to whom Ignatius was writing occasionally appeared in somewhat different forms also.

about the letters, an official letter could be businesslike, a letter of personal friendship very warm, one to a ruler or prelate quite courtly, counsel to a distressed penitent gently reassuring, admonitions to a recalcitrant Jesuit direct and stern. When giving advice on how to deal with such a Jesuit in a way that both demonstrates love and gives a salutary shock, Ignatius could be quite insightful.

High among the virtues Ignatius ranked gratitude: letters of appreciation and thanks went out to benefactors for gifts as grand as the founding of a college and as simple as a box of candles. Among other subjects treated, besides ones already mentioned, the following offer us only a sample of their variety: the desirability of frequent Communion, the problem of lawsuits against the Society, encouragement to the imperial army on an African military campaign, the program of studies for Jesuit colleges, a lengthy account of the calumnies against the early Jesuits in Rome, the health of Jesuits, the debts of the Roman Jesuit house "with 150 mouths to feed," and beautifully simple condolences on the death of loved ones. He revealed pastoral sensitivity in dealing with heretics and schismatics, but also at times employed sternness when this was called for. He taught various ways of praying, and discussed the manner in which members of the Society should deal with their superiors and the need for fundraising in order to support their ministries. He displayed reserve and skepticism at extraordinary physical phenomena when he saw them regarded as presumptive indications of holiness. He discussed food and drink and set down occasions when water, beer, cider, or wine would be most appropriate. He explained the reasons for literary studies; he expressed vehement opposition to dueling and emphasized the need for his men to learn the local language. He drew up norms for hearing the confessions of women and puzzled over the Theological Faculty in Paris and its unrelenting opposition to the Society. Two subjects that must surely count as unusual came up for consideration: the reformation of the "immured anchoresses" at Saint Peter's in Rome and, in a letter to Charles V in 1552, the desirability of commissioning a heavily armed fleet to sweep the Turks out of the Mediterranean. Ignatius did not hesitate to suggest ways of paying the expenses that this fleet would entail; one such proposals was to extract taxes from well-off religious orders. Finally, to offer some background to what can often appear Ignatius's extraordinary fixation on issuing detailed prescriptions, we note that in many of the letters he also advised, and in a letter to Peter Canisius specifically prescribed, a measure of prudence: "It is taken for granted that anything in the following directives can be disregarded or changed as he thinks best."

The twelve-volume collection of his letters critically edited in their original languages and published in the series Monumenta Historica Societatis Iesu, from which these present English translations have been made, includes 6,742 consecutively numbered letters, plus 73 others that were discovered later. These late arrivals, some of them not clearly dated, are now printed in the appendices of several of those twelve volumes.[2] That total of more than 6,800 letters makes it the largest such collection of the sixteenth century. It is, for example, larger than the collected letters of Erasmus and larger than the combined collected letters of Martin Luther and John Calvin. Even at that, other letters have undoubtedly disappeared.

It was only in the eighteenth century that deliberate attempts began to collect and organize Ignatius's letters. Before that time, only some of them, such as the famous one in 1553 to the Society in Portugal on obedience, had been published separately, while others had appeared in full or in part in lives of Ignatius, in books of prayer, or in histories of the Society of Jesus. An individual Jesuit might also at times out of personal devotion have collected whatever letters he could. Or a particular Jesuit house might have carefully preserved one or more original letters either sent to that house by Ignatius or later given as a present to an individual or to the community. Any such collections were usually small; moreover, at the suppression of the Society in 1773, they often disappeared or were confiscated by the governments of the cities and states that took over the property of the Jesuits.

Thanks to several individual former Jesuits who during the years of suppression had the opportunity to begin to search for such letters in various archives in Italy, a Spanish Jesuit, Roque Menchaca, was able to assemble the first sizable collection of Ignatius's correspondence, published in 1804 in Bologna, Italy, with a second edition following in 1837.[3] All ninety-seven letters in that edition were presented either in their original Latin or, if the original was in a contemporary language, usually Spanish, in a Latin translation. In 1848 a German Jesuit, Cris-

---

[2] One section of this series, known as Monumenta Ignatiana ex autographis vel ex antiquioribus exemplis collecta, includes *Sancti Ignatii de Loyola Societatis Iesu fundatoris epistolæ et instructiones*, 12 vols. (Madrid: Institutum Historicum Societatis Iesu, 1903-1911). These volumes were all later reprinted between 1964 and 1968 by the Institutum Historicum Societatis Iesu in Rome, and appear as volumes 22, 26, 28, 29, 31, 33, 34, 36, 37, 39, 40, and 42 of the series Monumenta Historica Societatis Iesu.

[3] Roque Menchaca, *Epistolæ Sancti Ignatii Loyola Societatis Jesu fundatoris libris quatuor distributæ. . . .* (Bologna, 1804 and 1837).

toph Genelli, published a life of Ignatius, to which he added an appendix of letters in Spanish and Latin.[4] In 1870 Marcel Bouix, a French Jesuit, put out a new collection in French of some 145 letters, a good number of them previously unknown.[5] The next step, and an important one at that, was the fruit of fifteen years of work on the part of several Spanish Jesuits who between 1874 and 1890 published a six-volume collection including 842 letters, all of them translated into Spanish with any non-Spanish original-language texts included in an appendix.[6] All of these collections culminated finally in the volumes of the Monumenta Historica series, critically edited according to the standards of modern historical scholarship (see note 1 above). More will be said toward the end of this introduction about the various editions and translations of the letters. But first it is important to say a word about their recipients and the purposes and contents of the letters themselves. Lengthy treatises have been written on those topics; here they need only be treated briefly because the letters will in most instances speak for themselves.

The largest number of the texts in those twelve volumes of the Monumenta series are in Spanish and Italian, almost 45 percent in each of those languages, with most of the rest in Latin and some few in Portuguese and French. More than five thousand letters are correspondence internal to the Society. By far the largest number of these letters appeared after 1547, the year that Juan de Polanco became secretary of the Society, quickly proving himself to be an invaluable assistant to Ignatius, as he helped draft his correspondence and the various preliminary versions of the Jesuit *Constitutions.*

Especially during those years while Ignatius was working on the *Constitutions,* both text and letters were mutually enhancing the structure and life of the Society. As has been said, if the *Constitutions* were establishing the spirit and laws of the Society, the letters were in a sense elaborating its jurisprudence. That may have been especially true in the letters that went out in the form of instructions—for instance, on such topics as the establishment of colleges or the vow and virtue of obedi-

---

[4] Cristoph Genelli, *Das leben des heiligen Ignatius von Loyola, Stifters der Gesellschaft Jesu* (Innsbruck, 1848), translated into English as *The Life of Saint Ignatius Loyola, Founder of the Jesuits.* In 1848 Genelli came to America, where for a time he taught church history at Saint Louis University.

[5] Marcel Bouix, *Lettres de S. Ignace de Loyola, fondateur de la Compagnie de Jésus* (Paris, 1870).

[6] Antonio Cabré, Miguel Mir, and Juan José de la Torre, *Cartas de San Ignacio de Loyola, fundador de la Compãnia de Jesus,* 6 vols. (Madrid, 1874-1890).

ence in the Society or the ways of living and working in so-called "mission lands." Among the most important of those means of structuring the Society and of contributing to its unity and to union among its members was this written correspondence itself. Ignatius wrote more than one letter describing, requesting, ordering, even pleading for the regular interchange of letters among his brethren.

His letters were written to a great variety of persons. They included, for example, parents quite happy or quite distraught that their sons had entered the Society; members of the Society overburdened by their responsibilities; extraordinarily generous benefactors and others who provided much, demanded more, and in reality gave little in return; scrupulous penitents hard to advise; and ardent Christians eagerly asking how best to love and serve the Lord. They ranged from people of importance and influence in the Church and civil society to novices newly arrived to join the Jesuits, from city councils to clerics and members of other religious orders, from later-to-be-canonized saints to self-confessed sinners, from individuals acting as financial agents for the Society to men and women who were benefactors or spiritual directees or personal friends. To cite only some examples, among Ignatius's correspondents were members of the hierarchy, Popes Paul III and Julius III; future popes Marcellus II and Paul IV; as well as cardinals and bishops of French, English, German, Italian, Spanish, Portuguese, and Flemish background. Ignatius wrote as well to the Holy Roman Emperor Charles V and to his son, King Philip II of Spain; and to Charles's daughters, Margaret, Eleonora, and Juana; to King John III of Portugal and Duke Albert V of Bavaria; to Claudius, negus or emperor of Ethiopia, and to Ercole d'Este, duke of Ferrara, and Juan de Vega, viceroy of Sicily. His Jesuit correspondents included Saints Francis Xavier, Peter Canisius, Francis Borgia, and Blessed Peter Faber, as well as many others of unsung sanctity and yet others who could be difficult to deal with, for example, Simão Rodrigues and Nicholás Bobadilla. But to these as to his other first companions he wrote regularly and often with affection, as was evident, for example, in the ending of one of his letters to Xavier, "Wholly yours, and always, in our Lord." The first extant letter after his conversion is a letter of spiritual direction to Agnès Pascual in 1524; many other such letters went in the following years to those who sought his spiritual counsel. Notable among them were such women as Isabel Roser, an early friend to whom he said he owed more than to any other woman in the world, and Eleanor Mascarenhas, who had first met Ignatius in 1527 at Alcalá or Salamanca and to whom almost thirty years later, in 1556, two months before his death, he wrote that he was "mindful, as I said above, how much I have had you and still have you in my inmost soul and would do so still more in the future if it were possible." He was uncharacteristically spare in writing to his relatives. His first letter to one of them, to his nephew, Martín García de Oñaz, by that time head of the house of Loyola, dates from 1528, some six years after his departure from Loyola; the next one was addressed to this relative four years later.

Whoever the recipient of a letter might be and whatever its subject matter, many of the letters have no literary style whatsoever. They are often convoluted in grammar and syntax and sentence structure. One writer speaks of the "nodosities" of expression and another of the "sinuosities" of Ignatius's sixteenth-century Spanish, not to mention, in the words of a third commentator, "the endless processions of gerundial platoons." At the end, the reader may understand what Ignatius wanted to say, but he will conclude that the writer seemingly had to labor very hard to achieve that end. This collection of Ignatius's letters has certainly tried to be faithful to his thoughts as expressed in his words and so has adhered closely but not slavishly to what he originally wrote. That has meant that it has not tried to polish what are sometimes rough-cut gems.

An exception to the difficulties of style can often be found in such letters as were written "by commission," especially by Polanco. But it is to be emphasized that even in those cases, Ignatius went over the secretarial drafts and corrected, added to, and subtracted from them, so that while sometimes the writing may be Polanco's, the thoughts are those of Ignatius. The secretary of the Society was supposed to be the superior general's companion, "his memory and his right-hand man" in everything that was entrusted to him. Several early Jesuits informally served as such secretaries in the first years of the Society's existence, until in March 1547 Ignatius chose Polanco for the task. For the next nine years until the death of Ignatius in 1556, he was daily at his side. Then for a total of twenty-five years he continued to serve as secretary of the Society. To him, for the devotion with which he performed his duties and for his chronicle of the Society's life during all those years, Jesuits in the generations to come owe an immense debt of gratitude.

Near its beginning, this introduction described the early steps in collecting the letters of Ignatius up to the critical Monumenta edition. Here, as we near its end, is the place to note various collections and translations that have appeared since then. Among the major ones are volumes of selections in French, German, Italian, Japanese, Polish,

Portuguese, and Spanish.[7] In 1959 William Young published in English a selection of 228 letters that for almost half a century, until this present volume, has been the major collection in this language.[8] Joseph Tylenda was the author of a 1985 volume of 40 letters and instructions.[9] In 1996, as part of a volume of selections from Ignatius's works that they entitled *Personal Writings*, Joseph Munitiz and Philip Endean translated and published 40 of the letters.[10] Hugo Rahner in 1956 published in German a collection of all Ignatius's letters to women, not to mention lengthy introductions for each of the women and each of those letters.[11] In 1959 that volume was translated into English.

This present book, with its 369 letters, is the largest such selection in the English language. It is the result of a collaborative effort among several members of the Institute of Jesuit Sources. Martin E. Palmer, S.J., selected and undertook to translate those letters from the twelve volumes of the Monumenta Historica edition. To the great loss of the Institute, however, he died in 1997, leaving behind an excellent draft version of all his translations. For several reasons further work on the volume could go forward only very slowly for some time and then had to be postponed until two years ago. At that time the undersigned author of this introduction went over Father Palmer's translations in detail, for the sake of clarity revised them when needed, and, in order

<hr>

[7] Paul Dudon, *St. Ignace de Loyola: Lettres spirituelles choisies et traduites* (Paris, 1933); Gervaise Dumeige, *Ignace de Loyola: Lettres* (Paris, 1959); Maurice Giuliani, ed., *Ignace de Loyola: Ecrits* [including a selection called "Lettres et instructions"] (Paris, 1991); Otto Karrer, *Geistliche Briefe und Unterweisungen*, ed. Hugo Rahner (Cologne, 1942), newly edited by Paul Imhof (Einsiedeln, 1979); Peter Knauer, *Briefe und Unterweisungen* (Wurzburg, 1993); E. Farinella and A. Tulumello, *Ignazio di Loyola: El messagio del suo epistolario*, 2 vols. (Rome, 1975); Mario Gioia, *Gli scritti de Ignazio di Loyola* [including an "Epistolario"] (Turin, 1977); V. Bonet, *Ignacio de Loyola: Shokanshu* (Tokyo, 1972); M. Bednarz and St. Pilipowiscz, R. Skóri, A. Bobera, *Pisma wybrane, Komentarze*, 2 vols. (Cracow, 1968); A. Cardoso, *Cartas de Santo Inâcio de Loyola: As primeiras cartas de uma vida nova* (Sao Paulo, 1998); A. Maciâ, *Cartas espirituales de San Ignacio de Loyola* (Madrid, 1944); Ignacio Iparraguirre, Cándido de Dalmases, and Manuel Ruiz Jurado, *San Ignacio de Loyola: Obras* [including "Cartas e instrucciones"] (Madrid, 1991).

[8] William J. Young, *Letters of St. Ignatius of Loyola* (Chicago, 1959).

[9] Joseph Tylenda, *Counsels for Jesuits: Selected Letters and Instructions of Saint Ignatius of Loyola* (Chicago, 1985.)

[10] Joseph Munitiz and Philip Endean, *St. Ignatius of Loyola: Personal Writings* (London, 1996).

[11] Hugo Rahner, *Saint Ignatius Loyola: Letters to Women*, trans. from the German by K. Pond and S. A. H. Weetman (New York, 1959).

to fill out several lacunae, added to the collection several letters that seemed very important. Father Palmer had not had the opportunity to write the specific introductions to the individual letters, without which in many cases their meaning and importance would have been obscure. The present writer, therefore, assumed responsibility for composing the introductions. He and John L. McCarthy, S.J., also of the Institute staff, edited the volume, for the index of which Father McCarthy was himself responsible.

One presentation after another by friends and foes of Ignatius have sought to portray him through his deeds and his writings. As for those writings, they have relied on one or more of important sources like the *Spiritual Exercises,* the *Constitutions,* and the *Spiritual Diary,* along with the so-called autobiography; but only to a lesser extent and more recently have they delved into his letters. One would have to read very much more than this selection of those almost 7,000 witnesses to Ignatius in order to plumb his character to the full. But what we have here is at least an attempt to present a representative selection of those letters, not only those considered "spiritual" but also those concerned with the ordinary round of everyday life within and outside the Society of Jesus. They, too, might be called "spiritual" in that they also are evidence of "finding God in all things." What has been assembled here comes with the hope that they will be an aid to understanding Ignatius in his undoubted complexity and his equally undoubted greatness. As has been well said,

> We are forced by them to the almost paradoxical conclusion that Ignatius, who was no literary man, who all his life handled the pen with difficulty, and who hid himself behind the awkward sentences of his *Spiritual Exercises* and the rough-hewn phraseology of the *Constitutions* of the Society, only in his letters becomes alive, with that humanity without which there is no holiness in the Church of God made Man.[12]

For the men and women of this twenty-first century who want to understand their own times, their world, their Church, their God, and themselves as well, these letters are as relevant as they were for their original recipients in the sixteenth century, four hundred and fifty years ago.

John W. Padberg, S.J.
Director
The Institute of Jesuit Sources

---

[12] Rahner, *Letters to Women,* 1.

CHRONOLOGY OF IGNATIUS

His Life and Times

Life of Ignatius	Date	Contemporary
Born (in October?) at Loyola, youngest of thirteen children	1491	Siege of Granada by Ferdinand and Isabella. Henry VIII of England born.
	1492	Columbus finds America. End of Moorish Kingdom in Spain. Alexander VI (Borgia) becomes pope.
	1494	Beginning of Italian wars. Suleiman the Magnificent born.
	1497	Vasco da Gama goes around Cape of Good Hope.
	1498	Savonarola executed in Florence.
	1500	Future Emperor Charles V born.
	1502	Spanish translations of Ludolph of Saxony's *Life of Christ*.
	1503	Julius II elected pope. Erasmus's *Enchiridion of the Christian Soldier*.
	1504	Luther enters the Augustinian order.

Life of Ignatius	Date	Contemporary
At Arévalo, probably in this year, enters service as page with Juan Velázquez de Cuéllar, treasurer of Ferdinand the Catholic.	1506	Construction of St. Peter's begins in Rome.
	1508	Michelangelo paints Sistine Chapel ceiling (to 1512).
	1509	Birth of Calvin. Henry VIII becomes king of England. Portuguese are in Southeast Asia.
	1511	Erasmus's *Praise of Folly*.
	1512	Council of Lateran V, abortive reform effort.
	1513	Leo X (Medici) elected pope.
"Atrocious crime" at Azpeitia.	1515	Francis I becomes king of France. Philip Neri and Teresa of Avila born.
	1516	Charles I becomes king of Spain (later on emperor, called Charles V). Machiavelli's *The Prince*; Erasmus's Greek and Latin New Testament; Thomas More's *Utopia*.
Service with the Duke of Nájera, viceroy of Navarre.	1517	Luther's 95 theses posted at Wittenberg.
Seeks permission to bear arms against death threat.	1518	

Life of Ignatius	Date	Contemporary
	1519	Charles V elected Holy Roman Emperor. Magellan begins his voyage. Cortez in Mexico.
	1520	Alcalá Polyglot Bible of Cisneros. Luther excommunicated.
Siege of Pamplona. Ignatius wounded, returns to Loyola.	1521	Suleiman the Magnificent and the Turks take Belgrade. Diet of Worms.
Aránzazu, Montserrat, and Manresa.	1522	Adrian VI, the reform pope, is elected, the last non-Italian pope—until 1978.
Barcelona, Rome, Venice, Cyprus on way to Jerusalem.	1523	Clement VII (Medici) elected pope.
Began study of Latin in Barcelona.	1524	Theatines founded.
	1525	Capuchins founded.
Studies at Alcalá and arrested there (1527) by Inquisition, on suspicion of being an *alumbrado*.	1526	Defeat of Empire by Turks at Mohacs in Hungary.
Transfers to Salamanca for studies and is arrested again there.	1527	Sack of Rome by the imperial army.
Arrives in Paris. Studies at Collège de Montaigu.	1528	Verrazzano off the American coast.
Meets and rooms with Pierre Favre and Francis Xavier. Studies at Collège Sainte-Barbe.	1529	Turkish siege of Vienna.

Life of Ignatius	Date	Contemporary
	1530	Charles V is crowned emperor. Lutheran "Confession of Augsburg." Henry VIII's break with Rome complete. Conquest of Peru.
Bachelor of Arts (Philosophy) from the University of Paris.	1532	Calvinist reformation begins in France.
Receives Licentiate degree. Begins study of theology.	1533	
Montmartre: Vows of the first companions: Ignatius, Favre, Xavier, Laínez, Salmerón, Bobadilla, and Rodrígues.	1534	Paul III elected pope. Cartier in Canada. Michelangelo begins the Last Judgment (to 1541).
Receives Master of Arts diploma. Ignatius leaves Paris for Spain. In Paris Favre receives Broët, Codure, and Jay among the companions.	1535	Thomas More and John Fisher martyred. Geneva adopts the Reformation.
In Venice Ignatius studies, gives the Exercises.	1536	
Ordination of the companions at Venice. Has vision at La Storta on way to Rome with Favre and Laínez.	1537	Venice and Turks at war.
Companions all together in Rome in ministries. Ignatius celebrates his first Mass.	1538	Theatines, Barnabites, Somaschi developing. Charles Borromeo born.
The "Deliberation" by these "First Companions."	1539	Coverdale's *Great Bible* in England.
Society of Jesus founded upon approval of Pope Paul III. Xavier departs for India.	1540	Angela Merici (founder of Ursulines) dies.

Life of Ignatius	Date	Contemporary
Ignatius elected superior general. First solemn professions. Begins work on *Constitutions*.	1541	Birth of EL Greco. Calvin's *Institutes of the Christian Religion*. Turks take Buda and Hungary.
Three established Jesuit houses: Rome, Paris, Lisbon.	1542	Roman Inquisition begins. Portuguese in Japan.
	1543	Copernicus's astronomical work *De revolutionibus orbium*.
Ignatius ill. Begins to write the first part of extant "Spiritual Diary."	1544	
Last extant part of "Spiritual Diary" written. Nadal enters the Society. Isabel Roser and two companions take Jesuit vows in Rome.	1545	Council of Trent opens.
Jesuits sent to Trent by Paul III. Death of Favre in Rome. Borgia secretly enters the Society. Isabel Roser and companions released from vows.	1546	Death of Luther.
Polanco becomes Secretary of the Society. Canisius enters the Society.	1547	Henry VIII dies. Ivan the Terrible begins reign in Russia. Cervantes born. Henri II becomes king of France.
Paul III approves the Spiritual Exercises; they are printed for the first time. Ignatius ill.	1548	Suarez born.
Xavier in Japan. Ignatius ill.	1549	First English "Act of Uniformity."
Society of Jesus again formally confirmed, this time by Julius III. Ignatius is gravely ill.	1550	Julius III elected pope.

Life of Ignatius	Date	Contemporary
Foundation of Roman College. Meeting in Rome on first version of *Constitutions*. Crisis in Society in Portugal. Ignatius is ill.	1551	Turkish threat at Vienna.
Ignatius completes "Autograph" (text B of *Constitutions*. Death of Xavier off coast of China.	1552	German College founded in Rome.
"Letter on Obedience" composed. Ignatius seriously ill. He begins to dictate so-called autobiography.	1553	Mary Tudor, queen of England.
Nadal elected vicar-general. Ignatius often ill. Construction begins on Jesuit church in Rome, initially entrusted to Michelangelo. Admits Juana of Austria, daughter of Charles V, secretly as a Jesuit.	1554	Cardinal Pole "reconciles" England to the Catholic faith.
Gonçalves da Câmara writes his *Memorial*.	1555	Marcellus II and Paul IV elected popes. Peace of Augsburg.
Ignatius ill much of the first half of the year. He dies on July 31. Laínez the vicar-general.	1556	Charles V abdicates as emperor. Palestrina's *Mass of Pope Marcellus*.

LETTERS INCLUDED IN THIS COLLECTION

Note: The first column below indicates the number **(NO.)** of the letter, as found in the Monumenta edition. The second column shows the recipient **(TO:)** of the letter. The third column indicates the date **(D.)** of the letter. The fourth column denotes the language **(L.)** of the letter **(F** = French, **I** = Italian, **L** = Latin, **S** = Spanish), and the fifth column indicates the page **(P.)** of this edition where the letter begins.

N.n. means that the letter has no number.

B.c. (by commission) denotes a letter written by someone authorized to do so by Ignatius.

---

¹ Vol. 12, app. 6, pp. 674–76.

² Ibid., app. 1, pp. 217–19.

³ Ibid., pp. 216–17.

NO.	TO	D.	L.	P.
81	King John III of Portugal	Mar. 15, 1545	S	118
83	Cardinal Marcello Cervini	April 15, 1545	S	120
89	Pierre Favre	July 16, 1545	L	121
102	Claude Jay	Dec. 12, 1545	S	122
106	Francis Xavier	Dec. 17, 1545	L	123
101	Francis Borgia, duke of Gandía	End of 1545	S	124
109	Doctor Pedro Ortiz	Early 1546	S	127
123	The Fathers of the Council of Trent	Early 1546	S	128
115	Pedro de Soto, O.P.	Feb. 20, 1546	S	131
n.n.[4]	Claude Jay	Mar. 6, 1546	I	133
121	Francis Borgia, duke of Gandía	April 23, 1546	S	135
124	Peter Canisius, from Jerónimo Nadal	June 2, 1546	L	137
131	The Fathers and Brothers at Coimbra	Aug. 8, 1546	S	140
132	Doimo Nascio	Aug. 10, 1546	S	142
133	Peter Canisius	Aug. 14, 1546	L	142
140	King John III of Portugal	Oct. 1546	S	144
141	Simão Rodrigues	Oct., 1546	S	145
137	Isabel Roser	Oct. 1, 1546	S	146
143	Miguel de Torres	Oct. 9, 1546	S	147
146	Francis Borgia, duke of Gandia	Oct. 9, 1546	S	149
147	Miguel de Torres	Oct. 13 & 18, 1546	S	151
149	Ferdinand of Austria, king of [the] Romans	Dec. 1546	S	154
2[5]	Diego de Eguia	Dec. 1, 1546	S	156

1547

152	Juan de Polanco	Feb. or Mar. 1547	S	157
153	Miguel de Torres	Mar. 2, 1547	S	159
172	Pope Paul III	May 1547	L	164
169	The Fathers & Scholastics at Coimbra	May 7, 1547	S	165
171	Manuel Sanches, bishop of Targa	May 18, 1547	S	174
174	Diego Laínez, from Juan de Polanco	May 21, 1547	S	176
176	Francis Borgia, duke of Gandía	mid-1547	S	181
179	The Entire Society, b.c.	July 27, 1547	S	183
180	The Entire Society, b.c.	July 27, 1547	S	188
182	The Jesuits of Gandía	July 29, 1547	S	195
185	Claude Jay	Early Aug. 1547	I	201
186	The Members of the Society in Padua	Aug. 7, 1547	I	203
192	Antonio Araoz	Sept. 1, 1547	L	207
214	Teresa Rejadell	Oct. 1547	S	208
202	Simão Rodrigues	Oct. 26, 1547	S	210
208	Antonio Araoz	Oct. 31, 1547	S	211
209	Antonio Araoz	Oct. 31, 1547	S	219
218a	Jerónimo Doménech, from Juan de Polanco	Oct. 31, 1547	S	221

[4] Ibid., pp. 733–34.
[5] Ibid., app. 6, p. 631.

NO.	TO	D.	L.	P.
230	Niccolò Lancilotti, b.c.	Nov. 22, 1547	L	224
234	Daniel Paeybroeck	Dec. 24, 1547	L	226

1548–1549

8[6]	Stefano Baroello	Early Jan. 1548	I	230
239	The Senate of Messina	Jan. 14, 1548	I	232
252	The Members of the Society in Rome	Feb. 2, 1548,	I	233
258	Nicolás Bobadilla	Feb. or Mar. 1548	S	235
281	Diego Laínez	Mar. 24, 1548	S	237
295	Andrés de Oviedo, b.c.	Mar. 27, 1548	S	237
302	Antonio Araoz	April 3, 1548	S	246
311	Dom Talpin, b.c.	April 12, 1548	L	247
382	Prince Philip of Spain	mid-1548	S	249
415	Jerónimo Nadal, b.c.	Aug. 4, 1548	S	250
419	Andrea Lippomani	Aug. 14, 1548	I	251
454	Antonio Araoz, b.c.	Sept. 4, 1548	S	252
466	Francis Borgia, duke of Gandía	Sept. 20, 1548	S	253
507	Diego Laínez, b.c.	Dec. 22, 1548	S	256
550	Juan de Avila\	Jan. 24, 1549	S	259
581	Mateo Sebastián de Morrano	Feb. 22, 1549	S	262
630	Jerónima Oluja and Teresa Rejadell	April 5, 1549	S	263
743	Andrea Lippomani	June 22, 1549	I	265
3[7]	Francis Borgia, duke of Gandía, b.c.	July 1549	S	266
760	Jerónimo Nadal, b.c.	July 6, 1549	S	283
776	Juan Alvarez, b.c.	July 18, 1549	S	285
790	Francis Borgia, duke of Gandía	July 27, 1549	S	290
18[8]	The Members of the Society Leaving for Germany	Sept. 24, 1549	L	291
893	Francis Xavier	Oct. 10, 1549	L	298
957	Andreas Iseren, b.c.	Dec. 2, 1549	L	299
958	Girolamo Croce	Dec. 4, 1549	I	300
959	The Whole Society, b.c.	Dec. 8, 1549	S	302

1550–1551

1005	All Superiors of the Society	Jan. 13, 1550	L	305
1145	Juan de Vega	April 12, 1550	S	306
1146	Isabel de Vega	April 12, 1550	S	307
1145 bis	From Juan de Vega, to Ignatius of Loyola	May 1, 1550	S	309
1211	Juan de Vega	May 31, 1550	S	310
1225	Miguel Ochoa	June 9, 1550	S	311
1228	Carlos Borgia	June 13, 1550	S	313
1246	Paschase Broët	June 21, 1550	S	314
1263	Juan Bernal Díaz de Luco	July 8, 1550	S	315
1267	The Army in Africa	July 9, 1550	L	316

---

[6] Ibid., app. 1, pp. 226–28.

[7] Ibid., app. 6, pp. 632–54.

[8] Ibid., app. 1. pp. 239–47.

NO.	TO	D.	L.	P.
1275	Isabel de Vega	July 19, 1550	S	317
1300	Charles de Guise, cardinal of Lorraine	Aug. 11, 1550	I	319
1326	The Jesuits at the House in Rome	Aug. 24, 1550	I	320
1362	Jacqueline de Croy, marchioness			
	of Bergen-op-Zoom	Sept. 15, 1550	L	321
1392	Juan de Vega	Sept. 27, 1550	S	322
1427	Carlos de Borja	Nov. 1, 1550	S	324
1428	Juan de Vega	Nov. 1, 1550	S	325
1429	Isabel de Vega	Nov. 1, 1550	S	326
1444	Francisco Villanueva	Nov. 13, 1550	L	327
1481	Urban Weber	Dec. 9, 1550	L	328
1554	The Members of the Society	Jan. 30, 1551	S	329
1587	Isabel de Vega	Feb. 21, 1551	S	330
1721	Ferdinand of Austria, king of [the] Romans	April 1551	L	332
1831	Arnold van Hees, b.c.	May 23, 1551	L	333
1848	Urbano Fernandes, b.c.	June 1, 1551	S	335
1854	Antonio Brandão, b.c.	June 1, 1551	S	339
1882	Antonio Araoz	June 1, 1551	S	345
1899	Jean Pelletier	June 13, 1551	I	346
1957	Girolamo Croce	July 14, 1551	I	351
1985	Claude Jay	Aug. 8, 1551	I	352
2048	Elpidio Ugoletti	Early Sept. 1551	S	356
2061	Ettore Pignatelli, duke of Monteleone	Sept. 12, 1551	I	357
2226	Antonio Araoz	Dec. 1, 1551	S	360
2271	Claude Jay	Dec. 15, 1551	I	363
2300	Simão Rodrigues	Dec. 27, 1551	L	365

1552–1553

2383	Manoel Godinho	Jan. 31, 1552	S	367
2384	Francis Xavier	Jan 31, 1552	S	368
2481	Queen Catherine of Portugal	Mar. 12, 1552	S	369
2517	Mary of Austria, governor of Flanders,			
	queen of Hungary and Bohemia	Mar. 26, 1552	L	370
49[9]	Everard Mercurian, b.c.	June 1552	I	372
2624	Juan Martínez Guijeño, archbishop of Toledo	June 1, 1552	S	373
2627	Prince Philip of Spain	June 3, 1552	S	375
2652	Francis Borgia	June 5, 1552	S	376
2769	Claude Jay	July 30, 1552	L	377
2774	Jerónimo Nadal, from Juan de Polanco, b.c.	Aug. 6, 1552	S	379
2816	Juan Esteban Manrique de Lara, duke of Nájera	Aug. 26, 1552	S	384
2861	Cesare Aversano	Sept. 10, 1552	I	386
2867	Silvestro Landini and Manoel Gomes	Sept. 10, 1552	I	387
24[10]	Those Sent on Mission	Oct. 8, 1552	I	393
3002	Diego Laínez, b.c.	Nov. 2, 1552	S	395

[9] Ibid., app. 1, pp. 309–11.

[10] Ibid., app. 1, pp. 251–53.

NO.	TO	D.	L.	P.
3014	Juana de Aragón	Late Nov. 1552	S	397
3104	Diego Miró	Dec. 17, 1552	S	401
3105	Diego Miró	Dec. 17, 1552	S	402
3107	The Members of the Society throughout Europe	Dec. 24, 1552	I	405
41[11]	An Unknown Prelate	[ca. 1553]	S	406
3165	The Rectors of the College in Italy, from Juan de Polanco, b.c.	Jan. 21, 1553	I	409
3220	Diego Miró	Feb. 1, 1553	S	409
3304	The Members of the Society in Portugal	Mar. 26, 1553	S	412
3316	Jerónimo Nadal	April 12, 1553	S	421
3335	Thomas of Villanueva, archbishop of Valencia	April 16, 1553	S	423
3417	Simão Rodrigues	May 20, 1553	S	424
3449	King John III of Portugal	June 6, 1553	S	425
3453	Diego Miró	June 7, 1553	S	427
3505	Francis Xavier	June 28, 1553	S	429
3547	Simão Rodrigues	May 20 & July 12, 1553	S	431
3561	Gaspare Gropillo	July 22, 1553	I	432
3562	John Baptist Viola	July 22, 1553	I	433
3578	The Whole Society	July 23 & Aug. 7, 1553	L	434
3605	Diego Miró	July 24 & Aug. 3, 1553	S	435
3584	Diego Miró	July 26, 1553	S	436
3620	Giovanni Ottilio, from Juan de Polanco, b.c.	Aug. 5, 1553	I	437
3627	Cardinal Reginald Pole	Aug. 7, 1553	I	438
3640	Nicolò Pietro Cesari	Aug. 13, 1553	I	439
3706	Nicolò Pietro Cesari	Aug. 27, 1553	I	440
3708	Hannibal coudret, b.c.	Aug. 27, 1553	I	441
3731	Giovanni Battista Tavono, from Juan de Polanco, b.c.	Sept. 9, 1553	I	442
3756	Juan Luis González de Villasimplez	Sept. 16, 1553	S	444
3768	Leonora de' Medici, duchess of Florence	Sept. 23, 1553	S	445
3794	Giovanni Ottilio, b.c.	Sept. 30, 1553	I	446
3913	Margaret of Austria, duchess of Parma	Nov. 17, 1553	S	447
3920	Nicolò Pietro Cesari	Nov. 19, 1553	I	448
3924	Nicholas Floris (Goudanus), b.c.	Nov. 22, 1553	I	449
3983	Ettore Pignatelli, duke of Monteleone	Dec. 10, 1553	I	450
3991	Andrea Galvanello	Dec. 16, 1553	I	452
4008	Luis, Infante of Portugal	Dec. 24, 1553	S	452
4010	Gaspar Berze	Dec. 24, 1553	S	453
4020	Filippo Leerno	Dec. 30, 1553	I	454

1554

4247	Pope Julius III	Rome, 1554	I	456
4031	Teotonio de Braganza	Jan. 1, 1554	S	457
4054	Magdalena Angélica Doménech	Jan. 12, 1554	S	458

[11] Ibid., pp. 290–93.

NO.	TO	D.	L.	P.
4066	Jerónimo Doménech, from Juan de Polanco, b.c.	Jan. 13, 1554	S	459
4094	Maria Frassona del Gesso	Jan. 20, 1554	I	461
4097	Girolamo Muzzarelli, O.P.	Jan. 23, 1554	I	462
4115	Signora Cesari	Jan. 28, 1554	I	465
4116	Fra Francesco de Mede	Jan. 28, 1554	I	466
4131	Filippo Leerno, from Juan de Polanco, b.c.	Feb. 3, 1554	I	467
4181	Doimo Nascio	Feb. 22, 1554	I	469
4182	Diego Laínez, b.c.	Feb. 22, 1554	I	470
4184	Gian Andrea Schenaldo	Feb. 24, 1554	L	471
4193	Gaspar Berze, b.c.	Feb. 24, 1554	S	472
4206	Rector of the College of Coimbra	Feb. 26, 1554	S	474
4222	The Rectors of the Society's Colleges	Mar. 3, 1554	I	475
4231	Emperor Charles V	Mar. 3, 1554	S	476
4251	Giovanni Battista Viola, from Juan de Polanco, b.c.	Mar. 10, 1554	I	477
4260	Maria Frassona del Gesso	Mar. 13, 1554	I	480
4271	Diego Miró, from Juan de Polanco, b.c.	Mar. 15, 1554	S	481
4284	Tarquino Rainaldi and Gaspar Ruiz	Mar. 18, 1554	I	482
4306	Antonio Enríquez, b.c.	Mar. 26, 1554	S	483
4336	Diego Miró	April 5, 1554	S	486
4340	John III, king of Portugal	April 6, 1554	S	488
4351	Francesco Mancini, b.c.	April 7, 1554	I	489
4454	Catalina Fernández de Córdoba, marchioness of Priego	May 15, 1554	S	490
4485	Enrique de La Cueva	May 22, 1554	S	492
4619	Bartolomé Hernández	July 21, 1554	S	494
4645	João Nunes Barreto	July 26, 1554	S	495
4654	Fernando Vasconcelhos, archbishop of Lisbon	July 26, 1554	S	496
4705	Simão Rodrigues, b.c.	Aug. 11, 1554	S	497
4709	Peter Canisius	Aug. 13, 1554	L	499
27[12]	Peter Canisius	Aug. 13, 1554	I	504
4713	The Widow of Jon Boquet	Aug. 16, 1554	S	507
4721	Francis Borgia	Aug. 20, 1554	S	509
4735	Miguel de Nobrega, b.c.	Aug. 25, 1554	S	510
4736	Miguel de Nobrega, b.c.	Aug. 25, 1554	S	512
1[13]	The Jesuits Leaving Rome for Portugal and Thence Traveling On to Ethiopia	Sept. 15, 1554	S	512
4788	Giovan Francesco Araldo	Sept. 16, 1554	I	514
4809	Filippo Leerno	Sept. 22, 1554	I	515
4812	Teotonio de Braganza	Sept. 22, 1554	S	516
4813	Teotonio de Braganza	Sept. 22, 1554	S	517
4814	Teotonio de Braganza	Sept. 22, 1554	S	518
4821	Giovan Francesco Araldo from Juan de Polanco b.c.	Sept. 23, 1554	I	518
4870	Juan de Mendoza	Oct. 14, 1554	S	519
4909	Giovan Francesco Araldo, b.c.	Oct. 28, 1554	I	520

[12] Ibid., app. 1, pp. 259–62.
[13] Ibid., VIII, app. 1, pp. 677–79.

NO.	TO	D.	L.	P.
5[14]	How to Ask for Alms	Nov. 1554	I	521
4921	Ercole Purino	Nov. 3, 1554	I	522
4959	Cristóbal de Mendoza	Nov. 17, 1554	S	524
4979	Bartolomeo Romano, b.c.	Nov. 24, 1554	I	526
4997	Juan Ignacio Nieto	Dec. 1, 1554	I	526
5024	Ascanio Colonna	Dec. 8, 1554	I	527
5041	Violante Casali Gozzadini	Dec. 22, 1554	I	528

1555

5[15]	For the Jesuit Superior in Ethiopia, regarding Ethiopian Affairs	1555	S	530
5061	Antonio Araoz	Jan. 3, 1555	S	531
5066	Princess Juana of Spain	Jan. 3, 1555	S	532
5120	Cardinal Reginald Pole	Jan. 24, 1555	I	532
5130	Bartolomeo Romano	Jan. 26, 1555	I	535
5154	Juan de Avila	Feb. 7, 1555	S	536
5174	Ponce Cogordan	Feb. 12, 1555	S	537
5197	Jerónimo Nadal and Diego Laínez	Feb. 18, 1555	S	541
5205	Claudius, negus of Ethiopia	Feb. 23, 1555	S	544
5210	Melchior Nunes Barreto	Feb. 24, 1555	S	549
5218	Melchior Carneiro	Feb. 26, 1555	S	550
5248	Gaspar de Borja, bishop of Segorbe	Mar. 12, 1555	S	552
5251	Robert Claysson	Mar. 13, 1555	L	553
5252	Paschase Broët, b.c.	Mar. 14, 1555	I	554
5280	Gerard Kalckbrenner (Hammontanus)	Mar. 22, 1555	L	556
5288	Jerónimo Doménech, b.c.	Mar. 24, 1555	I	558
5313	Juan Pérez de Calatayud	April 4, 1555	S	560
5329	Simão Rodrigues, b.c.	April 6, 1555	S	561
2[16]	João Nunes Barreto, patriarch of Ethiopia	April 7, 1555	S	563
5360	Everard Mercurian	May 2, 1555	I	571
5400a	Procedure for Dealing with Superiors	May 29, 1555	S	572
5427	Francis Borgia, b.c.	June 13, 1555	S	574
5446	Manuel López, b.c.	June 17, 1555	S	575
5471	Diego Miró	June 20, 1555	S	578
5500	Alberto Azzolini	June 29, 1555	I	579
5525	Francisco Jiménez de Miranda, b.c.	July 11, 1555	S	581
5535	Cristóbal de Mendoza	July 14, 1555	I	583
5544	Jerónimo Doménech, b.c.	July 18, 1555	S	584
5564	Alfonso Salmerón	July 27, 1555	I	586
5653	Pedro Camps	Aug. 29, 1555	S	589
5683	Juana de Valencia	Sept. 5, 1555	S	590
5736	Francis Borgia	Sept. 17, 1555	S	591

---

[14] Ibid., XII, app. 6, pp. 656–59.
[15] Ibid., VIII, app. "De reus Aethiopicis," pp. 696–98.
[16] Ibid., 680–90.

NO.	TO	D.	L.	P.
6[17]	Points Dictated to Juan Felipe Vito	Oct. 1555	S	592
5799	Simão Rodrigues	Oct. 12, 1555	S	594
5816	The Relatives of Silvestro Landini	Oct. 18, 1555	S	595
5817	Those Sent from Rome	Oct. 18, 1555	I	596
5825	Isabel de Vega	Oct. 20, 1555	S	598
5834	Jerónimo Nadal	Oct. 21, 1555	S	600
5846	Philip of Austria, king of England	Oct. 23, 1555	S	602
5863	Pedro de Zárate	Oct. 29, 1555	S	604
5919	Girolamo Vignes, b.c.	Nov. 17, 1555	I	605
5945	Girolamo Vignes, b.c.	Nov. 24, 1555	I	607
5947	Juan Luis González de Villasimplez	Nov. 26, 1555	S	608
5953	Enrique de La Cueva	Nov. 28, 1555	S	610
5954	Francis Borgia	Nov. 28, 1555	S	612
5981	Alejo Fontana, b.c.	Dec. 7, 1555	S	613
5991	Bernard Olivier	Dec. 9, 1555	I	614
5998	Juan Pérez	Dec. 12, 1555	S	615
6007	Girolamo Vignes	Dec. 15, 1555	I	617
6009	Lorenzo Scorzino	Dec. 15, 1555	I	618

1556

6068	The Rectors of the Society, b.c.	Jan. 1, 1556	I	620
6087	Juana de Valencia	Jan 7, 1556	S	621
6099	Luis Gonçalves da Câmara, b.c.	Jan. 15, 1556	S	622
6110	Girolamo Vignes, b.c.	Jan. 18, 1556	I	627
6116	Albert V, duke of Bavaria	Jan. 20, 1556	L	629
6155	Nicoló Pietro Cesari	Feb. 2, 1556	I	631
6177	Juan de Mendoza	Feb. 7, 1556	S	632
6205	Those Going to Begin the College in Prague, b.c.	Feb. 12, 1556	I	633
6216	Alejo Fontana, from Juan de Polanco, b.c.	Feb. 16, 1556	S	640
6230	Olivier Mannaerts	Feb. 22, 1556	I	642
6243	Andrés de Oviedo	Feb. 27, 1556	S	643
6281	Nicolás Bobadilla	Mar. 8, 1556	I	644
6282	Francis Borgia	Mar. 9, 1556	S	645
6295	Miguel de Torres	Mar. 15, 1556	S	646
6327	Alfonso Ramírez de Vergara	Mar. 30, 1556	S	647
6330	Alejo Fontana	Mar. 31, 1556	S	648
6371	Pedro de Ribadeneira, b.c.	April 14, 1556	S	650
6386	Antonio Soldevilla	April 19, 1556	S	651
6434	Gaspar Loarte	May 7, 1556	S	653
6443	Ottaviano Cesari	May 10, 1556	I	654
6452	The Jesuits Going to Clermont	May 11, 1556	I	655
6454	Adrian Adriaenssens	May 12, 1556	L	661
6463	Francis Borgia	May 14, 1556	S	662
6465	Gaspar Loarte	May 14, 1556	I	663
6481	Lorenzo Bresciani	May 16, 1556	I	663

---

[17] Ibid., XII, app. 6, pp. 659–62.

SELECTED LETTERS

OF SAINT IGNATIUS OF LOYOLA

❋ 1518–1540 ❋

To Charles I of Spain

December 20, 1518

(Unnumbered Letter, *Archivum historicum
Societatis Iesu* 44 [1975]: 136; in Spanish)

*A request, made a few years before his conversion, to bear arms in self-defense
against a man who was trying to kill him. According to the license granted the
following year for Ignatius himself and one bodyguard, Francisco de Oya had
wounded Ignatius, sent word he would kill him, stalked him several times, and paid
a woman to help trap him (she warned Ignatius and he escaped).*

Most Puissant Sir:

Iñigo López de Loyola declares that he has an enmity and difference with Francisco de Oya, a Galician and servant of the Countess of
Camiña, who says that he is going to kill him and, acting upon this, has
several times laid ambush for him, and has always refused friendship
even though this has many times been requested of him. For this reason
[the petitioner] Iñigo López has great need to bear arms for the protection and defense of his person, as he will explain if this should be necessary. He petitions Your Highness to grant him license to bear these
arms, and he will give sureties against his injuring anyone with these
arms; and Your Highness will thereby be granting him a favor.

✠

To Agnès Pascual

Barcelona, December 6, 1524

(Letter 1: I:71–73; in Spanish)

*Agnès Pujol of Manresa was one of Ignatius's earliest benefactors after his conver-
sion, having met him in 1522. From 1524 to 1526, following his return from
Palestine, she lodged Ignatius in the Barcelona house of her husband, the cotton-
dealer Bernardino Pascual. In this letter Ignatius urges her to bear up under
bereavement and obloquy, assuring her that "he wishes you to live in joy in him."*

1

I decided I ought to write you this because of the desires for the Lord's service that I have known in you; and I expect that at present, because of the absence of that blessed servant whom the Lord was pleased to take to himself, and your having there so many enemies and hindrances for the service of God, and because of the enemy of human nature who never ceases his temptations, you are probably feeling sorely pressed. For the love of God our Lord, aim always at going forward—always avoiding things that are a hindrance; for if you avoid them well, temptation will have no power against you. This is what you should be doing always, placing the praise of the Lord before all things—particularly since the Lord does not command you to do anything exhausting or harmful to your person. On the contrary, he wishes you to live in joy in him, giving to the body whatever it needs. And your speaking, thinking, and acting should be directed to him, and to the needs of your body for this purpose, while giving prior place to the Lord's commandments, for he himself wishes this and commands us this. And anyone who considers this carefully will find there is more trouble and pain in this life . . . [several words missing].

A pilgrim named Calixto is now staying there.[1] I would very much like you to talk with him about your affairs; truly, you may discover there is more in him than appears.

And so, for the love of our Lord let us strive hard in him, since we owe him so much. For we much sooner weary of receiving his gifts than he of giving.

May our Lady be pleased to intercede for us poor sinners with her Son and Lord and obtain for us the grace that, with our own toil and effort, he may transform our weak and sorry spirits into ones that are strong and joyful in his praise.

Barcelona, St. Nicholas's Day, 1525 [sic]

The poor pilgrim,

INIGO

✠

---

[1] Calixto de Sá became a follower of Ignatius and remained with him until his stay in Salamanca (*Autobiog.*, 64). He then left Ignatius and made his fortune in America, finally settling in Salamanca.

To Agnès Pascual

Paris, March 3, 1528

(Letter 2: I:74f.; in Spanish)

Ignatius reports to Agnès on his arrival in Paris, gives advice to her son Joán, and sends thanks for a benefactor.

May the true peace of Christ our Lord visit and shield our souls.

Considering the great goodwill and love which you have always had for me in God our Lord and have demonstrated to me in deeds, I decided to write you this letter and in it let you know of my travels after leaving you. With favorable weather and in complete good health, by the grace and goodness of God our Lord, I arrived here in the city of Paris on February 2, where I am engaged in studying until the Lord ordains otherwise for me.

I would very much like you to write me whether—and what— Fonseca replied to the letter you wrote, or whether you talked with him.

Remember me sincerely to Joán, and tell him always to be obedient to his parents and to observe the holy days; for if he does he will live long upon the earth and in heaven as well.

Remember me to your neighbor: tell her that the jewels got here, and that her love and goodwill for the sake of God our Lord never leaves me. May the Lord of the world repay her, and may he be in our souls through his infinite goodness, so that his will and desire may be always fulfilled in us.

Paris, March 2, 1528

Poor in goodness,

INIGO

✠

To Martín García de Oñaz

Paris, June 1532

(Letter 3: I:77–83; in Spanish, with numerous phrases in Latin)

Studying at Paris, Ignatius writes to his elder brother, now head of the Loyola family, about the marriage of Martín's daughter and arrangements for his son to begin university studies at Paris. He then offers a defense for the distance he had hitherto kept from his family; at the same time he urges his brother to greater concern for his spiritual responsibilities.

May the grace and love of Christ our Lord be always with us.

I received your letter and was delighted in his Divine Majesty at his service and love in the matter of your daughter, and at learning of the decision you came to regarding your son. May the sovereign Goodness graciously grant you to sustain and constantly advance all our plans ordered to his service and praise when you do so order them. Moreover, unless you judge something else better, I think it would not hurt to put him more in theology than in canon law; for it is a subject more pertinent and suitable for gaining everlasting riches that will last forever and give you greater comfort in your old age. For this purpose, I doubt you will find anywhere in Christendom greater advantages than at the university here. For his maintenance, tutors, and other academic needs, I think fifty ducats a year, properly provided, will suffice. I imagine you will not want your son, in a foreign, different, and chilly country, to suffer any want that might hinder his studies. If you consider the cost, you come out ahead with him at this university: he will accomplish more here in four years than anywhere else I know in six. Indeed, I do not think I would be departing from the truth if I said even more. If you are of a view to send him here, a view no less my own, it would be highly advisable for him to get here a week before the feast of St. Remi, this coming October 1, since that is when the arts [philosophy] course begins; if he is well grounded in grammar, he could begin his course on the feast of St. Remi. If he comes any later, he will have to wait until St. Remi's day of the following year, when the arts course starts over again.

I will do my best to steer him through his studies so that he applies himself, and also to keep him away from bad company. You write (these are your exact words): "If you think it best for him to go where you reside, please write me what it will cost me per annum; and if you could relieve me of this, it would be a favor to me should there be a suitable opportunity." I think I get your literal meaning (unless there is a slip of the pen): you would be pleased to have your son study here and to have me exert myself for a time so that you would have no expense from him. Regarding what I take to be the meaning, I do not see well enough where it comes from or what it aims at. Explain yourself if you think it pertinent; for in matters of justice and reason, I do not think God will let me be wanting, since my only motive is his most

holy service, your comfort therein, and your son's progress—if this is
what you decide you want done. You say you are very pleased that I have apparently given up my
practice of not writing to you. You should not be surprised: serious
wounds are treated with one type of salve at the start of a cure, another
in the middle, and still another at the end. Thus, at the start of my
journey I needed one sort of remedy; a little further on I am able without danger to use another—or at least there is no doubt I would look
for no second or third sort if I saw they were dangerous. It is not
strange that it should have been this way with me, since St. Paul, shortly after his conversion, said, "There was given to me a sting of my flesh,
an angel of Satan to buffet me" [2 Cor. 12:7]; and elsewhere, "I see
another law in my members fighting against the law of my mind" [Rom.
7:23]; "the flesh lusts against the spirit and the spirit against the flesh"
[Gal. 5:17]. The rebellion in his soul was so strong that he came to say,
"The good which I will, I do not; but the evil which I will not, that I
do" [Rom. 7:19]; "I do not understand what I do" [Rom. 7:15]. At a
different time later on he said, "I am certain that neither death, nor life,
nor angels, nor things present, nor things to come, nor any other creature shall be able to separate me from the love of God which is in
Christ Jesus our Lord" [Rom. 8:38–39]. I did not fail to resemble him
at the start; may it please the divine Goodness in my middle and end
not to deny me his complete and most holy grace, so that I may resemble, imitate, and serve all those who are his true servants; and should I
be about to offend him in any way or waver in a single point of his
service and praise, may he take me out of this life first.

But to come to the point: it is now a good five or six years that I
would have written you oftener except for two obstacles. The first was
the hindrance of my studies and constant conversations—not, however,
of a temporal nature. The second was that I did not have enough
grounds or evidence for thinking that my letters would result in any
praise and service of God our Lord or that it would give comfort to my
kin according to the flesh in such a way that at the same time we would
also be kin according to the Spirit and assist one other in the things
that will last forever. For the truth is this: I am able to love a person in
this life to the extent that he is striving to go forward in the service and
praise of God our Lord; for a person does not love God with his whole
heart if he loves anything else for its own and not for God's sake. Where
two persons, one a person connected with me and the other not, serve
God in equal measure, God wills us to have a greater closeness and
attachment to our natural father than to somebody who is not; to a

benefactor or relative than to one who is none of these; to friend or acquaintance than to someone who is neither. This is why we revere, honor, and love the chosen apostles more than the other inferior saints, because of their ever greater service and love of God our Lord. For charity, without which no one can attain life, is defined as the love by which we love the Lord our God for his own sake and all other things for his sake; it is even God himself whom we ought to praise in his saints, as the Psalmist says [Ps. 150:1]. I desire greatly—and more than greatly, if one may speak thus—to see intensely present in your own person, relatives, and friends this genuine love and strenuous effort in the service and praise of God our Lord, so that I might love and serve you ever more; for in serving the servants of my Lord, the victory is mine and glory is mine.

With this wholesome love and sincere and open goodwill, I shall now speak, write, and admonish just as I myself would wish and desire to be advised, roused, and corrected—with sincere humility and no profane or worldly pride. For a man in this life to spend sleepless nights, anxiety, and care upon putting up extensive buildings and enlarging his walls, income, and estate in order to leave behind a great name and reputation is not for me to condemn; but I cannot praise it. For according to St. Paul we ought to use things as though not using them, own them as though not owning them, even have a wife as though not having one; for the form of this world is of short duration [see 1 Cor. 7:29–31]. It could be; indeed, if only it were! If any of this has been your view, either in the past or in the present, I beg you by the reverence and love of God our Lord to strive with all your strength to win honor in heaven, remembrance and fame before the Lord who is to be our judge, by using earthly goods, since he has left you with an abundance of them, to gain the goods that are eternal—by giving good example and sound instruction to your children, servants, and relatives; by bestowing holy words on one person, just punishments on another (yet without anger or rancor); by granting to one your house's patronage, to another money and property; by doing much good to poor orphans and the needy. A person to whom God our Lord has been so generous should not himself be miserly. We will receive as much comfort and good as we ourselves have afforded in this life. Since you are able to do much there where you live, I beg you again and again by the love of our Lord Jesus Christ to strive hard not merely to think in this way but also to will and to act. To those who will, nothing is hard, especially if it is done for the love of our Lord Jesus Christ.

Don Andrés de Loyola has written me a letter.[2] The fact is that I would prefer face-to-face encounters to a lot of letter writing at the present time, when it is not called for. Hence, this letter will dispense me from writing to all the others: they should take this as addressed to themselves.

I decided to write you this once at length to answer the specific points in your letter and also to let you know better how things are.

To the lady of the house and her whole family, together with whoever you think will be glad to hear from me, please commend me heartily in the Lord who will one day judge us. I close, begging him by his infinite and supreme goodness to grant us grace, so that we may know his most holy will and entirely fulfill it.

The year 1532

I received your letter on June 20. Since you ask me to reply immediately, I am sending you this and two other copies by three routes to ensure that what you have decided in our Lord will not turn out for nought. If you receive this letter in time, and if your son could get here three weeks before the feast of St. Remi, so much the better— or if possible even earlier, so that he can take some introductory elements before beginning the course. A nephew of the Archbishop of Seville who is here in the college of Sainte-Barbe to start the arts course on the upcoming feast of St. Remi is planning to do the same. They could both benefit by taking this introduction, as we have considerable contact and readiness. May the sovereign Goodness be pleased to ordain everything for his holy service and continual praise.

Poor in goodness,

YÑIGO

✠

To Isabel Roser

Paris, November 10, 1532

(Letter 4: I:83–89; in Spanish)

A prominent noblewoman of Barcelona, Isabel Roser was an early benefactor and spiritual daughter of Ignatius. Years later, widowed, she came to Rome and unsuc-

---

[2] Ignatius's uncle, rector of the parish of Azpeitia.

cessfully attempted to found a women's congregation under his direction. She eventually returned to Barcelona, where she lived out her life in a Franciscan monastery.

Writing to Isabel from Paris, Ignatius expresses gratitude for her financial efforts on his behalf, even if the results are less than she wishes. He consoles her for the loss of her friend Micaela Canyelles and responds to her complaints about her physical and social trials with an uncompromising reassertion of the teaching found in his Spiritual Exercises: *we are to judge goods and evils solely by whether they serve to unite us to God, and we should rejoice at being given a share in Christ's insults and humiliations. On the latter point we see a unique case of Ignatius reinforcing his teaching with a (somewhat lurid) pious story, that of St. Marina.*

May the grace and love of Christ our Lord be in us.

Through Dr. Benet I received three letters from your hand, along with twenty ducats. I both pray God our Lord to credit them to you on judgment day and intend to repay you on my own account; for I am confident in his divine goodness both that he will recompense you in his own good and sound coin, and also that he will never let me fall into the guilt of ingratitude so long as in some matters he makes me worthy of service and praise to his Divine Majesty.

You tell in your letter of how God's will was fulfilled in [Micaela] Canyelles's exile and departure from this life. Indeed I cannot feel sorry for her, but only for ourselves who abide in this place of immense weariness, sufferings, and calamities. For knowing how she was beloved by her Creator and Lord in this life, I readily believe that she will meet with a good reception and welcome, and will not much miss the palaces, pomps, riches, and vanities of this world.

You also write me of the apologies from our sisters in Christ our Lord. They owe me nothing—rather, I am their debtor forever if for the service of God our Lord they employ their means elsewhere to better effect. We ought to be glad they do so; and if they do not or cannot, I truly wish I had something I could give them, so that they would be able to do much for the service and glory of God our Lord; for so long as I live, I cannot help being indebted to them. However, I think that once we have left this life, they will be well repaid by me.

In the second letter you tell me of your earlier long ailment and illness, and of your continuing severe stomach pains. Of course, when I think of your present ill health and pains, I cannot help feeling it in my soul, for I wish you every imaginable well-being and prosperity which might help you for the glory and service of God our Lord. However, when I reflect that these infirmities and other temporal losses are often from the hand of God our Lord, so that we will know ourselves better, more thoroughly lose our love for created things, and better bear in mind how short this life of ours is and so adorn ourselves for the other which will last forever—and when I reflect that he visits these things upon those he loves much—then I cannot feel sadness or pain; for I believe that an illness can leave a servant of God with half a doctorate in directing and ordering his life to God our Lord's glory and service. You likewise ask my forgiveness if you fail to supply me more amply, since you have many obligations and not enough resources. There is no reason to mention forgiveness; I am fearful for myself because I think that if I do not do for all my benefactors what God obliges me to, his divine and just justice will not forgive me—and how much more considering my liability toward you. In the end, if I myself prove unable to fulfill my obligations in this regard, my only recourse is that the Lord himself, counting whatever merits I may gain before the Divine Majesty (through his grace, however), will disburse them to those to whom I am liable, to each person according as he has aided me in his service, and above all to you, to whom I owe more than to anyone else I know in this world. And while I know this, I hope in God our Lord that I will increase and grow in this knowledge. And so be sure that henceforth your sound and sincere concern will be received by me with as much spiritual delight and joy as if it were accompanied by all the money you could send me. For God our Lord requires us to regard and love the giver more than the gift, so that we always keep him before our eyes, in our soul, and in our heart.

You likewise ask what I think about writing to our other sisters and benefactresses in Christ our Lord for their help in the future. I would rather decide this by your opinion than by mine. Although in her letter [Leonor] Zapila volunteers and indicates a willingness to help me, for present I think it better not to write her for help in my studies. We have no certainty of getting from this year to the next; and if we do, I trust that God our Lord will give us understanding and judgment so as to serve him the better and always correctly discern his will and desire.

In the third letter you mention how many acts of spitefulness, intrigue, and untruthfulness have besieged you on every side. This does not surprise me in the least, even if it were much worse. For at the moment when you decide, will, and strive with all your strength for the glory, honor, and service of God our Lord, at that moment you join battle and raise your standard against the world, and prepare yourself to cast away lofty and embrace lowly things, resolving to treat equally the high or the low, honor or dishonor, wealth or poverty, love or hatred, welcome or rejection—in short, the world's glory or all its abuse. We cannot pay much attention to insults in this life when they are no more than words; all of them together cannot hurt a hair of our heads. Deceitful, vile, and insulting words cannot cause us pain or contentment except as we desire them; and if our desire is to live absolutely in honor and our neighbor's esteem, we can never be solidly rooted in God our Lord, nor can we remain unscathed when faced with affronts. Consequently, just as I was once glad at the world's abusing you, I was no less grieved to learn that because of these adversities, because of your suffering and distress, you had to seek help from medicine. May it please the Mother of God—provided you can maintain complete patience and steadfastness by considering the worse insults and affronts that Christ our Lord endured for our sakes, and there is no sin on the part of others —that you might meet with even worse abuse, so that your merit may be ever greater. And if we fail to find this patience, we have cause to complain more of our own sensuality and flesh, of our own failure to be as mortified and dead to worldly things as we ought, than of the persons who injure us. For the latter are giving us an opportunity to acquire merchandise beyond what anyone can obtain in this life, and wealth beyond what anyone can amass in this world—as was the case with a person in the monastery of St. Francis in this city. This is what happened.

A certain house was frequently visited by Franciscan friars. Their demeanor being very holy and religious, a grown-up young girl living in the house formed a great love for this monastery and house of St. Francis—a love so great in fact that one day she dressed as a boy and went to the monastery of St. Francis and asked the guardian to let him take the habit because he had a deep desire to serve not only God our Lord and St. Francis but also all the religious of that house. He spoke so winningly that they immediately gave him the habit. Living thus a life of great recollection and consolation in the monastery, it happened that on a trip made with their superior's permission, this friar and another companion stayed overnight in a certain house. In the house there was a young woman who fell in love with the good friar. Accordingly (or rather, because the devil entered her), she decided to accost the good friar while he was sleeping and get him to have relations with her. But the good friar woke up and threw her from himself. This so enraged the girl that she began plotting how to harm the good friar as much as she could. Accordingly, some days later this evil girl went to speak with the guardian, asking for justice, along with other claims, because she was pregnant by this good friar of his house. So the guardian seized the good friar and decided (since the charge had become so public in the town) to place him bound in the street at the door of the monastery so everybody could see the justice inflicted upon the good friar.

He spent several days like this, rejoicing in the injuries, insults, and obscene words he heard uttered against himself. He made no self-defense to anyone, but within his soul conversed with his Creator and Lord, since he was being given an opportunity for such great merit before his Divine Majesty. After he had been on show like this for some time and everybody had seen how patient he was, they all begged the guardian to pardon what had happened and restore him to his love and to the house. The guardian, himself already moved to pity, received him back. The good friar lived many years in the house, until God our Lord's will for him was fulfilled. When they undressed him for burial after his death, they discovered that he was not a man but a woman, and consequently what a calumny had been done him. All the friars were amazed, and their praises for his innocence and holiness exceeded their earlier curses against his wickedness. However, even today there are many who remember this friar—or nun—better than anyone else who lived in the house for a long time. And so I would be more attentive to a single failure of my own than to all the evil that people might say of me.

May the Most Holy Trinity, in all trials of this life and in everything else in which you can serve it, grant you all the grace that I desire for myself, and may it grant me none greater than what I desire for you.

Please commend me most sincerely to Mosén Roser, and to anyone else you think will be heartily pleased to hear from me.[3]

Paris, November 10, 1532

Poor in goodness,

IÑIGO

[Postscript:] In Arteaga as well as several persons from Alcalá and Salamanca I see much steadfastness in the service and glory of God our Lord, to whom be infinite thanks for this.[4]

As you direct, I am writing to [Guiomar de] Gralla[5] about the reconciliation; the letter is going with that to [Agnès] Pascual; also to [Leonor] Zapila.[6]

---

[3] Mosén Joán Roser was Isabel's husband.

[4] Juan de Arteaga, an early follower of Ignatius. He did not remain with him, and later became a bishop in America.

[5] Guiomar de Hostalrich de Gralla, one of Ignatius's benefactors.

[6] Leonor de Ferrer, wife of Severo Zapila.

To Agnès Pascual

Paris, June 13, 1533

(Letter 5: I:90–92; in Spanish)

A begging letter to Agnès, enlisting her aid with his other benefactors in Barcelona.

May the grace and love of Christ our Lord be always for our favor and our help.

It is a year now since I received a letter from you through Dr. Benet (may he rest in glory), when he brought me an alms and provision from there. From your letter and from what they told me here, I learned of the great efforts you have made in my behalf, with entire goodwill, as you have always demonstrated to me. You likewise promised to put forth the same efforts and concern in the future. It seems that you have not only made me liable for the past but would like me to be bound for the entire future as well. May it please God our Lord that the true Lord for whose love and reverence you do this may repay you.

Although I wrote you another letter in reply to the one you sent me, I decided to write this one not only because of your great kindness but also because my studies have become more expensive than hitherto. This Lent I took the master's degree and in doing so paid out in unavoidable expenses more than my authority required or could bear. I have thus been left quite short, and there will be great need for God our Lord to help us. Accordingly, I am writing to Zapila, who in a letter she wrote me made me a very generous promise to do a great deal on my behalf and said I should write her about whatever I needed.[7]

I am also writing to Isabel Roser, but not regarding this request, since she wrote me a letter telling me not to be surprised if she no longer helped me as much as she might wish, because of the many needs she finds herself in. I certainly believe and, if one may rightly make such a statement, state that she has done more for me than she was able, so that I owe her more than I can ever repay. I think it would be better for you not to speak to her in order to tell her about any of my needs, so that she will not be distressed at being unable to provide for me. When I left there, the wife of Mosén Gralla earnestly promised to help me during my studies, and has always done so. Doña Isabel de Josa made a similar promise, and so did Doña Aldonza de Cardona, who has accordingly been giving me help. I am not writing to the last three, so as not to appear importunate; but please commend me earnestly to

---

[7] Zapila was a benefactor in Barcelona.

them and their prayers. As for Gralla, I always feel that if she is informed, she will wish to share in any alms sent to me. With regard to her and all the others, do as you think best: I will consider that the best thing and will always be satisfied, for I am ever in their debt, a debt I can never be quit of in the future.

The bearer of this letter will tell you more of the news here; I trust him in all matters as I would myself. Regarding your son Joán, my old friend in love and true brother in the Lord, who will judge us eternally, I am most anxious for you to write me how he is doing, for you know that I cannot help being happy over his welfare and sorrowful over the contrary. May God our Lord be pleased to give him the grace always to know himself perfectly and to experience his Divine Majesty in his soul, so that, seized by his love and his grace, he may be freed from all the creatures of the world. I close, asking God our Lord in his infinite goodness to make the two of you in this life what he made that blessed mother and her son, St. Augustine.

Please remember me cordially to your neighbors, acquaintances, and beloved friends.

Paris, June 13, 1533

The person who was to bring this has been detained by a business matter. He is sending in his place the man who will deliver this to you and who is returning here at once.

Poor in goodness,
INIGO

✠

To Jaime Cassador

Venice, February 12, 1536

(Letter 6: I:93–99; in Spanish)

Jaime Cassador, archdeacon (and later archbishop) of Barcelona, was a generous benefactor of Ignatius during his time of studies in Paris. Replying to a letter from him, Ignatius treats six points: (1) the procedure for handling contributions for him in Paris; (2) three of Cassador's nephews in Paris; (3) advice to a friend, gravely ill; (4) Ignatius's desire to work apostolically in Barcelona; (5) the benefit of frequenting spiritual persons; and (6) the reasons God allows his servants to suffer trials and tribulations.

May the grace and love of Christ our Lord be always for our favor and our help.

Reading a letter from you dated January 5, I not only rejoiced over it but grieved deeply because of it, perceiving in it such contrary and conflicting things. Thus, it had different and opposed effects on me: joy at seeing the excellent zeal which God our Lord gives you for grieving with those who grieve, not only in their corporal but even more abundantly in their spiritual infirmities; and great pain at the thought of the disastrous matters about which you write to me. Regarding this, five or six matters occurred to me that I ought to respond to. And so I will begin with the lower ones, those which do less to quench the thirst of our souls, so that we will not end with the savor and taste of things that are less for our eternal salvation.

First, you say that you will not fail to make the usual contribution—I should just let you know when. Isabel Roser wrote me that by April she will supply me with enough to finish my studies. I think this is best, so that she can provide me for the entire year, both for some books and other needs as well. In the meantime, even though the country is expensive and my health at present is no help for enduring any want or physical hardship beyond those entailed in study itself, I am provided for well enough, since Isabel Roser has had twelve escudos given to me on her account in addition to the other help and alms which you yourself sent me from there for the love and service of God our Lord, who I trust will fully repay you in sound coin not only for what you do for me but also for the great concern you show for my want—I do not think parents could show any greater solicitude for their own children. Two weeks before Christmas I was laid up in bed for seven days in Bologna with stomach pains, chills, and fevers, and so I decided to come to Venice. I have been staying here for about a month and a half, very much improved in health, in the house and company of a very good and learned man. For my purposes I do not think I could be better situated anywhere in this whole country.

Second, I was not upset at learning that the three nephews are absent from Marable, though I wish I had some idea why. I expect to find out soon, since I have written to one of my Paris friends, asking him to look them up and call on them for me. I say I was not upset, because unless I am mistaken they are honorable fellows who are careful about their reputation, so that I am confident that, one way or another, they will give a good account of themselves. During my stay there I noticed that Losada had quieted down, and with the example of the other two older ones, especially Jacobo, I trust in God our Lord that they will behave as they ought. May it please him in his complete and sovereign goodness to guide them always with his hand.

Third, as you requested and commanded in our true Lord with regard to Mosén Claret's illness, I have written to him.[8] Since you will see everything in the letter, I need add no more here. I would only ask that you help him provide for his interior health and whatever else God our Lord has given him in this life, since I doubt he would take it from anyone better than from you. For unless he has children or similarly close relatives whom he is legally bound to make his heirs, I think beyond any doubt that it would be better and sounder for him to give what he has to the one from whom he received everything, our universal giver, ruler, and Lord, in pious, just, and holy causes—and as much of it as he can while still living rather than after death. That a man should leave his property to somebody else for the upkeep of horses and dogs, for hunting, honors, dignities, and worldly display is something I cannot approve. St. Gregory lists two degrees of perfection among others: one when a man abandons all he owns to his relatives and kin and follows Christ our Lord; the other (which he rates higher) when in abandoning everything he distributes it to the poor according to the text "If you would be perfect . . ." [Matt. 19:21]. My meaning is that it is better to give to the poor when the need of one's relatives is not equal to that of the poor who are not one's relatives—for, other things being equal, I ought to do more for my relatives than for those who are not.

Fourth, regarding the wish you express to see me in Barcelona and preaching in public, be assured that I have the same wish dwelling within me—not as though I flattered myself that I could do what others cannot, or could achieve as much as others do there; but [I wish] to preach as a lesser person on simple, easy, and lesser matters, in hopes that God our Lord would second these lesser matters and interpose his grace so that we may be able to do some good for his praise and rightful service. For this reason, once I finish my studies a year from this Lent, I do not expect to delay a further year to preach his word anywhere else in Spain before we see each other there as we both desire. For I have no doubt that I have a greater liability and debt to the people of Barcelona than to any other town in the world. This is to be understood (the key not erring) unless God our Lord places me outside of Spain amid greater humiliations and hardships.[9] I am not sure which it will be; but certainly my state will be that of preaching in poverty, with none of the

---

[8] Joán Claret was a man of means whom Ignatius had known in Barcelona.
[9] "Clave non errante"—a reference to the papal "key"?

abundance or encumbrances I now have during my studies. At any rate, as a token of what I say, when my studies are over I will send to Barcelona the few books I have or will have, since I promised Isabel Roser I would send them to her.

Fifth, you tell how you wrote to the religious woman and would like to see the two of us meet there, in the belief that we would find joy in telling each other about ourselves.[10] I certainly do find, and it is a general rule with me, that when I join with anyone, even though a great sinner, to talk about the things of God our Lord, I am the one who gains and profits thereby; how much more, then, when it is with persons who are servants and chosen ones of God our Lord, must I not be wholly the gainer in every way? Indeed, ever since Dr. Castro told me at length about this woman and I learned that she was under your direction, I have felt very much attached to her, glorifying God for what he has thus been working in her.[11] In him I trust that if it is for his praise and service and our greater advantage, he will bring us together soon.

Sixth, as for what you say about the Monastery of Santa Clara, I certainly would consider no one a Christian whose soul was not pierced through and through at the thought of so much harm done to the service of God our Lord;[12] and I am less concerned over a single person's failure in judgment than over the consequent harm to many other persons, and to others who might devote themselves to God's service. Indeed, through our misery, just as we find it so hard to overcome ourselves where the spiritual profit is greatest, so a slight occasion is all that is needed for our complete undoing. Indeed, I earnestly wish I could visit these religious to see if I could somehow lay a foundation for their exercises and way of proceeding, particularly for the woman who is in such anxiety and danger.[13] For I cannot readily believe that a person who had been living amid worldly pleasures or with less devotion to God our Lord and who was of sound judgment could, through serving

---

[10] The identity of these women is unknown.

[11] Dr. Juan Castro (1488–1556), a doctor of the Sorbonne, had been given the Exercises by Ignatius in Paris. He later became a Carthusian in Spain.

[12] A Benedictine (originally Franciscan) monastery of women in Barcelona. Some of the members of the community were women of conspicuous holiness, among them Ignatius's correspondent, Teresa Rejadell, while others did not share this fervor. The more fervent wanted the Society to undertake their direction, but Ignatius never allowed himself to be moved by their entreaties.

[13] Perhaps Teresa Rejadell, from whom Ignatius was soon to receive a letter.

our Lord better and drawing closer to him, be allowed to reach such a state of desperation. Weak human being that I am, if a person came to serve me out of greater love for me, I would never—if it were in my power to prevent it—let him come to such a calamity as this; how much more God our Lord, who, being divine, chose to become human and die solely for the salvation of us all! So I find it hard to believe that for having given herself to divine things, apart from any other interior or future reason, she should have fallen into such torment and misfortune. For it is God's way to bestow understanding, not take it away; to bestow confidence, not hopelessness. I say, "apart from any other interior reason," because it is possible that during the time of the exercises her soul was marred by sin; and there are so many kinds of sin that they seem numberless. Or she may have been making the exercises in a marred way: what seems good is not always so; and thus, since good could not abide in the person together with evil, or grace with sin, the enemy could have had considerable power to act. And I said "apart from some other future reason" because it is possible that God our Lord, disposing all things with order, weight, and measure, saw that, although in grace at the time, she would fail to take advantage of the graces and gifts she received and, not persevering, fall into greater sins and finally be lost; and that, seeing this, our most kind Lord rewarded her for her slight service by allowing her to fall into these fears and continual temptations, all the while preserving her from perishing. For we must always presume that anything the Lord of the world does in rational souls is either in order to give us greater glory or else so that we will be less wicked when he finds no better dispositions in us. In short, since we do not know the underlying causes, we can make no judgment about the effects. Accordingly, it is always good for us not only to live in love; it is also very wholesome to live in fear, for his divine judgments are altogether inscrutable, and we may not seek reasons for what he wills. We can only weep, and pray for the greater well-being of her own conscience and for those of all the other women. May his divine Goodness ordain this, and not let the enemy of human nature gain such a victory over these women, whom he has purchased so dearly and entirely redeemed with his most precious blood.

I conclude, praying that by his infinite goodness he will grant us abundant grace to know his most holy will and entirely to fulfill it.

Venice, February 12, 1536

Poor in goodness,

INIGO

To Teresa Rejadell

Venice, June 18, 1536

(Letter 7: I:99–107; in Spanish)

Teresa Rejadell was a Benedictine nun of the convent of Santa Clara in Barcelona. In this letter Ignatius gives her detailed advice on scruples and on the discernment of spirits. These remarks constitute an important commentary on the relevant rules in the Spiritual Exercises.

May the grace and love of Christ our Lord be always for our favor and our help.

I received your letter some days ago, and it has brought me much joy in the Lord whom you serve and desire to serve even more, and to whom we must ascribe all good that appears in creatures. You wrote that Cáceres would inform me at length about your concerns;[14] he not only did so but also told me the means or opinion he gave you for each of them. Reading over what he tells me, I find nothing to add, although I would prefer getting the information in a letter from yourself, since no one can explain a person's sufferings as well as the one undergoing them.

You ask me for the love of God our Lord to undertake the care of your person. It is true that, without my deserving it, his Divine Majesty has for many years now given me the desire to give whatever satisfaction I can to all—both men and women—who walk in the way of his will, as also to serve those who labor in his just service; and since I have no doubt that you are one of these persons, I long to be where I could demonstrate what I say through deeds.

You also earnestly beg me to write you what our Lord tells me, and to tell you conclusively what I think. What I think and have concluded in the Lord I will most willingly tell you. If on any point I seem harsh, I will be so more towards the one who is trying to upset you than towards yourself. There are two matters in which the enemy is causing you confusion, though not so as to make you fall into any sin that could separate you from your God and Lord; however, he does confuse you and draw you away from his greater service and your own greater ease. First, he is persuading you to have a wrong humility; second, he is producing an excessive fear of God, which you dwell upon and occupy yourself with too much.

---

[14] Lope de Cáceres had been a disciple of Ignatius during the latter's early years of study in Spain.

Regarding the first point, the enemy's general practice with persons who desire and have begun to serve God our Lord is to bring up obstacles and impediments. This is the first weapon with which he attempts to wound them; namely, "How are you going to live your whole life amid such penance, with no enjoyment from friends, relatives, or possessions, leading such a lonely life and never having any ease? There are other less perilous ways you can save your soul." He suggests that we will have to live a longer life amid all these hardships than any human ever lived. He does not tell us about the great comforts and consolations which our Lord is accustomed to give to such persons if the new servant of the Lord breaks through all these obstacles and deliberately chooses to suffer along with his Creator and Lord. Next, the enemy resorts to his second weapon; that is to say, pride and vainglory. He intimates to the person that he possesses much goodness and holiness, placing him higher than he deserves. If the servant of God resists these arrows by humbling and abasing himself and refusing to consent to the enemy's suggestions, he comes with his third weapon, a wrong humility. Seeing how good and humble the Lord's servant is, how while fulfilling what the Lord commands, he still considers it useless, looks only to his own weakness, not to any vainglory, he gives the person the thought that if he discovers anything that God our Lord has given him by way either of deeds or of resolves and desires, he sins through another species of vainglory by speaking in his own favor. He thus tries to keep the person from talking about the good things he has received from his Lord, so that he will not produce fruit in others or in himself. For to recall what one has already received is always a help towards even greater things—although this speaking must be with great moderation and only for people's greater benefit, that is, one's own or that of other persons one sees are properly disposed and likely to believe the speaker and be benefited. Thus, by getting us to be humble, the enemy manages to draw us on to a wrong humility, namely, to one that is excessive and flawed.

What you say bears apt witness to this. After recounting certain frailties and fears which are very much to the point, you say, "I am a poor religious; I think I desire to serve Christ our Lord." You do not even dare to say, "I desire to serve Christ our Lord," or, "The Lord gives me desires to serve him." Instead you say, "I think I desire to serve him." If you reflect carefully, you will realize that these desires to serve Christ our Lord are not from yourself but bestowed by the Lord. And so when you say, "The Lord gives me strong desires to serve him," it is the Lord himself you praise by making known his gift; it is in him and not in yourself that you glory, for you do not attribute the grace to yourself. Hence, we must be very careful: if the enemy lifts us up, we must put ourselves down by counting our sins and miseries; if he casts us down and depresses us, we must raise ourselves up by genuine faith and hope in the Lord, through counting the blessings we have received, and the great love and goodwill with which he awaits our salvation—whereas the enemy does not care whether he speaks truth or falsehood so long as he gets the better of us.

Reflect how the martyrs, when placed before idolatrous magistrates, declared that they were servants of Christ; and so, when you are placed before the enemy of all human nature to be tested by him in this way, and he tries to rob you of the strength given to you by our Lord and to make you weak and fearful like this with his tricks and deceits, you will not dare to say that you *desire* to serve our Lord; rather, you must say and fearlessly confess that you *are* his servant, and that you would rather die than depart from his service. If the enemy gives me thoughts of justice, I will immediately think of mercy; if he gives me thoughts of mercy, I will counter by thinking of justice. This is how we have to proceed if we are to avoid being upset, and if we are to delude the deluder. We should quote the text from Sacred Scripture: "Beware of being so humble that you fall into folly" [see Ecclus. 13:10].

Now for the second point. Once the enemy has made us fearful through a semblance of humility—a humility that is wrong—and has gotten us not to speak even of good, holy, and profitable things, he then comes with a far worse fear: that we are separated, estranged, and alienated from our Lord. This fear follows largely from the foregoing; for once he has won a victory with the previous fear, the enemy finds it easier to try us with this second one. To clarify this somewhat, I will mention another procedure that the enemy uses. If he finds a person who has an easy conscience and lets sins go by without weighing them, he does his best to make venial sins out to be no sins at all, mortal sins venial, and very grievous mortal sins small matters. He thus takes advantage of the failing he perceives in us, in this case an overly easy conscience. If he finds another person whose conscience is delicate (no fault in itself) and sees that the person not only repels all mortal sins and all the venial sins that he is able (for they are not all in our power), and even tries to repel every semblance of slight sin or fault against perfection, then the enemy attempts to trip up this excellent conscience by alleging sin where there is no sin and fault where there is perfection, so that he can confound and distress us. Thus, in many cases where he cannot get a person to sin and has no prospect of doing so, he will try at least to torment the person.

To clarify how this fear is produced, I will mention, although briefly, two lessons which our Lord gives or permits (he gives one and permits the other). The lesson that he gives is interior consolation, which dispels all confusion and draws to utter love of the Lord. Some persons he enlightens in this consolation, to others he reveals many secrets, and beyond. In a word, with this divine consolation all hardship is pleasure, all toil is rest. When a person is going forward with this fervor and warmth and interior consolation, the heaviest burden seems light, the greatest penances or hardships seem sweet. This consolation shows and opens up to us the way we ought to go, avoiding the opposite. It is not always with us; it always follows its own definite times as has been ordained; and all this with a view to our own progress. For when we are without this consolation, the other lesson comes; that is to say, our ancient enemy throws up every possible obstacle to turn us from what we have begun, sorely afflicting us in ways completely opposite to the first lesson: he frequently gives us sadness without our knowing why we are sad; we cannot pray with any devotion, we cannot contemplate, we cannot even speak or hear of the things of God our Lord with interior taste or relish. Not only this, but if he sees us weakened and cast down into these accursed thoughts, he suggests that we are utterly forgotten by God our Lord; we end up thinking that we are totally separated from our Lord, and that all we have done and desired to do is worthless. He thus strives to reduce us to total discouragement. Thus we can see that all this fear and weakness of ours comes from dwelling excessively at such times on our miseries and submitting so abjectly to his lying suggestions. Consequently, we must observe who is giving battle. If it is consolation, then we must abase and humble ourselves and remember that the trial of temptation will soon come. If temptation, darkness, or sadness comes, we must resist and not let it taint us; we must patiently await the Lord's consolation, which will dry up all confusion and outer darkness.

Finally, we need to say something about how to understand things which we experience as coming from God our Lord, and how, once understood, to make use of them. It often happens that our Lord moves and drives our soul to one action or another by opening the soul up, that is, by speaking inside it without the din of words, lifting the soul wholly to his divine love, so that even if we wished to resist his impression, we could not. This impression of his which we receive must be in conformity with the commandments, the precepts of the Church, and obedience to our superiors, and entirely filled with humility, for the same divine Spirit is present in all this. The way we can often go astray is this: *after* a consolation or inspiration of this kind, while the soul is still full of joy, the enemy approaches all under cover of joy and on a pretext of good to get us to add to what we have experienced from God our Lord, so as to bring us to disorder and total confusion.

At other times he gets us to abate the lesson we have received by throwing up obstacles and difficulties to keep us from fully carrying out what has been shown to us. Here more than anywhere else we need to be alert, often reining in our great eagerness for speaking about the things of God our Lord and at other times saying more than the impulse or movement prompts us; for in this we must look more to the other person's character than to my own desires. When the enemy acts in this way to get us to magnify or abate the good impression received, we need to feel our way so that we can help others, as in fording a river: if I find a good footing or path, or the prospect of producing some good, I go forward; but if the ford is turbulent and the persons will take scandal at my good words, I stay reined in, seeking the best time or moment to speak.

Matters have been brought up that cannot be written about this way, at least not without very ample treatment, and even then there would be things that are more readily experienced than explained, particularly in writing. Our Lord willing, I trust we will meet there soon, and then we can go more deeply into some matters. Meanwhile, since you have Castro closer at hand, I think it would be a good idea if you corresponded with him; no harm can come of it, and possibly some good. And since you ask me to write just what I think in the Lord, I say this: Blessed will you be if you can hold fast to what you have.

I close, praying that the Most Holy Trinity by its infinite and supreme goodness may bestow upon all of us abundant grace, so that we may know its most holy will and entirely fulfill it.

Venice, June 18, 1536

Poor in goodness,
IGNACIO

To Teresa Rejadell

Venice, September 11, 1536

(Letter 8: I:107–9; in Spanish)

For Teresa Rejadell see letter 7. Ignatius instructs her on how to pray without harming her health and on how to counter temptations with the thought of God's love.

May the grace and love of Christ our Lord be always for our favor and our help.

I received two letters from you at different times. I sent what I consider an ample reply to the first, which you should have received by now. In the second you tell me the same as in the first, except for a few words to which I will reply only briefly.

You say that you find in yourself great ignorance, timidity, etc. (to know this is to know much), and that you think this is partly due to the many indefinite opinions you have received. I agree with you that one who is indefinite understands little and helps less—but the Lord, who does see, himself bestows his favor.

Any meditation in which the understanding has to toil wearies the body. There are other orderly and restful meditations which are peaceful for the understanding, are not laborious for the interior faculties of the mind, and can be made without interior or exterior strain. These do not weary but rest the body—except in two ways. One is if it prevents the natural sustenance and recreation which you owe to the body. By sustenance, I mean when one is so taken up by these meditations that he forgets to give the body its natural food, skipping the proper hours. By recreation—religious recreation—I mean leaving the mind free to rove at will amid matters good or indifferent, so long as they are not bad.

The second is something that happens to many people given to prayer or contemplation: because they exercise their minds much, they cannot sleep afterwards because they keep thinking about the matters they have contemplated and pictured. Hence, the enemy tries hard to preserve good thoughts so that the body will suffer from the loss of sleep. This must be altogether avoided. With a healthy body you will be able to do much; with a weakened body I am not sure what you will be able to do. A sound body is a great help for doing either much good or much evil: much evil in persons of depraved will and evil habits, much good in persons whose will is entirely given to God our Lord and trained to habits of virtue.

Thus, without my knowing what meditations and exercises you make and how long you spend on them, and apart from whatever Cáceres has told you, there is nothing fuller I can tell you beyond what I wrote you and here reconfirm: that you should above all keep in mind that your Lord loves you, as I have no doubt that he does, and that you should respond to him with the same love, paying no heed at all to any evil, foul, or sensual thoughts, to any timidity or tepidity, when they are against your will. For not to have all or some of these thoughts come is something that neither St. Peter nor St. Paul ever achieved. However, even if it cannot be done completely, we achieve a great deal by paying no heed to any of them. For just as I am not going to be saved through the good angels' good works, so I am not going to be damned through the evil thoughts and frailties that are brought before me by the bad angels, the world, and the flesh. God our Lord requires only that my soul be conformed to his divine majesty; so conformed, it makes the body act in conformity to his divine will, like it or not—wherein is our greatest struggle, and the good pleasure of the eternal and sovereign goodness. By his infinite kindness and grace may he hold us always with his hand.

Venice, September 11, 1536

Poor in goodness,

IÑIGO

✠

To Gabriel Guzmán, O.P.

Venice, November 1, 1536

(Letter 9: I:109–11; in Spanish)

The war between France and Spain meant that Favre and the others would be in danger as they traveled from Paris to northern Italy. Accordingly, Ignatius enlists the aid of a friend in Paris, the confessor of the French queen, Leonor of Austria.

May the grace and love of Christ our Lord be always for our favor and help.

Recalling the excellent and wholesome goodwill which has always been shown to me for the service of God our Lord without my deserving any such good, I decided to write you this letter, not to repay or compensate you for it—that is quite beyond me—but to request new favors and gifts in service and praise of his Divine Majesty. While I had always known your charity, I became wholly aware of it when, speaking in my absence, you arranged for me to talk with that great religious to whom I ask now to be most cordially remembered.[15] For this I shall be obliged to you as long as I live; and I am very glad to be thus bound, provided, whether in person or any other way, God our Lord makes me worthy of being able in any way to please and serve you, as I am so deeply bound to do in his divine and supreme goodness.

Master Pierre Favre and a few companions are facing a rather difficult journey, about which you can learn more fully from him. I suspect that with these enormous disorders and wars going on in Christendom because of our miseries and sins, he and his company may find themselves in great, even dire, straits. He requests you, by the reverence and service of God our Lord, to be on the lookout for any help and favor God our Lord may move you to give them and may be possible. All of this will be done for the love and glory of his divine and supreme goodness; besides that, I will consider it as done for myself personally.

Our beloved Dr. Castro has written me several times from the Charterhouse of Val de Cristo in Segorbe, where he is now a friar, having made his profession this past feast of St. John. May God our Lord give him abundant grace to arrive from good to better in his most holy service and praise. He asks to be cordially remembered to Padre Fray Juan and good Master Jean, whose servant, Master Miguel, is here leading an entirely new life.[16] Regarding him and everything else you will enjoy hearing about I am writing at length to Favre, from whom you can get a complete report. I close asking God our Lord by his infinite goodness to grant us his abundant grace, so that we may know his most holy will and entirely fulfill it.

Venice, November 3, 1536

> Poor in goodness,
>
> IÑIGO

---

[15] The allusion is to Mathieu Ory, inquisitor of France. Ignatius had heard that he had been denounced to the Inquisition because of his responsibility in inducing Castro, Amador, and Peralta to adopt a life of voluntary poverty. Guzmán must have intervened on Ignatius's behalf.

[16] Juan de la Peña was Ignatius's professor of philosophy. Possibly Ignatius here refers to Jean Benoist, who is named elsewhere in his letters. Miguel Landívar, was a Navarrese who once tried to kill Ignatius at Paris, joined him at Venice, belonged for a time to the small band of apostles, but was sent away. In 1538 we find him associated with a group of calumniators whom Ignatius forced to acknowledge their lies in court.

To Doña María

Venice, November 1, 1536

(Letter 9a: I:723f. [Appendix 1]; in Spanish)

Nothing more is known of this lady, presumably residing in Paris, whom Ignatius asks to help Favre and the other companions about to leave for Italy.

May the grace and love of Christ our Lord be always for our favor and our help.

I wrote you another letter before this one which I know you received but did not answer. Quite clearly you are more present in my soul than I in yours; for I think you have as much reason to be mindful of me, in true love and charity of the Lord who will save us, as I of your own tranquillity and repose in the service and praise of his Divine Majesty. Giving him all the thanks that I am able, I find myself in good health and looking forward to Lent, when I will be able to leave my scholarly labors and take up others of greater moment and worth. Since the time is short and Favre, some friends of his, and I are eager to join together to dig and labor in the vineyard of the Lord here, if you have at other times employed yourself on my behalf and have had increased desires to do so even more, I now in recompense beg you for the love of God our Lord to do so for these men's time of departure—whether by any financial help you can give them or by also speaking to other persons who might wish to obtain a share in the merit—so that they will be able to leave Paris and come here, principally for a pilgrimage which is holy, rightful, and also quite full of hardships. I ask this because I am confident that, besides your having a soul that is lofty and disposed for such tasks, God our Lord will grant you a full determination to employ yourself in them. I conclude, praying that in his infinite and sovereign goodness he will give us grace to know his most holy will and entirely to fulfill it.

Venice, November 1, 1536

Wholly yours in the Lord,
INIGO

To Manuel Miona

Venice, November 16, 1536
(Letter 10: I:111–13; in Spanish)

The Portuguese Manuel Miona had been Ignatius's confessor in Alcalá and later studied at Paris. Writing to him there, Ignatius strongly urges him to make the Spiritual Exercises, calling them "altogether the best thing that in this life I can think, perceive, or understand for helping a person benefit himself as well as bringing fruit, benefit, and advantage to many others." Miona became a member of the Society of Jesus in 1545.

May the grace and love of Christ our Lord be always for our favor and help.

I am very anxious to hear how you have been doing—and no wonder, since I am so much indebted to you in spiritual matters as a son to his spiritual father. And since it is right for me to return the great love and goodwill which you have always had for me and shown in deeds, and since in this life I know of no way to repay even a particle of this debt except by putting you into spiritual exercises for a month with a person they will name for you, and since you yourself even promised me you would do so—I beg you by the service of God our Lord, if you have already tested and tasted these exercises, to write me about it; and if not, I beg you, by his love and by the bitter death he underwent for us, to enter into them. And if afterwards you regret that you did, then besides any penance you may wish to give me (and for which I am ready), take me for a hoaxer of spiritual persons to whom I owe everything.

Since I have written to one person for all, I have not written to you individually up till now. And so Favre will be able to give you any news about me you would like to have, and you can see it in my letter to him. For the second and the third time, and as many more times as I can, I beg you by the service of God our Lord to do what I have been saying to you—lest the Divine Majesty at the end demand of us why I did not beg this of you with all my strength, inasmuch as this is the very best thing that in this life I can think, perceive, or understand for helping a person benefit himself as well as bringing fruit, benefit, and advantage to many others; for even if you felt no need for the former, you will see how immeasurably and incomparably you will be helped with regard to the latter.

For the rest, I conclude, praying the immense clemency of God our Lord that he will bestow on us the grace to know his most holy will, and that he will bring us to fulfill it perfectly according to the talent entrusted to each, at least so he will not say to us, "You wicked servant, you knew . . . ," etc. [Luke 19:22–f.].

Venice, November 16, 1536

Entirely yours in the Lord,
IÑIGO

✠

To Juan de Verdolay

Venice, July 24, 1537

(Letter 12: XII:320–23;[17] in Spanish)

From Venice Ignatius wrote to a zealous priest friend in Spain, inviting him to join the little group of companions in Italy. He reports to him on their reception in Rome, their ordination to the priesthood, and their plans for the immediate future. Verdolay did join the Society some months after Ignatius's death, and later passed to the Carthusians.

May the grace and love of Christ our Lord be always for our favor and our help.

Since passing through those parts and writing to you about two years ago, I have had no letter from you or news until now, when Isabel Roser let me know some three months back about your health and your good and sound teaching. She also told me you had written me and wanted very much to hear from me. I am sure that in this regard I am not much in debt, for were I not so tied down here by my own choice and to matters I deem of no small importance, there is no footsoreness that would stop me from seeking you out where you are. And so, seeing the situation there and taking into account the situation here, if you were to find it for the greater service of our Lord, I greatly wish that we might meet in these parts. I expect to be here for more or less a year; what God our Lord will ordain for me after that I do not know.

And so that you may be better informed about myself and other brothers of mine and yours in Christ our Lord, and to satisfy your wish to know, I thought I would write you this letter at some length, being sure that it will please you to have accurate news.

---

[17] This is the original of the letter, replacing the copy reproduced in I:118–23.

In mid-January nine friends of mine in the Lord arrived here from Paris—all masters of arts and well versed in theology, four of them Spaniards, two Frenchmen, two from Savoy, and one from Portugal, all passing through numerous outrages of war and long travels on foot in the worst of the winter. They took up quarters in two hospitals, dividing up so as to serve the sick poor in the lowliest offices and those most contrary to the flesh. After two months spent in this exercise, they went to Rome, along with some others who followed them with the same resolves, to spend Holy Week there. Finding themselves in poverty, without money or favor from anyone by way of letters or anything else, trusting and hoping only in the Lord for whose sake they had come, they found—and without any trouble—far more than they looked for; namely, they talked with the Pope, and after their arrival a number of cardinals, bishops, and doctors disputed with them. One of the disputants was Doctor Ortiz, who has been extremely favorable to them, as have other distinguished scholars.[18] The result was that the Pope, together with all the hearers, was so pleased that he at once began granting them all possible favor. First, he granted them permission to go to Jerusalem, giving them his blessing once and again and urging them to persevere in their resolutions. Second, he gave them an alms of about sixty ducats; moreover, between the cardinals and other persons who were there, they gave them more than a hundred and fifty ducats, so that they brought two hundred and sixty ducats here in bills of exchange. Third, he granted the priests among them faculties to hear confessions and absolve from all cases reserved to bishops. Fourth, he gave to those who were not priests authorizations or dimissory letters, with no mention of title of patrimony or benefice, allowing them to be ordained priests by any bishop on three feast days or Sundays. And so on their arrival here in Venice, on the feast of St. John the Baptist, we completed receiving all the orders, including the priesthood. Seven of us were ordained; for this we found every imaginable favor and goodwill— so much so that we had our own choice whether to be ordained under title of voluntary poverty, sufficient learning, or both. We chose under title of both, and made a vow of perpetual poverty in the hands of the papal legate here, not constrained by him but moved by our own will. For this priestly ordination they gave us two bishops, each of whom wanted to ordain us; and we had some trouble in satisfying the one, since we could not be ordained by both. After we had thus completed all this, both in Rome and in Venice, and all gratuitously, without carry-

---

[18] Pedro Ortiz was Charles V's envoy in Rome.

ing any money, the same legate gave us full permission to preach, teach, and interpret Scripture in public and in private throughout the dominion of Venice, as well as to hear confessions and absolve from cases reserved to bishops, archbishops, and patriarchs.

I have mentioned all this in order to comply with what I said above, and also to show our increased responsibility and confusion if we were not to do all we can for ourselves when God our Lord does so much for us, since the things and means that we desired seem to fall into our hands without our asking or knowing it. May the divine Goodness fill us with his grace, that we may not bury in the ground the favors and graces which he continually gives us and which we trust he will always give so long as we are not wanting. Therefore, I beg of you for the sake of the service and reverence of his Divine Majesty to pray earnestly for us, and to ask this of the men and women who are devoted to you; for you see how great is our need, in that whoever receives more becomes more of a debtor.

This year, despite all their waiting for a passage to Jerusalem, there was no ship at all, nor is there one now, because of this fleet being put out by the Turks. So we have agreed that the bills of exchange which they brought for the two hundred and sixty ducats should be sent to Rome and the money remain in the hands of those who received the alms for them, since we do not want to use this money except for the proposed voyage, and also so that no one will think that we hunger and thirst after the things which the world dies for. Once this remittance has been made—for it has already been sent—and this letter written, they will leave here in pairs the next day to do whatever work each one may be able to obtain grace for from our Lord, for whose sake they go. Thus they will spread out over this part of Italy until next year to see if they can go to Jerusalem; and if God our Lord wills that they not go, they will wait no longer but will go ahead with what they have begun. Here a number of companions have wanted to join us, persons not without sufficient learning; and we find ourselves having to refuse them rather than grow, for fear of failures.

I conclude, praying God our Lord, through his infinite and sovereign goodness, to give us his abundant grace, so that we may know his most holy will and entirely fulfill it.

From Venice, July 24, 1537

Poor in goodness,
YÑIGO

I afterwards received a letter from you; and, as our Lord is to judge me, I believe and feel that if you have much to do there, you will have more here, and a way for serving the Lord more than you desire. So see that we meet soon.

✠

To Pietro Contarini

Vicenza, August 1537

(Letter 13: I:123–26; in Latin and Italian)

Pietro Contarini was a noble Venetian who later became bishop of Paphos, on the isle of Cyprus, a see he subsequently resigned. Urging detachment from worldly goods, Ignatius writes him from Vicenza, where he had gone with Laínez and Favre after their ordination to the priesthood in 1537.

Having written to Martín Sonorza at some length about our affairs and there touched on some points pertaining to Your Lordship, I will be quite brief here, less because there is need to write you than so that we will not be thought to have forgotten you.

So far, by God's goodness, we are still in good health and experience daily more and more the truth of "having nothing yet possessing all things" [2 Cor. 6:10]—that is to say, all the things that the Lord promised he would give in addition to persons who seek first the kingdom of God and his justice [Matt. 6:33]. Now if everything will be added to them who *first* seek the kingdom of God and his justice, can anything be lacking to those who seek *only* the justice of the kingdom and his kingdom—those whose blessing is not so much the dew of heaven and the fatness of the earth [Gen. 27:28] but rather the dew of heaven alone? I mean persons who are not divided; I mean persons who keep both their eyes fixed on heaven. May he grant us this who, though rich with all things, stripped himself of all things for our furnishing; who, although in the glory of such power, knowledge, and goodness, subjected himself to the power, judgment, and will of paltry man. But enough of this. It applies mainly to persons whom Christ may keep in a different degree; for yourself it is more appropriate to take care that what you possess does not possess you, that no temporal things possess you, and that you render everything back to him from whom you received everything. A person who cannot be occupied exclusively with the one thing necessary can do the next best thing, namely, properly order the many things about which he is concerned and anxious. But I stray too far from my original topic—back to ourselves.

Near Vicenza, a mile from the Santa Croce gate, we found a monastic site called San Pietro in Varnello, where no one lives. So the friars of Santa Maria delle Grazie are willing for us to stay there as long as we want. We are doing so and will remain here for several months, God permitting.

And thus we shall have no pretext for not being good and perfect, for God on his part never fails. So pray to the Lord with us yourself that he will give to all of us the grace to fulfill his holy will, which is the sanctification of all. And farewell in Christ Jesus our Lord; may he guide us all in the way of peace, which is in him alone.

Regarding Signor Gaspare, I earnestly implore that if any business of his that might have been accomplished through you is still unfinished, you will take steps to ensure he has no grounds for saying or even thinking that we are the cause of his being delayed in Venice.[19]

Your brother in the Lord,

+IGNATIUS+

✠

To Diego de Gouvea, from Pierre Favre, by commission

Rome, November 23, 1538

(Letter 16: I:132–34; in Latin)

Diego de Gouvea, principal of the college of Sainte-Barbe in Paris during Ignatius's stay there, had suggested to his king, John III of Portugal, that he apply to Ignatius and his companions for missionaries to the Portuguese Indies. Writing on behalf of the group, Favre explains why they cannot comply: they have committed themselves to go wherever the pope decides.

May the grace and peace of our Lord Jesus Christ be with us all.

A few days ago your messenger arrived with a letter from you. From him we received news of you, and from your letter we learned of your kind remembrance of us as well as of the longing with which you thirst for the salvation of the souls whitening for the harvest in your own Indies. If only we could satisfy you—and indeed our own souls as

---

[19] Probably Gaspare de' Dotti, vicar of the papal legate in Venice and later a member of the Society of Jesus.

well, since we are zealous for the same things as you. However, at present much stands in the way of our satisfying the desires of numerous others, let alone yourself. You will understand this from the following: all of us who are mutually bound in this Society have given ourselves to the Supreme Pontiff inasmuch as he is lord of the universal harvest of Christ. Now in this offering we signified to him that we are ready for whatever he may decide for us in Christ. Thus, if he sends us where you are calling us, we will be delighted to go. Our reason for subjecting ourselves to his judgment and will in this way was that we know he possesses a better knowledge of what will be good for universal Christianity.

There have not been lacking persons who for some time have been striving to have us sent to the Indians daily being acquired for the Emperor by the Spanish. Approaches on behalf of this have been made particularly to a Spanish bishop and to the Emperor's legate. But they have learned that it is not the Supreme Pontiff's intention that we leave here, since the harvest is abundant at Rome as well. We are certainly not deterred by the distances or by the labor involved in learning languages, if only what most pleases Christ be accomplished. Pray to him for us, therefore, that he make us his ministers in the word of life. For though "we are not sufficient to think anything of ourselves as of ourselves" [2 Cor. 3:5], we nevertheless trust in his abundance and riches.

You will find plenty of news about us and our affairs in the letter which we have written to our very special friend and brother in Christ, the Spaniard Diego de Cáceres, who will show it to you. There you will see what trials for Christ we have had to undergo at Rome and how we have come through them unscathed. Even at Rome there are not wanting those to whom the light of the Church's truth and life is hateful. Be vigilant, therefore, you and those with you; strive henceforth to teach the Christian people by the example of your living just as earnestly as you have hitherto exerted yourself in defending the Church's faith and doctrine. For how can we believe that our all-good God will keep us in the truth of our holy faith if we flee from goodness itself? It is to be feared that the main cause of wrong doctrine is wrong living, and that unless the latter is corrected, the former will not be eliminated.

It only remains—to bring this letter to a close—that we beg you to graciously remember us to our revered teachers, Barthélemy, Cornet, Picart, Adam, Wauchope, Laurency, Benoît, and all the others, who are

willing to be called our teachers and for us to be called their pupils and
sons in Christ Jesus. In him we wish you health.

Rome, November 23, 1538

> Yours in the Lord,
>
> PETRUS FABER and his other companions and brothers

✠

To Pietro Contarini

Rome, December 2, 1538
(Letter 17: I:134–36; in Latin)

*Ignatius thanks the noble Venetian for his intercession with his relative, Cardinal
Gaspare Contarini, in the matter of the Jesuits' defamation suit in Rome.*

May the grace and peace of our Lord Jesus Christ be with us all.

We received your last letter to us, together with the letter of
recommendation you sent in our behalf to His Most Reverend Lordship
[Gaspare] Contarini; for both we thank your kindness and goodness. In
the first we saw the remembrance you have of us; in the other we experienced your good offices.

Your most reverend kinsman no sooner read your letter than he
sent one of his servants to the governor urging him to resolve our case,
which lay before him. A few days later the whole matter was fully ended, and in the way which we thought would be most to God's honor
and the good of many souls: a verdict was given declaring that upon
diligent inquiry nothing suspicious had been found either in our life or
our teaching. The sentence just as it stands, if you are interested in
seeing it, is already in the hands of the imperial ambassador there; it
was sent to him by some friends of ours. Of course, we know that this
verdict will not ensure that no one ever reviles us again, nor did we ever
seek as much. We only wanted to protect our honor, sound teaching,
and spotless life. With God's favor, we shall never worry if they call us
ignorant, uncultured, ill-spoken—or even wicked, fraudulent, and unreli-
able. But we were aggrieved to see the doctrine we preach accused of
unsoundness and the path we follow considered evil, for neither of them
was our own: they were Christ's and his Church's. But enough of this.

All those whom you said in your letter you wished us to greet in
your name now return your greetings through me. All are in good
health; may they be strong and right in spirit also, as we trust through

Jesus Christ our Lord, who is our peace, our repose, our fullness and consolation, and altogether the entire good for which we were made and regenerated, and for which we have been preserved thus far in this world.

But now farewell in him, and continue remembering us as you do.

Rome, December 2, 1538

Yours in the Lord,
IGNATIUS

✠

To Isabel Roser

Rome, December 19, 1538
(Letter 18: I:137–44; in Spanish)

Ignatius gives a full account of the storm of calumny raised against him in Rome and of the legal measures he took to quell it.

May the grace and love of Christ our Lord be always for our favor and help.

I can well believe that you are very concerned and no less surprised that I have not written you often, as I would wish and wanted to do. For if I were to forget what I owe to our Lord through your hands, with such sincere love and inclination, I believe that his Divine Majesty would not be mindful of me; for you have always been so active on my behalf out of love and reverence for him

The reason, then, for my delay in writing was that we were waiting from day to day and from month to month for the conclusion of an affair of ours so that we could inform you more fully about how we are doing here. Here at last is my report.

For eight full months we experienced the severest opposition or persecution that we have ever experienced in this life. I do not mean that they have molested us physically or called us into court or in any other way; but by spreading rumor among the people and calling us unheard-of names, they were making us suspect and hateful to the people, causing great scandal, so that we were forced to present ourselves before the legate and governor of the city (for the Pope had then gone to Nice) on account of the great scandal caused among many people. We began naming and summoning some who were behaving outrageously against us, so that they might declare before our superiors the evils they found in our life and teaching. And to make the affair easier to understand by going back to the beginning, I will give you some account of it.

It is more than a year since three of us belonging to the Society arrived here in Rome, as I remember writing to you. Two began at once to teach free of charge in the Sapienza College, the one positive and the other scholastic theology, and this by command of the Pope. I devoted myself entirely to giving and communicating spiritual exercises to others, both in and outside Rome. We agreed upon this in order to get some learned or distinguished men for our cause—or, better said, for the cause, honor, and glory of God our Lord, since our own is nought else but the praise and service of his Divine Majesty—in the hope that we would meet with less opposition among worldly people and thereafter be able to preach his most holy word more freely; for we could smell how barren the earth was of good fruit and how abounding in bad.

Once we had, through the action of God our Lord, gained some to our favor and opinion by means of these exercises—persons of high learning and reputation—we decided, upon completion of four months from our arrival, to gather together all those of the Society in this city. As they began arriving, we took steps to obtain permission to preach, to exhort, and to hear confessions; this was granted us very fully by the legate, even though in the meantime many evil reports concerning us were being given to his vicar to prevent the issuance of the permission. After receiving it, four or five of us began to preach on feast days and Sundays in various churches and to teach boys the commandments, the mortal sins, etc. in other churches; all the while we continued the two classes in the Sapienza as well as the confessions elsewhere. The others all preached in Italian, only I in Spanish. There was quite a large gathering of people for all the sermons, incomparably more than we thought there would be, for three reasons. First, because the time was unusual: we began right after Easter when the other preachers for Lent and the great feasts were ending; in this region preaching is customary only in Lent and Advent. Second, because it is usual that once the austerities and sermons of Lent are over, many, on account of our sins, are inclined more to leisure and worldly pleasures than to other similar or new devotions. Third, because, while we have no claim to be furnished with elegance or grace, we are nevertheless convinced on the basis of many experiences that our Lord through his infinite and supreme goodness does not forget us, and that through us, lowly and of no account as we are, he helps and favors many others.

And so we presented ourselves; and when two of them were summoned and called, and one of them found himself before the judges in a position quite the opposite of what he expected, the others whom we named to be summoned were so fearful that, not wishing or daring to appear, they got a writ so that we would have to continue the case before different judges. As they were persons, one with an income of a thousand ducats and another of six hundred, and one of even greater importance, all of them curial officials and men of affairs, they raised such a stir among cardinals and many other persons of importance in the curia that they kept us busy for a long time with this struggle. At last the two most important among them, having been summoned, appeared before the legate and the governor and declared that they had heard our sermons and lectures, etc. and had found everything, both in our teaching and in our lives, in entire justification of us. With that the legate and the governor, who held us in very great esteem, wanted to leave the matter in silence as regards both these persons and others. We kept repeatedly asking, as we deemed was right, that whatever was evil or good in our teaching be set forth in writing so that the scandal given to the people might be lifted; but we were never able to obtain this, either through justice or through law. From this time on, with the fear they had of justice, the same things as before were no longer being said against us, at least not in public.

As we were unable to persuade them to render a sentence or declaration in our case, a friend of ours spoke to the Pope after his return from Nice, petitioning him to give a declaration in the case. Although the Pope granted it, nothing happened; so two members of our Society also spoke to him. As he then left Rome for a castle outside the city, I went there and talked with His Holiness alone in his room for an entire hour. Speaking to him there at length about our plans and intentions, I clearly related to him all the times when trials had been held against me in Spain and in Paris, and also the times when I had been imprisoned in Alcalá and Salamanca. I did this so that no one would be able to tell him more than I did, and so that he would be more inclined to make an inquiry concerning us, so that one way or another a sentence or declaration would be rendered about our teaching. Finally, since in order for us to teach and exhort, it was essential to be in good repute not only before God our Lord but also before the people, and not to be suspect in our teaching and habits, I petitioned His Holiness in the name of all of us to give orders for a remedy, that is, for our teaching and behavior to be investigated and examined by any ordinary judge whom His Holiness might commission: if they found evil, we wanted to be corrected and punished; if good, we wanted His Holiness to favor us. The Pope, while he had reason for suspicion from what I told him, took it very well, praising our abilities and the good use to which we put them. Then, after speaking to us for a while and exhorting us (indeed with the words of a true and righteous shepherd), he gave strict orders that the governor, who is a bishop and the chief justice of this city both in ecclesiastical and in secular affairs, should inquire immediately into our case. He carried out a new trial and did so with diligence; moreover, the Pope, frequently speaking publicly in our favor and before our Society when he came to Rome (for every two weeks the fathers regularly go to hold a disputation during His Holiness's meal), has dispelled much of our tempest. The weather improves daily, so that in my judgment things are going very much as we wish, for the service and glory of God our Lord. We are now besieged by certain prelates and others who would like to see us bear fruit in their lands, through the action of God our Lord. We are remaining quiet, to await a greater opportunity.

Now it has pleased God our Lord that our case has been judged and settled. Concerning this, something not altogether unremarkable took place here; namely, that as it had been said of us or published here that we were fugitives from many countries, and especially from Paris, Spain, and Venice, at the very time that the sentence or declaration was to be given concerning us, there happened to have recently arrived here in Rome the regent Figueroa, who arrested me once in Alcalá and twice carried out proceedings against me; the vicar-general of the legate to Venice, who also instituted proceedings against me after we began to preach in the signory of Venice; Dr. Ory, who also instituted proceedings against me in Paris; and the Bishop of Vicenza, where three or four of us preached for a short time. And so all of them gave testimony about us. The cities of Siena, Bologna, and Ferrara also sent their official testimonies here, and the Duke of Ferrara, besides sending testimony, took the affair very much to heart because of the dishonor done in our persons to God our Lord. He several times wrote to his ambassador and to our Society, making the case his own; for he had seen the fruit borne in his city and also in the other cities where we had been active—for in this city we barely succeeded in preserving ourselves and persevering. And for this we give thanks to God our Lord, because from the time we began until the present moment, we have never failed to give two or three sermons on every feast day and also two lectures every day; some were occupied with confessions and others with the Spiritual Exercises. Now that the sentence has been given, we hope to increase the sermons and also our teaching of children; and while the soil may be sterile and barren and the opposition we have encountered strong, we cannot say in truth that we have lacked for things to do or that God our Lord has not effected more than our own knowledge and understanding could achieve.

I do not go into details, so as not to run on too much. In general, God our Lord has made us very happy. I will only say that there are four or five who are determined to enter our Society and have already persevered for many days and months in that determination. We do not dare to admit them yet, because one of the points among others charged against us was that we were receiving people and forming a congregation or religious community without apostolic authority. But now, although we are not yet united in our way of proceeding, we are all united in a determination to come to agreement for the future. We hope that God our Lord will soon dispose this in such a way that he may be better served and praised in all.

Since you have heard how our affairs stand, I beg you, for the love and reverence of God our Lord, [to pray] that we be very patient, desiring that he will work in us whatever may be to his greater glory and praise; for certainly the situation now is of great importance and weight. I will inform you more often of what is happening; and I tell you without doubt that if I forget you, I expect to be forgotten by my Creator and Lord. For this reason, I am not so much concerned to discharge my duty or return thanks in words; but you may be certain of this, that besides the fact that all that you have done for me out of love and reverence for him lives before God our Lord, you will share fully all the days of my life in whatever his Divine Majesty may be pleased to work through me and make meritorious by his divine grace, just as you have always aided and so especially favored me in his divine service and praise.

I ask to be very much remembered and commended to all the persons known to you and me who are wholesome and devout in holy conversation and joined together in Christ our Lord.

I conclude, asking God our Lord through his infinite and supreme goodness to deign to give his abundant grace to us, so that we may know his most holy will and entirely fulfill it.

Rome, December 19, 1538

Poor in goodness,

IÑIGO

While this was being written, the Pope has ordered that provision be made through the governor that an ordinance be given to the city for bringing together the schools for boys, so that we might instruct them in Christian doctrine, as we began to do earlier. May it please God our Lord, since it is his affair, to deign to give us strength for his greater service and praise. I am sending the actual declaration that was given here concerning us to the archdeacon Cassador (because it is in Latin), who will communicate it to you.

✠

To Martín García and Beltrán de Loyola

Rome, February 2, 1539

(Letter 19: I:145–47; in Spanish)

When this letter was written, Martín García, Ignatius's elder brother and head of the house of Loyola, had already died and been succeeded by his son Beltrán. Ignatius transmits a copy of the verdict passed in Rome declaring him innocent of heresy, and in a postscript reports the celebration of his first Mass.

May the grace and love of Christ our Lord be always for our favor and our help.

Inasmuch as I sent you a letter some days ago with Rozas and Magdalena de Sendo, I will be brief. Since Rozas had so many things to do for us and would be delayed for so long on the road, it occurred to me that this letter might perhaps reach your house by the time they get there. I am therefore sending along with this letter the sentence or verdict that was passed on us here for you to give him in case he wishes to take it along, so that because of his association with us there may be no lessening of his own and the others' good wishes in our Lord, who is to be our eternal judge. Blessed are those who in this life prepare themselves to be judged and saved by his Divine Majesty—for whose love and reverence I beg that you will not delay in making earnest efforts to reform your own consciences, so that your souls will be secure at the hour of our strict and unexpected need. Sending my greetings and best wishes to everyone, I would like this letter to be taken as for themselves by all who desire to have news of us and profit to their own consciences.

I close, asking God our Lord by his infinite and supreme goodness to grant all of us his abundant grace, so that we may know his most holy will and entirely fulfill it.

Rome, February 2, 1539

Bachelor Araoz is remaining here; if God our Lord grants me what I desire for him, he will be rich in this life and in the next.[20] Last Christmas Day, in the church of St. Mary Major, in the chapel where is the crib in which the child Jesus was laid, with his help and grace I said my first Mass.

I earnestly desire and beg of you by the love and reverence of his Divine Majesty, that we remember each other in our devotions, each of us acting as if he were at the end and term of his days and about to give a full and strict accounting of his life.

Poor in goodness,

IGNIGO

✠

To Magdalena de Araoz

Rome, September 24, 1539

(Letter 21: I:151f.; in Spanish)

Ignatius sends his sister-in-law condolences on the death of her husband, Ignatius's brother, Martín García de Oñaz y Loyola, and commends the Society to her and to her son Beltrán, the new head of the house of Loyola.

May the grace and love of Christ our Lord be always for our favor and our help.

Upon learning that the good pleasure of God our Lord had been fulfilled by removing from these present toils the companion he gave you for a certain time in this life, I immediately did the best thing I could do for anyone: I said Mass for his soul at an altar where every time Mass is celebrated a soul is delivered from purgatory. We ought not to weep while he is rejoicing or grieve while he is glad. Instead, we should look to ourselves—for we will come to the same point as he—

---

[20] Antonio Araoz was a nephew of Magdalena Araoz, wife of Ignatius's elder brother, Martín García de Oñaz. He was born in 1515. After his studies in Salamanca he went to Rome in 1538. He entered the Society of Jesus and was later the first provincial of Spain. He died in Madrid in 1573.

and live in such a way during this life that we may live forever in the other. Of course, I am quite certain that you are fully convinced of this, since I have always known you to be a person who fears God our Lord.

It now remains for me to ask you, for the service of God our Lord, to assist us with your actions and prayers in an enterprise which we have undertaken for God's glory, and which—worthless as we are—we have carried forward. Regarding this I refer you to my letter to your son Beltrán, who I hope will in all things be guided by you, although I am confident that he who at another time knew how to squander both what he had and what he did not have will now be generous—if he is at all able—in a matter as religious, righteous, and holy as this.

I conclude, praying his Divine Majesty to dispose of us and of everyone in the way we may best serve him in all things and in all things give thanks forever and ever.

Rome, September 24, 1539

Poor in goodness,

IÑIGO

✠

To Beltrán de Loyola

Rome, September [24?], 1539
(Letter 20: I:148–51; in Spanish)

Ignatius writes to his nephew Beltrán, now head of the house of Loyola, urging him to take up the reform of the local clergy and recommending that he send his brother Millán to Paris for studies. He also reports on the establishment of the new Society of Jesus and urges his nephew to take it under his active patronage.

May the grace and love of Christ our Lord be always for our favor and our help.

By his love and reverence I beg you always so to act that my hopes may not prove vain, since it has pleased God our Lord that you should inherit your father's place (may he be in glory) in my confidence. And it is to be trusted in God our Lord that he has placed and preserved you there until now so that you might settle and reform the clergy of your town above all, and in so doing show them true love—far different from a love that is carnal and destructive. I beg you once more for the love and reverence of God our Lord to remember how often we talked about this and to bend all your efforts to it.[21] Just as our forebears strove to signalize themselves in other matters (and please God they were not useless ones), you ought to wish to signalize yourself in what will last forever, and not expend efforts on things we will later have to regret. Since I am confident that my confidence in our Lord and in you as his instrument will not be disappointed, I say no more on this head.

I have learned here of your brother Millán's good intelligence and of his desire to study. I would like you to give this a great deal of attention and thought. If my opinion is worth anything, the only place where I would send him is to Paris: you will have him accomplish more there in a few years than at another university in many. Moreover, it is the country where students best maintain decency and virtue. So far as my personal desire for his greater progress is concerned, this is the route I would want him to take. Please tell his mother the same. In case Araoz is not there, there will be other persons of authority and exemplary life who will take good care of him.[22]

As to our affairs here, you will know that, regarding the course which we were able—in repeated deliberations—to conclude upon in our own consciences and in our Lord as the most appropriate and needful to us for laying a firm foundation and genuine roots to build upon later, it has pleased God our Lord—who, we are confident, in his customary measureless grace exercises a special providence over us and over our affairs (or rather his own affairs, since we do not pursue our own in this life)—in his infinite and sovereign goodness to intervene with his own holy hand. He has thus brought it about that, in the face of great adversity, opposition, and divergence of opinions, the Vicar of Christ our Lord has approved and confirmed our whole manner of proceeding, with an organized form of life and full authorization to draw up for ourselves constitutions as we deem best for our manner of living. A fuller report of all this and of everything else can be had from Antonio de Araoz, the bearer of this letter, just as if I were there in person; for we have no less regard for him than for any of us in the Society itself. He has spent about ten months in our house here and is now being sent by us to Spain to attend to business of his own and ours, and after his trip to return to us here. And so, besides giving him full credence, I ask you for

---

[21] These conversations occurred during the three months of the summer of 1535 which Ignatius spent in Azpeitia.

[22] Millán studied in Salamanca, which he left for Rome in 1541. There he was admitted to the Society and was sent to Paris in 1542 by St. Ignatius to continue his studies.

the love of God our Lord to show him the face you always show towards the servants of the sovereign Majesty, or would to me if I were there myself. And so, with him as a living letter, I will write no more about this.

Please give our cordial greetings to everyone attached to you or to ourselves, with a request for their prayers—now more than ever, since so difficult a task has been laid upon us, for the carrying forward of which we have no confidence in our own strength;[23] rather, relying wholly on the supreme power and goodness of God as well as upon your prayers and those of all who love us in his Divine Majesty, we trust that we will never shrink from any toil in the rightful service owed to him.

I close, asking his Divine Majesty to dispose of us and of everyone in the way we may best serve and glorify him in all things for ever and ever.

Rome, September 2, 1539

I consider in our Lord that this undertaking, which I will be explaining further, ought to be more specially your own, for various reasons which I know you will see to be correct the more you examine and think about them. And since I recall how you urged me during my stay with you there that I should carefully let you know about the Society that I was looking forward to, I am also convinced that God our Lord looked forward to your own taking an outstanding role in it, so as to leave behind a different and better memory than did the others of our family. To come to the point: despite my unworthiness I have managed, with God's grace, to lay a solid foundation for this Society of Jesus, which is the title we have given it and which the Pope has approved; and so I am rightly bound to urge you, and urge you strongly, to build and construct upon this foundation, so that you will have no less merit in the buildings than I in the foundation—and all by the hand of God our Lord. I mean, of course, when a suitable occasion arises or presents itself to you, one that you judge right and holy, and when his Divine Majesty grants you his most holy grace for this.

I am writing in the same vein to Doña María de Vicuña, since I think she may be able to help you in this matter.[24] Please share this letter with my sister Doña Magdalena and with the Lord of Ozaeta,

---

[23] The care of the newly born Society of Jesus.
[24] She was a cousin of Ignatius.

since in my letter to them I refer them to yours. If you know anyone else willing to contribute, it will be for the Lord's sake, who knows well how to repay and compensate them. Please greet and commend me to the lady of the house, who should take this letter as addressed to herself.[25]

Poor in goodness,

YÑIGO

✠

To Juan Laínez, from Alfonso Salmerón, by commission

Rome, September 25, 1539
(Letter 22: I:153–55; in Spanish)

Salmerón had been a close friend of Laínez from their student days at Alcalá, and was known to Laínez's family. Hence, it was he who, on behalf of the Society, wrote to Laínez's father this letter of recommendation for Antonio de Araoz. In his life of Laínez, Pedro de Ribadeneira gives a particular reason for writing about Laínez to his family. One of his brothers, Mark, was so concerned that Laínez may have fallen among heretics that he later went to Rome himself to see his brother. There he was so impressed that he joined the companions. He died in 1541, seemingly the first to die in the Society after it was confirmed in 1540.

May the grace and peace of Christ our Lord be always for our favor and our help.

It may seem unusual for Your Worship to receive a letter from me after so many years. However, since no occasion or reason for it had arisen, any surprise should give way—and were I not to write now that there is one, you would have reason for it. I believe Your Worship already knows that he who joined together Master Laínez and me in your house there in Almazán has preserved us in his constant love, both in studies and in the same profession and manner of living, and now has united and joined us more inseparably than ever. Hence, I consider all his affairs as my own, and his business as mine.

Accordingly, when the Cardinal of Sant'Angelo was sent by the Pope as his legate to the territories of Parma and Piacenza, and when the cardinal insistently petitioned the Pope that two of our Society should accompany him to preach and dispute with certain heretics and Lutherans, and the Pope granted this and commanded us to do so, we

---

[25] Magdalena de Araoz.

judged unanimously that one of those to go should be Master Laínez.[26] He, together with another of the Society, left with the cardinal nearly three months ago. We get weekly letters from them, reporting (thanks be to his Divine Majesty) that they are well, preaching, and producing great benefit.

Meanwhile I received from Your Worship two letters addressed to him, dated July 17, in response to a very long letter which he had written first; I carefully forwarded both of them to him. I believe he has received them by now, and I too wrote him to send me his reply. So I am charged with this matter, and with replying in his name in case he cannot.

Now, with the occasion offered by the departure of the bearer of this letter, named Antonio de Araoz—whom we hold in no less account than those of us here who form a single Society, because he has been in our house for about ten months and now is being sent there by us on business of his own and ours, and will return to us after completing his journey—with the occasion of this bearer, as I said, I thought I would write you these lines in the name of the whole Society and of Master Laínez, to give Your Worship and all those of your house the pleasure of receiving full and authentic news both of Master Laínez and of his whole Society. This is Araoz's sole purpose in going to Almazán, and he will also be able to inform you quite fully about how the Pontiff, the vicar of Christ our Lord, despite so many oppositions, contradictions, and divergent judgments, has approved and confirmed our entire manner of proceeding in living in an organized way, and given us full permission to have constitutions of our own as we shall deem best for our manner of living. In short, he will be able to provide detailed information about everything that has happened to us—and in particular to Master Laínez—here in Rome and elsewhere.

Hence, in addition to giving him full credit, we request you all, for the love of God our Lord, to show him the face that is right for a servant of his Divine Majesty, just as you would to Master Laínez if he were there. Since his journey is long and we trust he will not suffer any want, we therefore also request that he be given some alms, up to five or six ducats. And since he will be a living letter with all that I cannot set down on paper, I will go on no longer, referring you to the bearer for everything else.

---

[26] The Cardinal of Sant'Angelo was Ennio Filonardi.

And so I conclude, asking his Divine Majesty to dispose of us and of everyone in the way that we may best serve and praise him in all things and in all things give him glory for ever and ever. Amen.

Rome, September 25, 1539

In the name of the whole Society of Jesus,
ALONSO DE SALMERÓN

✠

To Antonio de Araoz

Rome, late 1539 or early 1540

(Letter 22a: XII:215f [Appendix 1, no 1]; in Spanish)

The "aunt" referred to in this fragment is probably Magdalena de Araoz, Ignatius's older sister-in-law and Araoz's aunt.

If he who gave life to my aunt has taken it from her, may he be blessed in all things. For he is no less holy, no less good or merciful towards us, no less worthy of praise and thanks, when he wounds us than when he caresses us and does us favors; when he sends sickness and death than when he gives health and life—above all because both the first and the second of these things should be loved only to the extent that they are pleasing to his most wise and righteous will. . . .

✠

To Beltrán de Loyola

Rome, March 20, 1540

(Letter 23: I:155f.; in Spanish)

A letter of recommendation to Ignatius's nephew on behalf of Francis Xavier, traveling to Portugal en route to India in the company of Pedro Mascarenhas, ambassador of the King of Portugal.

May our Lord be always for our favor and our help.

Owing to the extreme pressure we are suddenly under to send some of our men to the Indies, some to Ireland, and others to different parts of Italy, I do not have time to write as fully as I would like. Master Francis Xavier of Navarre, son of the Lord of Xavier and a member of our Society, is the bearer of this letter. He is going at the command of the Pope and the request of the King of Portugal, in addition to two other men traveling by sea for the same king. Master Francis will give you full details and will tell you about everything in my name, as though I were present in person.

You should know that the ambassador of the King of Portugal, with whom Master Francis is traveling, is in a very great way entirely our friend and one to whom we are in a great way indebted, and who for the service of God our Lord is disposed to do us many favors with his king and with all the persons he can. And so I beg you for the service of God our Lord to show him all the courtesy and hospitality you can. If Araoz is there with you, he should consider this letter as written to him; and thus Master Francis will be given the same credit on my behalf that would be given to me. I ask you to remember me very especially to the lady of the house and the entire household.

May our Lord be always for our favor and our help.

Rome, March 20, 1540

Poor in goodness,

INIGO

☩

To the Townspeople of Azpeitia

Rome, August–September 1540

(Letter 26: I:161–65; in Spanish)

Five years earlier, Ignatius had spent several months in apostolic ministry to the people of his hometown. In this letter he recalls his stay with them, urges them to peacefulness, and reminds them to keep up the good practices which he had inaugurated among them. He then urges them to enroll in a newly established confraternity of the Blessed Sacrament, adding a strong plea for more frequent Communion.

May the sovereign grace and love of Christ our Lord be always for our favor and help.

His Divine Majesty well knows how much and how often he has given me the intense wish and very strong desire to render every satisfaction in his divine goodness and every spiritual service, however slight, to all the men and women sprung from the same land from which God, in his accustomed mercy, gave me my beginning and natural being, without my ever meriting it or ever being able to requite him. These desires, received from the universal Lord and Creator more than from any creature, led me five years ago, when my health was not very good, from Paris to your town, where he who brought me there, with his accustomed divine mercy, gave me strength to do a little work, as you saw. What I failed to do must be blamed on my own faults, which are still with me.

And now once more, since my desires remain what they were, namely, that your souls should be quiet and peaceful in this life with the true peace of our Lord and not that of the world—for the world has many princes both great and small who make outward truces and peaces while interior peace never enters their souls, but instead animosities, envy, and many other evil desires against the very persons with whom they have made outward peace, whereas peace in our Lord, being interior, brings with it all the other gifts and graces essential for salvation and eternal life; for this peace brings one to love one's neighbor for the love of one's Creator and Lord and, by loving in this way, to keep all the commandments of the law, as St. Paul says, "Whoever loves his neighbor has fulfilled the law" [Rom. 13:8], that is to say, has fulfilled the entire law because he loves his Creator and Lord and his neighbor for his Lord's sake—in view of all this, I began thinking whether there might not be some other way in which, though because I am absent, I cannot do so in person, I might in some way put my desires into effect. And now, on the occasion of a great work brought about by our Lord through a Dominican friar, a great friend of ours whom we have known for many years, for fostering honor and devotion towards the Blessed Sacrament, I decided to console and visit your souls in the Holy Spirit by means of this bull, which is being brought by the bachelor [Antonio Araoz] together with the other indulgences listed in the bull, which are so many and precious that I am incapable of prizing or extolling them. I can only urge and beseech you all, for the love and reverence of God our Lord, to prize and promote it as much as you are able and is possible, by having it preached to the assembled people, by holding a procession, or by taking other measures more suited for moving the people to devotion.

I remember well the time when I stayed with you, and the people's resolves and determination after they had laid down holy and praiseworthy ordinances—namely, that the bells should be rung for those who might be in mortal sin; that there should be no indigent beggars, but that they should all be given help; that there should be no card playing or sellers and buyers of cards; and that the abuse should be eliminated by which women wore the [married woman's] headdress without warrant and to the offense of God our Lord. I recall that the observance of these holy ordinances was begun and maintained all the time that I was with you, with no little grace and visitation of God which brought you to do these holy works. Subsequently, I have had no word as to your constancy or slackness in keeping up works so rightful and so pleasing to the infinite and supreme Goodness. Now, however, whether you have kept them up and gone forward or have failed and gone back to your earlier practices, I beg, beseech, and implore you, by the love and reverence of God our Lord, for your greater progress, to employ yourselves with much effort and enthusiasm in rendering great honor, support, and service to his only-begotten Son, Christ our Lord, in this great work of the Most Blessed Sacrament. In it his Divine Majesty, both as to his divinity and his humanity, is as great, entire, powerful, and infinite as he is in heaven. You can do this by adopting constitutions in the confraternity that will be formed obliging each member to monthly confession and Communion—although this should be voluntary and without any obligation under pain of sin if the person does not [comply with them]. For I am convinced and believe without any doubt that by acting and laboring in this way, you will encounter inestimable spiritual progress. Once, all persons of sufficient age, both men and women, received the Most Holy Sacrament daily. A little later, devotion began to cool somewhat and Communion became weekly. Then, after a long interval, as people grew even colder in true charity, all persons reached the point of receiving on three principal feasts of the year, it being left to each one's choice and devotion whether to receive oftener, either once every other day, once a week, or once a month. And after that we have ended up with once a year, owing to our great coldness and weakness, so that we seem to have but the name of Christians left——as you will see the whole world in large part if you are willing to look at it with a calm and holy mind. So let it be our part, by the love and spirit of this Lord and for the immense benefit of our own souls, to restore and renew in some way our forebears' holy practices; and if we cannot do so entirely, then at least in part by going to confession and receiving Communion (as I said above) once a month. And anybody who wishes to go oftener will without any doubt be acting according to our Creator and Lord, as is testified to by St. Augustine, together with all the other holy doctors, when, after saying, "I neither praise nor condemn daily Communion," he adds, "but I do urge you to communicate every Sunday."[27] And since I trust that God our Lord, in his infinite

---

[27] Gennadius, *De ecclesiasticis dogmatibus*, chap. 53 (*PL* 58:994A), ascribed at the time to St. Augustine.

goodness and his accustomed mercy, will abundantly pour his most holy grace into the minds of all the men and women among you for so rightful a service to himself and so clear and manifest an advantage to souls, I now close, begging, praying, and beseeching by the love and reverence of God our Lord that you make me always a sharer in your devotions, particularly that of the Most Holy Sacrament, just as you will always have a full share in mine, poor and unworthy as they are.

Rome, 1540

IGNATIO DE LOYOLA

✠

To Beltrán de Loyola

Rome, October 4, 1540

(Letter 27: I:165–67; in Spanish)

Ignatius congratulates his nephew on his behavior, and requests him to forward a letter.

May the sovereign grace and love of Christ our Lord be always for our favor and our help.

From Araoz I have heard of the abundant grace which his Divine Majesty imparts to you for his service, and of your excellent reputation and example in your province, for which I give ceaseless thanks to God our Lord, trusting that you will always continue to advance from good to better until you fulfill in your person what I always expected since the time I came to know you. Since I wrote you at length a few days ago when I sent the bull concerning the Blessed Sacrament, I will be brief here.

If Araoz is not there, you may open and read the letters to him for more detailed news of us.

Should Estéban de Eguía not be there in your province, I ask you for the service of God our Lord to send a special person for him with his packet, or to send his packet very securely so that he receives it with his own hands, for it is a matter of great importance for the service of God. If Estéban is no longer in this world, open the packet and take out the one inside it, which it is essential to deliver to the person it is for, a certain Rojas, who I think lives in Alava or nearby in Piedrola. At other times he is to be found in Bilbao; I think his name is Fanste de Rojas.

I wrote you in the other letters how greatly I desire to see Millán here in Rome.[28] Believing that this would be greatly for the service of God our Lord and for the honor of his relatives and friends, I repeat my request and ask you to trust me.

The lord of Ozaeta ——— *[words missing]* and all our relatives should receive this letter as addressed to them. I should like to have an answer to this and my other letter. Remember me to the lady of the house, and to the whole family of Doña María de Vicuña.

My best greetings in our Lord to any others you think would be glad to hear from me. May he in his infinite and supreme goodness be always for our favor and help.

Rome, October 4, 1540

Poor in goodness,

INIGO

✠

To Pietro Contarini

Rome, December 18, 1540, and March 7, 1541
(Letter 28: I:167–70; in Italian)

Ignatius reports to Contarini on the long-awaited issuance of the Society's bull of confirmation, Regimini militantis Ecclesiæ. *He thanks him for his own assistance and requests that he write thanking Cardinal Gaspare Contarini for his invaluable intervention in the matter.*

Most Honored Sir:

May the sovereign grace and love of Christ our Lord be always for our favor and help.

Some time ago I informed Your Lordship how our controversy has been concluded and the verdict handed down in our favor, to the praise of the Lord. Since we wanted to get our Society confirmed by the Apostolic See so that we could more sincerely and humbly serve and praise our Lord and Creator, through his grace and despite our great unworthiness, we spoke to the Pope—thereafter wholly through the mediation of the Reverend Cardinal Contarini—and fifteen months ago the Pope approved and confirmed all the chapters we requested. However, when it came to issuance of the document, there were some who disapproved,

---

[28] Beltrán's younger brother; he entered the Society.

and we met with heavy opposition. We were awaiting the issuance from week to week, and that is why I did not write Your Lordship until now. Finally, at the end of a year, on September 27, they sent us the official bull of our confirmation, issued altogether without charge, in the very form we had requested. A copy of it is enclosed with this letter.

Since, by God's grace, Your Lordship was the occasion for the Reverend Cardinal Contarini's first being concerned about us and favoring us in every matter of God's praise, and since he was wholly the agent in this matter that was so desired by us and so important for the greater service of God our Lord, we would like Your Lordship to write a letter of your own to His Reverend Lordship and thank him for the holy efforts he made and daily continues to make on our behalf. For, so very obliged to you as we are, it is our wish to be altogether your debtors, eagerly acknowledging how deeply obliged to our Lord we are, with His Reverence the Cardinal being in every way the instrument and mediator as regards His Holiness, and Your Lordship as regards His Reverend Lordship the Cardinal—so that, in whatever matters the Supreme and Divine Majesty shall deign to grace us for his own praise and glory, we might be more Your Lordship's and His Reverend Lordship's than we are our own.

From the time of my last letter, about a year ago, up to the present, God be always praised and thanked, everything has gone well and prosperously for his praise, and incomparably better than we deserve, especially being such worthless instruments. If Your Lordship would like to have detailed information from our old friend and brother in our Lord, Martín de Somoza, he will be able to show you a number of letters from our brothers spread throughout various regions and provinces at the command of His Holiness.

Since through God's grace I myself deeply desire, because of my own great need, ever to be roused and exhorted in anything pertaining to his greater praise and glory, I thought it would be the part of charity just to recall to your mind (though I do not consider it necessary), merely out of a desire to know something, whether that Marietta with whom Your Lordship and I conversed together has remained steadfast in her good desires to be a religious and proved worthy of Your Lordship's favor and help. For I am firmly convinced that such religious concerns are Your Lordship's habitual office—or rather, if I may go even farther without fear, your vocation from our Lord God and his grace dwelling in your soul, so beloved by his Divine Majesty, enabling you to be cheerfully and diligently active in every work that is for his praise.

M. Niccolò Mercante, the bearer of this letter, is a great friend and brother of ours in the Lord. He may be fully credited by you there as if I personally were present.

I end, praying God our Lord that by his infinite and supreme goodness he may give us his grace, so that we may always know his most holy will and entirely fulfill it.

Rome, December 18, 1540

Your Lordship's most obliged servant in our Lord,

IGNATIO

The person bearing this letter was held up until now by certain obstacles. In the meantime, the Reverend Cardinal Contarini has gone to Germany as legate; Your Lordship may pay your offices to him whenever you think right.

Rome, March 7, 1541

✠

Counsels of Our Blessed Father Ignatius

Undated

(XII:674–76 [Appendix 6, no. 11]; in Spanish)

Spiritual counsels, dating from the early or mid-1540s, attributed to Ignatius by his first biographer, Pedro de Ribadeneira, who wrote in his (unpublished) "Historia de la Assistencia de España," that "his sons in Alcalá used them, in those first years (as we say)." Unfortunately, the attribution is not entirely certain.

Counsels of Our Blessed Father Ignatius

[1] We will take care to preserve our hearts with great purity in the love of God, so that we love nothing but him, and desire to converse only with him and with the neighbor for his sake, and not for our own pleasure or entertainment.

[2] Do not speak unnecessarily, but only for one's own or another's upbuilding, avoiding topics which are of no benefit to the soul, such as wanting to hear news and affairs of the world; try always to speak of matters of humility and mortification of the will, not of matters which tend to provoke laughing or complaining.

[3] No one should want to be considered a clever talker, or pride himself on being polished, witty, and well-spoken; he should look at

Christ, who despised all this and chose for our sakes to be humiliated and looked down on by people rather than honored and esteemed.

[4] We should not want to see or do anything which could not be done in the presence of God and of his creatures; and so we will always keep aware in our imagination of being present before him.

[5] One should never argue with another obstinately; instead, we should patiently give our reasons with a view only to bringing out the truth and preventing our neighbor from remaining in error; it should not be to push forward our own ideas.

[6] One of the things we must firmly ground ourselves in, if we are to please our Lord, is casting from us everything which can separate us from the love of our brothers, whom we must labor to love with heartfelt charity; for supreme Truth has said, "By this they will know you are my disciples," etc. [John 12:35].

[7] If somebody does something disedifying and thinks that he will therefore be looked down on and less esteemed than before, he should not let his spirit become so downcast that he turns backward; instead, he should humble himself and ask pardon of those his bad example may have scandalized, requesting as well a penance from the superior. He should heartily thank God for letting him be cast down so that he might be known by everyone for what he is; he should not want to be held better in men's eyes than he is in God's. Seeing him, the brothers should recall that they can fall into greater frailties and should pray for their amendment.

[8] In our superiors and those who are over us, we should always contemplate the person of Christ whom they represent; we should turn to them in our doubts, holding for certain that through them God our Lord will direct us.

[9] We should not keep our temptations to ourselves, or even thoughts of ours which seem good, but should tell them to our confessors or superiors, for "Satan transforms himself into an angel of light" [2 Cor 11:14]. All that we do should be done by the opinion and advice of our spiritual fathers more than by our own; indeed, we should always be suspicious of our own.

[10] In conversation we should be well-mannered, making an effort to appear neither too gloomy and serious nor too mirthful and undisciplined; rather, as St. Paul says, "let your modesty be known to all men" [Phil. 4:5].

[11] We should never put off good works, no matter how small, with the thought of doing other and better ones at another time. It is a very common temptation of the enemy constantly to propose perfection in future matters to us, and lead us to despise present ones.

[12] We should all remain perseveringly in the vocation to which the Lord calls us, lest we "break our first pledge" [1 Tim. 5:12]. For it is the enemy's custom to tempt those living in the desert with desires to deal with and help the neighbor, while he tempts those who help their neighbor by proposing great perfection in the desert and solitary life. He thus seizes on what is far off to keep us from what is at hand.

✳ 1541–1543 ✳

To a Recluse at San Juan in Salamanca

Rome, July 24, 1541

(Letter 30: I:172f.; in Spanish)

Ignatius sends indulgenced beads to a woman recluse he had known during his short stay in Salamanca in 1527. At that time he came to know several such recluses living a cloistered life of prayer and penitence near one of the city's churches.

May the Lord be always our protection and help.

Inasmuch as I have been able to deem my poor spirit never absent from true and sincere love of your soul, but most continually present to it, I decided to send you a treasure that is greater and a stone that is more precious in my poor judgment for persons who seek only the love of their Creator and Lord and the salvation of their own souls, than could be found upon the entire earth or in all human power merely as human. His Holiness has granted to our Society numerous truly inestimable graces upon certain blessed beads, placing his own hand upon them as he blessed them. The graces granted to these beads are as follows. If one of the beads thus blessed is placed in a rosary or chaplet, anyone reciting that rosary or chaplet gains at every recital of it all the indulgences of all the stations and churches of Rome just as if he made and gained them in person. And since the graces gained at these stations are almost numberless, I send them separately so you can see them in detail. In addition, anyone who for his devotion recites this rosary or chaplet thirty-three times, for the thirty-three years that Christ our Lord lived upon the earth, delivers a soul from purgatory. I am sending one such blessed bead to you for your own consolation and spiritual benefit, plus another three; one is for your good companion and my dear sister in Christ our Creator and Lord, to whom I ask you to commend me earnestly in our Lord. The other two are for the women you consider most devoted to you and who will make best use of them in our Lord, for his greater praise and glory. May he by his infinite and supreme goodness be always for our favor and help.

Rome, July 24, 1541

Yours in our Lord,

IÑIGO

✠

To Paschase Broët and Alfonso Salmerón

Early September 1541

(Letter 31: I:174–79; in Italian)

The following three instructions were for one of the first tasks assigned to the Society by the Pope, the clandestine mission of Broët and Salmerón as papal nuncios to Ireland with the mission of trying to deal with the problems brought about especially through Henry VIII's break with Rome. Here detailed instructions are given for the dangerous journey there via Scotland.

Upon leaving Rome, and presuming that you go forward without delay, you should nevertheless because of certain imperfections in the bulls inform the Most Reverend Cardinal of England (to whom you will present my respects), leaving everything in his hands, both the interpretation and the negotiating, and then go forward.[1]

If the cardinal thinks you should visit the Pope, you could get letters from him to the Pope and to the Cardinal of Santa Croce, or at least to the Cardinal of Santa Croce, whom you will greet in my name.[2] If the English cardinal does not think you ought to visit the Pope, at least get credentials from the Cardinal of England for Ireland, testifying to what is happening and to His Holiness's intentions, so that this can be shown to the Irish in case they will recognize its authority. If you decide meanwhile that you ought to see the Pope in any case, have the cardinal send you with letters from him.

On the journey the following agreement is to be laid down by all four *(sic):* "We, N.N., promise and pledge our word that we will be faithful to one another, and will not disclose this mission to Ireland to

---

[1] The Cardinal of England was Reginald Pole, who strongly promoted this mission.

[2] Marcello Cervini, the future Pope Marcellus II, was the Cardinal of Santa Croce.

any person whatsoever, unless forced to by justice or unless all of us or the majority decide otherwise—except, however, to Jerónimo Doménech and Francisco Estrada, to whom we will reveal it in Paris." Then each will sign his name.

In Paris it will be well not to lodge at the university but in town, and if possible not to visit the colleges unless you go incognito, that is, on foot with the companion. Send secretly for Doménech and Estrada and tell them everything, so that they can take care of business. Then, on the day when you intend to leave, call together all the companions, or those you think proper, and converse with them in your room, providing a repast or supper for them and charging them to keep your departure from Paris secret until you reach Scotland. At the end also, if it seems advisable, you may also inform Picard; and there you might consider the advisability of speaking to the King of France about help for ports or for Scotland, as is done with the English.[3] But always adopt the least risky course if there is any fear of being discovered or other danger.

In Paris it will be more edifying to give something to them rather than to display any necessity small or great.

You should both dress alike, at least as regards what is worn outside.

Once you have word on your embarkation, you may find it wise, instead of going near the port, to rent a suitable place some six or seven miles out and stay there, taking along a French or Spanish companion or other reliable person to watch at the port till the ship is ready to sail, so that when the provisioning is done you can all three go straight on board.

When you reach Scotland and speak with the King, it will be very useful to ask the King for a letter of recommendation for the Irish to get you a good reception.[4] Stay at his court until you receive his reply. With this and with a letter from the legates, send an emissary to Ireland; if possible, this emissary should go with a commission from the King so as to have more authority and connection with the King, or in whatever way is more feasible.

While awaiting the reply, be as diligent as you can in hearing confessions and [giving the] Exercises as well as other exhortations.

---

[3] Referred to are Doctor Francis Picard, a friend of the Society, and Francis I of France (1494–1547).

[4] James V (1512–1542) was king at that time.

Master Salmerón should as soon as possible deliver a sermon in Latin, after careful preparation in spirit.

If would seem good that the King of Scotland be informed about your way of proceeding, especially how you may receive nothing for yourselves from letters of credit but must place whatever you accumulate with reliable persons for impartial distribution to the poor in hospitals and in other pious works as they think best for the service and glory of God our Lord.

On taking leave of Scotland, if things have gone well in the Lord, you should petition the King for an intermediary in his court to take care of receiving any letters you write from Ireland for Paris and Rome, and similarly of letters arriving from Paris and Rome, and also to pay all postal charges. Also inquire carefully in Scotland about bankers connected with Paris so that you can have other means of transmitting your letters.

As for how far to go or not to go in lodging, food, and drink, let yourselves be guided en route by Master Francisco, for God our Lord bestows his favor on you in him and through him.[5]

Decisions on which port to embark from, at which time, what dispensations to grant, with whom to speak, and other matters pertaining to the office of legates, will be made among the three of you by majority vote; in short, in any matter where the enemy might sow discord, decide by majority.

In speaking with princes and other persons of rank who recognize you as papal legates, let Paschase do the talking. And subsequently thereafter, if you decide anything different, it should always be by majority vote.

En route you will write us with great care and frequency: namely, from your point of departure, from the English cardinal's, from wherever the Pope is, from Lyon in France, from Paris, from your port of embarkation, from Scotland, then from Ireland; and subsequently, on the first of every month or two or three days before, from wherever you are staying, with great care and in two copies. The first time, write for the Cardinals of England, Brindisi, Santa Croce, and Carpi—all the news always on a single separate sheet so that we can make copies for showing to them and to others we choose.[6] Also, if is not too much trouble,

---

[5] Francisco Zapata, a Spanish priest and aspirant to the Society, who accompanied them. He entered and later left the Society, becoming a Franciscan.

[6] The Cardinal of Brindisi was Girolamo Aleandro de la Motta.

you might write them directly; your letters to them you may send separately under wax and seal, or closed; include copies and send the packet to us. In the principal matters you should recount the course of events for greater edification; other news without exhortations, taking into account that the letter will be shown to shrewd persons who will want concise accounts of many things done rather than a lot of words about few if the subject does not require much. About other matters you will write on separate sheets.

Item: The letter with edifying news should be sent with the sealed letters inside, and then the whole packet is to be enclosed within one cover and addressed: "To Master Jerónimo in Paris" (I refer to the packets that will go through Paris), so that Master Jerónimo may read the letter of news only and then forward it to me with the sealed letters. You can write to us by three routes, by Portugal through the residence of the King's preacher;[7] by Biscay to the Lord of Loyola in the town of Azpeitia, in the province of Guipúzcoa; or by Scotland—and this latter would seem to be the most regular and convenient.

Be diligent regarding the Masses for Guidiccioni, and when you write let me know how many you have said.[8]

If I bore the responsibility you bear, I would, upon arrival at a city or town where we had to reside, have dinner or supper and sleep, depending on when we arrived; on that day or the following, or after our reception as legates, I would immediately, on that day or the following, barring any impediment, before being provided with anything, take any money left over from what had been given you and distribute part of it to the poor, and deposit part for clothing and shoes against the cold and the varieties of local climate. Then I would beg alms for the love of God our Lord from door to door for a day or two, and subsequently as God may inspire you. I intend this only for the two legates; Master Francisco may act however he finds devotion and love in God our Lord.

If they give you a separate church or house, take as much care as possible that no women, young or old, live there.

Item: Do not have a mule or horse. Try to get some Spaniard or Frenchman who knows the language of the country. In attire and food always aim at an appropriate simplicity. As regards letters of credit, take off more or less a half or third of the usual rate, as you deem proper;

---

[7] João Soares, O.S.A.
[8] The cardinal responsible for examining the Society's proposed Institute was Guidiccioni.

and receive no money into your own hands or control, but place whatever you are given for any kind of certificate in the hands and control of local persons who seem to be most reliable or pious, to be distributed impartially by them to the poor or to any pious works as and how they judge best for the greater service of God our Lord.

Item: Should these same reliable persons wish to support you with this money or with part of it, make sure you do not receive money into your hands or even into your control. Rather, when necessity compels you to get your sustenance for the love of God our Lord in some place and to beg from door to door or wherever they may be willing to give to you for his love and reverence, then these persons and others may provide for you in whatever way or fashion they shall decide is for the greater service of God our Lord.

Item: If such persons refuse to let you place what they give you under the control of others outside the Society, so that they can render an account of what they spend and the Society not have to receive any funds or even give an account of them, except when they had to beg from other sources door to door—then: "Freely have you received, freely give."

✠

To Paschase Broët and Alfonso Salmerón

Rome, early September 1541
(Letter 31a: I:727–31 [Appendix 1]; in Italian)

The second instruction for the legates to Ireland deals with the work of reform and encouragement in that country, and with the legates' reports to Rome.

MEMORANDUM ON THE AFFAIRS OF IRELAND

The purpose of this mission to Ireland is in general to further the affairs of that province in spiritual matters and to relieve as far as you can the consciences of the Supreme Pontiff and of the most illustrious and reverend protector of that province.

With this object in view, we shall mention here certain points regarding what is to be done by those who are sent there, what they should inform us about here, and what help they may be given from Rome.

WHAT IT APPEARS THEY OUGHT TO DO IN IRELAND

First, visit the Catholic leaders, and especially four secular lords who are the principal men in the realm, praising in the name of His Holiness their constancy in and zeal for the Catholic religion, encouraging them to persevere, etc.

Visit also the Catholic bishops, and do the same for them. And if any of them have failed in their duty by giving the people of their dioceses bad example through their lives, or by not residing at their cathedrals, or by not visiting their flocks, or by not seeing to it that the divine office is said or the churches are kept in due order, or by making bad selections and promotions in the ministry, or by any other public and important shortcomings, admonish them and exhort them to better conduct, if they desire a good report of them to reach this see.

Similarly with priests, especially parish priests, do all the good you can, helping them in their way of living by exhortations of your own and by resorting to the hand of the bishops to correct them for either public sins or negligence in doing their duty as regards divine worship and the help of souls. With those of a lower estate, however, one might make more use of the authority and jurisdiction he possesses.

Give special attention to the administration of the sacraments, seeing how the priests behave in baptizing, hearing confessions, and administering Holy Communion, extreme unction, and matrimony, and how the bishops behave in confirming and conferring holy orders, so as to counsel them; and wherever possible make up for what is lacking in this regard yourselves, especially as regards confession and Communion.

See also whether the word of God is preached in a Catholic way; and give to other ministers whatever instruction and help you can. Moreover, teach the people yourselves and exhort them to lead Christian lives.

If you hear of any heretical preachers or parish priests, see that they are deprived of the opportunity of harming others; the persons themselves you should endeavor to reclaim by showing them the truth in a spirit of gentleness. If they are obstinate and yet might be helped by others with authority and power over them, you should try to secure this, as well as their punishment if necessary.

Take care to confirm in the faith those who are sick, and to exhort them to confession in such cases and manner as is suitable, without yielding to worldly fear or temerity.

Where you hear of good prospects who are fitted to instruct and govern others, bring them to the notice of the bishops, so that the latter may make use of them and give them the benefices which they are accustomed and able to confer.

If in some places you could establish schools of grammar, finding adequate Catholic teachers, it would be an excellent remedy against the great ignorance in the country. It would be necessary to urge parents to send their children to be taught letters and good morals and to learn Christian and Catholic doctrine.

See if steps could be taken to restore some monasteries of men and women, or to reform those presently in existence.

It would also be good to make efforts towards introducing (or restoring if they previously existed) public pawnshops for the assistance of the poor, hospitals, and other pious institutions such as are common in these parts and would have a place there.

In all the works of charity here mentioned, and in others customarily undertaken by members of this Society for the good of souls, proceed according to our Institute by accepting no remuneration or even alms in return for any work you may do. Of course, if it is necessary, you may use alms for your support; but you must not ask or even accept them in return for work that you do, thus endeavoring to give edification by the example of your charity and zeal for their salvation, etc.

And while wherever the glory of God and the common good require you to risk your life—without rashness or tempting God—you should not flee the danger, nevertheless, speaking generally, use all the skill and prudence you can to avoid being captured by the Queen's agents;[9] and consult with such Catholic gentlemen as you can to see how far you can go in dealing with people in those areas governed by English heretics.

MATTERS ON WHICH YOU SHOULD SEND INFORMATION TO ROME

First, you will give overall information about the state of the Catholic faith and obedience to the Apostolic See, both among ecclesiastical and secular leaders and among the people, and describe the daily gains or losses in this regard. The way of writing this information will be indicated separately.

---

[9] The reference to Queen Elizabeth is presumably an anachronism on the part of the later copyist.

If there are any prelates who cannot be constrained there and are seen to conduct themselves so badly that there is no other recourse but the Apostolic See for reforming their scandalous conduct, even though their faith is Catholic, you should faithfully and candidly advise what should be done.

Similarly with any of the chief temporal lords who behave badly in religious matters and for whose correction the usual resources of the locality are insufficient.

Send a list of those you think suitable for the episcopate. Especially when a see falls vacant, you should mention the particular person you think best fitted for it, giving your reasons.

When any come to Rome to apply for bishoprics or greater benefices, it would be good if you sent your opinion whether, considering the people of the country, you think them suitable for the benefices they seek. If you think them unsuitable, your writing nothing will indicate your opinion.

In general, if you think of any important measures that the holy Apostolic See could employ for the common good of that province, mention them in your letters.

[The final section, on ecclesiastical faculties and privileges for Ireland which could be supplied from Rome, is deleted in the manuscript.]

✠

To Alfonso Salmerón and Paschase Broët

Rome, early September 1541

(Letter 32: I:179–81; in Spanish)

The third instruction for the legates to Ireland gives general counsels on dealing spiritually with the variety of persons they would encounter and on avoiding direct involvement in money matters.

HOW TO DEAL AND CONVERSE WITH PEOPLE IN THE LORD

In dealings with anyone, especially with equals or those of lower rank and authority than yourselves, say little and be slow to speak. Listen long and willingly, until they have finished what they wanted to say. Then reply point by point, come to an end, and take your leave. If the person rejoins, cut the rejoinders as short as possible; your leave-taking should be swift and gracious.

In order to deal with and win the love of highly placed persons and superiors for the greater glory of God our Lord, first study their temperament and adapt yourself to it. With someone of choleric temperament, quick and merry in speech, adopt somewhat his own style of conversation in good and holy matters; avoid seeming grave, phlegmatic, or melancholic. With those who are by nature reserved, slow in speech, serious and weighty in their conversation, adopt the same manner, for this is what pleases them. "I have become all things to all men" [1 Cor. 9:22].

Remember that when one person of choleric temperament deals with another choleric person, unless they are completely of one spirit, there is serious danger of their conversations ending in a clash. Hence, as far as possible, anyone who knows that his temperament is choleric should if possible, in every detail of his dealing with others, be well armed with an examen or some other reminder to be patient and not get upset with the other, particularly if he knows that the other person is unwell. In his dealings with phlegmatic or melancholic persons, there is less danger of a clash arising from hasty words.

In any conversation where we are trying to win a person over and ensnare him for the greater service of God our Lord, we should adopt the same procedure the enemy uses with a good soul—he always for evil and we always for good. The enemy enters through the other's door and comes out his own. He enters the other's door by praising rather than contradicting his ways; he cultivates familiarity with the soul by drawing it to good and holy thoughts that bring the good soul calm. Then, little by little, he endeavors to come out his own door, drawing the person under the appearance of good to some harmful error or illusion, always for evil. In the same way, we, [acting] for good, can praise a person or go along with him on some particular good point, passing over in silence any bad points he may have. Once we have won his love, we will better get what we want. Thus, we go in his door and come out our own.

With persons we see to be suffering trials or discouraged, we should behave pleasantly, conversing at length and showing much contentment and cheerfulness, both interior and exterior, so as to counteract what they are feeling, for their greater edification and consolation.

In whatever we say, particularly when reconciling quarrels and conversing spiritually, we should be on our guard and presume that anything we say may or will become public.

In dispatching business be generous with your time; that is, if you promise something for tomorrow, do it if possible today.

While you retain the supervision, it would be better for Messer Francisco to have charge of the fees.[10] You will be better able to refuse or grant anybody's request if the three of you never touch the money but instead transmit it through someone else to the designated recipient. Or else you could grant the dispensation or facilitate the matter after the person requesting it has paid the fee to the designated person and brought you the receipt. Or adopt any other more convenient procedure, so long as all three of you can say you never touched any of the moneys of this mission.

✠

To Pierre Favre

Rome, September 20, 1541

(Letter 33: I:181–85; in Spanish)

News about the conversion and marriage of a Jewish man and a prostitute, and the comings and goings of Jesuits in Rome and elsewhere. This letter well illustrates the activities of several of the first companions as well as of new recruits to a Society approaching the first anniversary of its existence as a religious order.

May the sovereign grace and love of Christ our Lord be always for our continual favor and help.

Since the time that I wrote you at length on July 24, we have had a rather unusual celebration of two sacraments at the same time; so that you may give thanks with greater devotion to God our Lord for what his Divine Majesty is doing everywhere, I will go into some detail.

There was a Jewish man here, thirty-two years old, of good appearance and life and not lacking in material goods, who, touched by God our Lord, decided to become a Christian. Whereupon, some days later, by his own fault and weakness he fell into dealings and commerce with a public prostitute, continuing in his sin for several weeks. Hearing of this, the authorities seized the prostitute and imprisoned her for intercourse with a Jew (there are numerous penalties here for Jewish men uniting with Christian women or Christian men with Jewish women). The Jew went into hiding and could not be found by the authorities. When we learned of this, by the grace of God our Lord who rules and accomplishes all things, we succeeded, within five hours of

---

[10] Francisco Zapata, a Spanish priest and aspirant to the Society, acted as treasurer for the legation.

hearing the news, in getting her out of prison through the favor of God and other good persons who were his instruments, and in bringing the Jew to our own house. Meanwhile, she stayed in a respectable house where she was frequently visited, so she could go to confession and be a good catechumen for a decent life; and the Jewish catechumen wished to take her as his wife at the proper time, after he became a Christian, and the prostitute [was willing to accept] him as her husband.

After we had them for a suitable time, we decided that the two sacraments of baptism and marriage should be celebrated together, that is, the marriage immediately following the baptism. And so on a recent Sunday, there came to our church Madama (who has made a practice of being involved in charitable affairs, and in our own without fail), the Cardinal of Santiago, the Cardinal of Burgos, the ambassadors of the Emperor and of the King of Portugal, and numerous other bishops and noble personages[11]—I even strove to dissuade some other cardinals who were originally coming, to ensure that we all might proceed with greater peace and calm in our Lord. Master Laínez preached and Master Salmerón did the baptism. Then, in the presence of all, with the former prostitute—now become a lady—dressed and adorned as a bride, Salmerón took the hands of the new Christian and the newly converted woman and married them, saying the customary matrimonial Mass. We experienced much satisfaction and edification on all sides. May unending thanks be to God our Lord.

Masters Paschase and Salmerón departed on the tenth of this month as nuncios to Ireland; Francisco Zapata left everything and accompanied them. The Pope likewise ordered Master Laínez to accompany Madama to receive the Emperor, [so that he could be of] consolation to her and so that she could go to confession to him until they reach the place where the Pope and the Emperor will meet.

Five or six persons have come out of the Exercises, some to join the Society after their studies, some with other great plans for the service and glory of God our Lord.

Araoz got here about twenty days ago, bringing two well-disposed young men who have studied logic and are quite intelligent. One is from Toledo, the other a nephew of mine;[12] both plan to join the Society. In the course of this coming October, God willing, we shall send a couple of men for studies in Paris, one a master of arts from Alcalá and

---

[11] "Madama" was Margaret of Austria, daughter of Charles V.

[12] Martín de Santa Cruz and Millán de Loyola.

the other a rather good Latinist from Parma;[13] [we shall send] as well five others to Portugal, four for studies at Coimbra and the fifth, Cipriano, for the Indies, where Master Francis [Xavier] went. With these seven sent off, there will be eight of us left in the house. In the spring we plan to send another six. From Paris we have sent Rojas and two others to studies in Coimbra, since the King wants to start a college for us and they are requesting us to send students to study there. As I think I wrote earlier, Master Francis went to the Indies with two others. Master Simão remained in Portugal with three others by command of the King, so the that the spiritual benefit could be spread around and the college could be built. From our scattered companions we are always getting excellent news. Unending thanks be to God our Lord, and may he by his infinite and supreme goodness be always for our continual favor and help.

Rome, September 20, 1541

☩

To Beltrán de Loyola

Rome, beginning of February 1542

(Letter 36: I:188–90; in Spanish)

Ignatius urges his nephew, the lord of Loyola, to provide funds in Paris for his younger brother Millán, who is about to leave Rome for studies there.

May the sovereign grace and love of Christ our Lord always be for our favor and help.

Since I wrote you earlier at length and my health is not good at present, this letter will partially repeat what we wrote before and give further details about your brother's departure. With God's grace and his health permitting, without fail he will be out of Rome and on his way to Paris this month before the beginning of Lent. He will be traveling in excellent company and will in addition bear a safe-conduct from the French ambassador, who is always very well disposed toward us and in time of need regularly gives us safe-conducts for those [sent there. Araoz will also travel with][14] Millán for about two hundred miles from

---

[13] Andrés de Oviedo, who would eventually become patriarch of Ethiopia, and Giovanni Battista Viola.

[14] The text in the MS is somewhat corrupt at this point. Here we supply what seems to be the sense of the passage.

here, and then part company with those going (with God's guidance) to Paris; he will then proceed straight to Barcelona, where he will stay for several months giving exhortations in our Lord. If you write him, they will know his whereabouts at the house of Isabel Roser, who lives opposite the Church of St. Juste.

Accordingly, if you have not yet made provision in Paris for your brother by the time this reaches you, I beg you, for reverence of our Lord, to do this with great care as quickly as you can, so that by Easter—or earlier, since he may get there before then—he can find his allowance ready for him, in the same way you provided for him at Salamanca or however else you prefer. Without proper provision, students suffer a great deal in that country, as Doña María de Vicuña will have learned by this time from the son she has there. You could send him the provision to give to Millán when he arrives, or you could send it to Jerónimo Doménech, a canon from Valencia at the Lombard college, to whom I will direct Millán from here, so that he will get additional help from his conversation and learning. Certainly, to judge from what I have seen of him here in Rome and from the way he made the Spiritual Exercises—which you yourself tried for a while with a great deal of sweat—your brother has found and reaped quite great fruit from them—so much that if our Lord gives him some time of life, I hope to see him a lamp, to the great satisfaction and content of all of you who love him with a genuine love, for the enlightenment of many souls living in the darkness of love for the worldly and passing things of earth.

For this reason, and so that he may be a comfort to you all in the future, be sure to make provision for him at once without fail by sending him the whole sum you agreed to provide him with for a year. Fearing that, as times are, you might find difficulty in getting bankers to make him the advance, I made inquiries and inform you by the enclosed note of ways you can provide for him.

In events here and throughout the dispersed Society, we have constantly new grounds to give increasing and unending thanks to God our Lord. May he always be for our continual favor and help.

To the lady of the house and the entire household, and to all you think will be glad to be greeted by me, please give my warm remembrance and greetings in our Lord.

Rome

Poor in goodness,

INIGO

✠

To Antonio Araoz

Rome, February 20, 1542

(Letter 37:I:190f.; in Spanish)

A suggestion that Araoz visit Juan de Polanco's family in Burgos, who are ill disposed toward Ignatius and the Society.

Araoz:

Master Juan Polanco has a mother and father in Burgos; the father, named Gregorio de Polanco, is a magistrate of the city. Among other children, he likewise has a brother there, also named Gregorio de Polanco. Both father and brother are quite ill informed and have a very bad impression of me and consequently of the Society, to the point where he writes grievous things to him for joining us and, while not accusing us of actual sins against good morals, paints us as they please. Among other things, I regret that in their minds Polanco himself may not be safe from the Inquisition because of his association with us and our teaching. Therefore, if after examining the matter and commending it to God our Lord, it should seem appropriate to you that on one of your trips elsewhere you might go to Burgos to remove this scandal with the word of the Lord, or contrive to have the inquisitors write something about our teaching in case you have much or any intimacy with them, you should do whatever the Lord inspires you to. If by chance you do go to Burgos, remember that all, or at least the majority, of those who have had sons or relatives of theirs in Paris will have a bad impression of me, because when Master Juan de Castro, bachelor and later doctor of theology and from Burgos himself, went begging for the love of God through the streets of Paris after distributing his possessions to the poor, this was strongly resented by all his fellow countrymen there, and they blamed the whole thing on me. He later became a Carthusian friar. These persons whom I knew at the time in Paris were named

Garay, Salinas, Maluenda, and Astudillo; hence, be careful about all these families or houses. I thought it good to warn you in our Lord. However, as regards taking any steps in the matter, do not be moved by what I write you, looking always to the greater service of God our Lord.

✠

To Simão Rodrigues
Rome, March 18, 1542
(Letter 38:I:192–96; in Spanish)

John III of Portugal was the early Society of Jesus' strongest royal supporter. All the more painful to the Society was a serious quarrel which broke out between the Portuguese king and Pope Paul III when the Pope appointed the former ambassador of Portugal to be a cardinal. The King then recalled from Rome his current ambassador there. Writing to Simão Rodrigues, leader of the Jesuits in Portugal, Ignatius urges the Society's obligation to do all it can to heal the rift. He expresses the assurance felt in Rome that King John would never go the way of Henry VIII of England.

May the sovereign grace and eternal love of Christ our Lord be always for our continual favor and help.

Considering in his divine goodness (and ready to defer to better judgment) how, of all imaginable evils and sins, one that most merits the loathing of our Creator and Lord and of every creature capable of his divine and everlasting glory is the sin of ingratitude, being as it is the refusal to acknowledge the goods, graces, and gifts that we have received, and so the cause, principle, and source of every evil and sin; and how, on the other hand, acknowledgment and gratitude for goods and gifts received is so highly loved and esteemed both in heaven and on earth, I thought I should recall to you how since our arrival in Rome we have in numerous matters enjoyed the full and continuous favor of the Pope, receiving special benefits from His Holiness; and at the same time how clear to the entire Society—and to yourself, who are present there, most manifestly of all—is the extent of what we all owe to the King, your lord and ours in our Lord.

First, because of the many spiritual graces which God our Creator and Lord has bestowed upon him, choosing to raise him up in every way through his accustomed grace to his own greater service and praise, and looking with infinite love as Creator upon his creature, for whom, being infinite and making himself finite, he chose to die.

Second, who are we, or where did we come from, that God our Lord should have ordained that so distinguished a prince should take notice of us, and that either of his own initiative or at the suggestion of others, without our having in any way imagined or contrived it, and even before the Society's confirmation by the Apostolic See, he should have asked the Pope so insistently to have some of our men for his service in our Lord, showing us such great favor at a time when our teaching was under no little suspicion?

Third, since your arrival there you will have been more fully aware (not that it is concealed from us) of how he treats you with great affection and love, even with material subsidies such as not all princes are accustomed to give. From the abundance of his heart and his affection for us, he has offered to found a college and to build houses for this Society, so unworthy in the sight of our Creator and Lord in heaven and of such a prince on earth; even more, he has taken under his wing all the men we have sent from here to study there.

My purpose in recalling all of this to you is so that you there and we here—all sharing the same goal of serving our Creator and Lord ever more intensely, maintaining complete loyalty and utter gratitude towards persons to whom under God's supreme goodness we are so indebted—might strive with all the strength granted us from above to bear our part in the many spiritual and corporal travails which the enemy of human nature, for the opposite purpose, has tried to interpose between these great and important personages.

Now, since you doubtless are aware there just as we are here of what has been or is occurring, it only remains that, with all of us being so indebted and obliged, you there and we here should all zealously take up our spiritual arms (since we have relinquished temporal arms forever) and pray fervently every day, continuing to remember this especially in our Masses, begging and beseeching that God our Lord will deign to interpose his hand and the fullness of his grace in this affair, so difficult and so deserving to be earnestly commended to his infinite and supreme goodness. And while I am convinced that with God's grace the enemy will never prevail in this situation, no little harm and confusion to many souls would result if things were to go on like this for even a very short time.

In a long conversation about this with the Cardinal of Burgos, who in all our affairs has been our very special lord and advocate in our Lord, he said something to me in confirmation of my own view which brought no little spiritual consolation to my soul.[15] He said, "So-and-so was talking to me and said that it was rumored or that it appeared the King of Portugal was leaving the Pope's obedience." The good cardinal would not hear of it, and answered indignantly: "Who says so? Even if the Pope were to tread the King of Portugal underfoot, he would never do that. Do you think that the people there are like the people here, or that their king is like the English king, who was already halfway outside before he declared himself? Do not think such a thing of so Christian and so conscientious a prince."

Although I would like to write a letter to the King myself, I have held back, partly at seeing how slight and unworthy I am for such a step, and partly because, seeing you there on the spot, I consider myself excused: it is your place to show him complete reverence and to speak for all of us as well as for yourself. However, if you should judge otherwise, I would not wish or desire to be wanting even in the slightest detail in our Lord.

Since, at the Pope's command, Master Favre has left Spain, Master Bobadilla the Cardinal of England's legation, and Master Jay Cardinal Carpi's diocese, all bound for Germany, we have had letters from the latter two, dated February 15, reporting how they had arrived safely in Speyer six days earlier and were going about their preparations to enter the wilderness.[16] We have had no letter from Master Favre about his arrival in Germany. Regarding the nuncios [Broët and Salmerón] to Ireland, though they set sail, we have had no word of their passage or landing there.

Since I have written fully elsewhere about the dispersed Society and the spiritual fruit which our Lord is deigning to produce through them, there is no more to say here. May he always in his infinite and sovereign goodness be for our continual protection, favor, and help.

Rome, March 18, 1542

A week ago today the King's ambassador left for Portugal.

Yours in our Lord,

YÑIGO

---

[15] The Cardinal of Burgos was Juan Alvarez de Toledo, O.P.

[16] Reginald Pole was the Cardinal of England; Cardinal Carpi's diocese was Faenza.

To Simão Rodrigues

Rome, March 18, 1542

(Letter 39: I:196–99; in Spanish)

Concerned by charges in Rome that Rodrigues was abetting King John of Portugal in his conflict with the Pope over the cardinalate of the bishop of Viseu, Ignatius consulted canonists in Rome and sent Rodrigues the following confidential letter.

Doctors' letter for Simão:

I have Doctor Torres in my house and in my company. Handling the business of the university of Alcalá, with his great ability and generosity, he had taken first place in the licentiate and graduated doctor of theology. And since he is so great a lover of God our Lord and so fond of all his servants, especially all those of this Society of Jesus, we take great joy in all good news of success in the service of God our Lord and the benefit of souls, which we hear frequently from all over the dispersed Society.

Regarding anything the opposite, were God to allow it for our sins, we would feel a great deal of pain and sorrow; and so when we heard talk here of certain things (which we do not readily believe), we decided to write you this letter without saying or communicating anything to your companions here. What is being claimed is that the King has fallen under the bull *In cœna Domini* inasmuch as they say he has proceeded against the Bishop of Viseu, who is now a cardinal, and is withholding his revenues and not letting him receive or send letters to his church so that it can be provided for and God's worship attended to, and much more of the like; that you are hearing the confessions of excommunicated persons and absolving them, specifically, of persons who have aided the King, some by supporting him, some by advising His Highness to proceed against the Cardinal of Viseu; and that, furthermore, it was your duty to admonish the King and that by failing to do so and by absolving those who have been advising him, you are acting against the Apostolic See. So much so that we greatly fear that this is being talked of in the highest instance in Rome (although said instance does not have so easy a head as to believe lightly everything reaching its ears); so much so that there were not wanting persons who said that since the reforming priests have been in Portugal, no one is taking excommunications seriously.

A friend of yours has replied, "I cannot vouch for what I do not know." I am quite sure that the King in this case has not sinned mortally, and that, supposing that the King has fallen under the bull *In cœna*

Domini, as a prince it is not his profession to be a scholar or doctor in theology so as to make such distinctions, so that he may be very much in the grace of God our Lord, as I am convinced he is. Again, if some say that he has fallen under the bull and others deny it, then while the King remains in uncertainty, awaiting a clarification so as in all things to obey the Apostolic See as the most faithful and Christian king which he is and always has been, I am confident that he is still very much in the love and grace of God our Lord. Similarly with Master Simão: we do not even know if he is fully aware of the matter, since the King has his counsel and learned men for such matters, or whether he has admonished His Highness or not. Hence it is not for us to judge matters on which we lack complete information.

Concerning absolution given by Master Simão and those with him, I firmly believe without the slightest doubt that they have used and are using the keys of the Church within their powers and not exceeding them by absolving in matters of excommunication or other cases in which they have no apostolic authority to absolve. Otherwise, they would be acting against the service of God our Lord, of the Apostolic See, and of the King and his entire realm. Let each one say what he will: right proceeding and truth have great power in themselves, above all in those who order and direct everything for the greater glory of God our Lord. And so the members of the Society do not much trouble themselves about things being said by persons who are uninformed about them, both because they hold it as quite certain, out of great experience, that the sovereigns and princes of Portugal are so very Catholic and Christian, and also because their ears have been deafened by hearing so many contradictions over the last six years. "If the world has persecuted me, it will persecute you also" [see John 15:20].

We, then, moved with zeal for God our Lord and with the very special love which we have for all the members of the Society, have written you this letter out of a great desire to hear and be properly informed on the situation there, so that here with truth for a shield we might be able to answer anyone. Hence, for the service of God our Lord, we beg you to write to us at length of the good and holy will and of the good and holy words and works of the King and of all his house, for most certainly we are, like you, very much affected towards His Majesty; [write] also of your own innocence and sincerity in the matter of confessions and conversations. For this could do a great deal of good here with persons who go on at length about many matters which they ought to cut short.

To Simão Rodrigues

Rome, mid-1542

(Letter 42:I:206–10; in Spanish)

A letter on the policy for sending scholastics to Paris and to Portugal, as well as other topics.

Esteban departed from here in good health when he left for there.[17] It is not surprising that he fell ill on such a long and difficult journey. Inasmuch as concern about his illness became almost public matter, the steps you took in his regard seem excellent to me. He has arrived in good condition and in health at our house, where he will remain until we can make some arrangement for him. I believe you will be more satisfied with Villanueva and Giacomo.[18] While Villanueva may seem a little old and lacking in basic Latin, the more you deal with him, the more capable you will think he is. I myself am convinced that he is one of the best subjects from there. Of course, I leave it up to you.

I have already written how Angelo, Sbrando, and another man had left Paris for there;[19] likewise how on April 28 Santa Cruz, Ercole, Niccolò, Codure, and Antonio de Parma left for there.[20] They have written us that they got through Parma all right. They all left behind a holy odor and much edification in the house here, and the least knowledgeable among them has in my opinion already half completed his literary studies. I have in part restrained myself until now, since Master Francis wrote me for the two of you that any students I sent you should not come lacking what they need there, and that it would be good if they had basic Latin studies.[21] Hence, of the sixteen which we have sent you from Paris and from here, only one or two whom we sent lacked basic Latin, having others that were equivalent (subject to better judgment). Consequently, though I can claim excuse, if you deem it right I shall make whatever amends you lay on me.

---

[17] Esteban Baroëll, who had earlier been sent to Portugal and now returned to Italy for reasons of health. He then went to Padua for studies.

[18] Francisco de Villanueva was to become the founder of the college at Alcalá and a great apostle of the Society of Jesus. Giacomo Giovannello, a Roman, died in 1546, still a scholastic of the Society.

[19] Angelo Paradisi and Isidoro (or Sbrando) Bellini are referred to here.

[20] Mentioned here are Martín de Santa Cruz, Ercole Buceri, Niccolò Lancillotto, Guillaume Codure (brother of Jean Codure, one of the first companions, who had already died), and Antonio Criminali (later martyred in India).

[21] Ignatius refers to Master Francis Xavier.

I beg you for the love of God our Lord to write me more often from now on, so that we will not commit new errors in the future. Write clearly if I should not send you students, or how many and what kind I should send. If I had been informed earlier about what happened with Rojas and his companions, I would have acted with more restraint. However, as God our Lord disposes and acts, yourselves being only his instrument, I trust in his divine majesty that all will turn out for the best in the matter of sending students. So far our policy has been as follows.

If someone is wealthy, we send him to Paris so that he can help himself and a number of others, since we have no aid there from other distinguished persons to assist with studies. In this way several have gone there, and they have taken care to support those who are unable or lack resources. Anyone we knew, however talented, to be unsettled or not completely tranquil we have always preferred to send to Paris rather than to Portugal. Thus, according to our poor estimation and always open to better judgment, we have thought it more advisable to send to you there those we were able to judge more tractable, steady, and secure, so that they would not commit some imprudence there and ruin everything else. Even among those whom we have sent, we have taken and will take care that they be of good inward or outward aspect, that is, in intelligence or appearance. Since it is not easy to find all three qualities in every man—goodness, intelligence, and bodily appearance—we do not do as much as we would wish. However, doing what we can in our Lord, we trust that if they are good persons, their long studies will enable them to progress in natural qualities as well.

Considering the matter well, it would not be too little if out of sixty men going for studies, twenty ended up for the Society. Some will die over the long period of time; some, as happens, will contract serious illnesses; some will go back on their resolves, as happens in all congregations, especially among those who go to studies and are not yet members of any congregation and do not live under the customary regime of obedience. We have seen this by experience in the case of some at Paris who have turned back. Among them is a certain Carvajal: after some exploits of his, he was unwilling to stay there longer and set off for here without our permission, saying that he had some matters of conscience that he wanted to discuss with me and then do as I ordered him. Accordingly, he has written me from Bologna that in Paris he was very anxious to see me, that he now dreads the scolding I will give him, and that he would like me to send word ordering him back to Paris. I expect him here within three or four days, and I cannot make up my mind what to do with him, whether to receive him or let him go. My personal opinion is that all the men who have gone to study in Paris, together with all those we have sent to you, have not given us as much trouble as this fellow all by himself. So think what you have been spared by our not sending you people like him.

As for our manner of living and our daily bread, it appears through the grace of God our Lord that we have plenty of everything. However, we do not make use of all that we might. Our fare being what it was when you were here in the house, we are not criticized for too much or too little, unless I am mistaken—although this past Lent I was a little more liberal with Pietro Codazzo, since I thought that he had gotten a lot thinner since the time when you and Rojas and ourselves were together.

In the matter of sending you students, I beg you by the love of God our Lord to write me at length and clearly up to how many and what kind of men you think they should be, so that as far as possible I can comply with your judgment in our Lord. Regarding these men, I am anxious that you give them a very solid foundation in Latin, and then the complete arts [philosophy] course, without any break.

As to the hindrance in the matter of the Indies, unless I am mistaken and barring a slip of the pen, what I wrote was as if to my own soul. Should it appear otherwise—which I cannot concede—I would like you to send me the letter or whatever you remember that I wrote, so that I can give my reasons and you yourself can act as arbiter to decide the matter and, if you deem it fitting, order me to make an *amende honorable* if that is called for; for I have so far always been more yours than my own, am much more so now, and trust to be much more so henceforth in our Lord.

I had written you that I was going to speak with the Pope, Santa Croce, Don Miguel, and Madama, and write to Poggio;[22] I have done so and by the grace of God our Lord am quite happy with the whole outcome. I have now made arrangements for Madama and the Cardinal of Burgos to write there, and for the Bishop of Bergamo to go speak with them;[23] he will bring the letters as I have arranged with everyone. With all this—the nuncio going in person and your being present in the name

---

[22] Mentioned here are Marcello Cervini, cardinal of Santa Croce and later Pope Marcellus II; Juan Alvarez de Toledo, cardinal of Burgos; and Margaret of Austria. Giovanni Poggio was nuncio in Spain.

[23] Luigi Lippomani, papal legate in Portugal, was bishop of Bergamo.

of all your men there—my mind is at rest and free of its earlier anxiety or concern, since I trust in God our Lord that he will work all things there with his own hand.

Regarding the bull and the collection that you might have made, as I wrote you, with all related matters: since the Bishop of Bergamo is going, I think it can be dispensed with entirely. Hence, if you think it good, it will be better to pass over it in silence: with such a good and righteous prelate we have a very special obligation to behave towards him as inferiors to our superiors in the Church of Christ.

For remaining matters I refer you to Master Laínez.

✠

To Simão Rodrigues

Mid-1542

(Letter 44: I:211f.; in Spanish)

While insisting adamantly on obedience and humility, Ignatius hopes to save for the Society two scholastics whom Rodrigues finds restive.

Regarding Rojas, I very much wish, should there be room for mercy and if he is willing to humble himself and improve, that no change be made. However, should you see that this is not the case for reasons better known to you than to me here, I leave everything to what you think best, and will deem as most sound whatever you judge to be so. If it is not possible for him to remain with you and he comes here, he will find the doors open until we see what progress he has made and whether he shows any hope of improvement for the future. I did not do as much in Carvajal's case: it is some forty days since he arrived from Paris; and though he wants to stay in our house, he has not yet slept in it.

I desire the same for Villanueva if he is willing to abase and humble himself. But if he rebels and will not amend, I would not have him with me even if he were my father. Above all, I beg of you for the love of God our Lord to see that all your men there are completely obedient and humble. If they fail in this, they are not for you there and will not be able to last long here. So deeply have I felt what you have written that I am not writing to either of them and have no inclination to leniency.

From a conversation with Doctor Iñigo López, I believe he is writing about a certain person. "If anyone sins against you, take one or two witnesses" [see Matt. 18:15f.]; with this I propose to be quit. "Cursed is he who trusts in man" [Jer. 17:5].

✠

To Simão Rodrigues

Rome, mid-1542

(Letter 45:I:212f.; in Spanish)

Ignatius counsels against taking one man out of studies, and complains that another does not write him.

Regarding Angelo, I question why you want to take him out of studies altogether, even if only Latin and some topics of positive theology. If he is unsuited for that much, I fear the priesthood would make him even less capable of it. Similarly, if you propose ordaining him there without studies, I wonder if it might not be more appropriate for him to come here for that. However, while expressing my doubts, I leave it to you to decide what is best, since in regard to the men you have with you there, you can reasonably be expected to see further than we can here. Hence, I will await what you write me to carry out whatever determination you make in this regard.

The document authorizing the recitation of the new office accompanies this letter.[24]

Do what you think best about Cipriano; that will be best with me—even though he, with his ideas of government, does not deign to write me. At least get him to write to Gómez Vásquez; and if he would write to Don Francesco or the Cardinal of Burgos, so much the better, for they are all delighted to get good news of him.[25]

---

[24] The radically revised breviary of Cardinal Francisco Quiñones.

[25] Reference is to Francesco de Solis, bishop of Bagnoreggio.

To Francis Borgia, duke of Gandía

Rome, mid-1542

(XII [Appendix 1, no. 3]: 217–19; in Spanish)

The following passage from an unpublished life of Francis Borgia by Dionisio Vazquez, S.J., summarizes a letter of St. Ignatius to Borgia on frequent reception of Holy Communion.

"What Father Ignatius replied to the viceroy was that, on the one hand, no general rule could be given that would be equally applicable to all, since for some persons frequent Communion would be profitable and pleasing to God, while for others it might be harmful and a source of offense to his Divine Majesty. Nevertheless, in itself frequent reception of the Most Holy Sacrament of the altar is a holy and blessed practice and should therefore be encouraged wherever the requisite disposition and preparation for this heavenly and divine food are present in the soul of the person wishing to receive. This disposition of soul should be verified through examination by a conscience that is enlightened and undeceived, and purified from the passion of self-love; so that one will neither think the dispositions are present where they are not, nor be apprehensive where there is nothing to fear, thus through indiscreet timidity depriving oneself of the sweet and nourishing Bread of Life. It is wrong for a person to presume to sit at the table of the heavenly banquet when not invited by the Lord; it is also wrong for the soul to reject health and life when it can see itself needy and being invited by God. The first person sins by arrogance; the second sins by faintheartedness when through human respect and failure to take the trouble to prepare himself, he deprives himself of the grace of the Most Holy Sacrament.

"He then gave him some rules and criteria for avoiding errors. The first rule was that a person wishing to frequently receive the Blessed Sacrament should have a pure and upright intention. The second was that he have the advice of the chosen spiritual father or confessor. The third was that the soul be experiencing progress in its growth in virtue, especially in charity, humility, compassion, and devotion; for if the soul grows and becomes stronger in these virtues through frequent Communion, it must not be timorous or deprive itself of so great a good. He concluded his letter by saying that if at such a distance his own judgment regarding His Lordship's person had any weight, relying on what he had heard from many sources about His Lordship's life, example, practice of prayer, and works of charity, he ventured to advise him to trust in the mercy of God our Lord and, taking courage from the mercies he had already received from his blessed hand, to practice frequent reception of the Most Holy Sacrament. For he anticipated that this would result in no little fruit for his own soul and for those of others who by following his example would be encouraged toward the same virtue. He went on to promise him that since he was prevented by his many occupations from coming to Spain, he would procure to send one of his companions, a person of excellent spirit and knowledge of divine things, by whose counsel His Lordship would be able to decide this or any other question he might have."

✠

To the Members of the Society in Italy

Rome, June 1, 1542

(Letter 41: I:201-5; in Italian)

A newsletter: events in Rome and Italy, the sad experience of the legates to Ireland, and activities of Jesuits in Portugal and Germany.

The grace and peace of Christ our Lord be always with us.

We have already informed you elsewhere about how we are here, and of some affairs of the Lord, such as the brief allowing the Jews to become Christians and retain their property, the brief sent by His Holiness so that our companions can be legates also in Scotland, and the departure of five of our men to Portugal and of two there to yourselves.

We now mention again that by the Lord's grace we are still continuing with confessions and Communions, and similarly with the Exercises. A marriage dowry has been provided for three Jewish women who became Christians—a widow and two girls.

Another Jew from Bologna was sent to the house by Cardinal Farnese and Cardinal Santa Croce with strong recommendations, so that they could be instructed and baptized. The brief for the Jews was published in various cities of Italy, such as Bologna, Arezzo, Modena, and Parma, where there are Jews out in the villages; and we hope for good results.

In the house there are some young men by God's grace endowed with good qualities. One is from Arezzo, a servant of Cardinal Carpi; he has come to replace Master André [des Freux], who has gone with Master Polanco to study at Padua. There is another from Modena, quite qualified; more will be coming from there. Finally, there is no shortage of tasks for the Lord, though there is of companions; for they are now also being sought from His Holiness by the Signoria of Venice, which has written warmly to their ambassador that they be sent men; two also for Naples, being sought by Cardinal Santa Croce; one for the Bishop of Bergamo, who is going as nuncio to the King of Portugal, requested of the Pope by the Cardinal of Portugal [Miguel de Silva]. "Pray the Lord of the harvest that he will send workers into his vineyard" [see Matt. 9:38], and if His Majesty vouchsafes, will make you instruments for calling them exteriorly, himself subscribing in the lives of those who are called with the finger of the Holy Spirit, for otherwise there would be no way to get in the door.

We had a letter from the men in Ireland. Briefly, by the grace and special providence of their Lord, they reached Ireland, staying there thirty-four days during Lent, suffering a great deal for love of the Lord God and bringing remedies to numerous souls, bringing them to confession and granting them indulgences, giving dispensations gratis to the poor and imposing money penances on others, the entirety of which, in their presence and that of the bishop, they distributed for the love of God to poor persons and for the repair of churches. Nevertheless, for our sins things are going so badly that letters from Germany do not shock us. All the princes [in Ireland] but one (who was about to do it) have allied with the English king, swearing to have him as head in spiritual and temporal matters, to burn any apostolic letters which reach them, and "if they find any belonging to the way, to bring them bound" [see Acts 9:2] to England or to his deputy in Ireland. Consequently, with no hope of fruit, they returned safe and sound to Scotland, where they will remain if our letters reach them before they leave; otherwise they will come here because of the needs we have.

About the fruit being borne in Portugal we cannot write you in a few words. Besides the general fruit being achieved among the people, nearly all the young gentlemen of the King's court and the ladies are going to confession and Communion and hearing sermons every Friday. Master Simão has conversed in spiritual exercises with Her Majesty the Queen and many of her favorite ladies, with great fruit to their souls. His Majesty the King is so attached to the Society for love of the Lord that it cannot easily be described; and he spends on them whatever they want. He has given to them a monastery with an income of two hundred scudi; it is for founding a college, according to what we have learned through letters of Master Simão and from reliable reports by persons coming from there.

We are expecting letters from India in September.

We have so far not received a letter from Araoz, who went to Barcelona with Don Diego [de Eguía].

About Bobadilla, we learn that by the Lord's grace he has borne good fruit with some particular persons, giving exercises to some canons and other priests and hearing the confessions of many others in the court of the King of [the] Romans, who has wished him to accompany the campaign presently being mounted against the Turks. He has shown him great tokens of affection, etc.

Master Jay and the Scottish doctor [Wauchop] are, by commission of the nuncio and command of His Holiness, to stay in Regensburg and the other cities on the Danube, and so far they have borne good fruit.

Master Favre reached Speyer on April 13, and on the journey the Lord God has borne considerable fruit through him. He now has in exercises the Spanish chaplains he brought with him;[26] the vicar general of Speyer; Otto Truchsess, who is a nobleman, etc.; and a doctor of civil and canon law. The bishop [Philip Flersheim] would make them if he were not a German mile outside Speyer. The bishop sent a messenger to the Cardinal of Mainz [Albert of Brandenburg] informing him of Favre's arrival, since the cardinal had sent his own messenger with word that when Favre arrived he should go there. And so it is thought that he will, and he has an order to remain in the cities along the Rhine. He also has become acquainted with a countess who, along with her principal ladies, speaks French; and so there is hope of good fruit.

That is all, except that we commend ourselves to your prayers.

Rome, June 1, 1542

I.

✠

To Antonio Araoz

Rome, June 12, 1542

(XII [Appendix 1, no. 2]: 216f.; in Spanish)

Precautions against scandal regarding the trip to Rome by Isabel Roser

If Isabel Roser decides to come to Rome and intends to make her journey here public, consider whether it would not be good for her

---

[26] Juan de Aragón and Alvaro Alfonso, chaplains to the daughters of Charles V.

to say that she is coming to visit the holy places here and then either go to Jerusalem, remain here, or return to Barcelona—provided this can be said truthfully. For myself, I am inclined to believe that if she comes to Rome it will be for the greater perfection of her soul; but I do not say this so that you will do anything beyond the instruction that you bore, since it is better that she herself choose one course or the other. As to her journey, however, if she makes it, I do not know what route she can take, or when and with whom she can come without occasioning scandal, if only passive, and disedification. May God help you. Amen.

Unless it were to everyone's satisfaction, I am not sure it would be good for you to come together. May God deign to guide and rule you in everything. If, on the other hand, he does not provide his divine assistance, when you do come I would very much like for the city or the vicar to write about you to Cardinal Santa Croce seeking some pretext— either because he has charge of us as our protector or because he is taking you to Naples.[27]

Likewise, if Roser is coming here, I wonder whether it would not be better for you and Don Diego [de Eguía] (since he is not up to staying there alone) to come before winter, as had been said, and she when the winter is over, so that it will not appear that you are bringing her, and truthfully so. Consider this in the Lord, and whatever you decide will seem best to me.

✠

To Giovanni Battista Viola

Rome, August 1542

(Letter 52: I:228f.; in Spanish)

A reproof to a Jesuit scholastic for professing obedience yet seeking to impose his own solution to an academic difficulty that he had brought on by ignoring Ignatius's directions. Viola had gone to Paris with Andrés de Oviedo in October 1541.

May the sovereign grace and love of Christ our Lord be always for our continual favor and help.

I received a letter from you, and do not understand it. Speaking of obedience in two places in your letter, you say in the first that you are ready to obey my will, and in the second, "Since I would sooner

---

[27] The city referred to here is Barcelona; the vicar, Francis Borgia.

long for death than kick against obedience, I submit to Your Reverence's judgment." Now inasmuch as it seems to me that obedience seeks to be blind, I understand blind in two ways: (1) An inferior ought to surrender his own understanding (where there is no question of sin) and do what is commanded him; and (2) an inferior who is or has been given a command by the superior and perceives reasons against what is commanded or drawbacks in it ought humbly to represent to the superior the reasons or drawbacks that occur to him, without attempting to draw him to one side or the other, and afterwards tranquilly to follow the way that is pointed out to him or commanded.

Now, in reply to your own obedience, I cannot manage to understand it. For after giving me what are in your opinion many good arguments to convince me that you ought to change teachers, you tell me elsewhere in your letter, "I decided to write Your Reverence begging you to deign to let me know whether we should change teachers or waste our time." You yourself can judge whether you are seeking obedience or submitting your own judgment so that I can tell you what to do. If you so abound in your own judgment and are quite clear that you are wasting your time, where is your submission of judgment? Or do you perhaps think I am supposed to tell you that you should waste your time? May God our Lord never let me, where I cannot help, do anything to anyone's harm!

Elsewhere you say, "I am really sorry to have wasted these last eight months under this teacher, but if you still think we should go on wasting it, we will continue with him." As I recall, when you left here, I told you that by the time you got to Paris the *Summulæ* course would have been underway for two or three months, and that you ought to study Latin for four or five months to gain confidence and then spend a further three or four months on an introduction to the *Summulæ*, so that you could enroll in the course the following year with some preparation.[28] But since you preferred to follow your opinion rather than mine and to enter a course that was already two or three months advanced, you be the one to decide who is responsible for your wasting your time.

I close, praying God our Lord by his infinite and sovereign goodness to give us his abundant grace so that we may know his most holy will and entirely fulfill it.

Rome

---

[28] Probably the *Summulæ logicæ* of Peter of Spain, a text in one of the courses required for the bachelor's degree.

Faculties Sent to Simão Rodrigues

Rome, November 1, 1542

(Letter 54: I:232f.; in Spanish and Latin)

We, the ten first members of the Society, had from His Holiness and from the Apostolic See the following faculties: to preach anywhere in the world; to hear confessions and absolve from cases reserved to the Apostolic See, except those mentioned in the bull *In cœna Domini;* to administer the other sacraments, but without prejudice to pastors; to anticipate and postpone the canonical hours; to say Mass before daybreak and after midday because of some business or spiritual advantage; and to have and read heretical books. At the present time, the following petition having been made to His Holiness, it has been graciously granted to us. Hence, if there are any in your company who have the conditions named in the petition, you may impart the above-named faculties to them in the measure and manner you think best; and I give you the same faculty for this that was granted to me by His Holiness.

PETITION TO HIS HOLINESS

The Society of Jesus humbly petitions the Holy Father that all the faculties and graces already granted the Society by His Holiness and the Apostolic See may be granted to Antonio de Araoz, licentiate in sacred theology, who entered the Society this year. It also humbly petitions that His Holiness would bestow upon the present or future superior of the same Society the faculty of bestowing these already granted faculties and graces upon any other persons who shall enter the Society, or who have a vow of chastity and poverty together with a resolve to enter the Society, as and when the same superior shall judge it expedient for the salvation of souls, the increase of religion, and the glory of God, on behalf of those to come, so that the entire Society may enjoy these faculties.

Today, November 1, 1542

Yours in our Lord,

IÑIGO

To Simão Rodrigues

Rome, November 1, 1542

(Letter 56: I:234; in Spanish)

A firm reply to charges that he fails to correspond to what is being accomplished in Portugal.

I am delighted at the great charity and the holy zeal by which you would convince me that if I were fully aware of the realities being accomplished in Portugal, I would not spare my feet from traveling or my tongue from speaking and shouting, whichever were more suitable. If I have failed or am failing to do the very little of which I am capable, I wholly condemn myself. Thus you can be assured that there is no need to convince me on this score; you need only set forth and explain your view. In the matter of powers I yield to many, for I know how weak and frail are my own; but insignificant though they are, I am convinced that they have been employed to the full satisfaction of all who have anything to do with this matter. And it is my place, as I have written you on other occasions, that things be presented to me, and that if there are any opinions or proposals, it be left to me to judge and to decide whether to speak or remain silent on behalf of the person in charge of the entire affair.

✠

To Simão Rodrigues

Rome, November 1, 1542

(Letter 57: I:235; in Spanish)

Points for Pedro Doménech to discuss with Rodrigues: letter writing; financial negotiations, and the possibility of sending foreign Jesuits to study in Portugal.

MEMORANDUM FOR SPEAKING WITH MASTER SIMÃO:

1. He should write us a letter that can be shown to anyone—great, middling, or small, good and bad—and which avoids speaking prejudicially of any individual.

2. In other letters he can write whatever particulars he likes and judges profitable for what we all desire for the greater service of God our Lord.

3. Regarding the two churches there and their incomes, it appears more seemly that the King entrust this matter to Señor Pedro Doménech or to Senhor Baltasar de Faria and have them make the petition here; we ourselves could easily be criticized here, etc.

4. Senhor Baltasar de Faria told me that the King, wishing to provide an income for a college for the Society, was sending him certain faculties from certain prelates; in the absence of such a faculty, he said, he intended to write there to have it sent. If it is, it would likewise be more seemly for all negotiations on matters of incomes or houses to be done through other hands than ours.

5. Inasmuch as the King of France has expelled from his kingdom all subjects of the Emperor, including nine of our men who had gone to Louvain, while we have seven other men from Italy still in Paris and so ill supplied because of these changes that I do not think they will be able to continue their studies; and with us having other men here in the house who have ability for studies and a good beginning in them—I would like to know whether I can send any of them to you there, and how many and of what sort. Until you write me I do not propose sending you any, so as not to fall into some breach of courtesy, even though we know how very generous a will is present there in our Lord.

✠

To Pierre Favre

Rome, December 10, 1542

(Letter 58: I:236–38; in Spanish)

Ignatius enjoins that greater order and care be used in writing him regular main letters which can be shown to the Society's friends and benefactors; private matter, to be written on separate sheets, requires less care. This letter went not only to Favre but to the other far-flung members of the Society.

I recall telling you frequently face to face as well as writing you frequently when we were apart that any member of the Society intending to write us here ought to write out a main letter that can be shown to anybody; for there are many persons who are well disposed towards us and who want to see our letters, but to whom we dare not show them because they are disorganized and full of inappropriate matter; and since these people find out when we have received letters from this or that person, we incur considerable resentment and give more disedification than edification. Just recently I found it necessary, or at least quite useful, to show letters from two members of the Society to a couple of cardinals who would have to take care of what they had written me; but since the letters contained irrelevant, disorganized matter that was not suitable to be shown, I was hard put to it to let them see some parts and cover up the rest.

And so I will now repeat once more what I said previously, so that we will all fully understand one another. I beg, therefore, by the love and reverence of God our Lord, that we handle our correspondence in a way that will be for the greater service of his divine goodness and the greater advantage of our neighbor. In the main letter we should write what each man is doing by way of preaching, hearing confessions, [giving the] Exercises, and other spiritual works which God works through each man, in a way that will give the greatest edification to the hearers or readers. If the soil is barren and there is nothing to report, there should be a few words about health matters, a conversation with so-and-so, or the like. But extraneous matters should not be mixed with this; these should be left for the separate sheets, which can contain the dates of letters received, the spiritual joy or sentiments occasioned by them, anything about illnesses, news, business, and lengthier exhortations.

I will describe what I myself do and, I trust in the Lord, will continue doing in this regard so as to avoid mistakes when writing to members of the Society. I make a first draft of the main letter, reporting things that will be edifying; then, after reading it over and correcting it, keeping in mind that it is going to be read by everybody, I write or have someone write it out a second time. For we must give even more thought to what we write than to what we say. Writing is permanent and gives lasting witness; we cannot mend or reinterpret it as easily as we can our speech. And even with all this I am sure I make many mistakes, and fear doing so in the future. I leave for the separate pages other details that are inappropriate for the main letter or lacking in edification. These pages each one can write hastily "out of the overflow of the heart," with or without careful organization. But this may not be tolerated in the main letter: it must be composed carefully and edifyingly, so that it can be shown around and give edification. Since I see everyone falling short on this score, I am sending everyone a copy of this letter, with a plea in our Lord that you always compose the main letter as I have indicated above, revise it, and then recopy it or have it recopied. If people will write two drafts like this, the way I do, I am sure the letters we get will be better thought through and organized.

And so, unless I see you doing this from now on for the greater unity, charity, and edification of all, I myself, unwilling to have to answer to God our Lord for negligence in matters of such importance, will be forced to write and command you under obedience to revise and, after correction, recopy or have recopied any main letter that you send me. Having thereby done all that is in my power, I will rest easy, though I would much rather you did not give me cause to write you this way. I urge you, then, as I am obliged to do for the greater glory of God our Lord, and I beg you, for his love and reverence alone, to correct your faults in writing, making it a point of pride and having a real desire to edify your brethren and others through your letters. Let the time you waste on this be upon my head; it will be time well wasted in the Lord. I make the effort to write two drafts of any main letter so that it will have some order; I even do the same with many of the separate pages. Even this one I have written out twice in my own hand. All the more reason why each member of the Society should do the same. After all, you only have to write to a single person, while I have to write to all of you. I can honestly say that the other night we calculated that the letters we are presently sending out to various places run to two hundred and fifty. Busy as some members of the Society may be, I am sure that I am, if not overly so, at least no less busy than anybody else—and with poorer physical health. So far there is none of you I can commend in this matter, though I say this not to point blame but in a general way.

If the copies of others' letters that I send you appear to have some order and be free of useless matter, the reason is that with enormous loss of my own time, I extract the edifying parts, rearrange the wording, and edit out the irrelevant matter, so as to give some pleasure in our Lord to all of you and edification to those who hear them for the first time. And I once more beg you to work at this for love and reverence of his Divine Majesty, and with a wholehearted and serious effort; it is of no little importance for the spiritual progress and consolation of souls. It will be all right to compose a main letter, revised and corrected, every second week; together, this amounts to two letters' worth of work. You may go on as much as you like in the separate pages and when writing only to a single person. With God's help I myself shall write to all of you every month without fail, however briefly, and every three months at greater length, sending you all the news and copies of all the letters from throughout the Society. And so, for love of God our Lord, let us all assist one another. And give me your help by carrying and lightening somewhat the heavy burden which you placed on my back, along with other activities not lacking here by way of pious works and spiritual gains. If I could do the work of ten, or if all of us were here together in Rome, there would be more than enough for us to do.

If your memory fails you, as mine often does, keep this letter or some equivalent reminder in front of you when writing your main letters.

Rome, December 10, 1542

✠

To Juan de Verdolay (?)

Rome, sometime in 1543

(Letter 75: I:283–85; in Spanish)

An invitation to a friend in Spain, possibly Juan de Verdolay (see letter 12), to come and join the apostolic work in Rome.

May the sovereign grace and love of Jesus Christ our Lord be always for our favor and for our help.

Some days ago, through some good Portuguese fathers, I received a letter from your hand, though not in response to the one I had earlier written you. It brought me great joy in the Lord to learn that you were in good health and rendering continual service and praise to his Divine Majesty. On the fathers' behalf, in accord with their own and my disposition, I had regard, as was proper, to the greater service of God our Lord and to your letter and extended myself as far as lay in my poor powers.

I later received a letter from Esteban de Eguía, a Navarrese gentleman who passed through here; and through what I also heard from others, I picked up that you have some inclination to come here to these parts. As I thought about this, something previously dormant within me in this regard reawakened, and I decided to write this letter to give you some gesture from my side. And it is this: if you do come here (since I trust in God our Lord that it will issue in service and honor to his divine Majesty, and that even if you reject and count as naught any offer of mine—which would be fine with me—it is still right for me to make it, since I firmly think and believe that in so doing I serve my God and Lord), my offer is this: desiring for you to come here, where there is the head of the world and the greatest possible (or at least very considerable) need, I, with the poor old woman, will put my mite into the treasury; and it is this: upon your arrival here I commit myself to furnish (or get someone else to furnish) you, and two other persons whom you may bring with you, with whatever you need by way of food, clothing, footwear, and decent living quarters. In addition to this, if our Lord does not abandon me, I am confident of giving you certain cardinals who, for his greater service and praise, support the cause of truth; indeed, I am confident of even more cardinals. And so, I commend you to God our Lord; have no doubts about things at this end and do not waste the great talent which our Lord has given you. For anywhere else you go will be on brooks and streams; here it will be on broad gulfs of sea.

I conclude in our Lord, hoping less to hear from you than to see you.

Rome

☩

To Nicolás Bobadilla

Rome, 1543

(Letter 74: I:277-82; in Spanish)

A reply, combining firmness with humility, to Bobadilla's outspoken protests against Ignatius's regulations about letter writing. Ignatius once said that he would give his vote to Bobadilla for general if half of the Society did so; it is interesting in this regard that at the time Ignatius himself was elected general of the Society, Bobadilla's vote had not yet arrived in Rome.

May the sovereign grace and love of Christ our Lord be always for our continual favor and help.

While I find myself by his infinite grace more inclined to humble myself entirely rather than defend myself in part, I have nevertheless, judging it for his greater glory, decided to employ both measures.

1. Regarding a certain fraternal correction among ourselves which I decided to make for God's greater glory, you say that you understand my mind but fear that not all would take it with your own understanding and sincerity. By "all" I suppose you mean all who belong to our Society, since I wrote only for them. But if you see that some of them are not taking my remarks with your own sincerity and purity of soul, let me know, and I trust in our Lord that I will accommodate myself to each and every one of them, to your own and their complete satisfaction.

2. With the argument that styles of speaking and writing are quite different, you demonstrate the impossibility of my correcting everyone's

taste by my own. I recall writing that the main letter ought to be written out twice: after being written the first time and corrected, it should then be copied or handed over to another to copy a second time, so as to avoid the disadvantages of unconsidered writing which I felt some of us were guilty of. If we all did this—myself first of all, since I think I have greater need—we would be a greater help to each other in the Lord. I did not and do not mean that a person with one style needs to write in a different one, or that a person with first-level skills has to write in a second level. If I cannot raise my own poor and mean native understanding to a level higher, I can hardly do so for others, since to give much or little belongs to our Creator and Lord. I only meant that in the case of main letters everyone should write a first draft, correct it, and then recopy it or have it recopied, since in this way we each do what we ought for the other. Neither I nor anybody else can give to another more than he has, but by making this effort each of us gives the best of what he has received from his Creator and Lord. Consequently, I do not believe I am setting myself up as a universal norm.

3. You consider it a good idea to write summary or abbreviated letters, for making copies only, but not giving us the full account that we want. You are quite aware of what I wrote you and of what we are all agreed upon: that the main letter should give any matters that are at all edifying, according as God our Lord works through each individual for the spiritual good of souls; and that anyone wishing to give further information—about news, illnesses, problems, and the like—should write as fully as he wishes on separate sheets or in a separate letter.

4. You observe that in the copy of your letter I had said, "I try to expedite [expedir] my time," when I should have said, "expend [expender] my time." If you had looked closely at the letter, you would have seen that in my own hand I had written *expender*, not *expedir*. However, perhaps the copyist here did write *expedir* for *expender;* I did not personally check the final version but relied on someone else, since it was not a main letter that was to be shown to others. I confess myself as guilty as you may judge me to be in our Lord.

5. As for the blunder you point out in my addressing my letter to you "At the palace of the King of the Romans," that is indeed what I wrote, thinking that you would be better known in the palace, a house where you frequently appear, than in the court at large spread all over the city. Hence, since I blundered in writing "of the Romans," I shall in future address letters to you "At the court of the King of Romans." If, as you say, everybody had a laugh over this, I would have thought that when you saw people laughing, you would stop showing it around. I will

be very grateful in our Lord if you show this letter around too, so that, having been corrected because of the first letter, I can obtain further correction through this one. For this is my desire in this life—to be set straight and corrected in all my faults by being given loving fraternal correction for them all. Indeed, I recall that right after you all made your profession, I earnestly asked and implored the entire Society that whenever anyone detected anything amiss in me, after first praying to God our Lord and conferring about it with his Divine Majesty, he would let me know my faults so that I could be helped and amended in our Lord.

6. You say you think I should not waste time correcting such trivial matters, and that people who did not know me might think I had nothing better to spend my time on. I recall that, besides repeated discussion and agreement among ourselves, I wrote you at length begging you to write your main letters twice in the manner, and because of the difficulties, mentioned above. I wrote that unless you did this I would be forced, with a view to our common spiritual good and my own conscience, albeit much against my character, to command you under obedience to do so. I recall that you received my letter and answered with considerable edification and satisfaction. But then in your first letter after that you wrote opposite to the way I had so earnestly asked and begged you in our Lord to do. You wrote in your main letter all kinds of news about the situation there which we would all have been delighted to have if it came in a separate letter or on separate pages, such as information about your own person and how you had a touch of rash that was killing you—all of which could have been put on a separate page as we had often agreed among ourselves to do, so that everybody could have a dish to his own taste, and all for the good. For we have numerous friends and acquaintances who learn we have received letters from the Society's members; they want to see these letters and enjoy reading them. If we do not show the letters when asked, we alienate them; if we show letters that are disorderly, they are disedified. Actually, I was not so much anxious to correct the phrasing of your letters as desirous of your own entire perfection—assuming, of course, that a part of that perfection consists in your humbling yourself and obeying the one into whose hands you made a vow of obedience, particularly in matters that are good or indifferent and without sin. Hence, while deeming up until now that it was to the greater glory of God our Lord and our own spiritual good for me to expend some of my time on this matter, if you think otherwise I shall in the future be able to conform myself to what you think best in our Lord; for I am sure of receiving as much benefit in his Divine Majesty from you as from any of the others.

7. You write: "You imagine that everybody is edified by these copies of yours. I rarely show them around or read them myself—I don't have the time. Two letters could be made out of the superfluous matter in your main letter." Of course I never imagined that you would show them to everybody or that everybody would be edified. I thought you would show them to a few people who would take them in good part, as I have learned has been the case so far with all the others to whom I have sent this same main letter (unless I am deceived by what they write me)—even Doctor Ortiz and his brother Fray Francisco, and Doctor Picart of Paris. As for your not deigning to read my letters for lack of time: by the grace of God I have more than enough time and inclination to read and reread all of yours. To get you to read mine, I will cut out whatever you think superfluous and make whatever adaptation I can in our Lord; once I have got your opinion, I will work hard on this. I will do the same for all others to whom I have written who are of your view and complain of superfluous matter, provided you let me know about it. For it would be quite a mistake on my part to spend so much time and labor only to annoy people uselessly. I therefore beg of you by the love and reverence of God our Lord to write me how you think I can best write you, whether by myself or through somebody else, so that I will not go wrong but fully satisfy you. Meanwhile, not knowing the right way to do it, I will await a letter from you—or I will commission someone else to write, however I perceive is to your liking.

Similarly, since you already know my own wishes in the matter, I ask you by the same love and reverence of his Divine Majesty always to write me the best way you can—as I have repeatedly asked and implored you and now implore you once more in our Lord, being apparently unable to obtain my most urgent requests because of my utter unworthiness—or however you think best. If the Society, or one half of it, agrees, I give you my own vote—for what it is worth—offering you willingly and with the greatest joy of soul the charge that I hold. I not only give my vote to you but, if you prefer, I am ready to give it to anybody else named by you or by any of the others, considering that whatever was thus decided would be for the greater praise, reverence, and service of God our Lord and for the greater spiritual solace of my own soul in his Divine Majesty. For the very truth is that, absolutely speaking, I would prefer to remain lowly and to be free of this burden. Thus, completely and fully setting aside my own poor judgment, I constantly hold, and hope always to hold, that whatever you and the Society determine, or a part of it as mentioned above, will be far the better thing; and this determination I herewith approve and confirm in my own hand.

Meanwhile, with respect to providing for your personal needs there, while it is our profession to offer ourselves to be sent wherever and in whatever way the Vicar of Christ our Lord may decide, without ourselves requesting any provision, nevertheless, since I judged that I might lawfully, speaking through others, explain or intimate your need there so that they could provide for it or not as they deem best for the glory of God our Lord, in accord with what you wrote me I spoke to Cardinal Santa Croce [Cervini] and also to Cardinal Morone. If I were there, I would rest satisfied with this and accept what I needed from any hand that I thought came from God our Lord. If occasionally I seemed not to have enough, I would take it that God was deigning to try me thoroughly so that I could acquire greater merit in his greater service, praise, and glory. But I need enlarge no more on this, for I think I know your disposition for far more than this in our Lord.

I was late in writing you because I did not know where you were, since you had written me about the baths and I did not know where you would end up.

May it please God our Lord that this letter find you in entire health and in the place or situation where you can best serve him and always praise his most holy name.

✠

To the Members of the Society of Jesus
by commission
Rome, March 1543–June 1544
(Letter 62: I:248–53; in Spanish)

This is likely a combination of two letters over a year apart, reporting the progress of the houses for catechumens and converted women; the lifting of the restriction on the number of the Society's members; the entrance into the Society of the brilliant (but, as it turned out, unbalanced) Paris humanist, Guillaume Postel; and other items.

May the grace and peace of Christ our Lord be always for our continual favor and help.

Last February, as directed by our father Master Ignatius, we wrote you briefly about some things that had taken place here over the previous three months through the help of our Lord. In this present short letter, I would like to inform you about what our Lord has deigned to work here since then, so that together with ourselves you may give thanks. The earlier letter mentioned the house which has been established for catechumens, and how Master Giovanni del Mercato accepted an invitation to take charge of it, and how when he saw the need for persons to assist him, he obtained from Cardinal Crescenzi the formation of an association to take charge of this, he himself wishing to be one of the association, whereas he had previously been the head of the entire work. The cardinal took the association under his protection, and asked Master Ignatius to become a member. Once this association of nobles and persons of rank was formed and there were five catechumens to be baptized, the project was launched by their being sent to the house where the house has been founded. And so, numerous cardinals and high-ranking figures having been invited in order to encourage the other Jews, there was a great celebration on the octave of Easter; neither the church nor the square could hold all the people who came to the holy baptism. After the sermon, Bishop Cornelius baptized three men and two women. One of them was a rabbi very learned in the law, with a son of his. Since he had three or four little children in Mantua, we wrote to the Cardinal of Mantua to make sure that the other Jews should not take them but [instead] to have them baptized. Since then seven others persons have been baptized, five Jews and two Moors; and there are now more who also want to be baptized.

We also wrote you about the growth of the house for sinful women, otherwise called the Company of Grace. Since then we have arranged with Cardinal Carpi to be the house's protector. With this obtained from His Holiness, we have since had a number of ladies become members of the association and take responsibility for assisting the women in their needs; and in this way, through the grace of our Lord, this work is quite solidly established. The women who have withdrawn from sin so far are twenty-four, all of them with so much spirit and edification that they are all very edified. Many others would like to get in; but the place is small, and they are waiting till it can be expanded, if it please our Lord.

This week His Holiness increased the Society's number. The earlier concession in the bull had been restricted to sixty members; now it is unlimited. Later His Holiness granted issuance of a brief confirming all the privileges previously granted to the Society and authorizing the superior to give them to anyone he wishes who is determined to enter the Society. As soon as the brief is issued, we will send it to you without delay and without fail.

○   ○   ○

Last March, three Frenchmen from Paris arrived, accompanied by a Master who proposed to enter the Society. Among them was one named Guillaume Postel, a man of about thirty-five, a reader of the King in Paris and beneficed, an adequate Paris Master of Arts, quite learned in Greek, Hebrew, and Latin, and moderately so in Arabic. He speaks excellent Italian and has produced several books, partly translations from Greek into Latin, partly works of his own. He relinquished his chair and his benefice and came to let himself be guided and governed by the Society; and so after making the Exercises he has decided to become a member of the Society. He has gone through some experiments, such as cooking and preaching in the square, and is persevering to the great edification of all. The others are a pair of promising young men; one has begun arts and the other grammar, and both are resolved to enter the Society. We have had word from Paris that five persons have decided for the Society, one of them a master and regent of Paris.

An abbot of numerous monasteries, elected general of the whole order, made the Exercises with great profit to himself and, it is hoped, to all his monasteries.

Master Francisco Zapata has now decided to join the Society. He has already served in the hospital and is ready to do all the other experiments, etc. Others are about to make the Exercises, and many others would like to make them if we had the capacity.

Master Ignatius has undertaken recently to bring about some very important reconciliations, and by the Lord's grace they succeeded, with much edification. The work of hearing confessions is growing rather than diminishing.

Master Paschase left here at the command of Cardinals Santa Croce and Carpi to reform a monastery in Reggio in Lombardy; and we have heard that he has already reformed it.

Master Pietro Codazzo's construction is just about completed; he worked very hard at it and was aided by our Lord with substantial alms, coming chiefly from the larger number of the cardinals who were moved to assist him, together with the other bishops. One of them, His Holiness's vicar, summoned him recently and told him that he had sent him three hundred ducats from his own limited funds, and that of those three hundred they were giving him a hundred. Another person has given him two hundred, and others one hundred, so that we have much reason to thank the Lord, seeing how generously he provides for us.

These are the main points, so as not to irk you, although there are numerous other quite edifying details we might supply you; however, so as not to go on too long this will suffice for now.

For all this may thanks be rendered to the Lord, who "works all these things in all" [1 Cor. 12:6].

☧

To Diego Laínez

Rome, March 13, 1543

(Letter 61: I:246–f.; in Spanish)

While preparing the Society's Constitutions, Ignatius begins to implement some of the provisions initially agreed to by the first companions—in this case regarding the teaching of catechism and the manner of dress.

Here are the constitutions on children as signed by the six who were present with authority for those who were absent, until they can be further spelled out and put into decent form.[29] Wherefore, in conformity with the constitutions and their declarations, I give you, as I am required to do, two commands in virtue of holy obedience. The first is that you teach boys or men for forty days each year, reckoning the year as twelve full months from the day you left Rome or arrived at the country where you were going. If by this reckoning you have already completed a year, or once you complete a year, you may begin counting, for example, with the year 1543, teaching them any time you wish, and then any time you wish in 1544, and so on—counting not by twelve-month periods but by the calendar year. The second command is that you be clothed and shod in conformity with the enclosed chapters regarding the constitutions on clothing and footwear. I likewise urge you to observe exactly chapters 5 and 6 on clothing and footwear; and if you are unwilling to do so by my exhortation, I command you to in virtue of obedience. However, so long as my conscience is not burdened regarding the promise and vow I made to God our Lord on the day of our

---

[29] The six present in Rome in 1541 were Ignatius, Laínez, Jay, Broët, Salmerón, and Codure. Those absent were Xavier and Rodrigues in Portugal, Favre in Germany, and Bobadilla in the kingdom of Naples.

profession, and by the power of the constitutions, so far as I am able, I grant you a dispensation to be used at your discretion in our Lord.

✠

To Ercole d'Este, duke of Ferrara

Rome, April 15, 1543

(Letter 65: I:257f.; in Italian)

A letter of gratitude for the intervention of the duke's cardinal brother on the Society's behalf, and for the recommendation for Salmerón. Several years later, in 1547, Claude Jay was, at the duke's request, sent to Ferrara as a spiritual guide. It was thought important to do what one could for the court in Ferrara, in part because of the danger in the Protestantizing sympathies of his wife, Renée.

Ihus.

Our Lord in Christ Jesus

May the sovereign grace and eternal love of Christ our Lord visit and greet Your Excellency.

Long have I been wanting to do this, had I not been deterred by my slight being and scanty worth. But now, summoning courage in our Lord because one of our Society is traveling to Lombardy, I have seized this occasion to write Your Excellency. In doing so, I cannot but rejoice in our Lord and render infinite and unceasing thanks to his Divine Majesty at the thought of how much his divine and eternal Goodness has done for us (unworthy even to be named), choosing Your Excellency as his outstanding and elect instrument for this. When did we deserve that Your Excellency, at the time of the greatest opposition against us in Rome, should have been mindful of our unworthy selves, and, when we were thought to be charlatans, should have borne such good witness to us and written so many times in our continual favor? And later, during another period of not inconsiderable opposition, when, after His Holiness had confirmed our least congregation, certain cardinals who were officials were unwilling to put it into a bull, it was through Your Excellency's means and intercession, by the instrumentality of Your Excellency's brother, our lord the Most Reverend Cardinal of Ferrara, that our whole cause was dispatched, as we informed Your Excellency in another letter, which also manifested our great debt and perpetual obligation.

May it ever please the sovereign and divine Clemency to recompense and repay Your Excellency with his most holy consolations and spiritual blessings and eternal peace; and to us, both those of us now and those to come, may he deign to give his eternal and accustomed grace, so that, our actions and operations being rendered worthy, Your Excellency might hold and dispose of all that is ours, in keeping with all we owe Your Excellency.

I return now to the present occasion that gives me courage in our Lord to write. The Most Reverend Cardinal Morone wrote me asking to have one of our Society for a time, so that in his diocese, through our Lord's cooperation, he might be able to produce some spiritual fruit. In view of his making this request most insistently, we deemed it our just duty to make our first recourse and reverence to Your Excellency, so that Master Salmerón, the bearer of this, who has been designated for this trip, may perform whatever Your Excellency might command and order him, as you shall deem in any matter to be for the greater praise and glory of God our Lord and for Your Excellency's greater honor and service.

Desiring this with all my heart, I close, praying to God our Lord, by his infinite and sovereign goodness, that he will deign highly to signalize Your Excellency in heaven and on earth in his greater service, and praise, and that Your Excellency will always consider us his most affectionate servants in our Lord.

✠

To Cardinal Marcello Cervini

Rome, June 24, 1543

(Letter 67: 1, 261f.; in Italian)

Ignatius urges enforcement of decree 22 of the Fourth Lateran Council (1215), which required physicians to get the seriously ill to call in a confessor before receiving medical treatment.[30]

---

[30] "Since sickness of the body may sometimes be the result of sin—as the Lord said to the sick man whom he had cured, *Go and sin no more, lest something worse befall you*—we by this present decree order and strictly command physicians of the body, when they are called to the sick, to warn and persuade them first of all to call in physicians of the soul, so that after their spiritual health has been provided for, one might more healthfully proceed to medicine for their bodies; for when the cause ceases, so does the effect. This among other things has occasioned this decree, namely that some people on their sickbed, when they are advised by physicians to arrange for the health of their souls, fall into despair and so the more readily incur

My Most Illustrious Lord and father in Christ:

May the sovereign grace and eternal love of Christ our Lord greet and visit Your Illustrious Lordship.

I received your Lordship's letter of the sixteenth on the twenty-first. Yesterday I spoke with the Cardinal Legate about getting physicians to observe the decree of Innocent III, and he told me that to ensure and confirm this observance for the future, he expected that, having written to the court, once the colloquy of His Holiness with His Imperial Majesty was over, there would be a satisfactory resolution and reply from Cardinal Farnese, since His Holiness had already been well informed on the matter and highly praised it, approving the observance of this decree.[31] In view of Your Illustrious Lordship's own very favorable attitude towards this holy work, I decided to submit a memorandum on it, so that the Cardinal Legate, seeing a letter from your Lordship or Cardinal Farnese assuring him of His Holiness's approval, could put it immediately into execution.

I pray God our Lord that Your Illustrious Lordship may be guided and governed in all things by his Divine Majesty.

Rome, June 24, 1543

Your Illustrious Lordship's most humble and perpetual servant in our Lord,

IGNATIO

✠

Rebuttal of Objections to Decree 22
of the Fourth Lateran Council

Undated

Letter 68, (I:264f.; in Latin)

See previous letter.

It is not against charity to deny medical treatment to a sick person who refuses confession, even if he should die.

1. Laws and canonical sanctions envisage first and primarily the common and universal good rather than [those that are] private and

---

the danger of death. If any physician transgresses this our constitution, . . . he shall be barred from entering a church until he has made suitable satisfaction."

[31] Rodolfo Pio, left in charge of Rome during Paul III's absence, was the papal legate.

individual. But to deny medical treatment to a sick person who refuses confession is a particular matter; hence, for the sake of the common good, it is not against, etc., since for one person who refuses to go to confession an almost countless number will.

2. If this were against charity, it would follow that all justice would be abolished. But this would be extremely detrimental. Therefore.

Proof: It would not be allowed to punish any crime, many of which can be listed. Therefore.

Proof: First, a judge would not be able to hand over to execution a heretic who refused confession and persisted in his faithlessness, whereas, if he refuses confession being so enjoined, he rightly may and should be put to death, even though, by the same reasoning, if he had lived he might have repented. But this would be most detrimental. Therefore, for the sake of the common good, it is not against charity.

3. God's law is unimpeachable. But some persons were killed who might have repented had they lived, as is clearly the case with Dathan and Abiram, Ananias and Sapphira. Therefore it is not against, etc. Also the man who gathered wood [Num. 15:32–36].

4. A canonical provision which has been holily and lawfully ordained by a general council, under the influence of the Holy Spirit present in the council's midst, cannot determine or decree anything against charity. Therefore, the council's authority and fatherly charity is a sufficient proof; consequently, it is not against, etc.; for it is stated in the decree that after the sick person's spiritual health has been attended to, one is to go on to medical remedies for his body, since when the cause ceases, so does the effect.

See the *Summa Angelica,* the *Antonina, Tabiena,* and *Silvestrina* on any illness.[32]

---

[32] The *summa*s of Angelo de Clavasio, O.S.F., St. Antoninus of Florence, O.P., Silvestro de Prierio, O.P., and Giovanni Cagnazzo, O.P.

Arguments for Decree 22
of the Fourth Lateran Council
Undated
(Letter 69: I:265–67; in Italian)

See previous two documents. The decree was put into effect, at least for a time, in Rome, but was not extended beyond that.

Noting that countless sick persons are deprived of spiritual medicine and pass from this life having made a very poor confession or none at all, since they are commonly urged to do so only when the illness has become acute and there is little or no hope of life, at a time when memory is failing and the mind so weakened that the confession is very summarily and poorly made and often not made at all because of delirium or other fatal circumstances; and seeing, moreover, that to bring up confession at such a critical moment hastens their death through the fright it gives them; all of which could be avoided if they would make their confession at the beginning of their illness, when it can not only secure the sick persons' souls but can still alleviate and substantially contribute to their physical health, "since sickness of the body may sometimes be the result of sin—as the Lord said to the sick man whom he had cured, *Go and sin no more, lest something worse befall you*" [Lateran IV, d. 22]—in view of all this, the Most Reverend Legate, who had also earlier made provision for this very matter in his own diocese of Faenza, desires to have observed the decree and chapter "Cum infirmitas corporalis, de penitentiis et remissione" laid down by the Fourth Lateran Council in the time of Pope Innocent III.[33] However, His Reverend Lordship proposes to mitigate the observance of the chapter; namely, where it says that the sick person's soul must be treated first so that "after their spiritual health has been provided for, one might more healthfully proceed to medicine for their bodies, so that when the cause ceases the effect may cease as well," he proposes to publish that the physician may treat a person on a first and second visit even if he has not gone to confession, but may take no measures on a third visit unless the person has previously gone to confession or makes his confession within three days. Even with this mitigation there have been physicians doing all they could to upset this holy work, not only here but also by writing there.

---

[33] The legate referred to is Cardinal Rodolfo Pio.

Even though some members of this profession hold an opposed opinion, claiming that it is against charity to let an obstinate sick person die by withholding treatment if he refuses confession, since if he were treated and lived, he might later repent and be saved, persons of sound judgment reply that all law is made for the common and universal good, even if it is harmful to some individual person. Thus, we see that in the precept of sabbath observance, a man who was gathering wood was commanded to be stoned for the common good and the general observance of the law [Num. 15:32–36]. Similarly with Dathan and Abiram, Ananias and Sapphira, and many others who, it could be claimed, might have repented if they had lived.

Likewise, God our Lord knew well that many persons were going to commit fornication, but he nonetheless posited the precept against fornicating for the common good and universal welfare.

Finally, after consulting together and studying the matter, a number of leading theologians and canonists have affixed their signatures, as Your Lordship can have scrutinized in the enclosed copy, the original remaining in our house with the seal of the general chapter that was held in Sant'Agostino and the signatures of all the learned theologians and canonists, whose opinion, albeit with some verbal differences, is unanimous, as can be seen in the copies of their approvals. Meanwhile, His Holiness, having been informed, has highly praised the step of having the decree observed. However, as the physicians are raising so much noise here, and it is even likely that—for our sins and blindness—they will seek all the support they can obtain there to block this holy work; and even if it is promulgated and put into execution, it is very clear that in order to wreck it, they will never leave off crying in protest.

✠

To Margaret of Austria

Rome, August 13, 1543

(Letter 71: I:271–73; in Spanish)

A request for help in obtaining for a priest the restoration of his right to say Mass; previously the priest had committed but later expiated some serious crime. Margaret of Austria, natural daughter of Emperor Charles V and wife of Pope Paul III's grandson, had much influence at the papal court and was a close collaborator of Ignatius.

My Most Excellent Lady in our Lord:

May the sovereign grace and eternal love of Christ our Lord greet and visit Your Excellency.

Just as Pietro Codazzo, the Milanese canon who takes entire care of us and of the new house for sinful women, is going to the court to get the full or final document of the bull for them because of a certain need that has arisen regarding the house and the association of women, it happens that a father of the order of St. Dominic brings me letters in which he is strongly recommended by persons whom I deem that in conscience I ought not fail and may not refuse in any just and proper matter. And so I decided to write to Your Excellency for God's greater glory, especially since, as the father himself informs me, God our Lord has bestowed upon him the grace of having word of his trials and desolation come to Your Excellency's ears. Now, since one of the chief spiritual works of mercy is to console a soul weighed down with desolation and tribulation, I cannot resist humbly interceding with Your Excellency in behalf of this soul—and this all the more as I know from my own experience that Your Excellency is readily inclined and disposed to all works of mercy in our Lord. Moreover, so as not to prove importunate in intervening to ask for something that is not feasible or just and deserved, and to make sure that it would not be refused, I have, in addition to what I myself in our Lord was able to judge or learn, communicated with several learned men and penitentiaries; and they are all one in thinking the request worthy and deserving of support, especially as the poor man has spent three years in prison for his sin, has done much penance through the space of eight or nine years, and now comes with the permission of his superior and the approval of learned men of his order to try to be reinstated and console his soul with the Divine Sacrifice. Likewise, since it is understood here that to avoid scandal he would not celebrate in the place where the offense was committed, but elsewhere, either in public or private, as his superior and order judge to be for the greater glory of God our Lord, it will be a great deal easier and more gratifying to grant the dispensation and console this soul.

But since I refer Your Excellency in this matter as in all else to Master Pietro Codazzo as though I were present in my own person, I will conclude, humbly beseeching God our Lord that Your Excellency be guided and governed in all your actions by the divine and eternal goodness.

Rome, August 13, 1543

The Lady Countess of Carpi is recovering from her illness, though not yet entirely. Endless thanks to the Giver of all life, inward and outward, for his greater service, praise, and glory.

✠

To Stefano Caponsacchi

Rome, September 19, 1543

(Letter 72: I:273; in Spanish)

An urgent reminder to a Jesuit in Bologna that he needs to write to an irritated correspondent.

Master Stefano:

If I am to meet with Cardinal Carpi's secretary, for the love of God our Lord write him immediately and apologize for your not having written to him; for he says that you can have no excuse, since you write to others, for forgetting him. He means this so seriously that I am astonished to see how jealous and angry he is.

Rome, September 19, 1543

✠

To Teresa Rejadell

Rome, November 15, 1543

(Letter 73: I:274–76; in Spanish)

Consolation on the death of her sister, reassurance about the status of her rule, and guidance on the practice of frequent Communion. It had been almost seven years since Ignatius and Teresa had exchanged letters; but in the intervening years Araoz had gone back and forth to Spain, helping the Benedictine nuns at Teresa's convent in their reform efforts, and so she was not without news of Ignatius.

May the sovereign grace and love of Christ our Lord be always for our continual favor and help.

1.   Having learned that God's will for your sister and ours in our Lord, Luisa, has been fulfilled by her being taken and withdrawn from the travails of this present life, I have many grounds and signs for assurance that she is now in the other life, filled with glory for ever and ever. From there I trust that she, as we do not fail to remember her in our own prayers, however poor and unworthy, will favor and repay us with

holy interest. Hence, for me to go on at length with words of consolation would be, I think, a kind of insult to you, since I am sure that you entirely conform yourself, as you ought, to the supreme and everlasting providence which has only our greater glory in view.

2. With respect to the habit and observance: where you have received a judgment in your favor—and even if you had not but do have the confirmation of the Apostolic See—you should have no doubts: you are certainly in conformity with the service and will of God.[34] For any rule of a blessed saint binds under sin inasmuch as it is approved by the vicar of Christ our Lord or by another with his authority. Thus the rules of SS. Benedict, Francis, or Jerome have no force of their own to oblige under sin; they oblige only when they have the confirmation and authorization of the Apostolic See, by virtue of the divine authority which this imparts to the rule.

3. Regarding daily Communion, we should recall that in the primitive Church everybody received daily, and that since that time there has been no ordinance or document from our holy mother the Church or the holy doctors, either positive or scholastic, against a person's being able to receive Communion daily if so moved by devotion. And while St. Augustine said that he neither praised nor blamed receiving Communion daily (although elsewhere he said he exhorted all to receive every Sunday),[35] he states later on, speaking of Christ our Lord's most sacred body, "This is daily bread; therefore live in such a way that you can receive it every day."[36] It follows from all this that, even if such strong signs or salutary movements were not present, the judgment of one's own conscience is good and valid testimony. That is, since all things are lawful for you in our Lord, so long as you judge (barring obvious mortal sin or anything you can deem to be such) that your soul is more helped and more inflamed with love for our Creator and Lord, and you receive Communion with this intention, finding by experience that this most holy spiritual food gives you sustenance, peace, and tranquility, preserving and advancing you in his greater service, praise, and glory, and you do not doubt this, then it is lawful and will be better for you to receive Communion daily.

---

[34] Ignatius alludes to a jurisdictional dispute instituted by the Franciscans and settled by a bull of Leo X, which handed over the supervision of the monastery of Santa Clara to the Benedictines.

[35] This quotation is now attributed not to St. Augustine but to Gennadius.

[36] This text or the sentiment expressed is found in both Ambrose and Augustine.

On this and other matters I have spoken at length with Araoz, who will deliver this letter. Referring you to him in our Lord regarding all matters, I close, praying to God our Lord that by his infinite clemency you may be guided and governed in all things by his infinite and sovereign goodness.

Rome, November 25, 1543

Poor in goodness,

INIGO

✻ 1544–1546 ✻

To the Jesuits of Spain, by commission

Rome, early 1544

(Letter 76: I:285–91; in Spanish)

News about the decree for physicians, the house for converted women, the conversion of two Hebrews, and other spiritual doings in Rome. It is not completely certain who wrote this letter for Ignatius, but it is probable that Jerónimo Doménech took on this commission.

May the sovereign grace and love of Christ our Lord be always for our continual favor and help. Amen.

Inasmuch as Master Ignatius has been more than usually unwell for the last four months, his continual illnesses threatening to remove him from our eyes, it has seemed good to some that he be relieved of his burden of writing these letters, a burden which weighed much more heavily upon him than appeared, so that, disencumbered of this task, he might more freely employ whatever time God our Lord deigns to grant him on weightier matters. His Reverence agreed to this, and the task has been given to me, unworthy and insufficient as I am. Accepting it under obedience, however, I trust in God our Lord that he will help me to satisfy at least the charity of all my dear fathers and brothers in Christ.

And so, in fulfillment of my office, I shall compile as briefly as possible in this letter some of the many things that have happened here to which I myself am an eyewitness, for the honor and glory of God our Lord, who is the one who "works all in all" [1 Cor. 12:6], and for the consolation of them all and of whoever, looking favorably upon such works, is accustomed to take great delight in the Lord and bless him, who is blessed for ever, through them.

In the last letter you were informed about the steps then being taken for observance of the decree of Innocent III "Cum infirmitas corporalis, etc.," and the great efforts which Master Ignatius devoted to this. Since then, by the grace of our Lord, the decree has been published to the physicians here, under a fine of five hundred scudi for nonobservance, as you will see from a letter I am sending you. At present efforts are being made to extend it more universally.

You were also informed about the new monastery established for sinful women, entitled the Company of Grace; by the grace of our Lord, it is still going forward, the company growing not only in numbers but in spirit, to our great satisfaction and the edification of everyone.

Regarding the catechumens, while, as you were informed in the earlier letter, we have relinquished the entire responsibility to a Messer Giovanni del Mercato, who has taken charge of the work, we were unable to avoid accepting a few in the house at the urging (or better, command) of the vicar [Filippo Archinto] and the Cardinal of Trana [Cupis]. Among these was a son of Master Paolo, the Pope's physician, a man of twenty-five, of good character, learned in his own law and, I believe, one of the most deeply religious in it. About twelve years ago, when his father, mother, brothers, and sisters became Christians, he refused to do so and went to Turkey, staying there until just a short while ago, when he came seeking to become a Christian. We directed him to the new house of catechumens.

He stayed there for two months; but finding no peace, he wanted to come to our house, and got the request made to the Cardinal of Trana; and so we were forced to receive him. When we did, God knows what we went through with him before we could get him baptized. He caused difficulty and turmoil to the whole house because of his unwillingness to delay his baptism any further. After we got him baptized, he misbehaved by insisting against Master Ignatius's judgment on going to Ancona to pick up some belongings of his. However, when this trip turned out badly for him, he recognized his fault in having refused to obey, and has so humbled and abased himself and undergone such a transformation that it is cause for giving praise to God our Lord, showing that it is truly a "change by his right hand."

He has achieved such knowledge of our Lord and of the vanity of the world that, disregarding his father, mother, brothers, and sisters or what he might have had from them (they are rich and influential), he has firmly decided to leave the world and follow Christ in perpetual poverty, chastity, and obedience, placing himself in the hands of Master Ignatius to dispose of him as he deems best for the greater service of our Lord. It is amazing how eager he has been to serve in the house in some lowly service, and how, when he was assigned to the kitchen, he has comported himself so well up to now in bringing the portions, indicating that he wishes to be left in some lowly service for the rest of his life.

God our Lord has given him a spirit of mortification and of desire for all opprobrium and insults for love of him. Besides certain mortifications which he has made in the house and elsewhere preaching at the banks, he was not content with these, but one day, under an impulse of the spirit and without Master Ignatius's knowing anything about it, he walked through a good part of Rome from morning to past noon—in quite cold weather—wearing only a hairshirt and drawers and scourging himself severely. He would have continued these and similar mortifications if he had not been forbidden. He continues with much humility and no little fervor of spirit, to the edification of everyone.

Another Hebrew who came to Rome to become a Christian, a young man of twenty-five, was imprisoned for some misdemeanor committed earlier. His mother, a Christian of four years, learning that her son had come from Hungary for this purpose, induced the Cardinal of Trana to take him under his protection; he referred the matter to Master Ignatius, and so he had to take charge of the Hebrew. The latter, before leaving prison, as a sign of his goodwill, gave a two-year-old son of his to be baptized right away and a brother of sixteen or eighteen to be catechized. With his son baptized and his brother in our house, he was released from prison. The two of them are now in our house preparing to become Christians. The man's wife, and his sister-in-law with her husband, have agreed to become Christians. The two women's mother has also indicated a wish to follow them. May God our Lord give her grace for this, and may he deign to illuminate all other unbelievers, so that they may forsake the darkness and receive the true light.

Among those who have made the Exercises since the last letter, seven have stood out: six of them for the Society and one to become a friar at Montserrat. Four have already set out with Araoz for Portugal, likewise the other for Montserrat.

Master Salmerón's brother and Pedro de Ribadeneira are here to go with the first men to university studies. Two have arrived from pilgrimage; others are here to make the Exercises, although already decided to enter the Society.

When Messer Alessandro, about whom you were more fully informed in the earlier letter, saw that his wife was unwilling to become a Christian, he left a son of his in the house and went to Spoleto to take care of his business; he will then return to the house to decide about his life.

Master Ignatius, during the time when he is free of his illness, has been quite busy, his spiritual labors constantly increasing; he not only has responsibility for confessing Madama's household but also that of the wife of the Spanish ambassador, and this quite frequently; he is also involved in some very important reconciliations, in drawing up the Constitutions of the Society, and similar activities.

Master Salmerón preached this Advent before the ambassador and his wife, and regularly preaches on Sundays and feast days. It is amazing how attached to him they have become in that house, especially the ambassador's wife, who is a blessed soul and a model of every virtue.

The others in the house, through the grace of God our Lord, are never without work; however, they are sometimes unable to attend right away to persons who come seeking spiritual assistance in confessions and private conversations. There are times when they are occupied with confessions from morning to evening, without taking any bodily refreshment.

His Holiness has summoned Master Ignatius a number of times; he discusses important matters with him and shows much love to the Society. At the urging of the vicar, he has given us the church of Sant'-Andrea with its house, which, as you know, is next door to Santa Maria della Strada. And so Master Pietro Codazzo is presently hurrying to prepare some rooms so that we can be better accommodated for the service of God our Lord. To this end we desire all our affairs to be directed—not only ours but those of the whole universal world, so that he may be served, praised, and glorified by everything for infinite ages. Amen.

✠

To Cardinal Antonio Pucci

Rome, July 19, 1544 (?)

(Letter 78: I:293f.; in Italian)

A request to the chief penitentiary for faculties to absolve an irregular priest.

My Most Reverend Lord and father in Christ:

There is a gentleman who, at the age of eighteen, got himself ordained a priest without having Latin and without authorization. Subsequently, besides his never having said Mass, he has remained in secular garb until the present, when he is twenty-three. Should Your Reverend Lordship deem it for the glory of God our Lord to grant me full faculties to remedy this soul in the forum of conscience, I shall be able to act in Your Reverend Lordship's name, to the greater glory of God our Lord.

Today, July 19

> Your Reverend Lordship's most humble servant in our Lord,
> IGNATIO

✠

To a Troubled Person

Rome, November 28, 1544

(Letter 79: I:294f.; in Spanish)

Advice to a man with an unfortunate past who wanted to live with the Jesuits in Padua.

May the sovereign grace and love of Christ our Lord always be our continual protection and help.

Being unable in any way to fall short of the great affection and wholesome inclination my soul feels for your own, I will briefly state, in reply to your letter and that of Master Laínez, what has been granted me in our Lord to think.

First, with regard to your going and living in your own country, I can think of nothing that would be worse for you or from which you should more shrink, as I wrote you earlier at length, because of what past experience has shown.

Second, as regards your settling in and residing in the house there with our men, I am unable to agree or be satisfied that it would be a good thing, partly because you are not finding there the fruit you desire and which it would be reasonable to expect, and partly because of the unhappiness felt both by your own people and ours at your inability to be helped in both soul and body as they desire. All things considered, I still think it would be safer, better, and for the greater universal good in our Lord if you took lodgings apart from our men there, with some good companions, spending what you would spend at home and trying that out for a year, with frequent confession and occasional talks with our men during the week. Moreover, you could attend one or more lectures, more to strengthen and clear your spirit than to acquire scholastic learning for the sake of others. Give yourself to any conversations and recreations you like which will not sully your soul, for this is more important for us than being lord of all creation. Once you have succeeded in calming down and finding peace and quiet of conscience through internal consolations and spiritual relish, then it will be time to study for the benefit of others, as your inner and outer forces allow. Above all, I beg you, for love and reverence of God our Lord, to remember the past and to reflect, not from a distance but close up, that earth is earth.

May God our Lord in his infinite and supreme goodness be pleased to give us his abundant grace, so that we may know his most holy will and entirely fulfill it.

Rome, November 28, 1544

✠

To the Dispersed Jesuits of Cologne

Rome, end of 1544

(Letter 80: I:295f.; in Latin)

Fragment from a letter to the Jesuit students in Cologne, who had been dispersed by order of the senate.

Though separated from one another in body and in lodgings, still with God's help it will be easy for you to ensure that brotherly affection continues to exist and flourish among you, inasmuch as by the freely chosen pursuit of your disciplines, the goal you have set for your life, and the vows you have duly taken, you have linked yourselves so tightly to one another for the glory of Jesus Christ. By this cement of charity it is right that our whole family should be cemented and united together. For the rest, it will be for God's guardianship to ensure that he for whose sake you endure these things will one day gather together the dispersed of Israel.

To King John III of Portugal

Rome, March 15, 1545

(Letter 81: I:296–98; in Spanish)

To forestall suspicion that might hinder the apostolic effectiveness of this still quite new religious order, Ignatius recounts the series of ecclesiastical trials through which he had passed without taint against his orthodoxy. He ends asking the King's permission for Rodrigues to come to Rome.

May the sovereign grace and eternal love of Christ our Lord greet and visit Your Highness. Amen.

From not a few signs and indications—our Lord knows—I am confident that if certain things that have happened to me have not already reached Your Highness's ears, they soon will—things belonging not so much to me as to my Lord, to whom be glory forever. Desiring in their regard always to boast not in myself but in my Creator and Lord, I decided that sooner or later I ought to give an account, however brief, of them all to Your Most Christian Highness, to whom we are forever so deeply indebted.

After my return from Jerusalem, I was subjected at Alcalá de Henares to three trials by my superiors and then arrested and imprisoned for forty-two days. After another trial at Salamanca, I was not only imprisoned but put in chains, where I remained for twenty-two days. At Paris, where I later pursued my studies, they tried me again. Throughout these five trials and two imprisonments, by God's grace I never engaged or wanted to engage any other advocate or attorney than God, in whom, by his divine favor and grace, I have placed all my trust for both present and future. Subsequent to the Paris trial, another was held seven years later at the same university, still another in Venice, and a final one in Rome against the whole Society. In the last three trials, because I was associated with the members of the Society (more Your Highness's than our own), we insisted that justice take its course lest offense be given to God through defamation of all the Society's members. It happened that when the final sentence was being passed, three of the judges who had tried me before—one at Alcalá, one at Paris, and one at Venice—were present in Rome. In all eight of these trials, by God's sheer grace and mercy, I was not censured for a single proposition of mine, not a syllable or anything greater; I had no penance imposed on me nor was I banished. Should Your Highness wish to know why I was the object of all this scrutiny and investigation, you should know that it had nothing to do with schismatics, Lutherans, or *alumbrados*, persons I never associated with or knew; the reason was surprise at an uneducated person like myself, particularly in Spain, speaking and conversing so extensively on spiritual subjects. And the truth is—our Lord, my creator and eternal judge, is my witness—that not for all the temporal power and riches under heaven would I wish that all this had not befallen me; indeed, I wish far worse would befall me, to the greater glory of his Divine Majesty.

Accordingly, my Lord in our Lord, should any of these reports reach there, I would hope that Your Highness, with that boundless mercy and grace which his Divine Majesty has bestowed on you for his greater service and praise, will stop to recognize his graces and will be able to discern the good from the bad, turning everything to good use. For the greater a desire we attain (barring offense on the part of our neighbor) of being clothed in the livery of Christ our Lord, namely, insults, false witness, and every other kind of wrongs, the more we will advance in spirit and win spiritual riches, with which, if we are living spiritually, our soul longs to be wholly adorned.

Because of the great longing our men here have to see Master Simão and of our serious need to decide certain matters of importance to the Society, we humbly petition Your Highness, for God's glory, to give him gracious and loving leave to go, as His Holiness has already done. I anticipate that his coming here, along with others of us who expect to be gathering, will turn out for the service of his Divine Majesty and of Your Highness, whose Society this is more than it is ours. Addressing this letter also to Her Most Serene Highness the Queen, I earnestly commend myself in our Lord to her great benevolence and her prayers; and may he in his infinite goodness grant us his abundant grace to know his most holy will and entirely to fulfill it.

Rome, March 15, 1545

> Your Highness's most humble and perpetual servant in our Lord,
> Ignacio

To Cardinal Marcello Cervini

Rome, April 15, 1545

(Letter 83: I:300–302; in Spanish)

Ignatius reports that rumors about Simão Rodrigues in Portugal are untrue and that he wants to come to Rome. He comments on the desire of Cardinal Otto von Truchsess of Augsburg that Jay attend the Council of Trent.

JHUS.

My Most Honored Lord and father in Christ:

May the sovereign grace and eternal love of Christ our Lord greet and visit Your Lordship with the abundance of his mercies, with which he never ceases to visit, instruct, and console the souls he specially loves, particularly in times of such urgent need and supreme importance as the present.

May it please his Divine Majesty that all things have the holy outcome desired by Your Lordship and by ourselves (unworthy as we are of mention), for his greater praise and eternal glory.

Within the last four days I received three packets of letters from Portugal bearing different dates. One contained a letter from Araoz for Your Most Reverend Lordship, which I am sending along with this. I believe it is old, judging from the other letters which came with it. Later, in another packet of March 3, he wrote me that he and Master Pierre Favre had already been given leave by the King to go to the princess in Castile, and that they were on the point of setting out.[1] By God's grace, so far as I understand all that has taken place in Portugal, the members of our Society there (who are more Your Lordship's than ours) are proceeding quite properly, indeed with much filial fear and not at all as was being rumored here. Moreover, Master Simão, the chief of our men there, or the one about whom most of the rumors were circulating, writes us urgently that we should talk to His Holiness—or that I should write to the King—so that we can have him come here, because he is very anxious to meet with us in Rome. Since our wishes coincide with his on this point, I wrote him with the gracious permission of His Holiness, and we hope that he will leave there in September and arrive here in November, where Your Most Reverend Lordship will deign to take him, as all of us, under your protection and service in our Lord. May he in his infinite and supreme goodness keep Your Most Reverend

---

[1] The Portuguese princess Maria, first wife of Philip II, who was pregnant and would shortly die giving birth to Don Carlos.

Lordship in his hand, enlightening and favoring you to his greater praise and glory.

Rome, April 15, 1545

Your Most Reverend Lordship's humble and perpetual servant in our Lord,

IGNATIO

I received a letter from our Master Jay, who is with the Most Reverend Cardinal of Augsburg: His Most Reverend Lordship is so pleased with him that he wants to have him attend the council. Jay says that unless another command is sent him from here, he will wholly comply. While I personally would never have been for suggesting that he go to the council, despite how satisfied I am with him, I thought it best not to disagree, only commending him to God our Lord. Should Your Reverend Lordship go there, please hold him always in my own place as your perpetual and affectionate servant in our Lord.

✠

To Pierre Favre

Rome, July 16, 1545

(Letter 89: I:311f.; in Latin)

The very formal tone of the letter indicates that it not only officially "communicates" to Favre "the Society's wide-ranging spiritual faculties, to be used only with the approval of the local spiritual authority," but also that the letter could well be shown to such an authority.

Ignatius of Loyola, superior of the Society of Jesus, to our beloved in Christ Jesus Pierre Favre, priest of the Diocese of Geneva and member of the same Society: greetings and eternal welfare in the Lord.

Although Our Lord His Holiness has specifically granted us unlimited authorization to exercise all the ministries formally granted to us by way of a brief, even without our consulting or having the approval of the local bishop or any other spiritual authority, nevertheless, inasmuch as we desire to employ this talent granted to us soberly and to the praise of the Lord according to His Holiness's intention, and are concerned lest our undertaking the administration of the word of God and the sacraments without the goodwill and leave of the immediate superior should occasion scandal among the people and hinder their edification, it is our will that, after first consulting the local spiritual authority and showing him the faculties, you act in such a way that, having first asked and obtained his permission, you are able to carry out your divine task with the love of all, unto his praise.

Given at Rome in the house of the Society of Jesus, at Santa Maria della Strada, in the year 1545 on the sixteenth day of July, in the eleventh year of the pontificate of His Holiness our lord the Pope.

✠

To Claude Jay

Rome, December 12, 1545
(Letter 102: I:343f.; in Spanish)

Bernardino Ochino, elected vicar-general of the newly founded Capuchin Order in 1538, had become a prominent Catholic preacher before turning Protestant and fleeing to Geneva in 1542. His defection was a great shock, and several attempts were made to reconcile him to the Catholic Church. In this letter Jay was bade to make such an attempt, but it is not known whether he was ever able to contact Ochino.

This letter (which is to be kept secret) is being written solely for your information in helping you to undertake and negotiate the following work of charity, which will be of great importance if it turns out for the glory of God our Lord. Briefly, a very charitable person close to us who has known Fra Bernardino for a long time came to talk with me so that I would do something about his case through pursuing a middle course of merciful satisfaction, etc. I replied that if I had a letter from him—without which I do not know how I could talk to the Pope or various other parties—I would not fail to do everything in my power, etc. So this person offered to write and try to get a letter from him. Therefore, taking advantage of this, but without letting him know about it and as though acting on your own (since, as you write, he is staying so close by), we here think it would be good, if you concur in our Lord, for you to try to visit him in some way or other and sound him out, getting from him some statement so that we might with all charity help him in any way we can, and so that he himself might seize an opportunity to help himself with the help of our Lord. In addition, you might try to urge and press him by asking him: "What is it that you are doing? What are you hoping for?" etc.—telling him that everything will be favorable for him, and offering yourself for complete support from here. If he shows fear, promise him the Society: I am here, and Masters Laínez and

Salmerón are here. Regarding his person and all his concerns, he should be fully assured that we are all his own as truly as is his own soul, etc. See if you can get a letter out of him, or whatever you are able in God our Lord to manage there with him—without his learning that we wrote you from here, etc. As quickly as possible write us here in detail about what happens in this affair, etc.

Rome, December 12, 1545

The person must in no way learn of our communicating this to you.

✠

To Francis Xavier

Rome, December 17, 1545

(Letter 106: I:350f.; in Latin)

Formal delegation of faculties granted to the Society by the Pope.

Ignatius of Loyola, superior of the Society of Jesus, to our beloved in Christ Francis Xavier of Pamplona, member of the same Society: eternal welfare in the Lord.

Our Most Holy Father and lord Paul III, by divine providence pope, lately granted by way of a brief to the present superior and members of the said Society, and to any individual member found worthy and deputed by the Society's superior, faculties which include those of preaching and interpreting the word of God to the clergy and people in any place and of hearing confessions and administering the other sacraments at his own and the Apostolic See's good pleasure, in the form and with the restrictions contained more fully in the aforesaid brief. We, therefore, whose only aspiration is that the Catholic faith might everywhere flourish and increase and that with all diligence the souls of Christian believers might be gained for God, relying upon the authorization contained in the aforesaid brief for what follows, do by these present letters constitute and depute you, Francis Xavier, member of the said Society of Jesus, in whose religion, integrity, knowledge, morals, and experience we place great confidence in the Lord, [as recipient of] the above-mentioned faculties.

In witness whereof we have caused the present document to be drawn up and furnished with the impress of our customary seal, and have signed it with our own hand.

Given at Rome, in the house of the Society of Jesus, at Santa
Maria della Strada, in the year of our Lord Jesus Christ 1545, on the
seventeenth day of December, in the twelfth year of the pontificate of
His Holiness the above-mentioned Pope.

IGNATIUS

✠

To Francis Borgia, duke of Gandía

Rome, end of 1545

(Letter 101: I:339–43; in Spanish)

*Borgia had become Duke of Gandía in 1543 and was leading a deeply spiritual life
there; he had come to know the Jesuits and wished to found a college in his city. He
entered the Society in 1546, but this was kept secret for a time so that he could
carry on his official and family responsibilities until he turned over the duchy to his
son. Here Ignatius sends Borgia reflections on how God's presence is experienced by
a zealous soul and how the soul places obstacles to grace. He advises frequent
Communion and asks Borgia to take charge of the new college at Gandía.*

My Lord in our Lord:

May the sovereign grace and eternal love of Christ our Lord greet
and visit Your Lordship.

On the last day of October, I received a letter of July 24 from
your hand, and I was more than greatly delighted in our Lord at perceiving in it matters drawn less from anywhere else than from such
inward experience and converse as our Lord in his infinite goodness is
accustomed to give to souls who wholly ground themselves in his goodness as the source, means, and end of all our good. May his holy name
be forever praised and exalted in and through all creatures, which have
been created and ordained for this so rightful and proper end.

I come now to some particular points that are presented and
written to me. First, you ask that I not forget you in my prayers, and
that I visit you through my letters. Actually, by my having continuously
done the first, and doing so daily—trusting in our Lord that any favor
my prayers might win for you will be entirely from on high and coming
down from his infinite goodness, and considering only his eternal and
perfect liberality and Your Lordship's devotion and holy intention—I
was sure that in thus keeping you spiritually before my eyes every day, I
was also complying with the second part of Your Lordship's wish, that of
being consoled by letters from me. As I consider how persons who go

out of themselves and enter into their Creator and Lord possess a constant awareness, attention, and consolation, as well as a perception of the way in which our entire eternal Good is present in all created things, giving existence to them all and preserving them therein by his own infinite being and presence, I readily believe that Your Lordship finds consolation in the greater number of them and in many others as well. For to persons who love God wholly, all things are a help and aid for meriting more and being more closely united by intense charity with their very Creator and Lord. Nevertheless, as Your Lordship so well says, the creature on its own part often places obstacles to what our Lord wishes to work in the soul. This happens not just before these graces, gifts, and delights of the Holy Spirit are received; even after the graces have come and been received—visiting and consoling the soul, ridding it of all its darkness and restless anxiety, adorning it with these spiritual goods, making it wholly happy and wholly in love with eternal things that will last forever in perpetual glory—still, it happens that we disconnect ourselves [from these graces] with thoughts of little importance, not knowing how to preserve this great heavenly good. Thus, we place obstacles to this grace and working of our Lord before it comes, and to its conservation after it comes.

And even though Your Lordship mentions these obstacles in order the more to humble yourself in the Lord of all and to exalt us, whose desire is for our own greater humbling—stating on the basis of what you hear from Araoz in Portugal that this Society never hinders what our Lord desires to work in it—I am personally convinced regarding myself that both before and after I am totally obstacle. Because of this I feel increased spiritual happiness and joy in our Lord, inasmuch as I cannot attribute to myself even a semblance of good. For one thing of which I am convinced (remaining open to another opinion from persons of better understanding) is that there are few persons in this life—indeed there is not a single person—who are capable of fully determining or judging how much they themselves hinder and prevent what our Lord wishes to work in their souls. Indeed, I think that the more practiced and experienced a person becomes in humility and charity, the more he will sense and become aware of even the slightest thoughts and other subtle matters which impede and hinder him, though these may appear to be of little or almost no significance, being in themselves tiny. Even so, a full awareness of our resistances and faults is not something we can have in this life: the prophet prays to be freed from the faults he does not know [Ps. 19:12], and St. Paul, confessing he is unaware of any, adds that he is not for that reason justified [1 Cor. 6:4].

I strongly desire in our Lord, who is to be my judge for eternity, that inasmuch as he in his infinite and accustomed mercy is making Your Lordship too a scholar in this holy school—something you cannot deny when you look and enter into your own soul, as I am confident I can tell from your letters—Your Lordship would labor and make every possible effort to recruit numerous fellow pupils, starting with the members of your own house (to whom we have greater obligation), so as to bring them by the safest and straightest way to his Divine Majesty. And inasmuch as this way is Christ our Lord himself, as the Lord himself says [John 14:6], I give abundant thanks to his divine goodness that, according to what I have heard here, Your Lordship frequently goes to receive him. Besides the many other great graces which the soul gains by receiving its Creator and Lord, a very special and outstanding one is that it will not let it remain long or stubbornly in sin: as soon as it falls, even into quite small sins (though none can be called small, since what is sinned against is the infinite and indeed supreme Good), it quickly raises it up again with increased strength and a firmer determination to render greater service to its Creator and Lord.

With Your Lordship proceeding along this path by means of God's grace, winning our neighbors and brethren by thus employing the talent given you by the Divine Majesty through his infinite and accustomed mercy, I merit—without myself meriting it—through my desire of imitating Your Lordship. And as to what Your Lordship writes about wishing to share in the affairs that I handle, the kind [of affairs] that I have here and find so heavy a burden—since I have been charged, in conformity with our manner of proceeding, with the superintendence of this Society (whether by divine ordination or by permission of his eternal goodness for my great and abominable sins)—I would ask Your Lordship by the love and reverence of God our Lord that, while aiding me with your prayers, you would also deign to assist me by assuming the administration and completion of a house or college that it is desired to set up there for scholars of this Society (which belongs no less to Your Lordship and to the Lady Duchess and to her sister the lady Doña Juana than it does to us);[2] and that, since it was at Your Lordship's request and command that these scholars were received into the Society to our souls' great joy, you would bestow whatever favor and protection you deem best in our Lord and judge to be for his greater glory. We are all the more delighted in his divine Goodness now that a

---

[2] The references are to Leonora de Castro, Borgia's wife, who would die soon after, and to Juana de Meneses, the sister of Leonora.

relative of the Lady Duchess is in the college, as Your Lordship writes me, and that Her Ladyship is so pleased.[3] Begging to be commended in our Lord to her prayers and favor, as well as to those of the lady Doña Juana, I close asking the Divine Majesty to grant us his abundant grace so that we may know his supreme will and entirely fulfill it.

Rome, etc., 1545

IGNATIO

✠

To Doctor Pedro Ortiz

Rome, early 1546

(Letter 109: I:354–56; in Spanish)

Charles V's learned ambassador to the Holy See had made the Exercises under St. Ignatius and wished to arrange that a large benefice of his always be held by a member of the Society. Ignatius explains why he cannot accept it.

. . . With respect to this benefice to which only professed members of this Society could succeed, so that subsequently it would be possible to make abundant provision at little expense for the house or college to be established in Alcalá, it is true that in the case of any other advantage to the general good of souls or to this Society (which is wholly yours), I would, in order to comply with your good intentions and holy devotion, be delighted in our Lord to be able to accept it. However, since it is our lowly profession to possess no corporate or individual incomes, and this has been confirmed by several bulls of His Holiness, we would not dare to turn back from a more perfect to a less perfect manner of proceeding. Rather, it is our fervent wish that for his own greater service and praise, God our Lord would take us from this life rather than let us set such an example for those who are to come. If the episcopacy and the care of souls presuppose the attainment of perfection, and entrance into religious life is the commencement of it, then in the latter it is always more perfect not to have than to have fixed incomes, either corporate or individual. And should it perhaps be the case that all benefices which provide for religious persons are for the greater universal good of the Church—as they probably or surely would be if the persons stayed the same after receiving the benefices as they were before— nevertheless, since in God's providence there are many different ways of

---

[3] The relative was Antonio de Muñiz. He did not remain in the Society.

reforming his universal Church, our own safer and more appropriate course is to proceed as nakedly as we can in our Lord, after the example he himself gives to us who with all humility wish to understand. Consequently, welcoming as we always have your holy intention and will, so full of charity, and your wish to put it into action, we remain ever more deeply indebted to you just as if everything had actually turned out as you wished. To resolve this matter, despite our conviction as indicated above, we assigned a period of three days for all the priests in the house (twelve of us) to celebrate Mass and all the laymen (about twenty) to pray for our intention, namely, that if our own opinion or will diverged from God's, it might in no case be done, but that in everything God our Lord's greater service and praise might be fulfilled in us all. We ended unanimously approving and confirming our original view, which was to avoid entirely all revenues, corporate or individual, and to separate ourselves from lawsuits and litigations of any kind. Having discussed this and other matters with Señor Salazar, I understand from what he told me that he will write you at length.

Rome, 1546

IGNATIO

✠

To the Fathers of the Council of Trent

Rome, first months of 1546

(Letter 123: I:386–89; in Spanish)

Instructions on how Laínez, Salmerón, and Jay, whom Ignatius sent to Trent at the order of Paul III, are to deal with others there, carry out the full range of the Society's ministries, and assist one another. Favre died in Rome on August 1, 1546, after arriving there from Spain on his way to the council. Peter Canisius later joined the other three in that city.

INSTRUCTION FOR THE STAY AT TRENT

Ihs.

FOR DEALING WITH OTHERS

1. While with God's help much can be achieved by associating and dealing with large numbers of people for the salvation and spiritual progress of souls, nevertheless, such dealings can, unless we are vigilant and favored by God's grace, be attended by great loss on our own and

sometimes everyone's part. And since according to our profession we cannot avoid such dealings, the better we are furnished with and guided by some plan, the more serenely will we proceed in our Lord. The following points—or others like them, more or fewer—can be used to help ourselves in our Lord.

2. I would be slow to speak, deliberate and loving, particularly when expressing a judgment on matters that are or might be treated at the council.

3. I would be slow to speak and careful to listen, keeping still in order to grasp and understand the speaker's ideas, feelings, and inclinations, so as the better to respond or keep silence.

4. In discussions of these or other topics, I would mention arguments for both sides, so as not to appear attached to my own judgment, taking care not to leave anyone annoyed.

5. I would not appeal to any persons' authority, particularly if they are important, unless the matters have been very carefully thought through; I would keep on good terms with everyone and avoid all partisanship.

6. If the points being discussed are so right that one cannot or should not keep silent, I would express my view as calmly and humbly as possible, and conclude with "in the absence of a better opinion."

7. Finally, for conversing and dealing with people about acquired or infused doctrine, when one wishes to discuss these things it is very helpful not to take into account my own leisure, lack of time, or urgency—that is, my own convenience—but instead to adapt myself to the convenience and condition of the person with whom I wish to deal, so as to move him to God's greater glory.

FOR HELPING SOULS

1. For the greater glory of God our Lord, our main purpose during this stay at Trent is, while trying to live together in some decent place, to preach, hear confessions, and give lectures[4] while teaching children, giving good example, visiting the poor in hospitals, and exhorting our neighbors—according as each one possesses this or that talent for moving all the persons we can to devotion and prayer, so that they and we may all implore God our Lord that his Divine Majesty will deign to

---

[4] Instructional and devotional lectures for the general public, as distinguished from the more oratorical sermon.

infuse his divine Spirit into all those handling the matters of this high assembly, so that the Holy Spirit may descend upon the council with a greater abundance of gifts and graces.

2. In preaching, I would not touch upon any points where Protestants differ from Catholics; I would merely exhort to virtuous living and to the Church's devotions, urging souls to thorough self-knowledge and to greater knowledge and love of their Creator and Lord. I would frequently mention the council and, as indicated above, conclude each sermon with a prayer for it.

3. In lectures, I would do the same as in sermons, attempting to enkindle in souls a love of their Creator and Lord as I explain the meaning of the passage under discussion, and also getting the hearers to pray as indicated above.

4. In confessions, I would speak as if my words to the penitents were being said in public; and in every confession I would give them some penance by way of prayers for the above-mentioned intention.

5. In giving the Exercises and in other conversations, I would likewise be minded that I speak in public. To all I would normally give the exercises of the First Week and no more, except in the case of the few persons who are prepared to decide their life by means of the elections. During the elections and throughout the Exercises, I would not let people make promises. Nor would I place them in seclusion, especially at the beginning; I might do this later if time allowed, but always with restraint, particularly if I had occasion to give the complete Exercises. And I would recommend prayers for the council.

6. I would teach catechism to children for a suitable time, depending on the possibilities and readiness of each place. I would teach the basic elements, with more or less explanation depending upon the hearers. At the end of the instruction or exhortation, I would have them say a prayer for the same intention.

7. I would visit the hospitals at the hour or hours of the day most suitable for physical health. I would hear the confessions of the poor and console them, even bringing them something if I could. I would have them say prayers, as was said regarding confessions. If there were at least three of us, we could each visit the poor every third day.

8. I would urge everyone I could in conversation to frequent confession, Communion, celebration of Mass, spiritual exercises, and other pious works, recommending also that they pray for the council.

9. As was said above, when expressing a judgment on some point, it helps to speak slowly or sparingly; however, when urging souls to their own spiritual progress, it helps to speak at length, articulately, lovingly, and feelingly.

FOR OUR OWN GREATER HELP

We will all take an hour in the evening to discuss with one another what was done during the day and what should be aimed at for the next day.

We will come to agreement on past or future matters by vote or in some other way.

One man each evening should ask the others to give him any corrections they think needed; the one being corrected in this way should make no reply unless they ask him to give an account of the point on which he has been corrected.

The second man will do the same the next evening, and so forth, so that they can all be assisted in greater charity and good reputation on all sides.

We should make our resolution in the morning and examine ourselves twice during the day.

This order should go into effect within five days of our arrival at Trent. Amen.

☩

To Pedro de Soto, O.P.

Rome, February 20, 1546

(Letter 115: I:363; in Spanish)

A request to the Emperor's confessor that he obtain the Emperor's intervention to reconcile two feuding gentlemen.

IHS.

May the sovereign grace and eternal love of Christ our Creator and Lord greet and visit Your Paternity with an increase of his gifts and graces, for his greater service, praise, and glory.

While with my little being and less worth, I am deservedly unknown to Your Paternity, nevertheless, upon there arising a good and holy task that is highly worthy of Your Paternity, and at the suggestion and bidding of Don Juan de Vega, whom I hold in all things as my lord in our Lord and who is also writing, I cannot refrain from writing you this letter, relying more, or altogether, upon Your Paternity's great charity to obtain the desired favor rather than on any merits I might feel in myself. What has happened is that, for the separation of creatures from their Creator and Lord, as Your Paternity has doubtless heard, the enemy of human nature has made great efforts to bring about a fierce enmity between Señor Don Francisco Lasso and a Hungarian gentleman, inciting it more and more, to the point where their souls and bodies are about to be lost, along with all else, little as it is—as Your Paternity will see by the accompanying report—unless God our Lord intervenes with his own hand, either immediately or by means of other instruments suitable in the sight of his divine goodness. I am convinced that Your Paternity will be and is highly suitable for his greater glory, and that no other instrument will be as effective, particularly in a case like this, with His Imperial Majesty. If he will take up the affair and issue a command with a Christian spirit, as he does in numerous other matters of greater moment, he could quite easily reconcile this whole vehement quarrel, inasmuch as there is little or no difference between the injuries on either side. Hence I have decided in our Lord to present before Your Paternity this holy work, so worthy of you, wholly assured that the matter itself, with no great urging or supplication on my part, will in our Lord quite suffice to assure, for God's greater glory, achievement of the desired goal. Your Paternity's reward will come from him who can do all things, and I myself will remain forever beholden to you; with my own powerlessness and little worth, I may never be able to repay you in deeds, but I know that I will at least live in great desire to serve you; for in loving and serving those who are true servants of my Lord, I love and serve the same Lord of all in whatever lies within my poor power, to the greater glory of his Divine Majesty.

May he deign in his infinite and supreme goodness to give us his abundant grace to know his most holy will and entirely to fulfill it.

Rome, February 20, 1546

Would Your Paternity be so kind as to commend me earnestly in our Lord to Monsieur Andalot, and may he take this letter as for himself.

Your Paternity's most humble servant in our Lord,
IGNACIO

To Andrea Lippomani

Rome, February 22, 1546

(Letter 117: I:366f.; in Italian)

As a gesture of gratitude to Lippomani, who had assigned to the college at Padua half the income of his priory of Trinità, Ignatius requests that he retain complete control over this money during his lifetime.

Very Reverend Sir:

Seeing the eagerness and the ardent desire which the Lord God has given Your Lordship in a special way for assisting the scholastics of this congregation of ours, as we have seen by the effects so far, and knowing how greatly His Majesty loves gratitude and dislikes its opposite, I and the professed brethren of the Society present here, in the name also of those absent, humbly beg Your Lordship, for whatever time the Lord grants you life (which we pray will be long, for the service of His Majesty), to have charge of administering not just half of the income, according to His Holiness's concession, but the entire amount, with power to preserve, increase, or diminish that of the scholastics in Padua with all the freedom—or even more—that you enjoyed before making this sacrifice to the Lord. We shall therein count ourselves even more favored, seeing that in this way you offer not only your exterior goods but also something far more important, your own person, by deigning out of love of God to have a fatherly care of us, as we have hitherto so abundantly experienced. In witness of the above, I here sign with my own name and with the seal of the Society of Jesus.

Rome, February 22, 1546

DON IGNACIO, superior of the Society of Jesus

✠

To Claude Jay

Rome, March 6, 1546

(I [Appendix 1]: 733f.; in Italian)

Instruction on how to behave while in Trent for the council. The other brethren who are referred to in the letter are Diego Laínez and Alfonso Salmerón.

Jhus.

I cannot set out for you in a letter what you will learn by word of mouth from certain of our brethren when they get there; this is the reason why I am not surprised but edified by some things which you write. However, I do want you to know that your initial activity ought to be in matters that are pious, humble, lowly, and which can seem ill to no one. For if you visit hospitals and hear the confessions of the sick with the permission and love of those who govern them, and also hear the confessions of other persons even in other parishes, as you write you are doing, and give exhortations with the permission and love of the rectors, then there is no reason why these persons should fail to be edified. And, speaking in general, when other persons see you proceeding humbly in good works and getting people to pray for a matter of such importance to all Christendom, I am confident that the sacred council, if it takes up the matter of the Society, will rather praise God for it than the contrary. For even here various high personages (or the highest), having this opinion of the Society and believing that our men will perform creditable works such as I have mentioned, rejoice in spirit. And for this purpose, the thing most suitable and necessary for you is that you all stay together, now in a church, now in a hospital, or now in some other place, so that you can discuss what has been done each day and what is to be done the following day. If this cannot be done, you will have to be satisfied with what you can do.

Hence, as confidentially as possible and without resistance on this matter, I ask that you not fail to take every possible care to write me weekly about your efforts for this or that particular monastery, church, hospital, or other place where you may stay. I also ask you to make a fair start on some of these projects, so that when the others arrive and find them already launched, they may be better [helped] in performing services in some hospitals a few times a week and in other charitable works; your own opinion will be of no slight value here and there.

Since he was not pressed by Monsignor Archinto, Master Laínez[5] went to Venice; I believe that he and another will preach in the region. Since you think that only two should go for now, when the month is over the pair of them will leave for where you are.

The only difficulty we see here in your staying together there is that of bodily maintenance—and we would not like it to be said in this regard: "O you of little faith" [Matt. 6:30]; "the birds of the air," etc. [Matt. 8:20].

---

[5] Archinto was the Pope's vicar in Rome.

To Francis Borgia, duke of Gandía

Rome, April 23, 1546
(Letter 121: I:379–82; in Spanish)

Ignatius replies to spiritual questions from the duke, sends news about a wayward Jesuit relative of the duchess, and explains the difficulty in Araoz's visiting Gandía.

Ihs.

My Lord in our Lord:

May the sovereign grace and eternal love of Christ our Lord greet and visit Your Lordship.

It is about two weeks since I received Your Lordship's letter dated January 16. May it please our Lord, who is waiting to judge and to save us by means of his infinite mercies, always to give Your Lordship a full understanding of the great spiritual delight we derived from your letter, as from all the letters you continually send us.

In answer to it as a whole, or to the main part, which is entirely spiritual and regards the greater thirst for the ever living waters, I would say, not putting my hand to another's harvest, that it is wholly up to the one who gives this thirst, watering and planting, to bring it to fruition. Similarly, since he is all-powerful and all-willing with regard to souls who are disposed and desirous of his greater service, praise, and glory, and since I am persuaded that his Divine Majesty will, as he is accustomed to do, wholly provide for and console those who walk in purity of heart, I do not think I ought to enlarge on this matter.

As to the affairs of the college, when Dean Roca arrives, if it please God our Lord, we shall discuss them. I trust in his divine goodness that he will not let me go wrong in matters of such moment for his own and Your Lordship's service, and that everyone will be spiritually altogether satisfied and that Your Lordship's great love and confidence in our regard, unworthy as we are of this favor, will not be frustrated.

Regarding the fresh desires which God our Lord has given us (as we are able to feel and understand in his Divine Majesty) for aiding the reform of the monasteries of nuns in Catalonia, Your Lordship will be more fully informed by the enclosed memorandum. The more difficult and laborious the project seems, the more worthy it appears of Your Lordship and of all persons in whom fervor and zeal for the honor of God our Lord is present. And therefore, by his love and reverence, I beg Your Lordship and Her Ladyship the Duchess (who, as they tell us here and we are able to perceive, regularly and capably applies prudent and spiritual measures in ordinary affairs) to take very much to heart this holy enterprise of the divine goodness, and to be as vigilant and as earnest as possible about it, as is explained more fully in the enclosed instructions.

Muñiz, who I understand is related to My Lady the Duchess, having become a pilgrim and wearing a heavy and outlandish garment, unshod and well tried in poverty, arrived in Rome on the twelfth of this month and went to lodge in the Hospital of Sant'Antonio, belonging to the Portuguese nation. From there he wrote me a letter, which I am sending with some others. I had him leave the hospital at once, placed him as a guest in a house depending on Ours, and provided for all his needs—not, however, letting him eat or sleep in our house or "killing the fatted calf because he who was lost had been found." I have not yet consented to talk with him, the better to help him. And so, moved and repentant, without my knowing anything about it, he made the stations through Rome stripped to the skin down to his waist and taking the discipline—not at all gently, I am told, with the blood running down his body. On other days he tried to preach and begged alms from door to door throughout the city. Upon hearing of these exploits of his, I sent him word that he was to stop them and that tomorrow or the next day we would have a talk together. I hope in our Lord (retaining, as I do, a certain natural feeling, or better, a certain devotion toward My Lady the Duchess, since in part this touches her, to God's greater glory) that as his repentance has begun, the Divine Majesty will carry it forward and increase it.

As for what Her Ladyship bids me regarding the licentiate Araoz, whom she desires to pay his respects in your territory sometime: these last few days His Holiness has directed that some of our men attend the council; and since it remained up to me to name them according to my own conscience, after we had recourse to God our Lord for several days in our prayers and Masses, I appointed Masters Pierre Favre, Laínez, and Salmerón; moreover, one of our men, Master Jay, is at Trent already. I wrote to this effect to the prince, to the new archbishop of Toledo, and to Favre himself, who we assume is by now closer to Rome than to Gandía. Consequently, while nothing stands in the way of Araoz's visiting Your Lordship and Your Ladyship, I believe that he will have more to do everywhere, being left as he is alone in Spain. But as far as I am able, to God's glory, I will always be at Her Ladyship's service and will write her in accord with her wish and devotion. Sending greetings and commending myself earnestly to her and to Doña Juana, both of whom should receive this letter as their own, I close, asking the Divine Majesty by his infinite and sovereign goodness to give us his abundant grace so that we may know his most holy will and entirely fulfill it.

Rome, 1546

✠

To Peter Canisius, from Jerónimo Nadal
by commission

Rome, June 2, 1546

(Letter 124: I:390–94; in Latin)

Drafted as coming personally from Ignatius but then signed by Nadal himself, this letter praises Canisius and postpones a decision on his future. It then sketches a panorama of the rapidly growing Society.

Jhesus

May the grace and peace of our Lord Jesus Christ be with you and with all of us. Amen.

It is my joy in Christ Jesus when I see the name of the Lord, when I see Jesus Christ, speaking to all in the Church through his blood, bear fruit and grow to maturity in great numbers of persons. We give thanks to God for his ineffable mercy and kindness, which he brings to fulfillment in us for the sake of his glorious name. I am frequently moved in this way by what I hear—and partly see—regarding yourself and others who are called to our Society in Christ Jesus. Come then, take strength in God and in the might of his power [Eph. 6:10] who is Christ Jesus our Lord and God: he died for our sins [1 Cor. 15:3]; more, he rose for our justification [Rom. 4:25]. Thus he has also raised us up and made us sit together with himself in the heavenly places [Eph. 2:6] in God. Know and explore in your spirit the vocation and grace which has been given to you [Rom. 12:3] in Christ; exercise it, work hard at it, trade with it, and never let it remain idle or stationary. He is the Lord who gives us both to will and to accomplish according to his goodwill [Phil. 2:13], in and through itself infinite and superglorious and towards us inexpressible through Christ Jesus. For the Spirit of Jesus will in all things give you both understanding [2 Tim. 2:7] and strength so that through you the name of God will bear fruit and be glorified for many persons unto hope of a better life in Christ Jesus. We write you this to spur on a galloping horse, as they say. In any case, you have made us wholly yours in Christ by your eager activity in the vineyard of the Lord, and have aroused in us great hopes that Christ Jesus will be glorified in you unto the end. As to what I understood yourself and Doctor Leonard [Kessel] to wish, namely, that I write you my will and opinion so that you might not depart from it, I recognize your obedience in Christ. I would lay this before you now except that I expect the arrival of our companion and brother Pierre Favre from the court of the prince of Spain in fifteen or twenty days. The Sovereign Pontiff has decided that he should go to the council at Trent. We have heard that he arrived at Valencia in nearer Spain on May 1, and we know, or at least hope, that he will not go to Trent without visiting us first. Accordingly, since he is familiar with the customs and situation in those countries, I thought I would be acting in the best interests of you both in Christ if I consulted with him and some other brothers before making in your regard any decision in Christ Jesus as to what we deem for God's service and glory.

If you do not get letters from us as often as I imagine you would both enjoy, or as often as we have a right to expect them from you, do not be surprised. I assume you can guess this, but I will inform you briefly about it anyway. I have such an enormous load of work in Christ Jesus—one that grows daily—that I can hardly break free to turn my attention to answering the most essential letters. I am overwhelmed here with a daily increasing mass of matters that require replies or letters from me, so numerous are the regions where the Spirit of Christ is at work spreading our Society for the glory of his name. We have a college at Padua for which a noble Venetian has destined an annual income of a thousand ducats;[6] however, we have a dozen of our men to be supported there. There has lately been a prospect of starting a college at Bologna; we have sent Master Jerónimo Doménech there, where he is being supported along with three scholastics. Moreover, there recently emerged at Trent the prospect of founding an ample and noble college in Christ at the university of Paris, where we already have some of our men. A college has been started at Valencia in Spain, endowed with an income of three hundred ducats, and some other scholastics of ours are already there. At Gandía in the same region, the duke has started another college, with an annual income of seven hundred ducats. Eighty of our men are being supported at the college in Portugal, and the King plans to increase the number of scholastics to a hundred.[7] He

---

[6] The reference is to Andrea Lippomani.
[7] The college in Coimbra.

has already assigned them an income of 2000 ducats, besides supplying all their other needs.

In addition to these, there are a host of other places to which we must write: Barcelona, the Emperor's court, the court of the prince of Spain, Louvain, yourselves, Trent, India—about which we can hardly write you anything except that the King sent ten of our men there on the last fleet: so great is the fruit of our Society in those lands in Christ, so great the hope of future harvest.

I say nothing of Alcalá, Toledo, or Valladolid, where we have either scholastics or others who expect letters from us. So if you do not get frequent letters from us, take it in good part. However, we will make sure that we never fail to write when we think there is something for which it is worthwhile taking the time for Christ's glory and for our consolation in you. But don't you neglect to write us more often. We sent Master Jacques L'Host from Gelderland to Agrigento in Sicily after Easter. The bishop of the city there is Cardinal Carpi, our Society's protector, to whom the whole Society is utterly indebted in Christ.[8] He made infinite efforts to get us to grant him one of our men to work in his name for the reform of the Agrigento Diocese, and we thought it best to send Master Jacques there to comply with his hopes, for the glory of Christ. We hope that he will put the province in order within a few months and then return to us. We recently got news of the arrival in Trent of our companions and brothers, Master Diego Laínez and Master Alfonso Salmerón; I believe you knew they had been appointed to the council by the Supreme Pontiff. They were warmly welcomed by both the legates of the Apostolic See and the other bishops, as well as by the cardinal legate of Santa Croce, who gave orders that they should be supplied with whatever they needed by way of food or anything else.[9] We hope in God's mercy through Christ Jesus that their coming there will not prove fruitless. We are sending this letter by a Fleming whom we love in Christ, Daniel Paeybroeck, who has set out under our obedience; welcome him as a brother and refresh his spirit in the Lord [see 2 Cor. 7:13].

It remains that we pray and beseech the God and Father of our Lord Jesus Christ that he will vouchsafe to reveal in our hearts his most holy will, and in addition give us the strength to fulfill it. May the grace of our Lord Jesus Christ be with you. Amen.

---

[8] Rodolfo Pio de Carpi.

[9] The cardinal was Marcello Cervini, the future Pope Marcellus II.

Rome, June 2, 1546

By commission of Reverend Father Master Ignatius,

HIERONYMUS NATALIS, unworthy novice of the Society of Jesus

☩

To the Fathers and Brothers at Coimbra
from Bartolomeu Ferrão, by commission

Rome, August 8, 1546

(Letter 131: I:405–7; in Spanish)

A highly spiritual announcement of the sudden sickness and death of Pierre Favre, written at the wish of St. Ignatius by his secretary at the time, Bartolomeu Ferrão.

May the sovereign grace and everlasting love of Christ our Lord be always our help and support.

Inasmuch as the greater a good is, the more eagerly it should be chosen and, once chosen, rejoiced in; and this joy and happiness, when spiritual and eternal, cannot contain or be the occasion of any sadness or disturbance in our own or our neighbor's regard; and whereas the greatest good in this life is union of the creature with its Creator through the will, but a far greater and ultimate good is actual union through eternal vision and enjoyment—it follows that the latter must be supremely chosen, preferred, longed for, and welcomed when it is offered by the Giver of all good, being as it is the ending of evils, boundless plenitude of graces and glory, and the final will of God. Moreover, this Giver of all good, being the sovereign provider of all things, has no need of any person beyond whomever he himself may wish to choose for his service; and what he primarily wishes is to bring to himself all those who will prove good, this being the end for which he created them. And since the sovereign Good is able and knows how to dispose all things as he wills, placing no bounds to his infinite might, it is man's duty constantly to desire all this, since, after all, of ourselves we can only offend (for "the just man fall seven times a day" [Prov. 24:16.]), whereas it is proper to God to preserve and to bestow grace. It was St. Martin's awareness and reservation in this regard that led him to say conditionally, "O Lord, if I am still needed for your people . . ."[10]

---

[10] "O Lord, if I am still needed for your people, I do not refuse the toil" (from the office of St. Martin in the Roman Breviary).

Now since, for his greater glory in these our times, his Divine Majesty wills that this must be so among those whom God our Lord knows, indeed for Father Master Ignatius himself, it would seem that we must have patience—he in remaining here and we in not departing—but also a great deal of happiness at having such a guide remain with us here during our lifetimes and such a second forerunner and faithful intercessor of the Society depart and be already there, namely, the Reverend Master Pierre Favre of happy memory. On the feast of his patron St. Peter, August 1, he was by God's ordinance freed from the bonds of this death and took leave of us happily in the Lord—just as Master Jean Codure, our first forerunner, died on his own feast day, that of the Beheading of St. John the Baptist. Their souls are now united in heaven and their bodies in Our Lady of the Way here in Rome, where they keep us company. It took place thus, the divine Goodness so allowing. After a long absence from Rome of approximately eight years, traveling through many lands under holy obedience, he arrived in good health on July 17. For a week we and his friends all enjoyed his company in our Lord. Then over a week he was twice visited with a tertian fever. Finally, on the morning of Sunday, August 1, as I said, the Feast of St. Peter in Chains, having made his confession the preceding Saturday night, he heard Mass and received the Most Holy Sacrament and extreme unction. Then between noon and the time of vespers, in the presence of all of us in the house and a number of friends who had come, with many tokens of his past life and of the eternal life to which he looked forward, he rendered his soul to his Creator and Lord.

Since we have need of friends and saints to intercede for us everywhere, we all trust in the Divine Majesty—his will being now fulfilled—that he will help us no less there than he might have here. For all things and eternally may the divine and sovereign goodness be praised and glorified. Amen. Amen. Amen.

Rome, August 8, 1546

By commission of Father Master Ignatius.

Your least and unworthy brother in our Lord,
BARTOLOMÉ FERRÓN

To Doimo Nascio

Rome, August 10, 1546
(Letter 132: I:408f.; in Spanish)

Through a friend of the Society, Ignatius sent the following message to a Spanish Franciscan who was carrying on a drastic campaign against what he deemed the nefarious innovations of the Jesuit Institute.

Jhs.

Master Doimo:

Since Fray Barbarán says he is going to have all our men between Perpignan[11] and Seville put to the flames, tell him that what I say and desire is that he—together with all his friends and acquaintances, not only between Perpignan and Seville but throughout the world—should be set afire and inflamed by the Holy Spirit, so that they might all reach high perfection and be greatly distinguished in the glory of his Divine Majesty. Tell him likewise that an investigation into our affairs is underway before Their Lordships the Governor and the Vicar of His Holiness, and that they are about to pass judgment; and that if he has anything against us, I invite him to come and testify before these judges to prove his charges; for I would prefer to pay myself if I deserve it, and to suffer alone, without all those between Perpignan and Seville having to be put to the flames.

[IÑIGO]

✠

To Peter Canisius
from Bartolomeu Ferrão, by commission

Rome, August 14, 1546
(Letter 133: I:409–11; in Latin)

In 1543, during his travels in northern Europe, Pierre Favre had accepted into the Society the zealous and learned young Netherlander Peter Canisius, editor of the sermons of Johannes Tauler and a close friend of the Carthusians in Cologne. Canisius had written from there to Ignatius requesting a decision about his status.

Ihus.

---

[11] Perpignan is a town near the Spanish-French border.

Reverend Brother in Christ:

The grace and eternal love of Christ our Lord be with us always. Amen.

Having written to you several times and in accord with your wish, and having also frequently received letters from you, we are surprised that our letters have not been reaching you. Among other things, Reverend Father Ignatius had commissioned me to reply to your request, that is, to know what was to be done regarding your status. The matter had been postponed for the arrival of Father Favre (soon to be coming here from Spain for the council), who, being thoroughly acquainted with the situation in Germany, would be able from both sides to make a surer and more satisfactory decision regarding your request, to the praise of God. Father Favre finally arrived in Rome, and Father Ignatius began discussing your situation with him. Father Favre touched upon the needs in Germany, expecting to be able to continue the discussion more fully at greater length. But the matter was left undecided between them by the sudden event of Father Favre's blessed falling asleep in the Lord—as we have written more fully in a letter to Father Bobadilla, along with other spiritual news from various quarters—to the great consolation of all the brothers in Christ, etc.

With there thus being no further occasion to wait for our blessed Favre—who will surely aid us all more now than he ever could have in this life, the Lord inspiring this hope and joy in us—Reverend Master Ignatius did not forget you. Pondering all the details in his heart, he now through my unworthy offices sends you the following reply regarding his mind in the matter.

First, the Society will be most happy to accept you under any conditions, either if you have completed your studies or need to pursue them still further. This is taken for granted. Further, while you are better informed than we about conditions in Germany, it is our part to let you know about those outside Germany. The fact is that at present colleges of the Society are coming into existence at a number of universities: Padua, Bologna, Pisa, Paris, Valencia, Gandía; and we are certain that they will soon need to be supplied with personnel: students, teachers, men to administer the colleges.

With all this as background, Father Ignatius's judgment is that you should examine and weigh in the Lord all the facts, and then do whatever in your own conscience you deem best, just as if you were acting under his command (this has long been his expectation of you, namely, that you would labor tirelessly in Christ's service)—either staying where you are, going to studies, or coming to Rome. Whatever you decide in this way, Master Ignatius will consider right and good. Also let us know this immediately and inform us about everything and about your decision. Since I am completely taken up with writing to the Society in various parts, I have commissioned our brother James from Douay, should he have any leisure from his religious labors, to reply in the name of us all to your latest letter, which, as usual, brought us great consolation.

Master Favre—whom we feel less inclined to pray for than to pray to for ourselves—also saw your letter before his blessed departure.

Farewell, and commend us heartily in the Lord to our fellow companions in Christ. For this time, please share this with the men at Louvain. Again, farewell.

Rome, August 14, 1546

By commission of Master Ignatius.

Yours in Christ,
Bartolomeu Ferrão

✠

To King John III of Portugal

Rome, October 1546

(Letter 140: I:429; in Spanish)

Ignatius offers himself personally to the King for the mission to Ethiopia, should none of the other companions be willing to go.

I have decided in our Lord to write the following in my own hand. Unless the other companions in this same resolve and profession to which (so far as we may believe) we have been called by his Divine Majesty should prohibit me (so as not to show myself rebellious to them all—though I do not think they will do so), I offer you, in case none of our other men are willing to take up this enterprise of Ethiopia, to take it up myself most willingly, if so bidden.

jℏs

To Simão Rodrigues

Rome, October 1546

(Letter 141: I:429f.; in Spanish)

Ignatius suggests that the Society's prohibition against accepting prelacies will not prove an insurmountable obstacle to a Jesuit's being named patriarch for the mission to Ethiopia sponsored by King John.

May the sovereign grace and eternal love of Christ our Lord be always our continual protection and help.

I have received your letters of August 14, together with one from the King, in which he accredits Senhor Baltasar de Faria to me and bids me assist him in any way I can. When the latter spoke to me and, upon learning that Master Favre was past the travails of this wretched life, requested another of the Society in his place to be made patriarch of Prester John's lands, I was uncertain whether any of our men would be willing to accept. Master Jay and Master Bobadilla have refused to be bishops, as you will see by some letters which accompany this one. Master Paschase and another of the Society have refused to accept two bishoprics that were offered to them. For me to command anyone under obedience to accept the patriarchate would seem to go beyond my jurisdiction. Of course, in favor of accepting it is the great difference between the episcopacy as customary in these parts and the one offered for Ethiopia. The former presents pomp and ease, the latter toil and hardships. For this reason, I believe that my own disposition is to allow no disservice either to God our Lord or to the King, so far as lies in me. But I cannot go very far in this matter, since some are in favor of it and others opposed. Senhor Baltasar de Faria is trying to get the Pope to give us a command; I was told the same by Master Bernardino Maffei, namely, that if we should refuse, the Pope would eventually command us to accept. It is quite likely that the Pope will give us this command. Our reply will be to ask that our Constitutions be observed; these will have to be interpreted, and that will be the time for a discussion and decision about whether the patriarchal office is compatible with our Constitutions and, if it is, under what conditions it can be accepted. So long as it entails no dignities, there is no difficulty whatever in accepting this holy enterprise for the greater glory of God. Inasmuch as I am sending the King a brief reply to his letter, I ask you for love of God our Lord to give him a full report, in the assurance that so far as our consciences allow, we shall all be at His Highness's service to perform whatever he shall command us. And I am confident that we shall find a way of doing so to the edification of all involved.

To Isabel Roser

Rome, October 1, 1546

(Letter 137: I:424f.; in Spanish)

Isabel Roser, Ignatius's long-time benefactress from Barcelona, had come to Rome with two companions to assist his activities. There she had persuaded the Pope to have a reluctant Ignatius receive her under the obedience of the Society. She and her two friends pronounced their vows on Christmas Day, 1545, at Santa Maria della Strada. The project did not work out, and in the spring of 1546 Ignatius succeeded in convincing the Pope to release him from this burden. The apostolic mobility central to the nature of the Society and the unquestioned presupposition of "cloister" for women religious made such a vocation impossible for women at that time. Ignatius sent Isabel the following missive explaining his thinking on the matter. Isabel was very unhappy with the decision; but the two eventually parted on good terms, and she returned to Barcelona, dying there as a Franciscan in 1554.

It is true that, for God's greater glory, I have an inclination to comply with your good desires and continue having you under obedience as you have been for some time now, doing whatever is appropriate for the greater salvation and perfection of your soul. However, I find I do not have the disposition or strength that I would like, owing to my frequent illnesses and my occupation with what I consider my primary duties to God our Lord and to our lord His Holiness in his name. Moreover, I hold in conscience that this least Society cannot properly assume responsibility for ladies with a vow of obedience, as I also explained at length some six months ago to His Holiness. I have therefore determined, for God's greater glory, to withdraw and remove myself from this responsibility of having you as a spiritual daughter under obedience, but rather as the good and kindly mother that you have so long been to me, to the greater glory of God our Lord. And so, for the greater service, praise, and glory of his eternal goodness, so far as lies within my power—always pending any decision by higher authorities—I refer you to His Holiness's most prudent judgment, provision, and decision, so that your soul may enjoy complete tranquility and consolation for God's greater glory.

Rome, October 1, 1546

To Miguel de Torres

Rome, October 9, 1546

(Letter 143: I:433–37; in Spanish)

Reports about the documents for the reformation of monasteries in Barcelona; overtures by the negus of Ethiopia ("Prester John") to John III and the likelihood that the Society will have to supply a patriarch for the mission; Laínez's preaching at Trent; the cessation of the campaign of slander against Ignatius and his companions waged by the papal postmaster Mattia, who was irate because Ignatius had persuaded the man's mistress to leave him; changes in plans for the council; and the Emperor's war against the Lutherans.

Ihs.

My Very Reverend Father in our Lord:

May the sovereign grace and eternal love of Christ our Lord be always our protection and help.

On Don Juan de Vega's arrival in Rome, I spoke to him about the issuance of the brief on the reform of the convents in Barcelona; His Lordship thought that it should go directly to the prince, and that he himself would write His Highness suggesting that he send the brief to the two bishops of Barcelona and Alguer, along with an urgent letter for each; and that he himself, Juan de Vega, would also write each of the bishops. Thus the task falls to me to have the secretary write the letters, and also to have the prince write to the viceroy of Catalonia. I have given Ximénez the reminder to write, and I think that everything will be dispatched in this post.[12]

The Pope has returned, but the individual in charge of the register has not yet arrived, remaining behind at Foligno because he was sick. I have been awaiting him daily in order to get a copy of the brief from the register. If this cannot be done here, do the best you can where you are according to the terms of our talk here, to God's greater glory.

After your departure the King of Portugal wrote me a letter, a copy of which I enclose. When I spoke later with Senhor Baltasar de Faria, he showed me a long letter from him relating how Prester John has sent His Highness an envoy asking him to send a true patriarch, since he is quite pleased with the ways of Portugal; also that Prester John is ready to give obedience to the Apostolic See; that in his lands both men and women are circumcised; that they observe the Sabbath as

---

[12] Pedro Ximénez, Juan de Vega's secretary.

do the Jews, receive Communion every Sunday either after confession or not, are baptized every year, and many other things; further, that Senhor Baltasar de Faria was to speak with the Pope to get Master Pierre Favre (of happy memory) chosen as patriarch, and that I was to command him to accept under obedience. Learning, however, that he is beyond all the trials of this miserable life, His Majesty is now bending every effort to have another of our men go with the same office to Prester John. It seems that all our friends are condemning us to this undertaking, even Her Ladyship Doña Leonor Osorio. Earlier, upon learning that Master Bobadilla had refused a bishopric; and then that Jay would not accept the see of Trieste, with many sheep and a thousand ducats of income, despite strong written urgings by the King of [the] Romans and his sending his own confessor, the archbishop, to talk with him and get him to accept, Her Ladyship told me in the warmest terms that she would rather lose everything she had than see one of the Society accept a bishopric. Now, however, she thinks that for the help of so many lost souls we may not refuse, since this was different from accepting a bishopric. Master Bernardo Maffei says the same, although he himself had refused a bishopric. May God our Lord dispose our wills to do whatever is for his greater glory; for if we are to believe Cardinals Burgos and Carpi, they are going to exile some of us for this undertaking. We will not be able to take Master Laínez from the council until they have held the first session, in which they are to resolve the decree on justification. Apparently His Holiness is having scholars examine the decree both here and at Trent, since Master Bernardo Maffei told me that he would send it to me here to be examined in our house.

A fresh favor has been shown to our men at Trent: although up to the present neither bishops nor religious nor other preachers had been permitted to preach in Trent, the legates have ordered Master Laínez to do so, beginning the next Sunday. From another letter, a copy of which I am sending you, it appears that they have already begun to preach and to give exhortations, as you will see from the letter.

Our good Mattia went to speak with Her Ladyship Doña Leonor Osorio, asking her not to act against him and saying that he will have the sentence signed and beg my pardon; also that he will speak in our favor anywhere she wants, even in the Campo de' Fiori. The day before yesterday, Her Ladyship called me and said that both she and Juan de Vega thought Mattia's offer should be accepted. After giving them many arguments, I eventually concluded for the opposite. I told her that I did not think we should make any deal with Mattia, and that I did not wish for him to ask my pardon or for the sentence to be given through his intervention and support; I said I had no doubt the sentence would be given as it stands, to God's greater glory. Finally Her Ladyship agreed that this would be far the better way. Yesterday Mattia went to speak with the Pope's vicar and publicly made many statements in our favor and in condemnation of himself. He is going around making friends for fear that what might happen to him will indeed take place. May our Lord be pleased that everything come about in the way that will be more for his glory.

According to what Master Bernardo Maffei tells me, it is thought here that Cardinals Morone and Sfondrato will be going to the council in place of the Cardinal of England [Pole] and Monte, with Santa Croce remaining as before. Apparently the council depends on the outcome of the Emperor's campaign against the Lutherans. So far, since his leaving here, things have gone well for him and he has been making gains daily; he and his army have now reached within a mile of the Lutherans' army.

May it please the Divine Majesty that everything turn out for his greater praise and glory; may he always, with his customary infinite mercies, be our continual protection and help.

Rome, October 9, 1546, delayed until today, October 18

Your most humble servant in our Lord,

[IGNACIO]

✠

To Francis Borgia, duke of Gandía

Rome, October 9, 1546

(Letter 146: I:442–44; in Spanish)

Three months after Francis Borgia's wife died and after he had made the Spiritual Exercises, he vowed to enter the Society of Jesus. In this letter Ignatius formally welcomes Borgia as a member of the Society and gives directions for the period of transition before the news can be made public. The "building projects" refer to the college and the university that Borgia wanted to establish for the Society at Gandía.

Most Illustrious Sir:

The divine Goodness has consoled me with the decision that he has placed in Your Lordship's soul. May he be given boundless thanks by his angels and all the holy souls who enjoy him in heaven, since we here on earth are incapable of thanking him adequately for so great a mercy as he has lavished upon this least Society by bringing Your Lordship to it. I trust that from your entering his divine Providence will produce abundant fruit and spiritual good for your own soul and for countless others who will be benefited by your example. And we who are already in the Society will be stimulated to make a fresh start in serving the divine Father of families who gives us such a brother and has procured such a laborer for the cultivation of this newly planted vine over which he has given me, altogether unworthy as I am, some charge. Therefore, in the name of the Lord, I welcome and receive Your Lordship from this moment as our brother, and as such I will always have towards you in my soul the love owed to a person who dedicates himself so generously in God's household to serve him perfectly therein.

To come to the details on which you wished to hear from me, namely, the when and the how of your entering: after recommending the matter earnestly to our Lord by myself and through others, I think it advisable, the better to fulfill all obligations, that the change be made gradually and with considerable thought, for the greater glory of God our Lord. In this way things can be arranged there successively so that, without any seculars being informed of your decision, you would soon be freed of hindrances to do what you so much desire in our Lord.

In particular, I would say that, with your lady daughters now of an age to be situated in their own households, Your Lordship should see them honorably married in keeping with their station as your daughters. If a good opportunity presents itself, let the marquis also be married. As for your other sons, they should not merely be left with the support and protection of their elder brother to whom the estate will fall, but also have adequate settlements to enable them to attend a well-known university in honorable style and thus follow up the studies in which they have already laid such solid foundations. For it is to be expected that if they turn out as they ought—and I am confident they will—the Emperor will one day show them the favor which your services warrant and the love he has always had for you gives promise of.

The building projects that have been begun should also be pushed forward, for I would like all your affairs to be fully concluded by the time our Lord will be pleased to have you make public the change in your life.

And while these affairs are being wound up, since Your Lordship already possesses such a solid grounding in letters on which to build sacred theology, I should be very glad—and trust that God would be served—if you seriously applied yourself to the study of theology. If possible, I would like to see you take the doctorate in the university there at Gandía, but in complete secrecy for the present (the world's ears are not ready for such a shock), until with God's favor time and circumstances leave us complete liberty.

Other matters can be explained as they arise day by day, and so I will now say no more, except that I look forward to frequent letters from Your Lordship and that I will write regularly myself, and will beg the divine and sovereign goodness that by his favor and grace he will carry forward the mercies he has begun in Your Lordship's soul.

Rome, etc.

✠

To Miguel de Torres

Rome, October 13 and 18, 1546

(Letter 147: I:445–48; in Spanish)

Ignatius writes to Torres in Spain, still not publicly a member of the Society, about Benedetto Palmio, a young Italian recruit to the Society; difficulties raised by Isabel Roser, a change of heart in the hostile postmaster Mattia de Santo Cassino, the dismissal of Fray Barbarán's proceeding against the House of Santa Marta, the granting of a costly papal authorization free of charge, and the doings of Francis Borgia's envoy Roca.

Ihs.

My Lord in our Lord:

May the sovereign grace and eternal love of Christ our Lord be always our protection and help.

Today, October 13, I received two letters, one from Master Jerónimo Doménech dated September 25, in which he tells me that the letters of Joán Paulo and my own did not arrive at Bologna, and that I should write to Barcelona in duplicate.[13] As a matter of fact, on the very day on which we took leave of each other in the country, although only for a short time, I wrote two letters before going to bed and put them in the post. My letters then went under the same heavenly—or better, earthly—influence as Master Jerónimo's to me, which were written at Bologna on the twenty-fifth of September and reached here on the thirteenth of October, together with the other letter from Master Bat-

---

[13] Reference is to Joán Paulo Borrell, a coadjutor brother from Barcelona.

tista Pezzano, dated the twenty-eighth of September, and along with it one from you, interceding between Benedetto [Palmio] and his mother. Since you were so generous in your promises to the mother, I am quite satisfied with what you promised and will do my best to carry it out. I hope, and in fact am quite convinced, that you are readier to withdraw from your mother than Benedetto is from his. As I write this, I am told that he has gone through Rome making a collection on various sides. He went about begging alms in various spots without my learning anything about it beforehand. He seems to be a young man who, if he lasts, will do great things.

Since Señor Juan de Vega's return with the Pope, there has been no post or courier leaving for Spain. One was supposed to leave a week ago, and I gave him a long letter, but he has not left yet. Señor Juan de Vega thought that the brief for Barcelona would best be sent directly to the prince—with this mail, I believe. I have not been able to send you a copy at Barcelona because the one who keeps the register remained behind sick at Foligno. I am making two copies of this letter, one for Barcelona and the other for Valencia, with the hope that one or other will come into your hands.

I do not think that it is a good idea to give Joán Paulo's letter for Barcelona to his uncle; events here are still in need of clarification. I mean that the Señora Roser wanted two things. First, remaining as she did on quite friendly terms with me, she wanted me to give her a letter indicating I had not sent her away for any fault. Secondly, she reneged on the arrangements that had been made regarding temporalities when these were dealt with in the presence of Doña Leonor [Osorio], Roser herself, Joán Bosch, myself, and another person from outside. I say that she reneged in that three or four days after these arrangements were concluded, she made up her own version of her accounts and claimed that in her judgment our house owed her a considerable sum of money. In the end, I refused her first request until the second matter was cleared up, for I am quite convinced that right is on our side. Thus, at my request, although with difficulty, she accepted mediation, in which she would propose someone from her side and I one from mine; on any matter where the two of them cannot come to agreement, we are to abide by the judgment of some distinguished and learned person, perhaps an auditor of the Rota; and after this had been settled, the Pope's vicar should intervene to put an end to the great scandal here and the one expected in Barcelona, with some people speaking in her favor and others in ours. And, God our Lord willing, once we have cleared up all these matters of interests, testaments, and donations, we shall remove many offenses against his Divine Majesty which can be removed in no other way; and for us it will be a good example for the future.

Mattia has testified in our favor to the Pope's vicar, condemning himself and wishing to make peace with us.[14]

Barbarán has lodged a long written proceeding against the House of Santa Marta, and His Holiness has commissioned Cardinal Crescenzi to look into it.[15] I spoke with him yesterday, and he told me that the complaint was baseless. Specifically, it is that we conduct the business of Santa Marta without apostolic authority (His Most Reverend Lordship knows the contrary), and that we are bent on reforming the whole world; that we enact statutes for expelling all adulterous married women from Rome, and other such charges which have not the slightest foundation. Knowing all this, the cardinal himself told me how to go about talking with His Holiness so as clear this all up. I am convinced in our Lord that the preceding will be regarded at its real worth and weight.

After turning over this complaint to him, His Holiness has done us a new favor in the matter of the bulls for Padua:[16] after having remitted to us the part of the merger which would have gone to the Pope, he now has done the same with what would have gone to the chancery officials, expediting by private bull what, so Master Pietro Codazzo tells me, would have cost the college about two thousand ducats.

So that he can talk about them with His Holiness, I have given Dean Roca the petition for the indulgences requested by His Lordship the Duke for the Exercises, and also for the college and university which His Lordship wishes to found. And so I believe that, after speaking with him throughout this week, he will leave for Milan, where it seems His Holiness is sending him (as he himself told me the day before yesterday).

Commending myself to Master Cristóbal [de Mendoza], I close, asking God our Creator and Redeemer to grant us his Holy Spirit for ever and ever.

Rome, October 13, 1546

This was already written when Cardinal Crescenzi last Friday informed the Pope that Barbarán's lawsuit against the House of Santa Marta was groundless. Moreover, as the vicar Archinto is to present the

---

[14] Mattia appears in a former letter, no. 143 (pp. 147–49).

[15] See letter 132 (p. 142).

[16] Documents authorizing transfer of income from Andrea Lippomani's priory to the Jesuit college.

former in the Signatura and the dean is in a hurry, we gave him the petitions for the erection of the college and university so that he can present them.

✠

To Ferdinand of Austria, king of [the] Romans

Rome, December 1546

(Letter 149: I:450–53; in Spanish)

Ferdinand of Austria, brother of the emperor Charles V, attempted to obtain Claude Jay, one of the first Jesuits, as bishop of Trieste. Ignatius vigorously resisted all such attempts. Here he expounds his reasons to Ferdinand. The "four or five" who had already been offered bishoprics were Rodrigues, Laínez, Broët, Bobadilla, and Jay himself. The danger was serious: soon Canisius, too, would be offered a diocese, and a cardinal's hat hung as a threat over Borgia and then Laínez.

We have learned of the holy goodwill which Your Highness has always had towards this least Society and towards certain of its members in particular, and which Your Highness now wishes to put more into effect—with a view to showing greater service to God our Lord and greater favor to all of us—by designating and choosing our Master Claude for promotion to a prelacy. Everyone recognizes Your Highness's holy intentions in wishing to make provision for the souls committed to you, for God's greater glory and their own spiritual benefit, while displaying towards us, unworthy as we are, so great benevolence and charity in our Lord. For this, we render Your Highness unceasing thanks in the Divine Majesty—while praying that in his infinite mercy he may deign, as he fulfills Your Majesty's every desire, to place and engrave in your soul (as I trust he will) a far, far better way of fostering our progress in keeping with our least profession. This will truly be the case when Your Highness commands our services, as is our most earnest wish, yet without bestowing upon us any dignities. For we are convinced in conscience that for us to accept the prelacy would be to demolish the Society. Indeed, if I wanted to think up or imagine a variety of methods for overthrowing and wrecking this Society, one of the most effective—indeed the most effective of all—would be to accept a bishopric. I say this for three reasons among many others:

First: this Society and its members have been joined and linked together with a single spirit, that of journeying throughout various parts of the world among believers and unbelievers as the Supreme Pontiff directs us. Thus, it is the Society's spirit to pass from town to town and from region to region in all humility and simplicity, without becoming attached to any particular place. As an element of the Society's very spirit, this has been given the confirmation of the Apostolic See as we have it in the bulls, where it says of us: ". . . as is piously believed, by the inspiration of the Holy Spirit," etc.[17] Hence, for us to abandon our simplicity would be for us to undo our spirit and so undo our profession, and its undoing would mean the complete ruination of the Society. Thus it would appear that by doing good in a particular place, we would do greater harm on the more universal level.

Second: so long as the Society has proceeded in this spirit, God our Lord has manifested himself in it in a special way through great spiritual profit to souls. And if the soil of Germany has proved more arid, last year in the King of Portugal's Indies one of our men baptized eighty thousand persons. Another of our men in Portugal, besides accomplishing great good in the kingdom itself, has dispatched to the Indies more than twenty persons who had renounced the world, and he has a hundred more students resolved to go there or to wherever else they might better serve God our Lord.[18] Except that I do not wish to go on too long, I could speak at length of Castile, of Barcelona, of Valencia and Gandía, as well as of many regions in Italy, telling how much God our Lord has deigned to accomplish through this Society as it follows this spirit communicated to it by his Divine Majesty.

Third: so far we have only nine professed members. Four or five of them have been offered bishoprics, and we always refused. If one of these men accepted a bishopric now, another would soon do the same, and then the rest as well; and thus, besides losing our spirit, we would completely wreck the Society as well, a greater good thus being lost for the sake of a lesser.

Fourth: if one of us accepted a bishopric, particularly at present when the Society and its members enjoy such a good reputation wherever they have traveled, to the great edification of souls, this would all turn poisonous, to the disedification and scandal of those who love us and are advancing in spirit, to the deep regret of those who are undecided about us but eager to make progress, and to the great disedification and scandal of others who do not think well of us. We would furnish ample grounds for a great deal of criticism and detraction, to the

---

[17] Paul III in the apostolic constitution *Regimini militantis ecclesiæ.*

[18] The reference is to Simão Rodrigues.

scandal of many souls for whom Christ our Lord died on the cross. For the world is so corrupt that whenever one of us sets foot in the palace of the Pope, or of a prince, cardinal, or other high-ranking person, people think we are acting out of ambition; and if we were to accept a bishopric at this point, it would be extremely easy for them to talk, criticize, and offend God our Lord.

✠

To Diego de Eguia

Rome, December 1, 1546

(XII [Appendix 6, no. 2]: 631; in Spanish)

These instructions probably date from the period when the Society was encountering difficulties because of the St Martha house for converted women.

Don Diego:

You will be pleased to observe these points:

1. You will take less time in saying Mass, at your devotion, and always finish an hour before midday.

2. You will not give Communion to any of the women more than once a week without informing me or the person I place in my name.

3. You are not to preach or talk on the altar at Santa Martha without my commission.

4. You will not have any of the women imprisoned, nor meddle in the responsibilities of the presidents.

To Juan de Polanco

Rome, February or March 1547
(Letter 152: I:457–60; in Spanish)

A reproof to Polanco (who nonetheless would soon be called to serve as Ignatius's secretary) for presumptuously writing Laínez that there was no longer any hope of starting a college in Florence, after he himself had alienated the duke and duchess of that city by his imprudent zeal.

Ihus.

May the sovereign grace and eternal love of Christ our Lord be always our continual protection and help. Amen.

On February 21 I received a letter from Master Laínez in Trent, together with one from yourself dated the first of the month. From it I learn that you wrote Master Laínez telling him that other more important undertakings ought not be slighted in favor of the planned house and business at Florence, the latter being practically undone. I cannot help being concerned and surprised over two points here, wondering whether you may not have been prompted by your fine zeal and large charity more than by experience and prudence in the latter. Hence, it would give me much spiritual consolation if you could relieve me of my doubts on this matter.

Regarding the first: I fail to see how it could have been right, when I was trying to get Master Laínez free for Florence, that you should write him urging the contrary without letting us know here first.

As for the second: before the project came to this sorry pass, I gave the matter prolonged thought; I had Master André [des Freux] write you about a full month ago to modify your manner of dealing with the sovereigns there. When dealing with such exemplary rulers, who with good reason are highly sensitive to who is for or against them, to hand them sheets of paper with precepts or counsels for the reform of their consciences and state without first having obtained the requisite love, credit, and authority with them is a course more apt to ruin everything than to achieve your goal.

Likewise, we had written to you at Bologna on how to deal with the bishop and the duke if summoned by them: you were to be guided wholly by their wishes, with a view to producing greater spiritual benefit among the people. Now you can see what your attempts at reforming the duke and the duchess right away have led to in your relations with them. Knowing the great charity and ability which God our Lord has bestowed upon you, I am confident that this experience will serve as a good warning for the future and that his Divine Majesty will yet accomplish much for his greater glory with you as his true and faithful instrument. And so do not be discouraged, but endeavor to go forward in the Lord of all.

We have the reputation, particularly in Rome, through certain persons who miss the truth, of wanting to rule the world. And should Mattia, the papal postmaster, or some of his followers in ignorance have passed through Florence, it would not be surprising if they spoke against us to the duke, and this may have contributed to further undoing the greater service of God our Lord.

For love of our Lord, be so kind as to write me as soon as possible and in duplicate a long, detailed report on whatever you have ascertained or suppose are or may have been the reasons which have occasioned the undoing of this project. Meantime, wherever the worst disedification has been felt regarding either yourself or all of us, I would like you there to perform some acts of special humility, to the greater confusion of the world, the flesh, and the devil. You might spend some hours each day in the hospitals serving the poor and consoling their souls by means of confessions and exhortations. For even if this work were more damaged and undone than it is, I myself am even more convinced in our Lord that if we can free Master Laínez from the council, we should have him come there as soon as we can, as we have written you in another letter, and if not him, then others of our men. If you have occasion to write him in the future, it should be to encourage his coming, not the opposite. I am confident in our Creator and Lord that the damage will be repaired, to his greater glory and the great spiritual benefit of many more souls. With our men acting there with great humility and thus helping to prepare the ground, through God's grace, I have no doubt that his Divine Majesty will fully provide a means for his greater praise and glory, since this, by grace of his Divine Majesty, is our sole desire.

May he, by his infinite and sovereign goodness, give us his abundant grace, so that we may know his most holy will and perfectly fulfill it.

To Miguel de Torres
from Bartolomeu Ferrão, by commission

Rome, March 2, 1547

(Letter 153: I:460–67; in Spanish)

A description of the vigorous campaign waged by Ignatius against Ferdinand of Austria's attempt to obtain the appointment of Claude Jay to the See of Trieste. Although Miguel de Torres had already been received into the Society and had made his vows, he had not yet publicized these events in Spain, where he had business to conclude; hence he is addressed here as a secular.

May the sovereign grace and eternal love of Christ our Lord be always our continual protection and help. Amen.

In this letter I wish in our Lord to let Your Worship know, as if present here yourself, about a covert persecution recently raised by the enemy of human nature against the Society. I write to you as to someone who loves the Society deeply and will not be misled by this affair— for I know that the whole Society holds Your Worship in the greatest charity and veneration.

The matter is as follows. Before leaving here, Your Worship presumably heard, as I believe, that the King of [the] Romans had sent his confessor, the bishop of Laibach [now Ljubljana in Slovenia], to deliver a personal letter to Father Claude Jay of our Society, then residing at the council in Trent. The father had joined the bishop in Venice to share the journey with him, and there they met and talked together for two or three days. Upon Master Claude's opening the letter from the King, he saw that it contained no other than a request, with great charity and altogether loving intent, that he accept the vacant bishopric of Trieste, located on the borders of Venice and Slavonia, a territory with a large population and an income of two thousand ducats. But even though the Kings's confessor did all he could to persuade him to accept this dignity, the father, convinced that it was to the Lord's greater service for him to refuse, came to this decision and wrote to the King, pleading as best he could to be excused.

After three months had gone by, and we learned here one day from His Holiness's secretary, Master Bernardo Maffei, that a further attempt was underway to make the same father a bishop, our father Master Ignatius went to the palace the next morning to speak with the secretary. The latter read out to him a very strong letter from the King of [the] Romans to the Pope. It contained three main points. First, the King's reason for selecting Master Claude Jay for the vacant See of

Trieste was that, faced with the great need for a perfect pastor in that territory, so ridden with error and vice, he could think of no one better than Master Claude, whom he knew to possess great goodness and learning through having dealt with him and heard many of his sermons in Germany; he spoke of him with the highest praise. Second, when he had written to the father through his confessor asking him to accept the bishopric, the father had in his humility begged off. Third, His Holiness should therefore command him under obedience to accept the post, seeing how just and necessary the matter was, for the sake of the great spiritual fruit a man of his outstanding life and learning would produce. The King so expanded on these three points that the letter resembled a major petition of the sort submitted to the Signatura.

When he saw this, Father Ignatius went to the house of Don Diego Lasso, the King of [the] Romans' ambassador. The latter showed him a letter he himself had received from his lord the King, partly in the King's own handwriting, charging him in the most insistent terms to exert every care and effort to send on to the King the brief of episcopal appointment which he had commissioned him to request from the Pope. Our Father asked the ambassador to comply properly with the King's instructions but to avoid forcing the matter to a conclusion, lest the Society suffer the hurt that accepting the bishopric would bring upon it. But the ambassador, after a good many kindly remarks, replied that if Master Claude refused to accept the see and the Pope failed to excommunicate him, he himself would leave Rome.

Seeing the seriousness of the situation, Father went back to talk with Master Bernardo Maffei. There he learned that three of the cardinals expert in business had seen the King's letter to the Pope and had, with a good and holy intention, concluded that the matter should be handled differently. Although the Supreme Pontiff had directed, at the ambassador's request, that a brief be drafted commanding Father Claude to accept the bishopric, these cardinals proposed that to forestall further evasion His Holiness would do better to make him a bishop right away and send him the brief afterwards. However, the secretary said he anticipated that the body of cardinals would object to this; he mentioned that if any of the cardinals were on our side, it would be the Cardinal of England and the Master of the Sacred Palace, both of whom had recently refused bishoprics themselves.[1]

---

[1] Cardinal Pole is the Cardinal of England. The reference to the Master of the Sacred Palace is apparently to Cardinal Badía, O.P.

Our Father spoke to one of these, as well as to some others. But failing to get what he wanted, he decided to go to the source and to talk with the Pope, lest his conscience accuse him of not having attempted every possible means in this affair. This he did. Most humbly he gave His Holiness a long account of the entire affair and set forth numerous arguments showing why this sort of appointment was good neither for the Society nor for the welfare of souls. His first argument regarding the Society was as follows. This Society began with a spirit of lowliness and humility, and with this spirit it is obvious how much our Lord has deigned to accomplish through it. Hence, were it now to forsake its beginning and its first devotion, and act in a very contrary spirit, such as by accepting and rising in dignities, it is clear that it would no longer be able to maintain itself in its peace and good works, but would come to its destruction instead.

His second argument was that, with the Society having so few professed members, one could only think that acceptance of this dignity would end in wrecking it. For if Father Claude took this bishopric, another professed would do the same, another would follow him, and so on, until none were left. This was confirmed by the fact that over the last seven years four bishoprics have been offered to four of our members. If even one accepted, the others would quite probably follow suit—which God forbid.

The third argument regarded the good of souls. Much harm would come to them and to the universal good of the neighbor. After all, if Master Claude were to accept, the only souls he could help would be those of his own diocese; but if he did not, he would be able to produce much fruit in the Lord in many cities, provinces, and kingdoms. For if God's word is not welcomed in one place, it can be sown quite well elsewhere and yield a hundredfold, as is seen from what has been accomplished by individual members of the Society, with the Lord's cooperation, throughout Italy, Spain, Germany, Hungary, Portugal, and the Portuguese Indies.

The fourth argument: inasmuch as throughout all these areas the reason for the Society's enjoying great credit and veneration in our Lord is that it proceeds in a spirit of humility and simplicity and one far removed from greed, there is no doubt that for it to accept dignities now could well occasion a degree of scandal, disedification, and criticism wherever the Society is known that would surpass any good that might be done in an individual diocese.

The fifth argument: there is another serious harm that acceptance of this dignity could wreak on the Society. There are presently in the Society something like two hundred novices and scholastics who have left everything in the world and resolved to enter the Society in poverty, chastity, and obedience. Many of these might take scandal at seeing us change our policy by accepting bishoprics, and as a consequence turn back. Others would find a motive for remaining in the Society, or for entering it, in the unsettling notion that in time they too might become bishops. In this way the Society's devotion could be turned into faction and ambition.

Our Father laid great stress on this and many other arguments while alone with His Holiness during the initial audience and in the chamber after dinner. In the end, the Pope—Our Father believing that he had done everything he could—answered him most charitably, commending his arguments and his lengthy discourse and praising the Society. But he stuck at one point that was firmly fixed in his mind: that the King of [the] Romans' action in providing for the diocese with Master Claude stemmed from the Holy Spirit. He alleged such texts as "The heart of the king is in the hand of the Lord" [Prov. 21:1] and so on, and said this was His Holiness's own opinion.

Finally, at the end of quite lengthy discussions, Father Ignatius told His Holiness that if this bishopric were accepted, there would be such scandal and criticism regarding it that the Society's members would no longer be able to come and talk to His Holiness, to cardinals, or to other persons in high place without people's claiming that they came ambitioning dignities of this sort; and that Don Juan de Vega and Madama had both already sensed the same scandal and would eventually speak to His Holiness about it.[2]

Then the Pope replied that he should go and pray over it, and that he himself would study the matter. After asking His Holiness for certain favors, which were granted, Our Father resumed his quest for any possible means of preventing the matter, unable to rest until he got this as he wanted. First, speaking with Don Juan de Vega, he got the Emperor's secretary to try his hand at interceding for us with the Pope. However, though the latter carried out his errand with all possible warmth, he got no more favorable a reply from His Holiness than Our Father had—indeed he found the Pope even more inclined to give the bishopric to Master Claude. When Father Ignatius saw this, making use

---

[2] In Jesuit parlance of that time, "Madama" was Margaret of Austria, daughter of Charles V and wife of Ottavio Farnese, the Pope's grandson.

of Master Pietro Codazzo and as many others as he could, he "did the holy stations"—visiting and talking with as many cardinals as possible; for it was expected that the consistory in which the question was to be dealt with would take place in three or four days' time.

The efforts he made in this matter are incredible. Not content with laboring the entire day, he conferred during the night with three cardinals living a good mile from each other, such as Cardinal Gaddi, who lives in Montecitorio, and Cardinal Salviatti, who lives in the Borgo near the palace. So great were his efforts, with the Lord's cooperation, that half of the cardinals were of our opinion, and all of them favorably disposed towards us. For, apart from the former, the others—those who wanted the bishopric to be accepted—were motivated by the belief that good bishoprics should be given to men of goodness and adequate learning, such as they asserted our men to be, so that we had no right to decline them. A good number thought this way, even those with the greatest love and affection for us in the Lord.

There was not a single cardinal who was not approached in our behalf—with the exception of two: one who had been appointed to argue in the consistory on behalf of the episcopacy, so that there was no point in seeing him; and the other who, after initially renouncing a different bishopric out of devotion, had subsequently gone back and assumed it.

Seeing that we were encircled like this on every side, that the consistory was going to be held the next day, and that the Pope had not changed his mind, Our Father took the step of going to Madama and getting her to write His Holiness a note requesting him not to treat the matter in the scheduled consistory but to wait until she and Don Juan de Vega had written to the King about it; then, if the King did not give way and His Holiness so commanded, the Society would accept the bishopric. The note was sent that Thursday, the eve of the Friday when the consistory was to be held. The Pope answered Madama that he would do as she requested. However, the cardinal who was supposed to propose the measure was unaware of this, and proposed it the next day anyway. He made no headway with it, however, being opposed by one who was of our opinion, who adduced good arguments that he had brought along. Father Ignatius immediately got Don Juan de Vega, Madama, and our protector, Cardinal Carpi, to write the King, and did so himself in the name of the whole Society, with such weighty arguments and lamentations that we have always had good hopes for the outcome.

At the same time, he sent word that our men who were at the council, and Master Bobadilla wherever he was, should write and get as many others at Trent as they could to write His Majesty about this matter. However, at the council they could only get a single prelate to write, since opinions about the matter diverged there as well.

While all these measures were being taken here, Don Diego Lasso still kept making every effort to get the petition of his lord the King acceded to without delay; and in the next consistory a week later he got the cardinal mentioned above to propose his cause once more. But by God's grace this was held up just as previously, His Holiness announcing his intention to keep his word to Madama and await an answer from the King. This arrived just a few days ago: he instructed his ambassador not to insist or proceed any further with the matter, agreeing that this was the better course. Masses and a Te Deum were accordingly ordered here in the house in thanksgiving for our escape from this great affliction and plague, for we were convinced that acceptance of the bishopric would have tainted or besmirched us all. Infinite and ceaseless thanks be to God for this.

Your Worship's most eagerly awaited letter is being answered by Father Master Ignatius, who is entirely yours in our Lord.

May he in his infinite and supreme goodness bestow his perfect grace upon us so that we may know his most holy will and completely fulfill it.

Rome, March 2, 1547

Your Worship's servant in our Lord,
BARTOLAMÉ FERRÓN

✠

To Pope Paul III

Rome, May 1547

(Letter 172: I:515–17; in Latin)

Draft of a petition to have exemption from the care of religious women made formally a part of the Jesuit Institute. A reply from the Pope that same month granted the petition, noting that according to its Institute the Society's members had always to be "shod and ready for spreading the gospel of peace in accord with the decisions of His Holiness wherever on earth he should send them."

Most Holy Father:

Your Holiness's devout petitioners, the superior and priests of the Society of Jesus, which was erected, instituted, and approved by Your Holiness in the Church of Santa Maria della Strada in Rome, do not fail, with what strength and slight abilities they possess, to exert themselves in daily service of the Church of God and of our Lord Jesus Christ, and consequently of Your Holiness, his vicar on earth.

But inasmuch, Holy Father, as they are being solicited by certain great men, particularly in Spain, to take upon themselves the care of nuns and devout women desirous of serving the Lord; and inasmuch as the petitioners are even now aware that this single office would be a great hindrance to the other tasks incumbent upon them for the service of God by virtue of Your Holiness's principal design for it; and while this concern is still just beginning to arise and can be prevented, and a small hindrance in the present could grow in the future—they come humbly to Your Holiness's blessed feet and implore as a special privilege that in their institution and in the confirmation of their Society (and may this be considered as expressed in so many words and may it be possible to cite them), Your Holiness might declare and decree that it would be a great hindrance to the other duties and services to God incumbent upon them by virtue of Your Holiness's principal design if they were to assume any care of nuns, sisters, or any women whatsoever, or to receive any vow or obedience from them; and that they should in no way be bound to assume the care of such women, nor is it expedient for their Institute and Society. Notwithstanding . . . *[there follow clauses of legislative technicalities]*.

✠

To the Fathers and Scholastics at Coimbra

Rome, May 7, 1547

(Letter 169: I:495–510; in Spanish)

Ignatius addressed this "Letter of Perfection" to the flourishing scholasticate at Coimbra, in Portugal. At the time it was prospering with vocations and zeal, the latter at times quite indiscreet. Simão Rodrigues, the provincial, was too compliant in allowing the scholastics to become "fools for Christ," in such manifestations as self-flagellations and half-nude preaching on the streets at Coimbra, and loud nocturnal summonings of the population to penitence. Favre and Araoz had noted the situation with concern; Rodrigues finally sought a letter from Ignatius, who, on his part, would like to have called Rodrigues to Rome. The situation produced this long and well-crafted letter, probably drafted by Polanco but expressing accurately Ignatius's own views. He urges the scholastics to advance towards perfection by depicting to them the excellence of the vocation and gifts they have received, the value of fervor, and the great need of souls. However, he exhorts them to avoid indiscreet zeal and to hold to the guidance of obedience. He concludes by indicating ways in which they can serve God during their time of preparation and studies.

May the grace and eternal love of Christ our Lord be always our protection and help. Amen.

Through letters of Master Simão and also of Santa Cruz, I regularly receive news of you; and God, from whom descends everything that is good, knows what consolation and joy it gives me to see how he is furthering you in your pursuit of both learning and virtue—the good odor of which encourages and edifies many people even in places distant from your own land. And if every Christian ought to be glad at this because of our common obligation to love the honor of God and the welfare of his image that has been redeemed by the blood and death of Jesus Christ, I have good reason to be especially glad in our Lord, bound as I am to have a particular affection for you in my soul. May our Creator and Redeemer be always blessed and praised for all of this, since it is from his infinite generosity that every good and every grace flows. And may it please him to open wider every day the fountain of his mercies so as to increase and further what he has already begun in your souls. I have no doubt that his supreme goodness—so supremely disposed to communicate his goods and that eternal love by which he is far more eager to bestow our perfection upon us than we are to receive it—will indeed do this. Otherwise Jesus Christ would not encourage us to aspire to what we can get only from his hand, when he tells us, "Be perfect, as your heavenly Father is perfect" [Matt. 5:48]. So it is certain that on his own part he is ready, provided that on our part there is a vessel of humility and longing to receive his gifts, and that he sees us making good use of the gifts we have received and praying diligently and earnestly for his grace.

On this point I will not fail to put the spur even to those among you who are already running. For I can assure you that you must make enormous strides in studies and virtue if you are going to come up to the expectations that so many people have of you, not just in your own kingdom but in many other regions as well—persons who, when they see what helps and advantages of every kind, both interior and exterior, God gives you, justifiably anticipate a quite extraordinary result. No commonplace achievement will satisfy the great obligation you have of doing well. Examine the nature of your vocation, and you will see that what would not be slight in others would be slight in you. God has not only called you out of darkness into his marvelous light [1 Pet. 2:9] and transferred you into the kingdom of his beloved Son [Col. 1:13], as he has done with the rest of the faithful. Rather, to ensure that you better preserve your purity and possess a more single-hearted love in the spiritual matters of his service, he thought it good to draw you out of the perilous sea of this world, so that your consciences would not be imperiled amid the tempests raised there by the wind of desire for possessions, honors, and pleasures—or, on the other hand, by the fear of losing all these.

He has done this also in order to keep these base things from occupying, or from dissipating and scattering, your mind and love, so that you might single-heartedly turn and dedicate yourselves to what God created you for: his own honor and glory, your own salvation, and the help of your neighbor. While all institutes of Christian life are directed to these ends, you have been called by God to this one, where, not with a mere general intent, but with an investment therein of your whole life and all its activities, you are to make yourselves a continual sacrifice to the glory of God and the salvation of the neighbor, towards which you are to cooperate not just by your example and earnest prayers but also by the other outward means ordained by his divine providence for our helping each other. From this you can realize what a noble and royal way of life you have taken up: for not only among human beings but even among angels, there is no nobler activity than that of glorifying their Creator and bringing his creatures back to him to the extent of their capacity.

Therefore, study your vocation, so that on the one hand you can give many thanks to God for this great favor, and on the other beg him for special help so that you can respond to it and strive onward with the great courage and diligence which you so badly need for the achievement of these goals. Slackness, tepidity, and lethargy in studies and in your other activities for the love of our Lord Jesus Christ, these you must recognize as sworn enemies of your goal.

To urge himself on, each of you should keep his eyes, not on those he considers of lesser caliber, but on those who are most ardent and energetic. Do not let the children of this world outdo you by showing greater care and zeal for temporal things than you do for eternal ones. It should shame you to see them running towards death more eagerly than you do towards life. Think poorly of yourselves if a courtier renders more attentive service for the favor of an earthly prince than you do for that of the heavenly King, or if a soldier trains and fights more bravely for the glory of victory and a bit of booty than you do for a victory and triumph over the world, the devil, and your own selves, as well as for the kingdom and eternal glory.

And so for the love of God do not be slack or tepid. For, as they say, if tautness breaks the bow, idleness breaks the soul; whereas Solomon says that "the soul of those who work shall become fat" [Prov. 13:4]. Try to maintain a holy and discerning ardor in working to acquire both learning and virtues. In either of these, a single intense act is worth a thousand listless ones; an energetic person achieves in a short time what a lazy one fails to attain in many years.

In studies there is a clear difference between the hard-working and the negligent, but the same is true in overcoming the passions and weaknesses to which our nature is subject, and in acquiring the virtues. It is certain that the listless, by not struggling against themselves, only late in life or even never attain peace of soul or the full possession of any virtue, whereas the energetic and hard-working make great strides in both areas.

Experience shows that any satisfaction in this life belongs not to the slack but to the fervent in God's service—and rightly so; for by making every effort on their own part to overcome themselves and get rid of self-love, they thereby rid themselves of the roots of all passions and anxieties; as they acquire the habits of virtue, they become able to act in conformity to these naturally, with ease and alacrity.

And in relation to God, our most merciful consoler, these persons thereby dispose themselves to receive his holy consolations, for "to the one who overcomes I will give the hidden manna" [Rev. 2:17]. Lukewarmness, on the other hand, keeps a person living in constant anxieties, for it prevents him from getting rid of their cause—self-love—and makes us undeserving of God's help. So you should summon up great courage to work hard at your praiseworthy exercises; for even in this life you will experience the value of holy fervor, not only in the perfecting of your souls but also in your peace of mind during this present life.

For if you look to the reward of eternal life, as you should frequently do, St. Paul will easily convince you that "the sufferings of this time are not worth comparing with the future glory that will be revealed in us" [Rom. 8:18], for "our present momentary and light tribulation achieves for us above all measure an eternal weight of glory on high" [2 Cor. 4:17].

If this is true of every Christian who serves and honors God, you can understand what your own crown will be if you live up to our Institute, which not only [calls you] to serve God yourselves but to draw many others to work for his service and honor. Regarding such persons Scripture says, "Those who instruct many to justice will shine like stars of the firmament for all eternity" [Dan. 12:3]. This should be applied to themselves by those persons who strive to do their duty with earnestness and diligence, both later in the battle itself and during the time of preparation for it. From elsewhere it is clear that merely engaging in actions that are intrinsically good does not suffice. Jeremiah tells us, "Cursed be whoever does the work of the Lord negligently" [Jer. 48:10]; and St. Paul says, "Do you not know that many run in the race but one receives the prize?" [1 Cor. 9:24]—that is, the one who strives hard—and, "Only he gets the crown who competes legitimately" [2 Tim. 2:5]—that is, who strives hard.

But above all I want you to be stirred up by the pure love of Jesus Christ, by a longing for his honor and for the salvation of the souls he has redeemed. For you are his soldiers in this company, enjoying a special title and special wages. (I say "special" because there are numerous other more general motives which strongly oblige you to seek his honor and service.) His wages are everything that you are and possess in the natural order, for he gave to you and preserves for you your being and life, with all qualities and perfections of body and soul and all exterior goods. His wages are the spiritual gifts of his grace with which he has so generously and lovingly anticipated you, and which he goes on giving even as you oppose and rebel against him. His wages are the incalculable blessings of his eternal glory which, without his being able to benefit thereby, he has promised and prepared for you, giving you a share in all the treasures of his happiness, so that you, by a sublime participation in his divine perfection, may be what he is by his essence and nature. Finally, his wages are the entire universe and every material and spiritual reality that it contains; for he has placed at our service not only everything under the heavens but his entire high celestial court as well, exempting not even one of the heavenly hierarchies, who are "all ministering spirits for those who will receive the inheritance of salvation" [Heb. 1:14]. And as though all these wages were not enough, he has made himself our wage, giving himself to us as a brother in our flesh, as our salvation's price on the cross, and as the support and accompaniment of our pilgrimage in the Eucharist. Oh, what a poor soldier he would be for whom such wages were not enough to make him toil for the honor of such a prince! For there is no doubt that it was to oblige us to desire and labor for his honor with greater eagerness that His Majesty chose to anticipate us with these priceless and costly favors—his all-perfect felicity, in a sense divesting itself of its own goods so that we might share them, and taking on all our miseries so that we might be freed from them; choosing to be sold for our redemption, dishonored for our glorification, made poor for our enrichment; and accepting a disgraceful and painful death to give us a blessed and immortal life. How excessively thankless and hardhearted would a person be if after all this he failed to acknowledge himself deeply bound diligently to serve and seek the honor of our Lord Jesus Christ!

Now, if you recognize this obligation and long to engage in promoting this honor of his, you are certainly living in times that require you to show your desires in action. Ask yourselves: Where is the Divine Majesty honored today? Where is his infinite greatness venerated? Where is his wisdom known, where his infinite goodness? Where is his most holy will obeyed? See instead, with profound sorrow, how his holy name is everywhere unknown, despised, blasphemed. The teaching of Jesus Christ is rejected, his example ignored, the price of his blood in a sense wasted on our part because so few take advantage of it. See your neighbors also—images of the Most Holy Trinity, capable of possessing the glory of him whom the whole universe serves, members of Jesus Christ redeemed by him with so much pain, opprobrium, and blood—see how wretched is their state, in such deep darkness of ignorance and amid such storms of desires, vain fears, and other passions; assailed by so many visible and invisible enemies; in danger of losing, not their property or temporal life, but the kingdom and eternal happiness, and of falling into the unbearable misery of everlasting fire.

To sum up my meaning in a few words: If you thought carefully about how deeply you are bound to defend the honor of Jesus Christ and the salvation of your neighbor, you would see how much you are obliged to dispose yourselves for every toil and labor to make yourselves apt instruments of God's grace for this purpose, particularly nowadays, when there are so few real laborers, so few persons who seek "not the things that are their own but the things that are Jesus Christ's" [Phil. 2:21]; you need to strive all the harder to make up for what others fail to do, since God is giving you such a special grace in this vocation and resolve.

What I have said so far in order to arouse the sleeping and spur on those who linger and loiter on the way should not be taken as an occasion for going to the opposite extreme of indiscreet fervor. Spiritual illnesses arise not just from chilling causes like tepidity but also from hot ones like excessive fervor. "Yours should be a rational service," said St. Paul [Rom. 12:1], for he knew the truth of the Psalmist's words,

"The king's honor loves judgment" [Ps 99:4], that is, discretion; and of what was prefigured in Leviticus where it says, "With every work of yours you shall offer salt" [Lev. 2:13]. Thus, as St. Bernard says, the enemy has no more effective device for robbing a person of genuine charity of heart than by getting him to proceed therein heedlessly and without spiritual reasonableness. We should always observe the Philosopher's adage, "Nothing in excess"—even in justice itself, as you read in Ecclesiastes, "Do not be overly just" [7:17]. Without this moderation, good turns into evil and virtue into vice; and numerous bad consequences ensue, contrary to the intentions of the one proceeding in this way.

The first is that it makes a person unable to serve God over the long haul. If a horse is exhausted in the early stages of a trip, it usually does not complete the journey; instead, it ends up making others have to care for it.

Second, gains made too hastily in this way usually do not last; as Scripture says, "Substance got in haste will be diminished" [Prov. 13:11]. It is not only diminished, it causes a fall: "Whoever is hasty with his feet shall stumble" [Prov. 19:2]; and the higher he was, the more dangerously will he fall—not halting until he comes to the bottom of the ladder.

Third, there is disregard of the danger of overloading the vessel; for while it is dangerous to sail a vessel empty, since it will be tossed about by temptations, it is even more dangerous to load it so heavily that it sinks.

Fourth, in crucifying the old man, the new man is sometimes crucified as well and becomes too weak to practice the virtues. St. Bernard tells us that this excess causes four losses: "The body loses power, the spirit devotion, the neighbor good example, and God honor." He thence infers that anyone mistreating the living temple of God in this way commits a sacrilege and incurs the guilt of the above-mentioned losses. Bernard says that these persons deprive the neighbor of good example: one person falls, this produces scandal, and so on. Givers of scandal to others, says Bernard, are destroyers of unity and enemies of peace. Moreover, one person's fall scares off many others and makes them lukewarm in advancing spiritually. The persons themselves run the risk of pride and vanity by placing their own judgment above others', or at least by arrogating what does not belong to them and setting themselves up as judges in their own case, of which their superior is the rightful judge.

Besides these harms, there are also others: weighing oneself down with arms one cannot handle, like David with the armor of Saul; or using the spurs instead of the reins on a naturally impetuous horse. Thus discretion is needed here to hold a person's virtuous practices between the two extremes. St. Bernard well advises, "Goodwill cannot always be trusted; it needs to be bridled, it needs to be regulated, especially in beginners." Otherwise a person who wants to be good for others may prove bad for himself: "If a person is bad for himself, for whom is he good?" [Sir. 14:5]. And if you think discretion is a rarity and hard to come by, at least make up for it by obedience, whose counsel will be sure. A person who prefers following his own opinion should listen to St. Bernard's words: "Anything done without the spiritual father's approval or consent should be put down to vainglory and not to one's credit." And he should remember that according to Scripture "it is the crime of idolatry not to submit, the sin of witchcraft not to obey" [1 Sam. 15:23]. Consequently, if you want to preserve the mean between the extremes of tepidity and indiscreet fervor, consult the superior and stay close to obedience. If you have a yearning for mortifications, use it to break your own will and submit your own judgment to the yoke of obedience, rather than by enfeebling your bodies and afflicting them without due moderation, particularly now during your studies.

From all that I have just written, I would not want you to think that I disapprove of what I have been told about some of your mortifications. I know that saints have made good use of these holy follies and others like them, and that they are helpful for overcoming oneself and getting further grace, particularly at the beginning. But for a person who already has a certain mastery over his self-love, I consider what I have written above about returning to a discerning moderation and not deviating from obedience to be the better course. I particularly urge obedience, and along with it that virtue, the sum of all the virtues, which was so stressed by Jesus Christ, who called its precept his own commandment: "This is my commandment, that you love one another" [John 15:12]. I want you not merely to maintain this unity and uninterrupted love among yourselves but also to extend it to all persons, striving to enkindle in your souls lively desires for your neighbor's salvation, weighing the value of every soul by the price of the blood and life of Jesus Christ that was paid for it; so that, as you acquire learning on the one hand and grow in fraternal charity on the other, you will become perfect instruments of God's grace, and collaborators in the sublime work of bringing God's creatures back to him as their highest end.

And do not imagine that during this interval of studies you are not being useful to your neighbor. Over and above the advantage to yourself (which is demanded by well-ordered charity: "Have pity on your own soul, fearing God" [Sir. 30:14]), you are serving God's honor and glory in many ways.

First, you are doing so by your present labors along with your intention in undertaking and directing them all for your neighbor's upbuilding. When soldiers are busy furnishing themselves with arms and munitions for the expected campaign, no one would say they are not working in their prince's service. And even if death were to cut someone off before he began dealing outwardly with the neighbor, he would nonetheless have served him in the labor of preparation. Moreover, besides this intention for the future, he ought to offer himself to God on his neighbors' behalf every day: through God's deigning to accept this offering, the man might well be as much an instrument for helping the neighbor as he would through preaching or hearing confessions.

The second way is by becoming very virtuous and good; this will enable you to make your neighbor the same as yourselves. The process that God wills to prevail in material generation he wills analogously in spiritual generation. Natural philosophy and experience teach you that for the generation of a human being or an animal, in addition to such general causes as the heavens, there is needed another immediate cause or agent which is of the same species, so that it will possess the same form as the one it wishes to transmit into another subject. (Hence the saying, "Man is begotten by the sun and by man.") Similarly, to impart to others the forms of humility, patience, charity, and so on, God wills that the immediate cause which he uses as instrument, such as a preacher or confessor, should himself be humble, patient, and charitable. In this way, as I was saying, while you personally advance in every virtue, you are also greatly serving your neighbor. For you are preparing a no less fit instrument, but even a fitter one, for imparting grace to others by means of a good life than by the acquisition of learning (although both are required for a perfect instrument).

The third way of helping the neighbor is by the good example of your life. In this regard, as I already mentioned, your good odor has by God's grace spread abroad and given edification even in places outside your own kingdom. And I trust in the Author of all good that he will preserve and increase his gifts in you, so that you may advance in perfection daily, and so that—without your seeking it—your good odor and the edification that ensues from it may increase.

The fourth and very far-reaching way of helping your neighbor consists in holy desires and prayers. While studies do not leave you time for long prayers, the time can be made up for by desires when a person turns all his activities into a continual prayer by undertaking them solely for the service of God. However, for this and all other matters you have persons with you there whom you can consult in detail. And while for that reason I need not have written all this to you, nevertheless, since I so rarely do so, I decided this time to take consolation in you by writing at length.

That is all for now, except that I pray that as God our Creator and Redeemer has deigned to bestow such a great grace on you by calling you and giving you a firm resolve to employ yourselves totally in his service, he may also graciously continue and increase his gifts in you all, so that you will steadily persevere and grow in his service, to his great honor and glory and the help of his holy Church.

Rome

> [Yours in our Lord,
> IGNACIO]

✠

To Manuel Sanches, bishop of Targa

Rome, May 18, 1547

(Letter 171: I:513–15; in Spanish)

Manuel Sanches, or Santos, a friend of Ignatius from their time of studies in Paris, later became auxiliary bishop of Lisbon and inquisitor general. Ignatius writes encouraging him to bear up under the burdens of his office.

May the grace and eternal love of Christ our Lord come always to our protection and help, for his own honor and glory and for our salvation. Amen.

I received a great deal of joy and consolation in our Lord from Your Lordship's letter: it testifies not only how Your Lordship keeps us in memory but with what charity you desire the furtherance both of our own spiritual benefit and, through us, of God's honor and glory, for which all creatures were created and ordered by his eternal wisdom. I beg our same Creator and Lord, by whose love every other love should be undertaken and governed, that he himself will undertake to repay with very special graces the love which for his sake Your Lordship has for me and for the interests of this Society that bears his name. On my own side, I know of no other means for satisfying Your Worship's remembrance and good desires except by responding with remembrance and very intense desires that God, the author of all good, will multiply in you longings for his honor and service, with a continual increase of his grace for carrying them into effect, and that he may be pleased to relieve Your Lordship of those burdens which in your letter you rightly judge to be a great encumbrance for one who has to mount up to so lofty a throne as paradise. Moreover, even without a person's relinquishing offices that are accepted and carried out for God's honor, it is possible for the soul's weight—which is love—to be lightened when even amid base and earthly things a person avoids becoming base and earthly, and loves all such things for the sake of God our Lord and insofar as they are for his greater glory and service. For we owe it to our ultimate End, who is in himself supreme and infinite goodness, that he be loved in all other things and that the whole weight of our love go towards him alone; he deeply deserves this of us, for he created and redeemed us all, giving himself entirely to us; and he rightly wills that we not fail to give of ourselves to him who has so totally given himself to us and desires to give himself to us forever. Regarding the rule and statutes, I think you will be served by Master Simão, who is close at hand and can inform you personally, better than by myself at such a distance and through a letter. Therefore, on this topic I will leave to Master Simão the task of answering you.

Would Your Lordship be so kind as on my behalf to kiss the hand of the Most Reverend Cardinal, your lord and mine.

No more for the present, except once more to ask the divine Goodness to take possession in us of what belongs to him by so many titles and to increase in Your Lordship all of his most precious gifts and graces.

Rome, May 18, 1547

Your Lordship's most humble servant in our Lord,
IGNACIO

To Diego Laínez, from Juan de Polanco

Rome, May 21, 1547

(Letter 174: I:519–26; in Spanish)

Replying to an inquiry of Laínez at Trent about the studies of certain scholastics, Polanco, recently appointed secretary of the Society by Ignatius, picks up on a general remark Laínez had made about the detrimental effects of too much literary study. He presents a battery of arguments for a solid grounding in languages and letters before going on to philosophy and theology. Laínez had already participated in establishing Jesuit colleges at Padua and Venice and would go on to assist in preparing such a foundation in Florence.

May the grace and peace of Jesus Christ our Lord be always present and growing in our souls. Amen.

Your Reverence's letter to me was no small favor: writing to me as you do in the midst of the articles and your other tasks, you give me even more cause to be grateful for the testimony of your memory of me.[3] This makes me hope for a remembrance in your prayers, for which I have so much need and of which I take assurance from the same charity which prompts you to remember to write me. I look forward eagerly to the summary you promise when there is a lull in your occupations assumed for the common good, and I will receive it as a great kindness. For it, and for so many others received from Your Reverence, may you be rewarded by him who does so with generosity for the sake of his poor, for whose service all is done and received.

With regard to Ludovico, Pedro Ribadeneira, and Fulvio, I have laid your views and those of Master Claude [Jay] before our father Master Ignatius.[4] He has given me no definite answer about these individuals. It may be that he will make a more definite decision before the end of the summer: new factors might emerge that could affect the deliberation.

With respect to Pedro: I know and can see that Father Master Ignatius has for him—over and above his charity towards everyone and his special charity towards those of the Society—a very particular love. He is anxious for him to have every possible advantage for his progress in studies and everything else, being confident that God our Lord will

---

[3] Referred to are the fourteen articles on the sacrament of penance then being debated at Trent.

[4] Among the scholastics who were studying at Padua occur the names of Fulvio Cardoli and Pedro Ribadeneira. The name Ludovico does not appear.

make use of him. So far, however, he has not indicated to me much inclination either way as to changing him or keeping him where he is. He may be waiting for some further development before reaching a decision about him.

I now turn to Your Reverence's general observation that for a mind to nourish itself excessively on the humanities tends to render it so dainty and spoiled that it loses ability and inclination for profounder matters, particularly when the latter have to be sought in authors whose style offers no allurement. On the matter of excess I agree with Your Reverence, because of your own authority as well as because of the instances we have of men who, once entering higher studies, found themselves exhausted by even slight exertions. Such persons really are spoiled: they get used to studying only things easy and pleasant and end up afraid or reluctant to deal with anything showing the opposite qualities, as do the difficult and unappealing topics that we find in philosophy and scholastic theology. However, while in agreement about spending excessive time on these studies, I would not consider it excessive (again, as a general observation) to spend as much time on them as is needed to master humane letters, particularly the languages, in the case of students of the proper age and ability. My reasons are as follows:

First. There is the authority of those, both ancient and modern, who urge the study of languages as essential for Scripture. Moreover, I confess myself particularly impressed by the fact that Father Master Ignatius thinks the same as I on this matter. He is very set on wanting the Society's members to be good Latinists; and, over and beyond whatever human prudence and experience he possesses, it is my belief that God inspires him with particular inclinations and convictions of this sort, since it is the wont of divine Providence to bestow upon those charged with governance a special influx of his grace for the general good of those governed.

Second. We have the example of ancient authors, such as Jerome, Augustine, and other Greek and Latin fathers, whose study of the humanities certainly did not dull the edge of their minds for penetrating deeply into the knowledge of things—to say nothing of the Platos and Aristotles and other philosophers.

Third. A third reason is general usage. In not overly lofty matters of this sort (and barring deception or violence on the part of the sensual appetites), there will not be universal error. But from ancient times to the present day, the commonest practice has been to begin with humane letters—except for certain periods when barbarism rather than scholarship reigned in letters no less than in [manners]; except for these periods, we find in Greece and Italy (and I assume in other places as well) the practice of proceeding from a solid foundation in humane letters to the other disciplines.

Fourth. Experience shows us that because of their inarticulateness many highly learned men keep their learning to themselves and are frustrated of [achieving] what they should chiefly have aimed at with it, the help of their neighbor. There are others who communicate their learning, but lack the influence and success they might have if their powers of expression matched their knowledge or if they could put an outward luster on their ideas that matched the interior light of their insight. This I think can be seen even in the scholastic doctors: if they could trade a portion of their subtle and learned arguments for a certain skill in expounding the rest, they might achieve more widespread good with the latter than they now do with them all.

Fifth. A fifth motive for establishing a foundation in the humanities is a whole series of rational considerations which occur to me:

The first is that, just as one needs to embark upon physical exertions gradually, beginning with lighter exercises until becoming more used to the toil, so it would seem that before the mind launches into toilsome subjects like philosophy and scholastic theology, it needs to acquire the habits of work. It should do this on less difficult and forbidding subjects, such as the humanities: these are more proportioned to a mind that lacks training and strength; they open it up and render it capable of entering upon weightier matters.

The second reason for thinking that time dedicated to acquiring this instrument of humane letters is well spent is that as a person advances in years and his head fills up with larger impressions of reality, it is unlikely that he will have much success with language studies. Experience and reason seem to me to prove this. His memory is no longer empty as it was in early years, no longer as ready to receive impressions of even petty matters. He cannot apply himself to the study of conjugations and other elementary matters in the same way as can those who have had no dealings with more important matters. Such matters incline the mind, once it is habituated to large and noble operations, to scorn lowering itself to petty ones—as if someone used to administering and ruling the affairs of a kingdom were to be busied with those of a village.

The second [sic] is that languages are without doubt useful for understanding Scripture, so that the time spent until they are mastered is well employed.

The fourth is that, besides their importance for understanding all the natural, acquired, and infused gifts of God, languages, especially Latin, are essential if one wishes to communicate to others what God has given to him.

The fourth *[sic]* is that the times we live in are so fastidious in this regard that, with so many people wanting to know languages, anyone who does not will not have much influence on them.

The fifth is that this subject seems particularly necessary in our Society, not only for dealing with people of different languages through conversations and letters, but also for being equipped to preach and speak successfully to ordinary people: the humanities are more on their level and so are helpful in dealing with them.

The sixth is that, even during the time when they are studying subjects they will use in the future, such as history, geography, figures of speech, and rules of rhetoric, I have no doubt that these "work together unto good for those who love God" [Rom. 8:28], and that more than a little.

The seventh is that there is in fact opportunity to exercise their wits and powers when they engage in rhetorical disputations (for those expert at it) or in original compositions, whether in verses or in prose pieces, in speeches or in letters.

The eighth is my conviction that it is essential to master a language once and for all if one is to possess it later on and make proper use of it. The only way to get this mastery is to give the required time and effort once and for all. Many people carry the rock of Sisyphus to the top of the slope and then leave it there and go back to the bottom. I know something about this by personal experience. I began Greek three different times; I bore the weight and trouble of the grammar and was just beginning to have a fair understanding of the authors. But I never got to the point where I could say I really possessed the language and had sufficient training and practice, and as a result it all did me little good. With Hebrew it was even worse: I never had all that much to forget, but now seem to have been completely relieved even of that. All this was because I did not make the effort once and for all to master the language; otherwise it would not have left me so easily.

In addition to this, the objections we mentioned at the beginning can be solved: it can be argued that not everybody who stays with the study of Latin and Greek long enough to master them thereby falls into the disadvantage of inability or reluctance to take on deeper subjects. A certain inclination may be left in the mind and the will, but certainly no unshakable habit having the force of nature, especially in a person who does not grow old in these studies, provided he stops them when he has reached the goal that I mentioned. And assuming a moral probability that this inclination produces in many persons an apathy towards higher studies, a good will can overcome the inclination. Plenty of people overcome it for worldly designs and make themselves study subjects for which they have no personal taste.

So it would appear that any members of the Society who are somewhat so inclined could overcome this with a similar effort of the will for the love of God. For this they would have three aids which worldly people lack. One is their purpose in taking up humane letters and everything else: solely the greater service of God and the help of our neighbor. A second is obedience, which will not allow them to dawdle over language studies even if they want to. A third is God's grace, which, given the two preceding dispositions, can rightly be expected to be more abundant. So far my general considerations.

Returning to Pedro Ribadeneira, there are additional reasons for keeping him at these studies a little longer. First, it will not hurt him to know more Latin, although he is well along in it, by seeing more authors, getting more practice, and, as I said, mastering the language more thoroughly. Second, I assume there will be plenty for him to learn in rhetoric, history, etc. Third, he only began Greek a short while ago, and in what little is left of this year would not be able to get very far in it. If he stays another year, I anticipate that with his ability he will turn out a fine Greek scholar. Fourth, I think what he learns will equip him for any other subjects he may take up, and keep him from being easily daunted by difficulties he meets with. Fifth, I suspect that the prior [of the Trinità] may somewhat resent our removing the better students, or at least the more promising ones. Sixth, I do not see at present where else he could go. Master Ignatius does not think it would be good for him to be sent to Spain. The Duke of Gandía and others wrote asking that students be sent there, and Our Father replied that it would be better if they provide them from there, and they agreed. Hence, it might not be a good idea for us to send anyone there now, to say nothing of the difficulty of travel and so on. In Paris there are no accommodations either at the moment. If we wait a year, I am sure there will be more opportunity.

But an end to arguments: there is no use multiplying them until Your Reverence tires of listening to them, even if my letter reaches you in a moment of leisure.

If the articles are still going on, there is no urgency about reading this; it will keep for reading until after the feast—although it would have been better to mention this at the beginning of the letter.

No more for the present, except humbly to commend myself to the prayers of Your Reverence and of all my reverend fathers in Christ there, as well as of everyone else in the house.

May Jesus Christ increase his grace in us all, so that the honor and service of his Divine Majesty may increase continually in us all.

Rome, May 21, 1547

✠

To Francis Borgia, duke of Gandía

Rome, mid-1547

(Letter 176: I:528–31; in Spanish)

Ignatius felicitates Borgia on his recovery from a sickness and on the marriage arrangements he made for his children (which, as a matter of fact, eventually turned out otherwise), reports the approval being given the Spiritual Exercises, *promises efforts on behalf of the university at Gandía, places Borgia in charge of some men he hopes to send to Spain, approves Borgia's vowing to enter the Society, and reports on the stay in Rome of Fray Juan de Tejeda.*

I received two letters together from Your Lordship, one dated the last of April and the other May 7. They brought the customary great pleasure and spiritual joy in our Lord which they always do—increasingly so since I perceive that his Divine Majesty increasingly supports Your Lordship in advancing your holy thoughts and desires in his greater service, praise, and glory: with the one hand he brings and presents these desires and with the other ever more busily works in them and with them for his greater honor and glory. May it please his divine and supreme goodness, as he daily increases his most holy graces, gifts, and spiritual visitations in his beloved and chosen soul, to be always disposed to preserve and increase [the soul] in the service and praise that are owed him.

As for Your Lordship's recent bad health, I wrote you elsewhere that I learned at the same time of both your illness and of your recovery. Accordingly, I had no cause for sorrow; indeed it seemed to me I should be happy in the confidence that this was not without some abundant spiritual fruit. Now that I learn that your illness and the profit therefrom started on the feast of the glorious St. Ignatius, this makes me rejoice even more in our Lord, since I also am sure that Your Lordship will grow in devotion to the name of this blessed saint, for whom I have, or at least desire to have, very special reverence and devotion in our Lord.

As for the arrangements for joining in marriage your own son and daughter with those of the marquis of Comares, considering the care and devotion you give and find in this matter, the truth is that I seem to experience the same in my own soul, believing that it will be from the hand of him who cannot be wanting in anything that is good and holy and entirely for his own greater praise and glory. The blessing which Your Lordship asks to be given them here in the name of our common Lord and Creator of all things Your Lordship may impart to them; and if I seem somehow reluctant to be the instrument, since I feel myself so unworthy of any good, I wholly give my place to Your Lordship, to employ in my stead whatever is to Your Lordship's liking and the service of God our Lord. I would only ask that we be notified here of the date on which the marriages will take place, so that all the priests of the house may offer Mass and all the others their prayers that these marriages on earth may take place and become spiritual marriages in heaven; and that, becoming thus spiritual in heaven, they may become spiritual also on earth. If we cannot be notified in time, at least let it be soon after their conclusion, so that we can do the same and so be able to satisfy the devotion we all feel in our Lord.

The *Exercises* have been examined and approved by the Cardinal of Burgos, to the considerable satisfaction and edification of his Roman lordship [Pope Paul III]. Regarding this and the other matter of obtaining greater graces for those who confess to one of the Society, once Dean Roca arrives we will see what is the best tack to take in our Lord. May he in his infinite and supreme goodness direct and accomplish this wholly in conformity with his greater praise and glory.

As for the business of the university and matters connected with it which Your Lordship so earnestly charges and enjoins upon me, I will do all I can to make the petitions, both personally and through others, to the persons in charge of such affairs; and I will take very special care in this until I can be found capable of greater things in matters of this sort.

As for the brothers requested by Your Lordship for Zaragoza and Seville, I have written several times to Portugal, to Araoz, and to Master Andrés [de Oviedo], and I believe there may be some word from there. Your Lordship should arrange matters as you think best and judge to be for God's greater glory; whatever it is, I think and judge the same. All jurisdiction and authority I may be thought to have over these brothers I give entirely to Your Lordship, so that Your Lordship can carry out there whatever you think is for God's greater glory, without recurring to us.

What Your Lordship, referring yourself to Master Andrés, requests appears to me to be just and holy and to God's greater glory, and a very special favor which God our Lord is bestowing on all of us.[5] May he be pleased in his infinite and supreme goodness to confirm it all for his greater service, praise, and glory. For the rest I refer you to Master Andrés and to what I am writing to him.

Fray Juan de Tejeda is here in our (or your) house, and we are having him stay because of the heat. When it cools off a bit, he will leave for there. All his projects have turned out according to Your Lordship's wishes, to God's greater glory; he leaves and carries with him much good odor of himself in our Lord, to whom be glory forever.

May this letter be received as her own by Her Ladyship Doña Juana, to whose gracious kindness I ask and beseech to be earnestly remembered and commended, as well as to Their Lordships her children and my lords in our Lord; may he keep them always in his fear and love, to live always and die in the greater love and service of his Divine Majesty.

May he . . .

✠

To the Entire Society, by commission

Rome, July 27, 1547

(Letter 179: I:536–41; in Spanish)

A long rationale in Ignatius's unending campaign to get Jesuits to send frequent and regular reports to Rome. The following letter then gives practical directives on how to carry on such correspondence.

Yhus.

May the grace and love of Jesus Christ live always in our souls and show itself in our works. Amen.

Very Reverend Father in Christ Jesus:

---

[5] This refers to Borgia's wish to bind himself by vow to enter the Society.

Although we do not know each other personally, Jesus Christ our Redeemer and Lord has long held me closely united to Your Reverence, tightening the bond of common charity by which he joins us in himself as members of his body through the other more intimate bond of a single institute of life, the same resolves and desires for seeking in him his greater service and glory. And so I have no cause to consider myself a stranger or to make apologies for writing to Your Reverence as someone unknown to you, for you must consider me very much your own in Jesus Christ our Lord. This is all the more the case in that I would be dispensed from such trouble by obedience, through which I have begun to be and will in the future be animated (with the help and favor of God) to serve Your Reverence and my other beloved reverend fathers and brothers in this matter of writing.

And while, in consideration of my own small being and worth and the desire God has given me to serve his Divine Majesty by serving his servants in this Society, I ought to consider even the most lowly office as ample indeed for me, I am under special obligation to our father in Jesus Christ, Master Ignatius, who has placed me in this office of writing; for, aided by the prayers of Your Reverence and of all, I trust I shall have no slight opportunity to serve you to God's glory, the character of the office making up for my own uselessness. For this exchange of letters, both from here and from there, possesses so much good in itself and is so highly to be esteemed that it would be folly not to undertake it with great devotion as a matter of great importance for the good of this Society and so of all our neighbors, and for the honor and glory of God.

Indeed, it seems to me that in this aspect we are very much put to shame by merchants and other businessmen of this world, who with great care and forethought exchange letters and write books about their own wretched interests in order to augment their own trifles, whereas we in spiritual business, where the interest is our own and our neighbors' eternal salvation and the glory and honor of God—shall we begrudge a little care and forethought in writing what we know will be of so much help to us? Should anyone wish to be told what are the advantages in those outside writing to Rome and those in Rome writing to them about both the state of business and persons and news of edification, we can name numerous great advantages, each of which is another reason and motive for cheerfully and diligently keeping up this writing.

The first is the unity of the Society, which by its profession is spread out in many places and thus more than other orders needs communication to hold it together and unite it; and the means for this is regular correspondence.

The second, consequent upon the first, is the Society's strengthening: the more united anything is, the stronger it is—besides the fact that the things written serve to strengthen.

The third is mutual love, which by nature cools with distance and forgetfulness and, contrariwise, is preserved and quickened by remembrance, which supplies for actual presence. For among persons who are normally absent from one another as our men are, it is clear how essential it is for them to refresh their memory of one another in order to keep up their love. The same effect is had by the charity shown by the one writing, which, as it creates obligation, also helps to love. We can learn these three advantages from the heretics, who at great cost to the common good of Christendom are united to strengthen and love one another. Surely we ought not be less energetic in furthering the common good than they are in destroying it.

The fourth advantage is mutual encouragement and stimulation to holy rivalry in virtues and in holy labors; examples are a great help for this, particularly recent examples of the brothers of our own household.

The fifth is greater strengthening against the spirit of inconstancy or discontent in their vocation on the part of those being troubled by this spirit; for they recognize what a favor God does them by keeping them in the Society, where they can see that the effects of spiritual fruitfulness testify to God's approval and to his care for the members of this Society.

The sixth, which springs from this, is growth in hope and love of God as one experiences in such a special way his providence and love for the Society and for those who belong to it.

The seventh is self-abasement: when those who think they are doing a great deal see the work of others and [note] how God is making use of them, they have cause to humble themselves and acknowledge their own lukewarmness.

The eighth is enhancement of the Society's good reputation, which, as everyone knows, is highly necessary for our goals of greater service to the author of all good and the help of our neighbors' souls.

The ninth, besides these, is that the above brings an increase in the Society's numbers. This is shown by the experience of many who were attracted to join the Society by what they learned from such letters and news.

The tenth is that many men, being alone and caught up in a variety of activities with many occasions that can upset them, need advice for themselves and for their manner of proceeding. These men will be helped by the opinion of the superior if they keep him apprised of their affairs and open their souls to him; and this benefit will be even greater with information being given on the part of all the other members of the Society.

The eleventh is the great consolation and joy given and received by the Society's members through letters; were there no other reason, this one ought to make us all be diligent in this matter if we have love for one another.

The twelfth is increased diligence in the work of God; having to report about what one is doing from day to day can serve as a stimulus for being more alert to do something that can be written about.

The thirteenth is that good news encourages friends to assist the Society, preserves and increases their attachment to it, and wins new ones.

The fourteenth advantage to the Society from this detailed communication about its affairs and persons is that it makes it possible for the Society to see whether it is occupied to good effect in one work or would be better occupied in another, whether Ours would do more good remaining where they are or being transferred somewhere else.

Besides these fourteen advantages regarding the Society's own good, there is a fifteenth that looks to the good of the neighbor: when they hear news of what God is doing through the instruments he employs, they are edified and encouraged to do good themselves.

The sixteenth reaches further: they will be better served and helped, the more advisedly their good is attended to and the better are the means sought for this purpose; and this will be furthered by things being communicated and represented to the superior so that he can see how the entire work is proceeding; for in this way it will be better possible to devise things helpful to the one who is working at close hand and, being occupied and distracted by details, will probably not be aware of many things that might aid him in the work of God.

The seventeenth reaches ever further to the universal good of the Church: with a continual overview of what is happening in various places, it becomes more possible to come to the aid of larger needs and seize larger opportunities. For while in one place a certain amount is being done, in another place a great deal more might be done, with equal effort, to the honor of God and the good of the neighbor. I do not see how this is possible unless there are continual reports on what is going on where the members of the Society are; otherwise, we would often have to act at hazard. Of course divine Providence can often guide our actions without our knowing it, and even better than we could imagine or hope; yet it is clear that Providence wishes us to do all that we can on our part and then to trust in its unfailing help.

Besides the above, there are three advantages in relation to God.

The eighteenth is that we can pray for God's help for the undertakings reported and commended to us from various places, and through the news renew our own fervor for carrying them out more enthusiastically.

The nineteenth is that these reports give us matter and cause to render thanks in more places and through more persons to the divine Goodness for the favors done both to those of the Society and to others through their instrumentality.

The twentieth and last is that this brings an increase in the glory and praise of God (which is the end of the whole universe), both in the actions themselves, which, the better they are done, the more they are for his honor, and also in making known what he does through the instruments which his almighty hand chooses to employ.

Thus there are many strong arguments which invite us to be diligent in this matter of mutual communication through letters—indeed, oblige us to do so if we truly love the good of the Society and of all our neighbors and the honor of God our Creator and Lord. For this reason, our father in Jesus Christ Master Ignatius has deemed that in this matter all of us should reform our behavior, both here and there. Moreover, this will surely be easier for persons outside Rome than for us here; for while the former only need to report about themselves, here we have to satisfy all the places where the Society is scattered, by writing to each place about what is happening not just here but everywhere else. And considering that for the reasons given above three or four of us are here occupied with a good will in this work of writing as our main and almost exclusive activity, Your Reverence should not consider it too much to spend a little time and labor on this essential matter. And so that we would have less occasion both here and there to fail in this duty, Father Master Ignatius has decided to send Your Reverence and everyone else in the Society the rules which follow; and he directs that both this letter and the attached which follow be placed in a volume which will serve for this and other matters. And so Your Reverence will have a copy made and sent to the college, and have another copy made to keep for yourself.

For the love of Jesus Christ, for the honor of whom any work undertaken, even if lowly in itself, is of high value in his divine presence, let us all undertake this work cheerfully and diligently, since Your

Reverence cannot complain of your own share in it. I can tell you that here, although the labor is great for persons as busy as we are, yet because it is a matter of such moment for the good of the Society and our neighbors to the honor of Jesus Christ, and because of the singular merit of obedience, we have condemned certain persons full-time to this activity, with greater labor than Your Reverence could readily believe—although I find myself forgetting what I said at the beginning when I speak of myself as condemned to this duty which I prize so highly, recognizing the favor which God does me in it. However, both can be said truthfully: what I said last in view of the obligation and continuous toil, and what I said earlier in view of its purpose and fruitfulness.

Well, that is all for now, except humbly to commend myself to the prayers of Your Reverence and of all my dear fathers and brothers in Jesus Christ; for I expect this high salary from Your Reverence's and their kindness for myself and those who assist me in this office; namely, the prayers by which you will obtain for us the grace that in this work we may render good service to all the members of the Society, to the benefit of souls and to the honor and glory of Jesus Christ our Creator and Restorer, whose own love and service has so anticipated our own and laid us under such obligation; for even when we have toiled supremely in his service with all our being, we remain infinitely his debtors forever. May he be blessed and glorified for everything unto ages of ages. Amen.

Rome, July 27, 1547

> Your Reverence's servant in Jesus Christ,
>
> +Joán de Polanco+

✠

To the Entire Society, by commission

Rome, July 27, 1547

(Letter 180: I:542–49; in Spanish)

These are directives which accompanied the previous letter. They draw on the experience which Polanco had gained as "scriptor apostolicus" at the Holy See before entering the Society. His service to Ignatius and to the whole Society was outstanding in the years after 1547, when he became secretary.

RULES TO BE OBSERVED REGARDING THE WRITING OF LETTERS BY THOSE OF THE SOCIETY SCATTERED OUTSIDE ROME

1. Certain matters are to be observed regarding letters received, others regarding letters sent.

Regarding Letters Received

First, it would be good if in the town where you are you could find someone through whom letters could be sent to you, such as the prelate or a merchant with connections in Rome. You should let us know here who the person is so that with a cover for him or in some other way we could address the letters to you; also who his regular correspondent is here in Rome, so that we can send letters through that person; and if he has no correspondent, at least who the person there is. And so that this person will not be burdened with the postage, it will be paid here or there. This same procedure will serve not only for receiving letters from us but also for sending letters; and we can use a similar procedure here so that the letters can travel both ways securely.

2. When you have found such persons, you will need to visit or send someone to them from time to time to find out if there are any letters and to fetch them, particularly if there is a scheduled time for this—in Italy there is such a time, and it should be known—or, for those outside Italy, if there has been any news about mail arriving.

3. Look at the date and record it, along with the date you received the letter. In this way you can tell whether you have missed a letter when you see that we mention one with a date that is not in your record. Moreover, by always mentioning to us the date of our letters and the date of receipt, you will keep us clear on this and we will know whether we need to send the letter to you again.

4. Be careful not to show letters to anyone who could be hurt by them, especially what is written on the separate sheets, but also what is in the main newsletter sent from here, whether these are extracts or copies of letters from the brethren; not everything is for everyone. There is no general rule in this matter; discretion must determine in each case whether those to whom the letter is shown are likely to be edified, as are spiritual, goodwilled, and religious persons, or not edified, as are men full of the spirit of the world who lack a taste for such things or interpret them badly. And so discretion must see whether it would be good to show such persons nothing, or only the part by which they would be edified and not the rest.

5. As discretion must be employed in not showing letters to persons who could be hurt by them, so diligence should be employed in communicating news of this sort to persons who will be consoled, stimulated, and encouraged by them; and to others who are inclined to the Society, either to enter it, as in the case of young men, etc., or to assist it, etc. Thus—with a certain tact so that they will appreciate it—such persons should be shown the letters in whole or in part as is deemed suitable. Likewise, persons who have members of the Society close by, as the one at the King of Portugal's court does at Coimbra, Valencia does at Gandía, and the one at the prince's court does at Valladolid and Alcalá, should have copies made of what they think should be communicated and send these or the originals themselves.

6. If some point in the letter requires careful response or some commission is given to you, this may be specially noted; and if it might quickly slip from your attention, it would be good to do the thing or give what reply you can while the matter is fresh in your mind, even if the letter should remain in your room until you send it or until a fuller response occurs to you. In any case, do not fail to take care of the matter and to do what is directed or give us a complete answer. For this purpose, any matter of importance might be read several times to ensure comprehension. If letters and commissions for other persons arrive, be sure to pass them on. So much for letters you receive.

Regarding Letters Sent

First, what should be written:

Regarding letters sent here to Rome (you will see below what should be observed with regard to other places), three things should be considered. First, what ought to be written; second, in what way; third, what measures and cautions should be employed in writing and sending them, so that they will arrive securely and quickly. On the last point, we will give only the conclusions: the reasons can be given anyone who requests them.

As for what ought to be written, this, in general, is anything that it is important to know about matters currently being dealt with, about the Society's members, and about the writer himself. Thus, it is necessary to report on the entire state of our spiritual enterprise. First, what is being done and what is being attended to: preaching, lecturing, confessing, giving the Exercises, conversing, studying, etc.

2. Second, the fruit which God is drawing from all this, so far as it is known to the writer or told him by trustworthy persons. All this

should be written with complete truth, reporting what each person deems will be for the glory of God and the edification of those who hear, and so that it can be seen whether the labor is invested well at that place or would be better invested elsewhere.

3. What help is being given by the spiritual prelate and by those who govern in temporal affairs; and other details, such as the persons, if any, who brought them to the town, and other persons—whether they are becoming cooler or warmer, are persevering, growing or diminishing, etc.

4. How he is being assailed with opposition, and those who are obstructing him in the work of God.

5. What reputation he has among the people, what favor or disfavor with the crowd, apart from the points already mentioned in the third and fourth points.

6. What he thinks about the overall progress of his work. And in order to do this seriously, it would be good if every day, or at least a few days in the week, each one would take a look as if from on high at the overall progress of his work: how he is gaining or losing ground, which means are best for him in the service of God, and which ones he should therefore start, continue, abandon, or change; and [he should note as well], taking into account what seems to him for the greater glory of God, what he should do as he is able according to his commission, or else write to consult the father superior on the matter so as to be aided by his opinion. Moreover, since this requires that he obtain information about these things, it would be good if he had a friend to tell him about what is going on, or ascertained the facts in some other skillful way.

7. He will also write any matters which are connected with his spiritual business. However, in the main letter he should not enter into state and secular affairs, even notable ones like wars, except for purposes of edification, such as prayers made to God, etc. On the separate sheets he may mention the most notable points if he thinks any good can come from writing them—but only where there would be no danger even if it became known. However, if it does not concern our business and might cause offense to others, he should write it neither in the main letter nor on the separate sheets.

8. He should have these same points which he observes in writing observed also by those living near him, whether they write to us here or to the person nearby who will inform us about everyone, sending on either their letters or copies of them. So much for affairs.

9. Next, as regards the members of the Society: we need to have written to us from every place, especially the houses and colleges of the Society, an account of those entering for the first time or having made a vow to do so, with mention of such qualities as their bodily appearance, age, health, condition, property, speech, intelligence, learning, spirit; similarly for those who have made a decision but not a vow for the Society, and others who are connected with it.

10. We should be informed about the state of their health—whether improving or worsening—and any notable incidents of disturbance or defects, as far as is possible and judged useful for the superior to know; and this regarding the students as well as those working in the vineyard of the Lord. For, while another has their immediate superintendence, it is good for us to know the more important things here, to see if we can give aid by writing, dismissing, transferring, etc.

11. We should also be informed about those who cease to belong to the Society—those who leave, with the reason why if this can be fittingly mentioned, and those who die, etc.

12. The person should write about his own health and manner of living in bodily matters: food, clothing, house, etc.

13. He should write about his own spiritual state: where weaknesses and temptations, etc. enter in, and where special graces and favors of God—both insofar as they are edifying or reporting them would be helpful for application of a remedy, etc. Regarding the colleges: here we should be informed also about where there is tranquility and peace and where the opposite (should God so permit), how far along they are in their courses, and in general whatever one friend would want to know from another.

14. Those in a given region, even if not near one another, should correspond so that those in one place can know what is going on in another—such as those in Valencia with the court and Portugal, those in Bologna with those in Florence, etc., those in Louvain with those in Cologne, etc. They should report about themselves, not about others inside or outside the kingdom; about these they will be informed from here or by the persons themselves. Of course, if they are more closely connected, as Gandía is with Valencia, Alcalá with the court, Lisbon with Coimbra, they should give not only their own news but also the news from elsewhere; and we will need only to write to the men at one place and they will be charged with writing or sending it to the other, as indicated above.

The Method to Be Observed in Writing

Thus far about *what* should be written. Now about the method.

1. They should review the matter they want to write and decide what ought to go in the main letter—namely, what can be shown to numerous persons—such as matters of edification; and what ought to go on the separate sheets, that is, matters not suitable to be shown, whether edifying or not, such as one's own and others' defects, or some praiseworthy things which are nevertheless not for everyone.

2. If the separate sheets contain a variety of topics, some of which could be shown to one person and others to another, they should be put in separate headings so that they can be taken apart and shown individually.

3. In the main letters they should be moderate in their praise of activities and persons in case of reversals later, etc. Any criticism should be even more moderate and should display charity even when revealing the truth about something ill-done by others; and this should not be done except when it is important that it be known.

4. A person writing about his own labors and what God is working in souls should, while telling all the facts, remember to write as if everybody were going to see his letter; he should express himself in such a manner that the reader will see that he is seeking to further not his own but God's glory and the edification of the neighbor, and to obey by writing what he is commanded, attributing wholly to God what is God's, that is, all that is good, and to himself what is his own, namely, all that is evil, etc. If there is something so extraordinarily laudable that he does not wish to report it in his own words, it would be good if he had a friend who could write about it; if not, it should come on a separate sheet, or else in the main letter in such a way that even somewhat suspicious persons would have no room for suspecting him of vanity.

5. Matters having to do with the sovereign or prelate will necessarily go on the separate sheets. They should be written not just with the naked truth of passion but in such words that if the person himself were to read them (if this were possible), he would not be disedified about our intention or think that we are seeking "what is our own" [Phil. 2:21]; and where certain details could not help giving offense and it was essential to mention them, a method might be employed to signify one thing by writing another.

6. Care should be taken to write the main letter in such a way that only good and holy affections will shine through for those who read or

hear it. And besides mentioning and ordering the topics as best one can, the handwriting should be at least legible, correct, and distinct; moreover, while fully covering the required matters, it should not be prolix, etc.

Procedure for Writing and Sending Letters

1. Thus far about the content and method; now for the procedure in writing and sending letters. First, it would seem that those outside Italy should ordinarily write every month and those in Italy every eight days, whether or not there is news and whether or not a courier is available. If, as can occur outside Italy, this time elapses without a courier being available and there is something to be added, it should be done; if not, the letter should be dated and sealed. No one should fail to write this frequently; anyone wishing to write oftener may do so.

2. If something of extraordinary importance happens within a few days after writing, one should not wait out the month or regular time but write and make a copy immediately. Moreover, one should try to find the easiest way, when the labor of writing will not be painful and the copied letters can be ready.

3. For news of edification, what is currently being done can be reported each time; however, since many letters are lost, every four months one should write a letter summarizing the edifying events since the previous such letter. Note should be taken of whether we acknowledge receipt of letters, and if we do not they should be sent again.

4. For business matters or important letters, two or three mailings should always be sent. Even so, rather than referring back to these in subsequent letters, one might briefly summarize the main point given in the preceding letter until word is received that it arrived. Sometimes we do not have here the letter referred to by a writer.

5. The postage should always be placed on important letters even if they come through friends, unless they are persons quite close to us.

6. It is helpful for transmitting letters securely to be friends with persons who engage in frequent correspondence, such as merchants, and to send a packet to persons of this sort here, particularly if they are merchants, advising us who they are so we can get the letters. When there is suspicion that someone might intercept one's letters, it is even more important to address them to some friend who will pass them on to us.

To the Jesuits of Gandía

Rome, July 29, 1547

(Letter 182: XII:331–38, replacing the text given in I:551–62; in Spanish)

Writing to a community of scholastics at Gandía, one of the earliest Jesuit houses in Spain, Ignatius, in his first major text on religious obedience, details the advantages of living under such obedience; then, as a temporary expedient until a professed Jesuit is present and the Constitutions are promulgated, he instructs them on how to elect a superior for themselves. The person whom they chose was Andrés de Oviedo. Many of the themes advanced here will appear later and in greater detail in Ignatius's great letter on the subject, written in 1553 to the Jesuits in Portugal.

May the grace and love of Jesus Christ our Lord live always and increase in our souls. Amen.

The obligation laid on me by the great responsibility and burden which I have been given, and the love and desires which God our Creator and Lord, in accord with this obligation, deigns to give me so as to desire ever more intensely, and consequently give thought to, what will best advance the good of our Society and its members for the honor and glory of God—all this inclines and compels me to provide effectively, as far as in me lies, whatever I judge in our Lord to be expedient for the Society's greater good. One such thing which I consider to be of great importance is that, wherever a number of men belonging to the Society have to live together for some time, there should be among them a head or superior by whom the rest can be directed and governed as they would be by the superior general if he were present. And since this arrangement has been made in Portugal and Padua and is now about to be made at Louvain as well, I think it should likewise be made there in Gandía, as also in Valencia and other places where there may be students of the Society. Hence, in this letter I shall first explain my reasons in our Lord for thinking it right to have a superior there in my place, for God's greater honor and praise and for the greater good of the individuals and community residing there, as well as of the whole body of the Society in general. Then I will explain the manner of making the selection and of obeying the one selected, as it seems best to me in our Lord.

Actually, with regard to the first part—giving some account of my motives for putting a superior in my place—I propose to write more at length than would be needed to convince you of a thing so holy and so necessary. But my purpose is not just to prove the rightness of the arrangement I am now making, but much more to exhort you to welcome this obedience and then to persevere in it with joy and devotion.

And so, to come to the point, one of my many motives is the universal example presented to us by all peoples who live some sort of organized life in common: in kingdoms as well as municipalities, and in their individual social groupings and households, both in the past and in the present, it has been the ordinary practice to concentrate rule in a superior so as to prevent confusion and disorder and to govern the group well. Surely what all persons of judgment and reason agree in considering the most correct, natural, and fitting course must indeed be believed most correct, most natural, and most fitting. But much more convincing is the living example of Christ our Lord, who, when he lived together with his parents, was subject to them. Of his two parents, the virgin Mary, the lady of us all, was subject to Joseph. Hence, the angel says to Joseph as the head, "Take the child and its mother" [Matt. 2:13]. When Christ our Lord lived in company with his disciples, he deigned to be their superior; and when he had to depart from them physically, he left them St. Peter to be superior over the others and over his whole Church, entrusting their governance to him: "Feed my sheep" [John 21:17]. And so it was, even after the apostles were filled with the Holy Spirit. Now if those men needed a superior, how much more will any other congregation need one! We also know that the primitive Church in Jerusalem made St. James the Less its superior. In the seven churches of Asia, there were the seven superiors called "angels" by St. John in the Apocalypse. In the other communities also, superiors were appointed by the apostles; and St. Paul urged obedience to them: "Obey your superiors and be subject to them" [Heb. 13:17]. This practice has been preserved by their successors down to the present day. But you will always find it in a very particular way the practice among religious persons, beginning with the anchorites and the earliest founders of religious orders down to our times, that wherever a number of persons lived together, there was to be among them a head who had authority to direct and govern the other members.

Apart from examples, there are persuasive rational arguments. For if we have to consider as the best way of life the one in which God is given the most pleasing service, then we shall have to hold that it is this way of life in which all make the offering of obedience which is more acceptable to God than any sacrifice: "Obedience is better than victims, and to hearken is better than to offer the fat of rams" [1 Sam. 15:22]. And rightly so, for in offering him our own judgment, will, and liberty, which is the most important part of a person, we offer him more than if we offered him anything else. Moreover, this mode of life is so helpful in acquiring every virtue that, in Gregory's words, "Obedience is not so much a virtue as the mother of virtues."[6] And no wonder, for it enables persons to win from God whatever they ask, as Gregory also says: "If we are obedient to our superiors, God will obey our prayers."[7] Before him, the Scripture had recounted of Joshua, a man who was quite obedient to his own superior Moses, that not only did the sun obey him and come to a halt at his words, "Move not, O sun, toward Gibeon" [Jos. 10;12], but even God Almighty, creator of the sun and of all things, obeyed him, "the Lord obeying the voice of a man" (Joshua 10[:14]). Thus great benefit in terms of growth in the virtues accrues to those who are subjects, for they have the Author of the virtues obedient to their prayer; and also because, as the Wise Man says, "You will add to virtue what you withdraw from self-will." In addition, this form of life helps a person to avoid many errors of his own judgment, and many faults or sins of his own will, through following that of the superior. This holds not only for particular situations but for a person's entire state of life, inasmuch as the person places divine Providence under greater obligation (to use our way of speaking) to guide and direct him, the more entirely he resigns himself into God's hands by means of obedience to his minister, that is, any superior to whom he subjects himself out of love for him.

In addition to this, there is the help in resisting and overcoming all their temptations and weaknesses which is enjoyed by those who have a superior nearby to whose judgment they can conform themselves and by whom they can be guided: "For an obedient man will speak of victories" [Prov. 21:28]; the noblest of all triumphs will be his, the triumph over self. Without doubt it is a very straight road when a person practices subjugation of his own judgment and will by means of holy obedience; this advantage, however, would be forfeited if the superior were far off. Likewise, this way of life is singularly meritorious for those who know how to make the most of it, for it is a kind of martyrdom which continually cuts off the head of our own judgment and will, putting in place of our own that of Christ our Lord as made known through his minister. And unlike martyrdom, it does not just cut off a single will—the will to live—but all our wills together.

---

[6] Actually, St. Augustine, *Contra adversarium legis et prophetarum*, 1, 14 (*PL* 42:613).

[7] Actually, from the *Sermones ad fratres in eremo*, included in the sermons of St. Augustine (Sermon 61 [*PL* 40:1344]).

Our merit is also increased by the great value which is added to all our good works through their being done out of obedience.

Another consideration is that it lets you travel with greater ease and speed on the road to heaven, like a person who walks with the feet of another rather than those of his own understanding and will. In whatever you do—sleeping, eating, etc.—it lets you travel along this road meriting the whole time, like travelers on shipboard who even while resting move forward. And at the journey's end, which is most important of all, it enables you to win and possess more securely the key that lets you into heaven; this key is obedience, just as it was disobedience which caused, and still causes, heaven to be lost. But even while the travail of our pilgrimage and present exile continues, this form of life confers a great taste of the repose of the fatherland. For it not only delivers us from perplexities and doubts but also frees us from the crushing weight of our own will and concern for self, which it unloads upon the superior, thus conferring peace and tranquility. If anyone living under obedience and having a superior nearby does not experience this, he should examine closely whether it may not be his own fault for beginning to meddle in his own life again after once having abandoned himself into the superior's hands. He should listen to what Bernard says to him and to others like him: "You who handed over concern for your own affairs once and for all to us—why do you meddle with yourselves again?"[8] Thus, for those who recognize the favor God does them thereby, it is a great relief and rest to have at hand someone they can obey. It not only brings repose but also ennobles and raises us high above the human condition; it strips us of ourselves and clothes us with God, the supreme good, who enlarges our souls in the measure that he finds them empty of self-will. For such persons can say, if they are obedient from the heart, "I live, no longer I, but Christ lives in me" [Gal. 2:20]. And while it might be claimed that any one can partake of all this through the obedience he gives in Christ to the superior general of the Society, I am certain that this will be very far less the case than for those who live in a community and have someone nearby to obey in our Lord.

Apart from all these spiritual advantages applicable mainly to individuals, this way of living is essential for the preservation of the entire body of your community. For it is a fact that no group can be preserved as a single body without being united, or be united without order, or have order without a single head to which all the other mem-

---

[8] *In Cant.*, Sermon 19 (*PL* 183:866).

bers are subject in obedience. Hence, if you wish our community to be preserved in being, you must necessarily wish to have someone as your head.

Besides its preservation, it is also important for the effective governance of the community there in Gandía that there be someone on the spot who understands and can make all provisions as I myself would if I were there. Experience has already made it clear that there are many important matters which cannot be taken care of from here, partly because not everything can be written and reported to us here (since not everything can be committed to writing) and partly because many opportunities would be missed while decisions were being sought from here and sent back.

In addition, this is a great relief—not only quite proper but even indispensable—for the person who bears the heavy burden of my office. I am under obligation to take care of every individual, and since I cannot do it by myself, I can at least do it through others.

Even apart from the matter of preservation, there is no small extension of authority throughout the body of the Society. For it is of great benefit to the Society that its students and other members be well practiced in obedience and make no discrimination of who the minister is in himself, but instead recognize in each Jesus Christ our Lord, keeping in mind that it is he they obey in his representative. The reason why this is so valuable is that, while the virtue of obedience is essential in any community, it is especially so in this community. For its members are men of learning. They are sent on missions by the pope and by prelates. They are scattered in places far distant from the superior's place of residence. They associate with persons of high rank. For many other reasons as well, it would appear that unless such persons' obedience was outstanding, they could not be governed. Hence, I consider no practice more appropriate or necessary for the common welfare of the Society than that of obeying with great perfection.

Also, for a person to know how to govern and direct others, he must first have become a master of obedience. Inasmuch as it is very important for the Society to have men capable of governing, it is likewise essential that it have a procedure for learning obedience. This is why in the house here we have two ministers, one under the other; all in the house must obey each of them, even if he is a layman, just as they would obey me or whoever held my place. Finally, if the mistakes or successes of others ought to instruct us what to imitate and follow, we see that in many communities the lack of superiors with sufficient authority to govern the rest has resulted in defects neither few nor unimportant. Contrariwise, it is obvious how much better is the government in those places where all obey a single superior.

I have now expounded my first point, that is, how much reason and reflection lie behind this very valuable and necessary provision that there should be a superior, and with what readiness and devotion you ought to embrace it. There now remains the second part: how to select this superior, and how to obey him when he is selected.

For the selection, all of you residing there should recollect yourselves for three days, without discussing the election among yourselves. The priests should celebrate with the special intention of making a good choice, and the rest of you should commend the matter earnestly to God our Lord in your prayers. Throughout this time you should ponder who would be the best person for this office, your only consideration being the best governance and greater good of your community there in Gandía, to the glory and honor of God; you should do this as persons who take this election upon their own conscience and will be required to give an accounting to God our Lord for it on the great day when they expect to be judged. Thus on the third day each one should write and sign his vote. The votes should be put together in a chest or place where no one may touch them until the following day. Then they should be taken out in the presence of all, and whoever has the most votes will be your superior or rector; and I now give him my own approval, until you hear otherwise from me. You may make use of this procedure so long as there are no professed members there, and until final promulgation of the Constitutions.

Now, as for how you will obey this man after electing him, I think it should be in just the same way as you would obey me if I, or whoever held my office, were present. For it is my wish that the whole authority which I would want to have in order to help you if I were present, for the greater honor and glory of God our Lord, should be possessed for the same purpose by your rector. And so give him no different respect from what you would give to me—or would give, rather, neither to him nor to me, but to Jesus Christ our Lord, whom you obey in both of us and for whose sake you obey his ministers. If there is anyone who is unwilling to obey and let himself be ruled in this fashion, either among those presently at Gandía or among those to come later, either under the present rector or under another who may replace him by order of whoever is superior general of the Society, that man should make up his mind to follow another path and to leave your community and its common life; for no one belongs there who cannot or will not submit to the obedience set forth above.

For all residing there this letter will serve as an authentic testimony of my will in our Lord. I would wish, and do desire, that this be carried out for the greater spiritual advantage of the present students of the Society, to the greater service, praise, and glory of God our Creator and Lord. By his infinite and supreme goodness may he deign to give us his perfect grace, so that we may know his most holy will and entirely fulfill it. Amen.

Rome, July 29, 1547

IGNATIO

✠

To Claude Jay

Rome, early August 1547

(Letter 185: I:568–70; in Italian)

Jay is mandated to place himself unreservedly at the service of the Society's early benefactor, Duke Ercole d'Este of Ferrara.

Ihs.

May the grace and eternal love of Jesus our Lord be always our continual help and protection.

Through your letter of the second of this month, I learn that the Most Reverend Cardinal of Santa Croce [Marcello Cervini] had promised you permission to go to Ferrara once you had delivered your opinion on the Sacrifice of the Mass. I do not know if this will reach you in Bologna or in Ferrara, since I imagine that, once having the Cardinal of Santa Croce's permission, you would not have waited for my approval—which, however, I sent you at the same time that the Most Reverend Farnese wrote to the Cardinal of Santa Croce; I shall now send you another copy.

Indeed, I not only am willing and pleased to approve His Excellency's making use of you for this period, but would wish that all of us, the entire Society, could employ ourselves in his service. For it seems to me that we should eagerly seize the opportunity to satisfy in some measure the deep obligation which we have all had from the beginnings of our Society towards His Lordship the Duke of Ferrara. For by the testimony and letters which he so kindly and charitably wrote at the time of the first opposition against us, His Excellency furnished us so much support and, by recommending us as well to his cardinal brother[9] and other high personages at this court, gave us through their patronage and charitable urgings such great help in the Society's confirmation that I can truly say that no other prince or lord equaled him in this respect, nor are we similarly obliged to any other as regards the founding of the whole body of the Society, for the growth of which God our Lord was pleased to employ as his first and most effective instrument the benevolent patronage and assistance of His Excellency.

And so that the memory of these favors, so graciously and generously done to us in our hour of need, may spur us even more to loving service of His Excellency, for the honor and praise of God, I shall send you—although your own obedience and charity would suffice without it—a copy of His Excellency's testimony and other letters; and I strongly urge you to make every effort in our Lord to demonstrate in deeds, in whatever matter of God's service he may wish to employ you, the eagerness which not only you but the entire Society is obliged to have in our Lord for rendering service to His Excellency.

As for the instruction you request on whether you should try to preach or not in the cathedral or elsewhere, or teach Christian doctrine as our Institute prescribes, or assist people by means of the Spiritual Exercises—to all this there is only one reply: Inasmuch as His Holiness has sent you to His Lordship the Duke to be employed by His Excellency according to his devotion in matters which he shall deem are for the glory and honor of God, it is right for you to let yourself be ruled entirely by His Excellency, considering him your sole superior during the time that you attend to serving him in Ferrara for the service of God and the help of his subjects. When by his gracious leave and commission you are able to devote yourself to any religious work that he deems would be of benefit to souls there, I am confident in God's goodness that it will not allow you to lose the good opportunities which come your way in accord with our Institute.

With this I conclude, praying that same sovereign and infinite Goodness will always deign to make us know and perfectly execute his most holy will.

Rome, August 1547

---

[9] Ippolito d'Este.

To the Members of the Society in Padua
from Juan de Polanco, by commission

Rome, August 7, 1547

(Letter 186: I:572–77; in Italian)

The college of Padua was insufficiently supported by its founder, Andrea Lippomani. To the Jesuits there, suffering real deprivation, St. Ignatius sent the following enthusiastic panegyric of real poverty voluntarily endured for the sake of Christ.

May the grace and true love of Jesus Christ our Lord be always in our hearts and increase from day to day until our consummation. Amen.

Dearly Beloved Fathers and Brothers in Christ:

There comes to our hands a letter from our friend and yours, Pietro Santini, written to Father Master Laínez in Florence.[10] In it we learn among other things of your love for poverty, which you have chosen out of love for Jesus Christ poor. Moreover, you sometimes have the opportunity for its effects to be seen in suffering a lack of necessities, to the extent that the prior of the Trinità's resources do not reach as far as his generosity and charity.[11] I know that with persons who are mindful of their state of life and keep before their eyes Jesus Christ naked on the cross, there is no need for exhortations to accept suffering—particularly since the letter itself shows how well you all accept it if you have some experience of poverty. Nevertheless, by commission of our father in Jesus Christ Master Ignatius, who has a true father's love for you, I will take consolation together with all of you in this grace which his infinite Goodness gives us, both here and there, by granting us to experience holy poverty—I do not know how strongly where you are, but very much so here—in keeping with our profession. I call poverty a grace because it is a very special gift from God. Scripture tells us that "poverty and probity are from God" [Sir. 11:14]; and how much God loves it has been shown us by his only-begotten Son, who came down from his heavenly seat and chose to be born and brought up in poverty. He loved it not only in life—suffering hunger and thirst, having no place to lay his head—but even in death, choosing to be stripped of his clothes and deprived of everything, even of water for his thirst.

---

[10] Santini was a building contractor who aspired to enter the Society, but had to give up the idea later.

[11] Andrea Lippomani was the prior.

Wisdom which cannot err wanted to show the world, says St. Bernard, the great worth of the jewel of poverty—a worth unknown to the world—by choosing it for himself, so that his teaching "Blessed are they that hunger and thirst; blessed are the poor," etc. [Matt. 5:3, 6; Luke 6, 20] would not appear out of harmony with his life.[12]

We can also see God's high regard for poverty in the way that his specially chosen friends—particularly in the New Testament, beginning with his most holy mother and his apostles and continuing through the centuries down to our own time—were for the most part poor, the subjects imitating their king, the soldiers their captain, and the members Christ their head.

So great are the poor in God's sight that it was especially for them that Jesus Christ was sent on earth: "Because of the misery of the needy and the groans of the poor I will now arise, says the Lord" [Ps. 12:6]; and in another place, "He has anointed me to preach the gospel to the poor" [Isa. 61:1]—words recalled by our Lord when he sent to St. John his reply: "The poor have the gospel preached to them" [Matt. 11:5]. Jesus Christ so preferred them over the rich that he chose to pick the entire holy college of apostles from among the poor, to live and associate with them, to leave them as rulers of his Church, appointing them to act as judges over the twelve tribes of Israel (that is, of all the faithful) with the poor as their legal advisors. This is how high the poor rank.

The friendship of the poor makes us friends of the eternal King. Love of poverty makes us kings even on earth—kings not of earth but of heaven. This is shown by the fact that while the kingdom of heaven is promised in the future to other persons, immutable Truth promises it in the present to those who are poor and who suffer persecution for justice' sake: "Blessed are the poor in spirit, for theirs is the kingdom of heaven" [Matt. 5:3; Luke 6:20]. They have a right to the kingdom even now.

Not only are they kings themselves, they also make others sharers in the kingdom. Our Lord teaches us in St. Luke, "Make for yourselves friends with the mammon of iniquity, so that when you fail they may receive you into everlasting dwellings" [Luke 16:9]. These friends are the poor—particularly the voluntary poor—by whose merits those who aid them enter the dwellings of glory. For they, says St. Augustine, are

---

[12] Alluded to is St. Bernard's Sermon I for the Nativity.

the "least ones" of whom our Lord says, "What you did to any of these least ones, you did to me" [Matt. 25:40].

This, then, shows the nobility of poverty. It scorns to amass a treasure of dung or worthless earth; it spends the whole resources of its love to buy the precious treasure buried in the field of holy Church— whether Christ himself or his spiritual gifts. This treasure will never be taken from them.

But if we look to genuine advantages inherent in the means that are suited to help us attain our final end, we will see that holy poverty keeps us from many sins by removing the occasions for them, for "poverty lacks the wherewithal to feed its love."[13] Poverty crushes the worm of the rich, pride; it cuts off the hellish leeches of lust and gluttony, and many other sins as well. And if through weakness a person falls, poverty helps him to rise at once. For it is free of that love which, like birdlime, binds the heart to earth and to earthly things and takes away our ability to rise up again and turn back to God. Poverty enables us in every circumstance to hear the voice (that is, the inspiration) of the Holy Spirit better, because it removes the obstructions that keep it out. It makes our prayers more powerful with God, for "the Lord has heard the prayer of the poor" [Ps. 10:17]. It lets us go forward unimpeded on the path of virtue, like travelers freed of all burdens. It frees us from the slavery common to so many of the great ones of the world, where "everything obeys or serves money" [see Eccles. 10:19]. When it is poverty of spirit, it lets the soul be filled with every virtue, for the emptier the soul is of love for earthly things, the fuller it will be of God through his gifts. And it is certain that poverty must be very rich indeed, since a hundredfold has been promised to it, even in this life. While this is fulfilled in a temporal sense when it is for our good, in the perfect and spiritual sense it is unfailingly true. Thus, those who voluntarily make themselves poor in human possessions will necessarily be rich in the gifts of God.

Poverty is the land teeming with hardy men—*fecunda virorum paupertas*—of which the poet speaks, in words far truer of Christian poverty than of Roman.[14] It is the furnace which tests one's progress in fortitude and other virtues, distinguishing what is gold from what is not. It is the breastwork which secures the camp of our conscience in religion. It is the foundation on which Jesus Christ apparently erects the

---

[13] Ovid, *De remedio amoris*, 749.

[14] Lucan, *Pharsalia*, i. 165.

superstructure of perfection; for he says, "If you would be perfect, go, sell what you have, and give to the poor . . . and come, follow me" [Matt. 19:21]. Poverty is the mother, nurse, and guardian of religious life, which is given birth, nurtured, and preserved by it, while it is weakened, corrupted, and ruined by affluence.

Thus we can easily see how great is holy poverty's practical value, over and above its nobility, especially since it is poverty which wins our salvation in the end from him who "will save the poor and the humble" [2 Sam 22:28], and lets us obtain the eternal kingdom from him who declares that the kingdom of heaven belongs to the poor in spirit. Nothing else can compare to this advantage. Hence, no matter how bitter its taste, it seems that holy poverty ought to be welcomed gladly. But really it is not bitter; it brings great delight to those who embrace it willingly. Even Seneca says that the poor laugh more heartily because they have no cares.[15] Experience shows the truth of this in the public beggars: if you look only to their contentment of mind, you will see they live more cheerfully and contentedly than great merchants, magistrates, princes, and other high personages. If this is the case with people whose poverty is not voluntary, what shall we say of those whose poverty is [freely chosen]? Possessing and loving nothing earthly that they could lose, they enjoy unshakable peace and utter tranquility in this area which for the rich is so full of storms. And with their assurance and purity of conscience they enjoy constant happiness, a continual banquet—especially since through poverty they dispose themselves for divine consolations, which in God's servants are plentiful in the measure that their earthly possessions and comforts are not, provided they know how to fill themselves with Jesus Christ, so that he will make up for and replace everything else.

But I must not pursue this further. Let what I have said suffice to console both you and myself and urge us to have a love for holy poverty. For the nobility, advantages, and joyfulness I have mentioned are realized fully only in a poverty that is loved and voluntarily embraced, not one that is forced and involuntary. I will only add this: Lovers of poverty should also love her retinue as far as they can—poor food, poor clothing, poor sleeping accommodations, and being looked down upon. Otherwise, someone who loved poverty but was unwilling to experience any deprivation or effect of it would be a pretty dainty poor person. He would certainly give evidence that he loved the name

---

[15] Epistle 80 to Lucilius.

rather than the reality of poverty—or loved it with words more than with the heart.

That is all for now, except to beg Jesus Christ, the true teacher and model of spiritual poverty, to grant that we may all possess this precious inheritance that he confers upon his brothers and coheirs, so that we may have abundant spiritual riches of grace and, at the end, the indescribable riches of his glory. Amen.

Rome, August 6, 1547

✠

To Antonio Araoz

Rome, September 1, 1547

(Letter 192: I:584–86; in Latin)

Araoz, a nephew of Ignatius, is named first provincial of Spain. Portugal, twice mentioned in the letter, had been constituted a province the year before. Its king, John III, and Simão Rodrigues had opposed the idea of creating a single province for the whole of the Iberian peninsula.

Ihs.

Ignatius of Loyola, superior general of the Society of Jesus, to our beloved son in Christ, the licentiate Antonio de Araoz, member of the same Society: eternal welfare and greetings in the Lord.

Inasmuch as in his mercy Jesus Christ is furthering and spreading this least Society more widely for the greater glory of his name, we have decided in accord with our office (having received this authority from the graciousness of the Apostolic See) to create and depute provincial superiors who may assume and alleviate a part of our own toil and burden.

Moved by the large harvest which has been collected in the Lord over these few years through the labor and effort of Master Pierre Favre, who rests in the Lord, and your own, we call you to this burden for all Spain except Portugal. Colleges of the Society have already been erected and others are underway or definitely planned; scholastics of the Society have been placed for studies in various academies; numerous excellent minds have been aroused either to devote themselves to religious life and the evangelical vows in the Society or to change their way of life for better spiritual fruit through their advice and ministry.

Hence, since the name of the Society has become so widely known and so many communities of the Society already exist in those provinces to the greater glory of the name of Jesus Christ, and since both nature and the Spirit of Jesus Christ our Lord and God teach us that it is worthwhile when a multitude of persons are preserved in their duty through lawful power and unity, we have tested and found you worthy on many scores that we should confer upon you a share of our office and power in that place. For from the very beginning of your vocation, you have labored in the field of the Lord with outstanding fidelity, steadfastness, obedience, religion, and fervor of charity, both in all other works of charity and in the preaching of sermons to the people, not only, as presently, in Spain but wherever in the world you sojourned. In short, you have worked for the exaltation of the glory of the name of Jesus Christ with such eagerness and skill that you have through his grace borne great and copious fruit for the Church of God Almighty.

Wherefore, relying upon the kindness and counsel of the Holy Spirit, by authority from the Apostolic See according to our Constitutions, we create and depute you as provincial superior of all Spain outside of Portugal, and do declare you so created and deputed in the name of the Father and of the Son and of the Holy Spirit. Amen.

It will be your task in Christ Jesus, for the greater praise and glory of God, for a more abundant fruit of the many souls commended to you in the Lord, and for the common edification of the people, through this office to administer with all fidelity the talent which you have received from heaven, and with his grace ever to labor with your entire being as strenuously as you can in Christ Jesus our Lord; and it will be our task to commend you constantly to the grace of Jesus Christ through our prayers and Sacrifices.

✠

To Teresa Rejadell

Rome, October 1547

(Letter 214: I:627f.; in Spanish)

Responding to a letter from Teresa in which she expresses her despondency over her personal faults and the bitter divisions in her monastery, Ignatius consoles her and requests her prayers for himself and for the Society of Jesus.

Ihs.

May the grace and love of Jesus Christ our God and Lord live always in our souls. Amen.

Santa Cruz brought me two letters of yours in which, indicating your unhappiness over your own and your community's faults, you indicate the righteous desire God our Lord has given you that something be done to remedy both. May he in his infinite mercy hear you, for it is written of him, "The Lord will hear the desire of the poor" [Ps. 10:17].

Regarding personal faults, it is certainly necessary that anyone with self-knowledge should acknowledge them in himself. In our present wretched state, no one can help having them, until all the evil in us has been utterly consumed in the forge of the eternal love of God our Creator and Lord, our souls being permeated and entirely possessed by him and our wills entirely conformed to—or rather transformed into—his will, which is rectitude itself and perfect goodness. But may his infinite mercy at least grant us all that we may every day regret and detest more deeply all our faults and imperfections; may he bring us to have a greater share in the eternal light of his wisdom and therewith to keep before us his infinite goodness and perfection, so that in its presence our smallest defects may become evident and unbearable to us, and we may attack and substantially weaken and diminish them with the help of God our Lord.

As to the community's defects for which you ask some remedy from God's hand and hope that in his goodness he will provide it, I not only desire but also hope the same. I see a sign that God will deign to have this reform brought about in that the prince is so desirous of it and that active measures are being sought to effect it.[16] That difficulties should exist is nothing new; it is the usual thing in matters of great importance for God's service and glory. But the more difficult the work, the more pleasing will it be to God our Lord and the greater an occasion it will furnish to give him endless and heartfelt thanks.

As to our Society's affairs, you doubtless have someone closer at hand to inform you. I only beseech you, for the love of Jesus Christ, our Society's head (as well as universal Lord and Sovereign of all created things), to remember us earnestly in your prayers to his Divine Majesty, that he may deign to make use of and be glorified by our Society more every day.

---

[16] Prince Philip of Spain, later Philip II.

As for my health, it is poor. Blessed be he who by his blood and death won for us eternal health in the partaking of his kingdom and glory. May he grant us the grace of having our bodily health here in time, whether good or bad, and everything else he has bestowed upon his creatures be employed always in his greater service, praise, and glory. Amen.

Rome, October [?], 1547

✠

To Simão Rodrigues

Rome, October 26, 1547

(Letter 202: I:599f.; in Spanish)

Explaining why he thinks Paschase Broët would be the best choice as patriarch for Ethiopia, Ignatius makes some interesting remarks about his other first companions.

JHS

If God our Lord ordains that one of this Society is to go on this Ethiopian enterprise, I believe the lot will fall to Paschase. If the choice were up to me, after examining the universal and particular goods according to my conscience, I would choose no one else. Assuming that I would not venture to have this responsibility given to anyone who is not professed, I see three essential things that would be needed by whoever goes: first, goodness; second, learning; and third, a good appearance and constitution and a medium age. Nowhere in the Society do I see these three elements as well combined as in Master Paschase. If we mention Jay, he is too old. Master Laínez lacks the appearance and is quite delicate. Master Salmerón lacks the age; he is still almost the beardless youth you used to know. Master Bobadilla is too sickly and not all that suitable. That leaves only nine of us who are professed, of whom you are at the head of the list. All are doing useful work in their present places. If a single man is requested, I think Master Paschase most perfectly unites all the needed qualities. First of all, he is so good that we consider him an angel in the Society. Second, in addition to his learning, he has much experience in visiting and reforming dioceses and monasteries; having gone as nuncio to Ireland, he has a deeper grasp of such activities than anyone else in the Society, and has given an admirable account of himself in all his undertakings, since he is naturally conscientious and energetic; he has been constantly involved in cases of conscience and those reserved to bishops, which would be a special need there in Ethiopia. Finally, he has a rather good appearance, he has strength and health, and he is more or less forty years old.

May God our Lord by his infinite and sovereign goodness deign to order and guide this entire matter, and if necessary make with his own hand the choice that will be most for the service, praise, and glory of his Divine Majesty. May he be ever our continual protection and help.

Rome

✠

To Antonio Araoz
from Juan de Polanco, by commission

Rome, October 31, 1547

(Letter 208: I:609–20; in Spanish)

Following the advice he had given to Jesuits in other places to keep their brethren informed by letter about what they were doing, Ignatius commissions Polanco to write to the members outside Rome, for their information and consolation, about the activities of the Society in and around the city. The letter is a most informative catalog of their works, giving as it does a vivid picture of both the expected activities, such as Ignatius's work on the Constitutions and the formation of new members, and the unexpected, such as the reform of "immured anchoresses at Saint Peter's." All the works listed here were carried on by "thirty-four or thirty-five of us here in Rome that include twelve priests, although none of them except Our Father is professed yet." The others were "laymen," that is, scholastics or brothers.

May the grace and love of Christ our Lord be felt always, with true knowledge and love of him in our souls. Amen.

Since we send reports from here about what God our Creator and Lord is accomplishing in other places through the instrumentality of the members of this least Society—deeming that to do so is for the greater glory and honor of the sole Author of all that is good, as well as for our own consolation and encouragement in the same Lord by having news of one another—I know that you will be eager there to learn what the Lord is accomplishing through those here in Rome as well. For Rome, which is in one sense the head and in another the stomach of all Christendom, would appear to be both of these for this Society as well; and we might even add a third: that it is the Society's heart. For while it is the Society's head, inasmuch as the entire Society is governed and moved from here, and its stomach, inasmuch as from here there is dispensed and distributed to its members what sustains their well-being and fruitful action, it can also be called its heart, both because it is the active principle of the other members, and because it would seem to be the seat of life for the entire body of the Society and the place from which this life flows out to the other members. For without the activity of Rome, it would hardly seem that the Society, however much it might grow in quantity, could be preserved in its proper being. Hence, those who for this reason grasp the importance of the house here in Rome will rightly be eager to know what takes place here. Of course, the most important things done here are not normally written about, nor can they be except in a general way. For the comparison with the three abovementioned organs also holds in the sense that their functioning within the human body, because it is so fundamental, remains invisible to the outward eye. The nerves through which the head produces sensation and motion remain hidden; hidden likewise are the veins by which the stomach transmits nourishment, and the heart vital spirits, to the entire body. Similarly, the principal function of this house, that of founding, governing, preserving, and increasing the Society and the good works which are carried out in its various parts, remains hidden, particularly to anyone who looks only for the sort of works which are customarily reported from the other places. However, without going into great detail, I will mention both kinds of functioning in this letter, so that having been indicated here once for all, it may serve for many other activities to those desirous of having news of what takes place here for their own edification, etc.

Let us begin with our father in Jesus Master Ignatius. He considers it his first and most important work by far to obtain for us the favor of God (by which this Society might be maintained and increased and have success in its enterprises) through his desires and holy prayers before God.

Another activity which much engages him is his work on the Constitutions, which, with God's grace, are to preserve and advance the Society in all good. This work, of supreme importance and necessity, costs him a correspondingly great deal of time and labor.

Besides this, he assists and employs his influence in dispatching the affairs of the Society which flow into Rome from all places where the Society is spread out, such as the foundation of colleges, houses, etc. This is one of his important activities, even though His Paternity accomplishes what he does in this regard more by the authority and credit which God our Lord gives to him and to the Society with the Pope and all the cardinals and the principal figures of the court here, rather than by great amounts of outward effort or exertion either in the affairs themselves or in procuring the patronage and backing of important persons. The favor of divine Providence is all the more visible in that even though he hardly ever pays courtesy visits to such personages—regarding which some complain of him—and scarcely employs any human means in their regard, he finds them so well disposed toward him that when he does speak to them on some urgent matter, he is able to deal with them in the fewest words about whatever he is after for the service of our Lord. This is true of negotiations being held elsewhere and assisted from here in Rome, as presently in Sicily and Bologna, as well as of negotiations in Rome itself, as presently with the Cardinal of Coria [Francisco Mendoza], who, through his great devotion and love towards the Society, has been moved by God our Lord to wish to erect a college for the Society's students in Salamanca, with the present intention of applying an income of eight hundred ducats to it, while giving indications of wishing to go far beyond this sum not only in Salamanca but also in Toledo and elsewhere.

In addition to all this, there is his ordinary burden of governing and animating the Society, assigning persons to various places, keeping in touch with everyone by letter, and giving assistance to those in need of it wherever they may be, both as regards their persons and their business. His attention is so divided up among various places that he must have special favor and great assistance from God our Lord to do justice to this aspect of his office alone. Here in the house, too, besides its ordinary government, his dealing with, getting to know, and testing the great variety of persons from various nations and lands who come here with the intention of entering the Society is a task that demands no little concern and effort and is of no small moment.

All the above has to do with the Society itself. But His Paternity is also much occupied with taking care of many other religious matters where he is under obligation to commit his support, whether because they are urged upon him by persons who are of help to the Society or because they are for the service and glory of God our Lord. Thus, under charge from the Prince of Spain he has been and continues to be active for the reform of the monasteries of Catalonia; likewise, under charge from the Viceroy of Sicily (who with his wife and family is very devoted to the Society), he is working for the reform of the monasteries of Sicily—a project which, if all turns out as hoped, will be for the great service of God and the good of many souls. Likewise, at the urging of the Vicereine of Sicily and other persons, he has worked for the badly needed reform of a monastery at Gaeta. Similarly here in Rome, at the instance of Cardinal Farnese he has been involved in the reformation of the immured anchoresses at St. Peter's, giving help in organizing the statutes they are to observe and charging one of the priests in the house with the care of their souls. And even though the press of business led him to attempt to get out of the work of Santa Marta and leave it to others to carry on with what he had succeeded in launching with the help of God's grace, nevertheless, chiefly at the urging of our protector, Cardinal de Carpi, he was unable to do so and consequently continues to be involved, through himself and others, in helping to run this holy work, which has occasioned us so much trouble and opposition. However, he is repaid by the great service done to God our Lord on behalf of so many souls who are plucked from the claws of the enemy and from a life of prostitution. Over the last three or four years, more than a hundred women have already been reclaimed through the refuge offered by this house, becoming religious, marrying, or being placed in the households of respectable matrons—to say nothing of those presently at Santa Marta (who are many) and those continuing to enter, to the great loss of the enemy of human nature, who has accordingly worked so hard to thwart this holy work. Similarly, just as efforts have been made to establish a home for orphaned children in Barcelona, this has been accomplished for another [such house] at Palermo in Sicily. I could go on about numerous other pious and holy works which he aids with his counsel and patronage and, in some cases, with considerable expense of effort, and also, I trust, to the great service and glory of God our Lord, who in all matters gives him such a sure and effective hand through the assistance of his own almighty hand.

He also has been and continues to be involved in ministry to individuals, acting as confessor to persons (albeit few in number) of high station. I know of one whom he induced to make restitution in the amount of twenty-five or thirty thousand ducats, thereby not only disburdening his conscience but also remedying the extreme want of those from whom the money had been taken. Many other such individual cases could be mentioned. In bringing about reconciliations between certain persons, God our Lord has given him a special grace where great personages fail to find a way and leave it to him to find a remedy for great evils; and so he has lately been and still is involved in a number of reconciliations. I could also mention the assistance he has given to various persons outside the Society through his conversation and support, in temporal matters as well as spiritual, but it would take too long to speak of them. However, I will add that there is much occasion for giving praise to God our Lord in that Our Father, while so regularly ill and afflicted by his ailments, particularly of the stomach—at times so badly that he cannot move or help himself physically—God nevertheless gives him such vigor of mind that in his weakness he finds strength to go on working. Moreover, as we have often noticed, our Lord even grants him bodily improvement when an urgent matter arises that requires him to work. As a result, both within the house and outside it, he labors day and night like someone whose age and bodily health strongly seconded him. So much for what it occurs to me to mention regarding the activity of our father in Jesus Master Ignatius.

The members of the house engaged in ministry for the most part assist him in the above-mentioned activities. Indeed, these demand a considerable number of persons, who, however great their abilities and desires to serve God our Lord, can be put to good use in these ministries.

There are thirty-four or thirty-five of us here in Rome. These include twelve priests, although none of them except Our Father is professed yet. However, some of them, who have strongly followed the Society and have been known for some time to Our Father, will probably be professed in the spring after engaging in new probations this winter in addition to those done earlier. Among these priests there are persons to whom God has imparted many graces in virtues, learning, and the other qualities demanded by the Society's Institute. Among the laymen also there are great abilities and qualities which give considerable promise that they will be chosen servants of God. Day by day we are receiving others, as well as dispatching men in due time for studies. May the Lord preserve and increase what he has so generously bestowed on both groups with the same generosity, to his great praise and glory and the welfare of souls.

Our Father is very careful to admit no one who is unsuited to our Institute and to dismiss those who after admission prove difficult or unwilling to do their duty, although he helps such persons to strive to serve God better elsewhere. He refuses to tolerate not only actual sins obvious to all (which by God's grace never occur) but also others which, being interior, are often not known or avoided even by some who consider themselves spiritual persons and servants of God, such as stubbornness of one's own judgment and will, which, even if greatly counterbalanced by other good qualities, is absolutely not tolerated in this house. While there are plenty of occasions in the house for exercising one's desire for poverty and for the mortification of numerous impulses of self-love, there is special occasion for exercising humility, the subordination of one's own wishes and opinions, and in general all the elements of obedience. One must obey not only the father superior, the minister, and the subminister, who are regular superiors over everyone, but also occasional superiors among the lowliest officials in the house, such as the cook and others; everyone who comes to the house must go and serve under them, obeying their orders even though they may be persons on whom God has lavished his graces of all kinds, and even though they may at another time have themselves been served and obeyed by many. And thus this house (God, the author of all good, be blessed!) functions as an excellent school of obedience, and there are many occasions to grow in abnegation, particularly of one's own judgment and will, which is considered of capital importance for persons in our institute.

As for the neighbor, they are attended to as well by many means. One, common to all the priests of the house, is their administering the holy sacraments, hearing numerous confessions of persons great and small at all times, confessions both general and particular. It would take a long time to tell in detail the fruit which results from this and the working of God in his souls by this means, although it would be to the great praise of him "who accomplishes all things in all" (1 Cor 12:6), by whose assistance many abandon their sins and vices, are freed of burdens on their consciences, and return to a religious and Catholic way of living, with some, both men and women, deciding to serve God our Lord in religious institutes. However, it is our belief that the numbers of these would be even greater if the church were more suitable.

The instrument of preaching is also practiced in our church by one of the men in the house. This was done regularly on Sundays and feast days, and even before and after meals during earlier months; this has been suspended in recent months because of the heat and other obstacles, although it is done outside. The truth is that the church is not at all helpful for attracting people. It was in bad shape when we originally accepted it, having a view more to its good location and possibilities for rebuilding and enlargement than to its present usefulness; it is small and poorly equipped (though it was much worse before), so that those who frequent it regularly must make up for its defects with a great deal of spirit. Our own holy poverty can excuse our not rebuilding it; but I do not know for whom, among the many friends in the Lord of our Society, God our Lord is reserving the crown for rebuilding it. But there is no doubt that with the root and foundation of the Society being here in Rome, a place where its good reputation is so essential and must flow out to the entire world, this work on the church would be one of the most important that could be undertaken for the universal good of the Society and hence of all the neighbors for whose spiritual assistance the Society is ordained. But we readily remit this concern to the one to whom the Society belongs and whose honor and glory is sought in the Society and all its affairs, trusting that here as elsewhere God our Lord will let us feel and experience in his good time the very special providence which he has always hitherto shown to us with regard to the Society's affairs. Furthermore, because of this inadequacy of the church, we do not have lectures there. A priest of the house who has accepted responsibility for giving lectures on their duties to the priests and pastors of Rome, many of whom are extremely uninformed, is giving them in a different church, that of Sant'Eustachio, and this with complete support by the authorities and the approval of the priests themselves. We trust that this will produce a great deal of good, which will extend not only to the pastors and priests but also to their numerous subjects, to whom they will be able to pass on what they have received, and whom they will be able to benefit with what they themselves have been benefited by. Attendance by these pastors and priests has so far been considerable. May God our Lord be served in all. This same priest has arranged with some schoolmasters to go to their schools and there to teach Christian doctrine and morals and what is most essential for their salvation. Many of these boys are already going to monthly confession and seem to be making much progress in our Lord; we trust that this will see much more growth.

Exercises are also being regularly given to various persons, some of whom experience great spiritual fruit. Some decide for the Society, others reform their lives and take steps for the good of their estates, etc. God our Lord is also being served through conversations, in which we give advice and draw persons to receive the sacraments, improve their lives, abandon their sins, and give alms and many goods. Recently we have brought about reconciliations and peace between several important personages, in addition to those mentioned above. We also visit the sick, particularly in the hospitals, where some of us provide corporal and others spiritual help.

A member of the house recently visited a person wounded in body but even more so in mind. The man refused to go to confession and had not done so for a long time; he also refused to forgive his adversary. With God's help he was induced to give public forgiveness to the person and be reconciled with him, kissing him and embracing him with a great demonstration of love, and likewise to go to confession with much devotion and to the extraordinary benefit of his soul. We have also persuaded other persons who were near death to forgive and make peace with their enemies and so prepare themselves for a Christian death. I will mention only one particular case: a noble and powerful person who had fallen sick and who, according to some gentlemen who assisted him, had enmities amounting to twenty-five or more. A member of the house visited him and tried to help him. God our Lord so assisted him that the sick man reached a disposition to be reconciled with them all, and actually gave directions for the required satisfactions and restitutions to be made. Once the sick man had thus unburdened his soul, he was so relieved and happy that whenever the priest through whom God had shown him such mercy came to see him, he would kiss him with heartfelt love; and we thus duly believe that he died well disposed.

In this matter of getting people out of their evil state, when visiting the sick in hospitals, God our Lord has been much served and has given aid to his poor; effective help was given to a man among them who had not received Communion for thirty years and had no intention of ever doing so. There were others who had not done so for a long time; others who had made bad confessions or none at all. Among these was a person in despair who, believing that his sins were irremediable, refused to dispose himself to confess them. But in the end God our Lord deigned to visit this man, and a great number of others, with his divine mercy through a priest of the house.

Out of many cases of assistance to the dying, I will mention two that are noteworthy. One was a person in a palace who was so poorly disposed to die that for three days before his death he refused assistance, instead blaspheming bestially with great impatience and an utterly profane spirit, so much so that those who saw and knew him were greatly distressed by the fear that he would die not just temporally but also eternally. Nevertheless, while he was as I have described, the divine mercy visited him at the end through a priest of the house; he was converted and disposed himself to die a Christian death. The other case was a woman dying in childbirth. She did not speak or give any indication of sensation. She had not made her confession; in fact they were practicing various sorceries over her to get her to give birth. This woman was greatly helped by the same priest. He was called to visit her and found her without sensation or speech. But he took her hand and began shouting at her so vehemently that with God's help he got her to come to herself and, after being asked, to give signs of sorrow for her sins and of a wish to be absolved of them. The bystanders looked on this as if he had miraculously brought her back to life. Thus absolved, she died to her temporal life with greater assurance of attaining spiritual life.

But to go into details about those whom God our Lord helps to live and die through the members of the Society here in Rome would be more than this letter would allow, and there is no need for doing so.

May he who is the sole author of whatever good is accomplished be blessed in all; for while able to produce these same effects without any instruments, he has deigned to make use of the Society's members for this purpose. May his Divine Majesty be pleased to increase in the Society's members his holy gifts and abundant grace, so that in ourselves and in our neighbors his service, praise, and glory may be mightily increased. Amen.

Rome, the last of October, 1547

✠

To Antonio Araoz

Rome, October 31, 1547

(Letter 209: I:620–22; in Spanish)

Araoz, the provincial of Spain, a zealous laborer to the point of injuring his health, caused concern by his preference for acting independently on his own. Ignatius instructs him on appointing superiors for the Jesuit scholastics throughout Spain, and then orders him to have two companions to live and work with him.

May the grace and eternal love of our Lord Jesus Christ be always our protection and help.

A second letter will be written you about other business. This one is in pursuit of two purposes. I am obliged to write by the charge which God our Lord has laid upon me and by the need to make some provision for these purposes, for the greater service and glory of our Creator and Lord. The first has to do with the communities throughout Spain made up of those seeking to be members of the Society, over which it has been judged good in the Lord to give you the same superintendence and authority that I myself might have in their regard through Jesus Christ, our common Lord, as you will have seen in the letters appointing you provincial superior of all Spain outside of Portugal. I consider that a provision needs to be made that wherever these communities exceed two in number, there should be a superior or head to whom the others, many or few, should render obedience and by whom they should be ruled as they would be by you or by me—or rather, by Jesus Christ our Lord, for whom and to whom obedience ought to be rendered by all. And just as all those living in one place ought to obey their immediate superior, so the superiors of these places (besides Gandía and Valencia, there come to mind at present Barcelona,

Alcalá, Valladolid, and Zaragoza, or wherever else there are any number of our men) ought to obey and be ruled by you, so that, with this subordination well observed, the unity of this body of the Society will be maintained and it will be ruled for the greater service of God and good of all its members.

I hardly think I need to impress upon you the reasons why I consider this statute about local superiors necessary and of great importance for the ends of the Society; you yourself will readily be aware of them, and may have read them in the letters I wrote to Valencia and Gandía on the election of the superior.

I will also explain what I consider in the Lord to be the best way of choosing a superior. If in a given place where a superior is to be appointed, you know of one who seems to you best qualified for the office, appoint him with none of the others in that place giving their opinion—at least with no one but yourself possessing authority in the matter. But if you are uncertain who would be best for the position, you may first ask the opinion of each of those residing in the place. They should give this in all purity, writing what they think will be for the greater service of God our Lord after having reflected in silence for three days and recommended the choice to God, the priests saying Mass for this intention and thinking over who among them all would be the best choice. They should not exchange opinions and no one should know what another thinks, let alone try to influence him one way or another. They should seal what they have written and give or send it to you. Then you, or whoever has your office, having commended the matter to God our Lord and said Mass for the same intention, will appoint the one who, after examining their opinions, you judge will best carry out this office to God's greater honor and glory. From this moment, by the authority given me by the Apostolic See, I consider this man the superior; and the rest should do likewise.

The second point is this: It seems to me in our Lord that, wherever you take up your residence and there happens to be a more plentiful harvest of souls, you ought to have at least two companions, both of them priests, or one a priest and one not, to help you in all that you have to do. The one would be to help you with confessions and more important matters, the other with lesser but necessary matters, such as writing and looking after your personal needs. Did I not judge that you would take this opinion of mine as if commanded under holy obedience, I would so command it. In view of what is written to me about the multitude of your occupations and the new burden that has been laid upon you as provincial in those kingdoms, which will add to your duties, it is essential that you have help, so that you can carry on your business well and more securely than if [you were] all alone—and also so as not to harm your health so much. For, as I gather from the testimony of your illnesses and from those who know you there, such as Dr. Torres and Santa Cruz, you need to watch out more for your health, and to have someone there who will watch out for it when you disregard it beyond what well-ordered charity allows. For since the body, like the soul, is from God and its preservation necessary for the service of the Divine Majesty, you need to take appropriate care of both for love of our same Creator and Lord. Therefore, from among those you think suitable, select two companions to live where you reside, for these and for other considerations.

Trusting that what I have said will suffice to ensure promptness in the obedience which God its author has bestowed on you, I will not enlarge any further on the matter, begging the Divine Majesty to bring us all to know his most holy will in all things and to fulfill it with prompt and genuine obedience.

Rome, the last of October, 1547

> Entirely yours in our Lord,
> IGNATIO

✠

To Jerónimo Doménech, from Juan de Polanco

Rome, October 31, 1547

(Letter 218a: XII [Appendix 1, no. 7]: 223–25; in Spanish)

A scathing, if indirectly delivered, reprehension of the provincial of Sicily for failing to carry out urgent pieces of business enjoined on him. Polanco expressly says that this letter was not commissioned by Ignatius; nonetheless, the editors of the Monumenta Ignatiana, the critical edition of the letters, judged that because it expressed the sense of Ignatius and sometimes used his very words, "it seems that it ought to be mentioned among Ignatius's letters."

(Read this letter when alone.)

Dearest Father in Jesus Christ:

Although I am not commissioned by our father in Christ Master Ignatius to reply to your letters (in fact, I am commissioned *not* to reply to their contents but to send them back to Your Reverence), I shall nevertheless write these lines, which, without going against what I was ordered, I am able to send not as a reply but to let you know that Our Father is most annoyed about the slight care you show in your letters and the lack of awareness of what was so particularly enjoined on you. (I hope Your Reverence will forgive me if I am overly candid in what I say; I would not want you to speak any less clearly to me when advising me of my own faults.)

His Reverence had been eagerly awaiting the testimony which Her Ladyship the Vicereine was to give regarding Matthias;[17] Your Reverence was supposed to obtain this, but he found no mention of it in your letters.

He had also been awaiting what he so urgently requested for Bishop Archinto and which Your Reverence was supposed to request, but he saw that you made no mention whatever of this matter.[18]

He also thought that the letters of October 9 would be accompanied by one that could be shown to the majordomo of the curia, who is friendly to him and a person who could be of great help in the service of God; this is why His Reverence wrote that Your Reverence should talk to Doña Leonor and gather what she might have to say on the matter, and then write a letter which could be shown to the majordomo, placing other matters on a separate sheet. Regarding all of this he found no mention in the letters, just a line and a half saying that you would see to it. This could not be shown to the majordomo, since it would give the impression that his business was not being very energetically pursued.

Faced with this carelessness, he showed more annoyance with Your Reverence than I ever remember seeing him display towards anyone else in the Society. For, though he has so much to do here in answering and satisfying all the Society's members dispersed in so many places, he makes an effort to fail no one, whereas Your Reverence has only a single part to take care of, while showing so little concern to do so (to repeat what he says) that you fail to respond to his most urgent commissions. When I began pleading Your Reverence's heavy occupation in pious and important works, etc., he checked me, saying that you should consider as your prime duty what is enjoined by obedience—on the supposition that you acknowledge it and acknowledge him as your

---

[17] Matthias de Tassis, a teacher, became a friend of Ignatius after having been an adversary. See *Chron.* 1:169.

[18] Philip Archinto was vicar of Rome at that time. See *Epist. Mixtæ* 1:331 and 334.

superior in the place of God our Lord; for matters of duty and obligation should always take first place, and unless this is done (as St. Bernard says), nothing else can be accomplished that is pleasing to the Holy Spirit.

In fine, he was so indignant that he brought up two courses of action, remaining unsure which to choose. One was to write Your Reverence to write him a letter every week, even if there is no news or no courier available. The letter would have two parts: one would be a reply to whatever is asked of you in letters from us and the other would [consist of] a daily account of your activities; furthermore, [he would require] that upon perusal of this [present] letter, wherever it finds you, you should cease hearing confessions and preaching until you have replied to every point in our letters that requires a response. He would enjoin all this by virtue of obedience; this is something which he has so far never resorted to, but (as he said) he knew no other medicine he could apply to negligence of this kind. The alternate course of action would be to suspend writing to Your Reverence altogether, so that you would acknowledge and repent of your fault upon coming to a realization of it by yourself.

It is true that we later came across something you said which I used in further defense of Your Reverence, at least with regard to putting off the execution of the two courses of action and in part mitigating the charge of negligence. It is where you say that you had replied on September 27 to our letters of late August. I inferred from this that Your Reverence might have written at length about everything in this letter, which we did not receive. God grant it be so. However, you would still deserve a scolding because you forgot one of the rules of correspondence: that in important matters you should not just refer us to an earlier letter, which might have been lost or delayed, but should write the letter again, either a copy or the gist of it, until notified of its receipt. You did not do so in this case.

No more for now, except that for the love of Jesus Christ, Your Reverence should be more careful in the future about what you are enjoined by Our Father, whom we have in the place of Christ, and indeed make up for your past deficiencies in this regard—as well as pardon me for my freedom in telling you what I think. For we are agreed among ourselves to speak the truth to each other, and Your Reverence ought to repay me in the same coin for love of Jesus Christ, for whose sake I write you thus.

May he give all of us the grace always to know his perfect will and perfectly to fulfill it. Amen.

Rome, the last of October, 1547

Your Reverence's servant in Jesus Christ,

+JO. DE POLANCO+

✠

To Niccolò Lancilotti, by commission

Rome, November 22, 1547

(Letter 230: I:648–51; in Latin)

The Jesuits in India are to send one of their number (together with some young Indian converts) to Europe to provide information needed for making decisions and to help obtain both special ecclesiastical faculties from the Holy See and whatever else might be of help to the mission in India and the college in Goa. Lancillotti, the recipient of the letter, had been in India since the previous year, 1546.

Ihs.

The grace and peace of our Lord Jesus Christ be with you all. Amen.

Dearest Father in the Lord Jesus Christ:

Another letter is being written in reply to your own which reached us in November of 1546. Here, by commission of our father in Jesus Christ Master Ignatius, I will add a few points which we trust will be for the glory of God, for your own and the college's spiritual consolation and progress, and, indeed, for the not inconsiderable advantage of Goa and all India. For the charity of Jesus Christ compels Reverend Father Ignatius to give careful thought to your affairs; nor does the long intervening distance by land and sea make him clasp you less tightly in the embrace of love—indeed, the farther you are separated physically, the closer he holds you in his affections in Christ Jesus, in whom we are all made into a single body wherever in the world we may be.

Our Father, then, judges that you should send to us from there a competent man who can faithfully report on your own and India's affairs to the Sovereign Pontiff and dignitaries of the Roman curia, and whose coming would offer Father Ignatius an occasion for procuring provision for you from the treasuries of the Church, such that not only the college and your city but a large part of India would be able to abound with spiritual riches for the glory of our Creator and Redeemer and for the help of numerous souls. First, then, he deems that you should select a man suitable for this task, one able to keep in mind and expound what will be needed. Second, you should take care that, fully instructed on affairs there, he should also bring us in writing a full account of whatever it would be worthwhile to know in providing for you and for India: climate, food, customs, and mentalities of persons and places, as well as whatever you think is needed for the worship of God and the help of souls there and throughout India: all this should come written out carefully and methodically, accompanied by attestations from Your Most Reverend Father Bishop or his vicar and from other persons of particular authority there.

Moreover, you should obtain letters from the Reverend Father Bishop and other dignitaries, along with letters written in your own and in the college's name, to His Holiness, the Supreme Pontiff Paul III, humbly and earnestly requesting all the graces which you deem opportune, including the faculty of absolving in cases reserved by the bull *In coena Domini*, etc., together with relics of saints and anything else which might foster Christian religion and piety and which you think would be of help to your college and city and to those territories.[19]

In addition to these letters to the Supreme Pontiff, you should have others written to the reverend cardinals whose names I am sending you, and also to the Reverend Maffei, bishop of Massa, earnestly requesting them in your letters (which can be identical, with only the names changed) to favor your cause with His Holiness our Lord the Pope.[20] You will also send letters from these same persons to Father Ignatius for him to employ in better promoting your case with these prelates and with the Supreme Pontiff. Upon reaching Portugal, your envoy should obtain letters of recommendation to all the above persons from His Serene Highness the King. It will also be a considerable help, both for better understanding the mentality of the Indians and for making an impression on those vested with supreme power here, if the man who comes could bring with him five or six young men from India. These should be of good appearance, particularly fine looking; two or three should come to Rome and the rest remain in our college in Portugal. There, once your business has been completed, the other two could return to be formed among our men in learning and the adornments of Christian discipline and virtues, so that upon their return to their own

---

[19] This bull reserved absolution of certain cases to the Holy See.

[20] Bernardino Maffei, the Pope's secretary and a friend of the Society.

people, they can be of greater usefulness to them and to other regions of India by the example of their life and learning.

As for the manner of receiving boys in the college, supplications and public processions, funerals, and the constitutions for founders which you sent us, we will reserve a decision until we are more fully informed about affairs there by the man you send, and also until we learn what is the mind of the King of Portugal. Meanwhile, you can proceed as you have been doing.

If you carefully execute these directives, our father in Christ Ignatius is confident that great advantage will accrue to the college, to Goa, and to all India for the progress of souls and consequently also for the honor and service of God as well as of the King of Portugal, and to the progress of our own Society in those regions.

May the infinite goodness of our Lord Jesus Christ bring this about, and may he deign to fill us all with the knowledge of his will and increase in all of us his name and his glory. Amen.

Rome, November 22, 1547

> Your servant in Jesus Christ, by commission of Father Ignatius,
> JOANNES DE POLANCO
> I.[21]

✠

To Daniel Paeybroeck

Rome, December 24, 1547
(Letter 234: I:659–63; in Latin)

A group of students intending to enter the Society had formed a community in Louvain. Ignatius writes approving their procedure and promising to send Jacques L'Hoost to be their superior when he is available. He approves their temporary rule—the Society's Constitutions had not yet been promulgated—and suggests modifications to make it clearer that the Society cannot admit women and to require that all members of the community have a vow of entering the Society. The letter witnesses both to the structuring of the Society that was still in progress and to certain points that were already set. Finally, Ignatius defends his caution in communicating to them the Society's faculties.

---

[21] Ignatius personally initialed the manuscript of this letter.

May the grace and peace of our Lord Jesus Christ be present always and increase in our hearts. Amen.

We received two letters from you, dated March 7 and 17. They both brought us great joy in the Lord, a joy that compels us to love you and all the companions with whom you have so closely united yourself in the desires of your heart and purpose of your life, for the glory of our Lord Jesus Christ, whose love alone is rightly the glue which joins and holds our whole Society together.

I strongly approve what you tell me of your life together, as well as of the choice you exercise in admitting applicants to our Society; I trust both will redound to the honor and praise of our Creator and to the profit of many—provided, however, that your light so shines among men that they glorify your Father who is in heaven [Matt. 5:16] and are themselves challenged by your example to emulate you. However, you have laid upon yourselves a heavy obligation to live holy and pious lives: having separated yourself from others in your residence and way of life, you will be under everyone's observation and on everyone's tongue. Nevertheless, I have confidence you will do this in him from whom comes every good and perfect gift [Jas. 1:17], to whom you have consecrated yourselves, and from whose goodness you have your vocation and holy desires as a more-than-common pledge. But I also believe you yourselves will derive great benefit from your common life: brother will lift up brother when he falls, support him when he wavers, spur him on by word and example when he flags; in fine, as you administer to each other the grace you receive [1 Pet. 4:10], you will prepare yourselves for fresh grace from the Father of Lights. For when two or three agree in asking for anything, Truth has promised that they will be heard [Matt. 18:19].

I both approve the choices you have made so far regarding this form of life and urge you to continue the same in the future; for I would not want it possible for us to say with truth, "You have multiplied the people, but not increased the joy" [Isa. 9:3] or the virtue. Take care, then, that those you accept are recommended by their uprightness of life. If they are not all learned, they should at least have capacity and willingness to learn. Above all, they should have the bodily health needed for the labors of our way of life. While we should be quite ready to assist any infirm and weak persons outside the Society, we have learned from experience that we should definitely not admit them into the Society, where they would be more a hindrance than a help to this way of life which we have undertaken for the honor of God and the salvation of souls.

I quite agree with you in judging that it would be a good idea for Jacques L'Hoost of Gelderland to be your superior. He is laboring in the Lord's field in Sicily, but I promise that when he is no longer detained by occupations which he cannot abandon without notable loss, I will try to have him come to you without delay; for I am confident that there will be no less gain there where you are for souls and the glory of our God and Lord Jesus Christ. Regarding your community, I would only add that I think it important that you try to win the approval and love of your bishop, so that you will grow in numbers and in virtue with the blessing of your father, to the praise of him who created and redeemed us, our Lord Jesus Christ, who is blessed above all things forever.

I do approve the rules and regulations you sent me and consider them appropriate for these beginnings of your community. As time goes on, experience will point up any needed additions or alterations. If I myself think of any warnings I ought to give you, I will gladly do so. Meanwhile I will mention two points. The first is this. In constitution 4 you say, "No man or woman will be admitted to this congregation who has been under vow," etc. Here you seem to be envisaging the female sex, even though further down you correctly make it clear that women may not be admitted to obedience under a vow. I would like to remind you that our Society does not—indeed cannot—admit women under its responsibility, except by way of giving advice or other ministries which can be denied to no one of whatever condition or sex. We made great efforts to obtain this from the Supreme Pontiff, to ensure that neither we nor those who came after us would be obliged, for the sake of works that are less important and subject to many inconveniences, to forgo works of greater value for the honor of God and the good of souls. And this has now been granted us.

My second suggestion is that while you speak of vows of poverty and chastity, you speak of a "resolve," not a vow, to enter the Society. Now, while I have no wish to induce anyone to undertake our way of living unless called thereto by God, I want you to know that we are normally unwilling to exercise government over persons committed to our care unless they have confirmed by vow their intention of entering the Society; your government will be very weak over persons who are free to withdraw from it at will. So if you would like to have one of our men sent to be your superior, as you intimate regarding Jacques L'Hoost, I do not see how we could grant this without either our having to forgo a practice which we have with good reason held to or else your confirming by a vow your purpose of entering as the others do.

As for faculties and privileges granted to this Society for the good of souls, I do not want you to interpret my delay in communicating them as a lack of confidence in your uprightness or prudence in making use of them; my conscience is witness of how high are my opinion and hopes in your regard. But inasmuch as this treasury of graces has been entrusted to me by the Supreme Pontiff for building up and not tearing down, for me to share with individual men of Ours whom I find qualified and according to each one's needs, I am bound to make very gradual and moderate use of it, being careful to dispense, not dissipate, it. Moreover, there are many who, abusing the privileges granted them, have lately had their privileges withdrawn. I am not referring to our own men, who to my knowledge have by God's grace neither abused such privileges nor been deprived of them. This should also make us more cautious, so that by employing and dispensing with competence and moderation the privileges given us, we can ensure their permanence. As these faculties are quite exceptional, we could also incur the envy of others by failing to use them with restraint.

I have said this to let you know that it is no wonder that I should want to know what I am sharing and with whom. Thus, anyone wishing to share in these privileges for the upbuilding of the neighbor ought to write to me individually, indicating his personal qualities, desires, progress in studies, and what he considers his qualifications for employing these faculties. He should state which particular faculty or faculties he is asking for. And then if I confer them (as I expect to do), I will be able to give an account of my stewardship to God, and to men should any ask. Meanwhile, you should be advised that those not yet professed may not publicly claim these faculties which will be enjoyed by the Society's members, since we have this grant from the Supreme Pontiff only orally, not by a written document. This applies to those not yet professed in the Society; the professed may show their faculties in a brief or written document. However, in the forum of conscience it is just the same to have received them orally, both for the security of the one dispensing and the benefit of the one receiving. Enough on this subject.

Farewell in our Lord Jesus Christ; may he deign to fill us with the knowledge of his will and grant us the strength to carry it out by his grace.

Rome, December 24, 1547

Yours in our Lord,
IGNATIUS

To Stefano Baroello

Rome, early January 1548

(XII [Appendix 1, no. 8]: 326–28; in Italian)

Instructions for a priest sent to Sicily on probation to minister to children in the company of another priest who had belonged to a different order, but who, under direction of the Society, was engaged in apostolic work, including the setting up of orphanages.

Yhs.

Dearest Master Stefano in Christ Jesus:

Our father Master Ignatius wishes you to be given the following reminders.

1. First, you should not say anywhere that you are a member of the Society of Jesus, since you are in fact neither a professed nor a coadjutor; but you can say that you are sent on probation and that it is your wish to be guided by the obedience of this Society and to serve the Lord in it with your slight powers by assisting the others.

2. Since you are in Sicily, you will recognize as your superior Father Master Jerónimo Doménech, and you will do whatever he orders you in the matter of the orphans and universally in all matters, as if Master Ignatius himself commanded you; and if there is any other of the Society who is in charge of others, you shall likewise let yourself be ruled by him.

3. In any uncertainties while you are in Palermo or anywhere else in Sicily, you will have recourse by letter to Master Jerónimo. However, you will write here to Rome whenever you like and at least once a month, telling how things are going, etc. These three points will be common to both Master Florence and yourself.

4. As for your dealings with the neighbor, say a special prayer every day that God will grant you discretion and grace so as to build up and not tear down, etc.

5. Be universally careful to act with all humility in matters that are proportionate to your ability, and do not meddle with those that are beyond your powers; for God wishes to be served by each of us accord-

ing to the talents he has bestowed upon us, and he is not pleased with presumption. Yet this should not in the least lessen your courage for vigorously undertaking whatever is within your grasp.

.6. As to preaching while you are in Sicily, you shall do so only when and where you are so ordered by Father Master Jerónimo. However, with his permission you may, indeed should, teach children Christian doctrine and urge them to the virtues, as he will direct you. Keep your exhortations short, etc., so as not to burden your hearers, and be sure what you say is solid, etc.

7. You will teach children grammar and other appropriate subjects as carefully and methodically as you can, also as Master Jerónimo will direct you.

8. At Mass you will not use chants but an even and sober tone; you will do well to make Master Florence responsible for admonishing fraternally about what he thinks.

9. As for confessions, you will hear those of the children in the best way that divine grace assists you, as you yourself diligently cooperate with it to do your duty properly. If Master Jerónimo advises you to confess other persons of a simple or other character, you will also do that. And although it does not seem that you ought to try to hear persons with complicated confessions, you should still have examined a summa just in case, such as that of Cajetan, etc.

10. At the proper time and place you may make use of the faculties that were given to you orally, apart from the one for reading heretical books, and also the faculties obtained by the Duke of Gandía.

11. As to exterior posture, facial expression, and gait, try to observe a becoming modesty, and ask Master Florence to admonish you; for with men, "who see what is outside," it is essential to strive that one's outward appearance also edifies.

12. As for speaking or not speaking, preserve a mean between too little and too much. Out of respect for important persons, be careful to say what is seemly and likely to edify. Among other things, try to avoid saying anything that would reveal ignorance or vulgarity; but composedly speak out what the Lord inspires you to say and what will befit the persons you are talking to and the things you are talking about—"unto edification." "May the anointing teach you all things." Amen.

Having done these things, present them to Father Master Jerónimo Doménech, who will consider them and give you the advice he thinks best. Amen.

To the Senate of Messina

Rome, January 14, 1548

(Letter 239: I:679–81; in Italian)

Ignatius responds to a request by the Viceroy of Sicily and the Senate of Messina for a Jesuit mission to that city and, specifically, for the establishment of a college there. He authorizes Jerónimo Nadal to represent him in the negotiations, which eventually led in that same year, 1548, to the first Jesuit school specifically established for lay students.

Ihs.

Most Honorable Sirs:

May the eternal love of Jesus Christ our God and Lord always visit Your Lordships and your entire Catholic city with special favors and graces. Amen.

At a time when the knowledge and service of God our Creator and Lord is so badly wanting and when there are so few persons concerned with repairing the harm done to it, it must cause great joy to every person desirous of God's glory and honor to see any place where a way is being sought in our Lord to have his Divine Majesty better known and served. Accordingly, we (who, weak though our forces be and far inferior to the esteem which Your Lordships in your great charity show for us, are yet among those who by God's grace long for his honor and service) have received great satisfaction and deep spiritual joy in our Lord at learning from the testimony of His Excellency the Viceroy and from Your Lordships' own letters of your projects for ensuring that in the future your noble city may enjoy more copious instruction in letters and virtues, which are the means for reaching the end of perpetual happiness. This has afforded us such great satisfaction not only in itself but also because of the hope shown by His Excellency and Your Lordships for the glory and service of God and the help of souls, and also because it is evident that this is the initiative and desire of His Excellency, to whom our entire Society—or rather his Society in our Lord—is so bound by duty and affection. Moreover, in view of Your Lordships' so very pious and Christian urging and the great devotion and holy desires you display for increasing the light of learning and virtue in your noble city, charity compels us to desire to assist your holy aims so far as our meager forces allow. And so I trust in our Lord that, so far as the fewness of our least Society's workers and the multiplicity of its spiritual occupations allow, he will give us grace to satisfy Your

Lordships' wishes, in part if we are unable to do so entirely, as you will learn in more detail from our Don Jerónimo [Nadal].

Certainly, if the thing is to be solidly established and able to be of permanent rather than temporary benefit to the city and to those who frequent it, an essential step would be the erection of the college—as Master Jerónimo has written us that Your Lordships intend; indeed it seems clear that this should be the starting point of the work. But here, as in other matters too extensive to be handled by correspondence, I refer you to Master Jerónimo, a long-time member of our Society and a man especially experienced in the matter of colleges, since he had founded one in his native Valencia. I ask Your Lordships to give him your confidence and to deal with him as if I myself were there, on any matter which may arise for the glory of God.

I shall here add no more, except that in response to the devotion Your Lordships demonstrate to our Society, although little deserved by us, we shall acknowledge ourselves more obliged to make special commendation of your noble city to our Lord Jesus Christ in our poor prayers. And if this work is his, may he be pleased to direct it so that his Divine Majesty may in the future be better known, honored, and served in your Catholic and devout city and kingdom, and so that souls, redeemed by his blood and precious life, may be better instructed in the way of their salvation and eternal blessedness. Amen.

Rome, the fourteenth

Your Lordships' most eager servant in our Lord Jesus Christ,

✠

To the Members of the Society in Rome

February 2, 1548

(Letter 252: I:707–9; in Italian)

Before selecting a group of Jesuits to be sent to Sicily, Ignatius had all the Jesuits in Rome testify in writing to their own degree of indifference and readiness to obey in the matter.

Ihs.

These are the points which our father in Jesus Christ Master Ignatius proposed to everyone in the house on February 2, 1548. Giving each man a period of three, four, or five days to recollect and commend himself to God, he had them ponder these points, come to a decision, and write down how they stood with regard to them. Our father in Jesus Christ judged that a man would not be suited for the Institute of this Society unless he had attained readiness, as demanded by true obedience, on all the following points.

1. Whether he finds himself indifferent to going to Sicily if so commanded or not going, and would prefer whatever is enjoined on him by the superior to whose governance, in the place of Jesus Christ, he is subjected.

2. Whether, if he should go, he finds himself indifferent towards accepting any task that is enjoined on him—such as, if he is educated, going to serve in corporal matters and ministries; if he is without learning, going to teach theology, Greek, or some other subject he does not know; and whether therein he would judge that what is enjoined on him by obedience is the best thing he could do. Likewise, whether a man sent to be a teacher is ready to accept any of the four courses, that is, scholastic theology, positive theology, philosophy, or humane letters.

3. Whether, if sent as a student, he is ready to study whatever subject he is assigned, namely, language, philosophy, or theology, and under whichever professor is assigned him. In the same way, whether, if sent to serve, he is ready to work in the kitchen or at any other job.

4. Whether, in addition to carrying out whatever assignment he receives, he is ready to consider it to be the best, submitting to the yoke of holy obedience not merely his performance but also his private judgment and will, so that he looks upon the assignment as the best in itself, finds peace and consolation in whatever the superior shall judge most helpful for his own and the general welfare, and makes evident his faith that God's providence is to guide and govern him through the superior, etc.[1]

---

[1] Among those residing in the house at Rome at the time was St. Peter Canisius. The following is his reply to St. Ignatius's questions: "After having deliberated with myself for some time on the brief proposal of my reverend father in Christ and superior, Master Ignatius, I declare in the first place that, with the help of our Lord, I feel equally disposed to either alternative, whether I am ordered to remain at home always, or sent to Sicily, India, or anywhere else. Moreover, if I must go to Sicily, I affirm simply that I shall be satisfied with whatever office or ministry shall be given me there, whether it be cook, gardener, porter, student, or professor of any class, even of matter with which I am unacquainted. And from this day, February 5, I vow and swear that I will not concern myself with the future as far as it concerns my dwelling, mission, or any comfort, leaving once for all such care and solicitude to My Reverend Father General in Christ. And to him I submit fully my understanding and my will for the government of my soul as well as for my body, humbly offering and

To Nicolás Bobadilla

Rome, late February or March 1548

(Letter 258: I:719–21; in Spanish)

In earlier letters to Ignatius and to one of the cardinals, Bobadilla had indicated that he had been suffering want. Ignatius told him about provisions made to relieve his needs. He had also wished to be recalled from Germany; Ignatius instructs him on indifference.

Jhs.

May the grace and peace of Jesus Christ our God and Lord be always preserved and increase in our hearts.

Through two letters of yours, dated December 10 and 24, which I received together, I see that not all the letters written to you from here must be reaching your hands, since your own letters give no indication of receiving any from us. The present letter will be more by way of reply to one which you wrote to the Cardinal of Santa Croce than to those you wrote to me; for when I went to talk with him today about another matter, he showed me a letter from you in which you speak of the provision you wish would be made for you. With his customary charity, His Reverend Lordship attributed this to the fact that you must have been suffering want; indeed, I told him (as I believe to be true) that for purposes of greater edification you had declined to take anything from some persons who would have given it to you. In sum, the cardinal told me that he had spoken to Monsignor Maffei, and that arrangements would be made for Master Prospero di Santa Croce (who I understand is going there as nuncio) to provide you with whatever you may need; and he charged me to write you that you should not hesitate to accept from the nuncio whatever you need, indicating that whatever was spent on you would be charged to the Pope. I myself spoke about this to Maffei, and he told them that this arrangement had been made. Accordingly, you will be able to obtain assistance in your need from Master Prospero.

As for your being recalled from Germany by authority of the Pope who sent you there, if reports are received here that your stay in that country is producing fruit (as we are convinced it is, for the divine

confidently surrendering myself in Jesus Christ, our Lord.

"The year 1548. I have signed this with my own hand.

"Peter Canisius of Nijmegen" (Otto Braunsberger, S.J., *Beati Petri Canisii Societatis Jesu Epistulæ et Acta*, 8 vols. [Freiburg im Breisgau: Herder, 1896-1923], 1:263).

service), then I believe it would be difficult to bring about [your return]. The Cardinal of Santa Croce still thinks that you should stay there, and Maffei that you should not move until Master Prospero's report is received from there. If they inform the Pope from there that your stay in that country is producing little fruit, there would be little difficulty with the recall from his side; however, you can easily see how favorable that would be for your good name, a thing which ought to be taken into account for the greater service of our Lord. Nevertheless, in this matter of the recall, if you do consider yourself altogether obedient, as you say in your letter, then you would in my view take another course, and it would be this: Wholly abandoning your own will by which you find yourself inclined more in one direction than the other, and striving to keep before your eyes the sole end of the greater service and glory of God, you would ponder carefully whether your staying in that country or in a different one in these parts would be more fruitful for this end. And should you deem in our Lord that your residence outside that country would be more fruitful, it would be good for Master Prospero to write here that as regards your departure from there, he leaves it up to what you write to your superior. Then you should write me a letter indicating that you are indifferent as far as you yourself are concerned (as all of us in this Society ought to be) towards residing there or in any other place, since you wish only to be wherever you can be employed for the greater service and glory of God our Lord and the service of the Apostolic See. At the same time, you should represent in a general way what God our Lord gives you to think, indicating that you are ready to consider as better the course which holy obedience may point out for you. With you writing in this tenor, there will be grounds, should a change in your residence have to be made, for its being done more to the glory of God our Lord and more to your personal credit, which, as you know, is essential to the ministers of God our Lord for their greater effectiveness.

May God our Lord direct all this, and give to all the grace always to know his perfect will and perfectly to fulfill it.

To Diego Laínez

Rome, March 24, 1548

(Letter 281: II:35; in Spanish)

A further separate note with directions for a careful leave-taking from Duke Cosimo de' Medici and other dignitaries of Florence.

Florence: Father Master Ignatius himself writes the following:

Master Laínez, our brother in the Lord:

Attend to the following three points. 1. Receiving with customary humility the gracious permission of His Lordship the Duke and of Her Ladyship the Duchess (either personally or through someone else), of His Lordship Don Pedro [de Toledo], of Master Alessandro Strozzi, and of the others in whom you have encountered special love in our Lord, you should make sure to retain your bond of complete love and charity with all of them.[2]

2. Neither on your own part nor on that of the Society should you give any sign of preferring to receive from, rather than giving to, any person you speak with, leaving it to God our Lord to effect whatever will be for the greater service, praise, and glory of his Divine Majesty.

3. Pledging that as far as you and the Society are able, you will serve Their Excellencies particularly, as well as the other persons more devoted to you, in whatever ways we may be able to deem for the greater glory of God, you will take your leave in the name of our Lord.

As for other matters regarding Venice and the other places about which we will write you, I refer you to the other letters being sent you.

Rome, March 24, 1548

✠

To Andrés de Oviedo, by commission

Rome, March 27, 1548

(Letter 295: II:54–65; in Spanish)

Oviedo, rector at Gandía, had written to Ignatius asking permission to live as a hermit for seven years, spending his time in prayer and penance in order to cultivate his spiritual life. Even earlier, he had declared that he needed at least eight hours of prayer every day and that six hours of sleep was too much for him. He

---

[2] Don Pedro was the father of Duchess Leonor de Toledo.

had been told that such a request was scarcely compatible with the Jesuit vocation. Ignatius had Polanco send him this extended discussion of obedience. Many of its paragraphs reappeared almost verbatim five years later in the famous letter on obedience to the Province of Portugal (letter 3304).

My dearest Father in Christ Jesus:

1. Since the inquiries in your letters have been replied to elsewhere, this letter will be devoted particularly to a number of things which Our Father specially commissioned me to say, His Paternity himself indicating the main points I should write. You will therefore take what follows as coming not from me but from His Paternity.

2. Regarding the spiritual exercises and studies of the scholastics there, nothing special will be said at present. Our Father has already seen what is being done by the scholastics of the Society in various places, such as Valencia, Coimbra, Louvain, Padua, and Bologna, besides what you write of your own men. He is now recommending this matter to God our Lord, with whose help I believe he will soon complete the constitutions to be observed in colleges throughout the Society regarding the men's conservation and progress in spirit and virtue as well as their progress in studies and in everything connected with them.

3. I have also been directed to tell Your Reverence to keep in constant communication with Father Araoz; for as you see, the Society by God's mercy is growing, and it is hoped that with the same grace it will continue to grow daily. May the divine and sovereign Goodness grant that it may not be merely in numbers and temporal matters but much more in spirit and all the virtues, and that thus his Divine Majesty may be served and glorified in them all.

4. With the Society increasing like this, the task of caring for it inevitably increases as well. Since it is not feasible for one man to attend to so many matters, the care has to be divided up in order the better to provide the proper direction for each man and to render the responsibility bearable and thus long lasting for the one who carries it. And since, with any large number, order is needed if confusion is to be avoided, in cases where there needs to be a large number of local superiors, there must be some among them who are higher and some lower, so that by this subordination unity among them all may be maintained, and with it the well-being and good government of the Society.

5. Almost all of creation teaches us that this must be so and that it is in keeping with the dispensation of divine Providence. For in all moving bodies we see how lower movements are successively subject to higher, all the way to a highest. In the angels we see the same holy

subordination of one hierarchy to another, as divine Providence thus brings all to their ends, the lowest by the midmost and the midmost by the highest, their mutual unity being preserved by this bond of subordination.

6. We are taught the same by the various secular subordinations in the Old Testament, with tribunes, captains of hundreds, of fifties, and of tens, under a single head wielding supreme power. We see the same in the polities of today, all well regulated, as well as in the ecclesiastical hierarchy and subordination of prelates beneath a pontiff. Moreover, we see that the good and—where it exists—bad condition and governance of states consist largely in the good or ill observance of this subordination.

7. In view of all this, Our Father desires very much in our Lord that the proper subordination of some superiors to others be observed in the Society, and that private individuals have recourse to their immediate superiors and give them obedience, and the immediate superiors to the provincial, as also the provincial to the general, and the general to him whom God gave him as superior. For this reason he earnestly recommends in our Lord that you have recourse to Licentiate Araoz in all matters and obey him as Jesus Christ our Lord, since you have him in his place. Any time Father Licentiate is in doubt about something, he will write to our father Master Ignatius, and all will be helped in our Lord. As to writing him, Your Reverence should do so when and as he directs.

8. As to the retirement and solitude of seven years which you ask, Father Ignatius thinks that as the matter is serious and may be a dangerous precedent in the Society, it needs further thought.

9. But as to the great insistence with which you press your petition, I sense that Our Father considers it quite unneeded. If His Paternity deemed the thing to be for God's greater service and glory, he would agree to it without much urging; and if he did not, even stronger urging would not avail. Speaking generally, I have often heard him say that it ought to suffice for the inferior to represent his reasons and open his heart to the superior, without making efforts to draw the superior to his own view or wish. For in many persons this is commonly a sign that one's own will and judgment are alive—indeed are setting themselves up as the rule by which the superior must be directed and to which he must be drawn.

10. He also said that he had never read that St. Francis or any of the holy fathers had ever given any of their religious permission to retire to the desert before their profession or before they had come to be very

thoroughly known. However, the situation is mended by the promptness and indifference Your Reverence shows for accepting whatever obedience ordains; this is a firm anchor which will make the soul steady and secure.

11. However, if one wished to test himself on such indifference—in the case of Your Reverence—he would do so by asking himself the following questions in God's presence. First: is he prepared effectively to accept or relinquish this retirement? Second: does he believe he will feel satisfied and consoled both in accepting or relinquishing it? Third: will he judge that both accepting it or relinquishing it will be the better thing, depending on whether the superior orders the one or the other? Anyone finding himself thus disposed can claim to possess the indifference demanded by true obedience.

12. It is certain that if obedience is a holocaust in which the entire person offers himself in the fire of God's love to his Creator and Lord without the slightest reserve, and a complete surrender of himself in which one renounces possession of his whole self and places himself in the hands of God through his minister—it is certain, I say, that if this is the case, then the range of human acts comprised in obedience includes not only effective execution but equally acquiescence of the will, together with acquiescence of the judgment, so that one approves what holy obedience commands to the extent that by dint of the will the judgment can bring itself thereto.

13. But this obedience demands that one cast far off any idea of the superior as a man subject to errors and miseries. Instead, one must behold in the superior him who is infinite Wisdom and Goodness, to whose divine providence the obedient man will subject himself and by which he will let himself be governed through the medium of his ministers, confident that he will be conforming himself wholly to his most holy will, the first and universal rule of all rectitude and justice, if out of love for him he conforms himself to the will of the superior he obeys in his place, which is for him a second, more immediate, and more easily known rule. He will be convinced that this rule, insofar as it commands him, will be in accord with God's rule, and indeed identical with it, since Christ our Lord said in the Gospel, "Whoever hears you hears me, whoever despises you despises me" [Luke 10:16]. St. Paul, writing in the same spirit to the Ephesians who owed obedience through human subordination, says, "Slaves, obey your masters according to the flesh with fear and trembling, in the simplicity of your hearts, as to Christ; not serving to the eye as if pleasing men but as slaves of Christ, doing the will of God from the heart, serving with a good will as

to the Lord and not to men" [Eph. 6:5–7]. Similarly to the Colossians, "Whatever you do, do it from the heart; serve Christ, as to the Lord and not to men" [Col. 3:23–24].

14. Now, if is true in worldly subordination that a person does the will of God in doing that of the superior, and obeys Christ in obeying the superior, what shall we think is the case when we do the will of spiritual superiors, of whom Christ himself says, "Obey your superiors and be subject to them" [Heb. 13:17]? And with how much more reason ought we to regard their will as that of Christ our Lord? For whoever sees the superior, in his role of superior, as Christ will easily subject his own will and judgment to him and conform them to that will which he took for the rule of his actions in the confidence that divine Providence would direct him by it, so that he will not fail to be conformed solely to the divine will.

15. To conform with this rule only in execution is the lowest degree of obedience. To conform one's will, making one's own will that of the superior, is more perfect. To conform oneself, over and above execution and will, in thinking the same is perfect obedience, which submits the judgment to the superior to the extent that the will can bend the understanding.

16. I say this because, while the understanding lacks the freedom which the will has, and gives its assent naturally rather than freely to objects that are presented to it as true, still, in many cases where the evidence does not compel the understanding, it can incline itself this way or that by focusing on the arguments for one side rather than the other. In such cases every obedient man ought to incline himself to think what the superior thinks and to seek arguments for the side towards which he sees him inclined rather than for the opposite.

17. There is also another method of subjecting the understanding to obedience, one that is easier and surer and practiced by the holy fathers. It is to take for granted (as is done in matters of faith, for example) that whatever the superior orders is the ordinance of God and his most holy will; and then, blindly and without any inquiry, with the impetus and alacrity of a will avid to obey, to proceed to the carrying out of what is commanded. This is how we are to believe Abraham obeyed when commanded to sacrifice his son Isaac. Likewise, in the new covenant, some of those holy fathers of whom Cassian speaks, such as Abba John, who did not consider whether what he was commanded was useful or not when he toiled so hard for a year watering a dry stick, or whether it

was possible or not when at a command he strove so earnestly to move a rock which many men together could not have moved.

18. To confirm this kind of obedience, we see that God our Lord sometimes accompanied it with miracles. Maurus, St. Benedict's disciple, went into the water at the command of his superior and did not sink. Another was told by his superior to bring home a lioness; he took hold of her and brought her to his superior. You know of other examples. What I mean to say is that this manner of subjecting one's own judgment by taking for granted that what is commanded is holy and in conformity with God's will is practiced by the saints and should be imitated by anyone wishing to obey perfectly in all things where there is no manifest sin.

19. Would to God that this obedience of the understanding were better understood and practiced, for it is certain that it is extremely useful, indeed necessary, for anyone living in religion, and very pleasing to God our Lord. I call it necessary; for just as in celestial bodies, if the lower is to receive movement and influence from the higher, it must be subject and subordinate, the one being ordered and adjusted to the other, in the same way when one rational creature is moved by another, as takes place in obedience, it is necessary for the one moved to be subject and subordinate to the one moving it if it is to receive influence and power from him; and this subjection and subordination cannot be had without conformity of the inferior's understanding and will to the superior's.

20. For if we look to the purpose of obedience, it is just as possible for our understanding to be mistaken about what is good for us as it is for our will. Hence, if we think it is right to conform our will to the superior's to keep it from going wrong, we should also conform our understanding to the superior's to keep it from going wrong. "Do not rely upon your own prudence," says Holy Scripture [Prov. 3:5].

21. This counsel is even more necessary in persons and things spiritual, inasmuch as the danger in the spiritual life is great when one races ahead in it without the bridle of discretion. Hence, Cassian says in the conference of Abba Moses, "By no other fault does the devil so draw a monk headlong to his death as by persuading him to ignore the advice of his elders and to trust his own conclusions and judgment."[3]

22. Thus, even in other human affairs the wise commonly say and consider that it is true prudence to distrust one's own prudence, partic-

---

[3] *Collationes* 2.11 (*PL* 49:541B).

ularly in matters regarding personal interest, where because of bias people are usually not good judges.

23. If, then, in his own affairs a person ought to follow the judgment of another, even someone not his superior, rather than his own, how much more the judgment of the superior whom he has taken to govern him in God's place as interpreter of the divine will?

24. On the other hand, without obedience of the judgment it is impossible for obedience of the will and execution to be what they should. For, as reason and experience prove, the appetitive powers of our soul follow the apprehensive; and so it would be an act of violence for the will to obey, over the long term, against one's judgment. If someone obeyed for a time under the general apprehension that one ought to obey even when commanded amiss, this cannot, at the very least, be long-lasting; and thus perseverance is lost, or at least the perfection of obedience which consists in obeying with love and cheerfulness. At least this much is lost: no one who acts against what he thinks can obey with love and cheerfulness as long as such opposition remains. Promptitude and alacrity are lost; without full conviction these will be missing, and instead there will be doubts about the rightness of doing what is commanded. The much extolled simplicity of blind obedience is lost when one debates whether the command was good or bad—perhaps even condemning the superior because what he commands is not to one's liking. Humility is lost when on the one hand we submit, but on the other place ourselves above the superior. Fortitude in difficult tasks is lost and, in short, all the perfections of this virtue.

25. On the contrary, obedience without submission of judgment is marked by dissatisfaction, pain, reluctance, slackness, criticism, excuses, and other imperfections and obstacles of no small moment which deprive obedience of its value and merit. For, as St. Bernard rightly says of those who are distressed when the superior commands something not to their liking, "If you begin to be upset at this, to judge your superior, to criticize in your heart, even while outwardly fulfilling the command, this is not the virtue of patience but a veil over your wickedness."[4]

26. For if we regard the peace and quiet of mind of the person obeying, it is certain that no one will ever possess these if he has in his own soul the cause of his disquiet and unrest, namely, a judgment of his own opposed to what obedience enjoins him.

---

[4] Sermo III, *De circumcisione.*

27. Moreover, that unity, which is what sustains the existence of every society and which is had through subordination of some members to others and made firm by the bond of obedience, cannot avoid being broken if this bond of obedience of will and judgment is not complete. It is for this reason that St. Paul so earnestly exhorts all to think and say the same thing [Rom. 15:5; 1 Cor. 1:10; Phil. 2:2], so that by union of judgment and will they may be preserved. Now, if head and members must think the same, it is not hard to see whether it is right for the head to agree with the members or the members with the head. And so, from what has been said it is clear how necessary is obedience of the understanding.

28. But if anyone wishes to see how perfect it is in itself and how pleasing to God, he can do so by consideration of how valuable is the noble offering which is made of so worthy a part of man; how one makes his entire being a living sacrifice pleasing to his Divine Majesty, holding nothing of himself back; and also how difficult it is for a person to overcome himself out of love for him and to resist the natural bent which people have for following their own judgment. Thus, while obedience is properly a perfection of the will which renders it eager to fulfill the will of the superior, yet it must also, as we have said, extend to the understanding, inclining it to agree with what the superior thinks, so that in this way one can proceed with the full force of the soul—will and understanding—to a prompt and perfect execution.

29. I have spoken at some length about this holy virtue, beyond what I had intended, by commission of Our Father, who, while he holds it necessary in all religious orders, deems it particularly necessary in ours. He desires that the members of the Society signalize themselves in it. With our common way of life, we cannot equal the austerity of others in garb or in fasts and other mortifications. But in this obedience and genuine abnegation of will and judgment, he is very desirous in our Lord that we go forward and signalize ourselves.

30. I also express myself on these matters rather freely by commission from Our Father, who bids me do so because he relies confidently on the devotion to obedience displayed by Your Reverence, and because, when through obedience a person gives himself to God and not to a man as such, Our Father feels obliged to act on behalf of what he thinks in our Lord belongs to his honor and glory. And for this reason, after having first set forth the dispositions which the obedient man ought to have in those parts of himself which are offered to God through his minister—namely, in will, judgment, and execution—we shall now set forth some matters in which this obedience is rendered, so that the

obedient man may test himself regarding this disposition in the presence of God our Lord, and beg him to bestow the proper dispositions upon him should he find himself lacking them.

31. First: since it is a matter of obligation for every religious to obey the one he takes for superior in what is laid down in his Institute, and it is (as the learned say) a matter of perfection to obey in all things, even when they are difficult and opposed to one's self-will (but where one sees no sin), you should examine whether you find yourself disposed to do what is merely sufficient or what is perfect—that is, to make the superior's will your rule only in certain things or in all things.

32. Second: should you be disposed in a general way to the more perfect, then examine in particular whether, where you judged something as proper for God's service—and desired it as such—but not as necessary or obligatory for salvation, you would be disposed to give it up if the superior thinks you ought to, and would incline your will and judgment to whatever the superior shows himself inclined.

33. Third: again, if he told you to do something under obedience and a doubt arose whether you ought to obey, and you could not tell whether it would be a mortal or a venial sin but had a doubt about it, examine whether you would be disposed to take the side of obedience, trusting that God, whom you obey in his minister, would give him greater light and rectitude for knowing and conforming himself to the divine will.

34. Fourth: inasmuch as the superior sometimes gives a command with the intention of obliging and at other times not, although with a clear expression of his will or some sign so that the subject will understand it, you should examine whether you would be disposed to obey not only in the first instance, which is obligatory, but also in the second, which pertains to the perfection of obedience.

35. Our Father would like Your Reverence to examine yourself in our Lord on these points of obedience with respect to Father Araoz or whomever else God gives you as superior, just as those who owe obedience to you ought to do concerning their obedience to you.

To Antonio Araoz

Rome, April 3, 1548

(Letter 302: II:71–73; in Spanish)

At the university of Alcalá, students customarily voted in the elections for academic chairs and university administration. Ignatius here directs that Jesuit scholastics studying there and at other Spanish universities, while doing their best in disputations and degree examinations, should avoid university politics and all outward signs of academic standing.

As to your asking me about whether our men at Alcalá should take part in the elections for the academic chairs as is customary for students there—you should not allow this but should forbid it altogether. This will be better for the security and peace of their consciences, as well as for our own Institute, which is to avoid every appearance of ambition, maintain peace and love with everyone, and not come into conflict with some by siding with others. Direct also that in Valencia and wherever else those under your charge take degrees, they should not accept placing by rank, either first or last. They should perform their disputations and stand for their examinations in a way that will show whether or not they have studied well, but should avoid placings and not be present when others are being named; they can take their turn later, outside the number. This is what I judge most suitable for us in our Lord so as to avoid all ambition and disquiet and give good example and edification to others. Although they may take part in disputations and receive degrees in order to spur themselves on in study and have greater authority for giving to others what God has imparted to them, this business of special placings, because it has more dangers than advantages, seems to me in our Lord inappropriate for our men and not in conformity with the spirit of poverty and humility by which we ought to proceed.

Rome, April 3, 1548

Yours in our Lord,

IGNACIO

To Dom Talpin, by commission

Rome, April 12, 1548

(Letter 311: II:83–86; in Latin)

Talpin, a learned young humanist in Paris, had made the Exercises under the Jesuit superior there, Paolo Antonio d'Achille, and taken his vow to enter the Society. Ordered to accompany d'Achille to Rome, Talpin demurred because of concerns about his health. Ignatius sent word to d'Achille that unless Talpin's ill health was extraordinary, he should be dismissed if he refused to obey the summons to Rome. To Talpin himself Ignatius had Polanco send the following message for reflection and encouragement.

May the grace and peace of Christ Jesus increase in us all. Amen.

Your letter, beloved Master Talpin in Christ, was received by our father in Christ Ignatius. As is his practice, he communicated his mind to me and charged me with answering you, a charge I take up the more gladly in the confidence that, with your charity being elicited by our correspondence, I will be the more united with you in the Lord and have a greater place in your prayers.

I turn now to my task of answering your letter. You write that you have put aside the thoughts which tempted you to desert the God under whom you serve—and we are convinced this was the case, no matter how the devil may have presented these thoughts under the appearance of good. We thank God and give you heartfelt congratulations, for we recognize that you have been delivered through God's goodness from a formidable assault of the enemy and from extreme peril. Indeed, the greater was the peril of your struggle, a struggle over forsaking a state of life you had rightly and properly undertaken, abandoning your calling from God, violating your first faith and the vow by which you had bound yourself, and returning to Egypt after having passed through the Red Sea, whereas God's truth declares that no one is fit for the kingdom of God who puts his hand to the plow and then looks back—the more perilous, I say, was this struggle of yours, the more ought we to exult over your victory through Christ's grace and pray that he will stabilize and confirm you more and more every day.

However, when you write with such anxiety and concern about your health and about the doctor's injunctions, my dear Talpin in Christ, you seem to me (charity will not let me conceal it) to be cheating yourself of the finest fruit of obedience. For although it has been granted us by very special gift of God to be unburdened through obedience of a most vexatious load—that is, care and concern about our own persons—you have, despite your weakness, of your own accord taken this troublesome pack upon your own shoulders; and you will see how you thereby not only retreat from perfection but do yourself a distinct disservice.

If, my dear Talpin in Christ, you perceive that you are begrudging yourself the peace, liberty of spirit, and cheerfulness enjoyed by those who dedicate themselves wholly to God through his minister and who thereby free themselves of all concern about their own persons—after once having offered yourself as a living sacrifice to God, having dedicated your mind and body as a holocaust to Christ, and having entrusted yourself to God's providence through the hands of his minister to be guided towards blessedness—why is it that you unreasonably ask to have yourself back, wrongfully withhold a part of yourself, and again meddle in the governance of yourself by preferring your own providence to God's?

"But my health has suffered badly." Nevertheless, even if it were utterly despaired of, surely you ought to imitate him who for your sake became obedient unto death, even to the death of the cross [Phil. 2:8]—even though, rather than lose obedience, you were to lose your life with him. I ask, what ought to be more desirable for you than to meet death through obedience to God in the person of his minister? Do you rate this poor, brief life, which in any case must be given up, so highly that you would be unwilling to exchange it for one that is eternal and full of happiness, even though you hear Christ saying, "He who loves his life shall lose it, and he who hates his life in this world keeps it unto eternal life" [John 12:25]? Rather, dear brother, with all your courage and confidence, cast your care upon God; throw all your concern upon him [1 Pet. 5:7]. With Paul's thought that whether we live or whether we die, we belong to the Lord [Rom. 14:8], and trusting that both in life and in death Christ will be glorified in your body, cheerfully prepare yourself even for the worst.

These, in my opinion, are the weapons, worthy of a man, with which you should fight; I have no intention of tarrying to tell you of the charity and prudence of your superior in ruling those whom God has committed to his care, each to be employed according to his strengths, talents, and inclinations in the various functions of our Institute, provided they deny their own wills; nor that I hope that your health will improve as well. Any such considerations I dismiss as weak and feeble. I would rather have you trust the God in whom you have believed and make ready for the worst.

So gird your loins for the journey at the date indicated in another letter to Paolo Antonio that sets forth the mind of our father in Christ Ignatius. If you have not got your affairs in order or cannot do so this summer, start the journey anyway and appoint an executor to take care of them as though you were going to die (for we must die completely to the world and the flesh). You should have the idea that it would be better to lose some of your property than to lose yourself; and so, if you cannot undo your chains, break them.

Farewell in the Lord Christ Jesus. Remember us in your prayers.
Rome

☩

To Prince Philip of Spain

Rome, mid-1548

(Letter 382: II:149f.; in Spanish)

Ignatius had met Prince Philip in 1535 when the latter was nine years old. Here, presenting his respects to the crown prince in the courtly rhetoric of the sixteenth century, Ignatius requests his help in reforming the women's monasteries of Catalonia.

My Lord in our Lord:

Being by reason of my lowly and humble profession in no way my own master, I have decided to do as best I can through this letter what I have intensely wished to do in person; that is, to express the genuine and heartfelt reverence and gratitude that I so profoundly owe to Your Highness in our Lord—a gratitude long since deeply engraved upon my soul and present at every moment. With all my strength—little indeed, I know—I beseech the Most Holy Trinity, in consideration of their measureless and infinite mercies, to console in every way and abundantly fill Your Highness with their most holy gifts and spiritual graces; may these graces always guide and govern Your Highness in this and in every other entirely good, just, and holy work, so as to bring true light and perfect brightness to as many nations as possible now lying in deep obscurity and darkness and in such tranquility and false peace of soul.

Among these works, by the love and reverence of God our Lord I humbly beseech Your Highness, when the proper occasion presents itself and tasks of greater importance permit, graciously to remember and take steps to ensure that Your Highness's absence will not prove detrimental to the reform of the convents of nuns in Catalonia, a project which Your Highness knows will be greatly to God's service.

May he in his infinite and sovereign goodness deign to bestow upon Your Highness all the grace and happiness, both in this life and in the next, that I myself wish for you—there being, in my poor judgment in our Lord, nothing greater that could be wished.

Rome

✠

To Jerónimo Nadal, by commission

Rome, after August 4, 1548

(Letter 415: II:182f.; in Spanish)

Notes for a letter to the head of the college in Sicily, dealing among other things with a troublesome subject of his.

Sicily: Master Nadal should be instructed that they ought to be very cautious about receiving persons into the house to live there, and that for thirty or forty days after receiving someone in the house, they should not receive anyone else—and this only after the person has made exercises and been examined. On this they should trust Master Ignatius that this is right. To maintain persons outside the house or to send them to Rome remains at his discretion.

2. In general, Our Father gives him authority to proceed as he thinks best in the matter of mortifications, the quality and number of classes and teachers, and the rest so long as he has not received any instructions to the contrary; however, he should inform us here of everything. Only he should look out for the others' health and make sure that they are of goodwill and that they carry on in that way.

3. He should examine whether it would be useful for furthering the progress in arts [philosophy] of some of the men there (for example, Canisius, Benedetto [Palmio], Hannibal [Coudret]) to plan for them eventually to teach the course themselves (this comes from me, not Master Ignatius).

4. Taking any money for the preacher who is to come will not be allowable, since he will come sent by [Alessandro] Farnese.

5. On increasing the income, Master Laínez will bring further instructions when he comes, and then you will have his summaries.

Regarding Isidoro [Bellini], Master Miona will write a letter on his own part and that of Our Father in which, after expressing pleasure at his improvement, he will charge him to write his opinion about all of the men there; this will still be useful even though Master Laínez will be going there soon on other business and have the office of visitor. And a copy of this will be sent to Master Nadal, with a reminder of what Our Father said to him here about appointing him minister and, if necessary, assigning him a difficult person who would not obey him very well but who would give satisfaction afterwards, etc.

Also to Nadal: he should write Pozzo [a friend of Nadal], etc.

✠

To Andrea Lippomani

Rome, about August 14, 1548

(Letter 419: II:187f.; in Italian)

A letter to the prior of the monastery of the Trinità in Venice, who was a friend of the Society, consoling him on the death of his uncle, the bishop of Verona.

May the sovereign grace and eternal love of Jesus Christ our Lord always visit Your Reverend Lordship with his sovereign gifts and spiritual graces.

From a letter of Master Laínez, I have learned that the news was correct which we received here about the passing of My Lord the Bishop of Verona from temporal life, as we trust in our Lord, to eternal. May the sovereign goodness of God, which for this end created and redeemed him, deign to grant him peace and perpetual blessedness.

Your Lordship shows, I believe, the genuine love and charity you bore him in the most useful way for him that you can, that is, by your devout concern for suffrages on behalf of his soul. For indeed, since this debt of death is common to all and the "way of all flesh," as the patriarch said [1 Kings 2:2]—a way every one of us will soon have to tread—we ought not show ourselves overly affected by it, especially since we know that "we have not here an abiding city, but seek for that which is to come" [Heb. 13:14]; rather, the true demonstration of love is to assist one another to enjoy eternal light and happiness more speedily. And although we are confident that his most powerful suffrages in the sight of God will be his own and Your Lordship's good works in the service of God and the Church, nevertheless, from our side, in order to pay in part the debt we owe, we gave orders on that very day for all the priests in the house to celebrate Mass for this intention and for all the rest to say special prayers; and this has continued until today. And it is most just that we should thus make far tighter the bond of charity we share with all that is Your Lordship's and with the entire house of Lippomani, who will always be in our Lord patrons of this Society, which is more Your Lordship's than our own.

I shall add no more here, but refer Your Lordship to the letters written to Master Laínez. I will only pray to Jesus Christ our Lord that he may give to all the grace of knowing and perfectly fulfilling his holy will.

Rome

✠

To Antonio Araoz, by commission

Rome, September 4, 1548

(Letter 454: II:222f.; in Spanish)

Polanco explains St. Ignatius's inflexibility in refusing admittance to the Society to those who had belonged to another religious order.

For Brother Villanueva:

As for Father Villanueva's controversy about receiving into the Society persons who had entered another order, I have read the reasons on both sides to Our Father. The matter stands thus: If you consider only the individual who without any fault of his own left another order before profession because he did not find there the greater service of God which he entered it to seek, there is no way to refute the arguments in favor of his being able to be received, assuming he has the qualifications, etc., and has made his probations, etc. However, if you consider the common good, taking a broader view which embraces the long-term consequences of allowing such admissions, Our Father is convinced that there is less harm in failing to receive a few good subjects of this kind than in allowing admission to many who would not be. Such persons can be saved outside the Society, and losing a certain number of good men who might enter by this route is less harmful to the Society than admitting a multitude of inconstant persons, etc., who would enter if this way were opened to them.

However, for Father Villanueva's consolation, I will tell you something I heard him say, making some little effort on behalf of those who have tried another order. He said that if there were an outstanding person with qualifications such that he seemed altogether suitable for admission, such a person might obtain a dispensation from the Pope to enter our order despite the constitution, etc. In this way the Society, while on its side remaining closed to persons [wishing to enter it from a different order], could be opened to some persons of this type. In addition, I see in practice that some men in this situation do come to the Society and assist it according to the talent God has given them. Although strictly speaking neither professed nor coadjutors nor scholastics, they still do the same work as the others who are, and can for their own part have the merit of obedience, etc.

As for changing this constitution, I know that Our Father is so firm that he will never be brought to consent to it during his lifetime. I myself would not dare to try, knowing with what light he proceeds in these essential matters. Enough on this subject.

✠

To Francis Borgia, duke of Gandía

Rome, September 20, 1548

(Letter 466: II:233–37; in Spanish)

Earlier in 1548 Borgia had made his profession in the Society of Jesus, but in secret since he was not yet able to renounce his dukedom. He was indulging his penchant for long hours of prayer and rigorous penance to such an extent that he was damaging his health. Ignatius himself had earlier in his life engaged in such excesses and knew the toll they took. Here he recommends that Borgia reduce the time spent on these exercises, devoting some of it to study and other activities, in all of which he should seek God. He urges Borgia to recuperate his health by eating as well as he can, and recommends that he seek the gift of tears and interior experiences of divine consolation, without which our thoughts and actions are "tainted, cold, and troubled."

My Lord in our Lord:

May the sovereign grace and eternal love of Christ our Lord be always our continual protection and help.

As I learned of your good order and mode of proceeding in spiritual matters and in corporal matters related to your spiritual progress, they indeed gave me fresh reason for great joy in our Lord. Thanking his eternal Majesty for this, I can ascribe it to his divine goodness alone, from which derives all that is good. However, knowing also in our Lord that we require different spiritual or bodily exercises at different times, since practices good for us at one time are not continuously so at another, I will state in his Divine Majesty what occurs to me regarding this matter, since Your Lordship bids me give my opinion.

My first thought, touching on the hours allotted to interior and exterior exercises, would be to cut them in half. For when and to the degree that there arise in us thoughts—either from ourselves or from our enemy—which move us to think or dwell upon matters which are extraneous, vain, or unlawful, and which we wish to prevent the will from taking delight in or consenting to—to that extent we ought normally to increase our interior and exterior exercises, taking into account individual persons and the different sorts of thoughts or temptations, and adapting the exercises to the persons in order to overcome them. On the other hand, the more such thoughts weaken and die out, the more there will arise in us good thoughts and holy inspirations, to which we should give unreserved admission and throw wide the doors of our soul. Consequently, from what I can judge in our Lord of Your Lordship's case, such weapons are no longer needed for overcoming the enemies; thus, I would deem it preferable to convert half of your time into study (for in the future there will always be need or use for acquired as well as infused knowledge), to administration of your estates, and to spiritual conversations—always taking care to maintain your soul in peace, quiet, and readiness for whenever our Lord wishes to work in it. For it is without doubt a higher virtue of the soul and a greater grace to be able to enjoy one's Lord in a variety of duties and places rather than in one only, and we should make great efforts in his divine goodness to obtain this.

As for the second point, regarding fasts and abstinences, my thought would be that for our Lord's sake you ought to preserve and strengthen your stomach and other physical faculties, not weaken them. For in cases where a soul, first, is disposed and resolved to prefer losing its temporal life altogether rather than offend the Divine Majesty by a single deliberate sin, however slight, and, second, is not being plagued by any particular temptations of the enemy, the world, or the flesh—and I am convinced that by God's grace such is the situation of Your Lordship (in the first case affirmatively and in the second negatively)—I very much wish Your Lordship to impress upon your soul that, inasmuch as both soul and body are your Creator and Lord's, you must give him a good accounting of the whole and hence not let the bodily nature become weakened; for if it is weak, the inward nature will no longer be able to function properly. Consequently, while I did strongly commend the fasts, rigorous abstinence, and retrenchment from ordinary food, and for a time was quite glad about them, I can no longer do so now that I see that these fasts and abstinences keep the stomach from functioning naturally and from digesting ordinary meats or other foods which supply proper sustenance to the body. Instead, I would seek every possible means to strengthen the body, eating any permissible foods and [doing so] as frequently as you find them beneficial (barring scandal to the neighbor). For we ought to cherish and love the body insofar as it obeys and serves the soul, and insofar as with the body's help and obedience the soul becomes more fitted for the service and praise of our Creator and Lord.

As for the third point, that is, inflicting hurt upon the body for our Lord's sake, I would completely stop any practices that could draw even a drop of blood. And if his Divine Majesty has bestowed grace upon you for this and the rest that I have mentioned (as I am convinced in his divine goodness that he has), I think that for the future (without giving reasons or arguments for it) it would be much better to give all this up and instead of seeking to draw any blood, to seek the Lord of all in a more immediate way; that is to say, his most holy gifts—for example, an infusion or drops of tears, whether (1) at our own or other people's sins, (2) at the mysteries of Christ our Lord in this life or the next, or (3) at the consideration and love of the divine Persons. These tears have greater value and worth in proportion as the thoughts and considerations prompting them are higher.

However, while in themselves the third sort are more perfect than the second, and the second than the first, for any individual person the best is where God our Lord most communicates himself through a manifestation of his holy graces and spiritual gifts. For he sees and knows what is best for the person and, knowing all things, points out to him the way. To discover this way it is useful for us, with the help of his grace, to seek out and try a number of ways so as to tread the one made clearest to us, as the happiest and most blessed in this life and wholly directed and ordered to the other everlasting life—whereby we are encompassed and made one with these most holy gifts. I refer to those that are not in our own power to summon up when we wish, but are sheer gifts of him who gives and can effect all that is good. Such are—with his Divine Majesty as their goal and scope—a deepening of faith, of hope, of charity; spiritual joy and repose, tears, intense consolation, elevation of mind, divine impressions and illuminations—along with all the other spiritual tastes and perceptions which are ordered to these gifts, with humility and reverence towards our holy mother the Church and her established rulers and teachers. Any of these most holy gifts should be preferred to all bodily acts; the latter have value only so far as they contribute to obtaining these gifts, or a part of them. I do not mean that we should seek these gifts merely for the pleasure or delight they bring, but so that our thoughts, words, and actions—which we know from personal experience to be tainted, cold, and troubled when these gifts are absent—might be warm, clear, and right for God's greater service. Thus we desire to have these gifts (or a part of them) and spiritual graces of this sort to the extent that they can help us for God's greater glory. Hence, when the body is jeopardized through excessive hardships, the soundest thing is to pursue these gifts through acts of the understanding and other moderate practices, so that not the soul alone will be healthy but, with a sound mind in a sound body, the whole will be more sound and more fitted for God's greater service.

As to how you should act in more particular matters, I do not think it advisable in our Lord to speak; I am confident that the same Divine Spirit that has guided Your Lordship to this point will guide and govern you in the future, to the greater glory of his Divine Majesty.

✠

To Diego Laínez, by commission

Rome, December 22, 1548

(Letter 507: II:274–77; in Spanish)

Detailed instructions for a visitation of Sicily

For Various Parts of Italy and Sicily, France, Flanders, and Germany
For Master Laínez:

On December 22 the following reminders were sent to Father Laínez for when he is in Sicily.

SOME DIRECTIVES TO BE OBSERVED IN SICILY REGARDING THE NEIGHBOR, THE SOCIETY, AND FATHER LAÍNEZ'S OWN PERSON

Regarding the Neighbor

1. In Palermo he will preach during Lent, attending as much as he is able to the other works of charity for the consolation and edification of that city, such as the children, etc.

2. At Monreale he will preach on Sundays and feast days after dinner, either going there to dine or after dining in Palermo, and always on

horseback, with another companion on horseback and a third following on foot; and Master Jerónimo should provide for this.

3. When there is a chance (as is likely after Easter), he will obtain information about the matters he was charged with at Monreale, and do whatever else he can to obtain the aim being sought, proceeding with both parts as far as possible in love and hewing to the middle, so as not to incur suspicion from either party.[5]

4. Both upon arrival, at the beginning, and afterwards he will write Cardinal Farnese whatever news he has to give.

5. He will do all he can to give satisfaction to His Lordship Juan de Vega and to his wife and house, striving to maintain and increase their goodwill and giving them what spiritual assistance he can.

6. He will confer with Master Doménech and see whether it would be good to make a visit to Calatagirona or some other part of the kingdom for which there might be a particular reason.

7. When he has come to some termination, or has done all that can be done at Monreale and Palermo, he will have to go to Messina, where he will see whether it would be good to preach the next Lent or Advent, etc.

8. In general, he should strive to do all the good he can in the island, remembering, for his manner of proceeding there, that "all islanders . . ."

Regarding the Society

1. He should remember to write a report to Rome weekly, or to have it written.

2. He should try to win numerous suitable subjects for God's service.

3. He should see how to decide about Masters Stefano and Florence and those in Messina as he judges best, just as if he had the office of Superior General, making use of the patent during his visitation as he deems best in the Lord.

4. If Masters Doménech, Nadal, and André [de Freux] have not yet made their profession, they may do so (if they are willing) into his hands.

---

[5] Cardinal Farnese wanted Laínez to reconcile the feuding secular and religious clergy in his diocese of Monreale.

5. He should consider how to organize the men in Messina so as to withdraw Masters André, Cornelius [Wischaven], and Canisius and replace them with others who will fill up their loss.

6. He should discuss with Master Jerónimo Doménech the latter's trip to Valencia, and see whether it would work out well for him to go from there to Portugal, and for Master Jay to accompany His Lordship Juan de Vega in his place. A separate sheet gives fuller information on this matter.

7. He should have special care, with God's grace, to foster the growth of the college in Messina in the love of the people, in authority, and in income (where this is possible). Similarly, he will help as much as he can with the new university.

8. For all this it would help, should he go through Messina, to take along the heads of the holy martyred women about which the city wrote so urgently to Master Ignatius, and also the bulls of the college and the university, which may have been sent by then, and the news from the Indies and other parts of the Society, which will be sent before his departure; also [it would help] if he can occasionally preach in passing. However, if it does not work out for him to go to Messina but straight to Palermo instead, he can make up for a visit with his letters, sending all or part of the above as he thinks best.

9. He should devote care to the colleges which have been talked about for Calatagirona and Palermo, and Master Doménech will inform him about the situation, etc. I do not mention Monreale, since we do not anticipate a foundation of the Society there.

10. On arriving in Palermo (which should be at least a week before Lent, God willing), he will write to the duchess or to Don Pedro de Toledo about his arrival, and he may mention the twelve that were supposed to be sent there; but this should be done so as to avoid the impression that we here are anxious to get them or trying to do so.[6] He might write, for instance, that, with regard to the agreement that had been made with Their Excellencies about sending twelve students to Pisa this March, it would be important, if this were to be done, to write to the Cardinal of Burgos or to Master Ignatius in Rome—and this whenever Their Excellencies pleased and not otherwise, etc. He could add that he both intends and hopes, upon completing the business for which he went to Sicily, to travel immediately to Florence, etc.

---

[6] Reference is to Duchess Leonor de Toledo of Florence and her father.

11. He should also see whether it would be advisable to write to some persons of greater influence in Naples to assist and advance the work that God our Lord will have inaugurated through his hand, even though Master Bobadilla is to go there for this purpose.

Regarding His Person

1. He should have no scruple about keeping Giovanni Filippo [Casini] with him or, if he prefers to place him in the college of Messina or elsewhere, about taking someone else as an assistant in his place.

2. He should travel on horseback, even if only from Palermo to Monreale, as indicated above.

3. He should look out for his health and not overwork.

4. For this, he should try to have lodging that is convenient and allows him freedom.

5. He should not let himself lack any necessities.

Regarding all these reminders and any others that may be given, Our Father (by whose command and order they are written) says that they are left to Your Reverence's discretion and to whatever the anointing of the Holy Spirit may show you.

☩

To Juan de Avila

Rome, January 24, 1549

(Letter 550: II:316–20; in Spanish, with citations in Latin)

The aims and projects of the zealous apostle of Andalusia, St. Juan de Avila, closely paralleled those of the new Society of Jesus, to which the saintly priest had steered a number of his followers. Here Ignatius expresses his gratitude and informs the saint of measures he feels compelled to take against calumnies by certain religious in Spain.

My Very Reverend Sir in our Lord:

May the sovereign grace and eternal love of Christ our Lord greet and visit Your Reverence with his most holy gifts and spiritual graces.

Having heard several times and from several of our men about the continual support, along with intense charity, which Your Reverence has given to this least Society, I resolved in our Lord to write you this, my motives being two. The first is to express our gratitude and deep appreciation; we give intense thanks to God our Lord, and to Your Reverence in his most holy name, for all your exertions for the glory of the Divine Majesty and for the greater increase and devotion of ourselves, Your Reverence's servants. Accordingly, in this acknowledgement I offer myself to Your Reverence, with all the devotion of which I am capable, as one of your adherents or spiritual sons in our Lord, to carry out most willingly whatever I may be commanded in the Lord of all and for which his Divine Majesty gives me strength. For to do so will, I am convinced, bring me great profit in his divine goodness, as well as let me satisfy in some measure the great obligation I feel; for I believe that in serving the servants of my Lord I am serving the Lord of all himself. My second motive is that, as Your Reverence has doubtless heard some favorable things in the Lord about our men, I thought it right in his Divine Majesty that you should also hear about the contrary ones—although I am convinced beyond doubt that with greater spiritual exercise on the part of those concerned, it will all turn out for God's greater glory. Namely, our men write us that in Salamanca they have met and still meet much opposition from certain Dominican fathers, who are motivated, I am convinced, more by well-intentioned zeal than by proper knowledge. This opposition has been going on for ten months. From recent letters of November 26 and December 2, we learn that it has now reached such an outrageous pitch that we have been forced to take steps in the matter, following the teaching of St. Augustine and numerous holy doctors. In his treatise on widowhood, St. Augustine states, "Our life is a necessity for ourselves, our reputation for others."[7] Commenting on Matthew, St. Chrysostom says, "Let us learn by his example to bear with magnanimity insults to ourselves; but insults to God we should not allow even to be heard."[8]

In his letter against Rufinus, St. Jerome says, "I do not want anyone to be patient under the accusation of heresy."[9] And St. Thomas (IIa IIæ, q. 72, a. 3) says: "We must be ready to endure insults if it is expedient. But there are times when we must repel a slander against us, especially for two reasons. First, for the good of the person offering the slander: to check his audacity and keep him from repeating his attempt in the future, as it says in Proverbs 26, 'Answer a fool according to his folly, lest he imagine himself wise' [v. 5]. Secondly, for the good of many other persons, whose progress might be hindered by the slander

---

[7] *De bono viduitatis*, chap. 27.

[8] Homily 5 on Matthew.

[9] *Ad Pammachium adv. errores Ioannis Hierosolymitani episcopi.*

made against us. Thus Gregory says in his ninth homily on Ezekiel, 'Persons whose lives are a model for the imitation of others must squelch the words of detractors when possible, lest people who might listen to their preaching fail to do so and thus, remaining in their evil habits, spurn to live a good life.'"

St. Bonaventure, in his *Apologeticus*, q. [12], raises the question: "When you ought to put up patiently with all wrongs done to you without making or raising any complaint about them, why is it that you not only fail to do this but even, not satisfied with the verdicts of bishops, procure from the Apostolic See judges and protectors, before whom you cite, at great labor and expense to themselves, persons who are a source of even slight annoyance to you, until they have given you full satisfaction? This is in contradiction to the Apostle, who says to the Corinthians, 'It is a fault among you that you have lawsuits with one another' [1 Cor. 6:7]. My reply is this: Religious should calmly endure wrongs and annoyances which issue in no evil beyond what is felt at the moment, as with offensive words, loss of property, blows, or the like; for these cause no further harm. But when graver damage may result, namely, grave harm to souls, it is no longer right to be patient."[10] Cajetan says in his *Summa:* "To disregard the calumniation of one's own good name is sinful when this harms or may be feared to harm others; our reputation is necessary to us for the good of others. St. Augustine says in such a case, 'He who, confident of his innocence, pays no heed to his reputation commits an act of cruelty, for he kills the souls of others.'"[11]

And so this is what we decided should be our course for God's glory: first, with all courtesy and love to have a letter sent them by a cardinal who it appears might have some influence with them;[12] second, likewise to present them with a writ from their own general; third, if both the first and second measures do no good, then for the sake of what God our Lord and charity toward our neighbor demand of us, and in order to repress the power of the enemy of our human nature, who prompts and persuades in this way even learned persons and religious who have been created for God's greater glory, we will resort to a peremptory lawsuit and papal brief, as Your Reverence will see. We inform Your Reverence of all this so that you may have full matter for praying earnestly to God in your holy Sacrifices and devout prayers that his Divine Majesty may deign to bestow his favor and aid on that quarter

---

[10] Op. XIII: *Determinationes questionum circa Regulam Fratrum Minorum*, ii. q. 12.

[11] Cajetan, *Summa*, Pars I.

[12] Juan Alvarez de Toledo, O.P.

where his greater praise and glory may redound forever—for by his grace this is the only thing we seek and desire.

To him be eternal glory for ever and ever from this and from all things; and may he deign, by his infinite and sovereign goodness, to give his perfect grace to us all, so that we may always know his most holy will and entirely fulfill it.

Rome, January 25, 1549

IGNATIO

✠

To Mateo Sebastián de Morrano

Rome, February 22, 1549

(Letter 581: II:345–47; in Spanish)

*Ignatius explains to an official in Zaragoza why he cannot undertake the govern-
ment of the Religious of Santa Clara in Barcelona.*

My Lord in our Lord:

May the sovereign grace and eternal love of Christ our Lord greet and visit you with his most holy gifts and spiritual graces.

Although through letters from others I had knowledge before this of Your Worship's person, as well as of the special charity towards this our least Society imparted to you by the Author of charity and of every good, and so have felt specially bound to have a strong desire for serving Your Worship in our Lord, both the one and the other have been much increased through your letter of the third of this month, full of humility and devotion, which I received this week. The letter reveals these gifts of God in Your Worship to be all the greater, the less cause I see in myself for their being directed towards me. However, praying that God our Lord, to whose glory alone all well-ordered goods should be referred, will repay with his infinite charity and the spiritual gifts which proceed from it the charity towards us which he has imparted to you, I will only say that I have been greatly delighted in the Lord by the exchange of letters between us. I would be even more delighted if at the first command you send me, I were able to demonstrate the desire which the divine Goodness gives me to do Your Worship every spiritual service in keeping with my poor profession. But Your Worship must understand that the authority of His Holiness stands in the way of our Society's undertaking the task which you and the pious ladies of

St. Clare indicate you would like it to assume. For when we perceived the numerous serious disadvantages that would accrue to a Society that needs to have, so to speak, one foot in the air ready to hasten from place to place, according to our vocation and the Institute which we follow in the Lord, if it were to take responsibility for monasteries of religious women—in itself a holy work, but because of its encumbering character incompatible with a manner of living like ours—we earnestly petitioned His Holiness to exempt and exclude us entirely from such cares; and so he did through his Signatura. It is therefore no longer possible to contravene his decree and authority. But were the Society ever to have charge of religious women, then both on account of Your Worship's command and of our great attachment towards these ladies in our Lord, I would certainly wish to begin with them. Meanwhile, I have no doubt that persons who are so spiritual and such lovers of what most pleases God our Lord, and who must have such a lively faith and hope in his divine providence and so broad a view for the universal good will in the end hold the Society lawfully excused in this matter.

May the eternal wisdom and infinite goodness of Jesus Christ our Lord and God bestow on all of us his light and rectitude, so that we may always know his most holy will and entirely fulfill it.

Rome, February 22, 1549

Your Worship's most humble servant in the Lord,

IGNATIUS

✠

To Jerónima Oluja and Teresa Rejadell

Rome, April 5, 1549

(Letter 630: II:374f.; in Spanish)

The continuing disorders in Teresa Rejadell's monastery of Santa Clara in Barcelona led her and the former prioress, Jerónima Oluja, to petition anew for the Jesuits to take it under their direction. This present letter replies to at least seven letters that one or both women had written to Ignatius between early January and early April of 1549, begging him to take under the obedience of the Society the nuns at this convent who desired reform. Araoz, who was in Barcelona in the previous year as provincial of Spain, had held out hope to the nuns that Ignatius might do so. But his travails with Isabel Roser in Rome had led Ignatius to get a papal brief prohibiting the Society from having women under its obedience. He here communicates this to the two Benedictine nuns.

May the sovereign grace and eternal love of Christ our Lord be always our protection and help.

Through letters I have from various persons there, I see how our Lord is visiting you with trials, giving you no slight opportunity to practice the virtues imparted to you by his divine Goodness and to prove their solidity. For it is amid difficulties (of which I see many in your affair) that we can test the genuineness of our spiritual progress. May Jesus Christ, who did and suffered so much for us all, give us abundant grace, so that for his holy love we may suffer fruitfully whatever we may have to suffer, and that anything in need of remedying may be remedied in the way that is most pleasing to his divine Goodness. This remedy, I am certain, is not the one you have hitherto been indicating. For although our Society, in keeping with its many obligations of special love in our Lord, is quite eager to console and serve you in conformity with our profession, the authority of the vicar of Christ has closed the door against our undertaking the government or direction of religious women. The Society itself petitioned for this from the beginning, since it deemed that God our Lord would be better served if the Society were as unencumbered as possible, so that it could go to any place where obedience to the supreme pontiff and the needs of the neighbor might call us. Hence I believe that this remedy was in no way what pleased God our Lord, and am confident that apart from it, in his infinite goodness, some better way will be found to achieve what you and all of us desire in our Lord regarding your peace and particular consolation.

While deferring to what may be judged best there, you will see my own thinking in Master Polanco's letter; I will not go into details here. I will only say that I wish you would believe me that for the end we all have in view, the greater service of God our Lord, it would not be right for us to accept what is being proposed there—although, if we did undertake care of any religious women, our ministry would be offered to you before anyone else.

May the divine Wisdom grant to all of us always to perceive his holy will, find peace and happiness in it, and perfectly fulfill it.

Rome, April 5, 1549

Your servant in our Lord,

IGNACIO

✠

To Andrea Lippomani

Rome, June 22, 1549

(Letter 743: II:445–47; in Italian)

Lippomani, a learned man, was instrumental in the foundation of the Jesuit college in Venice. Ignatius here suggests to him an expurgated edition of the Latin classics which could be safely and profitably placed in the hands of schoolboys. Lippomani in his reply was quite reserved about whether such a tactic was possible, not to mention desirable.

My Very Reverend Lord in Christ:

May the sovereign grace and eternal love of Jesus Christ our Lord greet and visit Your Reverend Lordship with his most holy gifts and spiritual graces.

I have for some weeks delayed writing to Your Lordship, having nothing of importance to mention. But I decided to write now, not only to offer you my respects, with a prayer that during these feast days the Holy Spirit has enriched you much with his spiritual treasures, but also to communicate to you a desire which our Lord has given to me for many years now and about which I would very much like to have the opinion of Your Lordship, who can also furnish considerable help in its realization. It is this: I have observed how receptive and retentive young people naturally are of the first impressions that are made on them, whether good or evil, so that these first notions, as well as the good or bad examples and models that are set before them, have a great influence on the rest of their lives. On the other hand, I have seen how the books, particularly those of humane letters, commonly taught to young people—Terence, Vergil, and the like—while containing many things that are useful for learning and not useless but helpful even for life, also contain some things that are quite profane and immodest, the very hearing of which is harmful, since, as Scripture tells us, "the imagination and thought of man's heart are prone to evil from his youth" [Gen. 8:21]—all the more so if such things are placed before them and inculcated in them by the books which they hear expounded, study, and have regularly at hand.

In view of this, it has long been and still is my thought that it would be very opportune to remove these immodest and harmful passages from such books, substituting others that would be more edifying—or at least to keep the good passages and get rid of the bad ones, even if nothing is added. For the last few years it has occurred to me that this would be of great value for Christian morals and for the proper training of youth. However, seeing no means of accomplishing it, I never got beyond the desire. Now, seeing how much our Lord is spreading this work of his, our Society, by means of his servants, not only through colleges but also through universities—of which two, at Gandía and Messina, are now under the Society's direction—it would appear that this project is becoming more feasible and easier to realize, at least in those places where the Society possesses authority. However, I would much appreciate knowing Your Reverend Lordship's opinion, because, if it is the same as ours, you could greatly assist us, for the glory of the Lord God, as I shall explain to you later.

That is all for now, except to tell you that we are well, God be praised, and that we earnestly commend ourselves to Your Reverend Lordship's prayers, praying that God's supreme and infinite goodness may give to all of us abundant grace always to know his holy will and perfectly to fulfill it.

✠

To Francis Borgia, duke of Gandía, by commission

July 1549

(XII [Appendix 6, no. 3]: 632–54: in Spanish)

At Gandía, partly under the influence of the Franciscan Juan Tejeda, two Jesuits became convinced that a spiritual life required lengthy hours of prayer every day. One of them, Andrés de Oviedo, even petitioned St. Ignatius to let him go live in the desert for seven years. The other, Francisco Onfroy, issued a document, now lost, consisting of thirty-two propositions regarding the reform of the Church and the Society and about Francis Borgia's role as "the angelic pope" in such a reform. A dossier about the two men was submitted to Rome, and Ignatius had Polanco send Francis Borgia the following lengthy assessment. It impugns Onfroy's prophecies on numerous grounds and rebuts the two Jesuits' claims about the indispensability of prolonged prayer. The document is a precious example of Ignatius's practice of the discernment of spirits.

Polanco's original text is here given along with Ignatius's handwritten corrections printed in italics. Material deleted by Ignatius is printed as ~~struck out~~.

1. Before descending to details, ~~it will be good~~ *we have deemed it wise in the Lord of all* to say some things which ~~will be useful~~ *may be useful, to the greater glory of his Divine Majesty,* in dealing with this matter.

First of all, it is clear that while we should not reject all prophecies made after the time of Christ, since we see them in St. John [Rev.

22:6], Agabus [Acts 11:28], the daughters of Philip [Acts 21:9], etc., and since St. Paul warns us, "Do not despise prophecies" [1 Thess. 5:20], neither should we give credit to all who say they are prophets, nor should we accept their prophecies, in view of the many kinds of deception in this matter and of the same apostle's admonition, "Do not believe every spirit, but test the spirits to see if they are of God" [1 John 4:1].

It is likewise clear that with regard to contingent future events, we cannot assert with assurance that a given eventuality is impossible; still, we would at the same time be ~~thoughtless~~ *rash* to believe that everything that might happen actually will—as the Wise Man says, "Whoever believes too quickly is light of mind" [Ecclus. 19:4]. This would be even less excusable in persons who have experience in these deceptions, of which we have numerous great examples nowadays.

Thus, it is ~~needful~~ *very useful and extremely necessary* to discern and examine such spirits. For this God our Lord, as for a matter of some importance, gives his servants the special "gratia gratis data" of the discernment of spirits, as the Apostle tells us [1 Cor. 12:10]. And this grace makes use of and operates through human means, especially prudence and learning.

Proceeding in this way, we may religiously accept some of the prophecies or revelations going around if they contain nothing opposed to reason or sound doctrine, are edifying rather than otherwise, and particularly if the person who delivers them and the quality of their contents render them plausible. Even so, spiritual and prudent persons commonly suspend judgment in such cases and await the outcome before deeming them genuine, even though they may not condemn them. For even the prophets themselves do not always see everything in their prophetic light as clearly and absolutely as they may assert. Thus, Jonah stated absolutely, "In forty days Nineveh will be destroyed" [Jonah 3:4], without there being, or at least without his expressing, the condition implied within the statement in God our Lord's eternal disposition, namely, unless they should repent. It can also happen that a genuine prophet is mistaken when, not seeing the matter of which he speaks in the prophetic light but in the natural light of his intellect and reason, he makes an assertion which is not correct. Thus Nathan was mistaken when he told David that in God's name he should build the Temple. But later, in the true and certain supernatural light, he saw the contrary, and so informed David that because he had shed so much blood, he would not be the one to build it, etc. [2 Sam. 7]. With such warnings given us by the Scriptures themselves, it is obvious how much more circumspect we ought to be in crediting persons of whom we do not even know if they are prophets, there being so many ways of mistaking error for the truth.

2. If such revelations or prophecies (even when there is nothing in them against sound morals and doctrine) contain anything not in accord with reason, it is lawful and good not merely to withhold belief but also to oppose them, unless they are confirmed by miracles or other proofs that are superior ~~to reason~~.

If, therefore, these revelations contain something contrary to good reason or sound doctrine and morals and, if believed, would cause disedification rather than edification, then to give them credence would certainly be ~~thoughtlessness~~ *rashness* and ignorance; and it is right and meritorious to impugn and discredit them, for this would be to act for truth and rightness and thus would be pleasing to the Author of truth.

To come now to the point at issue, the prophecies or revelations of B. [Onfroy][13] on which we have been commanded by obedience to give an opinion after commending the matter to God our Lord: having considered the matter in his divine goodness, we are of the opinion that these revelations belong to the last category. The reasons underlying this opinion are partly extrinsic, partly related to his person, and partly based on the propositions themselves—although in fact, even apart from any arguments, a first reading of the prophecies inclined one's mind to think ill of them, albeit ~~with compassion and no little sorrow~~ *feeling much compassion* at seeing such a disposition in their authors, persons whom we love with the tenderness of Jesus Christ. Indeed, often truth as well as error, of their own accord and apart from any arguments, move the understanding to give or withhold assent. And for anyone who thought that God our Lord might have imparted to us some grace for the discernment of spirits, it is to this gift rather than to any other considerations that this judgment might be attributed. But the arguments which subsequently confirmed it are as follows.

3. The first is that this spirit of prophecies or inward perceptions, particularly regarding the reformation of the Church, an angelic pope, etc., which has been current there for many years now, rightly deserves to be regarded with much suspicion. By means of it the devil seems to have gone about deluding all those in whom he finds a disposition to be persuaded of such things—among whom are counted persons of excep-

---

[13] For reasons of prudence or charity, names in this document were often replaced by letters that referred to particular persons. B = Onfroy; C = Oviedo; T = Tejeda. The Society was at times designated by an asterisk (*).

tional gifts of nature, learning, and (as they thought) grace. We might recall Amadeo[14]—to go no further back—or Fra Jerome of Ferrara [Savonarola], a person of great and exceptional gifts. It is really enough to strike fear in anyone getting involved with such things to see deception overtaking a man so prudent and learned, and, as far as could be seen, so virtuous and devout, and who strove by so many means to test whether his spirit was from God. And yet he was deceived, as we can see by the passing of the times set in his prophecies.

But to come to our own times, it is amazing in our own days how many people have become involved in this, including cardinals such as Galatino, whose case is public knowledge[15] (those not publicly known I pass over for their reputations' sake), persons who held and hold as a certainty that there will be angelic popes to reform the Church. An eminent chamberlain of Pope Paul named Ambrosio had this fixed idea, and apparently would not have rendered up the papacy for anything less than what it was worth.

Recently also there was a man at Urbino with a similar spirit who went so far as to dress as a pope and create cardinals. He began having so many followers that the Duke of Urbino thought it no small accomplishment to get rid of him and expel him from his territory. Likewise in other parts of Italy, such as Spoleto and Calabria, where there has recently arisen another person, a descendant of St. Francis of Paola, who also claimed that there would be an angelic pope who would bring about a reform, etc. His election was supposed to be last May, but it did not happen.

Guillaume Postel let himself be possessed by a similar humor, and Your Lordship doubtless knows what excellent gifts he had. As a result they turned him out of our house here.[16] He is now in Venice awaiting the deadline he set for the fulfillment of his prophecies. King Francis of France, who he claimed would be the temporal monarch, has died; yet he is now finding evasions with which fraudulently to defend his prophecies, claiming that by refusing to believe him, King Francis had prevented what God had planned, and that it would be his son who fulfilled it, just as Joshua did in place of Moses, to whom it had been said that he would bring the children of Israel into the Promised Land,

---

[14] Perhaps Amadeus of Savoy, the antipope Felix V, but more likely a Portuguese Franciscan João de Meneses da Silva, born in 1431, confessor of Pope Sixtus IV, founder of the Congregaçam dos Amadeos, and author of *Apocalypsis nova*.

[15] Cardinal Pietro Colonna, author of *De arcanis catholicæ veritatis* (1518).

[16] Postel was asked to leave in 1544 after several months living at the curia.

and he fulfilled it. He is now as fixed in his ideas as ever, or even more so, and is beyond helping. Indeed, the poor man has fallen into other errors so intolerable that they clearly demonstrate what his spirit is—to the point where they have not only given him up for lost but have forbidden him to preach; even the Inquisition wants to get hold of him.

A few days ago there also arrived a man from Portugal who was going to reform the Church; here in the house Our Father worked to bring him to his senses.

Another man from the same nation says that toward the end of the coming August he will infallibly be elected pope. He was trying hard to get an otherwise quite inconvenient church as his residence, because he thought he would make a very impressive exit from it when he was elected pope.

But not to go on at length about so many cases, I will only mention someone who recently came to speak with Our Father, a person demonstrating considerable spirituality; he claimed that at a distance of over two hundred miles, he had been elected pope. He asserted that Cardinal Farnese, among others, had in spirit been present at his election; apparently all he had to do now was take possession of the papacy. I think Our Father gave him an astute answer, suggesting that since a papal election is held only when the see is vacant, he ought to find out if Pope Paul was still alive to see whether his election was genuine, etc.

But to return to my point of departure: the first reason that moves us is seeing these and similar examples; things of this sort, even if they had far more solid foundations, would deservedly be rendered too suspicious to get involved in.

4. The second reason moving us is that neither Father Doctor Araoz in Spain nor our father Master Ignatius here approves any of this; rather, they consider it an error and a deception ~~of the devil~~ *of the enemy of human nature*. The simple fact of the approval or disapproval by such men has great authority with us. First, because they are superiors; for as it is a part of their office to rule, they ordinarily receive a greater influx of the gifts of God needed to govern those under their responsibility. Second, because they are such servants of God our Lord; and in doubtful matters it is more reasonable to hold with such persons even without reasons than with others who have many reasons, in order to discern specifically whether or not a spirit is from God. Our Lord says, "If anyone will do the will of him who sent me, he will know whether the teaching is from God," etc. [John 7:17]. Certainly rectitude is very pertinent to discernment. Third, because they both ~~possess through the~~

~~gift of Jesus Christ~~ *appear to have—and it is much more fitting and reasonable that they should have—through the special gift of Jesus Christ*, the Author of all good, this grace of discernment of spirits *regarding their own subjects more than others outside;* and when we add their great prudence and experience, there seems to be *much* cause for believing them on a matter which they consider so certain and indubitable, when it is their responsibility to know this, especially in the case of our father Master Ignatius.

5. The third reason is that when God our Lord makes such supernatural revelations, he usually does so for some good purpose and has in view some advantage for mankind. It belongs to the nature of these "gratiæ gratis datæ" to be for the good of the neighbor, according to St. Paul and the doctors. But if we examine what purpose or aim these particular prophecies and revelations might serve, instead of advantage we find harm and disedification for the members of the Society should they believe them, as well as for those outside. For surely to say that the Society was instituted defectively and should be instituted better would lead anyone who believed it to lose his peace in the Society. Keeping his eyes on the future, he would fail in his observance during the present. And finally, just as it is a great help for making progress in the Society to have esteem and love for it, so to occasion the loss of either would produce harm. And as for those outside, to claim that at its very beginnings the Society is already declining in spirit as it increases in numbers, and that it is in such dire straits, etc., would obviously be disedifying. Thus the harm in publishing such ideas is clear, while there is no apparent advantage at all—particularly as there is no willingness to tell the superior of the Society just how it should be reformed. All told, our position is that, just as in uncertain matters we ought to be more inclined to believe whatever helps and edifies when believed, rather than its opposite, so we ought to be inclined to consider these claims, which are of no help, to be false—as indeed they are. Summing up these reasons then: In view of the nature of these notions which ~~at every step~~ *so frequently* deceive many people nowadays, and in view of the opinions of Father Araoz there and Father Master Ignatius here, who are superiors and such servants of God our Lord and endowed with such prudence, and taking into account that no good but rather harm ensues from these revelations, they are not deemed to be from the good spirit.

Considerations Drawn from His Person

6. Then there are reasons stemming from the person of B. [Onfroy] for disapproving these claims. It is to be presumed that just as in nature a natural agent requires a subject that is properly disposed to receive its influence, the same holds in supernatural matters—although here with some individuals the contrary may occur, since the infinite Power has no need that the matter be properly disposed; but here we refer to what holds in the majority of cases, even though a properly disposed subject might not be necessary. Consequently, just as seeing a subject who is disposed for such graces would rightly incline us to credit their presence in him, similarly, evidence that he is not, but rather is disposed to let himself be deluded, inclines us in the opposite direction. That B. [Onfroy] has this disposition to be deceived is evident, first of all from consideration of his mind. To judge his natural disposition for the gift of prophecy by the way he speaks of C. [Oviedo], he is not suited for it, since his mind is muddled—as C. [Oviedo] himself informs us, saying that he is therefore not capable of teaching others. For to receive prophetic illumination, it would be more appropriate to have a clear and distinct mind not only so as to receive the illumination but also to be able to tell which aspects of it are absolute and which conditional, and to tell what he knows by the natural light from what he knows by the prophetic—for, if confused, the one could easily be mistaken for the other.

7. A second argument for his having been deceived is the fact that, as is evident from no. 24 and several others, he is a man who is quite pleased with his own judgment and excessively fixed in it. This settledness or stubbornness in his own opinion has likely been fostered by his continuous prayers *without order* and mental exercises, along with bodily mortifications. For it is natural that the more a rational creature withdraws from material realities, the more settled its understanding becomes in what it apprehends as true or false. Often such persons, particularly when blinded by the fumes of some passion, as seems to be the case here, come to hold uncertain or even false notions as utterly true ~~and to cling to them almost unmovably, particularly melancholic persons, in whom the earthy character of this humor fosters the settledness of their positions; and this is thought to be what is happening with B. [Onfroy].~~

8. Third, also contributing to his deception is his mistreatment of his body by indiscreet corporal and mental exercises (we have heard that he coughs blood and has other ailments). In this way, I am afraid—

and it seems clear—that he has ruined the organ of his imagination and damaged his estimative or cogitative power, which serves for judging particular matters and for discerning true from false and good from evil. This disorder of the cogitative power often leads to aberrations, *etc.*; and a further indication of this would be if he has an excess of melancholic humors, as I said. By the time this document arrives, he may have shown (God forfend it!) clearer signs of this *or of worse errors in this regard*.

9. Fourth, on the side of his will and affections, we can also see how easily this deception could happen. For as the will tends in one way or another, it pulls the understanding after it and does not leave it free to judge correctly. This is why people are generally not good judges in their own affairs. Now, B. [Onfroy] obviously had a strong tendency to prolonged meditations and prayers, to the point where he wanted to go into the desert and was apparently aggrieved at having his self-love thwarted in this. This seems to be the root of the prophecies and opinions listed in nos. 8, 9, 10, 26, 27, 30, and 31, in all of which this self-love seems to shine through.

10. Fifth, as it helps against being deceived, and is a sign that one is not, when a person can be seen to be walking straight in the Lord's presence in all things and seeking his entire will, so the lack of this rectitude that is visible in B. [Onfroy] suggests the opposite. I say "lack of rectitude," for we consider it certain that his will is not in conformity with God's will, the highest rule of rectitude, since it does not conform itself through obedience with the superior's will, as may be seen in nos. 10, 30, and the rest; rather he judges and condemns it.

11. Sixth, as it is a sign that a spirit is good if it leads to the observance and love of whatever one is obliged to for the service of God our Lord, so it seems to be an evil spirit that leads to the opposite. This can be seen in no. 9 and elsewhere, where he shows how small is his devotion to the Institute of life he has embraced and has vowed to follow. For he thinks that the Society has not been well established and wants to see it reinstituted to his own liking. There is no doubt that when a person does not think well of a thing, he is generally not very diligent or thorough in fulfilling it.

12. Seventh, as it is a sign that a spirit is from God when it makes the soul more humble and lowly, with greater self-knowledge in the light which God our Lord imparts to it, so this spirit seems to be from the devil, who is evidently raising *shows that it is from his adversary and ours, as can be seen from his prompting and raising* B. [Onfroy] to consider-

able pride, whereby he judges and condemns ~~his superior~~ *the one he has taken as superior in the place of Christ our Lord*, the superior's commands, the Institute of the Society, etc.

13. Eighth, just as the mortification of spiritual vices, ~~for example,~~ *such as* ostentation and vainglory, is a sign of a good spirit, so when we see these appetites unmortified, it is a sign of the evil spirit. This lack of mortification shines through in many of the statements written about him, especially nos. 20 and 21, where he speaks of those who are in a supernatural state, or soon will be. If he had a revelation of these things, it *seems* he should not so readily make them public. Persons who have such supernatural and extraordinary favors from God *our Lord* usually apply to themselves Isaiah's words, "My secret to myself, my secret to myself" [see Isa. 24.16], my secret to myself *[sic]*—and if they do disclose anything, it is with moderation and to the degree that they deem it God's will for their neighbor's edification, or that they are commanded to.

14. Ninth, to this reason is added the next, which regards inquisitiveness, rashness, meddlesomeness, as will appear in the third part, which will follow shortly, all of which are strong indications of his bad spirit, as their contraries are of the good.

Thus, as far as his person is concerned, the confusion of mind *indicated*, the stubbornness of judgment, the damage to the bodily organs and in particular to the cogitative power, the will biased and not upright in obedience or devoted to the fulfillment of his obligations, the pride and empty show, the inquisitiveness and rashness apparent in his statements—all these lead to the conclusion that the spirit inspiring them is bad and should be opposed *as the adversary, father of lies, and enemy of all good*. But let us go on to the third set of arguments, having to do with the things themselves.

Considerations regarding Some of His Propositions

Nos. 1, 2, and 3. These and other numbers dealing with prophecies, while themselves not impossible, deserve rejection per se because of the other inappropriate or erroneous statements which have been or will be mentioned. If the spirit were good it would uniformly speak well. Second, if we examine for what purpose these revelations were made, we can find no useful purpose, rather the contrary: disquiet, etc. Third, from a ~~human~~ *rational* viewpoint, as matters stand today there is no ground for believing novelties like these. For if they are supposed to be accepted as higher than or contrary to reason, any circumspect person ought to be given arguments that would satisfy an understanding grounded in reason, to convince him that these are revelations from God *our Lord*. For unless this is clear, it is wrong to run the risk of error ~~thoughtlessly~~ *recklessly*—so much so that we are not even obligated to believe everything that genuine prophets tell us, since in matters that have not been shown to them, clearly they can be mistaken, and sometimes what they say is not what was shown them in the prophetic light, but what they understood by their own natural reasoning, as in the case of some of the persons mentioned above. Now, if this can happen with genuine prophets, how much more cautious must we be in believing persons of whom we do not know if they possess the gift of prophecy, but who rather appear ~~to be recounting the visions of their own head, etc.~~ *to be recounting visions from our adversary or from their own humors*, as with so many cases today?

15. Nos. 4 and 5. First, it does not seem right to offer opposition or resistance to the Vicar of Christ, nor indeed is martyrdom much to be desired if it is to come from this quarter. Second, neither does it seem probable ~~that God would so abandon the Pope~~ *that the Creator and Lord of all should so abandon the Pope* in the general affairs of the Church when he has never done so in spiritual matters. Third, neither is it likely that he will persecute this Society, which is so much his own and so devoted to his service—even though in itself this might be possible.

16. No. 8. As for the * [Society] having declined in spirit over the last three years as much as it has grown in numbers, ~~this is a proposition that one would have to be very familiar with God to know for certain; but as far as can be humanly judged, we think the opposite is true~~ *so far as can be reasonably judged, we believe without possibility of doubt in our Lord that the opposite is true*. First, because experience makes evident—speaking of those about whom we have knowledge here, both professed and nonprofessed—that over the last three years there has been rather a growth in spirit and virtue, in the inner man. Second, this is indicated also by the edification given at the council and in various cities here in Italy and Sicily, and in the great fruit that God *our Creator and Lord* has produced in many souls through the members of the Society in Venice, Padua, Billom, Verona, Ferrara, Bologna, Florence, Perugia, Foligno, Rome, Naples, Messina, Palermo, and many other places, as can in part be judged by the reports currently being sent and from those sent at other times. This is known also where you are—nearby in Spain as well as in the more distant Indies, Congo, and Africa, where we can readily see that ~~God~~ *his Divine Majesty* is making much use of members of the Society. And since he himself teaches us the signs for knowing the

quality of persons when he says, "By their fruits you shall know them" [Matt. 7:16], it appears we are not without grounds for supposing there has been a growth in spirit and inward goodness, since we see the extent of the outward fruits. Third, this is also Our Father's opinion, and I consider him a good witness in this matter because of his responsibility, concern, and ability to be well informed about this.

17. No. 9. As for the claim that the * [Society] is not well instituted and will be better instituted in spirit, ~~this was not, it appears, dictated to him by the Holy Spirit~~ *it is not reasonable that as confirmation of this we should be persuaded that this was dictated by the Holy Spirit,* who "is the spirit of truth" and "has knowledge of the voice" [Wis. 1:7] and can be ignorant of nothing. Rather, it is ~~apparently his own~~ *the contrary or—as it appears—his own* spirit which does not know the actual condition of the Society, which is still coming into being (apart from its *necessary and* substantial elements). For the Constitutions are partly completed and partly still being worked on, and even in the bulls some points have begun ~~to be reformed~~ *to be reviewed, the whole matter being commended to God our Lord with not a few Masses, prayers, and tears, [all this] not to mitigate what has been well founded, but to perfect it even more, so that we may proceed from good to better for the greater glory of God*—without waiting for the fulfillment of his prophecy, which seems to proceed on the assumption that the affairs of the Society have now been settled once and for all. Second, as B. [Onfroy] can see from the bulls and briefs, the Society's institution contains nothing against the spirit even as he understands it, that is to say, taking the spirit to mean longer or shorter prayer, ~~besides the fact that no limit is set for the members of the Society, not even the students, now, nor is there anything decided~~ *for until now no limit has been set for the members of the Society or for its students, nothing having been decided.* This being so, which element of the institution appears to be defective and in need of more reformation in spirit? Third, the Holy Spirit does not dictate or command to be published something that offers no advantage for the future and would do harm in the present to those who believe it, making them lose their devotion to the Society's Institute and so observe it less well. For no person would be eager to comply with what he disapproves or be careful about observing it.

18. No. 10. His refusal to communicate anything about this reformation even to the superior smacks, first, of a bad (or at the least a very low) opinion of his superior, whom he considers incompetent to receive his revelations. This does not seem deserving of credit, since God has made him the origin of the Society, not in dream (or imagination), but in reality and truth. All the higher is the opinion of himself that B.

[Onfroy] exhibits, as the only person competent, etc. Second, it smacks also of the spirit who "hates the light" [John 3:20] and thus avoids such spiritual persons, who he knows are not ignorant of his trickery and will expose his deceits. Third, one can sense a spirit of very slight obedience and respect towards those whom he obeys in the place of Christ. Fourth, this revelation seems fruitless, since it is not communicated to any person ~~who could do anything about it~~ *or in any place where some spiritual good might result.*

19. No. 13. Besides his appearing to manifest here his earlier opinions and desires regarding the desert and his personal attachment to those about whom he prophesies, the matter in itself does not seem to be properly treated. First, because when God wishes to confer the gift of prophecy, he does not usually wait to confer it until the persons give themselves totally to him in prayer, as can be seen with Moses, David, and the other prophets, who had public activities, etc. How little previous disposition God needs is visible in the case of Balaam: he was an evil man, and we are told that, although his will was bad, his intelligence was apt, etc. And did his ass have the dispositions which he demands for prophesying? Second, this disposition would be either natural, such as a great and clear understanding, etc. (and of this sort of disposition more will be found in others than in C. [Oviedo]); or it would be supernatural, a "gratia gratum faciens" or one of the gifts of the Holy Spirit, such as the gift of understanding or wisdom. Now, it has never been found that any of these was ever judged or called a disposition for prophecy. Many who were never prophets have had them, and others have been prophets without being in the state of grace or possessing these gifts of the Holy Spirit. Therefore, it is not easy to see in what way C. [Oviedo] possesses the disposition for prophecy. In fine, these seem to be imaginings, entertained and uttered in a ~~reckless~~ *rash* manner.

20. No. 14. These also seem to us to be imaginings stemming from his attachments and quite implausible, although with God everything is possible. And to say no more than is necessary, we will not expand on this, observing only that it seems that if T. [Tejeda] was supposed to be an instrument for the reform of his order, he should not have failed as he did ~~in the points of obedience~~ *in certain points of perfect obedience.* This failure he himself did not deny while here, etc.—unless this may even be a hidden dispensation of God, one which it would be rash to believe until it is made clear, as with C. [Oviedo] and B. [Onfroy], to whom something may have stuck from association with him ~~as completely disciples of his.~~

21. No. 15. Since he is uncertain, he obviously has no revelation on these matters, but a mere opinion, one in which, first, there seems to be irreverence in comparing living and mortal persons with the saints, particularly a saint like St. Francis. Second, there is rashness in such a judgment. For although he may know great things of T. [Tejeda], *he does not know everything about St. Francis. Third, from what we have learned about T. [Tejeda] here,* and whatever further qualities he may be thought to possess, we would have no difficulty answering which of the two has done greater things. Rather, a blind attachment seems to lie behind this uncertainty.

22. No. 18. ~~That R. [Raphael = Borgia] is to be the angelic pope, and so on: it is possible, and here we would yield to no one in our joy over any great enterprise in which God our Lord might make use of him; but as for the papacy, until we see it, we do better to stand apart and leave it to God our Lord.~~ *That R. [Raphael = Borgia] is to be the angelic pope: this is possible and would be quite easy for the Lord of all; and we here would hardly or not at all yield to anyone in rejoicing in our Lord over whatever great enterprise in which his Divine Majesty might make use of him; but as for this dignity, until time brings it to light, we do better to stand apart from such thoughts and leave everything to be done by his divine Goodness.*

23. Nos. 20 and 21. First of all, it displays great rashness, to say what he says in these numbers, for it is only God who weighs merits, and it is not believable that he should have revealed and reveal such interior matters to him at every step, things done and things still to be done (he says, for instance, that "he will soon advance to a supernatural state," etc.), particularly when there are so many contrary elements in him. Second, even if these things had been revealed to him, he had no business so cheaply disclosing such deep and secret matters. Third, there is no advantage in making such things known, and consequently they deserve to be condemned for vainglory and presumption. The saints, when such things were revealed to them, did not talk about them like this, for no good reason. *St. Paul went fourteen years, so far as we know, without disclosing the revelation God made to him when he was rapt to the third heaven.* Fourth, what he says about the supernatural state and continuous presence of God seems fantastical and false, for we do not read this even of the great saints, although some servants of God have a more continuous memory and more frequent actual thought of God than others. Fifth, this seems impossible in the ordinary course of things even for highly spiritual and holy persons, because such a presence requires an actual and fixed—indeed unmovable—attention in the intellect, something incompatible with our state as wayfarers. Even very

devout servants of God complain about wanderings and instability of the mind, and we read that St. John occasionally relaxed his contemplations ~~and took a bit of enjoyment with a cat (if I recall)~~ *by lowering his attention to a bird he held in his hand,* saying to a follower of his who was disedified that, just as the bow cannot remain always bent, so neither could the understanding, etc.[17] It is true that sometimes, even many times, numerous servants of God have a great and vivid awareness, quite certain and stable, of his eternal truths; but for them to remain permanently in this state ~~would seem to be a kind of perpetual ecstasy which, to our limited knowledge, the doctors have yet to mention or the saints to experience; and as for his saying, "He will quickly advance to a state, etc.," I refer to what is said above~~ *is impossible to believe.*

No. 22. This fear of his is founded on a mistake. We have had no other information here than what has come from there, partly from C. [Oviedo] himself and partly from Father Araoz. If, then, the spirit tells him there are other tares, ~~we fear, indeed, we are quite certain, that it is the one~~ *it is rather to be feared that this was dictated to him by that spirit* of whom it is written that he is a liar and the father of lies [John 8:44].

24. No. 23. This liberty of which he speaks was taken in obedience to the superior and with the sole intention of helping C. [Oviedo]; if it went beyond the bounds of moderation, this at least did not spring from tares. Of this Master Polanco is sure, and if B.'s [Onfroy's] spirit claims that he was the devil's instrument in sowing such tares, this would make it evident and certain to Polanco himself that this is not the spirit of truth. For his conscience is witness before God our Lord that he loves and has always loved C. [Oviedo] sincerely in the Lord, and that by God's grace he is and always has been far from such a practice of sowing tares. Second, what he says of Master Polanco is either a revelation or a suspicion. If it is a revelation, beyond what has been said, he should have no fears—he should know it for certain, since it was revealed to him. If it is a suspicion, he should beware that it is not against charity, or at least rash judgment.

No. 24. Here is displayed, first, the spirit of disobedience and pride in his not submitting his understanding even to his highest superior. Second, there is vanity in his seeking to give the impression that he knows all this supernaturally. Third, as we have said previously, we here consider as both fantastical and false the continuation of what he says, etc.

---

[17] See Cassian, *Collationes ss. patrum,* collat. 24, chap. 21.

25. No. 25. He either considers this a revelation—and it is certain that those who know something through the prophetic light take no other grounds of their knowledge for their own sake, even though for the sake of others they may seek the support of reason and authority—or else not a revelation, in which case we see that he had no reason for being so obstinate, since the three authors he produces are capable of error and are not all of such weighty authority. And though what they say may be well, he may not be understanding and interpreting them well. Certainly some of them, like Henry Herp, require commentary in some passages if their meaning is to be acceptable[18]—as can be seen from an author who wrote a long preface to a little book of his; I do not recall his name but, though favorable to him, he certainly says this.

Nos. 26, 27, 28. Some remarks have already been made in no. 8 about what he says here. When all is said, there is no doubting our need that God increase us in spirit and virtue from day to day, and we hope that he will do so. But he is not excused of temerity in saying what he does not know, and it is hard to escape the note of pride, as he considers himself so very spiritual, to the point of despising the Society.

26. No. 29. He says that in no religious order is there less prayer. If he means that the Institute of the Society has limited its prayer to a shorter period than do the others, he is wrong, because up to the present there is no limitation. If he means that in no order do individuals pray less than in ours, he says what is untrue, as the facts show. Moreover, he should always keep in mind that living in the colleges for studies is different from being in the residences of the Society and outside of studies.

No. 30. Here he displays where he is hurting and where so many of his prophecies arise. What he says is wrong. First, he is ready presumptuously to condemn his superior for being mistaken on a point about which he himself knows nothing. In fact, those who know anything about this know that the superior is quite right. He certainly does not forbid prayer (which Christ commands to be made and is necessary for our salvation), although he may restrict it for some individuals who spend too much time on it. And this is in keeping with God's will, for he is pleased with whatever is reasonable, moderate, and in conformity with his wisdom. Second, he shows that he does not have his judgment mortified and does not really know what obedience is.

---

[18] Henry Herp, a Franciscan spiritual writer much read in the sixteenth century. His *Theologia mystica* was published in Cologne in 1538.

27. No. 31. To say that a meditation of one and two hours is no prayer and that more hours are required is bad doctrine and opposed to the opinion and practice of the saints. First, consider the example of Christ: although he sometimes spent the night in prayer, at other times he did not spend so much, as in his prayer at the supper or his three prayers in the garden. He is not going to deny that these were prayers, nor will he claim that they each exceeded one or two hours. They probably did not exceed an hour, considering how much of the night needed to be left over for the other mysteries, etc. Second, this can be seen from the prayer Christ himself taught us: he called it a prayer even though it is short and does not take more than one or two hours to say; ~~B. should not~~ *one should not deny* that this is prayer. Third, this can be seen from the example of the holy desert fathers, who regularly practiced prayers that did not reach an hour in length, as Cassian tells us;[19] they would recite as many psalms at a time, etc., as is done in the public services and offices of the Church—unless he maintains that these are not prayer either. Fourth, the same is seen today in the practice of the faithful, and even of devout persons, of whom ~~few and they rarely~~ *not all but only a minority—in fact, very few*—exceed two hours of prayer at a time ~~in particular, and even few that long; and it would be quite true that if more time were necessary, there would be, as he claims, little prayer in the Society or outside it either~~. Fifth, if prayer is "asking God for what is proper" and, to give it a more general definition, "the elevation of the mind to God with pious and humble affection,"[20] and if this can be done in less than two hours and even in less than a half hour, how can he claim to deny the name or reality of prayer to anything that does not exceed one and two hours? Sixth, the ejaculatory prayers so much praised by Augustine and the saints would not constitute prayers.[21] Seventh, the students who study for God's service and the common good of the Church—how much more time than this does he think they should give to prayer if they are to keep their mental faculties in condition for the work of learning and preserve their health? He would do well to reflect that it is not only in prayer that God makes use of a person; otherwise, anything less than twenty-four hours of prayer a day, if such a thing were possible, would be too short, since every person should give himself to God as totally as possible. But the fact is that there are times when God is served more by other things

---

[19] *De coenobiorum institutis,* 1. 2, chaps. 2, 4, 10; 1. 3, chap. 3. 2.

[20] St. John Damascene, *De fide orthodoxa,* I. 3, chap. 24.

[21] St. Augustine, *Ad Probam,* lett. 130, chap. 10, no. 20.

than by prayer, so much so that for their sake God is happy that prayer be relinquished—and all the more that it be shortened. Thus, we should indeed "pray always and faint not," but we should understand this rightly, as the saints and doctors understand it.

No. 32. Whether this is correct or not ~~Your Lordship will better be able to see on the spot, should you wish to investigate it, in case you think it important, etc.~~ *can better be seen on the spot, in case Your Lordship thinks it important.*

This will suffice, *it would seem*, on the character of B. [Onfroy] and for the statements attributed to him. Now we will make some briefer remarks about the opinions of the person C. [Oviedo].

The Opinions of C. [Oviedo]

28. Nos. 1 and 2. We here do not fully grasp this new species of miracles: we do not see how his conversation is beyond nature and so exceptional and deserving of this name. For the name "miracle" is attributed to certain exceptional works of God outside the course of things established by his divine wisdom, and so we do not see how it should be applied to T.'s [Tejeda's] conversation. Second, it was never said of St. Paul or of St. Peter, or even of our Lady, that their dealings or communication with people was miraculous—nor even of Christ himself. Third, here we observe an excessive attachment in C. [Oviedo] which apparently impedes his understanding.

No. 3. On this the remarks made above about the continuous presence of God suffice. We here consider this matter unworthy of belief if "continuous" is understood as it stands—unless by "continuous" he means "frequent."

29. No. 4. "To hear T. [Tejeda] speaking advisedly is the same as hearing God speak." First of all, this statement seems to display an attachment and esteem for a creature that derogates from the glory of the Creator, who we know infinitely surpasses in every respect all that he has created: so we should think and speak. Second, his saying "when he speaks advisedly" is even worse. It implies speaking with greater deliberateness and personal reflection, whereas it would be less unreasonable if he claimed that hearing T. [Tejeda] was like hearing God when God was speaking in him, moving his organs, etc., rather than when he spoke on his own with deliberation. Third, [I ask] C. [Oviedo] if he means that he hears God speaking mediately (as when he spoke to Abraham and the other patriarchs through the assumed person of an angel) or immediately (as his words seem to imply)—we could ask in

either case whether he himself has ever heard God speaking. If not, how can he make such a comparison without knowing what he is comparing? Looking at this statement superficially, one would judge that the familiarity of God's conversations with C. [Oviedo] has resulted in little esteem for them—or, more accurately, that he has not genuinely experienced them, inasmuch as he compares them to the conversation of a creature. Fourth, the statement is false, for if we make a comparison of power, no one will say of T. [Tejeda] that "by his word the heavens were established," etc.; if this [statement deals with] truth, uprightness, or, in fine, any form of perfection, this comparison is unacceptable and does not appear to come from a man who is truly spiritual or thoughtful in his opinions and statements.

Nos. 5, 6, 7, 8. These things are easy for God, and if he wishes to communicate them to his creatures, he can easily do so. But to believe that they are so (as with the prophecies mentioned above), a person who is religious and prudent in the Lord would want more adequate evidence before responsibly believing them—all the more so since some of them (such as the four-month rapture) are so rare, indeed unheard-of, and hence unbelievable. Second, we ourselves can testify that here, where he did converse with us somewhat, presumably showing the best he had to offer, he did not leave in us any admiration of him, nor did he confound those who dealt with him on any topic, as is claimed in no. 8. The contrary was true: he himself acknowledged [making] certain substantial moral errors, to say nothing of possible speculative ones.

✠

To Jerónimo Nadal, by commission

Rome, July 6, 1549

(Letter 760: II:462–64; in Spanish)

Part of a memorandum for a letter to the Jesuits in Messina, listing numerous advantages of the Society's having sole governance not only of the college that had been started there but also of a proposed university. This latter project came to naught because the government at Messina wanted control of such a university. The Jesuit college, however, was a lasting success.

Messina: 4. This will also be written to Messina; and the tenor of the letter sent for showing to the city was as follows: The Society was not requesting to have the superintendence or to be burdened with so many classes and other business of the university; and the form and terms of the establishment had been sent by the viceroy, to whom the city had referred the matter. Consequently, there are no grounds for complaint about the Society, which did not accept the exception, even though it took on this enterprise out of love for Juan de Vega and in the belief that it would be greatly for the service of God and the good of the city and island if the Society were to have charge of the studies. That this would be very beneficial for them, even if burdensome for the Society, can be seen (1) from the side of teachers: if the Society takes charge of the university as something wholly its own, it will be, so to speak, constrained to keep a sufficient number of good men there, which it would not do if anyone else had overall charge. (2) There would be a consequent loss of spiritual advantages deriving from the preaching and confessions of the Society's men there, since—on the same grounds—if they did not have the main responsibility, their numbers would diminish. (3) If others had governance over the Society, it is likely that they would not employ the same highly religious statutes that those of the Society employ and wish to employ, and the results would be less, etc. (4) It is likely that with others having the governance, the lectures would not be as regular, as can be seen from the way things go in other Italian universities. (5) Peace and unity would be less well maintained, since the members would not all have the same head: either those of the Society would be under someone else, a thing incompatible with their exemption; or the others would be under the Society's governance; or one group, with so many teachers and students, would be by themselves on one side and the others by themselves on the other; and this division is not good or the way to harmony—unless they shut themselves up in the college and do not get involved in public affairs. (6) They ought to take a close look at what happens in the conduct of other universities and in that of their own insofar as it has been led by the Society; and they will see the difference in conduct and learning, etc. (7) How many dissensions will be avoided by this governance and by not seeking exemptions. (8) More exercise in letters. (9) More scholars of the Society, and hence better examples, etc. (10) More concern for their sons. (11) More honor and praise and merit for erecting a university where religion and letters are learned together. (12) If they have been satisfied so far, then there will be no change. (13) In giving degrees they will act conscientiously, well, gratis, etc.

5. As for sending an arts [philosophy] instructor to Messina: if N.[22] is dismissed, someone will be sent in his place; otherwise, so long as the

---

[22] The troublesome Isidoro Bellini.

erection of a university remains undecided, etc., it would be unwise to send any more teachers, since there are already plenty.

6. As to the plan for the house of probation: Father finds it excellent, and says that for more than eight months it has been in the [draft text of the] Constitutions that there should be one, even here in Rome; but he is happy that this one should be the first. As for Nadal himself living in it, he leaves that up to him; but he rather inclines to the contrary—that Master André should stay there and he in the college.

7. As for N., Our Father refers to what was said last Saturday.

✠

To Juan Alvarez, by commission

Rome, July 18, 1549

(Letter 776: II:478–84; in Spanish)

Ignatius had authorized several Jesuits in Salamanca to take legal action in response to the attacks on the Society by the Dominican Melchior Cano. Alvarez thought this use of human means was "bending the knee to Baal." Polanco relays to Alvarez reproofs from St. Ignatius regarding his letters to Rome and his disdain for the use of such human means in God's service: God, the source of both grace and nature, wants both employed to the full.

It will come as no surprise to you that reproofs are sent out from Rome.[23] Nor do I think that you will be displeased to receive these which I have to send you on behalf of Master Ignatius—indeed, I assume you will treasure them above rubies. If I go into them at some length, lay it not solely to what you deserve but also to our idea of your fortitude, which lets us say to you whatever we think is needed. And since I am only the pen, you should take none of this as coming from me (I would have to do the same in censuring myself), but from Our Father, who ordered this for you.

First of all, while it is fine that you displayed obedience in the matter of writing every week, you did so rather haphazardly in that you kept the letters in the house. After writing the letters, you should also have tried to find someone to carry them. At least they could have been sent to Valladolid, where there are usually a good number of persons leaving for here. Our Father thinks that from now on it will suffice to

---

[23] *Capello*, here translated "reproof," also means "hat"; hence, we find here a pun on the cardinals' hats dispatched from Rome.

write every other week (unless for a particular reason someone wishes to write oftener) and that some way of sending them should be looked into every week.

Second. As to the manner of writing, the Society's practice is to include in letters that will be shown to others only matters suitable for anyone to see. Matters relating to business, or items not for everyone, are written on separate sheets or secondary letters which accompany those that can be shown around. Since you did not do this with your letters, we could not show them here. In accord with Our Father's instructions to me, your letters are being returned to you with lines drawn so that you can see what you should have written on separate sheets—that is, all the material outside the lines. We still have here everything that was marked, and which was removed for showing to the Cardinal of Coria, etc.

Third. You should also pay more attention to your spelling, particularly in Latin; and you should use Latin with ever increasing moderation and at the proper time.

Fourth. As to what you repeatedly mentioned when speaking of the letter of the licentiate Madrid, the fact is that nobody in the Society saw it;[24] having seen your letters and others with the remarks about Father Cano of which you are aware, he must have been moved to write the letter out of the abundance of his heart and because of his friendship with the Society. In consideration of his good intentions at least, he did not deserve all the heavy blows you deal him in nearly all your letters.

Fifth. You further declare, as you will see by your letter, that you decided not to make use of the documents we had sent you: having examined the matter after commending it to God, you deemed this preferable because of altered circumstances, etc. All well and good. But in giving your reasons why these means should not be used, your philosophizing appears faulty to us. You take so spiritual an approach that you seem to lose a proper grasp of the matter. You write as if you thought it was a base and human spirit to employ such measures and seek such favors, as though this were bending the knee to Baal, and so on. In another passage also, speaking of a different letter written by Our Father to Master Gallo at the request of Don Diego de Acevedo, when he himself wrote to his relatives, you say that they experienced the purest

---

[24] Referred to here is Cristóbal de Madrid, who later entered the Society.

joy, etc., at its being unleavened by this sort of means, as you will see at greater length in your letter.[25]

There are many things wrong with this manner of writing, if I am to speak the truth as obedience bids me. First, you are evidently judging and censuring your superior, who supplied these means, as having a base and human spirit. It would be no small matter if he were thought to be bending the knee to Baal or, worse, inducing others to do so. Thus by your being so very spiritual, you fail to be such in a matter so important and substantial as the spirit of humility and obedience.

Second, even if these were your personal thoughts, it would have been a matter not just of respect for your superior but of common courtesy not to write it in this way to the very person censured—at least not so openly and in a letter destined to be shown to everybody.

Third, you seem to forget, or not to know, that these helps were requested in great part, if not entirely, from there, partly by Father Doctor Torres himself and partly by Father Master Estrada[26]—and that you yourself indicated a desire for them, writing about how they were rising up against our saintly father and about so heavy a cross. The Cardinal of Coria here thought that there was a great deal of anger in the letter. Hence, since it was mostly requested from there and partly offered to us here by persons devoted to us, it does not appear that we were bending the knee to Baal or worshiping him when we accepted these means and sent them to you.

Fourth, even if we examine your spiritual philosophy itself, it does not seem very solid or correct—namely, that to employ human helps or resources and take advantage or make use of human influence for purposes that are good and pleasing to our Lord constitute bending the knee to Baal. On the contrary, it would seem that a person who deems it wrong to use such means or to invest this talent among others bestowed by God, claiming that this would be to contaminate the higher spiritual means of grace with the leaven of lower ones, has not correctly learned how to order all things to God's glory or to make the most of all things and means for the ultimate end of God's honor and glory. A person might be said to bend the knee to Baal if he places a higher value and more reliance on such human means than on God and on his gratuitous and supernatural helps. But if, while grounding his hope wholly in God, he carefully uses for God's service the gifts that he

---

[25] See *Ep. Mixt.*, III:644f.

[26] Miguel de Torres and Francisco Estrada.

bestows, both interior and exterior, spiritual and physical, in the conviction that his infinite power can accomplish what he wills with or without such means, but that he is pleased by such efforts when properly
undertaken out of love for him, then this is bending the knee not to
Baal but to God. He acknowledges God as the author of nature as well
as of grace—an acknowledgment that appears not to be given when a
person fails to render pure thanks to God and rejoice purely in him
when human means have intervened in the events that occasion his joy
and thanksgiving. Rather, such a way of speaking seems to suppose
there is one principle of grace and another of nature. God our Lord was
quite capable of sustaining the children of Israel in Egypt without Joseph's human power and influence, but Joseph was not wrong to use his
power and influence for this purpose. Similarly, there was little need of
the power of Esther and Mardochai to deliver and save the same people,
but their using that power does not mean they worshiped Baal. It is
true that when God wishes to bestow his grace in an overflowing and
extraordinary way in order to show himself superior to all of nature,
there was little need of human help—as in the time of his primitive
Church, when he told his disciples not to think of what they were going
to say before princes, etc., since the Holy Spirit, whom he wished to
communicate to them in a special manner, had no need of their natural
abilities. But even in those days, we see that the Holy Spirit made use
of the human qualities of some members of the primitive Church, as
with Apollos or with St. Paul himself. The latter did not think he was
bending the knee to Baal when he took advantage of the animus of the
Pharisees against the Sadducees and declared, in order to free himself
from them, "I am being tried about the resurrection of the dead" [Acts
23:6]; or took advantage of his Roman citizenship when they wanted to
deal harshly with him; or told King Agrippa that he considered himself
fortunate in being able to plead his case before him; or in his letters to
various persons employed measures of great human prudence, assisted
by superhuman prudence, which the author of both the one and the
other imparted to him.

After the time of the primitive Church, when things were more
established, we see that this was the common practice of the Greek
doctors, Athanasius, Basil, Gregory Nazianzen, and Chrysostom; of the
Latin fathers, Jerome and Augustine, and Ambrose before them, and
afterwards of Pope Gregory and the others who followed him. They
employed human talents and efforts—learning, eloquence, skill, and
even the arms of the mighty—for holy purposes in God's service. They
did not think they were worshiping Baal but God almighty, whom alone

they served with both natural and supernatural means. Thus, it is a conclusion of the Scholastic doctors that human means should be employed and that it would often be tempting God if, while not seizing the means that God places in our hands, we always looked for miracles instead. But this should suffice. In sum: the use of human means at the proper time, when directed purely to God's service, is not wrong, provided we keep our hope firmly anchored in God and in his grace. However, with regard to not using such means when God dispenses from them by providing otherwise, or when there is no expectation that they will be of avail for his greater service, we are all in agreement.

Sixth, as regards the document from the Dominicans and the two clauses which it ought to contain, it will not be difficult to have them supplied—unless, of course, this would be bending the knee to Baal, etc. As a matter of fact, nobody from the Society spoke to the aforesaid general to obtain it, or for the similar one that was issued there in Valladolid by the Franciscan general. Who requested it I do not know, but I am certain it was no one from the Society. I inform you that as many copies as are wanted can be made of either document.

Because of what is said in all or part of the above, our father master in Christ Ignatius says that you are not to function as secretary until you learn how to do it better, unless your letters have been shown to Father Doctor [Torres] or Father Estrada and come signed by the hand of one or the other.

This is what I had to say by His Paternity's commission and mandate. I know there will be no more need of compliments at the end than there was of courtesies at the beginning. As for me, I commend myself to your holy prayers.

Rome, July 18, 1549

Your servant in Jesus Christ,

JUAN DE POLANCO, by commission of our father Master Ignatius

To Francis Borgia, duke of Gandía

Rome, July 27, 1549

(Letter 790: II:494f.; in Spanish)

Besides the foregoing long report about the vagaries of Fathers Oviedo and Onfroy, Ignatius sent Borgia the following solemn attestation of their errors and request that he take steps to prevent further harm.

If what is written us is correct, it seems that B. [Onfroy] and C. [Oviedo], one more than the other, have found the desert they originally sought and are preparing themselves to find an even greater desert unless they can humble themselves and let themselves be guided according to each one's profession. It is evident that some remedy is essential; it can come to them immediately or by the instrumentality of one who is willing on his part and possesses complete sway. The former solicits us to prayer and Sacrifices before the divine Goodness; the latter would be if, by God's favor, Your Lordship is able by some means to achieve a good deal by your authority and presence.

Hence, looking to my obligation in conscience, and believing, moreover, without the slightest doubt and affirming before the tribunal of Christ our Creator and Lord, my eternal Judge, that they are wandering from the way, misled and in error, sometimes on and sometimes off the track under the influence of the father of lies, whose work is to declare or intimate one or even many truths so as then to come off with a lie and ensnare us in it—I ask Your Lordship, by the love and reverence of God our Lord, commending the whole affair to his supreme goodness, to give the matter much thought, keep watch, and take appropriate measures, not showing indulgence where so much scandal and harm can be caused on all sides, but seeing to it that everything turns out so that his Divine Majesty may be served in all things and the men themselves entirely restored for his greater service, praise, and glory, for ever and ever.

Rome, July 27, 1549

To the Members of the Society Leaving for Germany

Rome, September 24, 1549

(XII [Appendix 1, no. 18]: 239–47; in Latin)

William IV, duke of Bavaria, had appealed to Pope Paul III and to Ignatius to send several Jesuits as professors of theology to the university of Ingolstadt, an institution that had fallen into severe decline. Salmerón, Jay, and Canisius were chosen for the task. For them Ignatius wrote the following instruction, urging them to fulfill the specific mission for which they were called but at the same time to carry out the full range of the Society's ministries, concentrating their efforts on persons of influence and likely future ministers, and doing all they can to promote the founding of a college of the Society in Bavaria. The actual establishment of the Jesuit college took place only in 1556 under the next duke, Albert V, after lengthy and complicated negotiations (see letter 6226).

Helps for Those Departing for Germany

The goal to be chiefly kept in sight is that intended by the Sovereign Pontiff in sending this mission, namely, to help the university at Ingolstadt and, as far as possible, Germany itself in matters related to correctness of faith, obedience to the Church, and solid, wholesome doctrine and life.

A secondary goal will be to promote the Society in Germany, in particular by endeavoring to start colleges of the Society at Ingolstadt and elsewhere, for the common good and the glory of God.

The means for pursuing these closely related goals are themselves closely related; however, some contribute equally to both, some more to the first, and others more to the second. Hence, we shall treat them in that order.

Means Common to the Pursuit of Both Goals

1. The first and most important help will be if, placing no confidence in yourselves at all, you trust courageously in God and have a strong desire, aroused and nourished by charity and obedience, for achieving your goal; this will ensure that you keep your goal always in mind and before your eyes, commend it to God in your prayers and holy Sacrifices, and make diligent use of every appropriate means.

2. The second is a life that is excellent in itself and hence a pattern for others. This means avoiding not just evil but every appearance of evil, as well as showing yourselves models of charity and every virtue. This will be of great help to Germany, so much in need of such models.

Moreover, in this way, without your saying a word, the Society will be promoted and God will fight on its behalf.

3. You should have and display a sincere charity towards all, particularly persons of greater consequence for the common good. Among these is the duke himself; you should apologize to him for your late arrival and signify to him the love in which he is held by the Sovereign Pontiff and the Holy See, as also by the Society; and you should earnestly promise to work hard on behalf of his subjects, etc.

4. You should display your love in word and truth and render good services to large numbers of persons, by both spiritual assistance and exterior works of charity, as indicated below.

5. People should be able to see that you seek, not your own interests, but those of Jesus Christ, that is, his glory and the salvation of souls; and that for this reason you accept no stipends for Masses or for the ministry of the word or sacraments, and may possess no revenues.

6. You should make yourselves beloved by your humility and charity, becoming all things to all men. You should adapt to the local customs insofar as the Society's religious Institute allows, and as far as possible never let anyone depart from you unhappy (except if it contributes to his salvation). In your efforts to please, however, you should respect your conscience and not let excessive familiarity breed contempt.

7. Where factions and party strife prevail, you should not take a stand against either side, but instead show that you remain in the middle and love both parties.

8. It will help very much if, in the opinion of everyone, but particularly of the prince and notables, you yourselves and the Society as a whole enjoy solid authority and a reputation (grounded in fact) for sound teaching. This authority will be much fostered by outward as well as inward gravity in your gait and gestures, the propriety of your dress, and especially the circumspection of your speech and the maturity of your counsel on both practical and doctrinal matters. This maturity entails not hastily giving your opinion on any question (unless it is quite easy), but taking time to think about it, study it, or consult with others.

9. You should cultivate special bonds of goodwill with those who exercise supreme power. It will be of considerable help in this regard if you are able as much as possible to assist both the duke himself and the more influential members of his household through confessions and the Spiritual Exercises. You should also try to win over the university profes-

sors and other dignitaries by your deep humility and modesty and by rendering them becoming acts of service.

10. Hence, if you know of anyone, especially among the more influential persons, who has an unfavorable opinion of the Society or of yourselves, you should take prudent countermeasures, supplying the person with information about the Society and yourselves, to God's glory.

11. It will be helpful to have a good idea of individual persons' ways of acting and to plan ahead for various contingencies, especially in more important matters.

12. It will be advantageous for all the companions not only to think and to say the same thing but also to dress alike and act alike in ceremonies and other external matters.

13. The brethren should individually reflect on how best to achieve the above-mentioned goals, and confer with each other; and the superior, after hearing the others, will decide what should or should not be done.

14. They will take care to write to Rome either for advice or to report on the state of affairs. This should be done very frequently, for it could be of no little help in all matters.

15. You should occasionally reread these and the following guidelines, along with any others that may be added, so as to refresh your memory of them in case it fades.

Means Chiefly for the Primary Goal, namely, the Upbuilding of Germany in Faith and in Christian Doctrine and Life

1. The first thing is to do well in your public lectures; these are the main thing for which you were requested by the duke and sent by the Sovereign Pontiff. You should give solid doctrine without too much Scholastic terminology, which tends to put people off, particularly when abstruse: the lectures should be learned but comprehensible. They should be regular but not too long or too rhetorical. Prudence will dictate how much use to make of disputations and other academic exercises.

2. To increase your audience and be of most benefit to them, you should not only nourish the mind but also add things that will nourish the religious affections, so that the hearers go home from your lectures not just more learned but better persons.

3. In addition to the Scholastic lectures, it would be good to have sermons or biblical lectures on feast days. The aim of these is less to

instruct the intellect than to move the affections and shape behavior. They can be given either in Latin in the schools or in German by Master Canisius in the church where crowds of people attend.

4. So far as these essential occupations permit, you should devote time to the hearing of confessions, in which one ordinarily reaps the fruits of the plants that have been cultivated in lectures and sermons. You should hear the confessions not so much of women and common people (they should be sent to others for this purpose) as of young men of good character who might themselves become pastoral workers, as well as of other persons who, if given spiritual aid, could make a greater contribution to the common good. For when we cannot satisfy everyone, preference should certainly go to those who promise a greater return in the Lord.

5. You should endeavor to draw your students to spiritual friendship, and if possible to confession and the Spiritual Exercises; these should be the full Exercises for those who appear suited for the Society's Institute, while you should admit and even invite larger numbers to the Exercises of the First Week, and teach them as well a method of prayer, etc.—mainly, however, [these should be] persons from whom a greater good may be expected and whose friendship should be sought for God's sake.

6. For the same reason, great importance should be given to conversation and familiar dealings with persons of this sort; and while on occasion you may digress to a merely human topic because of their individual interests, you should return to the goal of their spiritual improvement, lest your conversations be useless.

7. You should also devote some time to more visible pious activities—hospitals, prisons, or other ways of helping the poor—which beget a good reputation in the Lord.

Such also are the reconciling of those involved in disagreements and the teaching of catechism to the uneducated where these are appropriate; prudence will dictate whether, depending upon the place and the disposition of the people, this should be done by yourselves or through others.

8. You should attempt to win the friendship of any leading adversaries and of the more influential among those who are heretics, or suspected of heresy, and are not altogether obdurate. You should try to withdraw them from their error tactfully and lovingly; some guidelines for this are being written elsewhere.

9. You should be competent in cases of conscience. With particularly difficult cases, you should take time, as was said above, for study or

consultation. For while you ought to avoid excessive scrupulosity and anxiety, you should not be overly lax, indulgent, or unconcerned, to the peril of your own and others' souls.

10. You should all try to have at your fingertips the matters regarding dogmas of faith controverted with the heretics, particularly nowadays where you are and among the people you deal with, so that where appropriate you can assert and defend Catholic truth, attack errors, and strengthen the doubtful or wavering, both in lectures or sermons and in confessions or conversations.

11. As to the manner of doing this, remember that, adapting yourselves to the character and inclinations of persons, you should act with prudence and proportion, not putting new wine into old wineskins, etc.

12. In defending the Apostolic See and its authority and bringing people to sincere obedience thereto, be careful that you do not, by incautious defenses, lose credibility as "papalists." Conversely, your zeal in pursuing heresy should evidence above all love for the heretics' persons, desire for their salvation, and compassion for them.

13. It will help to make good use of the Society's faculties and of those granted by the Sovereign Pontiff; these should be dispensed for building up and not for tearing down, generously but wisely.

14. It will help to dispose people as far as possible for God's grace by exhorting them to a desire for salvation and to prayers, alms, and all kinds of charitable works, which contribute to the reception and increase of grace.

15. To help your hearers to grasp, retain, and practice what you set before them, you should consider whether something might be given in writing, and to whom.

16. It is important that, either through the duke, Eck, or other friends, a convenient site be selected for celebrating Mass, hearing confessions, preaching, and being available to people who seek you out.[27]

17. It will help for the priests of the Society to confer with each other on their studies and sermons, and to criticize each other's lectures; in this way, any shortcomings in your lectures can be corrected at home, so that they will be more acceptable and helpful to your hearers.

---

[27] Leonhard Eck was a counselor of the duke, friendly to the Society; the duke sent him to Rome to ask for the three Jesuits for Ingolstadt.

Means for the Secondary Goal, the Society's Promotion in Germany

Besides the above measures, which would perhaps suffice without recourse to any others, a few more specific ones will be mentioned here. They come down to convincing the duke and other influential persons of the desirability and feasibility of having seminaries of the Society in their dominions.

1. The first is that efforts to found a college should not appear to be of our own doing, but that they should clearly stem from concern for the good of Germany and in no way from ambition or self-seeking on our part. We should make it clear that the Society appropriates to itself from the colleges nothing but toil and the exercise of charity, and that the college's revenues will be spent on the education of poor students, so that after their education they can be more useful laborers in the vineyard of Christ.

2. Regarding those in a position to influence the Duke of Bavaria and the persons around him (such as Eck) to found a college, let them take care not to speak of the college itself but to influence their minds in such a way that they themselves will gradually come to this conclusion.

3. For this it will help if they have a good opinion of the Society's Institute, being informed about those aspects of it more likely to please them and about the progress which by God's grace the Society has made over just a few years in so many parts of the world. This account will be all the more effective if the duke has already begun to experience some of these results in his own dominion.

4. Show the duke how valuable it will be for his own subjects, and indeed for all of Germany, to have seminaries of men who, unmotivated by ambition or avarice, will help others by sound teaching and the example of their life. Tell him the experience of the King of Portugal, who from a single college of the Society has provided spiritual workers for numerous places in the Indies, Ethiopia, and Africa, even outside his own kingdom.

5. Indicate to him how advantageous it will be for the university at Ingolstadt to have there, as at Messina and Gandía, a college where not only theology but also languages and philosophy are taught with Scholastic exercises after the mode of Paris.

6. Show him what a great crown awaits him if he is the first to introduce into Germany colleges of this sort for the advancement of sound doctrine and religious practice.

7. To convince him of its feasibility, he should be informed that colleges of this kind may be founded and endowed by allocating the income of benefices, abbeys, or other pious works that are no longer useful, especially given the strong approval of the Sovereign Pontiff and the leading cardinals for the establishment of such colleges.

8. If others join the Society's Institute and increase the body of men living there at the duke's expense, this might make it easier to induce him, in order to be free of this burden and the teachers' salaries, to take steps for getting a perpetual endowment for the college.

9. Many of these matters could be more conveniently and fittingly handled by persons having influence with the duke, such as Eck and others of the duke's friends, especially magnates such as the cardinals, who can write to the duke about the Pope's mind. All this will be more effective if early results of our work have begun to justify it.

10. If the duke or others seem inclined to want the colleges to be more open, and even have others besides religious living in them, they should be told that the college can include both religious and others so long as the administration remains in the hands of those who by their teaching and example can advance others in both studies and religion.

11. Investigate also whether there may not be private persons of greater income or property who are being moved by God to start the college. Steps should be taken to interest these persons and other magnates in this, for the common good of Germany.

12. Besides the colleges, the Society's cause can be promoted by attracting young men (and older ones, if educated) to its Institute. This can be done by the example of your lives, by getting them to know us better through the Exercises and spiritual conversations, and by other means discussed elsewhere. If these persons cannot be supported there or would be better off not remaining there, they should be sent to Rome or other parts of the Society. Similarly, we can, if necessary, transfer men from other places—Cologne or Louvain, for example—to Ingolstadt.

To Francis Xavier

Rome, October 10, 1549

(Letter 893: II:557f.; in Latin)

In this letter, rather formal and solemn in tone, probably because it was meant to be seen or heard publicly, Ignatius appoints Xavier provincial superior of all the Jesuits in the Indies.

Ignatius of Loyola, superior general of the Society of Jesus, to our beloved brother in Christ, Master Francis Xavier, priest of the same Society: eternal welfare in the Lord.

Inasmuch as, with the daily growth in the number of those who by the grace of our Lord Jesus Christ follow our Institute in various lands, there grows also the need on our part to provide for a multitude of affairs and consequently to share this burden with others, we have decided in the Lord to name one of our brothers as our representative to be the superior of all those living under the obedience of our Society in India and the other overseas territories, both under the rule of His Serene Highness the King of Portugal and beyond, and to invest this superior with all other attributes of our office.

Wherefore, deeply confident in Christ Jesus of the piety and prudence you possess in him, we name and establish you as provincial superior of all our men dwelling in the above-mentioned territories, with the entire authority granted us by the Apostolic See and vested in us by the Society's Constitutions. Moreover, we direct you in virtue of holy obedience that, accepting this share in our responsibility and authority, you make the fullest use of it for investigating, ordering, reforming, commanding, and forbidding; for receiving whomever you see fit into the Society on probation and for dismissing them; for placing men in any office and for removing them—in short, for taking any measures which we ourselves, if present, would have the power to take regarding places, things, and persons having to do with the Society, as you shall judge to be for the glory of God.

Considering the grace of God in you, we trust in the Lord that this will be for his honor and for the spiritual advantage of those committed to our care, as well as for the universal welfare of souls.

Given at Rome on the tenth of October, 1549

IGNATIUS

✠

To Andreas Iseren, by commission

Rome, December 2, 1549

(Letter 957: II:602f ; in Latin)

A Dutch Jesuit at Louvain, Iseren was unhappy studying under obedience because of what he considered his special calling to preach. Polanco attempts in this letter to urge the prior claims of obedience. A year later Ignatius opposed the ordination of Iseren, and after that there is no evidence of his remaining in the Society.

Beloved in Christ Master Andreas:

We congratulate you in the Lord on your progress in theological studies and other gifts of God. But we are uncertain whether we ought to congratulate you on the spirit of preaching and on the fervor and grace which you write that God has bestowed on you, since we know that St. Paul tells us not to believe every spirit [1 John 4:1]—although in Christ Jesus we both wish and hope for whatever is best. But if you should ask how to test whether such a spirit is from God, I think you should explore whether you find it hard and painful to submit to obedience in this matter. And if you are unable to find peace in the directions of Masters Adrian [Adriaenssens] and Cornelius [Brogelmans], then you should convince yourself that this spirit is not from God. For God, having no need of our goods in order to bring souls back to himself, employs as his ministers those whom he himself deigns to call to this. But how can you think that God is calling you to what you are called away from by obedience, which you have chosen for yourself as the interpreter of God's will? I will also add, dear Andreas, that after listening to the matter, Our Father in Christ replied to me that you really need to work harder at learning obedience. Come then, abandon the unsure and perilous path of your own judgment and follow the sure and safe path of obedience. Make up your mind that what your fathers and brothers tell you is what pleases God and will also be best for you and for your neighbors.

Please be sure to take care of your health also, and not to strain yourself in your spiritual exertions.

Farewell in the Lord Jesus Christ, and commend us to him in your prayers.

Rome, December 2, 1549

✠

To Girolamo Croce

Rome, December 4, 1549

(Letter 958: II:603–6; in Italian)

Ignatius writes to an angry father, firmly defending the decision by the latter's nineteen-year-old son to seek admission to the Society.

Honored Sir:

The sovereign grace and eternal love of Christ our Lord be always our continual support and help. Amen.

I recently wrote Your Lordship at length; but discovering that my letter was not delivered to you, I am writing it to you a second time. I had learned that Your Lordship was complaining of us and displaying no little resentment on account of Lucio, your son. And since I am convinced that this comes from your not having accurate information about everything that happened, I wish to provide it for you now, so that you will realize that our intention was to render service to God and to Your Lordship as well in a matter that touches you so closely. And although I have no need to offer excuses wherever the counsels and teaching of Jesus Christ are known, nevertheless, for Your Lordship's consolation and in order to satisfy the friendship in our Lord that we have with Your Lordship, I decided to write you this and the previous letter.

Your Lordship should know that Lucio came to confession in our church. He was unknown and had not otherwise spoken to the confessor or to anyone else in the house. He indicated that he wished to betake himself apart in order to serve God following our manner of proceeding. He urged the confessor to intervene with me to get him admitted. The confessor reported this to Master Polanco, who customarily examines those wishing to follow our Society, and on the following day brought Lucio to talk with him. Master Polanco asked him his age, his intentions, his motives for his decision, and how long he had felt this desire. Lucio replied composedly that he was nineteen years old; that his devotion impelled him to follow our Institute in order to remove himself from the sins of the world and better save his own soul by greater service to God our Lord; that he had felt inclined to the good all his life, although he had been led astray somewhat by companions; and that he had felt this desire for a year more or less. Similarly, when questioned about other points regarding religious life and the difficulties it entails, he showed himself quite willing and eager even to serve in hospitals and to go on pilgrimage as a beggar without money, or serve in the kitchen or in other humble offices.

In view of his excellent dispositions and the testimony of his confessor and believing that God was inspiring him, Master Polanco reported to me. He informed me that during the examination he had learned that Lucio was Your Lordship's son. In spite of all this, in order to test his constancy, we deemed it good to have him return to the house of My Lord the Bishop and remain living there as usual for a number of days, during which he could visit our house to be examined fully.[28] This he did, staying for eleven or twelve days. Then Master Polanco asked him (I myself did not speak with him) if he wished to enter our house. He indicated a wish to get farther away from his own house, so that he would not be disturbed in his resolution. When asked if he would like to go to Bologna or to Padua, he indicated a desire to get even farther away.

Consequently, since it so happened that we were about to send two men from our house to Sicily, where our Society has two colleges, in Messina and in Palermo, we sent Lucio along with them, at his expressed strong desire and request. On that same day they received the Blessed Sacrament at St. Sebastian's and set off on horseback with the courier as far as Naples. There they embarked, and we have learned that they arrived safely in Sicily, where he will have every opportunity to acquire not only virtue but learning of every sort: humanities, philosophy, and theology—all of which subjects are taught very seriously in our colleges by quite learned persons. Inasmuch as Your Lordship and your brother the bishop had destined your son for the Church, it seems to me that you should consider it a service on our part to relieve you of worry and expense in his regard and to place Lucio where he can become virtuous and learned, as I trust he will, bringing honor and great consolation to Your Lordships as well as spiritual aid (as I trust) to his city there, for the spiritual assistance of which it may be that God wishes to employ this instrument. Moreover, as far as we ourselves are concerned, Your Lordship can see that we have no other interest than the service of God and the help of Lucio's own soul and those of others who may be helped through him. Furthermore, he has not yet been admitted to our Society, and he will not be able to make profession in it, even if he wished, for eight to ten years, until he completes his studies. Your Lordship may be quite certain that he will not be admitted to profession for many years, as I have stated, and that in the meantime you will be able to see him and have consolation from him in our Lord; at least nothing shall be wanting from our side. All this being understood, I

---

[28] Reference is to Lucio's uncle Marcantonio, bishop of Tivoli.

leave it to Your Lordship to reflect whether you have more cause to thank us for the service we have done you or to complain of us.

Señor Luis de Mendoza knew nothing about this until Lucio had left;[29] I subsequently informed him and the papal vicar in confession.[30] But later, in view of what had happened to the lamented Master Alessandro[31]—for whom we grieve as reason demands, although his excellent dispositions give us hope that the Lord God has transferred him from temporal to eternal life—in view, I say, of this, and wishing to spare Your Lordship one affliction on top of another, I gave them permission to inform you that your son was alive and well, and had him send you a letter, which he wrote to Your Lordship from Naples.

That is all for now, except that I pray God to grant all of us copious grace always to know his holy will and entirely to fulfill it; and may he grant Your Lordship such light and such burning charity for his service that you may render his divine Goodness heartfelt thanks for placing your son in the situation where he now finds himself.

Rome, December 4, 1549

✠

To the Whole Society, by commission

Rome, December 8, 1549

(Letter 959: II:606–8; in Spanish)

A letter on the death of Pietro Codazzo, the Italian cleric who had donated his property to the Society and became the first Italian Jesuit, serving as the Society's financial officer in Rome.

Very Reverend Father in Christ:

May the grace and peace of Jesus Christ our God and Lord be always present and increase in our souls.

This is only to let Your Reverence know that yesterday, Saturday, the feast of St. Ambrose, it pleased God our Lord to take our good Master Pietro Codazzo from this temporal life—as we trust in his mercy

---

[29] Luis de Mendoza, a good friend of the Society, allowed the Jesuits to use a house he owned near Tivoli.

[30] Filippo Archinto was not only papal vicar for Rome but also governor of the city and bishop of Borgo San Sepulcro.

[31] Lucio's brother, who had died.

and in the grace which he gave him for loving and serving him—and to transfer him to the eternal and most happy life. He had long been heavily burdened and indicating a wish that God our Lord might deign to shorten his pilgrimage. On Tuesday, December 3, he said Mass with much devotion. That same day he felt more than usually unwell; the following day he was worse, suffering three bouts of chills and fevers in less than a day. On Saturday he felt better and tried to go from his room into another one to visit those who were sick; as he entered he felt faint and then collapsed, uttering the words "Jesus! Jesus! Jesus!" Others called our father Master Ignatius, who had spoken with him shortly before; and in his arms and those of others of the house, he rendered his spirit to the one who had created and redeemed him, had given him much grace to labor in his holy service during his lifetime, and thus seems to have wished to shorten his death so as to bring him more quickly to unending rest. May Jesus Christ, our life and all our good, be blessed for everything. Amen.

It is right that we should remember him as a founder by saying the Masses and prayers which Your Reverence knows are customary according to the Constitutions, and with which we should be even more generous in his case, since he was a founder and had lived and died with such constancy in the Society's obedience, serving this house and the entire Society with his person as well as with his property, and receiving many trials, insults, and detractions for the sake of Jesus Christ; in addition, he helped many to abandon their sins and return to the service of God. And although his many good works will follow and aid him, we on our part should show him due gratitude.

Our Father took special care not only of his soul but also of the burial of his body;[32] and with regard to his debts (which, with the burden of the whole house and of the construction that he bore, we learned were large, over a thousand scudi), Our Father pronounced himself liable for them, having the preacher declare this from the pulpit; he is ready to go to prison if need be to ensure that good Master Pietro is less hindered from enjoying the repayment of his labors in the presence of God.

---

[32] Besides the usual Masses and prayers, Ignatius ordered a specially inscribed tombstone for Codazzo.

On other matters I wrote this past week, though the letters have not yet left; I believe they will go with this one. And so nothing else occurs to me except that we all earnestly commend ourselves to Your Reverence's prayers.

May Jesus Christ be pleased to give us grace always to know and do his holy will.

Rome, December 8, 1549

Your Reverence's servant in Christ,
+JUAN DE POLANCO+

✳ 1550–1551 ✳

To All Superiors of the Society

Rome, January 13, 1550

(Letter 1005: II:646f.; in Latin)

By the time Ignatius wrote this letter, the Society had been in existence for almost ten years; in Italy and in the three provinces of Portugal, Spain, and the Indies, it had established itself in twenty-two houses. This made it all the more important to send written reports to Rome on a regular basis. In order to achieve this goal, Ignatius here resorts to a solemn command in virtue of holy obedience.

Ignatius of Loyola, superior general of the Society of Jesus.

To my beloved brothers in Christ, superiors of the provinces, colleges, and other places and communities of the same Society: greetings and everlasting welfare in the Lord.

Experience has shown us how greatly care in writing to us and furnishing us with needed information contributes to the requisite carrying out of our own office, to the union and mutual consolation of the Society scattered throughout many different parts of the world, and to the more rapid and effective dispatching of affairs for the glory of God and the edification of souls; and, contrariwise, how negligence in this regard seriously impairs all of the above. Consequently, we have decided in the Lord that we ought to ensure this in the most efficacious manner possible.

Therefore, we address all of you who are constituted in the name of our Lord Jesus Christ as superiors over provinces, colleges, or any communities of the Society numbering three or more members, whether rectors or superiors under any other title; we urge you in the Holy Spirit and enjoin you in virtue of holy obedience that you write to us, either yourselves or through others, and take due care to see that your letters reach us; those in Italy and Sicily once a week, those in Germany, Flanders, France, Spain, and Portugal once a month; and those in the far Indies once a year. In view of the great importance of this matter, we have decided that it is in accord with the will of God that we should have recourse to this solemn and inviolable obligation of obedience, in order to close the door on negligence and arouse in all a sense of urgency.

Given at Rome in the house of the Society of Jesus, January 13, 1550

IGNATIUS

✠

To Juan de Vega

Rome, April 12, 1550

(Letter 1145: III:13–15; in Spanish)

A heartfelt letter of consolation to Juan de Vega, viceroy of Sicily, on the death of his wife, Leonor de Osorio. They both had been devoted friends of Ignatius when her husband was Charles V's ambassador in Rome, and she was both his "spiritual daughter" (as he himself called her) and one of his most effective collaborators in works such as the House of St. Marta for reformed prostitutes. Two of the early Jesuits, Diego Laínez and Jerónimo Doménech, assisted at her deathbed.

JHS.

My Lord in our Lord:

May the sovereign grace and eternal love of Christ our Lord greet and visit Your Lordship with his most holy gifts and spiritual graces.

Last night, Friday, I learned from a letter dated March 30 that God our Creator and Lord had taken to himself your dearly beloved lady, Doña Leonor, whom he had so loved and enriched in this life with special graces and virtues and had permitted to send such a great treasure of good and holy works before her to his heavenly kingdom. May our Lord be always blessed for all that his most holy providence disposes. And since, through the death of Christ our Lord and Redeemer, he undid our own death, making it the conclusion of our temporal miseries and the beginning of eternal life and happiness for those who die in his love and grace, may it please his infinite and supreme Goodness not only to have made Doña Leonor a sharer in the fruit of the blood and death of his only-begotten Son but also to fill up the emptiness that her absence might cause in us who remain here. For certainly, if we look only to Her Ladyship, the tenderer and truer is the love towards her to which she bound us while alive, the fewer are our grounds for grief, in that her life and works leave us no room for doubt that their most generous and merciful Rewarder has placed her among his elect and blessed saints. If we look to ourselves who are left behind, the absence of someone whose presence was so good and desirable cannot help leaving profound sadness—although I am convinced in our Lord that she will aid us all from heaven not less but far more than from here on earth, since her charity and power are magnified the more she is united with the infinite charity and power of her Creator and Lord.

As for Your Lordship's own person, I am confident that you will accept this visitation from his hand with that magnanimity and fortitude of mind with which the Author of all good has endowed you.

May his sovereign Clemency be pleased to communicate itself to Your Lordship and guide your household and all the affairs of your government in such a way that you may know and experience that this matter lies entirely in the providence and hand of his Divine Majesty, under whose rule and government Your Lordship can find rest and consolation in all your affairs.

As for ourselves—more by way of fulfilling in some measure the gratitude we all owe towards so much love and so many kindnesses than with the idea that a person who lived and died as she did needs this sort of assistance—over and above the Masses and prayers of the whole house here, we will write to every part of the Society to do the same, for all of them are aware of our immense obligation, one which we rejoice constantly to owe in our Lord.

May he in his infinite and sovereign goodness grant his most holy peace and never ending glory to those whom he takes from this world; to Your Lordship and to all of us still here in it, may he deign to grant his abundant grace, so that we may always know his most holy will and perfectly fulfill it.

Rome, April 12, 1550

✠

To Isabel de Vega

Rome, April 12, 1550

(Letter 1146: III:17–19; in Spanish)

A letter of consolation for her mother's death to the daughter of the Society's patron in Sicily, the viceroy Juan de Vega. Both Fathers Laínez and Doménech ministered to her in her grief, and this is one of several letters Ignatius wrote to her on the subject of her mother's death. Isabel had taken part in her mother's activities in Rome on behalf of the Society and continued to do so in Sicily. In the course of her life, she received more letters from Ignatius than did any other of his women correspondents.

JHS.

My Lady in our Lord:

May the sovereign grace and eternal love of Christ our Lord greet and visit you with his most holy gifts and spiritual graces.

As we were on the point of writing about the arrival of the candles and numerous other articles sent to us with her usual great charity by the lady Leonor, we learned that God our Creator and Lord had called her from the trials and miseries of this present life to the rest and happiness of life everlasting. If we consider this event in a merely human way instead of with the eyes of faith, it would bring to all of us a sorrow as great as was the loveliness and indispensability of her presence and company and the love that was owed to Her Ladyship's great virtue and goodness. But if we consider, as we should, the reward prepared by God our Lord in his holy kingdom for those who live and die in his service, and how for such persons the ending of this brief and toilsome life is the beginning of another that is everlasting and blessed, we have occasion instead to praise and bless our Creator and Lord Jesus Christ, our life and all our good, and to rejoice in the glory and happiness which he imparts to those he takes to himself, rather than to grieve for the loss of help and consolation that we experience in such a death. For while the flesh as flesh feels it deeply, the spiritual realization of what is better should cause the suffering of our own loss to be outweighed by the great gain to a person to whom we are so indebted, and by what is most pleasing to God our Lord, to whose service, praise, and glory life and all things else should be ordered. May it please the Holy Spirit, true comforter of the faithful, to console you with an abundant flow of his grace. Indeed, I trust that Doña Leonor will obtain this grace for you from heaven and will help us all in our reverence before God's sovereign majesty. For the less is her concern for herself—having already reached the term and fulfillment of all her desires, where the infinite Good communicates itself to her with complete satisfaction—the greater will be her concern to help those she has left here on earth to attain the same.

Here, in the Masses and prayers of all in the house, we have begun and will continue commending her soul to him who created and redeemed her and endowed her with so many special graces. The same has been ordered to be done in different monasteries in Rome and wherever our Society is scattered. However, I am sure that it is rather all of us who need to be aided and favored by Her Ladyship in the presence of God our Lord. May it please him to give us his grace to employ our entire life here in his holy service, so that at its end we may rejoice like persons reaching a port of rest and security after the trials and dangers of the sea. May he give to all of us his abundant grace, so that we may know his most holy will and perfectly fulfill it.

Rome, April 12, 1550

✠

From Juan de Vega, to Ignatius of Loyola

Palermo, May 1, 1550

(Letter 1145 *bis:* III:16f.; in Spanish)

Juan de Vega's moving reply to Ignatius's letter of consolation on his wife's death is at the same time a plea for reassurance and spiritual closeness. The response which it elicited from Ignatius is given below (letter 1211, p. 310).

Very Reverend Father:

Since the only place I could find a remedy against the adversity which God was pleased to give to me and to my house was in the hope that just as God has exercised his justice upon me by giving this great sorrow for my many present and past sins, with the same justice he will likewise have given rest and glory to her on whom he bestowed the grace to merit this by her deeds, Your Reverence can judge the consolation and strength brought me by your letter, so fervently and persuasively confirming me in this hope and thought, sufficing to give me assurance that just as I see her in heaven with my imagination, I would see her with my very eyes if I deserved it—or, better, were not so undeserving of it. What above all troubles me is the fear that God has turned his wrath against me, since he has deprived me of the means by which I was able to avoid many ill deeds according to my evil and wicked inclination and was able to do some good, contrary to my own nature. And so I ask Your Reverence for the favor of commending me to God with your customary great charity, and also of letting me know whatever convictions or motions you may have regarding the state of this soul, who was devoted to you and full of charity.

In this situation Father Laínez and Master Jerónimo [Doménech] have performed their office towards God and the world with such perfection and such fruit and edification that they seemed sent by God and by the hand of Your Reverence. They have been a great help and comfort in this evil. Likewise, the Masses and suffrages which Your Reverence informs me you have ordered everywhere, and particularly in your own house, will, I am sure, be heard kindly by our Lord. And for my own peace, and in order to draw some profit from this great sorrow in which I still remain, I shall strive to hold Your Reverence and the entire Society in the same place as she did who merited to know it. Accordingly, I beg Your Reverence, for kindness and charity, to assist me in this determination and commend it to God, whom I beseech to preserve Your Reverence in his holy service.

Palermo, May 1

> At Your Reverence's service,
> JUAN DE VEGA

☩

To Juan de Vega

Rome, May 31, 1550
(Letter 1211: III:63–65; in Spanish)

Ignatius had written the Spanish viceroy in Sicily a letter of consolation on the death of his wife (see above, letter 1145, p. 306). The viceroy's moving letter of acknowledgment, with it a plea for further reassurance regarding his wife's soul and himself, has been preserved (letter 1145 bis, p. 309). Here Ignatius answers.

My Lord in our Lord:

May the sovereign grace and eternal love of Christ our Lord greet and visit Your Lordship with his most holy gifts and spiritual graces.

From a letter of Your Lordship's dated the first of the month, I see that one of the effects aimed at by the Creator in his chosen creatures through this sort of visitations is being achieved in Your Lordship—that of humbling them in their self-knowledge, whereby they consider themselves deserving of even the greatest scourges, for which the ill deserts of human weakness always provide more than enough cause. I was also consoled in our Lord to see another fruit which the servants of God our Lord reap from their trials, the raising of our love above the things of this life through a desire for everlasting life; for according as earth attracts and holds our love in its embrace, we need to experience earth's distresses if we are to rise heavenward. Blessed be our most wise Father, so kind in his chastisement and so merciful in his anger; may it please him to increase daily in Your Lordship what he seeks above all through these means: an increase in love for him and for all perfection, which will grow in the measure that it is not taken up with any other creature. Thus I am certain that the means ordained for this by his eternal providence through her blessed companionship on earth has been rendered far more effective by him for Your Lordship and your whole house by her being transferred to heaven. There, the less she has to desire for herself, being filled with the supreme Good, the more she will devote her now perfect charity to obtaining from the overflowing Fountain of every grace and good those graces that are needed for the attainment of the same end by the persons she once loved so much, and now loves even more and is far more able to help. This should indicate to Your Lordship the conviction inspired in me by God our Lord regarding the state of that blessed image of his who now rests from all her trials in felicity in his glory. There she is followed by her good works (which alone accompany us there, all else remaining below); indeed, she possesses in them an eternal treasure, which is a cause of endless joy in the divine presence for one who performs them for love of him.

As for the eagerness to further our least Society (which belongs wholly to Your Lordship) which Your Lordship states that you have and wish to have even more in our Lord: may Jesus Christ, our God and Lord, who placed it in your soul, perfect it in his divine love and reward it eternally. I make no offering on our part because we are already entirely yours in our Lord and have nothing that we can offer anew, albeit we can increase our eagerness to fulfill what we owe in the Divine Majesty.

May he in his infinite and sovereign goodness give to all of us his abundant grace, so that we may always know his most holy will and perfectly fulfill it.

Rome

✠

To Miguel Ochoa

Rome, June 9, 1550

(Letter 1225: III:74f.; in Spanish)

While still a scholastic, Miguel Ochoa gained renown as a healer. Polanco himself at one time experienced Ochoa's help. Because of the crowds who flocked to him, St. Ignatius had him ordained early so that he could hear their confessions. Because

Miguel's own health was fragile, Ignatius stationed him at the salubrious resort town of Tivoli and sent him this set of regulations. It has been preserved in Polanco's original draft with St. Ignatius's autograph corrections (printed as ~~struck out~~) and additions (printed in italics). These are reproduced here. They give an idea of St. Ignatius's attention to detail—in life as well as in letter writing.

The regulations to be observed by Micer Miguel Ochoa in Tivoli are as follows:

1. He will eat regularly two times a day—unless on some weekday, such as Friday, he should be moved by devotion to fast, taking a collation in the evening instead of supper. By eating two times I mean two meals, with bread, wine, and meat or something equivalent, such as eggs or fish—unless need dictates otherwise.

2. He should have a scheduled time for dining before noon and should be home before then. In cases where he cannot get back because of urgent matters for God's service, he should stay out and eat at any place he judges ~~most edifying~~ *decent*. Those at the house should not wait for him longer than until *an hour before* noon, and should eat with or without him at their scheduled time.

3. He should return home in the evening at the Angelus or *before it is rung* and check the house, closing the doors, etc.

4. He should go to bed at a scheduled time *and see that the others do too*, and should remain in bed at least six to seven hours, in order to sleep and rest.

5. Besides the office and Mass (when he says it), he should spend no more than an hour on meditation, prayer, *and examen, counting morning and evening together;* and during the day, particularly after eating, he should not make any protracted prayer~~, though he may use short elevations of his mind as often as he wishes~~.

6. In general, he should devote himself to the service of his neighbors in such a way that he takes into account his own bodily health for love of him for whose sake he serves his neighbors.

Monitor: Michele Bressano

✝
JHS

To Carlos Borgia

Rome, June 13, 1550
(Letter 1228: III:79f.; in Spanish)

A letter of spiritual congratulation and encouragement to Francis Borgia's son and heir.

Jhs.

My Lord in our Lord:

May the sovereign grace and eternal love of Christ our Lord greet and visit Your Lordship with his most holy gifts and spiritual graces.

Although for many years now I have had your entire blessed house inscribed upon my soul, and in particular Your Lordship as its chief pillar, desiring that Jesus Christ our God and Lord may keep you all inscribed in the book of life, I have not yet had occasion to write an individual letter to Your Lordship. I find one now in the spiritual joy caused me in our Lord by what Master Andrés writes of the great favors which he who is infinitely and supremely good bestows with such liberality upon you, as well as of the disposition encountered by these holy gifts in Your Lordship's soul as they make it feel and move it so efficaciously to desire and carry out what is for his holy service and glory. Endless blessings to him who has made Your Lordship heir not only to the lord duke's estate and temporal possessions but also to his virtues and spiritual riches, a far more precious and significant inheritance. For it is this, not the former, which must make Your Lordship heir to the kingdom of heaven, possessor of a wealth not restricted in worth and time but in itself infinite and supreme and in its enjoyment unending and eternal. For the rest, I am persuaded in our Lord that, as Your Lordship's great example and virtue at such an age edifies everyone and furnishes us with a great occasion to praise and bless the Author of all good, so will he not only preserve but daily add to Your Lordship's virtue and thus give us new and greater occasions for glorifying and praising his infinite clemency.

No more for the present, except heartily to offer myself and our least Society for the perpetual service of Your Lordship in our Lord. May he in his infinite and supreme goodness deign to give all of us his abundant grace, so that we may always know his most holy will and entirely fulfill it.

Rome, June 13, 1550

To Paschase Broët

Rome, June 21, 1550

(Letter 1246: III:90–92; in Spanish)

A young cleric from Bologna, Bartolomeo Boattiero, had spent a year with the fathers, during which time he had renounced his benefices in favor of a pious work, the Society receiving nothing. Upon leaving the house, he threatened to sue to recover the benefices. Ignatius answers threat with threat, an example of the firmness with which he could act.

Bologna: As for Bartolomeo, it is no surprise that he should be claiming I deceived him; he is not the first to render evil for good.

2. He should understand what he was told many times after the other time he left the house: that if he does not stay, nothing that belongs to him will stay.

3. However, we are here consulting qualified persons about what should be done regarding his benefices. It would not be right to return them to him; he would misuse them for his own damnation. If he claims he trusted me as a spiritual father and that I ought to be concerned for his salvation, it is certain that one should not give them to him for his damnation, as he was told here when he left the first time. We are investigating the advisability of assigning these benefices to the city there or to some person who will use them properly.

4. His claim that he did not give his consent in the chancery is patently false, as can be seen by the enclosed copy of the petition. Actually, when he gave his consent no one from the house was with him; he and a solicitor went.

5. As to his claim that he did not burden my conscience in the matter of the benefices and that he left the whole affair to me, this is as true as his claim that he did not give his consent.

6. With regard to his claim that he will defend himself in court, he should know that if the Society wants to proceed against him, it can do so, and so vigorously that it will astonish him. His absolution will have no standing before God or the world when it is shown how he has been telling the Pope lies, without which they would never absolve him, even in the external forum.

7. But even if he is absolved, we could well have him forced to come here because of all the things he took from the house when he was in charge of it; however, looking, as we have been doing, to his

reputation, we are not disclosing this foul deed of his, for which they say here that the galleys would be too slight a punishment.

8. And let him be quite certain that he has to make restitution. He cannot claim he brought the goods to the house: what he ate, wore out, and took away was more than he brought.

9. As to fear of infamy, we may not abandon what is just because of such dangers. He and his house are the ones running that danger when we prove our cause there before public officials and when his own actions, where the real infamy lies, come out.

All this should be written to him in a way that demonstrates love and gives him a shock.

✠

To Juan Bernal Díaz de Luco

Rome, July 8, 1550

(Letter 1263: III:107–9; in Spanish)

Juan Bernal Díaz de Luco, a high ecclesiastical official, had met Favre in 1541 and thereafter remained a close friend of the Society. When he was named bishop of Calahorra in 1545, he made every effort to bring the Jesuits to his diocese.

JHS

My Lord in our Lord:

May the sovereign grace and eternal love of Christ our Lord greet and visit Your Lordship with his most holy gifts and spiritual graces.

I received from Your Lordship a letter of June 4. I consider and will continue to consider it no small favor and mercy in our Lord that Your Lordship should look upon me as someone who—with great goodwill albeit with meager powers—employs himself in your spiritual service, to the glory of God our Creator and Lord.

I spoke to His Holiness about the matter Your Lordship charged me with, and enclose herewith the decision.

As to Your Lordship's joy over the success bestowed by God's providence upon this least Society's activities in his holy service and the help of souls, I would not expect otherwise from Your Lordship's zeal and holy charity. I beseech you to remember this Society in your prayers and holy sacrifices, asking that the infinite and supreme Goodness which has begun it may deign to accept the lowly instruments who make it up, rendering them daily more suitable for his greater service and glorification in the help of his souls.

As to the care for the Basque people which Your Lordship urges upon me, I am sure that as prelate of such large numbers of them, Your Lordship himself must have great care for them and show this in deeds.[1] Nevertheless, I trust in God our Lord that with whatever little we are able to do, we will not fail in the duty of charity.

Dr. Araoz has been in your region recently to organize a college to be started at Oñate, and may still be there. If this project finds support (which I am confident that God through his ministers will give it), there is reason to hope it will be of great spiritual benefit to that region, which badly needs teaching and spiritual exhortation, as Your Lordship well knows.

[There follows a report on complications encountered in trying to negotiate authorizations in Rome for a religious institution in Valladolid.— ED.]

I most willingly pledge the prayers which Your Lordship so insistently requests. May the infinite and supreme Goodness deign to hear them, and to give all of us his abundant grace, so that we may know his most holy will and perfectly fulfill it.

Rome, July 8, 1550

☩

To the Army in Africa

Rome, July 9, 1550

(Letter 1267: III:113f.; in Latin)

A letter to the army besieging Tunis in North Africa. This army comprised troops from Spain, Naples, Sicily, Malta, and Florence, along with papal troops, all under the command of Juan de Vega, viceroy of Sicily. Ignatius announces that he has obtained from the Pope an extension to them of the jubilee-year graces granted pilgrims to Rome. Diego Laínez accompanied the fleet as a chaplain.

Jhs.

Ignatius of Loyola, superior general of the Society of Jesus.

----

[1] The greater part of the Basque provinces then belonged to the Diocese of Calahorra.

To the illustrious lords, noble and valiant gentlemen, captains, soldiers, and all Christians campaigning against the infidel in Africa: may the help and protection of Jesus Christ and everlasting welfare in him be with you.

At the bidding of a letter from His Excellency Don Juan de Vega, viceroy of Sicily and captain-general of this holy expedition, I presented a request in his name and that of the whole army to His Holiness, our lord Julius III, by divine providence pope, asking that the treasury of the jubilee which has been opened for the faithful coming to Rome and visiting a certain number of churches be opened to you also, who are kept away by your war against the infidel for the glory of Christ and the exaltation of the holy faith. In his apostolic kindness His Holiness has gladly granted this grace to all of you (on the condition of contrition and confession). Thus, you will fight the more energetically, courageously, and bravely against the foes of the holy Cross, the more lavish you understand to be the generosity of God all-high and of his bride the Church, and the more happy the outcome of the war—whether victory for those who live or blessedness and the obtaining of pardon for all their sins for any who may die. To communicate to you the granting of this grace, we have thought it proper in the Lord to write you the present letter and to seal it with the seal of our Society.

Given at Rome, July 9, 1550

✠

To Isabel de Vega

Rome, July 19, 1550

(Letter 1275: III:121f.; in Spanish)

Assurance of prayers to the daughter of the Viceroy of Sicily for her choice of a state of life, for her deceased mother, and for her father's naval campaign to Africa. Interestingly, Nadal later noted in one of his talks in Portugal that "for a fortnight Ignatius was ill after having said three Masses at the request of the daughter of Juan de Vega." This may have been an instance of the illness sometimes resulting from the strain that Ignatius experienced while celebrating Mass.

Jhs.

My Lady in our Lord:

May the sovereign grace and eternal love of Christ our Lord greet and visit you with his most holy gifts and spiritual graces.

Since Your Worship's last letter was a reply to one of mine, I have been in less of a hurry to write again; but I have not been remiss in continually commending Your Worship's affairs to God our Lord, as one who is very desirous in his Divine Majesty to see a continual growth of his gifts in your soul. With the greater light and knowledge of spiritual and eternal things which comes from these gifts, corporal and temporal things will have less power to make you feel them. For you will not only make less of your loss in God our Lord's taking from this world to the next the blessed soul of Lady Leonor, and find consolation in the thought of Her Ladyship's repose, but will even see that it cannot be called a loss to yourself. For where she is now, she will be all the better able to help you reach the same blessedness that she possesses, inasmuch as her desires and prayers will be the more efficacious in the divine presence. You will even miss her presence and companionship on earth the less, the more with the thought and love of heavenly things you dwell in heaven. May it please Christ Jesus our God and Lord so to raise Your Worship's soul to himself and possess it completely with his holy love, that whatever state you choose, you will be a chosen vessel filled with his spiritual treasures. Amen.

For the rest, I trust that the holy inspirations and desires which God our Lord has given you and must continue to give you will not lose their power, and that you will always be ready to follow his divine will and call, and in him to render great service and glory to his holy name. May it please his infinite and sovereign goodness to direct you with his special providence in all your affairs, and especially in these which have so important a bearing for the whole of life. I for my part will not fail to beg this constantly from his Divine Majesty.

I have taken care of the Masses which Your Worship enjoined me to have said at privileged altars; in addition to them we have already said three hundred here in the house. But as I felt almost ashamed to pray so much for a soul who has already been so long in glory and is helping us by her intercession, I arranged that all the Masses and prayers said in this house should be directed to asking the divine favor for Juan de Vega and his naval forces; and I am having this written to the other parts of the Society.

May it please God our Lord to hear our prayers so far as it will be to his service and glory, and give to all of us his abundant grace so that we may always know his most holy will and entirely fulfill it.

Rome, July 19, 1550

To Charles de Guise, cardinal of Lorraine

Rome, August 11, 1550

(Letter 1300; III:139–41; in Italian)

Consolation for the death of his father, the Duke of Guise, and prayers for divine help as Charles assumes the responsibilities of his deceased cardinal-uncle, together with a discreet plea for the cardinal's active patronage in France. Guise had founded the university of Reims (1547–49) and, after his brother was assassinated in 1563, became head of the family, which was ardently Catholic in the conflict with the Huguenots. He was a patron of men of letters, such as Rabelais and Ronsard.

Yhs.

Most Reverend Lord and our honored protector in Christ:

May the sovereign grace and eternal love of Christ our Lord greet and visit Your Illustrious Lordship with his most holy gifts and spiritual graces.

Some days ago, to render Your Reverend Lordship my obedience in this matter—as I desire in our Lord Jesus Christ to render it in every other matter—I wrote Your Lordship a letter. It will have been delivered somewhat late by Don Battista [Viola], since he was awaiting an opportunity when he saw you less occupied after completing the pious duties connected with the funeral of My Lord of Guise of happy memory, whose passing from this short and miserable life to that which is happy and eternal I am sure Your Most Reverend Lordship has accepted from God's hand not only with the fortitude of a true Christian, who according to the Apostle should not be saddened by such a passing "as others who have no hope" [1 Thess. 4:12], but also with the fortitude of a true prelate and pillar of the Church, of whom Jesus Christ our Lord says, "You are the light of the world" [Matt. 5:14]—you who by the example of your living faith and hope and love of the life of heaven, instruct all not to esteem the life of earth except insofar as it contributes to meriting and attaining the other life. This having with God's help been fulfilled in My Lord of Guise (as we should believe from the sweet odor of his genuine piety, religion, and Christian virtues), and the fruits he had brought forth in God's service in this life on earth having reached maturity, God our Lord's divine and sweet providence chose to harvest and reward them in life eternal. And while I know that Your Most Reverend Lordship's great piety and charity will not fail to make use of the suffrages with which the Church militant is able to help those who are on their way to the Church triumphant, yet, considering that plenty in this matter can only help, I have ordered that the priests and all others in this house offer special prayers for His Excellency, and that all the Masses in the house be said with this intention, and that other Masses be said at privileged altars throughout Rome, entreating the divine Clemency to bestow on him its unfailing and most blessed light, so that he may know God's eternal truth and enjoy his infinite and most happy goodness with glory and joy unending. For over and above the universal obligation of charity, all of us feel strongly bound in his Divine Majesty, looking as we do upon Your Most Reverend Lordship as our true protector and patron in Jesus Christ our Lord, to have a special devotion and affection for Your Lordship's person and entire house, and to bring them all continually before God our Lord, praying that his supreme goodness will abundantly impart to you his most holy gifts in this world as well as in the next, for his greater service and glory.

We have also learned that Your Lordship's burdens have increased since the passing away of the Cardinal of Lorraine of happy memory (may he be in glory); however, we also trust that the giver of every good thing will bestow increased spiritual strength, so that you will be able to bear them for the advantage of all and for the benefit of his Church; and this we will beg of His Majesty.

Regarding our Society (entirely Your Most Reverend Lordship's), Master Viola will be able to supply some news of God's service being performed in various parts of the world and which we hope will be performed in France also, when the divine Wisdom, in its own time and place, so disposes through Your Most Reverend Lordship's instrumentality. May he grant to all of us abundant grace always to know his most holy will and perfectly to fulfill it.

Rome, August [11], 1550

✠

To the Jesuits at the house in Rome

Rome, August 24, 1550

(Letter 1326: III:156; in Italian)

These directions were given personally by St. Ignatius. Obedience should be prompt and blind, leaving any occupation on the instant.

Reverend Father Master Ignatius wishes, for God's greater praise and the greater spiritual progress of all of us—as he has already partly set forth in other constitutions—that from now on when he calls anyone, or the Father Minister calls any priest or lay member, or the subminister any lay member, the one called should come immediately as to the voice of Christ our Lord, obeying in the name of his Divine Majesty. Thus, the obedience should be blind and prompt to such an extent that if one is at prayer, he should leave his prayer; if one is writing and hears the voice of his superior—or, more accurately, the voice of Christ our Lord—and has begun a letter, that is to say, an *A* or a *B*, he should not finish it. Similarly, if he happens to be with anyone at all, even a prelate (unless he owes that person obedience), he should come if he is called by any of his superiors. In cases where a person is called while taking a bodily restorative of any kind, that is, is either at table or in bed; or while busy with a sick person, serving him a potion or medicine or engaged in some service which could not be interrupted without harm to the sick person, or is helping to bleed him; or if the person called is making his confession, or about to receive Communion, or hearing the confessions of others if he is a priest—in these cases he should send to the superior asking whether he wishes him to leave his meal, get out of bed, or leave whatever else it may be.

Given at Rome, August 24, 1550

Received at Messina, September 12, 1550

✠

To Jacqueline de Croy, marchioness of Bergen-op-Zoom

Rome, September 15, 1550

(Letter 1362: III:174f.; in Latin)

Ignatius explains to a noblewoman in the Netherlands why her brilliant and zealous pastor, Nicholas Floris of Gouda, now a Jesuit, cannot be returned to her town. In contrast to her brothers, who were very hostile to the Society, she was a great friend to it and had several times asked that Floris be sent back to Bergen.

Jhs.

Most Honored Lady in Christ:

May the grace and true peace which is in Christ Jesus be always preserved and increased in us. Amen.

I received Your Excellency's letter of July 1, in which, with persevering devotion and, I am convinced, no small desire for bringing help to the population committed to you by God, you request that our brother Master Nicholas be sent back. And indeed, when I see what is both Your Excellency's religious desire and my own desire to comply with your wish, and how nevertheless what we both desire does not take place, I conclude that God himself is preventing this for reasons perhaps unknown to us. A short while ago, when his mission to Poland was canceled upon the departure from life of Paul III of happy memory, Master Nicholas was dispatched to Venice so that he could help with the beginnings of the newly erected college there, serve the needs of his neighbor in that celebrated city (for he had already learned Italian), and since he was on his way to Germany, have that stretch of his journey behind him. When Your Excellency's letter reached me, the Supreme Pontiff, at the request of the new duke of Bavaria, who declared himself about to start a theological college, had already decided to send Master Nicholas to Ingolstadt to replace another theologian brother of ours whom he was calling away from there. He thus left Venice about the middle of August for Germany, where he will have a vast harvest which is badly in need of such workers as he, and where we may expect fruit of no mean dimensions and of lasting character both among the people and among the students, once the college is begun there. Meanwhile, it grieves me that, as I said, it is not possible to comply with Your Excellency's religious desire and devout request. However, such is your charity and kindness that I trust you will take this in good part and calmly accept everything coming from God's vicar in the same way as from God himself; for when the time is right, God, who is all-rich and almighty, will easily be able, through this or some no less suitable instrument, to fulfill the desires for his honor and the salvation of souls which he inspires in Your Excellency.

May Your Excellency fare well in the Lord Jesus Christ; and may [the Lord] deign to bestow his abundant grace upon us all, so that we may know his most holy will and always fulfill it. Amen.

I believe Your Excellency received the jubilee which we obtained for you and for a certain number of others of your choice.

✠

To Juan de Vega

Rome, September 27, 1550

(Letter 1392: III:190f.; in Spanish)

Congratulations to the Spanish viceroy of Sicily on the success of his arms in Africa. See also the earlier letter of July 9, 1550, to the army in Africa (p. 316).

Laínez had preached a victory sermon at Tunis on the occasion of the triumph of Vega's expedition.

JHS

My Lord in our Lord:

May the sovereign grace and everlasting love of Christ our Lord greet and visit Your Lordship with his most holy gifts and spiritual graces.

The purpose of this letter is to join with Your Lordship in giving many thanks to God our Lord, the chief author of every good, for the very successful issue that he has deigned to give this undertaking in his service under Your Lordship's direction. Besides the joy which we share with all the faithful at seeing a remedy put to the great evil that came from Africa to afflict your lands, and the beginning, as we trust, of the great benefit of the exaltation of our holy faith and the defeat of her enemies—besides this common joy, we feel one that is altogether special in that Your Lordship was the main instrument in this work, and that you together with Don Alvaro have returned safely.[2] May it please his divine and sovereign Goodness to preserve you, and ever add to his holy gifts, for his own service and glory and the universal good of his Church.

Regarding Master Laínez, who we are happy to know is in good health, I have nothing to report, assuming that in accordance with Your Lordship's orders, he will have left there in compliance with His Holiness's command.

2. Regarding the university at Messina, I would ask, solely for the service and glory of God our Lord, that Your Lordship direct that great attention be given to its freedom and its ability to act on the part of the Society (wholly Your Lordship's), as Master Jerónimo Nadal will inform you in full.

3. Enclosed Your Lordship will find the bull for the orphans, issued without charge.

May it please God to inaugurate and advance such good works by means of Your Lordship as will prepare for you in heaven and on earth a rare and enduring crown and to his Divine Majesty much service, praise, and glory.

✠

---

[2] Alvaro was the viceroy's son.

To Carlos de Borja

Rome, November 1, 1550

(Letter 1427: III:216f., in Spanish)

On the occasion of Francis Borgia's trip to Rome, while he was still outwardly Duke of Gandía, his eldest son, the marquis of Lombay, wrote a touching letter to Ignatius. In it he expressed grave misgivings about his ability to carry the burden of the dukedom that was about to fall to him. He also urgently warned Ignatius that his father could not be trusted to care properly for his own health and would need the vigilance of obedience if he was to preserve it. Ignatius replied as follows.

JHS

My Lord in our Lord:

May the sovereign and everlasting love of Christ our Lord greet and visit Your Lordship with his most holy gifts and spiritual graces.

From other letters Your Lordship will have heard of the lord duke's arriving in this country in good health and of the great joy and spiritual consolation which God gives us through his being here. This letter will merely be an answer to one of Your Lordship's, in which you mention being burdened by the weight of the gifts of God our Lord and fearful of not being able to bear it without special help—by this very concern disposing yourself all the more to receive such help in abundance from the one who laid the weight upon your shoulders for the great honor and glory of his holy name and the universal good. For he knows that he must take from his own house what he could not find in Your Lordship's or in anyone else's—I mean the gift of his wisdom and holy charity, so needed for the government of such an estate as yours. And because I strongly trust in the divine Mercy that he will bestow these gifts most liberally on Your Lordship, I have no fears about the weight of the other [burdens]. Indeed, I am quite sure that in bearing this burden well, as in all other matters, Your Lordship will show yourself the son of so great a father and the heir of the virtue and the grace which the author of these has placed in him. May it please the sovereign Goodness to listen in this regard to the desires and prayers of this least Society, which I am sure, in view of our great debt to your blessed house in the Lord of all, he will never permit to be remiss in offering such prayers to his Divine Majesty for Your Lordship. Especially will the order of charity oblige the lord duke himself to do so—and we will take care, as Your Lordship bids us, to keep him quite mindful of his bodily health.

I trust also that God our Lord will not permit us to be remiss if there is any occasion on which we may serve Don Juan.[3]

For the favor and help granted by Your Lordship to our work here in Rome we give thanks to God our Lord, the author of every good. May he make Your Lordship a sharer in any service that may be done him in this college and church, which, with his divine favor, we trust will be much. Any renewed offering of ourselves, being as we are wholly Your Lordship's by inheritance, so to speak, I consider superfluous.

May it please God our Lord to give all of us his abundant grace always to know his most holy will and perfectly to fulfill it.

✠

To Juan de Vega

Rome, November 1, 1550

(Letter 1428: III:219–f.; in Spanish)

Ignatius consoles the Spanish viceroy of Sicily on the sudden death of his eldest son, Fernando, who died as the viceroy was returning victorious from the war in Africa. One of the early Jesuits, Paolo d'Achille, who had been at Fernando's deathbed, sent a detailed report of it to Ignatius, and Pedro de Ribadeneira preached a panegyric in Rome on the occasion.

Jhs.

My Lord in our Lord:

May the sovereign grace and eternal love of Christ our Lord greet and visit Your Lordship with his most holy gifts and spiritual graces.

The grief we inevitably feel over Señor Fernando de Vega's leaving us here in this temporal life after being transferred to eternal life by him who created and redeemed him for that purpose does not prevent us from recognizing the very great attention and special love which God our Lord displays towards Your Lordship in sending such visitations upon your house and taking to himself such precious pledges, so that he might detach Your Lordship from all love of earth in the measure that you have greater reasons for fixing it wholly in heaven. Blessed be his inestimable providence and charity, by which he governs all our affairs; and may he be pleased to grant Your Lordship to perceive and to taste the fruit of his visitation, bestowing the grace to understand in what a

---

[3] Juan was the brother of Carlos, and had come to Rome with his father.

better and higher state than before you now have your good and Christian son, and to be content with all that his divine and supreme Goodness reveals as more pleasing to him and for his greater glory.

The Society here, wholly Your Lordship's and his, has given and will continue to give whatever help for his soul it can by way of suffrages in Masses and prayers. May it please the Lord of us all to accept them, and may he divert to us who live in this mortal life those not needed by him who lives in immortal and eternal life, so that in all things we may always know his most holy will and perfectly fulfill it.

Rome, November 1, 1550

✠

To Isabel de Vega

Rome, November 1, 1550

(Letter 1429: III:220–f.; in Spanish)

Consolation on the death of her young and favorite brother.

Jhs.

May the sovereign grace and eternal love of Christ our Lord be always our help and protection.

Although not by any letter from your city [Palermo], news has reached us that God our Lord, after granting the father so great a victory on earth, has willed to give the son a more perfect victory in heaven, where His Lordship Fernando de Vega, having conquered all opposition from the frail body and the soul, will with his few years attain and securely enjoy the supreme good which, with many years or few in this life, we all seek. I have no doubt that the tenderness of natural affection will have performed something of its work in Your Worship, but I am also confident that the grace with which God our Lord supplies for and perfects the weaknesses of nature will have given you such conformity with his divine dispositions and so much remembrance and love of eternal things that you would rather be with your mother and brother in the heavenly home, whenever it so pleases God our Lord, than bring either of them back to the trials of this pilgrimage or exile. For we may certainly trust that with a life and death like his, and even more with the death that our Lord Jesus Christ endured on his behalf, the divine and supreme Goodness will have already granted what your prayers and ours have begged for his soul, even anticipating all or much of the suffrages we offered.

May he be pleased to grant to all of us remaining here below his abundant grace, so that we may also know his most holy will and entirely fulfill it, and so all rejoice forever in his most blessed presence.

Rome, November 1, 1550

I ask to be earnestly remembered to Their Lordships Don Alvaro and Suero.[4]

✠

To Francisco Villanueva

November 13, 1550

(Letter 1444: III:230f.; in Latin)

The rector at Alcalá is officially mandated to prosecute a calumniator of the Society. Here as elsewhere, Ignatius was adamant in protecting the good name of the Society; such vigorous steps were necessary because the Society was so new and unusual a religious order.

Ignatius of Loyola, superior general of the Society of Jesus.

To our beloved brother in Christ, Francisco Villanueva, rector of the college of our Society at the university of Alcalá: greetings and everlasting welfare in the Lord.

Inasmuch as we have learned from reports and various letters of trustworthy persons that a certain Doctor de Las Casas, resident there, has been unleashing against our Society and its Institute a flood of injurious statements, we have judged it our duty, without passing condemnation upon his intention, to see that this license and excessive liberty of speech, which results in a lessening of honor to God and of edification to the neighbor—indeed, results in scandal to the latter—be repressed and restrained by such opportune means as have been provided by the Apostolic See. Wherefore, in the name of our Lord Jesus Christ and in virtue of holy obedience, we command you to make use of the apostolic letters sent to you and the faculties contained therein and to take steps to have the aforesaid Doctor de Las Casas (and any other person like him) cited before a magistrate or procurator to be chosen by you in our name and by the authority of the Apostolic See; and should

---

[4] Isabel's brothers.

he be unable to justify or prove the truth of his statements, [you are] to see that he is subjected to the punishment of ecclesiastical censures and penalties, for his own amendment, for the removal of scandal, and as an example to others, according to the righteous demands of justice.

Farewell in the Lord Jesus Christ.

Rome, November 13, 1550

IGNATIUS

✠

To Urban Weber

Rome, December 9, 1550

(Letter 1481: III:250f.; in Latin)

Ignatius politely informs the Bishop of Laibach (Ljubljana in Slovenia) that Claude Jay is for the time being unavailable for service in his diocese.

. . . be increased. Amen.

From the letter I received from Your Most Reverend Lordship, I learned both of the painful religious situation in Germany and of Your Lordship's own deep religious concern to provide help for that country and for the flock entrusted to your own care in particular. I pray the supreme and all-good Shepherd of the entire Church to take pity on his Germany and send it effective aid through his ministers—indeed, through the power of his own Holy Spirit—and that he may grant Your Lordship, along with your desire to remedy the situation, the effective achievement of this through a lavish outpouring of his grace.

As for sending our brother Master Claude, I want Your Reverend Lordship to know that I am inwardly inclined to do what you ask—and even far more. He who is eternal Wisdom knows how deeply I desire to do all I can to provide help for your flock and to comply with Your Lordship's wishes. However, in view of Master Claude's having been sent by His Holiness's authority to Ingolstadt, and from there for a half year to His Excellency the Bishop of Augsburg, I do not see—in consideration of the Sovereign Pontiff who sent him and the personages who obtained this from him—how I can send him elsewhere. If I did so without consulting the Pope, I would be acting against our Institute and holy obedience; if I privately requested the Sovereign Pontiff for a change in this mission, I would incur the just resentment of princes to whom we are deeply indebted. But if we are ever free to do so, Your Reverend Lordship will find me most ready to obey you.

May the sovereign and infinite Goodness grant all ever to know and carry out his perfect will and good pleasure. Amen.

Rome, December 9, 1550

✠

To the Members of the Society

Rome, January 30, 1551

(Letter 1554: III:303f.; in Spanish)

At the request of Ignatius and on the occasion of the jubilee year, the senior professed members of the Society had gathered in Rome at the end of 1550. During the ensuing weeks, while they were discussing the draft of the Constitutions that he and Polanco had prepared, Ignatius presented them with the following request to be relieved of his office. It was rejected.

Ihus.

1. Having reflected and pondered over various months and years, with no inward or outward agitation that I could perceive to be at work in me, I will state before my Creator and Lord, who will judge me forever, what I am able to perceive and understand for the greater praise and glory of his Divine Majesty.

2. Upon examining the matter factually and, so far as I could perceive within myself, without any emotional bias, I have come on many and varied occasions to the factual conclusion that because of my many sins, many imperfections, and many inward and outward infirmities, I lack to an almost infinite degree the qualities required for the responsibility over the Society which I presently hold by the Society's appointment and imposition.

3. I desire in our Lord that this matter be carefully examined, and that another person be elected who can carry out my present office of governing the Society better, or less poorly, than I.

4. Voting for this same person, I likewise desire that the office be given to him.

5. And not only does this desire of mine stay with me, but it is my well-grounded judgment that this office should be given not just to

whoever would carry it out better or less poorly than I, but to whoever would perform it equally well.

6. All this being taken into account, in the name of the Father and of the Son and of the Holy Spirit, my one God and my Creator, I lay down and resign, simply and absolutely, the office I hold, requesting and with all my soul beseeching in our Lord that the professed, along with whomever they shall prefer to add for this purpose, would accept this offering of mine, so justified before his Divine Majesty.

7. Should any disagreement arise among those having to allow and judge this petition, to God's greater glory, I request them, by the love and reverence of God our Lord, please to commend the matter earnestly to his Divine Majesty, that in all things his most holy will be done, to his own greater glory and to the greater universal good of souls and of the entire Society, and that he may receive all of this for his divine and greater praise and glory forever.

Rome, this day of Friday, January 30, 1551

IGNATIO

✠

To Isabel de Vega

Rome, February 21, 1551

(Letter 1587: III:326f.; in Spanish)

A letter of thanks to the daughter of the Spanish viceroy of Sicily, Juan de Vega, with further words of consolation on her brother's death.

Jhs.

My Lady in our Lord:

May the sovereign grace and eternal love of Christ our Lord greet and visit Your Worship with his most holy gifts and spiritual graces.

I received your letter of January 11 and the gifts you sent with it for this coming Lent. May he who gives you such mindfulness and charity accept it, rewarding you with ample increase in this life and with the perfection of life in his eternal glory.

You write that, on the one hand, you envy Señor Fernando de Vega, now in glory, at seeing him no longer in danger of offending God our Lord in this evil world; and, on the other hand, that you cannot help being concerned about him because he was summoned at the age he was. I would say that your envy is good and holy, and likewise your concern, provided that your envy betrays no lack of conformity with God's will that you stay on in this pilgrimage, however toilsome it is, for as long as it suits his greater service; and that your concern betrays no lack of sure hope that God our Creator and Lord has the departed Señor Fernando de Vega in his holy glory or on the way to arriving there very soon. For before God, just as old age does not of itself augment, so does youth not diminish one's merits in eternal life. Rather, at whatever age, the richest person is whoever makes himself most a sharer in Christ's merits with the charity which he bestows; and many make up for the want of time or works in his service by their great eagerness to serve. And so I am confident in his infinite kindness that Señor Fernando de Vega will have made up for anything wanting. This confidence is rightly grounded in the tokens of himself he gave in his life and in his death. In fine, we have so good a God, so wise and loving a Father, that we should never doubt that in his kindly providence he takes his children from this life at the best moment for them to pass to the other. And so I shall say no more of this.

As for Señor Juan de Vega, you are right in saying that I do not need much reminding in letters to keep His Lordship present in my poor prayers and sacrifices. May it please the divine and sovereign Goodness to hear the continual prayers which I offer for His Lordship, his house, and his concerns.

Master Laínez left for Florence at the time of the departure of the duke [of Gandía, Francis Borgia]. I will see that what you say in your letter is written to him.

We are in health (although my own has been rather poor lately), by the grace of God our Lord.

May he in his infinite and sovereign goodness give to all of us abundant grace always to know his most holy will and perfectly to fulfill it.

Rome

To Ferdinand of Austria, king of [the] Romans

Rome, April 1551

(Letter 1721: III:401f.; in Latin)

Through his contact with Claude Jay, the Austrian ruler determined to found a college of the Jesuits in Vienna. As the first Jesuits were about to leave for that city, Ignatius wrote Ferdinand the following letter.

Most Serene King:

May the sovereign grace and eternal love of our Lord Jesus Christ always protect and perfect Your Majesty with a continual increase in his gifts.

Inasmuch as the care and solicitude of Christian princes can be bestowed on nothing more momentous, noble, or worthy of themselves than is the defense and promotion of the Christian religion, Your Most Serene Majesty rightly gives careful thought to ways of restoring this religion where it has fallen and of shoring it up where it is tottering, striving as well to do whatever can be done to remedy the situation. For all this we give thanks to God, the author of all good; and we earnestly beg him always to preserve this excellent disposition of mind which he has bestowed on Your Majesty, enkindling an ever more ardent desire for his glory and the salvation of souls, and bestowing the strength to achieve it.

But, among other remedies to be employed against the disease which is sweeping Germany, that remedy should be pursued which consists in having men at the universities who by their example of religious life and integrity of Catholic teaching will work for the help and improvement of others—this seems to be not merely a wise and useful but an altogether necessary idea or, rather, inspiration of God. Let us hope that with the help of the divine Clemency, this will be partially realized through the college which Your Majesty writes he is going to establish in Vienna for our Society. We have the firmest hope in the divine Goodness that it will, and we ourselves shall duly endeavor, to the best of our weak powers, not to disappoint Your Majesty's devotion.

In accord with the view of Your Majesty's ambassador, we shall be sending to Vienna at the first opportunity two theologians and some scholastics who will be able to further this work by their learning and example. Meanwhile, if it is decided that Master Claude Jay should come earlier, he will be ready to obey Your Majesty, as all of us are most ready to do in our Lord Jesus Christ. May his boundless kindness grant Your Majesty to know what is his good and perfect will in all things, and to fulfill it for his glory and the universal good of the Christian commonwealth. Amen.

Rome

✠

To Arnold van Hees, by commission

Rome, May 23, 1551

(Letter 1831: III:484–86; in Latin)

Instructions and recommendations for a young Jesuit going from Rome to join Leonard Kessel in Cologne, where they are to complete their ecclesiastical studies and take steps to establish the Society in that city. This is a good example of a letter that is explicitly directive, while at the same time leaving specific decisions to a discerning judgment.

Jhs.

Dear Father and Brother in Christ:

I shall set down briefly in writing what I told you orally on Our Father's commission, as a written memorandum in case you forget.

1. Since the physicians think that your health requires a change from the air here in Rome, you are to go to Bologna along with the brothers traveling to Ferrara. If you think it best to remain for a while in Bologna, stay with the brothers there as long as you like. If you think you should go farther, or want to move to Padua and wait out the summer heat there, you are free to do as you please. My one caution is that in whatever you do, you take your health into consideration.

2. If you decide to go straight to Cologne without stopping, be sure not to overtax your body on the journey. Go by carriage, horse, boat (where you have a chance to travel by water), or whatever other means will best preserve your health. If you find agreeable company for making this trip, by all means take advantage of it.

3. When with God's grace you get to Cologne, prepare yourself to undertake the functions of the priesthood. In the interim, as is customary with members of the Society who do not yet say Mass and communicate themselves, go to confession and Communion once a week if you have access to a priest. And—to come back to where I left off—make use at Cologne, or wherever you are, of the spiritual arms granted you by Father General, in whatever way you judge best in consultation with

Father Leonard [Kessel]; Father General has considerable confidence in the Lord in the discretion of you both.

4. Warn Father Leonard (and consider the same as said to yourself) not to overwork himself, even out of genuine charity, to the point where he appears to be neglecting his bodily health. Even though situations sometimes occur where an extra exertion is unavoidable, he should nevertheless not deprive himself of sleep by spending the night in prayer or staying up much of the night, as those close to him report to us he is doing. What holds for sleep applies also to diet and whatever else is needed, as I have said, for the preservation of health. Moderation has staying power; what puts excessive strain on the body cannot last. Understand, then, that Father General's mind on this matter is that, in whatever spiritual, academic, or even bodily exertions you undertake, your charity should be guided by the rule of discretion; that you should safeguard the health of your own body in order to aid your neighbors' souls; and that in this matter each of you should look out for the other, indeed, for both of you.

5. As for studies: you should complete the philosophy curriculum or whatever part you have not finished, so that you can approach theology with a more adequate preparation—whether you attend classes or study privately at home (usually a less productive method). The procedure and amount of time is left to the discretion of the two of you. I shall say nothing at this point about Father Leonard's studies; charity itself and the anointing of the Holy Spirit will show him to what extent he should subordinate them to his priestly ministries.

6. As you have been doing with some success already, you should make efforts to call new soldiers of Christ to his banner. You yourselves know what means to use. Father General, however, does strongly recommend the custom of preaching and of giving oratorical discourses on the virtues, in order to impress their beauty upon young men and bring them to aspire to religious life out of love for them. He also recommends receiving into our house men you deem suitable for the Society's Institute; should they turn out to be unsuitable, they should be sent away with due courtesy. Cultivating contact with students in class, drawing them to frequent reception of the sacraments and to spiritual exercises, and winning over to our Institute those touched by God's inspiration—all this is commendable. You should keep there with you the men you think will prove useful to you; any others—provided they have a frank and presentable appearance, sound health, good minds, and virtuous character—you may send to us.

7. Furthermore, should God, the author of every good, present the opportunity to start a college where his glory could be pursued as you are doing now but on a permanent basis, be sure not to let the chance slip, whether coming from the side of the municipality itself, the bishop, or private persons—and whether from secular or ecclesiastical resources (for instance, we hear that in some parts of Germany there are monasteries which are altogether, or nearly, empty).

✠

To Urbano Fernandes, by commission

Rome, June 1, 1551

(Letter 1848: III:499–503; in Spanish)

The newly appointed rector of the scholasticate at Coimbra, the successor there of Simão Rodrigues, had proposed a number of questions having to do with the performance of his office. Here Polanco sends his understanding of Ignatius's mind on the matters inquired about. Besides the perennial question of letters to Rome, these include the qualities sought for admission to the Society, obedience, mortifications, prayer, subjects of study, indifference, differences of opinion, purity of intention, and the observance of rules.

Jhs.

In this letter I shall reply, dear Father, to yours of March 8. First of all, as regards Our Father's wishes about writing, you should understand that he does not wish to be supplied only with edifying news and the spiritual fruits reaped in confessions, sermons, etc.; it will suffice to give these things in a letter every four months (as has been written) and there is no need to treat them in detail in a monthly letter. Rather, what he wants to be informed about is whatever, as far as possible, he ought to know in order to fulfill more effectively the responsibility which God has given him. However, since there are countless small matters which one could write endlessly about and which can be sufficiently taken care of through the action of local superiors and provincials, Our Father would like to be given information about things that are of greater importance and present greater difficulty. Thus, he wishes to be kept informed of the number of the brethren and the names of those who enter, leave, or are dismissed; and for this he has asked that a list be sent every four months with their names and qualifications. Once we have a full list here, it will suffice afterwards to mention any changes over the preceding four months.

He would also like to know anything special about the brethren's mode of proceeding in their studies and spiritual progress, such as whether anyone is notably agitated by this or that significant temptation, and what means are used with him; similarly regarding those who are moving forward securely and strongly in God's service. It would be good to mention briefly the mortifications being used to cure various attachments, and what success these have—speaking in a general way or with only a brief delaying upon details. Mention should be made of those who are progressing and distinguishing themselves more than others in the doctrine and grace of preaching; of those who are in readiness to be sent to various places, having completed the ordinary course of study; of those who, without having completed [those studies], are sent out temporarily as an experiment or to satisfy some request that could not be denied; and so also of other things which I have mentioned in a memorial which I gave to Father Brandão and of which I think I sent you a copy, or will send one along with this.[5]

As for your request that you be sent some "maxims" for government, etc., I find myself unqualified to speak even of "minima." However, may the Holy Spirit, whose "anointing teaches all things" [1 John 2:27] to those who dispose themselves to receive his holy light, particularly regarding the responsibilities of one's office, instruct Your Reverence; and I am confident that he will, seeing that he gives you so much eagerness to do what is right for his greater service. Nevertheless, in order to say at least something of what I have been able to understand of Our Father's mind and mode of proceeding, I observe, first of all, that he desires members who are fit for something, who have a natural vigor and aptitude either for the study and practice of letters or for helping in external religious works; and they should not lack competence for either the one or the other. Moreover, he will sooner take one who gives hope of distinguishing himself in these external matters of service, even if he is not for letters, rather than one with no inclination or aptitude for external matters and poor ability for letters, though he has some such ability.

2. He wishes that they be past boyhood and of a height which I here indicate, with exceptions being made for rare gifts or extraordinary cases. As a rule, they should have a decent outward appearance, because of the dealings with the neighbor required by our Institute and manner of life. Hence, do not be satisfied with persons of bad external appear-

[5] See letter 1854 below (p. 339).

ance unless they have other rare gifts from God which can compensate for this and perhaps even render it edifying.

3. He is unwilling to accept persons not fully grown, youths, for example, if their bodily health is poor. With persons of learning or particularly good judgment, he is more tolerant of poor health: even half-dead, such persons can be useful.

4. As for those already admitted, I notice that the one thing he strives the most to have truly observed and is most pained to see not observed (I do not refer to mortal sins, which it is supposed are absent) is obedience—an obedience that extends not merely to execution but even to making the superior's will one's own and thinking the same as he in whatever one cannot positively affirm to be sinful. He considers obedience imperfect when the subject rests content with doing what is commanded and with willing to do it, and does not also think that it is the right thing to do, overcoming his own judgment and making it captive to holy obedience—always to the degree, I mean, that the will's writ extends to the understanding, as in cases where there is no compelling evidence, etc. Hardheaded persons who occasion upset and turmoil to others, even in slight matters, he does not tolerate.

5. With regard to mortifications, I notice that he prefers and values more highly those that touch honor and self-esteem rather than those which afflict the flesh, such as fasts, disciplines, and hairshirts. Regarding these, he seems not only not to apply the spurs, but actually to rein in persons who are not experiencing troublesome or dangerous assaults of the flesh—particularly students, who, so long as they are making progress in learning and virtue with no notable harm, he is more inclined to leave to their studies, holding that the better time for mortifications is before beginning their studies or after completing them.

6. As to prayer and meditation, except where there is a special need because of bothersome or dangerous temptations, as I said earlier, I notice that he approves endeavoring to find God in everything one does rather than spending long blocks of time on prayer. This is the spirit he desires to see in members of the Society: that, if possible, they should find no less devotion in any work of charity or obedience than in prayer or meditation. For they should not be doing anything at all except for the love and service of God our Lord, and each one should find greater satisfaction in doing what he is commanded, because he can then have no doubt that he is conforming himself to the will of God our Lord.

7. He desires in the members of the Society a surrender of their own wills and an indifference toward whatever they may be commanded.

This indifference he signifies by an old man's staff, which lets itself be moved entirely at his will, or by a dead body, which goes without resistance wherever it is carried. And although he normally inquires about a person's inclinations—for example, for studies or for some other kind of service—he is nevertheless happier sending to studies those who have no particular preference for anything but doing the will of God our Lord as interpreted by obedience, than he would be if they had a great inclination for studies.

8. As to studies, he uniformly wishes that all be well grounded in grammar and the humanities, especially if age and inclination are in one's favor. After that, he excludes no kind of approved learning, not poetry, rhetoric, logic, natural philosophy, ethics, metaphysics, or mathematics—especially, as I said, for those who have the proper age and ability. For he is happy to see the Society furnished with all possible arms for building up the neighbor, so long as those who possess them are ready to employ them or not as shall be judged best.

9. As to opinions, so far as possible he wants no divergences among members of the Society even in more important speculative matters, and all the more so in practical matters. Moreover, he makes much use of having a person set aside his own judgment and permit himself to be judged by others in cases where a person shows himself more stubborn than he should be.

10. As to intention, he would like all to have a very upright intention of seeking God's glory in their soul, body, and every operation, and of seeking earnestly to help souls, one by this means and another by that, one by himself and another by assisting other persons to do it, always looking more to the universal than to the particular good.

11. Concerning those who are assigned to something, such as studies, for which they are suited but which is unsuitable for them, I observe that Our Father's practice is to remove them from it; he considers it more important that they advance in virtue than in learning when the two things prove incompatible. He has thus withdrawn a number of men from studies because they were restless and not benefiting spiritually. The same would apply to practical activities.

12. As for strictness regarding observance of the house rules, I do not find that he employs it with those who fail to keep them for some special reason, such as ill health or occupations. In fact, he frequently makes exceptions as discretion requires. He does make those who are not so excepted observe the rules, and gives certain penances to those who do not as a reminder and warning to others who do not keep them.

For since there is no sin in not keeping them and it is right that they should be kept, there needs to be some sort of penalty for those who do not. With less substantial rules the penalty is lighter, and in general it is not harsh unless some point of obedience or other matter of greater importance is involved.

This will have to do for a letter. Our Father's Constitutions, which we hope to be able to send you soon, will have more to say on everything.

No more for now, except to commend myself to the prayers of Your Reverence and of all our dear brothers.

Rome, June 1, 1551

Your Reverence's servant in Christ,

JUAN DE POLANCO

✠

To Antonio Brandão, by commission

Rome, June 1, 1551

(Letter 1854: III:506–13; in Spanish)

Replies of St. Ignatius to a number of questions from a Portuguese scholastic who had accompanied Simão Rodrigues to Rome. The replies form a complement to the advice that Ignatius had written to Urbano Fernandes, the new rector at Coimbra, in a letter of the same date as this instruction (letter 1848, p. 335).

Jhs.

INSTRUCTIONS GIVEN BY OUR FATHER IGNATIUS, OR AT HIS DIRECTION, TO THOSE LIVING OUTSIDE ROME, AND OTHER SIGNIFICANT MATTERS THAT SHOULD NOT BE FORGOTTEN

For Portugal: These are the points on which a scholastic of the Society [Brandão] desires to have information according to Our Father's mind:

1. How much should someone studying in a college devote to prayer and how much to conversing with his brethren, supposing the rector sets no limits to either?

2. Should he omit Mass on some days or say it every day even if it hinders his studies somewhat?

3. After finishing philosophy, which branch of theology, speculative or moral, should he concentrate on more if he does not think he can devote himself fully to both in the college?

4. What should he do if he finds himself sometimes having inordinate desires to acquire knowledge?

5. Should he offer himself for some task without the superior's asking him, or leave it all up to the superior's disposing?

6. On which topics that would be more useful for our vocation should he work preferentially in meditation?

7. In confession, should a person mention his imperfections in minute detail or only the larger ones, so as to keep the confession short?

8. In hearing the confession of members of the community, should he question them even about matters not related to sin? In which cases should he ask the penitent's permission to tell the superior about what was said in confession?

9. How should he deal with the superior regarding the temptations experienced by others? Should he report them in full even if some of them may be over and past?

10. Should one correct an imperfection noticed in an individual member of the Society, or leave him with the delusion that it is no imperfection?

11. If before God one believes that his superior—say, the rector—is wrong about something, should he inform the provincial (and similarly with other subordinate superiors) or should he blind his own judgment?

12. What rule should be followed as regards writing to externs or members of the Society, not because of need or a command of obedience, but merely out of charity or courtesy?

13. In dealing with externs or certain members of the Society, should one use language they will find courteous or instead employ a certain religious bluntness?

14. What rule should be observed in giving a person information about the Society, and how should this be gone about?

15. In dealing with people outside the Society, may one advise them to enter a particular religious order? And is it proper to counsel an extern, or someone in the house without vows, to take vows?

[16.] What considerations enter into using or not using a privilege of the Society in dealing with a penitent?

[The following is placed in the margins:]

In the two margins the following brief replies are given, drawn from a number of things which the same scholastic saw in Our Reverend Father.

[Reply to Question 1:] The answer to the first of the two parts of the first question is to remember that the purpose of a scholastic at his studies in the college is to acquire knowledge with which to serve God for his greater glory by helping his neighbor. This demands the whole man, and he would not be devoting himself completely to his studies if he gave himself to lengthy periods of prayer. Hence, for a scholastic who is not a priest (barring the intervention of disturbing agitations or exceptional devotion), one hour besides Mass is all that is needed. During Mass he can make some meditation while the priest is saying the silent parts. During the allotted hour he may as a general rule recite the Hours of Our Lady or some other prayer, or else meditate, as the rector determines. For a priest-scholastic all that is needed are the obligatory office of the hours, Mass, and the examens. He could take an additional half hour in case of exceptional devotion.

The second part of the first question will be answered by considering the purpose of conversing with others: to influence for good those with whom we converse. This is hindered by talking either too little or too much. Hence one should avoid the extremes and try to strike a mean.

In connection with this second part, Our Reverend Father mentioned the great importance that should be given to obedience. His wish was this: Just as individual saints have preeminences that others do not, it is the same with religious orders; he wanted the Society to have one outstanding characteristic that would put it on a par with any other religious order, even though other orders might have characteristics that our Institute cannot have (although in some things, like poverty, we might well be able to equal them). Our Reverend Father wanted our outstanding feature to be obedience. He said that we have a greater obligation in this regard because of the fathers' extra vow of obedience to the Supreme Pontiff and because they are not allowed to decline carrying out any command of obedience. He also said that this obedience cannot be perfect unless the subject's understanding is completely conformed to that of the superior; otherwise, he will have a continual purgatory and cause for instability.

[To 2:] To the second question Our Reverend Father answered that, considering the purpose of the studies of one of our men, in cases where (1) obedience, (2) the common good, or (3) exceptional devotion do not dictate otherwise, it suffices to say two Masses a week besides Sundays and feast days.

[To 3:] As to the third question, preference should be given to speculative theology, since after his time in the college, he will be forced to spend time on moral theology, needing it for talks and other situations, whereas speculative theology is more suited to the classroom, where truths and their underlying grounds are examined.

[To 4:] The fourth question will be answered with the sixth.

[To 5:] The fifth. It is good for a person to place himself once and for all at the superior's disposal for our Lord's greater glory, leaving all concern about it to him as one who holds the place of Christ our Lord on earth, and not making frequent representations to him unless something occurs that might especially move the person to do so.

[To 6:] The sixth. In view of the end of our studies, the scholastics cannot engage in long meditations. Over and above the exercises for growth in virtue (daily Mass, an hour for vocal prayer and the examen of conscience, weekly confession and Communion), they can practice seeking the presence of our Lord in all things: in their dealings with other people, their walking, seeing, tasting, hearing, understanding, and all our activities. For his Divine Majesty truly is in everything by his presence, power, and essence. This kind of meditation—finding God our Lord in everything—is easier than lifting ourselves up and laboriously making ourselves present to more abstracted divine realities. Moreover, by making us properly disposed, this excellent exercise will bring great visitations of our Lord even in a short prayer. In addition, one can practice frequently offering to God our Lord his studies along with the effort that these demand, keeping in mind that we undertake them for his love and setting aside our personal tastes so as to render some service to his Divine Majesty by helping those for whose life he died. We could also make these two practices the matter of our examen.

To these exercises may be added that of preaching in the colleges. For after the example of a good life, one of the things that afford most help to the neighbor (which is the Society's special purpose) is preaching. Our Reverend Father thought that considerable benefit could be derived from the scholastics' getting practice in preaching: they should preach on Sundays on a subject of their own choosing; moreover, by way of practice, so as not to lose study time, two or three of them could declaim at supper the formula of the "tones" that they had been taught, starting off with the formula we use in Rome, so that, after working it through, they could more easily go on to a different one, adding to or subtracting from the Roman formula in accord with local practice.[6] The advantages of this excellent exercise are very great, but for brevity's sake are omitted here.

[To 7, on confessing imperfections:] On the seventh point, to avoid being misled, he should notice from which side the enemy attacks and tries to make him offend our Lord God. If the enemy is making mortal sins easy for him, he should strive to weigh even the least imperfections of that species and confess them. If the enemy tries to bewilder him by making sin out of what is not sin, the person should avoid going into details and mention only his venial sins—and of these only the more important. And if by God's grace the person has reached peace with our Lord, he should confess his sins briefly without going into detail but striving to feel confusion for his sins in God's presence by reflecting that since the one against whom venial sins are committed is infinite, this imparts infinite gravity to the sins themselves, but that through God our Lord's sovereign goodness they are venial and can be forgiven by using holy water, striking one's breast, detesting them, etc.

[8:] Regarding the first part of the eighth question: The confessor sometimes may and should ask questions about venial faults, for in this way mortal sins are brought to light and the penitent manifests his conscience more fully and is thus more benefited.

The second part of the eighth question: For greater clarity, Our Father stressed the importance of the superior's being aware of everything that is going on in his subjects, so that he can provide for each according to his needs. In this way the superior will not, being ignorant of his subject's affliction, place a person experiencing temptations of the flesh next to the fire by assigning him, say, to hear women's confessions, etc.; he will not put someone lacking in obedience into a position of authority. To prevent such things, Our Father reserves certain cases to himself, namely, all mortal sins and strong temptations against the Society's Institute or head and against perseverance. In view of this, the confessor, discreetly and taking into account the matter and particular circumstances, may ask permission to tell the matter to the superior, from whom there is reason to believe the afflicted person will receive more help in the Lord than from any other source.

[9:] The ninth: The answer to the ninth may be gathered from the foregoing: the superior ought to be fully informed about everything,

---

[6] The "tones" were a short stock sermon devised for exercising the gamut of "tones"—expository, threatening, consoling, etc.

even things over and past—provided that ill will plays no part and that due charity toward the neighbor is maintained.

[10:] The first part of the tenth question, on the correction of another: Success in this matter depends largely upon the authority enjoyed by the person giving the correction, or upon his love and the perception of this love. Lacking either of these, the correction will produce no effect of amendment. Correcting others is thus not for everybody. Moreover, no matter how a person gives an admonition, deeming that it will lead to the person's amendment, it is better not to state things too forthrightly, but indirectly under some pretext; for one sin can engender another—the sin originally committed may incline a person not to accept the alms of correction well.

As to the second part of the tenth question—on whether a person ought to leave another under the false impression that something is no imperfection—Our Reverend Father said that for the person's own good this was the best course, and that the more one attends to others' faults, the less likely he is to dwell within himself and look at his own faults, and so the less progress he will make. However, when a person is becoming more perfect and has his own passions under control and in good order, and our Lord enlarges his heart to help others as well as himself, that person may well correct another's fault, observing the procedure indicated in number 11 below.

[11:] In response to the eleventh question, Our Father recounted what he had told the first fathers after six of them had made their profession together. He told them that there were two ways they could help him perfect his own soul: first by their own perfection, and secondly by drawing his attention to anything they judged was not according to God. However, they should follow this procedure: their admonition should be preceded by prayer; then, if they still thought and judged the same in the presence of the Lord, they should tell him about it privately—a procedure he himself follows now. To do this well, Our Reverend Father said that it would be a great help if the superior entrusted this duty to certain of his subjects—the priests, for example, and persons who give edification. A person concerned only to benefit himself would do well to blind the eyes of his judgment. If someone has to express his opinion, he should take care first to place himself before our Lord, so as to know and decide what he ought to do; then he should courteously tell the person if he deems it will do him good; if not, he should tell the person's superior. Here Our Father mentioned the great advantage of having an admonitor to report things to the superior; also of having one or two men who would function as vice-rectors, one under the other, to assist the rector. In this way the rector can be of much greater help to different persons and be more loved by his subjects, who will see him as someone they can turn to if in some matter they feel ill-used by the vice-rectors.

[13:] I found Our Father's reply to the thirteenth question quite striking; namely, that in dealing with another we should do as the enemy does when he wishes to draw a person to evil: he goes in by the way of the one he wishes to tempt to evil, but comes out by his own. Similarly, we may accommodate ourselves to the inclinations of those we deal with, adapting ourselves in our Lord to everything, only to come out later with the good we were laboring for. Our Father made another remark about how to break free from a person whom there was no prospect of helping: talk to him vigorously about hell, judgment, and the like. The person will then not come back—or, if he does, it will presumably be because he has felt himself touched in some way by the Lord.

The third thing he mentioned was to adapt oneself to the temperament of the person being dealt with (whether phlegmatic, or choleric, etc.)—doing so with moderation.

The remaining questions are more dependent on circumstances than those discussed here.

✠

To Antonio Araoz

Rome, June 1, 1551

(Letter 1882: III:534f.; in Spanish)

Nephew of Ignatius's sister-in-law Magdalena, Araoz entered the Society in 1539 and devoted himself tirelessly to preaching and spreading the order in Spain, where he had been provincial since 1547. His health suffered, and after a series of fruitless attempts had been made to get him to moderate his labors, Ignatius sent him the following command under holy obedience.

JHS.

May the sovereign grace and eternal love of Christ our Lord be always our protection and help.

I have received reports about how necessary it is for you to attend carefully to your health—and have some personal experience of this also, since I know that although your health is poor, you let yourself be carried away by charity to take on labors and hardships beyond what your health can endure. Judging before God our Lord that it is more pleasing to his Divine Majesty that you behave with moderation in this matter so as to be able to labor in his service over the long haul, I have decided in our Lord to command you that in all matters of food (diet and mealtimes) and sleep (amount and times of rest), you should follow the judgment of the physician. For the next three months, until September, you are to give no sermons, but instead attend to your health (unless the lord duke or Don Juan think you might be able to preach once in a month without harm to your health).[7] To forestall useless caviling and to let you know that I really mean this in our Lord, I order you in virtue of holy obedience to observe this directive.

I beg God our Lord to give to all of us his abundant grace always to know his most holy will and perfectly to fulfill it.

Rome, June 1, 1551

✠

To Jean Pelletier

Rome, June 13, 1551

(Letter 1899: III:542–50; in Italian)

This is one of the fullest outlines of the overall apostolic activity of the Jesuits in a city. As the title below suggests, the instruction was frequently used, with adaptations, for new Jesuit establishments. Jean Pelletier, to whom this letter was addressed, was the rector of the Jesuit community at Ferrara.

IHS.

AN INSTRUCTION ON THE MODE OF PROCEEDING SENT TO FERRARA, AND IN ABOUT THE SAME TENOR TO FLORENCE, NAPLES, AND MODENA, WITH SOME MODIFICATIONS

Three things should be aimed at in [. . .]. One is the preservation and increase of the members of the Society in spirit, learning, and numbers. The second is the edification and spiritual advancement of the city. The third is the consolidation and increase of the new college's temporalities, so as to provide for the better service of the Lord in the first and second areas.

---

[7] Reference is to Francis Borgia and his son Juan.

Part 1

The first part, regarding the members of the Society, provides the foundation for the others. For the better they themselves are, the more suitable will they also be for acceptance by God as instruments for the edification of externs and the permanence of the foundation.

1. Therefore all should strive to have a right intention, seeking exclusively "not the things that are their own but the things that are Jesus Christ's" [Phil. 2:21]. They should endeavor to conceive great resolves and desires to be true and faithful servants of God and to render a good account of themselves in whatever responsibilities they are given, with a genuine abnegation of their own will and judgment and a total submission of themselves to God's government of them by means of holy obedience, whether they are employed in high or lowly tasks. They should pray as fervently as they can to obtain this grace from the Giver of every good. Moreover, the one in charge should from time to time remind them of these things.

2. So far as possible, the order and method of the college here [in Rome] should be followed, particularly in the matter of weekly confession and Communion, the daily examination of conscience and hearing of Mass in the house, the practice of obedience, and not conversing with externs except according to the regulation of the rector, who will decide how much each man may be entrusted with for edifying others without danger to himself.

3. Within the house they should practice preaching daily during dinner and supper, a different man on each day of the week, with no, or at most an hour's, preparation for these sermons in the refectory. In addition, sometimes during the week they should practice preaching in the vernacular or in Latin, being assigned a topic to speak on extempore; there should be sermons in Greek also, making use of the "tones" (though this latter may be varied according to the capacity of the student).[8]

4. Each one should strive to advance in learning and assist the others, studying and teaching what is assigned him by the rector. Care must be taken that the lessons are accommodated to the students, and that all the students get a thorough grounding in grammar along with training in composition, with careful corrections by the masters. They should engage in disputations and conferences.

---

[8] See footnote 6 above.

5. They should strive by means of academic and spiritual conversations to draw others to the way of perfection. With their younger pupils, however, this should be done only with the greatest tact; and not even older students may be received [into the Society] without their parents' approval. If it is deemed proper to receive an older student into the house (when he has made this decision for himself) or to send him to Rome or some other place, this may be done. However, discretion and the anointing of the Holy Spirit will point out the best course; or for greater security in cases of doubt, they should write to the provincial or to Rome.

6. For these purposes, it will be useful to have some of the more advanced students carefully compose Latin discourses on the Christian virtues and deliver them publicly in the presence of all every week or every other week on Sundays and feast days. They should invite young men and others, especially those who seem suitable for the religious life, to hear these talks. This will be a good way to dispose those whom the Lord may call, [preparing them] to take the path of perfection; at the least it will make a good impression and give edification, and those in the house will obtain progress in literary practice and in the virtues.

Part 2

Regarding the second aspect, that of working for the edification and spiritual profit of the city (over and above helping outsiders by means of prayer):

1. The first means is by providing an education in Latin and Greek to all comers, according to their ability, by giving class lectures and having the students practice disputation and composition.

2. By taking care to teach Christian doctrine to the children every Sunday or on a weekday; and on another day having them memorize some little bit according to the program of the Roman College or however they deem best. This will be done in the house or in their own church or in any suitable nearby place that they think most appropriate. This practice could well produce more spiritual benefit than preaching.

3. By seeing to it that the pupils form good habits through having them hear Mass daily if possible, attend the sermons given on feast days, go to confession once a month, and cease blaspheming, swearing, and using indecent language.

4. Thought should be given to whether it would be good to have preaching on Sundays and feast days, or only have one of the men teach

catechism classes in the church or in a public place while some of the men practice preaching in the monasteries.

5. Thought should be given to the advisability of lectures on Holy Scripture or Scholastic theology for priests—for example, on the sacraments or a manual of conscience cases—if not at the beginning, at least later.

6. They should give special attention to heresies, and be properly armed against heretics. They should know by heart the topics of controversy with them and try to engage with these so as to uncover and cure their infections; or, if this is not possible, to impugn their wrong teaching—skillfully, however, and not antagonizing these persons, but lovingly attempting to rescue them.

7. They should strive to draw people to the sacraments of penance and Communion, and be prepared for administering these.

8. Through spiritual conversation all of them can assist those they deal with, particularly when they find them so disposed as to give hope of good results. The exercises of the First Week could be given to large numbers, but the remaining Weeks only to those who show themselves suited for the state of perfection and are disposed to be genuinely helped by devoting themselves totally to the exercises.

9. Where there is time, they should take care to assist prisoners, visiting the jails if possible and having one of the men preach there, urging them to go to confession and turn to God, and hearing their confessions when this is called for and can be done without detriment to tasks that are more obligatory and pleasing to God.

10. They should also remember the hospitals—if, as I say, they occasionally have time left over—striving to console and spiritually assist the poor as far as they can. Here also occasional exhortations will be profitable unless an examination of all the circumstances indicates otherwise.

11. In general, they should try to be aware of the pious works in the city where they reside, and do what they can to further them either by their own efforts or through others. Moreover, they should show diligence and charity in starting new works that do not exist.

12. But while numerous means of helping the neighbor and numerous pious works are suggested, discretion will also guide them in which alternatives to embrace when they cannot undertake them all, as they keep their eyes always on the greater service of God, the common good,

and the Society's good reputation, together with the special interests of the college and the characteristic concerns of the Society.

Part 3

The third part consists in striving skillfully to put on a firm basis and increase the temporal goods of the new college. For this, over and above the sacrifices and prayers which should be offered by all in the house for this intention insofar as it is for God's glory, the observance of the points mentioned in the first and second aspects will be more effective than any other means on our part. But in regard to a few means special to this third aspect, the following will be helpful:

1. They should work to maintain and increase the goodwill of the cardinal and of the municipality, complying with their wishes wherever this is possible according to God, and serving them in the pious works in which they particularly wish to employ them, where this offers no prejudice to God's greater service. They should have a care for their own good reputation and authority with these persons, and speak so as to convince them of the Society's intention to expand its work, even though it ordinarily begins from the ground up so that it may later grow rather than diminish.

2. They should also strive to win the goodwill of private citizens and benefactors and converse with them about spiritual matters. Special help given to such persons would be quite suitable and pleasing to God, whose affairs are at stake.

3. Besides the benefactions that they can envisage from His Excellency[9] and his household, they should hold in high esteem and spiritual friendship that most illustrious lord, the Duke of Monteleone,[10] as head of this work, and the other persons who support it. Besides the fact that they will be helped, this will augur well that the service of God will always continue in the efforts of the college which they are helping.

4. The better to preserve needed authority in spiritual things, they should try if possible to have their friends make requests and handle temporal affairs with His Excellency or with others less closely bound to them, rather than [carry on these activities] by themselves, or they should at least do this in such a way that there is no wrong appearance of greed.

---

[9] Ercole II d'Este.
[10] Ettore II Pignatelli.

5. They should give special attention to eventually acquiring, if they do not yet have one, a good, sizable piece of land, or one that can be expanded sufficiently for a house, church, and school; if possible, it should not be too far away from the activity of the city. And once this has been acquired, it will be a good beginning for the rest.

6. They should write here weekly, so that they can be given assistance and information on various matters.

✠

To Girolamo Croce

Rome, July 14, 1551

(Letter 1957: III:580f.; in Italian)

Ignatius had earlier (letter 958, p. 300) defended himself against Croce's angry charge that the Jesuits had inveigled his son Lucio into the Society. Here he once more tries to placate the furious father.

Jhs.

My Most Honored Sir in Jesus Christ:

May the sovereign grace and eternal love of Christ our Lord be ever our help and protection. Amen.

I recall having written to inform Your Lordship how little I contributed of my own to the vocation of Master Lucio. God our Lord willed that this calling should appear to be—as it in truth was—from himself. None of us was aware what great efforts he was making to be admitted. At no time, either before or after, did I speak with him. I say this, not because I think there is anything wrong in inducing any qualified person soever to greater and more perfect service of God, but because in truth the thing happened in such a way that the Holy Spirit willed no one to receive the credit for what his infinite goodness clearly accomplished by itself.

I can say the same to Your Lordship about this move of his from Palermo to Valencia in Spain. In truth, not only was I not the person behind it, I was not even aware of it. Two or three of our men happened to be sailing to Spain, and Master Lucio, wishing not to be hindered or troubled by Your Lordship in his good determinations, insisted so strongly and with so many arguments that he be taken to Spain in the same ship that he persuaded them; as a result, they had already left many days before I received first notice of it. Later we learned by letters from our men in Valencia and Gandía that they had been there and by God's grace had arrived safe and sound in Valencia.

I wanted to let Your Lordship know this, so that in things which are effected by God's sovereign wisdom you might strive rather to conform yourself thereto than grow angry at men and wrongly blame them. For the rest, I myself, certainly, and this entire house and Society deeply desire for Your Lordship all consolation and happiness and peace of spirit, which I know not how to have other than by giving up whatever in our own wills is in conflict with the will of God. For in all else Your Lordship will always find us most eager to content you to the limit of our poor strength for the greater glory of God. And so I beg Your Lordship by the love of Christ to let bygones be bygones; between us may there be from Your Lordship's side that same charity and love which we on our side have always had toward Your Lordship, and will continue to have in the future.

May the sovereign goodness of God deign to give all of us his abundant grace always to know and carry out his most holy will.

Rome, July 14, 1551

✠

To Claude Jay, by commission

Rome, August 8, 1551

(Letter 1985: III:602–5; in Italian)

A Jesuit college had been established in Vienna with the generous patronage of the ruler, Ferdinand, king of the Romans. Its success led to discussion of ways to restore the decayed faculty of theology at the University of Vienna, in order to provide Germany with educated priests. In this letter, Ignatius suggests a refinement of Ferdinand's initial plan for this restoration. It includes ideally the study of languages (Latin and, if possible, Greek and Hebrew) and then of philosophy, both as preparation for theology. He bases his plan upon the "modus Parisiensis," which the first members of the Society had experienced at the University of Paris.

Jhs.

May the grace and peace of Christ our Lord be always present and grow in our souls.

From Your Reverence's letter of July 21, our father Master Ignatius has been informed of His Majesty the King's very holy intention to reform theological studies at the university of Vienna—or rather to restore them, since, as we understand, they have been practically abandoned for lack of students in that faculty. And certainly, given the present times and conditions in Germany, this measure seems highly appropriate and necessary. Our Father and all of us would be delighted if the Society could serve His Majesty in this. However, I will tell you freely what our thinking is here (and you should represent to His Majesty whatever part of it you think proper) about the means for achieving this goal of the restoration of theological studies in Vienna.

Three approaches might present themselves to someone reflecting upon this problem. The first is the one which you write that His Majesty wishes to employ. This is to have each province send a number of theology students, including some men of our own, and to have frequent lectures and exercises, etc. This would be an excellent procedure provided there could be found in Vienna, or sent there from the provinces, a good number of students ready to take up theology and study it with success; the plan apparently presupposes this as an indispensable condition. But there is reason to fear that such readiness is lacking, on two counts. The first is that, as we have learned, there is at present among the Germans little inclination of will and little devotion for the study of theology, particularly Scholastic theology. Without such inclination and devotion, any exercises will be coldly done and result in little progress. The other reason is that, even if well-disposed, the students will be insufficiently provided with the indispensable foundation in logic and philosophy, perhaps even in languages. Even if some are found, they will be very few, and theological exercises require a goodly number of suitable and well-grounded students; otherwise, as experience in other universities shows, the whole thing quickly grows cold, the best program being useless if there are no students to follow it; and thus the goal aimed at would fail to be attained.

If it is claimed that our own scholastics could form a student body, there would still not be enough of them. Moreover, others might get the idea that theology should be left to religious, and this would thwart the purpose of furnishing educated pastors for the churches or parishes, since our own men are unable to accept such curacies. The first plan, then, seems to suffer under these disadvantages.

The second plan would be, with a view to restoring the study of theology, to begin with a more long-range preparation and motivation of the students. Thus, the provinces would send young men destined for the study of theology who would first receive a grounding in Latin and, where there is aptitude or talent for it, Greek and Hebrew. Once a substantial number—say a hundred or so—were solidly grounded in the humanities, they could begin the arts [philosophy] course and be carefully trained in it. In the following years good numbers of others with a solid grounding in humanities would also enter succeeding courses, theology always being kept in view as the goal, for which the teachers of the humanities and arts should steadily inculcate in their students an enthusiasm and love. Thus, upon completion of the arts course, out of the hundred who started at least fifty, and perhaps more, will be suitable for the theology course. With a sufficient number of students who are really eager to study theology and solidly grounded in the lower disciplines, they will make real progress in theology.

Excellent as this plan appears, certain problems with it may be pointed out. The first is having to wait so long to see the results of all this effort—although a delay of five or six years should not be a major consideration when the result will go on indefinitely. The second difficulty is that there are many students in the university already advanced in the languages, and some even in philosophy, who would be disinclined to take the lower subjects. The third is the embarrassment of having a university like that of Vienna go without the higher disciplines being taught during the period while students are being grounded in the lower ones.

To avoid these difficulties a third plan might be employed. It is the following. While allowing the lectures in philosophy and theology to continue as they have in the past, stress should be placed, as indicated above on the second plan, on efforts to lay a solid foundation for the future study of theology. This would be done by preparing and training the students in the lower disciplines of languages in such a way that those who will be sent from the provinces for theological studies and all others studying languages at the university devote themselves to getting a good foundation in the humane letters, under teachers who will take care to enkindle in them a longing for sacred doctrine and instill in them a love for it. Once a sufficient number are far enough along in languages, an arts [philosophy] course should be started with solid and regular exercises according to the method of Paris. This would be continued in succeeding years, until, with the completion of the arts or philosophy course, there are a good number of well-trained students eager for theology. Then it will be possible to inaugurate a theology course given according to the method of Paris and continued in subsequent years. Thus the public lectures would have a larger attendance and an audience capable of profiting by them. For this third plan, the college being founded by His Majesty the King for our Society could be of considerable help. In the first place, the college will appoint instructors in humanities and languages who, over and above their lectures, will devote special attention to ensuring that the students do exercises, make progress in scholarship and good morals, and have a love for the study of theology. Once there are enough well-prepared students, the college can also furnish lecturers in philosophy who will proceed as we have indicated, preparing their students for theology. Once these are ready, the college will likewise be able to supply masters in theology itself, who will give the courses according to the method of Paris, where the Society first did its studies and with whose procedures it is familiar.

This plan seems to be free from objections. The first disadvantage mentioned above, the delay, can be more easily tolerated (especially being unavoidable), there being no interruption of the university's usual lectures. The second difficulty—the presence of students who are already advanced—disappears for the same reason: if they are unwilling to lay a better foundation, they can go on as they are doing. The third— embarrassment to the university—is no longer a problem because things will continue there just as before. Moreover, if university lecturers leave and cannot be replaced, a class in Sacred Scripture and another in cases of conscience or the like could be provided from the college until there are students prepared (as outlined above) to start Scholastic theology with a solid grounding. While it might seem an excessive commitment for the Society to provide teachers first in humanities and later also in philosophy and theology, so great is our debt to His Majesty the King, and so great the public good likely to result, that we may in no way fail to do this.

Hence, Your Reverence should discuss all this with the bishop of Laibach and, if he approves, with His Majesty the King.[11] At least by explaining his thought and offering to do what he can, Our Father is partially paying his general debt of charity and the special debt of service he owes to His Majesty the King for the glory of God our Lord. May he in his supreme and infinite wisdom guide and govern us all as is best for the salvation of souls and for his praise and honor. Amen.

Rome

---

[11] Reference is to Urban Weber, bishop of Laibach (Ljubljana in modern Slovenia) and confessor to the king.

To Elpidio Ugoletti

Rome, early September 1551

(Letter 2048: III:638f.; in Spanish)

A college of the Society in Florence ranked high among Ignatius's priorities. The city was important intellectually as a center of humanism, and its ruling family, the Medici, enjoyed great prestige. It took long and patient negotiations to achieve Ignatius's goal of a college there. Two other letters to Ugoletti precede this one; the first is a set of instructions, the second a set of reasons for founding the college in Florence rather than in Pisa. On the occasion of founding the college in Florence, Ignatius describes for the superior two ways of sending the initial group of scholastics, leaving it to the Duchess of Florence to choose which she prefers.

Jhs.

Instruction for Don Elpidio on the Manner of Sending the Scholastics

In one of two ways our scholastics have on other occasions been sent to colleges started by our Society. The first is in the manner of the apostles, without money, traveling poorly clad like the pilgrims that appear here, but without going to present themselves to the Pope. The place where they go then clothes them as is usual for the Society's scholastics. This is the practice when the founders leave it up to the Society, because she thus acts in conformity with her poverty. This is what was done for the college of Padua and that of Venice, founded by the prior of the Trinità.

The second way is when those inspired by God our Lord to found colleges write to the General and also to the Pope (or to one who will speak with him) and request that the work be inaugurated with his blessing—out of devotion to the Apostolic See and to give good example in the court. In this case, they arrange for them to be clothed here as they would there, so as to make a more presentable appearance both here, when they go to kiss the Pope's foot, and there. They likewise furnish some travel money, so that they can go more comfortably. This procedure was followed by the cities of Messina and Palermo, the letters being written both by them and the viceroy, Juan de Vega. This was also done a few months ago by the King of [the] Romans; and from Naples His Excellency the Viceroy writes (as does the Duke of Monteleone) that the same provision will be made for the twelve who within a few days are to be sent to begin a college there.

What you should do is to propose these two ways to Her Excellency the Duchess (either orally or in writing, as opportunity offers), so that she can choose which she prefers, inasmuch as the scholastics are Her Excellency's own, as is indeed the entire Society. Whichever way seems to her to be best for the glory of God our Lord will seem most correct to all of us, for we do not consider the Society's work or its members so much our own as they are Her Excellency's.

✠

To Ettore Pignatelli, duke of Monteleone

Rome, September 12, 1551

(Letter 2061: III:646–49; in Italian)

Ignatius explains to the duke, who was vigorously promoting the founding of a college in Naples, that it was the overall activity of the Society's colleges, not the presence of a few well-known scholars or preachers, which underlay their effectiveness.

JHS

My Most Illustrious Lord in our Lord:

May the sovereign grace and eternal love of Christ our Lord greet and visit Your Lordship with his most holy gifts and spiritual graces.

I have received the second copy of Your Lordship's letter of the sixth of this month, and from it I learn the effect of the holy charity imparted to Your Lordship by the Author of charity and of every good. This charity, prompting you to subordinate every other consideration, even bodily health, to the hastening of the work of God our Lord, testifies how much more powerful than anything else in Your Lordship is the love of him and of his glory and service. May God's sovereign goodness deign to communicate itself intimately to Your Lordship and repay this charity of yours by daily inflaming it more until the consummation in his kingdom.

As for the favorable disposition that has been found in His Excellency [the Viceroy], with God our Lord guiding the work through Your Lordship's hand, we expected nothing else. All this month there will be time to write His Holiness, since they say he will not be leaving until the beginning of next month.

As for the persons to be named in His Excellency's letter, if Your Lordship objects to what we wrote as our preference, the order could be changed.[12] Thus, one of the men could be Doctor Alfonso Salmerón and the other Doctor Andrés de Oviedo. But since Salmerón is already at the council in Trent, we could add (if Your Lordship agrees) that since he is presently much occupied with other matters, he will come to Naples as soon as he has dispatched them, being sent without delay once released from the council. Meanwhile, another priest could be requested in his place. I beg Your Lordship to entrust the selection of this man to me, and also to have patience for at least half a year and see how the work goes. I am hopeful and confident in the divine and sovereign Goodness that Your Lordship will be satisfied. Moreover, I can say in all truth that seeing Your Lordship's devotion increases our own for having a very special care of the college in Naples. It has been our experience that the great spiritual benefit and common good which we see being produced through God's grace by our colleges throughout Sicily and Italy and in other places derive less from the preachers than from the witness of exemplary life given by those in the colleges and from the zeal shown for aiding souls in letters and Christian virtues without any appearance of avarice, in particular through the public classes and exercises in letters. These draw the young not only to secular learning but also to the knowledge that a Christian ought to have, as well as to frequent confession, the daily hearing of Mass, and sermons every Sunday. Thus they are led to love the virtues and are drawn away from all vices and sins. Moreover, through their sons the parents as well are drawn to piety. In addition there are of course also the regular sermons on Sundays and holy days and the teaching of Christian doctrine, which do not merely console and move people's hearts but reap a great and steady harvest of change of life for the good and growth in spirit and virtue.

I would also add that in works of this kind, we find that the way of humility—of starting without a great deal of noise but growing steadily day by day—produces better results. Actually, it frequently happens that the scholastics themselves receive from God our Lord a greater grace for preaching than do the doctors. Thus, in Messina and in Palermo, where we have learned priests and theologians, the little ones have other, younger men who attract a large audience, give great satisfaction, and reap much spiritual profit. This shows clearly that the author of every good is God, and that all things come from him; thus greater glory is given to his most holy name.

---

[12] Ignatius had originally suggested Bobadilla, but the duke asked for Salmerón or someone else who could preach fluently in Italian.

Nevertheless, we do not on our side fail to send some men of solid learning. Thus we proposed, until Master Salmerón comes, to send (together with Master Andrés de Oviedo) Master Bobadilla, who, learned and excellently versed in theology and the governance of souls, seemed quite suitable. In fact, we had announced his appointment and ordered his departure from Brescia before receiving any communication from Your Lordship in his regard. We expect him in Rome at any moment. Since His Holiness has sent many of our men to other places, we really have no one else competent in Italian to send right now—that is, no one such as Your Lordship and the work would require.

But, as I did at the beginning, I humbly beg Your Lordship to be content for a time to let us manage this holy work, as regards assigning our brothers, on the basis of our own knowledge and experience of them. Please believe that at present we are doing our best to comply with Your Lordship's holy intention and desire. I am well aware that there are some persons who are more attached to Master Salmerón than to Master Bobadilla; Your Lordship will be aware of some of these. On the other hand, I know that many are pleased and delighted at the news that Master Bobadilla is coming. May it please God our Lord that Your Lordship will soon have experience of the value of the scholastics' classes and the edification given by the priests. Regarding the latter, I have promised Master Bobadilla to the Archbishop of Palermo for his archdiocese (at his insistent request) as soon as Master Salmerón gets to Naples. I trust this will be soon, at most within a year, given the letters Your Lordship will have written. Indeed, at its present pace the council will soon be done—or rather undone, given all the disagreements they have there, because of our many sins.

I shall say no more here, except that I, together with this entire least Society, which is more Your Lordship's than our own, humbly commend and offer myself to Your Lordship's service. And I pray the divine and sovereign goodness of God our Lord to grant all of us the grace always to know his most holy will and perfectly to fulfill it.

Rome, September 12, 1551

To Antonio Araoz

Rome, December 1, 1551

(Letter 2226: IV:5-9; in Spanish)

The following program for a Jesuit college, sent by Ignatius to the provincial of Spain, is in many points a remarkable epitome of Ignatius's spirit in the work of education. It is a central document in determining the purpose that Ignatius had in mind in moving the Society into the work of education.

Jhs.

The peace of Christ.

Seeing that in your region as well as here in our own, God our Lord is moving his servants to start various colleges of this Society, it has seemed to Our Father that it would be a good idea to give an account of the method and advantages which have been found through experience in the colleges here [in Italy], those of the colleges there being already well known; his intention is that this be carefully studied and, so far as the matter is in our power, nothing be left undone for God's greater service and the aid of our neighbors.

The manner or method employed in founding a college is this. A city (such as Messina and Palermo in Sicily), or a ruler (such as the King of [the] Romans and the Dukes of Ferrara and Florence), a private individual (such as the prior of the Trinità in Venice and Padua), or group of persons (as in Naples, Bologna, and elsewhere) furnish an annual sum of money—some of them in perpetuity from the beginning, others not until they have come to know and verify the advantages of this work. A suitable building is procured and two or three priests of more solid learning are sent, the rest being students of our own who, in addition to advancing their own education, can aid that of others and, through their good example, personal contact, and learning, also assist them in virtue and spiritual progress.

The procedure in such places is this. At the beginning three or four teachers in humane letters are appointed. One starts off with the elements of grammar, accommodating himself to beginners; another is assigned to those on an intermediate level; another for those advanced in grammar; and another for the more advanced humanities students in Latin, Greek, and—where there is readiness for it—Hebrew. When the school has been announced, all who so desire are admitted free and without receipt of any money or gratuity—that is, all who know how to read and write and are beginning Latin grammar. However, if they are young boys they must have the approval of their parents or guardians and they must observe certain conditions, as follows.

They must be under obedience to their teachers regarding which subjects they study and for how long.

They must go to confession at least once a month.

Every Sunday they must attend the class on Christian doctrine given in the college, as well as the sermon when there is one in the church.

They must observe decorum in their speech and in all other matters, and be orderly. Where they are not or fail to behave as they ought, in the case of young boys for whom words do not suffice, there should be a hired extern corrector to punish them and keep them in awe; none of our own men is to lay a hand on anyone.

The names of all these pupils are registered. Care is taken not only to provide various kinds of classes but also to have them exercise themselves in debating, writing compositions, and speaking Latin all the time, in such a way that they will make great progress in letters along with the virtues.

When there are a fair number of students already grounded in humane letters, a person is appointed to inaugurate the arts [namely, philosophy] course; and when there are a number of students well grounded in arts, a lecturer is appointed to teach theology—following the method of Paris, with frequent exercises. From then on, the whole arrangement is continued. For experience has shown that it is inadvisable to begin by teaching arts or theology: lacking a foundation, the students make no progress. This plan applies where there is a readiness for more than humane letters. This does not exist everywhere; in such places it is sufficient to teach languages and humane letters.

Beyond this, the priests in the colleges will aid in hearing confessions, preaching, and all other spiritual matters; moreover, in this work the young men sometimes have grace that equals or exceeds that of the priests, God our Lord being greatly served thereby.

So much for the method. Now I shall mention the advantages which experience has shown to accrue from this kind of college for the Society itself, for the extern students, and for the people or territory where the college is situated (although this can in part be gathered from what has already been said).

The advantages for our own men are these:

1. First of all, those who teach make progress themselves and learn a great deal by teaching others, acquiring greater confidence and mastery in their learning.

2. Our own scholastics who attend the classes will benefit from the care, continuity, and diligence which the teachers devote to their office.

3. They not only advance in learning but also acquire facility in preaching and teaching Christian doctrine, get practice in the other means they will later use for helping their neighbors, and grow in confidence through seeing the fruit which God our Lord allows them to see.

4. Although no one may urge the students, particularly young boys, to enter the Society, nevertheless, through good example and personal contact, as well as the Latin declamations on the virtues held on Sundays, young men are spontaneously attracted, and many laborers can be won for the vineyard of Christ our Lord. So much for the advantages to the Society itself.

The benefits for the extern students who come to take advantage of the classes are the following:

5. They are given a quite adequate grounding in letters through the great care which is taken to ensure that everyone learns by means of classes, debates, and compositions, so that they are seen to profit greatly in learning.

6. Persons who are poor and unable to pay the ordinary teachers, much less private tutors at home, here obtain gratis an education which they could hardly succeed in obtaining at great expense.

7. They profit in spiritual matters through learning Christian doctrine and hearing in the sermons and regular exhortations what they need for their eternal salvation.

8. They make progress in purity of conscience and consequently in all virtue through the monthly confessions and the care taken to see that they are decent in their speech and virtuous in their entire lives.

9. They draw much greater merit and fruit from their studies, since they make a practice of directing them all to the service of God from the time they begin studying, as they are taught to do.

For the people of the country or territory where these colleges are established, there are also the following advantages:

10. Financially, parents are relieved of the expense by having teachers to instruct their children in letters and virtue.

12. Aside from the schooling, they also have in the colleges persons who can preach sermons to the people and to those in monasteries and who can assist them through administration of the sacraments to quite good effect, as has been seen.

13. The people themselves and the members of their households are drawn to spiritual concerns by the example of their children, and are attracted to going more often to confession and living Christian lives.

14. The people of the country have in our men persons to inspire and aid them in undertaking charitable works such as hospitals, houses for reformed women, and the like, for which charity also impels our men to have a concern.

15. From among those who are at present only students, various persons will in time emerge—some for preaching and the care of souls, others for the government of the land and the administration of justice, and others for other responsibilities. In short, since young people turn into adults, their good formation in life and learning will benefit many others, with the fruit expanding more widely every day.

I could elaborate further, but this will suffice to explain our thinking here about colleges of this kind.

May Christ, our eternal salvation, guide us all for his better service. Amen.

Rome, December 1, 1551

✠

To Claude Jay

Rome, December 15, 1551

(Letter 2271: IV:36–38; in Italian)

Negative and positive criteria, mostly in terms of apostolic work, for admission to the Society. Ignatius sent this to Jay in Vienna to assist him in deciding whether to admit candidates to the Society.

Qualities of Persons Considered Apt for the Society of Jesus

Although the charity and zeal for souls practiced by this Society embraces all sorts of people according to its Institute, in order to serve and help them in our Lord to reach the infinite and supreme Good, the

Society does not do this for all persons by incorporating them into itself, but only those deemed useful for the end it seeks, that of helping the neighbor. Hence, there are certain impediments which entirely exclude from the Society, so that not even the general can admit persons having them.

The first is to have separated oneself for some time from the bosom of holy Church by denying the faith, as in the case of infidels, or by incurring errors against faith for which they have been subject to official condemnation, or by having severed themselves from union with the Church as schismatics. Of course, this applies to those in whom such heresy, schism, or unbelief are personal sins, not to those born among heretics, schismatics, or infidels.

The second is to have committed homicide or incurred infamy because of some heinous sin.

The third is to have taken the religious habit or lived as a hermit in monastic garb; it is an indication of inconstancy to abandon the way of perfection once taken.

The fourth is to be bound with the bond of matrimony or legal slavery.

The fifth is an infirmity of the head such that it is darkened or impaired in judgment, or shows any notable disposition towards this. These five impediments entirely exclude a person. There are others which, even if each does not exclude per se, nevertheless render a person less suitable; and the defect could be present in such a degree that no one having it would be deemed admissible for the service of God. Such are

▸ Uncontrolled sinful passions or habits, where there is little hope of amendment;

▸ Inconstancy, shiftlessness, and similar defects; indiscreet devotions which make certain persons fall into illusions or errors of importance, especially where the person is hardened in his own judgments, a dangerous trait in a congregation;

▸ Incapacity for studies through want of intelligence, memory, or speech, in the case of persons being admitted for other than domestic services;

▸ Lack of physical integrity, infirmity, weakness, or any other notable impairment of the body;

▸ Too tender or advanced an age; below fifteen is considered too young even for acceptance into probation;

▸ Debts or other legal obligations, etc.

Contrariwise, the qualities favorable for admitting persons to the Society (that is, for other than domestic service) are these:

First, a good education, or sufficient intelligence and memory to acquire one; and in practical matters either discretion or a sound enough judgment to acquire it in time. Second, they should have a good will, one inclined to their own perfection and the help of the neighbor. Third, they should have a certain gift of speech, since they will need to deal extensively with others as our Institute requires. Fourth, an appearance presentable enough for being able to edify the neighbor. Fifth, good health and sufficient strength to endure the strains of our way of life. Sixth, other external endowments such as authority, noble birth, and the like. As the latter do not suffice when the others are lacking, so they are not necessary when the others are present; however, to the extent that they contribute toward upbuilding the neighbor, they render even more suitable for admission someone who in any case was already qualified by the above-mentioned traits, which, when present in a greater or lesser degree, render the person more or less suitable for the aims of the Society's Institute. However, the mean to be observed in all this will be taught by the unction of divine Wisdom to those who have received responsibility for this, to his greater service and praise, etc.

✠

To Simão Rodrigues

Rome, December 27, 1551

(Letter 2300: IV:49f.; in Latin)

Ignatius formally relieves Rodrigues of his office as provincial superior of the Portuguese Jesuits. Troubles in Portugal had grown over the years while Rodrigues was provincial, so that finally Ignatius took the action noted here and appointed Diego Miró the second provincial of the oldest province in the Society.

Ihus.

Ignatius of Loyola, superior general of the Society of Jesus, to his beloved brother in Christ, Master Simão Rodrigues, priest of the same Society: everlasting welfare in the Lord.

Considerations of equity and prudence in Christ Jesus demand that the not inconsiderable labors entailed in administering the provinces of our Society should not weigh indefinitely upon the same persons, but, through occasional change, be divided among others who are qualified to bear them. Accordingly, inasmuch as you have for a long time been heavily engaged in the province of the kingdom of Portugal, which we entrusted to you and which has been given great increase by God, the author of all good, and inasmuch as with your present suffering from age and poor health, it does not seem proper to hold you any longer in these labors, we now, by the same authority by which we laid the burden upon you, so as to afford you some relief after all these years, release you from this office, in the name of the Father and of the Son and of the Holy Spirit.

Given at Rome, December 27, 1551

✳ 1552-1553 ✳

To Manoel Godinho

Rome, January 31, 1552

(Letter 2383: IV:126f.; in Spanish)

Appointed treasurer of the college at Coimbra, the austere Manoel Godinho, one of the brethren who had written to Rome with complaints about the government of Simão Rodrigues, found his involvement in finances and lawsuits incompatible with the spiritual life. He appealed to Ignatius, and received from him the following reply.

May the sovereign grace and eternal love of Christ our Lord be always our protection and help.

I received a letter from you, dearest brother in our Lord, informing me of your arrival from San Fins with the brethren you had under your charge there, [having given] entire edification through the grace of God our Lord.

Although responsibility for temporal business may appear and be somewhat distracting, I have no doubt that your holy intention and your directing everything you do to God's glory makes it spiritual and highly pleasing to his infinite goodness. For when distractions are accepted for his greater service and in conformity with his divine will as interpreted to you by obedience, they can be not only equivalent to the union and recollection of constant contemplation, but even more acceptable to him, since they proceed from a more vehement and stronger charity. May God our Creator and Lord deign to preserve and increase this charity in your soul and in the souls of all; and we shall rightly consider that all activities in which this charity is exercised for God's glory are very holy and right for us, particularly activities in which we have been placed by the infallible rule of obedience to our superiors. May the "double spirit" of which you say you stand in need be bestowed on you in abundance by him who gave it to Elisha; and I will not be remiss in desiring and begging it of his Divine Majesty.

If, however, looking only to the greater glory of God our Lord, you still think before God that this responsibility is unsuitable for you, confer with your superiors there, and they will do what is proper; and I will not fail to aid you from here, as one who holds you deep within my soul.

May Christ our Lord help us all with his abundant grace, so that we may always know his supreme will and perfectly fulfill it.

Rome, January 31, 1552

Yours in our Lord,

IGNACIO

✠

To Francis Xavier

Rome, January 31, 1552

(Letter 2384: IV:128; in Spanish)

Ignatius congratulates Xavier on his entrance into Japan. The concluding phrase, "wholly yours, and always, in our Lord," bears witness to the deep friendship of the two men.

Jesus

May the sovereign grace and eternal love of Christ our Lord be always our constant protection and help.

Our dearest Brother in our Lord:

We have not received your letter this year, which we understand you wrote from Japan but which has been held up in Portugal. However, we were very glad in our Lord that you arrived in good health and that a door has been opened for the preaching of the Gospel in that territory. May he who opened it deign to bring those peoples out of their unbelief through it and into the knowledge of Christ Jesus, our welfare, and of the salvation of their own souls. Amen.

The Society's affairs, by God's goodness alone, are going forward and constantly increasing throughout Christendom: these his least instruments are being made use of by him who—with them or without them—is the author of all good.

For other matters I refer you to Master Polanco; this note is to let you know that I am still living amid the misery of this woeful life.

May he who is the eternal life of all those who truly live grant us his abundant grace, so that we may always know his most holy will and perfectly fulfill it.

Rome, January 31, 1552

Wholly yours, and always, in our Lord,
IGNATIO

✠

To Queen Catherine of Portugal

Rome, March 12, 1552

(Letter 2481: IV:183f.; in Spanish)

Charles V's younger sister Catherine may well have been the object of Ignatius's chivalric daydreams as he lay on his sickbed in Loyola. Years later, as Queen of Portugal, she made the Spiritual Exercises and became a great patroness of the Society. Here, in the only letter to her that has been preserved, Ignatius sends some relics collected in Rome for her and her son, the heir apparent.

My Lady in our Lord:

May the sovereign grace and eternal love of Christ our Lord greet and visit Your Highness with his most holy gifts and spiritual graces.

When Master Simão was in Rome last year, he made great efforts to obtain authorization from His Holiness to send a number of relics for Your Highness and for His Highness the Prince; and while His Holiness graciously granted the favor, it had not been put into effect when Master Simão left Rome. Hence, deeming it would be a service to Your Highnesses for the glory of God our Lord, I renewed the petition to His Holiness. Having received his authorization, I myself and some other men from this house went to remove all the relics we were able to obtain. Your Highness may dispose of them all as seems best in our Lord; for as regards his own share, His Highness the Prince will be content with the division made by Your Highness, according to His Holiness's intention.

I shall add no more, nor shall I make any fresh offering of myself and all the members of this least Society to Your Highnesses in our Lord, since we have for many years so rightly considered ourselves—as I trust Your Highnesses consider us—wholly your own in our Lord. May his infinite and supreme goodness deign to grant all of us his abundant grace, so that we may always know his most holy will and entirely fulfill it.

Rome, March 12, 1552

✠

To Mary of Austria, governor of Flanders, queen of Hungary and Bohemia

Rome, March 26, 1552

(Letter 2517: IV:202–4; in Latin)

Close to the heart of Ignatius was the founding of a college of the Society at Louvain in Flanders, site of one of the great universities of Europe. But such a foundation could not legally be made without the permission of the governor of Flanders, Mary of Austria, second-youngest sister of Emperor Charles V and widow of Louis, king of Hungary and Bohemia, who had been killed at the great Turkish victory over the Christians at Mohács in 1526. In 1530 her brother had installed her as the regent of the Netherlands, a post that she still held at the time of this letter. While her sister Catherine in Portugal was extraordinarily favorable to the Jesuits (see letter 2481), Mary followed the advice of her counsellors, Granvelle and Van Zwichum, who were unfavorable to them. In this letter Ignatius presents to the regent a brief sketch of the Society, its purposes, members and activities, and asks for permission to establish a college at Louvain. The letter received no reply. Ignatius did not live to see a house established there. It was only after Charles V abdicated as emperor and his sister left the Netherlands that the Jesuits were formally established at Louvain in August 1556, a few weeks after Ignatius had died.

JHS.

Her Sacred Royal Majesty

Most clement Lady:

Since the founding a few years ago and confirmation by the Apostolic See of the Society of the name of Jesus, whose protector is Cardinal Carpi, it has pleased Almighty God that a number of learned and pious men should leave their homelands, renounce their own property and all worldly goods, and dedicate themselves to God in this Society. They have been joined by numerous young men of good character and outstanding promise, natives of various places, who have embraced the discipline of this Society in order to serve spiritually as soldiers under the banner of Jesus. For the Society was founded with the intention that its professed members, rendering obedience to the Holy Apostolic See, should work for the general good of souls; namely, by public preaching of the word of God, practice of works of Christian charity, proclamation of the Christian faith to any and all unbelievers when sent to do so, and finally by strenuous opposition to the efforts of heretics, each according to the talent he has received from the Lord. However, since this can be carried out only by persons who join knowledge of the sacred writings with piety, divine Providence has prompted a number of illustrious and most religious princes, as well as numerous other God-fearing, noble, and generous men similarly well affected towards the scholastics of this Society, to establish colleges for them. These have been successfully founded in a number of important places, such as at Catholic universities in various countries, where there are numerous such persons who can be formed to decent and truly Christian behavior and at the same time be brought with outstanding trustworthiness and care to solid learning in Holy Scripture. There are a number of such colleges in Spain, one in Portugal, several in India, two in Sicily, as well as in Rome, Bologna, Padua, and Venice.

Yet from the Society's earliest confirmation there were not lacking in it studious young men who had already studied for a number of years in various places, but particularly at the flourishing University of Louvain. There a number of them made such progress in their studies that, with Christ's favor having successfully completed their studies there, they supply useful workers for the vineyard of the Lord. Some have not yet finished their studies there.

Meanwhile, it has pleased the divine Goodness to inspire certain honorable men to take steps for the benefit of these scholastics, who are living there in poverty. That is, there are persons who, as in other places, are eager to see a college of the Society of Jesus established at the famous academy of Louvain. For this purpose one such person would be quite willing to offer and assign possessions of his own, including real property. However, this cannot be done without the approval, without the kind consent and kindly patronage, of Your Sacred Majesty. Wherefore Ignatius of Loyola, a priest of Spain and superior of said Society, most humbly and obediently petitions Your Sacred Majesty to vouchsafe to grant such permission for erecting this college at the great University of Louvain, and likewise to permit real property to be assigned to it, together with such annual income as the generosity of good friends may sustain, up to the amount of a thousand ducats.

Should Your Sacred Majesty grant this favor, you will be performing an act of undoubted piety and one most pleasing to the Lord Jesus. Moreover, you will render this entire Society—already indebted to Your Majesty on so many scores—even more closely obligated to you, so that for as long as it endures it will continue pouring forth prayers to God for Your Majesty's security and well-being and for the happiness of all your realms.

✠

To Everard Mercurian, by commission

Rome, June 1552

(XII [Appendix 1, no. 49]: 309–11; in Italian)

An outline of the aims and methods of a Jesuit college, for use in Perugia. (For a similar outline, see letter 2226, pp. 360–63.) Mercurian, then about thirty-eight years old, had entered the Society in Paris only four years before, in 1548. He was later rector at Perugia and Loreto, served as provincial of France and then of Flanders, and finally was elected the fourth general of the Society in 1573.

Jesus

Information about the Colleges of the Society of Jesus

The Society's goals for its colleges come down to two heads. The first is that the country or territory where the college is erected should be aided in letters and in spiritual matters by the example and industriousness of those in the college. The second is to educate the Society's own students, so that they may become useful laborers in the vineyard of God our Lord; this too will redound to the benefit of the country inasmuch as, besides the edification they give by their good life and behavior, they will be able, once their education is completed, to contribute to the commonweal by teaching, preaching, hearing confessions, and performing other works of charity; thus the college will be a kind of seedbed continually producing fruits of this kind.

For this purpose, when beginning a college we customarily send some men to attend particularly to the aid of souls by means of the sacraments, exhortations, instruction in Christian doctrine, and other spiritual means; there are usually two or three priests to attend to this.

Second, we send a number of schoolmasters to teach the boys Latin, Greek, and Hebrew: they give classes and carefully exercise the pupils in composition, debate, and other literary exercises.

Third, a certain number of scholastics are sent to pursue their own studies and also to assist the others in domestic tasks and in the classes as well.

Fourth, the classes are open gratis and without any remuneration, direct or indirect, to all, both rich and poor, who wish to make progress in letters and virtue, so long as they can read and write well enough to start learning [Latin] grammar. However, they must comply with the following requirements.

Young boys who come must have the approval of their parents or of whoever is responsible for them.

They must be obedient to their masters as to deciding which studies and exercises they are to do.

They must go to confession at least monthly.

They must attend the weekly class in Christian doctrine once it is taught, and to the sermon when one is given.

They must, if possible, hear Mass in the college daily.

Finally, they must observe decorum in word and deed, and let themselves be formed in good behavior and in interior and exterior virtues.

Fifth, since with small boys words are sometimes not enough, it will be necessary, when other punishment is needed, to take on a corrector from outside the Society, inasmuch as it is not fitting for the masters to administer other than verbal chastisement; however, when this is required, they can tell the corrector what to do, and he must follow their directions completely.

Sixth, all the pupils will be enrolled by name, so that they can be properly kept track of.

Seventh, when students have progressed to the point where they can leave the college in sufficient numbers to inaugurate an arts—or philosophy—curriculum, the Society regularly supplies the needed instructors; and after that similarly with theology, which will not be started at present (I refer to Scholastic theology) since, so far as we know, there are no qualified hearers, and also because it is the Society's practice to make a lowly and humble beginning, and then to increase with God's help.

This is more or less the practice in the college in Rome and elsewhere; it can be followed in Perugia.

✠

To Juan Martínez Guijeño, archbishop of Toledo

Rome, June 1, 1552

(Letter 2624: IV:263–65; in Spanish)

Originally favorable to the Jesuits, Guijeño, the archbishop of Toledo and primate of Spain, turned against them, denying Jesuits the right to administer the sacraments and withdrawing faculties from any priest who had made the Exercises. One of his griefs was the Jesuits' admission into the Society of New Christians, converts from Judaism or Islam or their descendants. The Church of Toledo forbade giving any position of responsibility or dignity to such converts or their descendants. The papal nuncio, Poggio, persuaded the archbishop to back down on the refusal of faculties; but Ignatius, concerned about maintaining the Society's existence in Spain, capitulates to the archbishop's demands about the New Christians, at least in Spain.

Ihs.

My Most Illustrious and Reverend Lord in our Lord:

May the sovereign grace and eternal love of Christ our Lord greet and visit Your Illustrious Lordship with his most holy gifts and spiritual graces.

Although it is something new for me to write Your Lordship, it should not be new to feel and demonstrate gratitude for benefits received; hence, learning of those lately done by Your Lordship to our least Society, I consider myself not only deeply bound to pray to the divine and sovereign Goodness to recompense them with lavish and everlasting repayment, but also to write you—not indeed to render thanks, for I leave that to him for whose love you have done us these favors—but to give Your Lordship a sign that you have not done or promised your favors, about which I have been informed, to thankless or ungrateful persons. And although, to someone whom God our Lord has placed in so great and lofty a position in his Church, the service which our poor profession can offer is paltry indeed, nevertheless, I beseech Your Lordship to consider us wholly yours in our Lord, and as such to make use of us for the greater glory of his Divine Majesty. And in token of our holding Your Lordship as our lord and father and of our always doing so, I am writing to our men there that neither in Alcalá nor elsewhere in that realm should they accept anyone for our Society who is not according to Your Lordship's intention or indication.

And although the Apostolic See has granted us numerous faculties for the help of souls, I am also writing them to employ these only insofar as Your Reverend Lordship shall deem they ought to employ them in order to help carry some small portion of the great burden which God our Lord has placed upon Your Lordship. For just as I attribute to Your Lordship's great spirit and zeal for souls what happened in our regard in the past, before you possessed information about our way of proceeding, by the same token I am convinced that once Your Lordship is so informed, you will be our true protector and lord and father and be more helpful to us than any other prelate of that realm, so as the better to fulfill the desires for God's service and the help of souls which the Author of all good bestows upon us. May it please his infinite goodness and wisdom to communicate himself abundantly to Your Reverend Lordship, and to grant all of us his abundant grace, so that we may always know his most holy will and entirely fulfill it.

Rome, June 1, 1552

✠

To Prince Philip of Spain

Rome, June 3, 1552

(Letter 2627: IV:268f.; in Spanish)

A letter of thanks for Philip's support in canonical difficulties encountered by the college at Alcalá because of the archbishop of Toledo, Juan Martínez Guiyeño (see letter 2624, pp. 373f., noting the different spelling of the name). Ignatius repeats his request for the Prince's assistance in the reform of the monasteries of Catalonia. The "present public disturbances" to which Ignatius refers were the battles then going on in Germany against the emperor, Charles V, the father of Prince Philip.

Ihus.

My Lord in our Lord:

May the sovereign grace and eternal love of Christ our Lord greet and visit Your Highness with his most holy gifts and spiritual graces.

Although the great indebtedness, love, and affection that I bear to Your Highness's service cause me to keep you every day very present before God our Creator and Lord, I decided to write this letter and by means of it humbly to kiss Your Highness's hands for the favor, in addition to many others, that you have shown us all by supporting our cause, as a true protector and lord, with the lord archbishop. May Your Highness's unending and blessed reward be God, our supreme and eternal good, whose service and glory moved, and I hope will continue to move, Your Highness's royal and Christian soul always to show gracious favor to this least Society, which is entirely Your Highness's own.

In addition, I deem I should not altogether fail to request that when the present public disturbances allow, as I hope in our Lord they will, Your Highness might graciously remember to command the furtherance of the Christian and holy work of reforming the monasteries in Catalonia. Moreover, trusting that I will thereby render a great service to God our Lord and to Your Highness, I shall not fail to mention this again at the proper time.

May it please the divine and sovereign Goodness to give all of us abundant grace, so that we may always know his most holy will and perfectly fulfill it.

Rome, June 3, 1552

Your Highness's most humble and perpetual servant in our Lord,

IGNATIO

✠

To Francis Borgia

Rome, June 5, 1552

(Letter 2652: IV:283–85; in Spanish)

Ignatius describes a three-day process of interior discernment in the matter of opposing a proposed cardinal's hat which the emperor, Charles V, had asked Pope Julius III to confer on Francis Borgia. In setting out what happened to him as he tried to decide his own position, Ignatius described elements of all three "times" of election as set forth in the Spiritual Exercises. *This letter also includes the famous statement that the same Holy Spirit could move one person to favor something for a particular reason while moving another person to oppose it for a different reason. Ignatius confesses that while he has no doubt that God wanted him to oppose the cardinalate, it might still be God's will that Borgia receive it. When Ignatius asked for Borgia's own opinion, the latter hesitated until finally, in 1554, he decided against accepting any such dignity.*

IHS.

May the sovereign grace and eternal love of Christ our Lord be always our constant protection and help.

In the matter of the cardinal's hat, I thought I would give some account to you, as if to my own soul, regarding what took place within me, for God's greater glory. As soon as I learned for certain that the Emperor had nominated you and that the Pope was willing to make you a cardinal, I immediately had this impulse or spiritual movement to oppose it in any way I could. However, being unsure of God's will because of the many reasons that occurred to me on both sides, I ordered all the priests in the community to say Mass and those not priests to offer their prayers for three days that I might be guided wholly to God's greater glory. Over this period of three days, there were times when, as I reflected and conferred about the matter, I experienced certain fears, or a lack of that freedom of spirit for speaking out and opposing it. I thought, "How do I know what God our Lord wants to do?" and did not find within myself total certainty about opposing it. At other times, when I went to my regular prayers, I felt within myself that these fears receded. Repeating this petition at intervals, sometimes with this fear and sometimes with the opposite, I finally found myself, during my regular prayer on the third day and continuously thereafter, with a judgment so complete and a will so calm and free to do all I could with the Pope and the cardinals to oppose it that if I failed to do so, I would be, and am, quite certain that I could give no good account of myself to God our Lord, but instead a wholly bad one.

However, I held then and hold now that there would be no contradiction in its being God's will for me to take this course while others take a different one and the dignity be conferred upon you. The same divine Spirit could move me to this course for one set of reasons and move others to the opposite for different ones, with the outcome being what the Emperor indicated. May God our Lord act everywhere as may be always for his greater praise and glory. I believe it would be useful for you to answer the letter Master Polanco is writing about this on my behalf, and to state what intention and will God our Lord has given or may give you, so that, receiving it in writing, we could show it where needed, leaving the whole matter in the hands of God our Lord, so that he might fulfill his holy will in all our affairs.

Your last letter, dated March 13, is being answered in another. God our Lord grant that your journey and the entire outcome have gone as we had hoped for here in his Divine Majesty, and that this letter may find you in perfect health, both interior and exterior, as is my desire and constant petition to God our Lord in my poor unworthy prayers, for the greater glory of his Divine Majesty. May he in his infinite mercies always be our constant protection and help.

From Rome

✠

To Claude Jay

Rome, July 30, 1552

(Letter 2769: IV:348–50; in Latin)

An account of the German College to be inaugurated that winter, and a formal mandate to recruit students for it. The five cardinals referred to in the letter were Pio Carpi ("protector" of the Society of Jesus), Alvarez de Toledo, Marcello Cervini (later Pope Marcellus II), Giovanni Morone (legate and presiding officer at the Council of Trent), and Giacomo Puteo. The "Cardinal of Augsburg" was Otto

Truchsess, one of the most important proponents of the reform in the Catholic Church in Germany.

Jesus

May the grace and peace of our Lord Jesus Christ be ever preserved and increased in us. Amen.

My dear Brother in Christ:

I think that you have heard more than once about the German College to be established here in the city of Rome. It is to receive selected young men who display good character and the promise of Christian piety and virtue, for education in good morals and the cultivation of all kinds of learning. Under the protection of the Supreme Pontiff and a board of five cardinals, they will live in the college under the care of our Society, so that they will lack no necessities in regard to lodging, board, clothing, books, and furnishings—in short, all the customary accommodations for students. Upon making creditable progress in learning and virtue, they would be sent back to Germany and given ecclesiastical benefices; indeed, those who have been conspicuous for special attainments in virtue would be promoted to bishoprics and the highest dignities. Persons who yearn for Germany's salvation envision, as the surest and almost the only human means for shoring up and restoring its tottering—and, unfortunately, in many places collapsed—church, the possibility of sending there large numbers of faithful and energetic men of that nation and tongue, models of studious life and solid learning, who by preaching the word of God, by lectures, or at least by personal conversations, will be able to tear away the veil of ignorance and vice and open the eyes of their fellow countrymen to the light of the Catholic and orthodox faith.

Those, therefore, who come to Rome to this college, which has been erected for the benefit of Germany (as can be seen from the transcript or copy of the apostolic letter enclosed), will have instructors to train them carefully in Latin, Greek, and Hebrew. If they have completed their humanities, they will follow courses in logic, physics, and other liberal arts, and at the end get a good training in theology, by means of lectures and regular exercises. They will also have persons to care for them in spiritual and domestic affairs and to govern the college; these will be members of our Society, men both learned and pious, largely from Germany or neighboring countries. Since we would like to commence this noble work this year, the most reverend and illustrious cardinals who have undertaken the protection of this venture, and especially the Most Reverend Cardinal of Augsburg, whose zealous charity is remarkably active in it, decided that we ought to write you and Master Canisius and other dear brothers of the Society in Vienna, to have you send to Rome as soon as possible a number of young men of German birth and language, to arrive here if possible throughout October, or at least November. We, then, upon whom it is incumbent most willingly to take up this burden with all due zeal, seriously enjoin you to employ in recruiting and sending these young men all the energy and zeal that you would use in a matter of the greatest import for the glory of God and the salvation of souls.

Rome, July 30, 1552

> Yours in our Lord,
> IGNATIO

✠

To Jerónimo Nadal from Juan de Polanco by commission

Rome, August 6, 1552
(Letter 2774: IV:353f.; in Spanish)

Polanco relays to Nadal in Sicily a strong spiritual impression that has come over Ignatius: that Emperor Charles V ought to organize an enormous fleet and drive from the western Mediterranean the Turks and the corsairs who were ravaging its coasts. Not completely sure that the inspiration is from God and uncertain whether he would have any credit with the Emperor because the Jesuits were not held in high esteem at the court of Charles V, Ignatius asks Nadal's opinion. Ignatius's willingness in such an important matter to set out for the Emperor's court is reminiscent of the willingness, expressed in an earlier letter to the King of Portugal, to go personally on a mission to Ethiopia if such was necessary. The accompanying letter of the same date (no. 2775, pp. 380–84) systematically presents Ignatius's arguments for this grandly conceived plan and his detailed suggestions on how it could be financed.

Jhs.

The peace of Christ.

Dearest Father in Jesus Christ:

I shall not fail to communicate to Your Reverence, being so commissioned by our father Master Ignatius, an impression he finds himself with these days, so that you may write what you think about it—although were God our Lord to give His Paternity some more effective interior sign than he has so far, or if he were certain of enjoying credit with His Majesty, he would await no one else's advice. It has to do with these Turkish fleets which he sees arriving in Christian lands year after year and inflicting so much harm by carrying off so many souls who are going to perdition because they deny their faith in Christ, who died to save them. In addition, the Turks learn and get experience of these waters, and burn various places. He also sees the damage the corsairs so commonly wreak in the coastal areas upon the souls, bodies, and property of Christians. Seeing all this, he has come to the strong conviction in our Lord that the Emperor ought to muster a great fleet and assert mastery of the sea, thereby preventing these evils and bringing about other great advantages of importance for the universal welfare. He feels himself moved to this not only by zeal for souls and charity but also by the light of reason, which shows that this project is highly necessary and can be executed with the Emperor spending less than what he now does. Our Father is so set on this matter, as I said, that if he thought he could find credit with His Majesty or had a stronger sign of the divine will, he would gladly devote to it what is left of his old age, undaunted by the hardship of the journey to the Emperor and Prince, the dangers of the road, his own ailments, or any other obstacle. Your Reverence should recommend this matter to God, ponder it carefully, and let us know soon what in the sight of God you think.

Rome, August 6, 1552

> Your Reverence's servant in Christ,
> by commission of our father Master Ignatius,
> JUAN DE POLANCO

✠

To Jerónimo Nadal, by commission

Rome, August 6, 1552

(Letter 2775: IV:354–58; in Spanish)

See the introduction to the previous letter. Not only does Ignatius want Nadal's advice in the plans he suggests for Charles V to send an armada against the Turks, but he also sets out those plans in detail in this letter, which he probably wanted Nadal to give to Juan de Vega, the viceroy of Sicily, who was both a very good friend of Ignatius and an equally good friend of the Emperor. The letter is a vivid example of Ignatius's willingness to take advantage of politics, not only the Turkish menace but the French-Spanish rivalry, as one of the human means to advance the glory of God. It was nineteen years later that a Spanish and Italian fleet under the command of Juan of Austria, brother of Philip II, won the great naval victory over the Turks at Lepanto in October 7, 1571.

Jesus

The peace of Christ.

Dear Father in Jesus Christ:

In my other more general letter, I related briefly how Our Father was being moved, not only by the zeal of charity but also by the light of reason, to believe that a large fleet both should and could be raised. In this letter I will show in greater detail, first, that this fleet ought to be raised and would be highly advisable and, second, that this can be done at little expense—in fact for less than what His Majesty currently spends on naval affairs.

The reasons underlying the belief that this ought to be done are as follows:

1. God's honor and glory suffer badly when Christians, great and small, from so many places are carried off among infidels, where many of them, as experience shows, renounce their faith in Christ, to the great pain of those who are zealous for the preservation and advancement of our holy Catholic faith.

2. It will lie heavily on the consciences of those who are able but fail to do anything about so many people being lost, from children through all ages, who, unwilling to bear the harsh slavery and countless other evils which they suffer from the infidels, become Moors or Turks. These number in the thousands, and on the day of judgment our princes will see whether they should have placed so little value upon many souls and bodies that are worth more than all their own incomes, dignities, and signiories, since Christ our Lord paid the price of his life's blood for every one of them.

3. All Christendom will be rid of the great peril it incurs from this coming and going of the Turks. So far they have not been aggressive on the sea, but they are beginning to get experience and acquire a taste for it, and are starting to employ on what little remains of Christendom the tactic they used in taking the empire of Constantinople: that of abetting one prince to oppose and keep engaged with another so that they wear each other out, and then intervening themselves to take what belongs to both. Thus, with them making use now of this way of acting with France, there is danger that they will eventually come in without being called, placing Christendom under great pressure by land and sea. This

problem and those mentioned above would be removed if His Majesty mastered the sea with a strong navy.

4. This fleet would largely rid the kingdom of Naples of the occasions for its disturbances and agitations. Without hope of help from the Turk, the insurgents would have no prospect of achieving their aims. In addition, neither would they be allowed to hope for support by sea from France, and they would fear immediate reprisals upon the rebels from the fleet. This would pacify not only Naples but all of Italy, Sicily, and the other islands of this sea.

5. With the fleet strong enough to convince him that the Turks would be unable to come here, the King of France would be deprived of their help in diverting and depleting His Majesty's forces, and see that his best policy was to keep the peace. Even if he did not do so inside his own kingdom and frontiers, he would have no motivation for raising havoc in Italy. Kept permanently inferior at sea and deprived of help from that quarter, he would be weaker and thus more inclined to peace.

6. It would end the continual material devastation by the Turks and corsairs all along the coasts of Spain, Italy, and other places, as well as the expense of fortifications along all the coasts because of never knowing where the Turkish fleet will strike. The high costs of all this are evident from the past two years in the kingdom of Naples and Sicily and elsewhere; but with a fleet serving as a universal bulwark, these would be unnecessary.

7. It would secure and facilitate passage from Spain to Italy; this is clearly of great importance for the general welfare of these kingdoms and that of many individuals who suffer severely from the interruption of this traffic.

8. With a powerful fleet and mastery of the sea, it would be easy to recoup our losses and much more, along all the coasts of Africa and Greece and in the Mediterranean islands. A foothold could even be gained in many lands belonging to the Moors and other infidels, opening a broad path to their conquest and consequently to their being made Christians. On the other hand, without a fleet other positions important for Christendom might be seized, as Tripoli was.

9. His Majesty's honor and reputation, of crucial importance among both believers and infidels, would be greatly enhanced by this fleet. He would be seeking out the enemy in their own lands and doing something more than defending himself with so much difficulty here in his own, thereby losing much of the credibility and authority with which,

even without arms, he might in some fashion protect his subjects in many places.

These are the motives which move Our Father by way of reason to the conviction that a fleet should be raised.

And now for the second part: how to accomplish this. His ideas are as follows.

Assuming that His Majesty will have no lack of manpower, being by God's grace better supplied therewith than any prince known in the world, the funds could be raised from a variety of sources:

1. Numerous wealthy religious orders in His Majesty's dominions, which could do with far less than they have, might be ordered to provide a fair number of galleys. Thus, the Hieronymites could be assessed so many, the Benedictines so many, the Carthusians so many, etc. This includes the abbeys in Sicily and Naples that have no religious.

2. A second source would be the bishoprics throughout his domains, with their chapters and benefice holders; these could contribute a large sum of money to outfit a good number of galleys for the benefit of Christendom.

3. Another source could be the four orders of knights, all of which, like that of St. John, ought by virtue of their institutes to assist this fleet against the infidel with their property and persons. To accomplish this in due form, the Pope could be persuaded to sanction the levy, or else the superiors there in Spain and in his other dominions could be dealt with, since it is for the universal good of Christendom.

4. A fourth source would be certain of the grandees and secular nobles of his realms. What they expend for the sake of grandeur on hunting and feasting and extravagant retinues would be more appropriately and honorably spent fitting out ships against the infidel, for the glory of God. If they do not serve personally, they should be eager to help and serve with their property. This could produce a large number of galleys.

5. The merchants could band together and finance a good number of sailing ships or galleys; apart from the good of Christendom, it will be of benefit for their own business.

6. A further source would be the towns and municipalities of his realms and dominions, particularly the coastal cities which suffer so many depredations from the Turks, Moors, and other corsairs. What would be lost to this robbery would be far better spent on galleys, so that there would be no robbers. What they are used to spending on

defenses ought to be spent on the fleet; then there would no longer be need for the expense and drain on their business for self-protection. The regions that would benefit most from this, such as the kingdom of Naples and Sicily, could contribute more.

7. The King of Portugal could help; he could finance from his own realm, in an identical or similar way to that proposed for His Majesty, a certain number of galleys and other sailing vessels.

8. There are the signiories: that of Genoa, which could pay for a few galleys, and those of Lucca and Siena, which will always contribute even if that of Venice cannot.

9. The Duke of Florence, who ought to help for the sake of his own dominions, over and above the common good. He too, as was suggested for the King of Portugal, could draw on ecclesiastical and secular sources similar to those listed above.

10. A tenth source could and ought to be the Pope and the lands of the Church, should God so inspire him. If not, he could at least permit the measures outlined above, which would be no small contribution.

There you have, dear father, what occurs to Our Father here on this subject by way of reason. Over and above what the Emperor could contribute from his own considerable revenues, these ten sources would seem to yield enough to maintain a large fleet. With additional help from the royal revenues, it would seem possible to maintain without much effort upwards of two hundred or, if needed, three hundred ships, mostly or nearly all galleys, to the great benefit of what little is left of Christendom, which in this way could be expected to expand mightily, whereas at present we rightly fear its diminution and notable loss.

Study all this and let us know your opinion, for if other more qualified persons do not speak out on this, perhaps one of the poor members of the Society of Jesus may undertake to do so.

May God, eternal wisdom, grant to His Majesty and to everyone in all things to know his most holy will and the grace perfectly to fulfill it.

Rome, August 6, 1552

✠

To Juan Esteban Manrique de Lara, duke of Nájera

Rome, August 26, 1552

(Letter 2816: IV:385f.; in Spanish)

The house of Loyola had close relations with that of the Dukes of Nájera, Ignatius having served there as a youth. Upon being applied to for help with a projected marriage between the daughter of Beltram, Ignatius's nephew, and a relative of the Duke of Nájera, Ignatius wrote the following letter. He recalled his service with the reigning duke's father, and explained why he had not kept up relations even with his own family and had declined to become involved in the marriage negotiations. As a matter of fact, the grandniece had, unknown to Ignatius, married Francis Borgia's second son, Juan, three weeks earlier. Ignatius was later unhappy at the rumors that the Loyolas were trying to move up in the world by such a marriage alliance with a ducal family and the suggestion that he had supported it.

My Lord in our Lord:

May the sovereign grace and eternal love of Jesus Christ our Lord greet and visit Your Lordship with his supreme gifts and spiritual graces.

A letter of yours dated January 22 was given to me yesterday by Don Juan de Guevara.[1] I will not delay to apologize for my neglect in writing, since it has been my manner of proceeding, and that of all who leave the world for Christ our Lord, to forget as much as possible the things of earth, so as to be more mindful of those of heaven, and to have all the less concern for human courtesies as we are obliged to have more complete concern for what regards the service of God. Nevertheless, had there arisen an opportunity of serving Your Lordship to God's glory, I would not have failed—in conformity with my profession of poverty—to show the affection which I owe Your Lordship's person and house for the favors and love by which your forebears bound me thereto. So in my poor prayers, the only means available to me for serving you, I have commended and through the grace of God will continue to commend Your Lordship and all your affairs to God our Creator and Lord, whose special protection and most abundant grace I desire may always be experienced by Your Lordship and all your house, to the glory of the Divine Majesty.

As for the business of the marriage about which Your Lordship writes me, this is a thing of such a nature and so alien to my least profession that I would consider any involvement on my part quite out of keeping with it. In fact, it is ten or eleven years since I have written to anyone of the house of Loyola, accounting that I had abandoned it, together with the whole world, once and for all for Christ and that I should in no way start again regarding it as my own. However, if Your Lordship thinks that it will be to God's greater glory that the union of

---

[1] A nephew of the duke.

these two houses be brought about, and that it will turn out well for them in terms of the end we all ought to desire, I think it would be well to write to my nephews, the Lord of Oceta and Martín García Loyola, to meet with Your Lordship and discuss the matter in person. I believe that as far as that side is concerned, the matter is entirely up to these two, as I explained fully and at length to Don Juan.

And so I have nothing further to say on this matter, except to defer to whatever Your Lordship may judge best in our Lord. I beg of him by his infinite and supreme goodness to give to all of us his abundant grace always to know his most holy will and perfectly to fulfill it.

Rome, August 26, 1552

✠

To Cesare Aversano

Rome, September 10, 1552

(Letter 2861: IV:408–14; in Italian)

This instruction for the first rector of the college at Modena is substantially identical with that of June 13, 1551, to Jean Pelletier (letter 1899, pp. 346–51), with the addition of the following specific instructions for the Jesuits going to Modena.

For Those of Modena Alone

1. Father Master Cesare will take care, if necessary, to dispense any and all of the others at Modena regarding fasts and prohibited foods as well as recitation of the Office, freeing himself and them from all scruples in these regards, whenever he may judge such dispensation appropriate. For reasons of health, Father Cesare's collateral will be able to dispense him in the same fashion.

2. Father Don Cesare will hear the confessions of all the others of the Society in Modena, and will go to confession to Master Adrian [Witte], so that in this way mutual union and charity may be better preserved. However, should it be judged suitable for Master Adrian to confess all or some of the others, cases which are reserved in Rome shall be reserved to him as superior.

3. He may entrust Master Adrian with superintendance of the classes and the duty of visiting them; however, he himself should also be concerned to see that things go well.

4. There would not seem to be time at the beginning for preaching in large places, or in very public smaller ones. But, as they will see [being done] in Perugia, they should concentrate on the classes and on teaching catechism, interspersing exhortations, etc. They might also preach in some monasteries. Subsequently, they can gradually see what should be done.

5. Since the priests are quite young, they will need to compensate for their age with maturity of behavior, acting in such a way as to preserve holy humility and not incur contempt or lose the authority they require with the persons with whom they deal. Thus they should demonstrate humility in their external activities and, even if asked, not state that they have studied theology for this or that amount of time, but only that they have studied theology. They should preserve rather than lessen people's idea and opinion of their learning, without prejudice to truth or modesty.

6. Care should be taken that no one converse with externs without his express permission. If they are teachers, they should not talk with their pupils except in public places and without having special familiarity with any individual—except, as has been said, with express permission and for some important matter. No one should touch anyone else, neither a pupil nor any other sort of person, either on the ear or hand or any other part of the body; and the priests should diligently ensure the observance of this.

✠

To Silvestro Landini and Manoel Gomes

Rome, September 10, 1552

(Letter 2867: IV:416–22; in Italian)

Detailed instructions to an Italian and a Portuguese, both sickly, sent on a reconnoitering and canonical visitation to Corsica. The vice-legate was at that time the archbishop of Genoa, Geronimo Sauli. The cardinals were Bernardino Maffeo and Giovanni Riccio, the latter popularly called Cardinal Montepulciano from his birthplace. This letter gives good evidence of how careful Ignatius was about the protocol of visiting officials and presenting them with the appropriate documentation.

Instruction for Those Going to Corsica

The Journey

1. Master Manoel will leave Rome together with the others going to Modena. At Bologna they will all pay their respects to the Most Reverend Vice-Legate, and Master Manoel will give him the letter from Rome and ask him what instructions His Reverend Lordship wants to give for Father Don Silvestro during the time he will be staying in the Genoese state and in Corsica; he will also show him the brief for him from His Holiness and the note from the cardinals.

2. On arrival in Modena, he and Father Don Silvestro will leave for Genoa with the bishop's permission, and unless prevented by illness, make their departure quickly, leaving the new college in good order and giving them some instructions.

3. In Genoa they will visit the lord protectors of San Giorgio, presenting them with their letters and showing the brief of His Holiness as well as the note from Cardinals Maffei and Montepulciano, so as to reside for a time in the Genoese state.[2]

4. After this, or before, they will visit His Lordship the Vicar of the archbishop, give him his letter, and offer themselves for twenty or thirty days—or, in accord with the note from the reverend cardinals, a little longer—for any spiritual service inside or outside Genoa; and this they shall perform.

5. Before leaving, they will find out from a father inquisitor at San Domenico about what is known regarding the evil doctrine being sown in Corsica by a certain master, and any other matter. They should also find out if there is an inquisitor on the island; and whether there is or not, they should show the clause in His Holiness's brief about their faculties for reconciling heretics without prejudice to the inquisitors, etc. They should learn from him how to go about dealing with such persons without prejudice to the inquisitors, but rather according to their mind.

6. In Genoa they should endeavor to give a good odor and taste of the Society. When it is time to cross to Corsica, they should arrange with the lords of San Giorgio to inform them occasionally about whatever needs arise, and for the Signoria to send whatever assistance they can. They should get letters for the Signoria's officials in Corsica and for

---

[2] The "lord protectors" were the Signoria, or governing body, of Genoa. They had asked that Jesuits be sent to Genoa.

others if necessary; and they will sail to Corsica in whatever manner or way the lords indicate to them.

Regarding Their Persons While in Corsica

1. Although Father Don Silvestro and Master Manoel are companions, Master Manoel should have due respect for him like that of a collateral to a superior. If anyone joins them, Father Don Silvestro should have a superior's authority over him. Regarding matters of doctrine, he should let himself be advised by him, and also in the execution of this mission; that is, where and how they should proceed in visiting, preaching, confessing, or not; and generally in all matters for which they are sent to Corsica, the direction and governance of both should be vested in Father Don Silvestro.

2. Each should have charge and authority over the other in the treatment of their bodies, and consequently in dispensing, when needed, from the Office or from fasting, and similarly with regard to foods during the periods when they are prohibited, according as their health dictates.

3. It will be good if they can take on a person to help them with domestic matters, even if he is not suited for the Society.

4. As for their food and other necessaries, they shall accept what they need according to the arrangement that will be made for them, so long as it is not by way of compensation for penalties or dispensations or anything obviously belonging to their office, for according to the Society's Institute they may not make use of such. Since they are both sickly, they should take special care not to allow each other to suffer too much, so that they can last in the service of God and of their neighbor.

How to Proceed in Corsica regarding the Neighbor

1. They should carefully study the brief from His Holiness—particularly Father Don Silvestro—and have at hand a summary of it; and they can gauge their behavior by the authority granted them therein and the privileges of the Society, so as neither to exceed their powers nor lag behind in making what use discretion dictates they should of the arms granted them for the service of God and the good of souls.

2. Father Don Silvestro should recall that the purpose of this mission and visitation in Corsica is primarily to get information about its spiritual needs and to inform Their Most Reverend Lordships whom His Holiness has charged with these, [letting them know] both the needs and their recommendations for remedying them; their secondary

purpose is to apply what actual remedies they can with the means they deem appropriate.

3. In regard to the latter, their work will consist mainly in visiting, preaching, and hearing confessions, and in lovingly admonishing or even reprehending. Punishment, unless in great or urgent cases, they should employ sparingly and with much tact in the beginning; however, where they judge that the larger and better part of the inhabitants approve and there is no fear of opposition to their actions, they may proceed to impose punishments.

4. If they find many spiritual needs for which they ought to provide and are unable to satisfy them all, they should choose the undertakings which are most important and practicable and without danger of impeding God's greater service.

5. Although they must follow whatever directives they receive from the lords of Genoa regarding which places to visit, yet if they receive no such directives and the matter is left to their own choice, they should go first to the more important places from which their good example and reputation can be extended to the others; or else to the places which are in greater need and can least suffer delay; or else to where they find the greatest support and the least difficulty.

6. Given the great importance of the goodwill of the people, and especially of the principal personages whose being helped spiritually redounds to the greater good, they should strive to be loved by all through a demonstration of genuine charity and the purest zeal for the salvation of their souls. This holds especially for the officials of the Signoria in Corsica and for the bishops and the lords in Genoa themselves; they should work to increase their devotion towards themselves and the Society, so that they will not fail in matters of their office and duty.

7. Regarding the importance of their being seen to be far from any appearance of greed, they should take care not to receive with their own hands any moneys by way of penalties, fees for dispensations, settlements with usurers, or the like; these should be held in deposit by good persons of standing, so that they can be spent on the poor and on pious institutions, either for their current financial needs or for similar needs as they arise, thus promoting the edification of all.

8. Because there is said to be great ignorance among the priests on the island, they should see whether to set up regular schools or colleges, at least one to a diocese, or even a university in one or two of the principal localities, where along with good morals and humane letters, the

other disciplines could also be taught, at least cases of conscience. This latter might be as good as a number of colleges; and the localities could contribute support for both the teachers and a number of their students, who would subsequently receive ecclesiastical benefices and alleviate the ignorance of the people and aid them by their example. However, discretion will dictate if this second course is preferable to the first one of founding colleges in each diocese—or perhaps setting up classes of Christian doctrine in each town, larger colleges in the main dioceses, and a university in one of the biggest ones.

9. If among the secular clergy who are without benefices they find any persons apt for cultivating the vineyard of the Lord, they should see how to put them to work in accord with their talent, in preaching, teaching Christian doctrine, or acting as assistants to those who have curacies of souls; and they should supply information about such persons, so that they can be given benefices that fall vacant.

10. If none such are found among the secular clergy, but there are some apt for these duties among the religious, they should see how to put them to work according to their talent. If they find no one in either clergy, they should write to the lords of Genoa and ask for help.

11. While they should not get entangled in matters of temporal government, they may, when necessary, admonish the officials of the Signoria with due charity; and if this does not suffice and they see that something needs to be done, they should suitably inform the lords of Genoa.

12. They should diligently write to the Signoria, [telling them] how things are going, and also to Rome—letters which will give edification to whoever sees them as well as private letters for the superior of the Society.

Reminders for Those in Corsica

1. In Bologna Master Manoel may accept the travel money offered him by the Most Reverend Vice-Legate.

2. They should get information in Genoa about the college which the Sauli family is said to be arranging for the Society.

3. Since Father Don Silvestro is rather unwell, he should take care of himself and not let himself get overtired or exhausted; he should prefer taking a longer time to accomplish his goals rather than overtiring himself in order to get everything done quickly.

4. Master Manoel should also remember that he is sent not only to assist Father Don Silvestro but also to preserve and strengthen his own health. This they should do, not working to excess in any corporal or spiritual activity.

5. In traveling from one place to another, they should have no scruple about using horses; and while they should be ready to beg alms if there is no other arrangement, when they are given them, they should accept enough for themselves and for one servant.

6. In case Master Manoel cannot travel beyond Modena, Father Don Silvestro will proceed to Genoa, and if Master Manoel does not arrive by the end of his stay there, one of the less-occupied students at Modena, perhaps Juan Nieto or some one like him, should go in his place, with Master Manoel remaining as his substitute.

7. While in their enclosed messages they should tell things the way they are, in their showable letters they should have an eye to the edification of the reverend cardinals who will see them, etc.

8. They should take special care to have the goodwill of the episcopal vicars as far as possible, so that their reports to Rome will not be damaging; and even if they see some great evil in them, they should write to Rome before breaking with them. Of course, they may employ loving and humble admonition, but they should take care to leave them friendly and contented.

9. If they write to anyone besides ourselves in Rome, the letters should be sent unsealed, so that we can read them; they should also send some signed blank sheets, so that we can change anything that needs to be changed—in accord with the truth, of course—should it be deemed expedient for God's greater glory. Even when they write to us, it would be good to send some signed blanks for the same purpose.

10. With regard to informing the lords of Genoa about shortcomings in their officials, they should do this only in easy matters and with great tact, so as not to get embroiled in controversies, unless they have first advised us in Rome with full information so as to have our opinion and judgment from here.

11. For greater union and mutual charity, they should make their confessions to each other as long as they are together and are the only priests of the Society.

✠

To Those Sent on Missions

Rome, October 8, 1552

(XII [Appendix 1, no. 24]: 251-53; in Italian)

This instruction extracts points from Part VII of the Constitutions, *which had not yet been fully promulgated throughout the Society. It is divided into three sections: on care for self, on dealing with the neighbor, and on responsibility toward the Society.*

Jhs.

One sent out in this Society to labor in the vineyard of the Lord should have three concerns: one is himself, another is the neighbor with whom he deals, and another is the head and entire body of the Society of which he is a member.

In the first place, with regard to himself, he should take care not to neglect himself for the sake of helping others. He should be unwilling to commit even the smallest sin for all the spiritual gain that could be had, nor even place himself in danger of such. For this it will help to converse only sparingly and in public with persons from whom he has reason to fear anything. In a general way, he should prescind from the outward person and look upon the creature, not as good-looking or attractive, but as someone bathed in the blood of Christ, an image of God, a temple of the Holy Spirit, etc.

To defend himself from all evils and acquire all virtues—to which he will be able to draw others in proportion as he himself is filled with them—it will be helpful to take some time for himself each day for examination of conscience, prayer, the reception of the sacraments, etc.

He should also give suitable attention to his health and bodily strength.

In the second place, with regard to the neighbor, he should consider (1) which persons he deals with: they should be the ones from whom the most results can be foreseen—supposing he cannot deal with everybody. Such would be persons in greatest need and those possessing great authority, learning, or temporal goods, and others who are suited to be laborers—in general those who, if helped themselves, would most be able to help others, for God's glory.

2. He should consider which religious works he spends his time on. He should prefer before any others those for which he is specifically sent. Among other works, he should prefer those which are better—that is, the spiritual over the corporal, the more urgent over the less urgent,

the universal over the particular, the permanent and lasting over those that do not last, etc.—in cases where he cannot do both. He should also remember that it is not enough to get a good and religious work started: he must as far as possible complete it and put it on a permanent footing.

3. He should consider the instruments he ought to employ. Besides his example and prayer full of desires, he should consider, for instance, whether to make use of confession, or spiritual exercises and conversations, or catechism teaching, or lectures, or sermons, etc. And he should select those arms (if he cannot make use of all) which are deemed likely to be most effective and which each individual is best able to employ.

4. He should preserve the proper manner of proceeding, aiming at humility by starting from below and not getting involved in higher matters except when invited or asked, unless discretion should dictate otherwise, taking into consideration time, place, and persons. This discretion cannot be confined within any rule. The manner also includes working to obtain the goodwill of the persons with whom he deals, by a manifestation, grounded in truth, ———— in virtue and love;[3] also by trying to have credit with them, and adapting himself to all with holy prudence. This is chiefly taught by the anointing of the Holy Spirit, but we contribute to it by reflection and careful observation. Thus, the examination of conscience mentioned above could also be applied to such reflections, and some time during the day would need to be devoted to them. It is particularly important that in cases of conscience and difficulties where he does not have the solution clearly and confidently in mind, he not give a reply or solution hastily, but only after adequate study and reflection.

In the third place, as regards the head and body of the Society, he should (1) let himself be directed by the superior, keep him informed of whatever he ought to know, and be obedient to any orders that he is given.

2. He should be concerned for the Society's good name and reputation and for any way in which he can further it for God's glory, chiefly through foundations (especially of colleges wherever opportunity or favorable circumstances are seen) and by recruiting good prospects for the Society, such as persons who are educated, or very active, or young, when they have good appearance, health, intelligence, good inclinations, and no apparent impediments, etc.

---

[3] The original manuscript is worn away at this point in the letter.

To Diego Laínez, by commission

Rome, November 2, 1552

(Letter 3002: IV:498–500; in Spanish)

Ignatius, so considerate of the feelings of others of his first companions, particularly Simão Rodrigues, had no such scruples with the man who was to succeed him at the head of the Society. Here he has his secretary Polanco send Laínez a harsh letter of reproof for shortcomings in his dealings with his superior in Rome. Laínez responded by asking forgiveness, by seeking to be relieved of his responsibilities as leader of the Society in Venice, and by suggesting that he be brought back to Rome, where he would willingly carry out the lowliest tasks in the house, or if he was incapable of doing that, he would teach the entry class in Latin grammar.

JESUS

To Father Laínez (confidential)

The peace of Christ.

Father mine:

This letter should be received, not as coming from Your Reverence's son that I am as Polanco, who owes you all respect and reverence, but as from an instrument or pen of Our Father, who has ordered me to write what is herein contained. He has been intending to have it written for some time, but because of your quartan fever put it off until now that you have recovered from it.

Our Father is not a little displeased with Your Reverence; all the more so in that faults in someone who is loved are always more serious to the one who loves him, and are felt the more keenly the less they had been anticipated. And so he has charged me to write you about some of them so that Your Reverence may know yourself and not continue in them but correct them instead, as will be easy for someone with as great goodwill as God our Lord has given Your Reverence. First of all, the prior of Trinità wrote Our Father along with Master André [des Freux], strongly urging that Master Girolamo Otello be sent in the latter's place.[4] To quote his own words, "For many reasons our dear son in Christ, Master Girolamo Otello, would be quite suitable, according to what Reverend Father Laínez has told me." This was no slight error, though no doubt done with a good intention. You should not have encouraged or advised the prior to ask Our Father for what he was not going to grant him. You might at least have ascertained Our Father's mind before giving an opinion like this to the prior. And even though I

---

[4] The prior is Andrea Lippomani; the house was in Venice.

should wish to add reasons for this and for what follows, Our Father's judgment was that I should not; the submission of your own judgment that Your Reverence owes your superior in whatever pertains to his office should be all you need. But there is likewise an express prohibition against anyone's urging important persons, among other things, to write to Our Father and request particular individuals without consulting him first, because of the many untoward consequences when he has to refuse.

This error was caused by a second one (over and above your personal failing): Your Reverence's disagreeing with your superior over the removal of Father des Freux from Venice. You not only disagreed, but you made it clear to des Freux himself, as well as to Fathers Salmerón and Olave, that you disagreed, or that you did not approve Our Father's order. How appropriate it is when someone upon whom the most recent arrivals are supposed to model themselves lets them see that he considers bad what the superior considers good, this Your Reverence can conceive. And after Master André wrote a number of considerations which he and Fathers Salmerón and Olave deemed sufficient for removing him from Venice to Rome, Our Father was also not pleased with some of the remarks in your reply, such as about the bad repercussions out in the villages and so on—also indicating a divergence of your own judgment from your superior's. Advice or representation is good at the proper time, but a dissenting judgment is not.

The third error which has caused Our Father no little pain is your having sent Gaspare here without first reporting his condition, merely saying, "since they are Paduans," etc. Your Reverence should not have concealed such a matter when sending a person like him to the house here. Our Father looks upon any such withholding of information from the superior, whom one is supposed to aid with one's knowledge and not hurt, as a very bad thing in this Society or any religious order. Neither was Our Father pleased that after the man was sent to Your Reverence to be dismissed by you from there, you approved his wish to return here, with the remark that you think him deserving of mercy and other statements which Our Father calls "decrees." He does not enjoy your writing him such decrees; it is no way for anyone to speak to a superior. Rather, he has told me to write you and tell you to mind your own office; if you carry it out as you ought, you will be doing not a little. You are not to trouble yourself in advising him about his office. He wants no such advice from Your Reverence unless he asks for it— and wants it even less now than before you took over your charge, since the way you have administered it has not won you much credit with him in matters of government.

Your Reverence is to examine these errors in the presence of God our Lord, dedicating some prayer to this over a period of three days. Then you are to write whether you consider them to be errors or faults. You should also choose the penance you think you deserve and send it in writing; however, you are to do nothing in that regard before receiving Our Father's reply.

No more for now, except to beg that God our Lord will grant to all of us (especially the writer of this letter as needing it more) much light to know and humble ourselves, and the grace to know and do his holy will in all things.

Rome, November 2, 1552

By commission of our father Master Ignatius

JUAN DE POLANCO

✠

To Juana de Aragón

Late November 1552

(Letter 3014: IV:506–11; in Spanish)

Juana de Aragón, who had married Ascanio Colonna, duke of Palliano and Tagliacozzo in 1521, had been sensationally estranged from her choleric husband since 1535. In addition, their son, Marc Antonio, had vigorously rebelled against his father and sided with his mother. At the Pope's instance, both Bobadilla and Araoz (see letter 63, not included in this collection) attempted to reconcile them, but in vain. On November 2, 1552, Ignatius himself, making one of his rare trips from Rome, met with the duchess for two days in the kingdom of Naples and urged her to take the initiative in the reconciliation. Upon his return, he sent her the following memorial. Ignatius's mission was unsuccessful in part because a year later the duke was arrested on suspicion of being anti-Spanish. Juana herself gave cause for concern because of her friendliness in Naples with the "evangelical" humanists around Juan de Valdés, himself of Erasmian and Alumbrado tendencies.

Jesus

My Lady in our Lord:

Although I have already informed Your Excellency in conversation about the way of coming to agreement with Signor Ascanio which I deem in our Lord to be more conformable with his holy will and more suitable than any other for Your Excellency's own good, nevertheless, prompted by the attachment which his infinite Goodness has given me to Your Excellency's service and complete perfection, I shall not fail— though against my usual custom—to set down in writing my reasons for this view, in the hope that, by reflecting upon and weighing them from time to time with the good and holy inclination which God our Lord has given you, and above all through his grace, you may perhaps come to a different opinion and decision from your present one. I say then, my lady, that the best means I can think of, all things considered, is for Your Excellency to make up your mind, with great courage and with trust in our Lord, to go to Signor Ascanio's house and place yourself completely in his power, without seeking any guarantees or compacts, but freely, in the way that a wife is, and ought to be, under her husband's authority. My reasons for thinking this are as follows:

1. If the reconciliation is to be perfect and complete, there is no other way than by winning Signor Ascanio's entire heart and love. This will be done, not by negotiating compacts and seeking guarantees, as between enemies, but by showing love, humility, and confidence in him as your husband; and this will be achieved in the way I have indicated.

2. This way will display greater perfection of humility in Your Excellency than will any other. The fact is that unless one of the parties bends and behaves humbly, no permanent reconciliation of hearts can be reached. And if one of the two has to bend and act humbly, how much more reasonably should a wife distinguish herself in humility than a husband, and how much less excuse will she have before God and mankind if because of her refusal to humble herself, the unity that ought to exist between herself and her husband fails to be achieved.

3. Moreover, this would be the more courageous and great-hearted course, one befitting Your Excellency's blood and noble soul. You would show thereby that you do not fear even the danger of death, which many would fear; it is this that reveals a truly great heart. On the contrary, all these sureties and guarantees are not the mark of a person of courage.

4. The harder this course is, the more heroism does it show on your part in overcoming yourself and putting down any past or present high feelings toward Signor Ascanio. It would thus be of more lofty merit before God our Lord if you do it for love of him. Consequently, even if an easier course were open to you, you ought to prefer this one as more perfect.

5. This would be an act of greater perfection and consequently more pleasing to Christ our Lord and more in keeping with his counsels. If he is so much a lover of peace between all persons, even strangers, that he wants them to suspend their offerings and sacrifices until they are reconciled, how much more will he want it between those he has joined in the union of matrimony, of which he says in the Gospel that what God has joined together no man should put asunder, that the two will be one flesh, and that to make a life with the other, each must leave father and mother, etc. [Matt. 19:5f.].

6. It will be more in keeping with the laws which his Divine Majesty has laid down for holy matrimony, as numerous passages in Scripture make clear, where it says that the husband is the head of the wife and that wives should be subject to their husbands, a model being given in Sarah, who called her husband her lord [Eph. 5:22f.; 1 Pet. 3:6].

7. It would be an act of greater trust in our Lord, who is delighted when we rely on his providence over us. This would not be tempting his Divine Majesty, since it has been judged by prudent and learned persons that this trust would be highly commendable, entailing in any case little or no danger.

8. It would be all the more pleasing to God in that it would more completely rob the devil of means for offending his Divine Majesty; in your present situation (which would to God our Lord were less visibly seen), these are many on both Your Excellency's part and that of others.

9. It would be an act of greater charity toward Signor Ascanio if you proposed in this way to win him over (as I am confident in our Lord you would) and restore him to a condition less dangerous to his salvation and one where he can live more in God's grace and service, since your own act of high virtue will also oblige His Excellency to strive to distinguish himself more in all Christian virtues.

10. It would be a great act of charity towards him for you not only to relieve him of domestic concerns by running his household, as he desired, but also to contribute to his spiritual peace and contentment and a good old age (from which, at sixty, he is not far), so that he can finish his life in loving union with his wife and children.

11. Again, this way of reconciliation would be the best and quickest means to remedy the situation of your lady daughters, thereby stealing Signor Ascanio's heart.

12. Even Signor Marcantonio will be more fully reconciled with Signor Ascanio, for his peace with his father depends on that of Your

Excellency; this would end certain difficulties he is likely experiencing now.

13. Your Excellency would put an end to many high feelings, sins, and difficulties of your own and Signor Ascanio's servants, as well as of the friends and partisans on either side, bringing them all great cause for consolation in our Lord.

14. All wives will be given a commendable example of the submission, humility, and charity they should have towards their husbands.

15. To the public at large, both great and small, to whom this breach has afforded so much cause for talk and gossip, Your Excellency would give great edification and cause for praising God our Lord through this act of high virtue and nobility of spirit.

16. If Your Excellency's honor and reputation ought to be brought into account—as they should—I am confident that you will highly enhance them by this action. Honor is, properly speaking, the reward owed to virtue. Hence, the more generous and perfect the act bringing about this reconciliation, the greater the honor that should and will be accorded it by all good people. The more universally public and notorious this case is, the farther will Your Excellency's reputation for magnanimity therein spread, to your great glory in heaven and on earth.

17. Your Excellency's good and noble heart should be moved by the thought that this act will also repair and enhance Signor Ascanio's honor, which you and your children ought to hold as your own.

18. If Your Excellency takes into account your temporal advantage, be assured that this is the course you should follow, for thereby Signor Ascanio becomes your captive and remains your slave. As a consequence, besides giving your daughters a dowry, he will pay your debts and provide for your future necessary expenses; for you will be mistress and administrator of all he owns, as I have understood from Signor Ascanio. I am sure it will be a great relief to Your Excellency not to have to burden your friends any longer in this respect.

19. Your Excellency would also be relieved of a certain amount of expense, since you will be able to dismiss part of the personal guard you maintain in your house.

20. As for Your Excellency's personal safety, this is the best way of all that I can see to assure it. For it would completely heal the wound to Signor Ascanio's spirit, win you his goodwill, and remove all occasion of his hurting you and so of your fearing him. No one fears anything from a person who loves, and he will have to love Your Excellency when he

sees how you trust and honor him in this way. Thus, all his efforts will be directed towards your protection rather than otherwise.

21. Even if he retains some resentment (which I consider impossible if you take this step), it is unlikely he would abuse your person. Even if he did not fear God, he would fear the Pope, the Emperor, his son, and the entire Spanish nation. He would see that it would ruin his reputation, his station in life, everything that he has. And he would be all the less inclined to risk this if you humble yourself, as I said, and render him due obedience.

22. If we look to Your Excellency's own happiness and peace, the way to obtain it is by procuring your own safety through removing the fear and mistrust, the suspicion and alarm, that you will inevitably have if you need to protect yourself from your husband, refusing to surrender and place yourself fully into his hands.

23. It will also contribute to Your Excellency's quiet and peace of mind to get rid of the many vexations you now have, since you will be living in the material and spiritual comfort of your own home.

24. Moreover, as for ease in achieving the reconciliation, my suggestion is surely the easiest of all, avoiding all haggling, complications, and intermediaries.

25. As for speed, the matter could be concluded today, or at any time Your Excellency decides to conclude it in this way; I do not know when it will be concluded any other way.

26. Finally, may Your Excellency reflect that this is the advice of those most devoted to your service in Christ our Lord, and that in one's own case it is right to trust others more than oneself.

☩

To Diego Miró

Rome, December 17, 1552

(Letter 3104: IV:558f.; in Spanish)

Named provincial of Portugal in mid-1552 after Simão Rodrigues and at a particularly difficult time for the province, the over-anxious Miró intervened excessively in the minutiae of the Jesuits' community and academic life, down to prescribing how the community bell should be rung and what rooms should be used for various functions. In what may be only part of a letter, Ignatius warns him of the distance which higher superiors should keep from such matters.

It is not the business of the provincial or general superior to keep such close account of the details of affairs. Indeed, however capable he might be of doing so, it is better that he assign them to others; these can later report to the provincial what they have done, and he, having heard their opinions, can make whatever decisions are his responsibility. In cases where he can leave to others both the handling and the decision, this would be much better, especially in temporal matters, but also in many that are spiritual. This is the procedure that I follow, and I experience that it gives me not only help and relief but even a greater peace and security of soul. And so, as your office demands, devote your love and concern to the overall good of your province, and when making necessary arrangements in individual matters, listen to those who in your opinion might have the soundest judgment on the topic.

Do not meddle with the execution of orders or get personally involved in them. Instead, act as a universal mover, setting the individual movers into motion. In this way you will get more things done, and better done, than otherwise—and things more appropriate to your office. Moreover, if your subordinates do anything badly, it will be less harmful than if you do. It is more appropriate for you than for them to rectify their mistakes—or for them to rectify mistakes made by you, which would happen all the time if you meddled more than you should in the details of execution.

May Jesus Christ, our God and Lord, grant to all of us the grace always to know his most holy will and perfectly to fulfill it.

Rome, December 17, 1552

✠

To Diego Miró

Rome, December 17, 1552

(Letter 3105: IV:559–63; in Spanish)

There is a breakdown of obedience in the Portuguese Province that arose in part because the previous provincial (Simão Rodrigues) proved himself unable or unwilling to take the necessary corrective measures. In the face of the problem, Ignatius, on the same day as the previous letter, mandates the provincial to dismiss from the Society those who are unwilling to obey their superiors, or to send them to Rome if there is any reason to hope for their amendment. He was careful to ask that the Portuguese monarch be apprised of these measures and the reasons for them, because there would be political implications in dismissing some of the members who were well connected at the Portuguese court.

Jhs.

May the sovereign grace and eternal love of Christ our Lord be always our help and protection.

According to reports I have from Dr. Torres, whom I sent in my place to visit you in our Lord in that kingdom, I understand that there is a notable failing among not a few of our men in that virtue which is more necessary and essential in the Society than any other, and in which we are solemnly urged to distinguish ourselves to the greatest extent possible by the vicar of Christ in the bulls of our Institute. I mean respect, reverence, and perfect obedience to superiors, who hold the place of Christ our Lord—or rather, to the Divine Majesty in them. Moreover, from what you have heard about how I must and do desire this virtue in my brethren, you can well imagine how happy I have been to hear that there is among you anyone who without any respect says to his superior, "You should not have commanded me that," or, "It is not good that I do this"; or who refuses to do what he is commanded, or who by signs and actions shows the lack of interior reverence and submission that has been reported to me towards one whom he ought to reverence as holding the place of Christ our Lord, and to whom as such he ought to humble himself in all things before his Divine Majesty. This matter has apparently gone so far because of the fault of a person who was responsible for correcting it but did not do so. May God our Lord forgive him. How much better it would have been to remove from the Society any diseased members and protect the healthy, rather than let them infect many others with so grave a malady by example and association with them! On another occasion I had a letter written about how pleased I was that Master Leonard [Kessel] in Cologne had at one blow dismissed nine or ten men who were behaving badly. He later did the same thing again, which I likewise approved—although, had measures been taken at the start of the trouble, it might have sufficed to dismiss one or two. And now, although late, the remedy is being applied there: better late than never.

I command you in virtue of holy obedience to have the following observed for me with regard to obedience. If there is anyone who is unwilling to obey you—not just you, but any of the local superiors or rectors there—you are to do one of two things: either dismiss him from the Society or send him here to Rome if you think that a particular individual can be helped by such a change to become a true servant of

Christ our Lord. Communicate this to Their Highnesses if necessary; I have no doubt that they will be content, in view of the spirit and holy intentions with which God our Lord has endowed them; for to keep among you someone who is not a true son of obedience does no good for the kingdom. Nor can it be believed that a person whose own soul is so destitute of help will be able help others, or that God our Lord would be willing to accept him as an instrument for his service and glory. For we see from experience that men of average or even below-average talent are often the instruments of remarkable and supernatural achievements, because they are completely obedient and through this virtue allow themselves to be moved and possessed by the mighty hand of the Author of all good. Conversely, we see great talents laboring harder without achieving even average results; the reason is that, being moved by themselves—that is, by their own self-love—or at least not letting themselves be properly moved by God our Lord through obedience to their superiors, they produce results that are proportionate, not to the almighty hand of God our Lord, who does not accept them as his instruments, but instead to their own weak and feeble hands. Understanding this, Their Highnesses will, I am confident, be satisfied. And while we have plenty to do here without having to deal with persons coming here from there, we shall, because of what charity demands—a charity which God our Lord gives us in an even more special way toward Portugal—not refuse this labor.

No more for now, except that I beg the divine and supreme Goodness to give to all of us his abundant grace always to know his most holy will and perfectly to fulfill it.

Rome, December 17, 1552

The mandate which I am sending you to dismiss or send here those who are disobedient, you will have published in the colleges and houses throughout your province. You will see that the King is informed of it, so that it will not appear that the men being sent outside the kingdom because they need help are being removed from Portugal because of a desire on our part to have here persons who would be valuable workers in His Highness's territories, but rather that they are being sent elsewhere to make them such, so that upon their subsequent return there, they will be as His Highness and everyone else desires, in the service of God and the care for souls in his kingdom.

Yours in our Lord,

INACIO

To the Members of the Society throughout Europe

Rome, December 24, 1552

(Letter 3107: IV:564f.; in Italian)

A warm encouragement to Jesuits suffering the effects of poverty. Such poverty often arose when those who founded colleges for the Society could not or would not fulfill their obligations or promises to support them. Typical of Ignatius was his special concern for those who were ill, even when confronted by scarce resources.

The peace of Christ.

From various letters we have learned that God our Lord is visiting Your Reverences with the effects of holy poverty, that is, hardships and the lack of certain temporal things which would be necessary for bodily health and well-being. It is no slight grace that the divine Goodness deigns to confer on us in letting us have a real taste of what we ought to be constantly longing for so as to be conformed to our leader Jesus Christ, in accord with the vow and holy Institute of our order. Actually, I know of no place in the Society where a share in this grace is not being felt, although more in some places than in others. However, when we compare ourselves with our brothers off in India—amid great physical and spiritual toils so ill provided with food, in many places never eating bread or drinking wine, subsisting on a bit of rice and water or equally unnourishing fare, poorly clothed, and in general suffering much hardship in the outward man—I do not think our own suffering is too severe. We may account ourselves in our own Indies, for they can be found everywhere. In any case, if whoever is ordinarily responsible for supplying our needs fails, we can have recourse to holy mendicancy and in that way supply our want. And should God our Lord still wish us to have something to suffer, the sick should not lack for anything; the healthier will be better able to practice patience. And may this virtue be granted all of us by him who made it so lovable through his example and teaching, Jesus Christ our Lord; may he give us love for him and delight in his service in place of everything else.

Rome, December 24, 1552

✠

To an Unknown Prelate

Rome [ca. 1553]

(Letter 41: XII:290–93; in Spanish)

In February 1551 the Society of Jesus opened a school in Rome where classes in "grammar, the humanities, and Christian doctrine" were to be taught free of charge. This was the beginning of the Roman College. In the autumn of 1553, Ignatius decided to establish classes in the "higher studies" of philosophy and theology, faculties appropriate to a university. The need for financial support for such an ambitious enterprise was obvious. This letter was probably written at that time on behalf of such an institution. It is not clear whether this was simply a general draft document that set forth the reasons for funding, that is, endowing, such an institution or whether it was meant to be directed to a particular person capable of such munificence. There were certainly friends of the Society, such as Cardinals Alessandro Farnese and Ippolito d'Este, whose resources were sufficient for the task, and some have thought that the letter might have been intended for one of them.

Jesus

Considerations for Motivating N. to Be a Founder of Our College at N.

1. If he takes into account his debt to God, who with so little exertion or merit on his part has granted him so many favors of every kind, both interior and exterior, he will have a great opportunity to show his gratitude to God's generosity by employing himself in a work so much for God's service and glory as is this college. None of the Society's colleges throughout Christendom is thought likely to offer greater or more universal service to God than this, as experience has already begun to demonstrate.

2. If he has zeal for the common good and the help of souls and for the increase and spread of the Christian religion, this is a work expressly ordered to that purpose. It will not only provide teaching for the youth of Rome, with instruction in letters and morality, but might eventually be attended for the same purpose by students from all Italy and points beyond, and probably would be as its reputation spreads. In addition, it will provide a formation for many students from Germany and the other northern regions ravaged by heresy. These men can then be sent home as faithful workers, who by their example and teaching will strive to restore their nations to the bosom of holy Mother Church. Formation will also be provided for numerous workers of our own Society, whose education is entirely directed to this goal of the common good. From

here they will be sent throughout Christendom, wherever there is need, as well as among heretics and schismatics, Moors and pagans. And while our institute is present everywhere, the men formed here under the eyes of the Sovereign Pontiff and the Apostolic See will naturally be more extensively employed than others in such work. Thus, this college will be a continual seedbed of ministers of the Apostolic See for the service of holy Church and the good of souls.

3. If zeal for the divine glory and the universal good ought to move him, so should considerations of his own advantage. Advantageous is whatever helps a thing toward its proper end; and for human beings, the most advantageous things are those that help toward their final and blessed end. Now, since these, according to Catholic teaching, are good works meritorious of eternal life, it is obvious how advantageous it will be for him to share in, indeed make his own, all the good and meritorious works that will issue from this college for the glory of God and the good of so many souls.

4. Furthermore, founders of the Society's houses and colleges enjoy other great advantages, both in life and in death, through the suffrages of our entire Society by way of Masses and prayers, as prescribed by our Institute and as can be seen from the attached document about the remembrance of founders.

5. Another consideration is the advantage for N., as well as for his entire house and his successors, in having this group of good men bound on special grounds to their perpetual love and service. In many spiritual and temporal eventualities that they may meet, they will be well served by them not only out of freely given charity but also as a debt.

6. He will also derive substantial intellectual and spiritual benefit for himself. Having as his own a college with professors in every discipline who are also virtuous servants of God, he cannot but find it extremely valuable to have contact with them and the opportunity to make use of their labors. Moreover, should he wish to spend a few days with them in retreat, he would be doing so in his own house.

7. Nevertheless, the main advantage is that, if N. should undertake this excellent work, God, the lavish rewarder of whatever is done for love of him, would repay him with an abundance of his spiritual gifts in this life and in eternal life.

8. A work like this would also be very important in discharging his own conscience. N. has great ecclesiastical holdings, and he is obliged to dispense their income well. According to the learned commentators, this means taking out what is needed for his own decent support according

to his state in life and spending the rest on the poor and on religious works. Accordingly, in this religious work, which will help so many poor in Christ, he would have an excellent means of discharging his own conscience as well as of aiding the soul of the one who left him all these ecclesiastical holdings.

9. These are the motives which most ought to move him. However, if a person's state of mind is such that he is motivated by other considerations as well, such as respect for his authority and reputation, or his honor and fame, then this work will be one of great importance. It will be the most outstanding of the Society's colleges; it will be their head, just as the house here is the head of the other houses of this order, which God our Lord has raised up in these days for his great service. It will be continually before the eyes of the Pope and the entire papal court, which is quite well informed about it; and it will be located in Rome, from which its good reputation would spread everywhere. Thus, even a person deeply concerned for his good name would, as founder of such a work, have greater and more rightful grounds for distinction than any other that I now know.

10. If he is also concerned to leave a remembrance of himself after his own days, this work would clearly be a perfect means, and a great and lasting adornment to his entire house: with the enterprise being so widely known and of such universal benefit, its founder cannot help but be renowned in many ways.

11. If present happiness and gratification motivate him, this work will abundantly and immediately afford him such. He will be able to enjoy it right away, although its growth as time goes on will also increase his motives for happiness, as he sees the results of his efforts.

12. He might also be attracted by the ease of doing this: the completed building will be paid off gradually, and the college can be supported largely by financial help from other sources. At his own pace and according to his own devotion, being a young man, he will be able to spend progressively whatever God inspires him to.

May the divine Wisdom deign to grant him the understanding to see and the effective will to hit upon what will be most pleasing to his Divine Majesty, as this is our only goal, etc.

✠

To the Rectors of the Colleges in Italy
from Juan de Polanco, by commission
Rome, January 21, 1553
(Letter 3165: IV:601f.; in Italian)

Corporal punishment of students was not unusual in the sixteenth century. What is somewhat unusual is Ignatius's solemn prohibition, "in virtue of holy obedience," against Jesuits' being the ones to inflict such corporal punishment on pupils in their schools. If an external "corrector" could not be found, one of the more mature or older students was to inflict the corporal punishment. This prohibition against Jesuit involvement appeared also in the definitive 1599 Ratio studiorum *(no. 364).*

The peace of Christ.

I believe we have written on other occasions that our men should not personally strike the boys who come to school when they need correction. For, granting the need for the boys to be punished in this way, it is not fitting for us to punish them with our own hands. But since we hear that in some places, because of the difficulty in getting a corrector, this procedure is not being observed and instead some of our men are performing this office, Our Father has given me orders that in virtue of holy obedience a command be issued in his name throughout the Society in Italy to the effect that none of our men should lay hands on any pupil to punish him, but that they should take steps to obtain a corrector from outside the Society when they have a difficult pupil, or should look for some other method, such as having one of the older pupils be the one to strike the others. In any case, a means should be found so that our men will not do what is unbecoming to them.

Other subjects will be handled in separate letters.

May Jesus Christ be with everyone.

✠

To Diego Miró
Rome, February 1, 1553
(Letter 3220: IV:625–28; in Spanish)

King John III of Portugal had requested that Diego Miró and Luis Gonçalves da Câmara serve as confessors for himself and his family. This was the first instance in which Jesuits were asked to be royal confessors. They firmly declined, considering such a lofty post incompatible with the Jesuit Institute, and also because of the delicacy of the situation in which Ignatius had recently removed Simão Rodrigues from that office; the latter was a close friend of the King and former provincial of Portugal.

Ignatius here gives his reasons for overriding their decision. He may have been too sanguine about the ease with which one of the reasons against taking the post, "seeking out honors and dignities," could be countered. One of the longest-lasting criticisms of the Society was that its members were royal confessors and therefore, willy-nilly, had secret power without public responsibility.

May the sovereign grace and eternal love of Christ our Lord be always our help and protection.

From various letters which we have received from there, we learn that His Highness has with insistent devotion requested you, and also Father Luis Gonçalves, to be his confessors, but that you have both begged off, not out of any fears for your own consciences in dealing with that of His Highness, which, as you write, you consider holy, but because you think that this is an honor which should be avoided no less than a bishopric or cardinal's hat in those realms; and I understand that for the same reason Father Luis Gonçalves has even given up acting as confessor to the Prince [Sebastian, the son of King John III]. Certainly, I myself, when I consider your motives, grounded on humility and safety, which are better found in lowliness than in prominence, can only approve and be edified by your intention. However, all things considered, I am convinced that you did not make the right decision, if we look to the greater service and glory of God our Lord. First, because it is your profession and Institute to administer the sacraments of confession and Communion to persons of every condition and age; just as you are bound to assist persons of the lowest degree, so are you bound by the same duty to give spiritual consolation and help to those of the highest degree. Second, given that from its very origin and commencement our whole Society has been under more particular obligation to Their Highnesses than to any other Christian prince, whether in view of their good works or of the special love and charity which more than anything else ought to win over your hearts, I can think of no excuse to justify our not trying to serve Their Highnesses in a matter which is so appropriate to our profession and which they indicate will bring them spiritual consolation and satisfaction. Then, if we look to the universal good and God's greater service, these will, so far as I can perceive in the Lord, ensue more strongly from this. For the good of the head is shared by all the body's members, and the good of the sovereign by all his subjects, so that spiritual benefit given to the sovereign should be rated above that which might be given to others. To give one instance by which you can judge others, consider how important would have been a reminder from a confessor to come to a conclusion in the matter of the patriarch of Ethiopia, involving as it does the salvation not just of many souls but of numerous cities and provinces. Moreover, whether one of you hears His Highness's confessions or not, be sure to keep on reminding him of this matter and reporting to me, whenever you write to Rome, about what you have done.

However, coming back to the reasons why you should not decline this task, I do not think that even the one about your personal safety is pertinent. If all we looked for in our vocation was to walk safely, having to place the good of souls second to keeping far from danger, we would have no business living and dealing with our neighbor. But it is our vocation to have dealings with all people. Indeed, as St. Paul says of himself, we should make ourselves all things to all people in order to gain all for Christ [1 Cor. 9:22]. If we proceed with a pure and upright intention, not seeking our own interests but those of Jesus Christ [Phil. 2:21], he himself in his infinite goodness will protect us. Indeed, unless his mighty hand held our profession fast, no avoidance of such dangers would avail to keep us from falling into them and worse.

As for the possibility that people would claim you are seeking out honors and dignities, it will collapse of itself under the weight of the truth and the evidence of the facts when people see you preserving the lowliness that you have chosen for Christ our Lord. Thus, you should not allow any considerations or talk from the crowd to keep you from what could turn out to be of great service to God and to Their Highnesses and for the common good. In conclusion, to satisfy my conscience in this matter, I command you and Father Luis Gonçalves, in virtue of holy obedience, that one of the two should comply with whatever Their Highnesses may command you in this regard—unless someone else in the Society seems preferable to you and is also acceptable to His Highness for this post. Have confidence in the divine Goodness that whatever is done this way through obedience will be for the best. You are to make this command known to His Highness and show him this letter, should he wish to see it, or at least give its main points.

Since Master Polanco will write at length on other matters, I will say no more here except that I earnestly commend myself to your prayers and sacrifices. I beg God our Lord to give us all his abundant grace always to know his most holy will and entirely to fulfill it.

Rome, February 1, 1553

Yours in our Lord,

IGNACIO

To the Members of the Society in Portugal

Rome, March 26, 1553

(Letter 3304: IV:669–81; in Spanish)

After the Spiritual Exercises, perhaps until the publication and translation of his "autobiography," St. Ignatius's "Letter on Obedience" to the Province of Portugal was for long his best-known writing. Generations of Jesuits heard it read at table once a month in their refectories. The letter was written in the context of the split in the province between the supporters and the opponents of the former provincial, Simão Rodrigues, and of the tension brought about by his successor, Diego Miró, a good but rigid individual. Even an official visitor sent by Ignatius, Miguel de Torres, could not reestablish peace and unity. About thirty men left the Society during this restless period. At one point Ignatius even asked Gonçalves da Câmara, "Who is provincial?"

This is the fullest of Ignatius's several treatments of the subject (see letters 182, 243, and 295). The letter urges the crucial importance of obedience for Jesuits (paragraph 2), centers obedience upon the person of Christ (3), insists that it must extend beyond mere execution to conformity of the will and understanding with those of the superior (4–19), suggests ways of acquiring and practicing the virtue (one being "blind obedience") (20–24), approves representing to one's superior difficulties against a command (25), and shows how the Society's welfare depends upon obedience being observed at every level (26–29). It concludes with a ringing final exhortation (30).

The ascetical perspective that underlies the development of the letter is different from the apostolic perspective in which obedience is developed in the Constitutions. *The ideals in the letter are certainly those of Ignatius, who signed it personally; but in its development Polanco surely had a hand, as evidenced by the breadth and variety of quotations from the Scriptures, the Fathers, and ecclesiastical writers.*

Jhus.

May the sovereign grace and eternal love of Christ our Lord greet and visit you with his most holy gifts and spiritual graces.

1. It gives me great consolation, my dear brothers in our Lord Jesus Christ, to learn of the lively and efficacious desires for your own perfection and his divine service and glory bestowed on you by him who in his mercy has called you to this institute, preserves you in it, and directs you to the blessed end at which his chosen ones arrive.

2. And although I wish you all perfection in every virtue and spiritual grace, it is true (as you will have heard from me on other occasions) that it is more particularly in obedience than in any other virtue that God our Lord gives me the desire to see you distinguish yourselves.

This is not only because of its own extraordinary worth, so emphasized by word and example in Sacred Scripture, both Old and New Testaments, but because, as St. Gregory says, obedience is a virtue which alone implants all the other virtues in the mind and preserves them once implanted.[5] To the extent that this virtue flourishes, all the other virtues will be seen to flourish and produce in your souls the fruits which I desire and which are demanded by him who through his own obedience redeemed the world which had been lost through lack of it, "becoming obedient unto death, death on a cross" [Phil. 2:8].

We may let other religious orders outdo us in fasting, night-watches, and other austerities which each one, following its own institute, holily observes. But in the purity and perfection of obedience, with genuine resignation of our wills and abnegation of our judgment, I am very desirous, dear brothers, that those who serve God in this Society should distinguish themselves, and that its true sons may be recognized by this—never looking to the person whom they obey, but in that person, to Christ our Lord, for whose sake they obey.

3. For the superior is not to be obeyed because he is highly prudent, very good, or qualified by any other gift of God our Lord, but rather because he holds his place and authority—as eternal Truth has said, "He who hears you hears me, and he who despises you despises me" [Luke 10:16]. Nor, on the other hand, should he be any less obeyed in his capacity as superior if he is less prudent, for he represents the person of him who is infallible wisdom and who will make up for any shortcomings in his minister; nor if he is lacking in goodness or other excellent qualities, since Christ our Lord, after saying, "The scribes and Pharisees have sat on the chair of Moses," expressly adds, "Do all that they tell you, but do not act according to their works" [Matt. 23:2f.].

Therefore I would like all of you to practice recognizing Christ our Lord in any superior, reverencing and obeying his Divine Majesty in him with all devotion. This will appear less strange to you if you recall how in writing to the Ephesians St. Paul enjoins obeying even temporal and pagan superiors as Christ, from whom all well-ordered authority derives: "Be obedient to your masters according to the flesh, with fear and trembling, in the simplicity of your heart, as to Christ; not serving

---

[5] *Moralia* 14.28 (Jacques-Paul Migne, *Patrologiæ cursus completus: Series Latina* (Paris: Garnier, n.d.) 76:765B. Hereafter this collection of the Fathers of the Church will be cited as *PL*, followed by the volume number, the page(s) number(s), and, when needed, the column number.

to the eye, as if pleasing men, but as servants of Christ doing the will of God, rendering service from the heart and with a good will, as to the Lord and not to men" [Eph. 6:5–7].

4. From this you can infer, when a religious takes someone not only as his superior but expressly in the place of Christ our Lord to direct and guide him in his divine service, to what degree he ought to hold that person in his soul, and whether he should look upon him as a man, and not as the vicar of Christ our Lord instead.

5. I also desire it to be firmly fixed in your souls that the first degree of obedience, which consists in the execution of what is commanded, is quite low. It does not deserve the name of obedience or attain the worth of this virtue unless it rises to the second degree, which consists in making the superior's will one's own, in such a way that there is not just effective execution but a conformity of wish, an identical willing and not willing. This is why Scripture says, "Obedience is better than sacrifices" [1 Sam. 15:22]; for as St. Gregory explains, "In sacrifices the flesh of another is slaughtered, in obedience our own will."[6] And as this will possesses so high a value in a human being, so also does the oblation by which it is offered to one's Creator and Lord through obedience. What a great and dangerous deception it is for persons to think they may lawfully deviate from their superiors' will—not only in matters pertaining to flesh and blood but even in those which are of themselves quite spiritual and holy, such as fasts, prayers, and other religious works. Such persons should listen to what Cassian well says in the "Conference of Abba Daniel": "It is one and the same sort of disobedience whether one ignores the elder's command out of eagerness for labor or longing for ease; as harmful to violate the rules of the monastery in order to stay awake as to sleep; as bad to neglect the abbot's command in order to read as to disregard it in order to sleep."[7] Holy was Martha's activity, holy was Magdalene's contemplation, holy the penitence and tears with which she bathed the feet of Christ our Lord; but all this had to be done in Bethany, which is interpreted as "house of obedience." As St. Bernard remarks, Christ our Lord apparently wanted to show us that "neither the effort to perform good works nor the leisure of holy contemplation nor the tears of penitence would have been pleasing to him outside of Bethany."[8]

---

[6] *Moralia* 1.35, 14.28 (*PL* 76:765B).

[7] *Coll.* 4.20 (*PL* 49:609).

[8] *Ad milites templi* 13 (*PL* 182:939).

6. And so, my dear brothers, try to make the surrender of your wills complete. Through his ministers, freely offer to your Creator and Lord the freedom he has bestowed on you. Think it no small fruit of your free will that you are able to restore it totally in obedience to the one who gave it to you. In this you do not lose it; instead, you perfect it, wholly conforming your own to the most certain rule of all rectitude, God's own will—the interpreter of which is the superior who governs you in his place. Thus, you should never attempt to draw the superior's will (which you should consider the will of God) to your own; for this would not be making God's will the rule of yours but yours the rule of God's, subverting the order of his wisdom. It is a great delusion and a mark of persons whose understanding is darkened by self-love, to think that obedience is preserved when the subject tries to draw the superior to what he himself wishes. Listen to St. Bernard, who had much experience in this matter: "Anyone who makes efforts, openly or covertly, to get his spiritual father to command him what he himself desires is self-deluded and flatters himself as a follower of obedience. He is not obeying his superior; instead, the superior is obeying him."[9] And so I conclude that anyone who wants to rise to the virtue of obedience will have to ascend to this second degree, which, over and above the execution, consists in making the superior's will one's own—or rather in stripping off one's own will and clothing oneself in God's will as interpreted by the superior.

7. But whoever aims at making a complete and perfect oblation of himself must, in addition to his will, offer his understanding. This is a further and the highest degree of obedience. He must not only have the same will as the superior but also be of the same mind as he, submitting his own judgment to the superior's to the extent that a devoted will is able to influence the understanding.

8. For while the understanding does not enjoy the same freedom as the will and by nature gives its assent to whatever is presented to it as true, nevertheless, in many matters where the evidence of the known truth is not compelling, it can, by the will's intervention, incline to one side rather than the other; and in such matters every truly obedient person should incline himself to think the same as his superior.

9. It is certain that since obedience is a holocaust in which the entire person offers himself without the slightest reserve in the fire of charity to his Creator and Lord through the hands of his ministers, and

---

[9] *Sermo de diversis* 35.4 (*PL* 183:636A-B).

a complete surrender of himself in which one renounces possession of his entire self so as to be possessed and governed by divine Providence through his superiors, it cannot be held that obedience includes only effective execution and the will's acquiescence; it must also include the judgment's thinking the same as the superior commands—to the extent, as I have said, that by dint of the will it can incline itself thereto.

10. Would to God our Lord that this obedience of the understanding were as fully grasped and practiced as it is necessary to anyone living in religious life and highly pleasing to God our Lord. I call it necessary; for, just as in celestial bodies, if the lower is to receive movement and influence from the higher, it must be subject and subordinate to it, the one being adjusted and ordered to the other, in the same way, when one rational creature is moved by another, as takes place in obedience, it is necessary that the one moved be subject and subordinated to the one moving if it is to receive influence and power from him; and this subjection and subordination cannot be had without conformity of the inferior's understanding and will to the superior's.

11. For if we look to the purpose of obedience, it is just as possible for our understanding to be mistaken about what is good as it is for our will. Hence, if we think it right to conform our will to the superior's to prevent it from going wrong, we should also conform our understanding to his to keep it from going wrong. "Do not rely upon your own prudence," says Scripture [Prov. 3:5].

12. Thus, even in other human affairs wise persons commonly consider that it is true prudence to distrust one's own prudence—particularly in matters of personal interest, where, because of bias, people are usually not good judges.

13. If, then, in his own affairs a person ought to follow the judgment of another—even someone not his superior—rather than his own, how much more the judgment of his superior, whom he has taken to govern him in God's place as interpreter of the divine will.

14. There is no doubt that this guidance is even more necessary in spiritual persons and matters because of the great dangers in the spiritual life when a person races forward in it without the bridle of discretion. Hence Cassian says in the "Conference of Abba Moses": "By no other fault does the devil so draw a monk headlong to his death as by persuading him to ignore the advice of his elders and trust to his own conclusions and judgment."[10]

---

[10] *Collationes* 2.11 (*PL* 49:541B).

15. On the other hand, without obedience of judgment it is impossible for the obedience of the will or execution to be what they should. For our soul's appetitive powers naturally follow the apprehensive, so that it will be an act of violence for the will to obey over the long term against one's judgment. And if someone obeyed for a time under the general apprehension that one ought to obey even when commanded amiss, this cannot, at the very least, be long-lasting; and thus perseverance is lost, or at least the perfection of obedience, which consists in obeying with love and cheerfulness; for no one who acts against what he thinks can obey with love and cheerfulness as long as such opposition remains. Enthusiasm and alacrity are lost; without full conviction these will be missing, and instead there will be doubts about the rightness of doing what is commanded. The much-extolled simplicity of blind obedience is lost when one debates whether the command was good or bad—perhaps even condemning the superior because what he commands is not to the person's liking. Humility is lost when on the one hand we submit, but on the other place ourselves above the superior. Fortitude in difficult tasks is lost and, in a word, all the perfections of this virtue.

16. On the contrary, obedience without submission of the judgment is marked by dissatisfaction, pain, reluctance, slackness, criticism, excuses, and other imperfections and obstacles of no small moment which deprive obedience of its value and merit. For, as St. Bernard rightly says of those who are distressed when the superior commands something not to their liking, "If you begin to be upset at this, to judge your superior, to criticize in your heart, even while outwardly fulfilling the command, this is not the virtue of patience but a veil over your wickedness."[11]

17. For if we look to the peace and quiet of mind of the person obeying, it is certain that no one will ever possess it if he has in his own soul the cause of his disquiet and unrest, namely, a judgment of his own opposed to what obedience enjoins on him.

18. For this reason, and for the sake of the unity which is what sustains the existence of any society, St. Paul earnestly exhorts all to think and say the same thing [Rom. 15:5], so that by unity of judgment and will they might be preserved. Now if head and members must think the same, it is not hard to see whether it is right for the head to agree with the members or the members with the head. And so, from what has been said, we can see how necessary is obedience of the understanding.

---

[11] *Serm. 3 de Circumcisione* 8 (*PL* 183:140C).

19. But if anyone wishes to see how perfect it is in itself and how pleasing to God our Lord, he can do so by consideration of how valuable is the noble oblation which is made of so worthy a part of man; how one makes his entire being a living sacrifice pleasing to his Divine Majesty, holding back nothing of himself; and also how difficult it is for a person to overcome himself out of love for him and to resist the natural bent which people have for following their own judgment. Thus, while obedience is properly a perfection of the will that renders it eager to fulfill the will of the superior, yet it must also, as we have said, extend to the understanding, inclining it to think what the superior thinks, so that in this way one can proceed with the full strength of the soul—will and understanding—to a prompt and perfect execution.

20. I think I hear you say, dear brothers, that you see the importance of this virtue but would like to know how you can acquire it perfectly. I answer with Pope St. Leo, "Nothing is hard for the humble, nothing rough for the meek."[12] Be humble and meek, and God our Lord will give you the grace always to maintain sweetly and lovingly the offering you have made to him. Apart from these, I will suggest three specific means that will be very helpful for you in reaching the perfection of obedience of the understanding.

21. The first is that, as I said at the beginning, you look not to the person of your superior as a human being subject to errors and miseries, but instead to the one whom you obey in him, Christ—who is supreme wisdom, measureless goodness, infinite charity; who you know cannot be deceived and will not deceive you; and whose utterly faithful charity—since you are certain that you have placed yourself under obedience for love of him and have submitted yourself to the superior's will, in order to be more conformed to God's will—you know will never fail to guide you by the means which he has given you. So do not consider the voice of the superior, insofar as he gives you a command, as anything but the voice of Christ—as St. Paul said to the Colossians, exhorting subjects to obey their superiors, "Whatever you do, do it from the heart, as to the Lord and not to men. . . . Give your service to Christ" [3:23f.]; and as St. Bernard said, "Whether God, or man his substitute, commands anything, we must obey with exactly the same care and submit with exactly the same reverence (so long, of course, as man commands nothing contrary to God)."[13] Thus, if you look, not upon the human being with your outward eyes, but upon God with your inward eyes, you will find no

---

[12] *Serm. 5 de Epiphania* 3 (*PL* 54:252A).
[13] *De præcepto et dispensatione* 9.19 (*PL* 182:871D).

difficulty in conforming your will and judgment to the rule of action which you have chosen.

22. The second means is that you always be quick to seek out reasons to defend what the superior commands or is inclined towards, rather than reasons to disapprove of it. A help for this will be to have a love for whatever is enjoined by obedience. This will beget an obedience which is cheerful and free from any unpleasantness. As St. Leo says, "We do not serve under harsh necessity when we love what is commanded."[14]

23. A third means for subjecting the understanding is even easier and surer, and employed by the holy fathers. It is this: taking for granted and believing—very much as we do in matters of faith—that whatever the superior enjoins is the command of God our Lord and his holy will, one proceeds blindly to the execution of the command, without any inquiry and with the force and promptitude of a will eager to obey. This is how we are to believe Abraham obeyed when commanded to sacrifice his son Isaac [Gen. 22]. Similarly, in the new covenant with some of those holy fathers mentioned by Cassian, like Abba John, who did not examine whether what he was commanded was worthwhile or not, as when he laboriously watered a dry stick for a whole year; or whether it was possible or not, as when he strove so earnestly, when so commanded, to move a rock which a large number of persons could not have moved.[15]

24. To confirm this kind of obedience, we see that God our Lord sometimes seconded it with miracles, as when St. Benedict's disciple Maurus, entering the water at his superior's command, did not sink;[16] or when another, being commanded to bring back a lioness, seized and dragged her to his superior;[17] and other cases with which you are familiar. My point is that this manner of subjecting one's own judgment without further inquiry, taking for granted that the command is holy and in conformity with God's will, is in use among the saints and ought to be imitated by anyone who wishes to obey perfectly in all things where no manifest sin is evident.

25. However, this does not mean that where something occurs to you different from the superior's opinion, and you have prayed and

---

[14] *De ieiunio septimi mensis*, serm. 89.1 (*PL* 54:444B).

[15] *Inst.* 4.24 (*PL* 49:183C-184A); 4.26 (*PL* 49:186A).

[16] See St. Gregory, *Dialog.* 1.2.7 (*PL* 66:146A-B).

[17] *De vitis patrum* 1.3.27 (*PL* 73:755D—756A-B).

come to the conclusion in the presence of God that you ought to represent the matter to the superior, you may not do so. But if you want to proceed in this matter without suspicion of self-love or attachment to your own judgment, you must maintain, before and after making this representation, not only an indifference towards actually undertaking or relinquishing the matter in question, but one such that you are even more pleased with, and consider as better, whatever the superior may ordain.

26. What I have said about obedience applies to individuals with reference to their immediate superiors, to rectors and local superiors with reference to provincials, to these with reference to the general, and to the general with reference to the one God our Lord has given to him as superior, his vicar on earth. In this way subordination will be fully preserved and, as a result, unity and charity as well, without which the welfare and governance of the Society, or of any other congregation, cannot be preserved.

27. This is the way divine Providence gently disposes all things, bringing to their ends the lowest by the intermediate and the intermediate by the highest. Thus, among the angels there is subordination of one hierarchy to another; and also in the heavens and in all bodily motions, subordination of the lower to the higher, and of the higher in turn to a supreme movement.

28. And we see the same on earth in well-ordered states, and also in the hierarchy of the Church, brought under the one universal vicar of Christ our Lord. The better this subordination is kept, the better the governance. It is for lack of this subordination that we see such notorious defects in any society.

29. That is why in this society, over which our Lord has given me some charge, I want the perfection of this virtue to be pursued as if the Society's entire well-being depended on it.

30. I would like to end this topic without digression just as I began it, imploring all of you for the love of Christ our Lord—who not only gave us the command but went before us with the example of obedience—to make every effort to attain it through a glorious victory over yourselves, overcoming yourselves in the highest and most difficult part of yourselves, your will and understanding, so that in this way true knowledge and love of God our Lord may wholly possess and guide your souls throughout this pilgrimage until he brings you, and many others by means of you, to the final and most happy end of his own everlasting bliss.

I commend myself earnestly to your prayers.

Rome, March 26, 1553

> Yours in our Lord,
> YGNATIO

✠

To Jerónimo Nadal

Rome, April 12, 1553

(Letter 3316: V:13–15; in Spanish)

Here Ignatius instructs Nadal as to what he was to do in Portugal and Spain to which the former had sent him as "Visitor" with full powers. It is a sign of the great trust that Ignatius had in Nadal.

What I have in mind for Master Nadal to do in Portugal and Spain—without prejudice to his doing whatever else he deems good in our Lord—is the following.

1. In all places where the Society resides, he will explain the part of the *Constitutions* appropriate for that place.

2. He will examine the domestic rules, order, and manner of proceeding of the house and bring them into line with what he understands our mind to be; and while taking into consideration the circumstances of places, persons, and so on, he will leave in each place an order in conformity with our Institute, by which they will be regulated.

3. In all colleges where it can be done, he will introduce the method of the colleges in Italy as regards classes and languages, and will give them their structure, particularly in the more important places and where greater spiritual profit and edification can ensue from this. It is believed that introducing this in the universities will be more difficult.

4. Where there are courses of studies, he will examine how they are faring, either where our men attend the public schools or externs come to ours, so that both the members of the Society and those outside of it may progress in letters and virtues.

5. He should also examine their procedures for dealing with and providing profit to their neighbor in spiritual matters, as well as those used by the members of the Society for their own advancement in conformity with the Society's Constitutions.

6. In providing for material things, he should also examine what should be done; and should recourse to alms be suitable in some places, for how long and in what manner.

7. In decisions about temporal matters that require our authority, he should have the same as I and may substitute others as he judges best.

8. He will have authority to accept colleges and houses for the Society or to direct that they not be accepted, as he deems best in our Lord.

9. Within the same province he may move subjects from one place to another as he thinks best.

10. He should see how to ensure that good subjects who present themselves for the Society are not allowed to get away for lack of support, since it has been written that many have failed to be admitted for this reason; if they have a solid knowledge of Latin or are even more advanced, he can send them to Rome.

11. If he thinks good, he may demand an accounting of their persons and offices from any persons, even rectors or superiors; and each one should give it. However, in the cases of Father Francis [Borgia] and his men, Doctor [Antonio] Araoz, Master [Francisco] Estrada, Doctor Miguel de Torres, and Don Teotonio de Braganza, he may make representations but not dispose with authority. And in the case of the college at Oñate and whatever else is under the charge of Father Francis and Doctor Torres, he will also not make use of the above authority, for we deem this best in our Lord, but will deal with those who are in charge. And if they are of a different opinion, he should not do anything in opposition to Father Francis or Doctor Torres until I have been advised here.

12. He will decide as he sees fit in our Lord any uncertainties about the bulls [pertaining to the Society] and other matters connected with the Society's manner of proceeding.

13. He may grant the privileges of the Society in the same way as myself, and empower others to grant them. He may likewise revoke any that I may have given and which he thinks ill-placed at present, even though they were appropriately conferred at the time; and he shall effectively suspend or revoke by the authority of our bulls any privileges received from the Apostolic See through any hand but our own among the men under our obedience and among those who have left the Society; and this should be made public.

14. He may admit to the profession of three or four solemn vows those he judges qualified, after consulting the principal men there. Similarly for spiritual and temporal formed coadjutors, for scholastics, and for [those in] first probation. He may also dismiss [men], acting altogether as God our Lord inspires him and getting information from those best in a position to give it, such as Doctor Miró in Portugal, those who placed him [Miró] in that office, and other good and faithful servants of God.

15. He should give special attention to the college of Santiago to make that sure persons of quality are sent there, as the Cardinal of Santiago requests.[18]

16. For the combining [of benefices] granted by His Holiness at the time when Father Francis was there as Duke of Gandía, we never received the proper documents for the holders of the benefices to give their consent; and so we are awaiting their arrival—particularly in the case of the archdeacon of Jerez, or of another to give what he is supposed to for Oñate.

17. He should have them contribute there towards a procurator to negotiate the common business of the colleges.

☩

To Thomas of Villanueva, archbishop of Valencia

Rome, April 16, 1553

(Letter 3335: V:24f.; in Spanish)

Ignatius thanks St. Thomas, who was greatly devoted to the Society, for his patronage of the Society's college in Valencia and promises to send him Jerónimo Doménech or Diego Miró.

Jhs.

My Most Reverend Lord in our Lord:

May the sovereign grace and eternal love of Christ our Lord greet and visit Your Most Reverend Lordship with his most holy gifts and spiritual graces.

From Your Lordship's letter of October 9, which (together with its bearer) arrived quite late in Rome, I perceive what great concern and vigilance God our Lord gives to Your Most Reverend Lordship for seek-

---

[18] Juan Alvarez de Toledo, O.P.

ing out every spiritual help for the flock entrusted to you by his divine Wisdom, since you show such special interest in the very slight help that has been afforded by our college there. I know how great is the obligation not only of the college there, the recipient of so much help and favor, but of the whole of our least Society, upon which this favor overflows, to render Your Most Reverend Lordship service in our Lord. I have indeed a great desire not to fail in this just obligation, as far as lies in my power; and at the first opportunity which God our Lord sends us, I will try (if Master Jerónimo Doménech cannot go) to have Father Master Miró go there if I can get him free from Portugal, or someone else. I shall so charge Father Araoz, provincial of our Society in those realms.

Humbly commending myself and all our Society to Your Most Reverend Lordship's holy prayers, and offering myself, in accord with our lowly profession, to Your Lordship's service in our Lord, I shall merely pray his divine and sovereign goodness to give all of us abundant grace always to know his most holy will and perfectly to fulfill it.

Rome, April 16, 1553

Your Most Reverend Lordship's most humble servant in our Lord,

YGNATIO

⊕

To Simão Rodrigues

Rome, May 20, 1553

(Letter 3417: V:73f.; in Spanish)

After being relieved of his office as Portuguese provincial and commissioned to Spain, Rodrigues returned to Portugal, where his presence was a source of embarrassment. In an attempt to remove him from the scene, Ignatius wrote him on the same day both this letter and letter 3547 (below). He held off sending either of them for almost two months, and then dispatched the second with a postscript.

The sovereign grace, etc.

I received your letters of March 23 and 26 and April 12, and in view of what you write in them, together with numerous other matters which concern you, I see no other way of dealing with these things properly, dearest brother, than for you to come here to Rome. If you do come, however, I have confidence in Christ our Lord that he will let us find some means by which your soul will be consoled to the glory of God our Lord.

As to your reputation, I will only say that I will be as careful of it as you yourself could be, for I see the reasons for this. Indeed, by means that right now you could not easily imagine, your complete satisfaction is being sought. Trust me in this for the love of Christ our Lord and lovingly take this road. For certainly, should it please his Divine Majesty, it would be a great consolation to me if before departing from this world, I could see you and leave your affairs in a different condition. If I cannot help feeling such a desire toward all my brethren, all the more so toward those who were the first when God deigned to join us together in this Society, and particularly toward you, for whom, as you know, I have always had a very special love in our Lord. And do not be fearful about your infirmity; he who is eternal health will give you, through the power of obedience, all the health you need. After all, you made this journey once before with a quartan fever, when less bound to [do so] than now, and the Author of health gave you health. Moreover, Luis Gonçalves's coming (though he has not yet arrived here) gives you a good excuse there for wanting to come yourself.

I ask you once more to trust me; no matter what may be said, I will look out, as I should, for your consolation and reputation, to God's glory.

May his divine and sovereign Goodness be pleased to give all of us his grace always to know his most holy will and perfectly to fulfill it.
Rome, May 20, 1553

✠

To King John III of Portugal

Rome, June 6, 1553

(Letter 3449: V:98f.; in Spanish)

A letter of appreciation for the King's support of the Society, together with an announcement that Jerónimo Nadal will be coming to Portugal to set up colleges for extern students, that is, students other than members of the Society.

Jesus

My Lord in our Lord:

May the sovereign grace and eternal love of Christ our Lord greet and visit Your Highness with his most holy gifts and spiritual blessings.

I received a letter from Your Highness brought by Father Luis Gonçalves, who with God's favor arrived at Rome in good health on the twenty-third of last month. Both the letter, expressing satisfaction with the change of provincial, and the report from the man himself, on whom Your Highness commands me to rely totally as regards what he tells me on Your Highness's part, confirm what I have always been convinced of in our Lord; namely, that just as it was his Divine Majesty's will that among Christian princes Your Highness should be the first and chief instrument of his providence for inaugurating and advancing the affairs of this Society (which is entirely Your Highness's), similarly, in whatever regards the preservation and increase of this Society's welfare, he will always grant Your Highness to perceive and be pleased with the best course to be followed, in view of the zeal and sincerity with which Your Highness seeks the glory and service of God our Lord and the help of his souls, which is the only goal that we ourselves aim at.

Regarding certain points which Father Luis Gonçalves told me Your Highness would like observed in the colleges of that kingdom, Your Highness should have full assurance that they will be observed without the slightest deviation from Your Highness's will, not only in my days but afterwards as well; our Constitutions and the arrangements for matters in Your Highness's dominions will help ensure this. However, I shall not go into the details here; Father Luis Gonçalves will write what is necessary regarding them.

Realizing how much souls could be helped and God our Lord served through them in Your Highness's kingdom by having our men organize schools to instruct youth in letters and good behavior, and in this way draw parents and relatives to the service of God by means of their sons, I directed that wherever feasible in Your Highness's kingdom, our men should try to set up such schools, as has been our practice here in Sicily and Italy, to the notable benefit of the places where such colleges are located. Being repeatedly asked from there to send someone with experience and skill in setting up such schools, I have decided—in order not to fail in a matter so important for God's and Your Highness's service—to send there for a period of time Doctor Jerónimo Nadal, our provincial in Sicily and a man who is quite capable in many areas, including this business of organizing colleges and schools. He started the ones in Sicily, and we had called him for the same purpose to Rome. However, despite the great need for his presence in the new college here, I decided to set all our own concerns aside so as not to scant those of Your Highness's kingdom, to the glory of God our

Lord. I thought it best to inform Your Highness of this, in case reports have arrived about the coming of Father Nadal.

I shall say no more, except to beg the divine and sovereign Goodness to give all of us his abundant grace always to know his most holy will and completely to fulfill it.

Rome, June 6, 1553

✠

To Diego Miró, by commission

Rome, June 7, 1553

(Letter 3453: V:108f.; in Spanish)

When Jerónimo Nadal was sent as Ignatius's plenipotentiary representative to Portugal, Polanco wrote the provincial this letter in glowing commendation of him.

The peace of Christ.

To inform Your Reverence about the mission and person of Father Master Jerónimo Nadal, who is being sent by Our Father to Portugal, the reasons for his coming are as follows.

The first is for him to help you there with the new type of schools to be set up in that kingdom. He has a better understanding of this matter than anyone else we know of here, for he has had extensive practice and experience in this work, with excellent results. The best-founded and best-organized colleges of the Society here are the ones he organized in Sicily.

His second task is to explain the Society's *Constitutions.* He will be able to do this very well, since he is someone who has understood and penetrated the mind of our father Master Ignatius. He will also be able to afford much help with the domestic rules and all such arrangements there; he will also explain to you the rules observed in the house here, from which whatever is suitable there should be adopted, taking circumstances into account.

Third, he will be able to resolve uncertainties regarding the Society's bulls and many others about Your Reverence's present mode of proceeding which cannot be satisfactorily taken care of by correspondence. In general, he will be of help to you there in whatever matters may arise in that kingdom, where the advice and intervention of someone like him, according to our Institute and profession, can be of great assistance.

As for his person, I will say this. There are few if any men we could send who will be more sorely missed here than Master Nadal. He was taken out of Sicily, where he was provincial. Although quite indispensable there and esteemed by the viceroy (more than could be said in letters, for he knew him very intimately), he was nevertheless withdrawn from there because of the very great need of the colleges here in Rome (I mean our own and the German colleges) for a man like him. However, Our Father has set all this aside in favor of what he perceived to be needed for the Society's good in the realms where you are. He is a man of great speculative and practical intelligence, not merely gifted in every branch of scholarship and shrewd in government and the managing of practical affairs, but outstanding in both areas, as you will see there when you deal with him. Spiritually, he is a person who has truly allowed God's grace to take possession of him; and it would be a long story to recount everything about him since he entered the Society here in Rome some eight or nine years ago when he came for the council. He has extensive knowledge of our father Master Ignatius, for he has dealt much with him and seems to have grasped his spirit and penetrated the Society's Institute as much as anyone else I know in the Society. At the same time, in humility and perfect obedience not only of execution but also of will and understanding, he is one of those who have most steadily shown themselves to be true sons of this Society. In addition, he is a man of great courage in the service of God; and for great and wide-reaching affairs—indeed for all affairs—he is most energetic. I wanted to write this so that Your Reverence would be aware of what is thought here of his person. "Judge not according to the appearance, but make a just judgment" [John 7:24].

Since Father Master Nadal will be staying there in the kingdom for some time, Our Father, who trusts him as he does himself, has granted him the fullest powers he is able to confer, so that he will be able to be of greater help during the time of his stay there.

No more for now. May Jesus Christ be with us all.

Rome, June 7, 1553

To Francis Xavier

Rome, June 28, 1553

(Letter 3505: V:148–51, in Spanish)

Ignatius recalls Xavier from Asia for consultations with the King of Portugal and the Holy See. He was to inform the King how the faith was spreading in the "Indies" and to stimulate his interest in Ethiopia. Moreover, he was to give the Holy See accurate information and counsel on how best to proceed with the evangelization of the "Indies"; finally, he was to move suitable men to volunteer to go there as missionaries. At the time he wrote this letter, Ignatius did not know that Xavier had died in December 1552. It took almost three years, until around October 1555, for that news to get to Europe.

Ihs

May the sovereign grace and eternal love of Christ our Lord be always our help and protection.

Dearest Brother in our Lord:

We received here your letters of January 28, 1552, later than we should have because of the difficulty in transit from Portugal to Rome; hence, you will not have received a reply as soon as I would have wished. We have learned of the door which our Lord has opened to the preaching of the Gospel and the conversion of the people of Japan and China through your ministry, and we are greatly consoled in his Divine Majesty, hoping that his glory and the knowledge of him will spread further every day, also among peoples who with God's favor will be capable of preserving and carrying forward what they have won.

I also think it was a good idea for you to send Master Gaspar [Berze] and others there and to China. And if you have gone to China yourself, as you say you are inclined to do unless prevented by matters in India, I shall approve of it, being convinced that it is eternal Wisdom which guides you. Nevertheless, by what can be understood from here, I deem that God our Lord will be better served through your person if you have remained in India and sent others under your direction to do whatever you had planned on doing; for in this way you would accomplish in a number of places what you can accomplish personally only in one. I say more: in consideration of the greater service of God our Lord and the help of souls in those territories, and of how much their welfare depends upon Portugal, I have determined to command you under holy obedience that amid so many journeys, you set out on the one that leads to Portugal, with the first available good passage. I command you this in the name of Christ our Lord, even if [this means that you will] return shortly afterwards to India.

So that you can inform persons there who might want to keep you for the good of the Indies, I will give you the reasons here for this action, which regard the good of the Indies as well.

First, you are aware how important for the preservation and increase of Christendom in those lands, as well as in Guinea and Brazil, are the good arrangements which the King of Portugal is able to provide from his own kingdom. If a ruler possessing such Christian desires and holy intentions as the King of Portugal is given information by someone with your knowledge and experience of the situation there, you can imagine how he would be moved to do many of the things you might suggest to him for the service of God our Lord and the help of those territories.

Next, given that the Apostolic See has such need of full and accurate information about the situation in the Indies—and from a person in whom they have confidence—so as to make the spiritual provisions that are necessary or important for the welfare of this new Christendom and of the old Christians living there, you would also be much more suitable for this service than anyone else there because of the knowledge you possess and because of what is known about you.

You also know how important it is for the good of the Indies that those who are sent there be suitable for the goals that are sought in the various regions. Your coming to Portugal and here will be very helpful in this regard. Not only will far more persons be moved to want to go there; you yourself would see who among those so moved are suitable for going or not, and which persons should go where. The importance of doing this correctly you can judge for yourself. All that you write us from there cannot give us a sufficient understanding unless you, or someone with your knowledge, personally knows and deals with the men who are to be sent.

Over and above these reasons, all concerning the good of India, I feel that you could also fire the King's interest in Ethiopia; for years he has been on the point of acting, with no results being seen. From Portugal you could also be of considerable help for the Congo and Brazil, something you cannot do from India because of the lack of communications. And if your presence appears to be important for government in India, you will not govern any worse from Portugal than from Japan or China—in fact, a great deal better. And so, with all your even longer past absences, undertake this one; leave behind whatever rectors you wish and one person in overall charge of everything there, along with the consultors you judge best; and God our Lord will be with them.

For other matters I refer you to Master Polanco. I recommend myself from the heart to your prayers, asking the divine and supreme Goodness to grant all of us his abundant grace so that we may always know his most holy will and perfectly fulfill it.

Rome, June 28, 1553

On arrival in Portugal you will be under obedience to the King to do whatever he determines for you to the glory of God our Lord.

Wholly yours in our Lord,

IGNATIO

✠

To Simão Rodrigues

Rome, May 20 and July 12, 1553

(Letter 3547: V:189f.; in Spanish)

For this letter and its postscript, see the introduction to letter 3417 (above).

Master Simão Rodrigues, beloved son in our Lord:

I have read and pondered your letters of February 10, March 23 and 26, and April 12, and many others which I am receiving from there; and out of the conviction and knowledge that it would be highly expedient in our Lord for the greater spiritual peace and consolation of those who are persevering in our Society in the Portuguese realms, as well as for discussion of other general matters regarding the whole Society that cannot be handled otherwise than face to face, I have decided in our Lord to impose a little physical hardship on you by having you come to the house here in Rome. Wherefore, in virtue of holy obedience, as in a matter of major importance, I command you in the name of Christ our Lord to come—either by land or by sea, however you think best. And this is to be as quickly as you are able: within eight days after seeing this letter you are to set out and come directly here.

I ask God our Lord to guide and accompany you, and to give all of us the grace always to know and do his most holy will.

Rome, May 20, 1553

Son, Master Simão, trust me that your coming here will give consolation in our Lord to both your soul and mine, and that everything which both you and I desire for God's greater glory will turn out well. So with great devotion accept our seeing each other; and if you do not find much devotion, God our Lord will give it to you through your perseverance in coming here. Remember with what goodwill, because of my bidding at a time when I had no authority over you, you found yourself in Portugal with a quartan fever and then recovered. How much more now when it is under obedience and your illness is less severe.

Master Simão, set out immediately, as is indicated above, and have no doubt but that we will enjoy here both spiritual and bodily well-being, to God's greater glory. Trust me completely, and you will be very glad in our Lord.

Today is July 12.

✠

To Gaspare Gropillo

Rome, July 22, 1553

(Letter 3561: V:201f.; in Italian)

Gropillo, a priest from northern Italy who had lived almost as a hermit near Bolsano, later grew to know and love the Society. He gave his hermitage to Ignatius as a gift and provided hospitality at the hermitage for Simão Rodrigues, who was returning from Portugal (Ignatius was very grateful to him for having done so).

Gropillo had doubts about living under the obedience of the Society. Ignatius wrote several letters, now lost, to him on the subject and assured him that superiors would act responsibly in his regard. Gropillo came to Rome and under the direction of Ignatius took vows. Later, however, he left the Society.

May the sovereign grace, etc.

I have received two letters from you at once, brother mine in Jesus Christ, and learned of the reasons which move you to have doubts about your vocation. I am unwilling to call it into doubt, despite your reasons. I shall ask Master Don Diego Laínez to reply to them, and will refer to him everything else regarding your person, since he knows and has a special love for you. This much I will tell you for myself: Just as you or any other religious ought to be ready to do whatever he is enjoined with entire abnegation of his self-love and of his own judgment, in the same way it is my responsibility, or that of anyone else who is a superior, to make use of that care and prudence which are required by discerning charity in commanding one thing or another. And so, be always of good courage and strive every day to win from God our Lord the grace of denying yourself totally, so that you can be his true disciple.

And may his infinite and supreme goodness grant to all of us abundant grace always to know his most holy will and perfectly to fulfill it.

Rome, July 22, 1553

✠

To John Baptist Viola

Rome, July 22, 1553
(Letter 3562: V:202f.; in Italian)

Viola was superior of the first group of Jesuits to go to Paris in 1540. Among his responsibilities was serving as commissary for northern Italy under the provincial of Italy, Diego Laínez, who was frequently occupied with other matters. Ignatius urges the timid Viola to assert the authority over local superiors that was his as commissary.

May the sovereign grace, etc.

I have been reliably informed that in the exercise of your office as commissary you behave toward your subjects with more deference than you ought. While it is commendable for you to be humble and to subject yourself to everyone in your own heart, in outward matters you must remember that you represent Christ's person towards your subjects, who include all the rectors of colleges in the province of Italy and, consequently, the others under the rectors. When you think something should be done for the service of God, even if you see that the rectors have a contrary opinion or inclination, you should not let them follow their own ideas or wishes, but make them come over to yours by employing your authority over them, even if you have to reprehend or give them penances in the presence of everyone. And in order that neither you nor anyone else may claim ignorance of my will or of the authority vested in you, let them all know that it is our will that you possess the full authority of a provincial over the rectors and other subjects of the province, with power not only to give penances to the rectors and the others but also to remove them from office and to install those whom you see as more fit. Indeed, I command you to make use of this authority wherever needed, and always to have more regard for the general good than for the particular.

That is all, except that I pray God our Lord to grant all of us the grace always to know his most holy will and perfectly to fulfill it.

Rome, July 22, 1553

Although, to strike fear, Our Father writes Your Reverence to use the authority granted you for removing rectors, you should not do so without informing us first.

On the other matters, such as giving public or private penances, you need not consult, but may do whatever discerning charity dictates.

☩

To the Whole Society

Rome, July 23 and August 7, 1553
(Letter 3578: V:220–22; in Latin)

Peter Canisius, who was one among the many Jesuits whom Ignatius sent to Germany, asked him to order the entire Society to offer special prayers for that country, so imperiled by heresy. Ignatius did so in this letter, adding "England . . . and the northern nations" to the petition.

Jesus

Ignatius of Loyola, superior general of the Society of Jesus, to my beloved brothers in Christ, superiors and subjects of the Society of Jesus: everlasting salvation in our Lord.

Since the order of charity by which we must love the entire body of the Church in Jesus Christ her head requires that remedies be applied especially to that part of the body which is seriously and dangerously ill, we have determined that to the extent of our weak powers, we ought to devote the Society's efforts with particular zeal to the aid of England, Germany, and the northern nations imperiled by the grievous disease of heresy. And although we may labor earnestly for this end by other means, and although many of us have for years striven to assist these regions by the application of prayers and Masses, nevertheless, in order to extend and prolong this work of charity, we enjoin upon all our brethren—those under our immediate authority as well as rectors and superiors in charge of others—that they and those under their charge should each month offer to God the sacrifice of the Mass if they are priests, and prayers if not priests, for the spiritual needs of Germany and England, so that God may at long last take pity on these regions, and others infected by them, and lead them back to the purity of Christian faith and religion.

It is our intention that this continue as long as the needs of these nations continue to require this assistance. It is also our intention that no province where our Society is present, not even those in the farthest Indies, be exempted from this office of charity.

✠

To Diego Miró

Rome, July 24 and August 3, 1553

(Letter 3605: V:270f.; in Spanish)

Ignatius instructs the Portuguese provincial on how he is to use the documents (letters 3447 and 3584 below) commanding Rodrigues to leave Portugal for Rome under pain of dismissal from the Society.

Given the infrequency of the post leaving Rome for Portugal and Portugal for Rome, I have decided in our Lord to send you once and for all whatever documents might be needed in the business of Master Simão. Hence, the first thing you are to do is to give him the dispatch I am sending you, both the letter and the patent, showing the copy to His Highness. If this does not suffice, give him the copy a second time to serve as a second warning. Should he allege some indisposition, consult with some learned persons you think are competent, particularly of the order of St. Dominic. If they determine that he is under obligation to come to Rome, show their opinion to the King and tell His Highness that you have the enclosed document for dismissing Master Simão should he fail to obey after the third warning you give him, unless His Highness takes care of the matter by ordering him to obey and come to Rome. Then indicate this to Master Simão again for the last time, informing him of your authorization, should he not obey, to dismiss him from the Society as disobedient, obstinate, incorrigible, and a source of harm to the whole body of the Society. If all these warnings (with whatever intervals between them you deem best) do not suffice, after consulting His Highness and petitioning his approval, you will—with His Highness's consent—dismiss him on the authority of this letter of mine. And to prevent him from claiming that you have not adhered to my instructions, I declare that I leave it to your judgment, together with the other three or four others who ordinarily serve as consultors, or any that you choose, to determine whether you have proceeded properly; and I give my approval to whatever you shall do. However, even if you dismiss him, be sure that you petition His Highness to command

and compel him to come here; however, I hope that he will deign to do this before you resort to these penalties, and thus forestall much harm to that soul and others whom he hurts by his example.

May the eternal Wisdom give all of us the light we need to find the right course in whatever pertains to his service.

Rome, July 14, 1553

Once again I charge you not to execute what I have written about the dismissal of Master Simão without His Highness's consent.

Meanwhile, keep the above letter completely secret; except for Doctor Nadal and Doctor Torres, no one should know that you have such a document from me.

Sealed August 3, 1553

If the two whom I have named are there with you, let them know everything, and do everything in accord with their opinion.

☩

To Diego Miró

Rome, July 26, 1553

(Letter 3584: V:233; in Spanish)

As a last resort for getting Simão Rodrigues out of Portugal, Ignatius, gravely ill and fearing himself near death and thinking Rodrigues directly disobedient about leaving Portugal and coming to Rome, authorized the Portuguese provincial to dismiss Rodrigues from the Society should he refuse to obey. Unknown to Ignatius, Rodrigues was in fact sailing from Spain to Italy at the time this letter was written. For further instructions on how Miró was to use this document, and letter 3547 above, see letter 3605 immediately preceding.

May the sovereign grace and eternal love of Christ our Lord be always our protection and help.

In view of the obligation laid on me by God our Lord of looking out for the universal good of the whole body of this Society in such wise that when a member has become so diseased as to be not merely incurable himself but a source of harm to the healthy members, I am forced to cut that member off and, even with no little pain, separate him from the healthy ones; and whereas Master Simão is not only incorrigible in his obstinate disobedience but also a source of harm to others, as experience has shown me to my great sorrow, I have decided to command you —and do so command you in virtue of holy obedience—to give him three warnings as I have directed you, and then if he is still fails to obey, to dismiss and separate him in my name from the whole body of the Society; and to declare that he is dismissed on account of the faults of inconstancy in his vocation and obstinate disobedience, and that I judge him not only to be incorrigible but a source of great scandal to others in the Society with whom he has dealings.

May the sovereign and divine Goodness deign to give him grace and a path of salvation, even if he has drawn many others from theirs.

Rome, July 26, 1553

✠

To Giovanni Ottilio, from Juan de Polanco by commission

Rome, August 5, 1553
(Letter 3620: V:296f.; in Italian)

Here Ignatius renewed his efforts to counsel a scholastic at Padua severely tempted in his vocation. Several other letters followed this one in an attempt to save his vocation, including one giving him permission to go on pilgrimage to Loreto to ask God's grace. Increasingly it seemed that Ottilio was staying in the Society as a convenient place to do his studies. In addition, he began to urge others to leave. Finally, Ignatius dismissed him in September 1554.

The peace of Christ.

Dearest Brother in Jesus Christ:

Our Father has received the letter you wrote on the advice of Father Don Battista Tavono. After further consideration, it appears that nothing is more important for the salvation of your soul and the glory of God our Lord than that you should settle down in your vocation, and also strive as hard as you can to give greater edification every day, making use of the means decided on by your spiritual fathers. Be of good courage. God our Lord, who called you to his service in this Society, will also give you the grace to be edifying therein, even though sometimes persons achieve what they desire only with effort and time. But as long as a person tries to do his best, even if he recognizes many faults in himself, we cannot say that he is wasting his time in religious life. So commend yourself to Christ and stand firm in the essential things and make progress in the others, as I have said, and God will be with you. May his grace always be preserved and grow in your heart.

Rome, August 5, 1553

✠

To Reginald Pole, Cardinal of England

Rome, August 7, 1553

(Letter 3627: V:304f.; in Italian)

Ignatius congratulates Cardinal Pole on Mary Tudor's accession to the throne of England and the prospect of the full return of that country to the Catholic faith. Pope Julius III had appointed Pole legate to England.

My Most Reverend and Esteemed Lord in Christ:

May the sovereign grace and eternal love of Christ our Lord greet and visit Your Most Reverend Lordship with his most holy gifts and spiritual graces.

I recently was visited on Your Lordship's behalf by one of your gentlemen, with that great demonstration of charity and kindliness which we have always recognized in Your Reverend Lordship. The author of this and of every good, Christ our Lord, will himself be the reward of his own gifts in Your Reverend Lordship. In addition to this, however, I cannot help sending my congratulations and giving heartfelt thanks to God our Lord for this door which he has deigned to open for the restoration of the kingdom of England to the bosom of the holy Church and to the purity of the holy Catholic religion and faith. Our confidence in this regard is all the greater in that we are sure that it was not the bad will of the people but of their princes which occasioned their errors, and that with divine Providence now providing good rulers, there is every reason to hope for a return to their natural state on the part of the peoples there, where at other times the name of Christ our Lord was so highly exalted and glorified.

Moreover, we are confident that Your Reverend Lordship's going to England by order of this Holy See will be a most powerful instrument of divine grace, and that Your Lordship's holy and long-cherished desires will be heard by the divine Clemency, along with those of others whom we do not doubt God our Lord has preserved and "who did not bend the knee," etc. [Rom. 11:4].

As to ourselves, I promise Your Lordship the continual petition of our sacrifices and prayers in the presence of God's supreme goodness. And although before this time I had given orders that in every place where there are any of our Society, even in India, all the priests should offer Mass and the others say special prayers for the spiritual help and the restoration of those peoples, and that this should continue as long as the need lasted, I am now repeating the order inasmuch as we seem to be laid under a fresh obligation by this new beginning granted by divine Wisdom and this occasion for renewing our own desires with hope.

This is all, except humbly to commend myself with our entire house and Society to Your Most Reverend Lordship's holy prayers. May God our Lord grant to Your Lordship a happy voyage in his holy service, and to all of us abundant grace always to know his most holy will and perfectly to fulfill it.

Rome, August 7, 1553

✠

To Nicolò Pietro Cesari

Rome, August 13, 1553

(Letter 3640: V:326f.; in Italian)

Ottaviano Cesari was the young son of Nicolò Pietro Cesari, secretary of Ettore Pignatelli, duke of Monteleone. Against the opposition of his parents, Ottaviano left Naples to join the Society in Sicily. Hoping to undermine the vocation, his parents agitated to have him returned to Naples. On his own initiative, Ottaviano wrote to Ignatius that he was firm in that vocation, going on to say, "Send me to the ends of the earth," if Ignatius so wished. Here Ignatius rebuffs the attempt by the parents. There were to be further letters on the same subject as they persisted in their endeavors.

Jesus

Most Honored Lord:

May the grace and peace, etc.

To Your Lordship's letter which arrived this week, about having Ottaviano returned to Naples, I shall respond, albeit briefly, by saying that for my own part I am most inclined to render every service and give every consolation in the Lord to you and your spouse, all the more so since His Illustrious Lordship the Duke has written me about the matter. Nevertheless, as Your Lordship must be aware, upon my writing to Palermo I received answer not only from our own Don Paolo but from Ottaviano himself that he has justifiable fears that his coming to Naples might occasion him grave temptations, so that he earnestly begs

me not to put him in such peril.[19] And so I would be failing in my duty
if I did not accede to this reasonable request of his; were I to act otherwise, I could hardly answer to God our Lord. I am sure that Your Lordship will easily be able see this if you strip yourself of that natural
feeling which is so often opposed to the true love of charity with which
children ought to be loved.

If Ottaviano were loved in this fashion, neither you nor his lady
mother would seek, for your own consolation according to flesh and
blood, to put your son in danger of grave loss according to the spirit, as
it would be for him to be disturbed in his vocation, which many signs
show with great clarity to be from God our Lord. Seeing his firmness in
this regard, it would seem more right for you both to assist him in his
vocation rather than the contrary, as you have been doing.

Nothing further at present except that, as I have written to His
Illustrious Lordship the Duke, you can be assured that it will be many
years before Ottaviano makes his profession, which will give an opportunity for his firmness to be observed more clearly and for God our Lord
to be praised thereby. May his divine and supreme goodness grant all of
us the grace always to know his most holy will and to fulfill it.

Rome, August 13, 1553

✠

To Nicolò Pietro Cesari

Rome, August 27, 1553

(Letter 3706: V:418–20; in Italian)

*Two weeks after his previous letter to Ottaviano Cesari's father (see letter 3640
above), Ignatius, in a reply to another letter from the father, even more strongly
refuses the request that Ottaviano be sent back from Sicily to Naples. Ignatius
discounts the distress of Ottaviano's mother as an argument for moving him, and
even threatens to send him to distant Spain unless his parents stop troubling him.*

Jesus

My Most Honored Lord in our Lord:

May the sovereign grace, etc.

While I have nothing substantially different to say from what I
wrote Your Lordship two weeks ago, I will nevertheless reply to your

---

[19] Paolo d'Achille was rector of the college at Palermo.

letter. I am sure that you do express your views without bias; still, I cannot in good conscience order Ottaviano there so long as he has such well-grounded fears that it would disturb and hinder his spiritual advancement. Moreover, even if he himself had no such fear, reason daily shows us grounds for it, for my lady his mother would certainly not leave him in peace at Naples if she will not do so even in Sicily. Your Lordship should not be surprised that I do not think it right to give this consolation to the mother at such a cost to the son. This is the common teaching and practice of the saints and all the servants of God. If his mother were reasonable, she might be satisfied to know that he is well, advancing in studies and virtue, and that it is only a two or three days' trip to Naples and back to where he is living. She is not the first mother to have a son in religious life. She should not think of him as lost to her; indeed, she ought to think of him as won for her. If, having given him to the service of some prince, she would endure his absence, let her be patient with his absence for a few years, and leave him in the service of God until he is more a man; then, when he no longer fears opposition, it will be easier for him to be sent back to Naples—whereas now, if Ottaviano hears that his parents will not be at peace, he will urge that he be transferred to Spain or Portugal, where she might never see him again.

Therefore, let Your Lordship encourage her to take this matter of her son in a Christian way; Christ our Lord has a greater part in him than she does, and so she should not be surprised that her son prefers the service and will of Christ to her own or that of any other creature. Let Your Lordship promise her also that if she will remain at peace, I will give orders for her to have frequent letters from her son, whereas if she does not, she may receive none for a long time. In sum, I will do whatever I can for her consolation provided it is without detriment to her son's spiritual progress.

No more, except to ask God our Lord to give all of us the grace always to know and carry out his holy will.

Rome, August 27, 1553

✠

To Hannibal Coudret, by commission

Rome, August 27, 1553

(Letter 3708: V:421f.; in Italian)

Coudret was one of the early Jesuits sent to the college at Messina, the first to be founded explicitly and primarily for lay students and in many ways a model for later Jesuit schools. Some of the humanistic-classical texts adopted for study in the college raised questions. Polanco, on behalf of Ignatius, responded to the concerns, but he made a mistake about the book to which he refers, De octo orationis partium constructione. *As a matter of fact, this book was written by Erasmus.*

The peace of Christ.

Dearest Master Hannibal in Christ Jesus:

It is true that Our Father does not want works by Erasmus, Vives, Terence, or any other writers dwelling upon immodest *[disonesto]* topics to be taught. But I will say two things to relieve your scruple. First, this rule is not yet being rigorously observed outside Rome, especially where some have already started to use these books. Second, here in Rome we are endeavoring to adapt these authors as follows. The objectionable passages are removed from Martial, Horace, and the like, and the remainder is left under the author's names, etc. The little work on the eight parts of prayer is being printed without Erasmus's name, since he did not write it. We are also preparing an abbreviated version in verse containing what is valuable in Erasmus, and similarly with other authors. We will have these books printed and then they will be sent to you in Messina through our bookseller, who will print them. What you have been doing up till now is all right, and you may continue with that.

If Master Bernard [Olivier] should arrive there, in your charity remember us to him. When I learn where he is, I will write him.

I commend myself to your prayers.

Father Master Louis [Coudret] is well, and still has the same office.

May Jesus Christ be always the help and support of us all.

Rome, August 27, 1553

☩

To Giovanni Battista Tavono
from Juan de Polanco, by commission

Rome, September 9, 1553

(Letter 3731: V:451–53; in Italian)

Polanco writes to the rector at Padua about a change of air for one scholastic, the continuing problems of Giovanni Ottilio (see letter 3620), and those of another, Giovanni Battista, who is tempted against his vocation.

The peace of Christ.

From the letter of the first of this month, we learn that the air in Padua is bad for Guerrico during the winter, and so he can come to Rome with Father Don Elpidio when he returns to Rome. From here we will send him to Sicily, where we are told the air will be good for him both summer and winter, and where it will be possible to regulate his diet according to his needs. I imagine they will all agree to come as far as Ancona by sea, and perhaps this will also do him good.

As regards Giovanni [Ottilio], Our Father has made no decision different from his previous one. With the intelligence he has shown so far, it would seem that the Exercises would be of considerable help to him, and enable him to see his temptations. For as to his saying that the commandments are enough, it is clear that they are not enough for him or for anybody inspired by God to follow the way of the counsels, especially once he has so bound himself. As for his saying that he cannot keep or stand to hear the rules, these words are clearly not his own but from the devil, who is a liar and the father of lies. Soldiers and servants and the majority of lay people observe much heavier obligations. To say that he cannot preserve chastity would be heretical; and in any case failure to keep it, inside or outside religious life, would mean his damnation. His saying that he wants to live, not off the goods of the Church, but by his own labor is also crazy and seems to smack of Lutheranism—not that anyone thinks that Giovanni is tainted with heresy, but it is the same devil that persuades the heretics of these lies who persuades him of them also. I think that a person who labors at teaching others has just as much merit as a person working at the tailor's trade. In conclusion, since tepidity has spoiled him, fervor of spirit can cure him, and for this it would seem that the Exercises will be useful to him.

Father Commissary writes us of a Giovanni Battista from Ferrara who is also severely tempted. We are uncertain whether this is he or the one he sent us as dispensers. Whoever he is, he should not be sent to Rome, but helped there where he is. I am uncertain whether the one sent to be dispenser may have been put to work in the kitchen and the sacristy. When Father Don Elpidio gets here too, he will be able to provide information on a number of matters. During his absence, Your Reverence will take over his responsibilities.

May Christ, our Lord and eternal Wisdom, give to all of us light always to know and always to carry out his most holy will.

Rome, September 9, 1553

To Juan Luis González de Villasimplez

Rome, September 16, 1553

(Letter 3756: V:488f.; in Spanish)

González de Villasimplez was royal treasurer in the kingdom of Aragon. He often acted as a channel between St. Ignatius and the Spanish Jesuits. Ignatius writes him a letter of encouragement, urging him to ground his happiness in God alone.

My Lord in our Lord:

May the sovereign grace and eternal love of Christ our Lord be always our help and protection.

I received Your Worship's letter of the ninth of this month; were anyone to seek proof of the great love that God our Lord has given you for us, he would find it abundantly in this letter. May God our Lord, whose love ought to be the foundation and rule of every other love, repay you by so increasing his love in your soul that no one's absence would ever cause you pain except that of him who is the supreme and most perfect good. Just as there is nothing good without him, so neither is any good lacking where he is present, since all the good which is sought in his creatures is present in greater perfection in him who created them. I beg him always to make himself known and loved by Your Worship, and to place deep within your soul the example and teaching which Christ our Lord placed before the whole world. If you continue in your excellent and Christian practice of frequent confession and Communion, as well as of prayer and almsgiving, Christ our Lord will keep you from stumbling, let alone falling. For of all who act in this way it can be said, "He has given his angels charge over you, and in their hands they shall bear you up, lest perhaps you dash your foot against a stone" [Ps. 91:10]. So do not fear the stumbling blocks of which you write, but instead those which all Christians must fear if they are to keep themselves from occasions of falling.

It would not be right on our part to fail to remember you, and the love which God our Lord has given us for you will not permit it.

As for Spes, your servant, I suppose that he will have written you of his decision. He is now in our house, having been called, I think, by

God our Lord. His connection with you is a circumstance which increases the happiness of us all in his vocation.

Señor Pedro Zárate is much beholden to you for the special memory you have of him, and I do not think he will allow himself to be outdone in this respect, and in all eagerness to serve you.

Signor Tommaso Spinola and Signor Francesco Cattaneo will deliver this letter to you. In them you will recognize men of Christian zeal and great virtue, according to what we know here of them.

In Your Worship's last letter there was nothing about your going to Spain. May it please the divine Goodness that it be when and in the way that it will be best for you.

And so I will add no more, except to ask God our Lord to grant to Your Worship and to all of us his abundant grace, so that we may always know his most holy will and entirely fulfill it.

Rome, September 16, 1553

✠

To Leonora de' Medici, duchess of Florence

Rome, September 23, 1553

(Letter 3768. V:505f.; in Spanish)

The Duchess of Florence, the Jesuits' patron there, had intervened on behalf of Cesare Rinaldi, a lawyer at the papal court, who was campaigning to get his son Tarquinio out of the Jesuit order, because he considered it a blot on his family's honor that his son should have entered the Society. After trying to use the influence of cardinals and nobles who were benefactors of the Society, he tried force to extricate his son, all to no avail. Then he asked the duchess to come to his aid. She was a woman of strong will, not used to being thwarted, particularly by those who were dependent upon her, as were the Jesuits. Ignatius's letter to her mixes deferential acquiescence with a tactful but firm request that she not make such interventions in the future. Despite promises not to do so, Rinaldi continued to try to dissuade his son from remaining in the Society, but to no avail.

My Lady in our Lord:

In Your Excellency's letter of the sixteenth of this month, I learn your command and behest regarding Tarquinio, a scholastic of our Society; and I have no doubt that Your Excellency's compassionate and tender heart has felt sympathy for Master Cesare Rinaldi, Tarquinio's father according to the flesh—which he has shown himself to love more than the spirit or his son's progress therein, since he has been making such efforts to deflect him from the path on which God our Lord had placed him for his own service; and his wanting him brought to Rome could be with this intention. However, out of due respect for Your Excellency's letter, and having had occasion to assure myself of the young man's steadfastness, as well as having received certain promises from his father, I shall do as Your Excellency bids regarding Tarquinio so long as he feels courageous and confident that God our Lord will give him fortitude. At the same time I beseech Your Excellency not to intervene so readily with your authority in matters of this kind; it could be the cause of some soul's abandoning the service of God and being lost forever, which I know is the farthest thing from Your Excellency's holy intention. Inasmuch as in cases where people press their interests with little fear or love of God, it is better not to bend in any matter which might place no slight burden on one's conscience, and because I and our whole Society are Your Excellency's, it seemed to me that I ought not fail to give you this counsel, as one sincerely desirous of the service and the supreme and eternal gifts of God our Lord in Your Excellency.

May the divine Goodness grant all of us his abundant grace, so that we may always know his most holy will and entirely fulfill it.

Rome, September 23, 1553.

✠

To Giovanni Ottilio, by commission

Rome, September 30, 1553

(Letter 3794: V:538f.; in Italian)

See the earlier letter (3620) to the same restless scholastic. Ignatius was always both gracious and firm with him.

The peace of Christ.

Our Father received your letter, dearest brother; and though you write some things obscurely, you make it clear that you would like to be absolved from your vows. Our Father will always be pleased to give you consolation in whatever is lawful where he can do so without harm to your conscience or his; but he does not believe this possible in absolving you from your vow until you have spent a somewhat longer time in trial and have devoted yourself to the Spiritual Exercises for a number of days. We are writing Father Don Battista to try and help you, and you should make corresponding efforts, and keep up your exercises throughout this winter. And if in the coming spring you want anything from

Our Father, I know that he is ready to console you however he can. Try seriously, dearest brother, to pray Christ to dispose you for his grace, because much is at stake for you here, perhaps nothing less than your eternal salvation.

May Christ, the author of grace, teach you his most holy will and give you the grace to fulfill it.

Rome, September 30, 1553

✠

To Margaret of Austria, duchess of Parma

Rome, November 17, 1553

(Letter 3913: V:699f.; in Spanish)

Ignatius consoles the Emperor's daughter ("Madama") for the wars that were ravaging her duchy of Parma.

Jhs

My Lady in our Lord:

May the sovereign grace and eternal love of Christ our Lord greet and visit your Excellency with his most holy gifts and spiritual graces.

I received great consolation in our Lord from the visit by Master Adrian on Your Excellency's behalf, welcoming as a very special favor this token of the customary remembrance and special charity which he who is infinite and supreme charity has given to Your Excellency toward our Society. He likewise is the author of the attachment we all feel deep in our souls to Your Excellency's service for the glory of his Divine Majesty. His infinite wisdom knows how frequently I bring the remembrance of Your Excellency before his most holy presence, desiring that he preserve his gifts in you and increase them for his greater service and praise; and that from all these trials which he has permitted, he will draw the fruit which his divine goodness can and customarily does draw, for the great perfecting of Your Excellency's soul in this life and for the merit of a special and lasting crown in the next, where our supreme and most blessed happiness, unmixed with any toil or misery, is stored up for us by him who won it for us at the price of his blood and life. Meanwhile, may it please him to give us a great knowledge of the sweet dispositions of his providence, by which both in adversity and in prosperity he constantly provides us with occasions for advancing in the attainment of our everlasting blessedness and joy.

In the house and college here we are all well, and both here and elsewhere God our Lord bears us forward and makes use of this least Society, which is entirely Your Excellency's and always will be, to the glory of his Divine Majesty. May he be pleased to give all of us his perfect grace always to know his most holy will and perfectly to fulfill it.

Rome, November 17, 1553

✠

To Nicolò Pietro Cesari

Rome, November 19, 1553

(Letter 3920. V:710f.; in Italian)

Another refusal to send Ottaviano Cesari for a visit with his parents in Naples (see letters 3640 and 3706 above).

My Most Honored Lord in our Lord:

May the sovereign grace and eternal love of Christ our Lord be always our help and protection.

I have received Your Lordship's letter, in which, with all possible moderation, you indicate your desire to satisfy your lady wife's wish to see Ottaviano. Certainly, so far as it could be done without prejudice to Ottaviano himself and the service of God in him, I would dearly like to content a mother's heart, while also giving Your Lordship the double consolation that you would apparently receive from seeing the mother restored to calm and having the son before you. And any time we decided to bring him to Rome, this is what we would do—let him stay over for a few days in Naples and then continue his journey. But since it would be wrong to force Ottaviano's will or unsettle his mind by placing him in greater danger than he can easily endure, we will have to see his state of mind and will before determining whether he is to come. Consequently, I can only promise you my greatest readiness to perform, to the extent that I can in our Lord, what His Illustrious Lordship the Duke and also Your Lordship indicate to be your desire.

May the divine and sovereign Goodness deign to convert towards itself all our love and inclination, so that we may love all his other creatures in conformity to him and not otherwise; and may he give to all of us the grace to know and always to fulfill his most holy will.

Rome, November 19, 1553

To Nicholas Floris (Goudanus), by commission

Rome, November 22, 1553

(Letter 3924: V:713–15; in Italian)

Floris, a zealous apostolic Jesuit from Gouda in the Low Countries, lamented his spiritual dryness and lack of the gift of tears. Polanco relays to him Ignatius's assurance that sensible consolations are not essential to Christian holiness.

The peace of Christ.

My dear Father in Jesus Christ:

I received Your Reverence's letter of October 12 and am much edified to see your longing to help souls in Germany not only by preaching and other external means but also with your tears, the gift of which you desire to receive from the Giver of all good.

As to the first part—being of practical help to the neighbor by the external means of preaching and so forth—we may unconditionally beg Christ our Lord to deign to "give to his voice the voice of power" [Ps. 68:34] and to confer on the administration of the sacraments the wished-for efficacy. As for the gift of tears, one may not pray for it unconditionally, since it is neither necessary nor unconditionally good and suitable for everyone. However, I have brought the matter before Our Father Master Ignatius, and for my own part have asked and will continue to ask God our Lord to grant it in the measure that it is suitable for the purpose that Your Reverence seeks it, namely, the help of souls—your own and your neighbors'. Dear father, "it will go badly in the end for a hard heart" [see Sir. 3:27]; but a heart like your own, full of longing to help souls and serve God, cannot be called hard. When someone feels compassion for the miseries of the neighbor in the will and the higher part of his soul, desires to do what he can to relieve them, and performs the offices of a person who has this active will for taking the necessary means, he needs no further tears or sensible feelings in the heart. While some people may have tears because their nature is such that the affections in the higher parts of their souls easily overflow into the lower, or because God our Lord, seeing that it would be good for them, grants them to melt into tears, this still does not mean that they have greater charity or accomplish more than other persons who are without tears but have no less strong affections in the higher part of the soul, that is, a strong and efficacious willing (which is the proper act of charity) of God's service and the good of souls, just like that of persons who have abundant tears. Moreover, I would tell Your Reverence something of which I am convinced: There are persons to whom I would not give the gift of tears even if it were in my power to do so, because it does not help their charity and damages their heads and bodies, and consequently hinders any practice of charity. So Your Reverence ought not to be distressed over the lack of external tears; keep your will strong and good and show it in your actions, and that will suffice for your own perfection, the help of others, and the service of God. And remember that the good angels do all that they can to preserve human beings from sin and to ensure God's honor, but do not grieve when the contrary happens. Our Father frequently commends our own men's imitating the angels' manner in this.

That is all, except to commend myself earnestly to Your Reverence's prayers.

Rome, November 22, 1553

✠

To Ettore Pignatelli, Duke of Monteleone

Rome, December 10, 1553

(Letter 3983: VI:49–51; in Italian)

In the continuing battle over Ottaviano Cesari's vocation (see letters 3640, 3706, 3930, 4115, and 4116), Ottaviano's parents enlisted the support of their patron, the Duke of Monteleone. Here Ignatius again defends his decision to keep Ottaviano out of his parents' reach. (The struggle went on for five more years, and ended with Ottaviano's departure from the Society.)

Jhus.

My Most Illustrious and Honorable Lord in our Lord:

May the sovereign grace and eternal love of Christ our Lord greet and visit Your Most Illustrious Lordship with his most holy gifts and spiritual graces.

I received Your Lordship's letter of the sixth of this month from your courier. On the one hand, I am delighted that Your Lordship knows so well my desire to serve you, as I for my part promise to do insofar as it lies in my power for the glory of God our Lord; indeed, I do not think that reason and the very willing obligation we all feel toward Your Illustrious Lordship would allow me to fall short in this regard. On the other hand, it grieves me that I am not able to satisfy Your Lordship's wish have to Ottaviano brought back to Naples, not even to make good on a promise; for it is not to be thought that I could promise Your Illustrious Lordship something that was impossible for me, and among persons who fear and love God our Lord, what cannot be done in good conscience is considered as impossible. And in this matter I am convinced beyond doubt that I would offend God our Lord were I to give the unconditional command being sought by Ottaviano's mother, for whose mental and physical distress I have great sympathy. And from the heart I wish her its true cure, which consists in conformity to the will of God our Lord. But to satisfy her wishes with a bad conscience on my own part—this I certainly neither could or ought to do for any created thing. Moreover, we must not think divine Providence so short of resources that it cannot cure the mother except with the sight of her son, whom I do not think I could send to Naples without committing sin. Further, I wish to inform Your Lordship that our men in Sicily, seeing how the son was being bothered and fearing that as long as his mother was close by, she would be constantly unsettling him, had decided to send him to Spain or Portugal on the first good ship available. Indeed, the young man may have been sent there by now. I did not forbid this, being convinced that, besides the young man's being removed from danger, his mother would also be consoled and brought to a better spiritual state when she lost all hope of seeing her son for some time. This is the second reason why I cannot satisfy the mother by giving her son an unconditional command to come and see her. I know that Your Illustrious Lordship, with the light granted you by God our Lord, will realize that I can give no other answer, and also will know how much of what I say should be communicated to the mother.

I pray that the divine and supreme Goodness will graciously make itself known and loved as it should be, taking possession of this lady's heart so that she will love all other creatures in the divine Goodness and for its sake, and that the grace may be granted to us all to know and perfectly fulfill his most holy will.

Rome, December 10, 1553

✠

To Andrea Galvanello

Rome, December 16, 1553

(Letter 3991: VI:63; in Italian)

Galvanello had done much good in the northern Italian parish of Morbegno in the Valtellina, to which he had been sent at the request of Pope Julius III because that area was tinged with Protestantism from nearby regions. Its inhabitants did not want him to leave and threatened to call in a Protestant preacher if he did so. So Galvanello strongly recommended that he stay there and be appointed pastor. When it became clear that he was using a variety of means not in conformity with the Society's Institute, Ignatius sent a severe reply.

Father Don Andrea:

If Your Reverence wishes to be a member of this Society, you must grieve at any harm done to its whole body. It is a great harm to act against its Institute. Well-ordered charity for helping souls is highly commendable; but ill-ordered affection, even having the appearance of good, is reprehensible. And if you wish to know which affections are well ordered in a religious and which are not, examine whether they are in conformity with the rule of his obedience and Institute or not. A word to the wise . . .

✠

To Luis, Infante of Portugal

Rome, December 24, 1553

(Letter 4008: VI:85f.; in Spanish)

A letter of thanks to the brother of the King of Portugal for his favors to the Society, both those past and those offered for the future.

Jhs.

My Lord in our Lord:

May the sovereign grace and eternal love of Christ our Lord greet and visit Your Highness with his most holy gifts and spiritual graces.

To Your Highness's letter of September 27 I wish to be able to respond not so much with words as with gratitude, acknowledging and giving infinite thanks to God our Lord for the favor he does this least Society in giving Your Highness such eagerness to favor and help it in his divine service. While the worth of Your Highness's actions well shows the strength of your will to favor us, yet it is clear that far more remains hidden in the treasury of Your Highness's heart than can have been revealed by outward effects. It is with this impulse that Your Highness commands us to consider what you might do for us and what we might petition Your Highness to have done. This reminds us of the infinite and supreme goodness of God our Lord, who has impressed on Your Highness's soul this trace of himself: it is characteristic of him to wish to give us greater graces than we are ready to receive, and to move us to desire and hope from his divine liberality what will fulfill and even outdo our desires and hopes. May he be blessed and praised in all his creatures and all the good he has placed within them. Amen.

I am very glad that Your Highness has been so pleased with the coming of Father Francis Borgia and Master Nadal; I noted the same in their own letters as in that of Your Highness.

News of other matters Your Highness will doubtless have heard from our men, and I refer you to them, humbly commending to you this whole Society, which is less ours than it is Your Highness's.

May God our Creator and Lord give all of us his abundant grace, so that we may always know his most holy will and entirely fulfill it.

Rome, December 24, 1553

✠

To Gaspar Berze

Rome, December 24, 1553

(Letter 4010: VI:87f.; in Spanish)

Ignatius approves Berze's appointment as head of the Indian Mission during Xavier's absence in the East, and advises him to postpone his planned trip to Ethiopia.

May the sovereign grace and eternal love of Christ our Lord be always our help and favor. Amen.

We received your letter of January 12 of this year, together with others which our dearest brother, Master Francis, had left written there. From both we understand that you are in charge of the college there and the rest of India while Master Francis is gone. I am very satisfied with his choice, and I trust that the divine and supreme Goodness will supply for the weaknesses and lacks of his instruments and thus give you the grace to render him great service in your office.

I do not think that your desires to go to China and Japan have been unfruitful in the divine presence, for the offering of your will that you made will have been accepted; for the rest, you should take as the sure interpretation of the divine will whatever has been enjoined on you in obedience by Master Francis.

With regard to going to the land of Prester John, unless you have already done so by the time this reaches you, I think you should put off your journey until the patriarch is named and ten or twelve others are sent to Ethiopia. If this does not take place this year, you may be sure that it will by next year's sailing at least. However, if you see the situation to be such that you deem in our Lord that you ought to go without awaiting the arrival of those being sent from here, I can only defer to what you determine after listening to the other brethren with whom you are supposed to consult, as has already been written and as you will see in the *Constitutions* if they send you a copy from Portugal.

For other matters I refer you to Master Polanco, who will go into more detail, according to my instructions.

May it please the divine Wisdom to communicate itself to you in all you do and to give all of us his abundant grace, so that we may always know his most holy will and entirely fulfill it.

Rome, December 24, 1553

✠

To Filippo Leerno

Rome, December 30, 1553

(Letter 4020: VI:109f.; in Italian)

Leerno had been named rector at Modena earlier that year; while the financial situation was satisfactory, he thought that some of the young Jesuits in his charge did not want to change for the better and others were lacking in obedience. So Leerno thought that he was not the right person to hold the office of rector. In this letter Ignatius encourages him in his task.

The peace of Christ.

Dear Father Master Filippo:

The office of rector is in good hands with Your Reverence, and you must take care not to humble yourself to the point of yielding to a spirit of faintheartedness. God's gifts are not to be despised, even though we duly deprecate our own imperfections. Be of good heart, and take advantage of whatever help your companion, Master Giovanni

Lorenzo [Patarini], is capable of giving you. Do not demean yourself or be wanting in courage. Be assured that we have a higher opinion of God's gifts in you than you yourself seem to have.

As to the blindness or dryness of spirit which you think you find in yourself, it might easily stem from this diffidence or faintheartedness, and thus be cured by the contrary. Above all, remember that God seeks from us solid virtues, such as patience, humility, obedience, abnegation of our own will, and charity—that is, readiness to serve him and to serve our neighbor for his sake—rather than other forms of devotion, though his providence may grant us these when he sees that they are good for us. But since they are not substantive matters, an abundance of them does not make anyone perfect, nor the lack of them imperfect.

I will add no more about this, except to pray that Jesus Christ our Lord may be always the help and protection of us all.

Rome, December 30, 1553

✳ 1554 ✳

To Pope Julius III

Rome, 1554

(Letter 4247: VI:443f.; in Italian)

At the time of the Holy Year Jubilee of 1550, Pope Julius III had ordered the segregation of the sexes in visiting the stational churches in Rome, to prevent the less-than-edifying conduct that took place on those occasions. A stational church, originally dating from the fourth century, was the particular church where the Christians of Rome gathered for the liturgy on a certain day. Later, when jubilees were instituted, the major basilicas of Rome became the "stations" to be visited in order to gain the jubilee indulgences. Ignatius here asks the Pope to make permanent his order regarding the segregation of the sexes.

Jhs.

Most Holy Father:

The enormous devotion and spiritual benefit, greater than can be said, which resulted during the last jubilee from Your Holiness's new and holy regulation that the women and the men should go separately to different churches, has opened the eyes of many good persons zealous for the service of God and produced in them a desire to petition that during his pontificate Your Holiness would deign to leave as a perpetual ordinance this holy practice of separating the stations for the men and the women throughout the year, so that this spiritual treasure which is so lavishly dispensed by the Apostolic See in this city may not be stolen by the enemy of human nature, who is accustomed, in the times and places where remission is granted for sins committed, to cause countless new sins through the occasion of the men and women going together.

Wherefore, we humbly petition that Your Holiness would deign to instruct his vicar, or whomever he judges best, to provide for dividing up the ordinary stations in such a way that the men and the women earn the same indulgences on different days; and that this ordinance be established for the future, to the universal benefit of souls and perpetual memory of Your Holiness as the author of so great a good.

✠

To Teutonio de Braganza

Rome, January 1, 1554

(Letter 4031: VI:130f.; in Spanish)

Teutonio de Braganza was a member of the high Portuguese nobility, stepbrother of the Duke of Braganza. Once he had decided to enter the Society, he had to overcome the opposition of his family through a series of adventurous escapades. In the Society at last, he became a partisan of Simão Rodrigues in the troubles among the Jesuits in Portugal. His superiors decided to send him to Spain and thence to Rome. While waiting at Barcelona to sail, he became seriously ill. Ignatius here agrees to a postponement of his voyage and encourages him to interior peace and to the pursuit of his studies at Cordoba. Meanwhile, Teutonio had returned to Portugal.

May the sovereign grace and eternal love of Christ our Lord be always our help and our protection.

From letters of Master Nadal, the commissary, I learn, my dear brother, that God our Lord has visited you with a serious illness. I am sure that, in his divine goodness, this has all happened for an improvement in your health, for your merit, and for the exercise of your virtues, so that you will know how to find the fruit that God our Lord wishes to see gathered from such visits, he whose wisdom and infinite charity seek our greater good and our perfection, no less with bitter medicine than with the sweetest consolations. With that I hope, through his divine favor, soon to hear news of your health, which I am sure you will employ generously in his service.

Your coming here and the reality of seeing you would give me great consolation; but as I have already seen for a long time, there is no way open to fulfill this desire that each of us has, given your illness. Thus I think it good to postpone your trip at present. So that you can make progress in letters and at the same time enjoy greater consolation, stay at Cordoba and continue to carry on your studies there; and if there are other things which can cause you concern, put them aside, in the assurance that I will concern myself with them enough and that all will finally turn out for the great glory and service of God our Lord. May his infinite and sovereign goodness give to all the fullness of his grace to know and to do his most holy will.

Rome, January 1, 1554

To Magdalena Angélica Doménech

Rome, January 12, 1554

(Letter 4054: VI:160–62; in Spanish)

The sister of Jerónimo Doménech, provincial of Sicily, and daughter of Pedro Doménech, a major benefactor of the Society in Valencia, had been ailing physically and spiritually, as her brother had informed Ignatius by letter the previous month. Ignatius comforts—or, in a sense, braces—her in her sufferings.

My Lady in our Lord:

May the sovereign grace and eternal love of Christ our Lord be always our help and protection. Amen.

Through letters from Valencia I learn that God our Lord has been visiting Your Worship with bodily and spiritual trials—thus displaying, by these many occasions for merit that he gives you, his very special love for you, as well as his intention of repaying your good desires and works all the more richly in his eternal blessedness inasmuch as he shows himself unwilling to reward them in this world and temporal life. I certainly desire for you, madam, all the contentment and consolation of soul that I could wish for myself, and I sympathize with you in your trials as reason and the law of charity require of me; still, I cannot help regarding as a very special gift of God our Lord the opportunity he gives you to practice patience, faith, and hope in him, as you remain convinced that the divine and supreme goodness and charity of our all-wise heavenly Father is providing you with what is best for you. For it is in adversity no less than in prosperity, in afflictions as well as in consolations, that he displays his eternal love by which he guides his chosen ones to unending happiness.

His kindness and mercy are such that if it were for our good, he on his part would be inclined to keep us always consoled rather than afflicted, even in this world. But since the condition of our misery in this present state requires that at times he employ trials instead of comforts with us, we can at least see his fatherly and supreme mercy in his limiting these trials to the brief course of this life—not without an admixture of many consolations at the proper times—and in his rewarding our patience with inestimable happiness and glory in the eternal life that never ends, where there is no admixture of any affliction or sadness or unhappiness of any kind, heaven having none of these, but only utter fullness of joy and blessedness. Even so, if you strive to resign yourself into the hands of Christ our Lord by conforming your own will entirely to his and being fully ready to follow him in the trials he underwent in this world whenever he may wish to share them with you, so that you can follow him later in the glory of the other world, I have no doubt that your trials will largely cease and your fortitude in bearing them will so increase that you will hardly feel them. On my part, I and those with me here will not cease earnestly recommending Your Worship's concerns to God our Lord. If there is anything I am able to do to further your consolation, I would be most willing to do it, as one who loves you deeply in our Lord. May he deign to give to all of us his bountiful grace that we may always know his most holy will and entirely fulfill it.

Rome, January 12, 1554

✠

To Jerónimo Doménech
from Juan de Polanco, by commission
Rome, January 13, 1554
(Letter 4066: VI:178–80; in Spanish)

Doménech, the provincial of Sicily, had complained both to Ignatius in written form and also by word of mouth to others about the lack of manpower to carry on the works for which he was responsible there. The reply is a strikingly realistic account of the penury in quantity and qualifications of the men available to Ignatius, as he bore the responsibility of governing the entire Society and its works. Furthermore, the letter delivered a sharp reproach to Doménech for airing his complaints in public.

The peace of Christ, etc.

My dear Father:

I would prefer writing Your Reverence things that would console rather than wound you—but you would have to stop giving so much cause. Indeed, were he not restrained by certain considerations, Our Father would take action to display more clearly his displeasure with Your Reverence's complainings. They reflect discredit on him: not only do you not submit your judgment to his in the arrangements he makes regarding persons under him, but you also criticize his arrangements as bad in the presence of others, as you obviously did with the three men who have just arrived from Spain: you wanted to keep Master Pedro Canal there, and you complained to them that Our Father at first sent you some of the principal men in the Society and later withdrew them all, etc. Your Reverence overlooks the fact that you were given some recompense for those taken away; and you overlook something even more important, namely, that Our Father has an obligation to look out for the universal good. Thus, while leaving you the personnel that he does for maintaining and carrying forward the works there, he also takes care of other works in which God our Lord wishes to make use of the Society and its members. The college at Venice has only one priest, who has no philosophy or theology; that of Padua has two who have a not-very-good hold on literary studies and nothing above that; that of Modena has two who are barely average in Latin and still youths. At Ferrara, Pelletier, who was alone there, has been sent another man who has little by way of literary studies or anything higher. Master Francesco Palmio is at Bologna, but we cannot send him a priest to be his companion because there are none. Master Louis [Coudret] is at Florence, together with another who has scarcely made his literary studies. There are two men at Gubbio, neither of them a theologian. At Perugia there is a single theologian and another who is not. And the lack of masters to teach in these places is, I believe, equal to or even greater than the lack of priests. But this does not prevent them from producing fruit, God our Lord making up for what our slight forces cannot accomplish. In comparison with the rest of Italy, Sicily is without doubt better provided than any other place, even after making all necessary allowances.

This does not mean that Our Father wants you to refrain from representing what you think; rather, he wants you to. But he does not want you letting a single word escape you there to suggest that you criticize his actions. Indeed, so long as you do not voice in public the shortcomings you see, he is happy for you to let him know about them, leaving the matter up to him and preferring the universal to the local good, in the conviction that once Our Father has been informed—simply and without arguments or complaints—he will do what is best for the greater service of God our Lord and the general good. Indeed, we should all aim at this, even though the angels of particular places might have a special predilection for their own provinces or localities. And so that Your Reverence will not forget this practice of keeping confidential what you think is amiss there and of writing by way of representation, etc., you are to send in your own writing how you intend to do this, for this is Our Father's command. You ought also to think about giving him some consolation here occasionally. He has a great deal of trouble providing for so many places in Italy and in Ethiopia, besides maintaining the *studium generale* here in Rome, where there is so much illness among both professors and students. Dr. Olave was giving two lectures a day in theology, but got so exhausted that for his health's sake he has had to be relieved of one of them; it will be given by Master Jean [Couvillon], the one who came from there. But after all, God is our help; it is his glory that we seek in Sicily, in Rome, and everywhere. May he fill us with knowledge of him and hope in him, and may he dwell with perfect love in our souls. Amen.

Rome, January 13, 1554

✠

To Maria Frassona del Gesso

Rome, January 20, 1554

(Letter 4094: VI:223f.; in Italian)

Maria Frassona del Gesso, the widow of one of the ministers of Ercole d'Este, duke of Ferrara, was talented enough to be called one of his "ministresses." She was a very generous and exceedingly effective benefactor in founding the Jesuit college there, to the displeasure of her relatives. Anxious and in fragile health, she increasingly depended on the rector, Father Jean Pelletier, and wanted regular and frequent visits from him to give her spiritual guidance. Tongues began to wag. Ignatius had complete confidence in Pelletier; but to remedy the situation, he wrote to the rector, suggesting that he make no more than two visits a week, always with a companion, and that he introduce some other Jesuit who could at times be her confessor. Just when Pelletier began to put these suggestions into effect, Frassona became seriously ill and needed Pelletier more than ever. Ignatius then wrote this letter of consolation. The news that he would keep Pelletier there permanently revived her. She was generous enough to be so recognized publicly. She became equally generous to the Roman College.

Jhus.

My esteemed Lady in our Lord:

May the sovereign grace and eternal love of Christ our Lord greet and visit Your Ladyship with his holy gifts and spiritual graces.

Having heard in letters from our men that Your Ladyship has been visited by God our Lord with some bodily illness as well as with trials of soul, I thought I ought to pay you a visit by letter—no other way being possible—and remind you that it is usual with the providence of our most holy Father and all-wise Physician to act in this way towards those whom he loves much. Moreover, the more quickly after this present life he wishes to bring them to share in his own eternal happiness, the more he purifies them with such trials in this world, where he does not want us to be able to find any rest or repose for our love. For this reason he prods his chosen ones not only with heavenly longings but also with earthly vexations. However, the latter help increase our glory when they are received with the patience and thanksgiving with which we ought to welcome the gifts of his fatherly charity, from which come scourges as well as caresses. If there is any way to stir up trials and afflictions of mind in this world, it is by striving to conform our own will perfectly with God's. For if our hearts were wholly possessed by him whom we cannot lose except by our own willing it, nothing could happen to us that afflicted us very much, since affliction always arises from losing or from fearing to lose what we love. I am writing to our brother Master Jean [Pelletier] not to let his new additional duties keep him from visiting you as he has been accustomed, for your Ladyship is really the reason he is in Ferrara, and for Your Ladyship's satisfaction and consolation I intend keeping him there permanently so far as it depends on me and God our Lord gives him life.

No more, except to commend myself earnestly to Your Ladyship's prayers and pray God our Lord to grant all of us the grace always to know his most holy will and perfectly to fulfill it.

Rome, January 20, 1554

Entirely Your Ladyship's in our Lord,

IGNATIO

✠

To Girolamo Muzzarelli, O.P.

Rome, January 23, 1554

(Letter 4097: VI:229–33; in Italian)

This letter for Girolamo Muzzarelli, a Dominican friend of the Society and nuncio to the court of the emperor Charles V, dealt with the foundation of the German College in Rome. It was meant to assist Girolamo to inform the Emperor about this work, so dear to the heart of Ignatius, and to solicit his financial support. Ignatius had heard more than enough from letters of the Jesuits in Germany and Austria about the lamentable state of the Church there, about examples of an ignorant and loose-living clergy, and about the troubling lack of vocations to the priesthood, all of which were contributing to the spread of the Reformation.

Cardinal Giovanni Morone, a papal legate and a good friend of Ignatius, proposed in January 1551 an institution in which German seminarians, could be brought to Rome, trained there, and then returned to Germany as learned and devout priests. Several cardinals enthusiastically supported the idea, and Pope Julius III asked the College of Cardinals for financial help. Finally, in 1552 the school began operations.

Ignatius then turned to Charles V, saying that the Pope and his cardinals had thought it necessary for him to approach the Emperor, in order that the latter might provide financial help and also afford other princes an example of generosity to this new work. Finally, because Charles V had regularly held the Society of Jesus at arms' length, despite his personal friendship with Francis Borgia, Ignatius took pains to make clear that the Society would receive no material benefits from carrying out its responsibilities for this new institution.

The first point to make is that, given the present extreme scarcity of good and faithful apostolic workers in Germany, where there are no persons of suitable Catholic life and learning to whom the cure of souls can be entrusted, it has become evident that if what remains of religion is to be preserved and what has been lost through the bad example of Catholics and the bad teaching of the heretics is to be won back, there is urgent need to create for these nations and tongues a seedbed of fresh plants, where efforts will be made to take intelligent young men and give them training and formation in good morals and letters, so that from among them can be chosen bishops, pastors, preachers, and professors who will be both good and educated men, and in this way by contrary medicine cure the sickness which has been contracted in those nations, as already mentioned, through the bad example of their pastors, preachers, and professors.

To do this as it should be done was not feasible in Germany. For one thing, the Catholic religion is too much undermined not only among open heretics but even among many who are ostensibly Catholic; their bad example would have been most damaging to such young men, already too inclined to liberty. Another reason was the apparent impossibility of providing for the temporal needs of this college and of manning it with suitable teachers and administrators. In addition, because of the detestation for the name of the Holy Roman See in those nations, which makes them all too ready to remove themselves from her obedience and unity, the proper place to erect this college was Rome. There they could witness at first hand the Holy See's charity, generosity, and zeal for their salvation, and change their bad opinions and attitudes into good ones, and consequently be better disposed towards the requisite unity with her. Furthermore, to keep bad example from harming their morals, His Holiness and the leading cardinals determined that responsibility for this work should be given to the Society of Jesus, whose task it is in their colleges to teach letters and good morals simultaneously.

Since in both endeavors they have by God's grace had considerable success in Spain, Portugal, Sicily, Italy, and other more distant nations, there is every reason to expect that in this college they would have the same results which they have had, and are still having, in their other colleges.

Those who originated and volunteered to promote this work were Cardinals Morone, Santa Croce, Carpi, St. James, Pacheco, de La Cueva, and the Cardinals of England and Augsburg.[1] When the project was submitted to His Holiness, he judged (as they all had) that this was not only the best but also practically the only way to preserve what remains and restore what is lost of the Catholic religion. Consequently, the bull for the erection of this college was issued, and its protectors named by His Holiness. These include the Most Reverend Cardinals du Bellay, Carpi, St. James, Cervini, Morone, and the Cardinal of Augsburg. Statutes were drawn up, and a number of students of good intelligence recruited. There are already about fifty men in the German College, with two or three of the Society of Jesus to govern and accompany them, since the students are not allowed outside the house except in their company, so as to remove the occasion for possible untoward consequences of their going out alone.

Alongside the German College there is another college of the Society of Jesus where all the disciplines except medicine and law are taught with great seriousness and application. Here the Germans come for their classes and other academic exercises. Under this good example and training, they are already making so much progress in their lives and learning that it is cause to praise God mightily and to hope that they will be instruments of great service to him.

His Holiness and the cardinals have made contributions of their own to launch this work, so that there is a modest annual provision for expenses. But to be an effective help for Germany, it is estimated that this institution should maintain about two hundred students, not counting other personnel. This would require an income of eight or nine thousand ducats. Consequently, His Holiness and the above-mentioned cardinals have judged it necessary to apply to His Majesty, to whom God our Lord has granted not only such power but also such singular zeal for the restoration of the Christian and Catholic religion in his empire of Germany, so that just as His Majesty has done so much by

---

[1] That is, Giovanni Morone, Marcello Cervini, Rodolfo Pio di Carpi, Juan Alvarez of Toledo, Pedro Pacheco, Bartolomé de la Cueva, Reginald Pole, and Otto Truchsess.

arms as well as through the council to gain those nations for Christ, he might also help by this means, which may perhaps be more effective than any of the others can be. For it is not enough to subjugate Germany militarily or even win general acceptance of the council's definitions unless there are bishops, pastors, preachers, and professors who can uproot evil teaching by word and example and plant good teaching in people's hearts—which is precisely the aim of this college.

Hence, let His Majesty be entreated to deign to assist this work by some incomes that are at his disposal and some pensions, or however he thinks best.

The King of the Romans and the King of Portugal will also be asked for help, but it would be up to His Majesty to take the lead and assist not only by his contribution but also by his example, so that the other princes will help.

His Majesty might also be informed that the Society of Jesus chose not to assume temporal responsibility, but only the spiritual charges mentioned above. It can draw no profit other than the practice of charity towards those nations and the increase of the Catholic religion. To ensure this, every year it has the college's rector (a member of the same Society) swear that neither the house nor the college of the Society of Jesus has made any use, great or small, of the German College's temporal goods.

✠

To Signora Cesari

Rome, January 28, 1554
(Letter 4115: VI:251f.; in Italian)

This letter was to no avail. Ottavio's mother then turned to Cardinal Carafa, who ordered Ignatius to send the young man back to Naples. Pope Julius III invalidated that order. Ottavio's mother then obtained a personal meeting with the Pope, who set up a commission of cardinals to consider the case. They advised her to concern herself with her daughters, hardly the outcome she expected.

May the sovereign grace and eternal love of Christ our Lord be always our help and protection.

I have received a letter of the twelfth of this month from Your Ladyship, indicating your desire to have your son Ottaviano summoned to Naples to restore your health, which you believe will be improved by seeing him. I am sure Your Ladyship already knows that if in any way I could serve and console you without going against the will of God our Lord, I would be most eager to do so. However, a person of my profession cannot choose to comply with the will of a human being over God's will—something that not only a religious but every layperson should be far from doing. And since I believe that it would be against God's will to place the young man in danger, I cannot acquiesce in having him come to Naples at present—not until he himself is stronger and Your Ladyship more at peace and content with your son's choice. Moreover, I cannot believe that Your Ladyship's physical or spiritual health requires the presence of your son. To think this would be to do an injury not only to Your Ladyship but also to the divine and sovereign Majesty: we would seem to believe that he has no other way to assure Your Ladyship's inward and outward health than by an act on our part that was disordered and sinful, as it would be to bring your son at this time to where he could visit with you. Your Ladyship should remember that you are not the first mother whose son has become a religious, and that no fathers or mothers according to the flesh have as great a part in their children as does God, who created both parents and children and has restored them with the blood of his own only-begotten Son. So we must conform ourselves to his holy will; Your Ladyship's consolation depends more upon this conformity than upon seeing your son.

Otherwise, in whatever way I can give Your Ladyship satisfaction and contentment as God wills, I shall always do so—and even more willingly as I learn that you are submitting yourself to the will of God our Lord in a more Christian and patient manner.

May his divine and sovereign goodness grant to all of us the grace always to know his most holy will and perfectly to fulfill it.

Rome, January 28, 1554

✠

To Fra Francesco da Mede

Rome, January 28, 1554

(Letter 4116: VI:252f.3; in Italian)

Ottaviano Cesari's mother had also enlisted the intercession of a Franciscan with whom Ignatius had earlier had correspondence. Ignatius again refuses to send Ottaviano to Naples.

Jhus.

May the sovereign grace and eternal love of Christ our Lord be always our help and protection.

I have received Your Reverence's letter. As you were prompted to write it by tenderness, pity, and compassion towards Ottaviano's mother, I am confident you will be satisfied with the reason that compels me not to violate charity toward the son by putting him in peril for the sake of his mother's consolation according to the flesh. God our Lord is quite able to give her inward and outward health without disordered action on our part; and it would be no little disorder to let the son visit her. He is a young plant and may not have roots strong enough to withstand the storms of maternal affection. Please endeavor (as I am sure you will) to make her understand that her consolation and peace of mind depend upon conforming herself to God's will, not upon seeing her son. She ought to be striving for his perseverance, unless she wants to prove herself a mother only according to the flesh.

I earnestly commend myself to Your Reverence's prayers, and pray the divine and sovereign Goodness to grant that all of us may in all things know and fulfill his most holy will.

Rome, January 28, 1544

✠

To Filippo Leerno,
from Juan de Polanco, by commission

Rome, February 3, 1554

(Letter 4131: VI:280–82; in Italian)

This letter to the rector of the college at Modena deals with day-to-day matters in the life of the Society, first with an internal matter of governance, then with real estate and with several of the apostolates of the Society. The "collateral" was an unusual component of the Society's governance structure set up by Ignatius himself. The collateral was supposed to be a trusted companion of the superior, a support to him in his governance, but neither under the superior's jurisdiction nor, in turn, holding authority over the superior. However admirable as an ideal, the office eventually was discontinued in the face of the real difficulties it entailed for both the superior and the collateral. As for real estate, this is one of the many hundreds of letters Ignatius wrote dealing with that subject, setting forth the physical needs for property and buildings experienced by the growing Society and describing the rapidly expanding work of the colleges. Finally, the letter bears witness to how important in the eyes of Ignatius were the Spiritual Exercises.

The peace of Christ.

We received no letter from Your Reverence last Saturday.

We wrote you two weeks ago, sending you the *Directory for Confessors*.[2] We are sending our letters by the post, no longer by way of Bologna. We also sent the document or memorandum on points that needed to be observed, and on Your Reverence's duties toward your collateral, Master Giovanni Lorenzo, as well as the collateral's towards the rector, so that Master Giovanni Lorenzo will know how he ought to behave towards you, namely, by helping you in every way possible, acting as an angel of peace between yourself and our other men, and in general making efforts to be helpful in every respect. Seeing how highly Your Reverence wrote of him, Our Father has given him this office, which he gives to people in whom he has great confidence.

I also wrote that efforts should be made to obtain a church. I said that we could accept the chapel of Sant'Antonio with the responsibilities that go with it; accepting this chapel, I think, would be preferable to going to San Bernardino's or the church of the reformed women to preach and hear confessions.

In addition, I wrote that while it is looked upon here as a quite useful and holy practice to get people to go to confession once a week, it is not considered a good idea to urge men or women to reception of the sacraments every day, although it may be permitted to some especially good and devout persons. A single reception over and above the regular weekly one may more readily be allowed, especially on feast days.

Regarding the Spiritual Exercises, Our Father has commissioned me to send a reminder everywhere that we should endeavor to make use of them with both men and women (the latter, however, should come to the church to receive them). This refers to giving the exercises of the First Week and leaving the persons with some methods of prayer suitable to their capacity; and to Exercises where the person is not put into seclusion but takes a few hours each day for this purpose. In this way we can extend to large numbers of people the usefulness of the Exercises up through the general confession and methods of prayer, as already stated. Moreover, Our Father says he wants a weekly written report on whether anything is being done about the Exercises, giving the numbers of persons who have made them or been urged to make

---

[2] A handbook for confessors of the Society written by Polanco himself; it had just been printed.

them, just as with the number of the students. In giving the full Exercises, there is no need to be so expansive; in fact, these should be given only to particularly apt subjects, such as men suitable for our Society or other persons of importance, since for these persons they would be particularly valuable and the time devoted to them well spent. Your Reverence should not be surprised at Our Father's strong insistence on this matter of the Exercises. Among all the means used by our Society, this is in a special way the Society's own, one which God our Lord has made great use of for countless souls. The majority of good subjects in the Society today were drawn there from the world by this means. Thus, if we wish to increase the Society's numbers with good men, this would appear to be an excellent means. The Exercises, especially those of the First Week, are also of great value for married persons or others in secular or religious life. No more on this.

We all commend ourselves earnestly to the prayers of Your Reverence, Father Giovanni Lorenzo, and all the other beloved brothers.

Rome, February 3, 1554

☩

To Doimo Nascio

Rome, February 22, 1554

(Letter 4181: VI:343; in Italian)

Doimo Nascio was a very good friend of Ignatius. At a somewhat advanced age, he wanted to join the Society, but after a brief time as a novice, it was thought that he would better serve God as a layperson. At the time of this letter, Nascio, faced with the decision about a change of residence, is advised, in default of light from God on the matter, to abide by the desires of his earthly lord. In the present case, this was Ascanio Colonna, charged with treason against the Emperor, Charles V, and imprisoned in Naples. It is he and the Emperor to whom Ignatius refers in saying that there was "not too much prospect of . . . reconciliation."

May the sovereign grace and eternal love, etc.

Reverend and dear Master Doimo in Christ:

I received your letter and understand the hesitation you indicate about going to Venice. I have prayed over the matter as you bid me, and I will tell you what I think with all the lovingness which our friendship in our Lord demands.

If I had resolved to serve some lord, especially one with whom I was as pleased as Your Reverence says you are with yours, I would want, if faced with making a change, to know his will and to accommodate myself to it, for the service of God our Lord. And so, as regards whether or not to make this trip to Venice, I would want to know which way Signor Ascanio's will inclined in the matter, and conform myself to that unless I had some other source of clarity on what would be for God's greater service. If I had such, there would be no further need of deliberating: I would simply follow what I knew would be more pleasing to God. So this is my opinion. Although there is not too much prospect of the reconciliation which we all desired so much, you can leave this matter in God's hands and employ your charity in other things, for the glory of God our Lord. I ask you to commend me earnestly to him, and I pray the divine and sovereign Goodness to give us all the grace always to know and fulfill his most holy will.

Rome, February 22, 1554

✠

To Diego Laínez, by commission

Rome, February 22, 1554

(Letter 4182: VI:344f.; in Italian)

This letter was written to Laínez, who was at that time in Genoa. He was an excellent preacher and it was no wonder that he was much in demand for that work. Ignatius makes clear that he is not, however, to preach to the detriment of his health.

Ihus.

The peace of Christ.

We received Your Reverence's letter of the fifteenth, and understand from it that you are preparing to preach every day, beginning with the second Sunday of Lent. The gentlemen who are not satisfied with less than a sermon a day must be prompted by excellent zeal and charity for their church; but as Our Father is bound to have zeal and charity for yourself in particular as well as for the others under his care, he does not want you undertaking labors that your bodily weakness cannot bear. In this matter you should follow the doctor's advice. Otherwise, it can easily happen that through your excessive willingness to labor this Lent, you may be prevented from preaching for years to come and be unable to attend to other business in the service of God. This is perhaps insufficiently considered by those who want to have a sermon every day, looking only to the present.

In desires to die among infidels I know that Your Reverence has not a few companions; but in the end one must be better satisfied with whatever divine Providence ordains through superiors.[3] Your Reverence will have news of India through Florence, since Father Louis [Coudret] has directions to send them to you.

No more for the present, except to commend ourselves earnestly to Your Reverence's prayers.

I forgot to say that the King of the Romans has written rather eagerly about the compendium;[4] but we will talk about that when the labors of Lent are over. I am sending Your Reverence a copy of his letter.

Rome, February 22, 1554

Postscript: Although the other letter is written in absolute terms, so that you can show it where necessary, it is still left up to Your Reverence just as before whether to preach or not. But for the love of God, do not kill yourself; be content with what you are able to do, etc.

✠

To Gian Andrea Schenaldo

Rome, February 24, 1554

(Letter 4184. VI:347f.; in Latin)

A citizen of Morbegno, in northern Italy, had written opposing the removal of Father Andrea Galvanelli, who had worked fruitfully in that city. Ignatius explains that the Society's Institute forbids accepting permanent pastoral responsibilities. The technical Latin term that Ignatius uses in this letter is "cura animarum"; perhaps this term could be most clearly translated today as "permanent responsibilities of a pastorate." (For what Ignatius wrote Galvanelli himself, see letter 3991 above.)

Ihus.

---

[3] Laínez had written: "Concerning the news about . . . infidels, God knows how deeply pleased I am; for myself, there constantly come from time to time, however coldly, I know not what desires to go to Jerusalem; and although I know that the way to die well is to live well, when I see how I fail in living, I wish that our Lord might grant me by way of mercy to die well, as is the case when a person dies in confessing his faith or in preparing to do so."

[4] A compendium of theology Laínez was working on.

The grace and peace, etc.

Although little acquainted with the one to whom I am replying, I do not wish to seem wanting in my duty and so feel I ought to respond briefly to Your Charity's letter. In it you endeavor to convince me that we ought to take upon ourselves the cure of souls, and that therefore our brother Andrea Galvanelli ought to be kept there among you. Of course, our Society bends every effort to help and further the salvation of souls, impelled thereto both by charity and by our own Institute; moreover, the grave needs of souls throughout the world goad us constantly forward, adding the spurs to those already running of their own accord. It is not this which our Constitutions forbid us, but rather the obligations customarily attached to a cure of souls or pastorate. The members of this Society need to be free and unencumbered, so that they can fly off to any place on earth where greater hope of God's glory and the salvation of souls beckons us, not settling in any particular place (unless we happen to have a college or house there), but working for different people over limited periods of time, gratis and without being bound. It accords with modesty, and indeed with prudence, that one should approve—or at least not disapprove without considerable examination—what is done with forethought and system by other persons who fix their gaze solely upon the will of God. It should be permissible for everyone who serves Christ under the banner of holy Church and with her approval to abound in his own opinion. Nevertheless, I take your letter in good part, convinced that it is prompted by your piety and charity towards your own people.

I shall add no more, since I have written all that is necessary to the authorities of your city.

Farewell in the Lord Jesus Christ.

☩

To Gaspar Berze, by commission

Rome, February 24, 1554

(Letter 4193: VI:357–59; in Spanish)

Gaspar Berze (or Barzaeus), a Dutchman, was, along with Francis Xavier, one of the great Jesuit missionaries in India in the sixteenth century. Before entering the Society, he had served in the army of Emperor Charles V, lived as a hermit at Montserrat, and worked in the royal treasury of Portugal. Ignatius had Polanco write him that his apostolic exertions should not lead him to neglect his health.

However, when this letter was written, Berze had already died in 1553, after only five years of extraordinary labor in India.

From the earliest years of the Society, the news that its members sent back to Rome became of great interest, especially in non-European countries. It was not only Jesuits who were fascinated by these letters. Copies of them were quickly made and widely circulated and were very influential in making the Society known, in attracting vocations, and, in some instances, in helping to inaugurate fashions in such areas as architecture, furniture, and clothing.

The peace of Christ.

My dear Father in Jesus Christ:

May the grace and peace of Christ our Lord be always present and grow in our souls.

I did not expect to write any letters beyond those we already have for the present sailing, but on our later receiving from Portugal a letter written in Goa about Your Reverence's illness and about the labors of preaching and the like that you are undertaking in the midst of it, Our Father decided that this letter should be written to you, informing you from him that he does not consider such a manner of proceeding advisable or likely to last very long. While your holy zeal and love of austerities are most edifying, he thinks they are missing that salt which God our Lord wanted to be offered him in every sacrifice—that "reasonable service" which St. Paul wishes to be given him by those who offer themselves to God our Lord [Rom. 12:1].

There are two dangers in treating yourself so harshly. The first is that, barring a miracle, Your Reverence will not be able to last very long in the holy ministries you undertake. Rather, you will either be cut off by death or become too ill to continue your labors, which it is reckoned would impede great service of God and help of his souls, in which you could employ yourself for many years if in good health. The second danger is that, being so hard on yourself, you could easily become too hard on those under you; if only by your example, you might push others to excessive effort—the more so the better they are.

In a word, Our Father recommends moderation to Your Reverence. When you are ill, he does not want you to preach unless the doctor tells you that it will do you no harm. And since in your own case Your Reverence might be uncertain about where moderation lies, it would be good to choose someone there who lives or travels with you to serve as the superior over you in matters of food, sleep, and moderation in work, and for you to obey him in the Lord on these points. We have made use of this procedure here to moderate the activity of some of the

Society's leading men and holders of the most important offices. So much for the care of your person.

There are important persons in Rome who read the letters from the Indies with great edification and who frequently express a wish for geographical information about the countries where our members travel: how long the days are in summer and in winter, when summer begins, whether shadows falls to the left or to the right—in short, information should be furnished about anything else that is out of the ordinary, such as plants and animals that are unknown here, or of a larger size, and so on. Sauce of this sort for the palate of a harmless human curiosity can be sent either in the letters themselves or separately.

Since we have taken the pulse of persons of high quality and intelligence and learned that they find this more edifying, it would be good for the writer, when preparing letters for showing to people outside the Society, to dwell less on matters specifically related to members of the Society and more on matters of general interest. Otherwise, the letters cannot be printed here without considerable cutting. Of course, news about individual members of the Society are quite appropriate for the edification of our own members, but this can be sent separately. Any deficiency in this latter regard can be remedied here, even if with some trouble, but as regards the first there is no way we can make up for it here. Hence, Your Reverence can order the members of your province to write as indicated above.

Referring you to the other letters, I will add no more, except to say that here at the house, and in the Roman and German Colleges, we are by God's grace in good health. May he grant us interior health who is the world's true health and life, Jesus Christ our God and Lord. Amen.

Rome, February 24, 1554

✠

To the Rector of the College of Coimbra

Rome, February 26, 1554

(Letter 4206: VI:378; in Spanish)

Arriving in Rome in November 1553 after his removal from Portugal, Rodrigues received a warm reception from Ignatius, but there also remained serious questions that had preceded him regarding his governance as provincial in Portugal. Rodrigues requested that a commission of four fathers examine these accusations. After this group had found serious missteps in his governance of the Portuguese Province,

Rodrigues wrote the new provincial to that effect. The commissioners also proposed a set of severe penances. Rodrigues accepted them, but Ignatius remitted them all except for the prohibition against his returning to Portugal. To protect Rodrigues's reputation from his own self-accusations, Ignatius accompanied Rodrigues's letter with the following testimonial. (Rodrigues finally did return to Portugal in 1573, where he was received with great affection and evident joy.)

The sovereign grace, etc.

Enclosed is a letter of our beloved brother Master Simão. Even though in it he reproaches himself harshly for a number of things, I want you to know that in our opinion here his intention was good and that anything he did wrong, either when in office or afterwards, was done not with ill will but with the conviction that he was doing what was right. I am daily happier with his company and conversation. However, inasmuch as the Constitutions do limit the provincials to three years, and because he himself wished to be freed from this burden, and because we have judged it best, in view of the rigorous perfection required by the Society and its government, to change the superior in that kingdom, we have summoned him here, where he will have no lack of abundant opportunities to employ himself in the service of God our Lord.

If you show his own letter to anyone, you are ordered under obedience to show this one along with it, so that no one may be left with an incorrect impression.

May Christ our Lord give all of us the grace always to know his most holy will and perfectly to fulfill it.

Rome, February 26, 1554

✠

To the Rectors of the Society's Colleges

Rome, March 3, 1554

(Letter 4222: VI:410f.; in Italian)

As vocations to the Society arose from among the students in the Jesuit colleges, some parents were less than happy when their sons decided to become Jesuits, as the case of Ottavio Cesari among others shows in the letters in this collection. Hence this prohibition of accepting legal minors into the Society or encouraging them to enter without the consent of their parents or guardians.

Ihus.

May the sovereign grace and eternal love of Christ our Lord be ever our continual protection and help.

Inasmuch as our purpose in the colleges and schools is that youth be taught and formed in letters and good behavior, and their families edified by this as well as by the other works of charity—confessions, sermons, etc.—practiced by the Society, we have deemed it right in our Lord to order all of you and strictly command that no young man who is still under the authority of his relatives or guardians shall be admitted into our Society—whether in the college itself or by sending him elsewhere—without the agreement and consent of those under whose authority he is. And much less ought our men to urge or persuade students of this kind to enter our order. For while of itself it is lawful and praiseworthy to help persons who have reached the age of discretion, and even to urge them to the state of perfection (that is, to religious life), nevertheless, in our schools to urge or to admit persons in this way is not judged appropriate, for the sake of God's greater service and the universal good, which is our goal more than is the particular good, as reason demands. In order to promulgate this ordination and decree of ours, we have written to all our colleges to this same effect.

We commend ourselves to the prayers of all, and pray God our Lord to grant to all of us grace to know and always carry out his most holy will.

Rome, March 3, 1554

✠

To Emperor Charles V

Rome, March 3, 1554

(Letter 4231: VI:421f.; in Spanish)

This letter was to solicit the Emperor's intervention with his sister Mary, governor of the Low Countries, in the matter of founding and endowing a Jesuit college at Louvain. For reasons presently unknown, this letter was never sent.

TO HIS HOLY CATHOLIC IMPERIAL MAJESTY:

May the sovereign grace and eternal love of Christ our Lord greet and visit Your Majesty with his most holy gifts and spiritual graces.

Considering that the providence of God our Creator and Lord has placed Your Majesty in such a position and responsibility and also bestowed a mind that takes as its own the concerns of the universal good and of God's glory; and inasmuch as his providence has likewise raised up in Your Majesty's days this least Society of ours, of which it is making use and, I hope, will make daily greater use in Your Majesty's realms and in other parts of Christendom and beyond, it has seemed to me in our Lord that, faced with a great obstacle to this work in God's service, I ought to have recourse to Your Majesty, whose thoughts I am convinced are wholly directed to that service. Wherefore, I humbly petition Your Majesty graciously to hear certain information which will be provided him on our part, and to make whatever provision shall seem to be for God's greater glory—looking upon all of us as belonging very much, as we do in our Lord, to Your Majesty, to Your Majesty's children the King of England[5] and the Most Serene Princess,[6] to his brother the King of the Romans,[7] and to his sister the Queen of Portugal[8]—not merely as their vassals, as the majority of us are (some belonging to houses known to Your Majesty), but as deeply indebted to them for the kindness and goodwill which God our Lord, the author of all good, has inspired in them to raise up this Society in its beginnings.

May he be pleased to grant all of us his abundant grace always to know his most holy will and entirely to fulfill it.

Rome, March 3, 1554

✠

To Giovanni Battista Viola
from Juan de Polanco, by commission

Rome, March 10, 1554

(Letter 4251: VI:447–50; in Italian)

The commissary, or subprovincial, for northern Italy was a somewhat scrupulous person whom the responsibilities of the position had worn out and occasioned in him a prolonged illness from the summer of 1553 on. He worried about the special

---

[5] The Emperor's son Philip, consort of Mary Tudor and future king of Spain.

[6] Juana, daughter of Charles V and, as a scholastic, secretly a Jesuit from 1555 until her death in 1573.

[7] Ferdinand I of Austria.

[8] Catherine, wife of King John III.

treatment this had required and the extra costs to the Society. Ignatius tells him not to worry about the money and to do whatever may be needed to recover his health. Further letters followed this one; gradually Viola fully recovered his health, living for thirty-four more years, reaching the ripe old age of seventy-two.

The peace of Christ.

Dear Father in Christ:

We received your letter of the third of this month; I will now answer it.

First of all, Your Reverence should put aside the worry or vexation which you indicate you have at the thought that you cause the same to our Society. Be assured that the Society will never begrudge you any expense or trouble. It would show little trust toward her, or little confidence, to have doubts about this.

As for your going to Lunegiana or Sarzana, and occasionally visiting the fathers at Garfagnana, act entirely as best suits you and contents you—not, however, going against the advice of the physicians, whom it is reasonable to believe and obey up to a certain point in matters pertaining to their profession. In sum, in doing whatever you judge will be more restorative for you in the Lord and improve your health, you should be convinced that you are acting under obedience, since this is Our Father's mind, and you should have no scruples on this score.

On whether to take a companion or not, have more regard for what is best for you than for the cost. If the money from the houses is not enough, we will be quite happy to make up the rest. It is true that the reason you mention, which will be written about individually, rather inclines us to let you go without a companion from the Society, who might perhaps be less helpful than another in the matter of your service and bodily welfare. But arrange for whatever service you think best. Do not think that because of our many debts here we are unable to provide funds wherever they are needed; in these matters God never fails us.

I am sending you herewith an authorization for collecting money due, issuing receipts, and so on, as well as for naming a substitute so that you can collect the money at Parma by proxy. I am also sending a pair of testimonial letters, one about your expenses and the other stating that you are residing wherever you choose under obedience, for reasons of health.

If Master Giovanni Francesco [Brunello] of Parma does not bring funds with him on the account of the house but does bring money in any other way, take the amount you mention or more if you think you should. I will add: if he brings no money at all and the doctor says that you should leave right away, Your Reverence should instruct Father Don Francesco [Palmio] to borrow on my account whatever sum you want to take with you. I will make repayment within eight days of the presentation of letters to me, or however is customary. Or else they can take out a fifteen- or twenty-day loan in Bologna, and we will send repayment through a bank as soon as we are notified. It makes no difference to us whether you spend the money from the houses or any other money; it all belongs to the Society, and the Society will supply your expenses anywhere, whether they are greater or less than the price we get for the houses. We would never have mentioned this price except that we thought that the transfer of funds would take place and that Your Reverence would be staying at or near Parma.

As for your question about what to do if you find you are making no more improvement in your own country than you have so far in Lombardy—whether you should stay in those parts or return to Bologna, etc.—Our Father says that you are free to stay wherever you wish. You may return to Bologna if you wish, or go on to Genoa, or come to one of the colleges here closer to Rome—including Tivoli, which is about fifteen miles from Rome and has excellent air. Our Father would be agreeable to your coming to Rome, either for a long-term stay or leaving when you please for Tivoli, where we have a fine house and a few brothers—always, of course, barring objections from the doctors. So first try your native air. Then you will be free to move wherever you wish and think you will be most consoled. The only obligation we would lay on you is to let us know occasionally how you are. And if it will console you to have news of the Society, it will always be sent you from here or from the place nearest you. As for your assurance that you are not separating from the Society in spirit but only in body and for a time, Our Father says this is clear: even if you wanted to separate, we would hold you back with ropes. But you should not think you are separated even in body; the fact is that when a person is sent from one place to another by obedience, even alone, he is not separated from his congregation either in body or in soul so long as the bond of obedience persists. And if in the course of time you desire a companion so as not to appear to be living alone, write and summon someone to your liking from any of the colleges.

We are looking into the need for a priest at Bologna, and one will be provided, God willing, after Easter.

We have learned that Giovanni Antonio and Taddeo [Amaroni] reached Ancona and were on their way to Perugia to see if they could get from there to Florence and Siena respectively. We have heard nothing about them since.

We commend ourselves very earnestly to Your Reverence's prayers, however short.

May Christ Jesus be with us all.

Rome, March 10, 1554

I forgot to mention that you should consider yourself dispensed from the obligations of fasting and abstinence, the Office, and so on: do whatever suits your health. You may make use of any other indults granted to the Society in the measure that to the glory of God our Lord it will be for your consolation and that you judge best.

✠

To Maria Frassona del Gesso

Rome, March 13, 1554

(Letter 4260: VI:460f.; in Italian)

Upon receiving her letter of consolation from Ignatius (see letter 4094 above), Maria suddenly—and to her mind, miraculously—recovered her health. She renewed her efforts on behalf of the college at Ferrara, and sent a shipment of dry goods to the Jesuits of Rome. Thanking her, Ignatius reinforces his teaching about the grace of suffering. As for overwork on the part of the rector at Ferrara, Jean Pelletier, and Senora del Gesso's counseling him to moderation, she herself regularly demanded a lot of him.

My Most Esteemed Lady in our Lord:

May the sovereign grace, etc.

A few days ago I replied to Your Ladyship's letter of February 15; later I received another of December 18, together with a number of articles you sent as a gift and alms, which were most welcome in our Lord, since we see in them the great charity and devotion which prompted you to send them. God, for love of whom every well-ordered gift is given and received, will be Your Ladyship's most generous rewarder on behalf of ourselves and of all his poor.

As for Your Ladyship's wishing that you felt your soul readier for the cross, God will take care of that in his own time, that is, when patience will be necessary for you. There is no cause to doubt this, for we have the promise of his eternal truth that he will never let us be tempted or tried beyond what we can bear. Rather, anyone who reflects on his sweet providence rightly trusts that everything will work together for his good, and is confident that the divine and sovereign Goodness, now chastising his children and now caressing them, always acts with the same charity in pursuit of their greater good. Hence, we can conform our will to God's with full confidence, resolving to be content with whatever disposition of us he makes. We will thus in time of need not lack the patience to bear our trials not only uncomplainingly but even gratefully, in the conviction that adversity as well as prosperity is a favor from God our Lord, as it really is, especially for those who truly concern themselves with his divine service.

As for the exertions of our brother Master Jean [Pelletier], my intention is that they be moderate, and I have written him to this effect; and if he should behave otherwise, it would be contrary to our intentions and directions. I trust that he will not, although goodwill often prompts even God's servants to overshoot the mark, so that they need a reminder; and Your Ladyship does well to give him one occasionally.

Nothing else, except that we commend ourselves most earnestly to Your Ladyship's prayers.

May God our Lord deign to grant all of us his grace always to know his most holy will and perfectly to fulfill it.

Rome, March 13, 1554

✠

To Diego Miró
from Juan de Polanco, by commission

Rome, March 15, 1554

(Letter 4271: VI:474f.; in Spanish)

The scholastic Francesco Adorno, a noble Genoese who had entered the Society in 1550 in Portugal while he was with his father there, had been going too far in his efforts to detach himself from his family. Ignatius tells him to stop writing in ways that his parents might find wounding, to say the least. Adorno later became one of the most eminent Italian Jesuits, serving as rector, preacher, writer, and spiritual director of Saint Charles Borromeo.

Very Reverend Father in Christ:

The peace of Christ.

This letter is being brought by the same person who will bring Our Father's and Master Simão's, as well as a general letter. And since a direct post for there may be leaving soon, I will say only that it is a good while since we have had a letter from Portugal, the last being the one we replied to earlier. We would like to know if the dispatch for Ethiopia arrived, and what decision His Highness has taken concerning this undertaking.

The other thing is that Our Father would like our brother Francesco Adorno, from Genoa, to write to his family in Genoa and try to give them consolation by his letters. And although in token of his having left father and mother for the service of Christ, he may use the style of speaking where you are that is most edifying to himself and others, in writing he should follow the normal usage. He should not write "the man said to have been my father," as he is reported to have written—an expression which, in its usual acceptation, his mother could find insulting. He should write "my father," etc., and similarly with other expressions. When writing to persons in the world, he may accommodate himself to them so far as our profession allows and as is judged will be most edifying and consoling to them in our Lord. And he will be able to avail himself of this freedom of spirit all the more as with time he stands firmer in his vocation and runs less risk of excessive affection towards his relations according to the flesh.

Since that is all for this letter, I will merely commend myself to Your Reverence's prayers, asking God our Lord to grant all of us the grace to know and fulfil his most holy will.

Rome, March 15, 1544

✠

To Tarquino Rainaldi and Gaspar Ruiz

Rome, March 18, 1554

(Letter 4284: VI:491–93; in Italian)

Travel instructions for two scholastics sent from Rome to Valencia.

Jhs.

To be observed on their journey by the two who are being sent:

1. The weaker should walk ahead and the stronger behind or alongside him. If one rides and the other walks, the one walking should precede.

2. Also as regards stopping at one place or another and traveling more or fewer miles, the stronger will adapt to the weaker, in this case Tarquinio.

3. The one going on foot may beg along the way if he wishes, and also in the villages if he judges it becoming.

4. He may preach if he finds spirit for it; at least the two of them can exhort to doing good when they have the opportunity.

5. When they have extra time in the hostels, they can read some religious book or converse about religious matters.

6. If one is unwell, the other should serve him with charity and see to bringing him somewhere nearby where the Society is.

7. If either of them is more than eight days on the journey, he should not fail in the customary confession and Communion, if possible with one of the Society.

8. They should not travel in the heat of the sun, but preferably in the morning. They should refrain from traveling during the hottest hours, unless there is a cool breeze. During the night they should also look for some muleteers or other good and safe company, since it would be better to travel a good part of the night and rest during the day.

9. They should not sleep in a bed with any stranger.

10. They may hire a relay horse from one stage to another as they think best, so that the one traveling on foot can get some rest and they can finish the journey faster.

11. They should go by way of Perugia and rest there for a day. Gaspare should take the letters that Giovanni Battista forgot and give them to Father Everard [Mercurian].

12. Before dinner every day and before going to bed each night, Gaspare should take the mule's saddle off to see if it is hurting him, and he should take good care of him.

✠

To Antonio Enríquez, by commission

Rome, March 26, 1554

(Letter 4306: VI:522-25; in Spanish)

Enríquez was a friend of the Society in the service of the emperor, Charles V. Such service required a peripatetic life, since it was the practice at the time for European sovereigns to move regularly from place to place in their domains. In this case, the lands governed by the Emperor were numerous and extensive. Polanco transmits an exhortation to live as a spiritual wayfarer in those circumstances.

Honorable Sir in our Lord Jesus Christ:

May the sovereign grace, etc.

I was hoping to answer a letter of Your Worship which I received from Florence, and so had requested a friend of ours at His Majesty's court to let us know if you were there.

I have now received a further letter from Brussels, dated February 22, which resolved the question. To Our Father and the rest of us here, all so devoted to your service, this letter gave a great deal of consolation in our Lord. And although the letter about your journey which you say you wrote on arrival has not reached our hands, the trouble you take in writing so frequently is a favor which we should highly esteem, and one which shows the warmth of feeling which God our Lord has given you. May his divine and sovereign goodness be pleased to perfect with the gifts of his grace those of nature which he has so abundantly bestowed upon Your Worship, so that both may be employed always for his greater service and praise and may earn for you an outstanding crown of eternal happiness.

Our Father is in fair health and sends Your Worship his deepest respects. We shall continue commending your affairs to God our Lord, for beyond the journey to Brussels there lies the longer journey to our heavenly fatherland, and we should always remember that we are wayfarers until we arrive there, never getting so attached to the hostelries or countries through which we pass that we forget where we are going or lose our love for our final goal. For it was that we might better attain this goal that our eternal Father gave us the use and service of all his creatures, and not that we should be so delayed by love of them that for the temporal and imperfect goods of this short life we lose the perfect goods of that which will last forever. The unwisdom of this, while quite evident to anyone with an intelligence enlightened by our holy faith, is sometimes not realized even by the wise of this world. This is because they are exteriorly dissipated, hardly ever entering into themselves with due reflection—wasting the light of the understanding and busying it with irrelevant things instead of applying it to those which are of supreme importance for their blessedness. They thus let their whole lives slip past, trying to spend these few days of our present pilgrimage amid honors, enjoyment, and prosperity, with no provision—or no serious provision—for what must bring them incalculable and unending wealth, honor, prosperity, and satisfaction in our heavenly fatherland. Truly, the saying of the prophet fits such people: "They set at nought the desirable land" [Ps. 106:24]; for if they placed any value on it, they would at least do as much to ensure their living blessedly there as they do to live pleasantly on this pilgrimage where God our Lord has placed us so that we might journey thither.

I will not pursue this further, confident in God our Lord that Your Worship is not one of these persons. Yet, so deep is the wretched state of the old man that unless the new man, renewed by the grace of Christ our Lord, makes use of the proper means, he can easily slide into every kind of imperfection. And so, as Your Worship's true servant, I cannot omit recommending to you frequent reception of the holy sacraments, the reading of some spiritual books, and prayer with whatever recollection you can manage—setting aside for yourself some time each day, so that the soul will not lack its nourishment and Your Worship not repeat the complaint, "My heart has dried up because I forgot to eat my bread" [Ps. 102:5]. Likewise, Your Worship will be much helped by associating with good and spiritual persons, as well as by continuing and increasing your excellent practice of giving alms, which is a universal means for obtaining every kind of good from him who is the never-failing source from which everything must flow.

If I have spoken at too great length for a first letter, put the blame on my deep devotion to your service in Christ our Lord. May it please him to increase his spiritual graces more copiously every day in Your Worship's soul and in the souls of us all. Amen.

Rome, March 26, 1554

Postscript: I recall that Your Worship once indicated to me a desire to have some information about our Society: having heard it occasionally mentioned, you wanted to be better informed, so that you could respond and perform the offices required by charity and by the desire given you by God our Lord for showing it towards us. Herewith I am sending information about our house here in Rome, our college, and the German College. This report will give Your Worship a detailed idea of the situation; you may afterwards use any part of it as you think best. The house and college here at Rome will give you an idea of the usual practice in the others throughout Christendom, at least in the main ones, as well as in those among unbelievers in the Indies and in Africa, where God our Lord makes use of the ministry of these lowly instruments of his.

If Your Worship wishes me to write more detailed news, this will be done either by myself or by our men at Louvain—whom I beg Your Worship to consider as wholly your own, just as we ourselves are in our Lord Jesus Christ.

March 26, 1554

✠

To Diego Miró

Rome, April 5, 1554

(Letter 4336: VI:564–66; in Spanish)

Ignatius sends the King of Portugal two suggestions for making his law against dueling more effective. The unusually vehement terms that Ignatius uses in this letter to characterize dueling, such as "perverse and devilish custom," "impious abuse," "disordinate practice," and "attributed to the devil," may hark back to examples he had seen in his courtier days when, so he says in his so-called autobiography, "he was a man given to the follies of the world": or to his own indignation and desire "to go in search of the Moor and slay him with his dagger" for what Ignatius thought was an impugning of our Lady's honor.

May the sovereign grace, etc.

Referring you to the other letters that accompany this one, I will mention here only that having heard in a conversation that there are two brothers from Portugal here in Rome who were both involved in duels and had killed their opponents, and decrying as I do this perverse and devilish custom among Christians—a custom not even practiced among infidels—of jeopardizing both soul and body out of a vain sense of honor, I was delighted and highly edified to hear of the decree which His Highness has issued in his kingdom prohibiting challenges to a duel under pain of losing both property and life.

While deeming this a quite good and holy measure, if I were in His Highness's presence I would not fail to suggest two further points which, added to the first, would in my view assist greatly in achieving His Highness's holy and Christian purpose.

The first is that any person accepting such a challenge should be declared a traitor and publicly branded with infamy, and also lose his life and property. In this way the disease will be cured by its contrary: a man who would enter a duel in order not to lose a part of his honor would now decline it in order not to lose the whole of that honor.

The second is that His Highness appoint four prominent men (or whatever number he deems suitable) with authority to deal with disputes between men which stem from insults or affronts, the usual occasion of these challenges. Before it comes to a challenge, these officials could examine the issues of honor or dishonor on both sides and take what steps they deem best. In addition, His Highness could take upon himself the reputed affronts, so that the parties could be satisfied and reconciled.

This measure would contribute greatly to the service of God in thus ending this impious abuse, one so opposed to all reason either human or divine that it can only be attributed to the devil. If it pleases God our Lord that this project be effectively carried out, then it is possible that other Christian princes would follow His Highness's example. For they must all consider this disordinate and perverse practice to be evil, particularly since it is based on nothing but the wrongheaded opinion of worldly men, the majority of whom themselves admit that they feel tyrannized by this damnable custom and are unhappy being subjected to it. Thus, if it is publicly declared to be wrong and those who fall into it are labeled with infamy, it would be possible and, it would seem, not at all difficult to expel this tyranny of the devil from every Christian land. Of the many achievements for which His Highness will be remembered, this would surely be one of the most outstanding.

To prevent people from being quicker to wrong others because of the removal of this deterrent, it could be provided, as pointed out above, that the person committing the wrong should be punished, first with disgrace and then in his person and property as well, as shall be judged appropriate. If Christian princes would take the matter seriously in hand, it would be easy to bring men to this way of thinking, so much more in accord with all reason, not only Christian but even merely human, than is the contrary practice brought into the world by the devil.

And since I cannot do so in person, I charge you to represent this to His Highness. And may the supreme and eternal Wisdom impart to His Highness its holy light and clarity, so that he may in all things see what will be more for the divine glory and the universal good of souls; and may he grant us all to know and always to fulfill his holy will.

Rome, April 5, 1554

To John III, king of Portugal

Rome, April 6, 1554

(Letter 4340: VI:570; in Spanish)

Ignatius writes to console the King on the death of his only surviving son, Don João, who had been heir to the throne, and to congratulate him on the posthumous birth shortly thereafter of his grandson, Sebastian, now that heir. The mother of Sebastian was Princess Juana, now a widow who returned to Spain and later secretly became a scholastic. Thus she was the only woman Jesuit in the Society's history.

My Lord in our Lord:

May the sovereign grace and eternal love of Christ our Lord greet and visit Your Highness with his most holy gifts and spiritual graces.

The great sorrow that we ourselves have all felt at this loss—not for him whom God our Lord has taken to himself, for he is much the gainer in this exchange of a temporal for an eternal kingdom, but for ourselves whom his infinite wisdom has chosen to deprive of such a prince and lord—makes us understand well what must be the sorrow in Your Highness's paternal heart; and this itself is another source of no ordinary grief for us.

And yet, when one considers the great and royal spirit and singular gifts with which God our Lord has endowed Your Highness, it would appear that he has decided to test these through this extraordinary visitation and to give to the world in Your Highness a salutary lesson in fortitude and conformity to God's will—of which indeed the report we have received here already gives proof, with great admiration on the part of those who hear about it and grounds for exalting him who is the perpetual and unfailing source of every good. Through these visible effects he shows how greatly he loves Your Highness and trusts in your virtue, inasmuch as he sends you such great occasions of practicing it to his glory.

On the other hand, in his most gentle providence he has chosen to delight and console us all with the birth of the new prince, thus showing himself, as he truly is, the Father of mercies and the God of all consolations. Blessed be he for ever, and may he deign to preserve this gift of his for his greater service and the common good of all. We shall implore this often for him in our prayers and Sacrifices. Your Highness will understand even without our writing it that these prayers, as well as our care on behalf of the soul whom God now has in his glory, will be such as correspond to the obligations felt by this least Society, which is entirely Your Highness's.

May the divine and supreme Goodness be pleased to give to all of us his abundant grace, so that we may always know his most holy will and entirely fulfill it.

Rome, April 6, 1554

☧

To Francesco Mancini, by commission

Rome, April 7, 1554

(Letter 4351: VI:585–87; in Italian)

Seriously ill, Francesco came from Sicily to Naples. He wrote to Ignatius, saying that for his own spiritual consolation he judged it better to stay with his Jesuit brethren there than with his family. The superior, Alfonso Salmerón, realized he could not be properly treated in the college there, and had him go home to his family to recuperate. Ignatius writes to assure him of his abiding bond with the Society. (Francesco did recover, but then left the Society.)

May the grace and peace of Christ our Lord always abide and increase in our souls.

Dearest Brother in Jesus Christ, Master Francis:

You will have learned the answer given to your letter if you have been in Naples. Our Father desires for you every spiritual consolation, and since this would have consisted in staying among your spiritual brothers and fathers, he would have let you stay in Naples had your poor health been able to bear it. But since the physicians judged that your recovery absolutely required your native air, consolation had to give way to expedience. But be assured, dear brother, that although you may be separated from us in body, you are intimately united by the bond of charity on our side and, I am sure, on yours as well. Be confident also that you are united to us not only by this bond but also by that of holy obedience, which binds all the members of our Society into a single spiritual body, into which you are incorporated no matter where you are. Therefore, consider yourself under obedience in employing any medical remedies and aids that are suggested to you, as well as whatever forms of decent recreation, even physical, may be recommended to you; for in this way you will more speedily get past your present illness with God's help, so that you can dedicate yourself fully to his service. And you should not think that working to recover your health is an insignificant occupation when you desire it for no other purpose than to serve God, and in conformity with God's will. Nevertheless, you also need a great deal of resignation (even while using all reasonable means for recovery) in order to be content with whatever disposition God our Lord makes of you. As long as he visits you with illness, accept it from his hand as a very precious gift from the wisest and kindest of fathers and physicians; make up your mind to be content, both in soul and in body, in acting and in suffering, with whatever may please his divine providence. And write us once in a while, however briefly.

Master Pompilio told me that you had requested some spiritual books. It would be all right for you occasionally to read or have someone read to you for your spirit's refreshment and consolation. But avoid excessive reading or devotions, especially those that are mental; these would block the way to your recovery, which is the reason for your going home and that of obedience in sending you there. So be very moderate in any mental exercises, and assume that outward recreation, when well ordered, as I said, is also prayer and a means by which you please God our Lord.

May his grace always abound in your soul.

We all earnestly commend ourselves to your charity.

Rome, April 7, 1554

✠

To Catalina Fernández de Córdoba
Marchioness of Priego

Rome, May 15, 1554

(Letter 4454: VI:709–12; in Spanish)

Ignatius writes to console the marchioness on the loss of her eldest son, the count of Feria, and to praise her Christian spirit in happily approving the entrance into the Society of her priest son, Antonio. His entrance was an important event in helping to establish the reputation of the Society. The Cordobas, "grandees" of Spain, were one of the most illustrious Spanish families and one of the richest of Andalusía. One of Antonio's brothers, a Dominican, became the highly regarded bishop of Sigüenza; his uncle was Francis Borgia. Pope Julius III had already, at the behest of Emperor Charles V, made Antonio a cardinal "in petto." His mother was a great benefactor of the Society. Father Antonio came to be one of the most respected Jesuits in Spain.

My Lady in our Lord:

May the sovereign grace, etc.

I recently received two letters together from Your Ladyship, dated July 9 and December 18, and with them not only much graciousness in the concern shown by Your Ladyship to favor the college at Córdoba, but a very special consolation in seeing the spirit and complete conformity to God's will shown in your letter at God's taking for himself two such sons—one to the fullness of life in heaven, and the other to die from now on to the love and designs of earth, disposing himself to have no other business than that of bringing himself and many others to heaven, dedicating himself totally to his Creator's glory and service.

While it is a singular favor that God has conferred on Father Don Antonio—particularly since he had greater occasion to withhold his love, in part at least, for things below, whereas now he has entirely turned and dedicated himself to things on high—nevertheless, not every mother relishes such favors being done to her sons. God's grace must have profoundly shaped Your Ladyship's heart, engraving upon it a perception and love of eternal goods, for you to be consoled in this way by Father Don Antonio's relinquishment of temporal goods for eternal ones. May he who is the font of light and of all well-ordered love increase in you what he has begun to impart to you in his infinite and supreme generosity, and give you the true and Christian consolation of seeing all your children, each in the state of life to which he is called by God, employing themselves greatly in his praise and service, traveling always straight towards the final and blessed end which he has prepared for them.

With the business of uniting the benefices in the hands of such capable persons as Andrés Vela and the licentiate Casarubios, I doubt there is much we will need to do, except to beg God our Lord, in keeping with his infinite riches and liberality, to reward the charity that he himself has bestowed on Your Ladyship and Father Don Antonio by prompting you to take this step, along with other assistance given by Your Ladyship to advance this work in his divine service.[9] Still, I have told them that if there is any way we can help, we will not be wanting, at least in intention, although we do not usually get involved in business of this sort, as alien to our profession.

Regarding what Your Ladyship writes about having Father Francis [Borgia] stop in Córdoba and visit Your Ladyship and the countess of

---

[9] Antonio was planning to have the income from his benefices transferred to the Jesuit college at Córdoba.

Feria, I very much wish in our Lord I had received it earlier;[10] for at the urging of the count and countess of Ribagorza I already promised that Father Francis would go to Zaragoza on his way back from Portugal, and I wrote him some months ago to do so and stop there for a time. He is probably already there, or else en route. However, I will tell him that when he has somewhat fulfilled his duty to them and to Zaragoza, he should give close attention to the work in Córdoba and to the service and consolation of Your Ladyship and the countess.

We have been informed about the house that Señor Don Juan de Córdoba donated for the college, along with everything else. May the divine Goodness build it for him in heaven, and make him a full sharer in whatever good may accrue from this work to God's glory and the help of souls. Beyond doubt, his great devotion, charity, and generosity have placed the Society—not only there but everywhere—under great obligation to serve him in our Lord.

My deepest respects to my lady the countess. I most heartily commend myself and the whole Society to her prayers. As her example has been and continues to be so edifying to the world, I am confident that her prayers will be very powerful before God—before whom I also promise I will present Your Ladyship often, imploring his divine mercy to preserve and greatly increase the gifts he has granted you, until their glorious consummation in his holy kingdom.

May he give to all of us his abundant grace always to know and entirely to fulfill his most holy will.

Rome, May 15, 1554

✠

To Enrique de La Cueva

Rome, May 22, 1554

(Letter 4485: VII:43–45; in Spanish)

Enrique, natural son of Cardinal Bartolomé de La Cueva y Toledo, was a talented but emotionally erratic ecclesiastic who had taken a vow before Francis Borgia to enter the Society. His father strongly favored the step, but the Jesuits in Spain had doubts about his suitability, especially in view of his concerns about the treatment he

---

[10] The countess was the widow of Catalina's elder son.

would receive in the Society. As Enrique wavered, the cardinal pressed Ignatius to receive him, and in this letter he does so. After entering the Society, Enrique was an effective preacher, yet over the course of almost two years he vacillated in his vocation. At first his father, the cardinal, wanted him to stay, and Ignatius himself was doubtful about releasing him from his vows. Finally both his father and Ignatius decided that it was better that Enrique leave, and so he did.

My Lord in our Lord:

May the sovereign grace and eternal love of Christ our Lord be always our protection and help.

After replying to your letter a few days ago, I again consulted with our common father and lord, the Most Reverend Cardinal, concerning your affairs and state of life. The conclusion was the same as before, namely, to approve strongly and to consider as right and acceptable to God our Lord the sacrifice of your person which you have made to his Divine Majesty—and this taking into due consideration not only the spiritual talent and gifts received from his divine hand but also your physical constitution and all the other factors in Your Worship which should be kept in mind; for we have judged in our Lord that good use can be made in this institute, for his great service and glory, of what his divine goodness has bestowed upon you. Even if you have less strength and bodily health than would be needed for certain toils and hardships which are endured by those who have the health and strength to pursue their good desires, this does not mean you will lack ways of giving good service to God our Lord—or the comforts which may be deemed opportune even for someone living in his own house outside of religious life. For besides the fact that our Institute accommodates itself to what is best for each of its members in matters of work and bodily treatment, the respect and obligation felt by the whole Society toward the Most Reverend Lord Cardinal de La Cueva—whom, as I have said, we regard as our father and lord with a very special affection and devotion to his service and all his interests—means that we could not fail to take special account of everything concerning your person. Nor would whatever is required for this purpose fail to be provided by him who through his all-kind providence governs and daily increases this new plant which he has been pleased to place among the others in his Church.

As for the rest, I have written and will write again to Master Nadal to take careful thought about the best time and manner for relinquishing the unavoidable occupation which Your Worship has had for some time, and which is perhaps no longer so, so that we can all be conformed to our Institute not only inwardly but also outwardly. At that point I will adapt my manner of writing to what is customary among us.

Meanwhile, I earnestly commend myself to Your Worship's prayers and ask God our Lord to grant to all of us abundant grace so that we may know his most holy will and entirely fulfill it.

Rome, May 22, 1554

Entirely Your Worship's in our Lord,
IGNATIO

✠

To Bartolomé Hernández

Rome, July 21, 1554

(Letter 4619: VII:268–70; in Spanish)

The recently founded college in Salamanca included two priests and fourteen scholastics who were studying theology but who were also zealously engaged in other works, such as visiting hospitals, preaching, and teaching catechism. Writing to the new rector of the college there, Ignatius endorses his decision to have the Jesuit scholastics focus their outside contacts on fellow students at the university. He insists that lack of sensible devotion during studies is nothing to worry about.

The peace of Christ.

Since spiritual conversation cannot be extended to everyone, it is quite right that it should be concentrated on students of the university; it will benefit not only them personally but many others as well by means of them, since such persons are capable of communicating to others whatever they themselves receive for the glory of God.

It is no cause for wonder that not all of our own students experience the relish of devotion that one might desire. He who dispenses this grace does so where and when he thinks fit. During the time of studies, which impose considerable spiritual effort, we may presume that divine Wisdom sometimes suspends sensible visitations of this sort, for although they give great delight to the spirit, they sometimes excessively weaken the body. Moreover, the occupation of the mind with academic pursuits naturally tends to produce a certain dryness in the interior affections. However, when the study is directed purely to God's service, it is an excellent form of devotion. In sum, so long as one does not jeopardize solidity of virtue and gives the time prescribed by the Constitutions for prayer, with or without many consolations, he should not think there is anything seriously wrong, but should instead accept from God's hand whatever he disposes in this regard, always laying more store by the more important things: patience, humility, obedience, charity, etc.

I have nothing more to add now, except to commend all of us earnestly to the prayers of Your Reverence and of all in the college there.

May Jesus Christ our Lord be in our souls with an abundance of his spiritual gifts. Amen.

Rome, July 21, 1554

✠

To João Nunes Barreto

Rome, July 26, 1554

(Letter 4645: VII:313f.; in Spanish)

In 1546 the ruler of Ethiopia, the "Prester John" of legend, asked John III of Portugal for help in the form of troops and missionaries, for the surrounding Muslims were threatening his kingdom. Ignatius offered himself and the Society itself for the possibility of reuniting the land to the Roman church. It took until 1554, after repeated requests to Portugal from the king and from Ignatius, to start the project. At that point Ignatius assigned João Nunes Barreto, who had been laboring among Christian captives in Morocco, to lead the expedition. Barreto accepted gladly, but shrank from being consecrated a bishop, a requisite if he was to serve as "Patriarch" of the Ethiopian church. For his conscience' sake, he asked Ignatius to write him a few lines "which I will preserve all my life, for my own consolation and to thrust in the devil's face and say: All I know is how to obey as I am bound to." Ignatius replied thus to his request.

May the sovereign grace and eternal love, etc.

I received your duplicate letter of April 6. Regarding affairs in Africa, where you have worked for a number of years on behalf of the captives, we have all much occasion for thanking God our Lord that he has deigned to make use of your person and labors in so many ways and thereby prepare you to be worthy of entering upon even greater labors of greater and more universal advantage to souls. And do not, as you look at your own meager strength, be frightened by this great undertaking, for all our sufficiency must come from the one who calls you to this work. He must give you whatever is needed for his service; he laid this burden upon you without your own will, and no shoulders of human competence or effort could sustain it unless the divine hand helped to bear the load and guided the one who bears it. Hence, the less confidence you have in your own self, the more you should have in him who commands you through his vicar to assume this task, from which I trust in the divine and supreme goodness there will ensue notable spiritual benefit for all those regions through their being brought back to the true and genuine worship of God our Lord. If any scruple in this regard should trouble you, cast it off not only upon me, whose decision you are following, but also upon the Supreme Pontiff, at whose command, in the place of Christ our Lord, you will accept the responsibility being given you.

Regarding the persons you indicate in Portugal, a decision cannot easily be made here. Hence, when the eight who are to be sent from here and from Castile arrive in Portugal, the remaining men up to twelve can be selected there, as may seem appropriate—and God our Lord will wholly direct this work of his.

As to the instruction you request for better proceeding in the divine service on this mission, I trust that it will be given you more fully by the Holy Spirit with his holy anointing and the gift of prudence that he will give you in particular situations. However, should there be any reminders or guidelines which can be given you from here, based on information that is had about the condition of those territories, they will be sent to you; and if any questions occur to you there, you can write us and we will reply.

I earnestly commend myself to your prayers and sacrifices, begging our Lord to grant all of us the grace to know and perfectly fulfill his most holy will.

Rome, July 26, 1554

✠

To Fernando Vasconcelhos, archbishop of Lisbon

Rome, July 26, 1554

(Letter 4654: VII:327f.; in Spanish)

For several years a certain amount of tension had existed between the archbishop of Lisbon and the Jesuits there. To calm the waters, Ignatius offered to the archbishop of Lisbon the services of the Jesuits living in that city, and requests his patronage for them. He sent the letter to the provincial, Diego Miró, and told him to take the superior of the Jesuit church and the rector of the Jesuit college in Lisbon with him to visit the archbishop and present the letter. Relations greatly improved thereafter, with the archbishop now happy with the work that the Society was doing in Portugal.

My Most Reverend Lord in our Lord:

May the sovereign grace, etc.

Inasmuch as it is not only in accord with our Institute but particularly urged in our Constitutions that the members of this least Society, wherever they may be living, should have recourse to the bishop, recognize him as their father and lord, and as far as our weak powers and profession allow, offer to serve him in caring for the souls under his charge, I have for this reason seen fit not only to charge our men who have a house and college in your city to do their duty in this respect, but also to do so myself from here in the name of our whole Society. I accordingly beg Your Most Reverend Lordship to accept and consider us all, both there and here, as your sons and servants in our Lord; and to reckon that in all the members of our Society in your archbishopric of Lisbon you have so many faithful and obedient ministers ready, in conformity with their profession, to carry whatever little part they can of the burden which God our Lord has placed on Your Most Reverend Lordship's shoulders and which must be shared if it is to be borne. It will be a very deep consolation to me, both because of the character of the burden and of the great personal worth of Your Most Reverend Lordship, if you will consider us all as belonging to Your Lordship and take our men in Lisbon under your special protection, granting them the faculties which you judge they ought to employ for the help of the souls under your charge.

This will be all, except humbly to ask Your Most Reverend Lordship's blessing and prayers, and to pray to God our Lord that he will deign to give to all of us his abundant grace always to know and fulfill his most holy will.

Rome, July 26, 1554

✠

To Simão Rodrigues, by commission

Rome, August 11, 1554

(Letter 4705: VII:391f.; in Spanish)

Restless after leaving Portugal and then Italy, Rodrigues tried to get papal permission to return to live in Portugal, subject to no other superior than the general of the Society. When that plan did not succeed, he revived the first companions' original idea of going on pilgrimage to the Holy Land. Ignatius, who wished to found a college in Jerusalem, strongly encouraged him to undertake this pilgrimage and obtained papal permission for him to do so. Rodrigues began to worry about going. This letter gives further encouragement. The danger could be lessened by his passing as a citizen of France, then allied with the Turks who ruled Palestine. Henry II gave that "special privilege" of naturalization to the Society in 1550. It enabled the Society to possess real estate, from the income of which it could support Jesuit scholastics. The Parlement of Paris vigorously and for a long time opposed the King's decision.

The peace of Christ.

My dearest Father in Jesus Christ:

Since Our Father is laid up in bed, although improved somewhat, he is not writing Your Reverence; however, I conferred with him and here give the gist of what I understood to be his will and opinion.

Our Father thinks that unless there are Spaniards or Flemings on the pilgrim ship, Your Reverence should not travel on it; however, if there are either of these, he thinks that if he were in your place he would make the journey; all the more so in that all members of the Society can declare themselves natives of France, since the King has made us such by a special privilege to the entire Society. Moreover, those of us who are Paris masters are citizens of that city, so that we can truthfully say that we are Frenchman and from Paris. Since Your Reverence can talk a little French and look more French than Spanish, it would seem even from a human point of view that you could make the journey—moreover, Christ our Lord can be expected to aid his own pilgrims greatly. And since you have already written the King, etc., it is hard to see, with others going, how your staying behind would be taken. Your Reverence should commend this to God.

I say nothing about the scruple regarding litigation, for since this is college property, the petition can certainly be made.

If the news about the embarkation of the Turk should be true, that would be important. Let us know if it is confirmed.

No more, except that by God's grace we are well and all commend ourselves to Your Reverence's prayers.

Rome, August 11, 1554

✠

To Peter Canisius

Rome, August 13, 1554

(Letter 4709: VII:398–404; in Latin)

Protestantism had made great inroads in Austria, and Ignatius responded to a request for advice from Peter Canisius. Ignatius consulted five Jesuits about the matter and then sent this reply to Canisius. The five were Diego Laínez and Alfonso Salmerón, two of the first Jesuits and eminent theologians; Juan Polanco, the secretary of the Society; André des Freux, humanist and translator of the first "official" version of the Exercises *into Latin; and Martin Olave, theologian, organizer of the course of studies and professor of theology at the Roman College.*

In the first half of this letter, Ignatius takes a hard line against the Protestants, not unlike the line commonly taken by the principal reformers against the Catholics. Both sides called upon the secular rulers to use coercion against their opponents when persuasion failed, a not-uncommon position in the sixteenth century. In the second half of the letter, Ignatius suggests measures for furthering the Catholic faith, some of which he develops in the material in the following letter.

The peace of Christ.

Reverend and dear Father in Christ Jesus:

We have learned of the request which Your Reverence's religious concern prompted you to make in your letters of July 7 and 17; namely, that we should write what we think might be the best methods for preserving His Royal Majesty's territories in the Catholic faith, for restoring religion wherever it has collapsed there, and for shoring it up where it is tottering. This matter seemed to require our attention all the more in that His Majesty is deemed, as a true Christian ruler, ready not merely to seek advice but also to act on it. Otherwise, if painstaking investigation were not followed by vigorous execution, investing effort on our part would be considered ridiculous rather than worthwhile. It will be up to your own prudence to decide which of these proposals to place before His Royal Majesty. While all of them would appear quite useful if the circumstances of persons, places, and time allowed, nevertheless, some may need to be suppressed owing to the refractory disposition of the persons and countries concerned. Thus, it must be stressed that this document is addressed to Father Rector [Nicolas Lanoy] and yourself; you are to select and note whatever points seem applicable, ignoring those that do not. I shall undertake to inform you briefly about what is thought on this topic by several other solid theologians of our Society who are characterized by learning, judgment, and intense charity towards Germany.

In a bodily illness, it is necessary first to remove the causes of the disease, and then to take measures for reestablishing strength and health. Similarly, in this pestilence of souls that is raging in the King's dominions because of the various heresies, the first thing is to examine how to eliminate its causes, and then to see how strong and healthy Catholic doctrine can be restored and consolidated there. For brevity's sake, I shall here give only my bare conclusions; the underlying reasons in each case will be obvious to anyone.

First of all, if His Royal Majesty were to proclaim himself not only a Catholic—which he has always done—but also an implacable and fierce adversary of heresy, declaring open and not merely secret war on all heretical errors, this would beyond doubt be the best and most immediate of human remedies. This would lead to another highly important step, namely, his refusing to allow any heretic on his royal council, and even less his seeming to honor such men, whose advice must be assumed to aim, covertly or overtly, at fostering and nourishing the heretical wickedness with which they are imbued. Again, it would be of the greatest help if he refused to allow anyone infected with heresy to occupy governmental posts, particularly the highest office, of that province or city, or any magistracy or dignity at all. Finally—and it would be good if there were public notification of this—the moment any person is convicted or strongly suspected of heretical perversity, he should be ineligible for any dignities or emoluments but instead be expelled from them, etc. Moreover, if in order to show that the business of religion was being taken seriously, an occasional example were made by depriving a few offenders of life or property, or by banishing them, this measure would be all the more effective. All public professors and administrators in the universities at Vienna and elsewhere ought, it would seem, to be deprived of their status if they fall into bad repute with regard to the Catholic religion. We think this should also hold for rectors, prefects, and teachers in private colleges, to ensure that those responsible for training young people in piety will not corrupt them instead. Suspect persons—and much more open heretics—should not be retained in such posts, lest they infect the young. Even students who seemingly cannot readily be brought around, if there are such, ought to be expelled. All schoolmasters and tutors ought to understand and know from experience that there is no place for them in the King's dominions unless they are Catholics and profess themselves as such.

It would be useful either to burn or banish from every region of the kingdom all heretical books turned up, by a thorough search, in the possession of booksellers or private persons. Moreover, even books by heretics that are free of heretical content, such as works on grammar or rhetoric, or Melanchthon's logic, should be totally banned in hatred of their authors' heresy. It is not good even to cite such books, much less allow them to enjoy the esteem of young people, whom the heretics attempt by such works to draw to themselves. Other and more scholarly books can be found for them that are free from this serious danger. It would also help greatly if booksellers were prohibited under heavy penalties from printing such works, or from adding any commentary by a heretic that contained an example or word smacking of impious doctrine or bore the heretical author's name. It would also be good, under the same penalties, to prohibit any merchant or other person from importing into the King's dominions books of this sort printed elsewhere.

No pastors or confessors in ill repute for heresy should be tolerated. Upon conviction, they should at once be deprived of all ecclesiastical revenues. Better a flock without a pastor than one whose pastor is a wolf. Even pastors who are Catholic in faith but subvert the people by their gross ignorance or by the evil example of their public sins ought to be punished severely and deprived of their incomes by their bishops; certainly they should be removed from the official care of souls. It was their bad lives and ignorance that brought the pestilence of heresy upon Germany.

Preachers of heretical doctrine, heresiarchs, and others caught spreading this plague ought, I think, to be subjected to heavy penalties. A public proclamation should be made everywhere to the effect that those ready to retract within one month from the date of publication will receive indulgent absolution in both [internal and external] forums, but those convicted of heresy after that time will lose their civil standing and be disqualified from receiving any honor. If it seems advisable, it might be wiser for such persons to be exiled, imprisoned, or on occasion even punished with death. However, I say nothing regarding the extreme penalty or the setting up of the Inquisition, since such measures appear beyond the capacity of Germany in its present situation.

A fine might be exacted from any person who calls the heretics "evangelicals," so as to deny the devil the joy of seeing enemies of the Gospel and of the cross arrogate to themselves a name contradicted by their deeds. They should be given their true name, "heretics," so that even the mention of them will arouse repugnance, and so that their deadly poison will not be concealed under the cloak of a holy name.

Synods of bishops and the proclamation of dogmas and, particularly, of decrees in councils may serve, by instructing them in the truth, to bring around the less well-educated clergy who have been led astray by others. The ordinary people may be helped by the vehemence of good preachers, pastors, and confessors in openly denouncing and expressing their hatred of the heretics' errors. As long as the people believe what is necessary to salvation and profess themselves Catholics, it might be better to overlook other deficiencies that may be tolerated.

So much for how to root out errors. Now we will go on to methods for planting the solid teaching of Catholic truth.

The first help will be if the King has in his council only men who are Catholics and everywhere favors, honors, and endows [only such men] with secular and ecclesiastical dignities and incomes. Likewise, if only men who are Catholics and swear they will always remain Catholics are appointed to governorships, magistracies, or any other positions of authority over others. Great care should be taken to provide for the royal dominions, from whatever source, excellent bishops who will edify their subjects by their example and word. Care should also be taken to recruit large numbers of preachers and confessors from among the religious and secular clergy, men zealous for the honor of God and the welfare of souls, who will present Catholic teaching to the people with fervor and persistence, and will confirm their teaching by the example of their lives. Dignities and benefices should be conferred upon these men. On feast days they could tour the towns and villages teaching the people what is appropriate for the salvation of their souls, subsequently returning to their own churches. They will make a stronger impact if they give the Gospel without charge. Incumbents of curacies who are incompetent or suspected of unsound doctrine, if they cannot easily be deprived of their benefices, should be ordered to support at their own expense good and competent substitutes who can nourish the people by administration of the sacraments and of the word of God; and they themselves should altogether refrain from this office.

In the future, no one should be granted a beneficed pastorate unless he has first been investigated and found to be a Catholic of decent life and sufficient intelligence. The incomes should be sufficient to ensure that such men will not decline curacies.

All administrators and public professors in the universities, all rectors of private colleges, and even all schoolmasters and tutors should, by previous examination or private investigation, be proved to be Catholics and well attested by Catholics before being allowed to function. They should take an oath to remain Catholics in the future, and if any such persons are subsequently discovered to be heretics, they should be severely punished for perjury as well.

There should be officials charged with keeping track of what books are imported by merchants or printed within the royal dominions; they should ensure that no books are sold which have not passed the censors.

It will also help if young people are everywhere taught by their instructors some catechism or manual of Christian doctrine; it should contain a summary of Catholic teaching which children and uneducated people can have in their hands, etc.

It will also help to furnish poorly educated but intelligent curates and pastors with a manual instructing them what they need to present to the people to ensure that they will welcome or reject what ought to be welcomed or rejected.

It will also help to have a summary of Scholastic theology that will not be unacceptable to the learned of our own time—or to those who consider themselves learned.

However, given the extreme scarcity in the royal dominions of pastors, confessors, preachers, and teachers of this quality—Catholics of both learning and goodness—it would appear that His Royal Majesty ought to make strenuous efforts, on the one hand, to recruit such persons elsewhere, even at high cost, and, on the other, to set up inside his dominions the greatest possible number of seminaries (or perhaps a few very large ones) for the training of such persons.

The seminaries that could be provided are of four sorts. The first would be from among the religious who habitually perform these functions. It would be most helpful if His Majesty were to aim at increasing the number of Germans in the religious houses and colleges of the Society of Jesus and of other orders, both at Vienna and at his other universities, so that, pursuing their studies by means of His Majesty's generosity, their students would then emerge as hardworking preachers, teachers, and confessors.

Second, there is the German College in Rome. He could send a large number of talented young men to study there at his expense, all of whom would be sent home once they are properly formed in learning and virtue. Or His Majesty might prefer to found a similar college in Rome for his Austrian, Hungarian, Bohemian, and Transylvanian subjects.

Third, at his own universities he might establish new colleges similar to the German College in Rome, under the direction of learned and religious men. Upon completion of their studies, the students could become pastors, schoolteachers, or preachers.

These three types of seminaries could be financed partly from the revenues of depopulated monasteries; partly from the incomes of parish churches lacking incumbents; partly by modest assessments imposed upon the various populations to provide public support for the education, to their own spiritual benefit, of one, two, three, or more talented students of good character selected from their own areas; and partly from the pensions provided for bishops and other higher clergy; or from whatever sources His Royal Majesty thinks best.

A fourth kind of seminary might consist of colleges for educating the children of nobles and wealthy persons at their own expense, to equip them for later assuming even the highest secular and ecclesiastical dignities. However, it is essential that both this and the other three kinds of seminaries have rectors and teachers who are such that the students can receive from them piety conjoined with sound Catholic doctrine.

☩

To Peter Canisius

Rome, August 13, 1554
(Vol. XII, Appendix 1, pp. 259–62, no. 27; in Italian)

Although this letter lacks the name of the person for whom it was destined, and the date on which it was written, the editors of the Monumenta have judged it to be either a complement to or a further development of the previous letter to Canisius and therefore assigned it the same name and date. It is a program for offsetting Protestant propaganda in Germany and France: the creation of a "summary theology" to be taught at all educational levels, the spread of Jesuit schools, and the writing of popular tracts to counter the Protestant literature.

JHS.

Seeing the progress which the heretics have made in a short time, as they spread the poison of their evil teaching throughout so many countries and peoples and seize the initiative to go forward, "their speech creeping daily like a gangrene" [see 2 Tim. 2:17], it would seem that our Society, inasmuch as it has been accepted by divine Providence among the efficacious means to repair this great harm, should be concerned to come up with remedies that are suitable but quick acting and of wide scope, and can be employed as rapidly as possible for the preservation of what is still healthy and the cure of what has fallen sick with the plague of heresy, particularly in the northern nations. The heretics have made their false theology popular and adapted to the capacity of the common people. They preach it to the people and in the schools, and disseminate booklets which can be bought and understood by many, reaching with their writings where they could not through their ministers. And since through the negligence of those who should have done something about it and the bad example and the ignorance of Catholics, especially the clergy, they have wrought such destruction and ruin in the vineyard of the Lord, it would seem that our Society should make use of the following means to oppose and remedy the evils which have come upon the Church through these persons.

In the first place, then, alongside the full-scale theology taught in the universities, which requires a foundation in philosophy and hence a long time to acquire, and is suited only to good and alert minds, weaker ones being confused and little benefited by it, there needs to be another summary theology which quite briefly covers the essential matters not now controverted and treats controversial issues somewhat more fully in a way that is accommodated to the present needs of the people. It should solidly prove dogmas with good arguments from Scripture, tradition, the councils, and the doctors, and refute the contrary teaching. It would not require much time to teach such a theology, since it would not go very deeply into other matters. In this way numbers of theologians could be produced in a short time, and these could take care of the preaching and teaching in many places. Abler students could study the higher and more developed courses, and those who do not succeed in these should be taken out and put in this abbreviated theology.

The main conclusions of this theology, in the form of a short catechism, could be taught to children as Christian doctrine now is; likewise, [it could be taught] to uneducated people who are not too infected and are capable of fine points. This could also be done with our younger pupils in the lower classes, who could learn it by heart.

For those in the higher classes, such as the first and perhaps the second, and those in philosophy and theology, at an hour of the day when they are not at lectures it would be good to teach them this summary theology, as mentioned above, so that all possessing some aptitude will learn the most usual teachings and be able to preach and teach Catholic doctrine and refute its contrary sufficiently for the needs of the people. This would seem appropriate especially for the colleges in upper and lower Germany, in France, and in other places where the same need exists. In the case of persons who have no abilities for serious study or whose age will not permit it, it will be enough if besides the study of languages, they attend the classes of this summary theology and the cases of conscience, so as to be good and useful workers for the common good.

These theological lectures could be attended by the priests of the country as well as by foreign students in the higher institutions, in short, by anyone who wishes. By their means an antidote against the poison of heresy could quickly be provided in many places. Hearing the lectures and having the book in their hands, these persons will be able to preach to the people and teach in schools that will accept Catholic doctrine.

Another excellent means for helping the Church in these travails would be to multiply colleges and schools of the Society in many lands, especially in places where it is thought there would be a large number of students. However, it seems that there should be a dispensation for taking on colleges with fewer personnel than our Institute requires, or else for accepting charge of classes without the foundation of a perpetual college if there is among our men, or among those not belonging to our institute, someone to teach this theology to the students, preach sound doctrine to the people, and promote their spiritual welfare by the administration of the sacraments.

Not only in the towns where we have a residence but also in the nearby places, the better prepared among our students could be sent to teach Christian doctrine on Sundays and feast days. Extern students too, if there are any suitable among them, could be sent by the rector for the same service. By thus giving, besides their teaching, the example of a good life, and by shunning every appearance of greed, they will be able to refute the strongest argument of the heretics: the evil lives and the ignorance of the Catholic clergy.

Since the heretics write booklets and pamphlets aimed at discrediting Catholics, especially the Society, and shoring up their false dogmas, it would seem expedient that in such cases our men should pen short and well-written replies or tracts which can be brought out quickly and widely purchased, and in this way remedy the harm wrought by the pamphlets of the heretics and disseminate sound doctrine. These works should be modest but lively, exposing the evil behavior and deceits of the adversaries. Moreover, where needed, a number of these pamphlets could be gathered in a single volume. It is important, however, that they be written by learned men with a grounding in theology, and adapted to the capacity of the multitude.

With these measures, it would seem that we could do significant service to the Church and in many places quickly counteract the beginnings of the evil before the poison has gone so deep that it would be very difficult to remove it from the heart. We should employ in healing the people the same diligence as the heretics do in infecting them. We will have on our side something they cannot have: solidly founded and therefore enduring doctrine. The most gifted will be able to study more fully in the Roman College and in other colleges of upper and lower Germany, as also in France; sent afterwards to different places where our men reside, they will be the directors and instructors of others.

✠

To the Widow of Jon Boquet

Rome, August 16, 1554

(Letter 4713: VII:409–11; in Spanish)

Jon Boquet, an auditor of the Royal Council, had been one of the early and generous benefactors of Ignatius when he lived in Barcelona. He continued to be so in subsequent years to Jesuits who came to Catalonia. The letter, consoling the widow of Boquet, stresses the importance of hope in eternal life. It was signed by Ignatius, but Polanco, his secretary, was primarily responsible for the somewhat unctuous style of the text.

Ihs.

May the grace and eternal love of Christ our Lord be always our continual protection and help. Amen.

Of the many signs that we possess a lively faith and hope in eternal life, one of the surest is not to be overly saddened at the death of those whom we dearly love in our Lord. Such grief may be more permissible for those who think that with bodily death the one who had been alive is now lost and is no more, for according to their erroneous idea death is the worst of miseries. But this cannot be permissible for persons who hold with Ecclesiasticus that "death is better than life," knowing as they do that death is a brief passage from present toils and miseries to the repose and glory of life eternal, especially for those who live and die as Christians.[11] It was of them that God told St. John to write, "Blessed are the dead who die in the Lord" [Rev. 14:13]. Thus we see that if we should not bewail the blessedness of those we love, neither should we [mourn] their dying, which is the beginning of, or at least the certain way to, that blessedness.

I say this, madam, because if the death of Mosén Joán Boquet, our beloved friend in Christ Jesus, were an evil, I could not help sharing deeply in the sorrow over it as one who loved him dearly in Christ our Lord. But I am confident that he will dwell in the place of the elect through the mercy of the one who created him and redeemed him with his blood and had him be strengthened at his death with his holy sacraments, essential for eternal life. And so I do not grieve; instead, I rejoice in our Lord, who by his dying has removed the fear of death from us and by his resurrection and ascension into heaven has shown us what and where is true life (to which we go through death), in the sharing of his kingdom and glory. And so, from his side, I can find no cause to grieve.

Likewise, we would find no cause to grieve on your side or mine if we knew how to recognize God's providence and love for us, and to trust in what is ordained for us by the wisdom of our kindly Father, who so loves our greater good, convinced that in prosperity and in adversity, in life and in death, he desires and aims at what is best for us.

So it will be a help frequently to lift on high the love which tends to the things of earth, removing from before our eyes what we love on earth, so that with greater freedom we may turn our whole love to his infinite goodness and his heavenly gifts, centering it more on our Creator and Lord in the measure that we have less occasion to dissipate it on creatures. However, to avoid going on too long, I will only say that for our part we here are praying that the divine Goodness will grant Señor Jon Boquet peace and rest in his holy glory, and at the same time see fit to console you and take the place for you of him and of all things, multiplying in you and your family his very special gifts and graces—in which may it please His Majesty to make us grow daily in the way of his greater service, praise, and glory. Amen.

Rome, August 16, 1554

The bearer of this letter, a priest and a good friend of ours in our Lord, will deliver two Agnus Deis that I am sending you with him. He will be able to tell you about the graces attached to them.

---

[11] "Better is death than a bitter life" (Ecclus. 30:17).

To Francis Borgia

Rome, August 20, 1554

(Letter 4721; VII·422f.; in Spanish)

The Marian sanctuary of Aránzazu in the Basque country had burned down, and various people had written to Ignatius, asking him to get the grant of a jubilee indulgence from the Pope to help rebuild it. Recalling the night he himself had watched in the sanctuary after his conversion, Ignatius, seriously ill, explains the difficulty of the request and suggests a route for obtaining it.

Jhs.

May the sovereign grace and eternal love of Christ our Lord be always our help and protection.

I received your own letter of June 25, together with others from the provincial father minister of Cantabria and from the council of Oñate and Azpeitia.[12] Don Juan and our brother Dr. Araoz also wrote.[13] The sum and substance of all the letters was that I try to obtain a jubilee of several years for the bishoprics of Pamplona and Calahorra to help in the rebuilding of Our Lady of Aránzazu. Indeed, the fire there was a great misfortune, especially for those of us who know the devotion the place inspires and the great service rendered there to God our Lord. Hence, whatever measures are necessary for the restoration of the monastery should be eagerly undertaken. I may tell you that I personally have a special reason for desiring this. When God our Lord granted me the grace to make some change in my life, I remember having received some benefit for my soul while watching by night in the nave of that church. But you must know, my dear brother, that because of illness I have for the past two months scarcely spent four in twenty-four hours of the day out of bed, God be praised. Besides, this matter of a jubilee is obtained from the present pontiff only with much difficulty.[14] I think the best way of getting this jubilee would be to have the princess write to His Holiness and to Cardinal Carpi, the protector of the Franciscans, and to me also, if you think it well.[15] Then, if I am strong enough, I might be able to do something in the matter with the Cardinal Protector or with His Holiness. Since it would apparently be easy to get these

---

[12] The father minister was Francisco del Castillo, O.F.M.

[13] Don Juan de Borja, lord of Loyola.

[14] Julius III.

[15] Juana d'Austria, daughter of Emperor Charles V, currently regent of Spain for her brother, Philip II, and secretly a Jesuit scholastic.

letters written in Spain through yourself or Dr. Araoz or whomsoever you might suggest, and since the delay will be brief and there is no hurry, I would be of the opinion that the matter could be conducted in this way. A summary of what I have said, or this letter if that seems good to you, might be shown to those who have written to me on the matter, to whom I would rather reply with deeds than with a letter.

As this is all I wished to say, I will close, commending myself earnestly to your prayers and asking our Lord to deign to give all of us his abundant grace always to know his most holy will and entirely to fulfill it.

Rome, August 20, 1554

Entirely yours in our Lord,

IGNATIO

✠

To Miguel de Nobrega, by commission

Rome, August 25, 1554

(Letter 4735: VII:446–48; in Spanish)

Miguel de Nobrega, a zealous but also impetuous Jesuit, suddenly on his own decided to leave Goa and preach the Gospel to the Moors in a town on a neighboring island. Then he decided to return to Portugal, but before he could do so the Turks captured him. While in captivity, he helped his fellow Christians, assisted the dying, and even at some peril converted several Muslims. Finally, from Cairo he got in touch with Ignatius and asked his help in ransoming him from the captivity that he now found burdensome. While this letter exhorts Nobrega to Christian patience and tells him that the Society had few financial resources, Ignatius was working to free him as a shorter accompanying letter (no. 4736)) made clear. As a matter of fact, Nobrega was ransomed in September 1554 even before he received these letters.

Ihus.

May the grace and peace of Christ be always present and increase in our souls.

Dear Father and Brother in Jesus Christ:

Our Father has received three letters of yours from that city [Cairo], and from them learns of your captivity and that of the Portuguese and other Christians who were seized with you. Blessed be God our Creator and Lord; and since he gives you the grace to suffer in his service, may he also grant you the patience and fortitude he sees that you need to bear this heavy cross on your back with gratitude and awareness that his divine goodness sends hardships, trials, tribulations, and adversities with the same charity and love as he is accustomed to send repose, contentment, joy, and all prosperity. As an all-wise physician he knows, and as an all-loving father he desires, what is best for the healing of the secret or manifest diseases of our souls. He provides what is best even though it may not be the most pleasing to us. And though we may employ whatever measures ought reasonably to be used to lighten or remedy the temporal ills sent or allowed by God's hand, once having taken such steps we surely ought to be glad of the share in his cross imparted to us by Christ our Lord. We should remember not only that it is better to purge our sins in this life than in the next, but also that the momentary trials of this life earn an eternal reward—no common reward but a sublime one, as the Apostle says: "Our present momentary and light tribulation," etc. [2 Cor. 4:17]. We know of many saints who were brought by God our Lord along this path of captivity to the liberty and blessedness of his kingdom. And so, dearest brother, take courage in him who has created and redeemed you by his blood and life, and trust in his gentle providence, which will either free you somehow from this captivity or at least render it very fruitful—no less so than liberty—for the end at which we aim, which is the divine glory and service and with it our own everlasting salvation and happiness.

When it comes to human means, you know that the poverty of the houses of our Society is such that they neither have nor may have revenues or any possessions at all. We can help you with prayers, and should anyone offer to donate something for the redemption of captives, we could try to get some alms to ransom Your Charity and the other Portuguese Christians there with you.

In fact, one of our brethren who had been called from Spain to Rome was captured by the Turks and put to rowing in the galleys.[16] He is a priest and theologian, and an excellent servant of God. Because of the difficulty in raising the ransom, we have for some time been unable to free him. But God is great, and one way or another will help his own.

May he preserve you in the purity and firmness of your holy Catholic faith, and give to all the courage needed to make the most of all these trials.

Rome, August 25, 1554

---

[16] Jean de La Goutte (see letter 94, not in this collection).

To Miguel de Nobrega, by commission

Rome, August 25, 1554
(Letter 4736: VII:448f.; in Spanish)

See the introduction to the previous letter (no. 4735).

In the other letter, in case there should be need to show it, I hold out little hope for your ransom. This one is to let Your Reverence know that we have great sympathy for you. Even though you do not have the union of the Society, since Father Master Francis [Xavier] has dismissed you and Our Father will not readmit you, the union of charity still remains, and will move us to work for your release from captivity as soon as possible. We have spoken here with the King of Portugal's ambassador to get His Highness to help in ransoming the Portuguese there, and we hope he will help with a substantial alms. On our part, we will continue doing whatever we can, and as rapidly as we can. Keep up your spirits and be courageous in Christ our Lord—for he will return for those who are his own, and will not delay.

✠

To the Jesuits Leaving Rome for Portugal
and thence traveling on to Ethiopia

Rome, September 15, 1554
(Appendix de rebus Aeth., no. 1.: VIII:677–80; in Spanish)

These travel instructions were for five of the Jesuits whom Ignatius was sending to Ethiopia, a project dear to his heart. Two of them, Andrés Ovieda and Melchior Carneiro, were to be ordained auxiliary bishops to assist João Nunes Barreto, the newly ordained "patriarch" of Ethiopia. No date is given to this document but since they were near Rome on September 15 getting ready for the journey and had already left Rome on September 15, the editors assigned the date given here.

Instruction for Those Going to Portugal for Ethiopia

1. First, what they should do until they get to Portugal; then, what they should do en route to Ethiopia and upon arrival there.

The superior of the five leaving here will be Doctor Andrés de Oviedo. Father [Melchior] Carneiro will be his collateral and act as superior in the event of illness. As for setting out from inns and stopping, etc., the two will agree, taking into account the others who perhaps have less experience in walking.

2. One who seems the most suitable shall always see to it that the animals are taken care of, that their hooves are cleaned, and that they are washed down; and he should be present when they are fed their barley. He should not do these services by himself, but upon arrival at the inn promise something to one of the servants who will do it properly.

3. Another should be in charge of making sure they do not forget anything at the inns; and as far as possible they should sleep close to one another, so that nothing is stolen from them.

4. Father Carneiro will keep the money and pay it out himself or through another as needed.

5. The other three whom they will take with them are Father Fray Diego de Merlo, Don Antonio de Ulloa, and Doctor Arce's Master Pedro. If one of them drops out, they can take another in his place. But at the points of crossing where they can be asked an accounting of their safe-conduct, the three should go as servants of the patriarch-elect. He can give them whatever positions he wishes (though this will not be needed until León, nor afterwards if the King's safe-conduct does not name the three servants), such as chaplain, majordomo, etc. Don Antonio can take along the French servant that they say he has, even though he is not in the safe-conduct. The three should be treated companionably and charitably. If one of the five falls sick and it is a short matter of a day or two, they can wait. If it is longer and he cannot travel, he should be left, if possible, with a supply of money in some place of the Society; if this is impossible, someone should stay with him. A notarized copy of the safe-conduct should be obtained to leave with him; and then, with the money he still has or with credit, he should continue his trip as best he can. If circumstances suggest that some other course is preferable, they should follow that.

6. In case they should be robbed, they should continue on as best they can until they can get credit, and then fully resupply themselves as far as the credit will reach.

7. They may take any credits at the rate set down in them; and if there is need and they set a higher rate, they will still take them.

8. In Spain they should find out where Doctor Araoz is, passing through Oñate and Burgos. From him they should get the three priests destined for Ethiopia; and they will pay their travel costs to Portugal.

These men will be under the obedience of the two aforesaid throughout the journey.

9. They should consult among themselves on whether to go through Coimbra or Évora on the way to the court or to go instead straight to the court, and then do what they decide in the Lord. However, they should consult first with the provincial of Portugal [Diego Miró], and have themselves presented to the King by one of the infantes.[17]

10. If it has not already been done, they should quickly make the selection of the others who will be going from Portugal to Ethiopia. Even without them, however, the five sent from here and the three from Castille can present themselves to His Highness and kiss his hand on Our Father's behalf, hand over the letter from him, and speak about whatever is judged appropriate by the infante Don Luis or, if he is at court, by the cardinal infante.

11. The men from here should quickly get the needed dispatch from the King sent to Rome, unless he has already done so in accord with the letters that were written from here, of which they will carry a copy.

12. They should tell Father João Nunes to make the profession of four vows. If among the others there are any who have the learning required by the Constitutions, they should also make the profession of four vows; if they are not so qualified, then that of three vows; if they are lay, that of a formed coadjutor.

The three priests sent from here, Master Johannes the Fleming, Master Miguel, and Master Juan Tomás, will be engaged in cases of conscience while they are there by Father Master Andrés, Father Carneiro, or by someone else they prefer; the same holds for the others who may need this.

✠

To Giovan Francesco Araldo

Rome, September 16, 1554

(Letter 4788: VII:528; in Italian)

A Neapolitan lady had started a home for six or seven abandoned girls, whom she brought to the Jesuit church for the sacraments. Unfortunately, she rented a house next door to the Jesuits, where the girls' windows looked onto the Jesuits' rooms.

---

[17] The King's two brothers, Luis and Cardinal Enrique.

When she refused to move, the Jesuit superior, Alfonso Salmerón, threatened to deny the girls the sacraments in the Jesuit church. Araldo, their chaplain, wrote to Andrés de Oviedo, protesting this highhandedness and asking him to intercede with Ignatius to countermand Salmerón's action. He received the following reply, which must have disappointed him.

Dear Father in Christ, Master Giovan Francesco:

I have seen Your Reverence's letter to Father Master Andrés [de Oviedo]; and while I am convinced that you were led to write as you did by your good and fervent will to serve God, you nevertheless clearly step beyond the limits of holy obedience and of humility, her mother, in thus manifesting an opinion dissenting from and even opposed to that of Father Master Salmerón, whose decision you wish to change as though he stood in error. And yet, if you remember that he is the superior, and that, over and above the light of learning and prudence and experience that he possesses, God our Lord cooperates with a special influx of his light in guiding him because of his responsibility for governing the college, then you should think that your own judgment is more likely to go wrong than his, and that having represented your view, you should be quicker to submit your judgment to his than to set aside his for yours. For myself, I do not believe that Father Salmerón would have forbidden these ladies to receive the sacraments in your church except for a serious reason. While this was not written to us, I suppose that their being housed so close to the college is likely to engender some suspicion. Or perhaps there is some other reason, more visible to one with a universal rather than a particular view. Because of the special love I bear Your Reverence, I did not want to fail to bring this to your attention.

Therewith I commend myself to Your Charity's prayers and sacrifices, etc.

Sent September 16, 1554

✠

To Filippo Leerno

Rome, September 22, 1554

(Letter 4809: VII:558f.; in Italian)

Advice for the rector at Modena to pass on to a wealthy couple who were uncertain what to do with their estate now that their son had died.

Ihus.

The peace of Christ.

Regarding the wealthy childless couple who desire to serve God in peace of soul, the husband wanting to sell off his property while the wife wants to keep it and leave it after death for the benefit of her soul, I will say two things. The first is that without sinning either could carry out his or her intention—however they think best. Secondly, the husband's plan seems the more spiritual, especially if he is a man who is able and accustomed to employ himself on better things than possessions, and if he intends after his death, or even during his lifetime, to give what he has for the benefit of his soul and the service of God. I will add a third suggestion. In either case—whether they sell their property for investment or keep it—they might well be advised to leave as their heir the one who gave them all they have, by means of some pious work which they would adopt as their child and leave as their heir —as the Roman patrician John and his wife did in the time of Pope Liberius. Since both husband and wife are good and spiritual persons, they should realize that God took away their own son and gave him the eternal possession of his kingdom at an early age so that they would not have to worry about providing for him and could employ their good inspirations and desires from God, along with their resources, in pious works in his service, thus raising their thoughts and intentions to what pertains to the greater glory of Christ our Lord and the general good of their country.

For light regarding which pious work they ought to spend their means on and how to do it, they should earnestly commend themselves to God our Lord, and make an election worthy of spiritual persons. May Jesus Christ be their guide and enlighten them always to know and always to fulfill his most holy will.

Rome, September 22, 1554

✠

To Teotonio de Braganza

Rome, September 22, 1554

(Letter 4812: VII:562f.; in Spanish)

See letter 4031. Teotonio finally left Portugal for Rome in a ship escorting Philip II of Spain to his marriage to Mary Tudor of England. By way of that country and then passing through Flanders and Germany and Italy, he arrived in Venice, where he met Simão Rodrigues and once again delayed his departure for Rome. The following three letters moved him to start for Rome in early October.

The sovereign grace, etc.

Dearest Brother in our Lord:

I received your letter of the fifteenth, with the copy of the patent from Father Francisco [Borgia]. The lord comendador mayor [Afonso de Lencastre(?), ambassador of the King of Portugal in Rome] also sent me a letter from His Lordship the Duke [Teodosio de Braganza] and from Her Ladyship the Infanta Dona Isabel for Master Nadal, both of which I opened and took as for myself.

Upon learning of your arrival in these parts, I rejoiced in our Lord—though I would be a great deal happier if I knew that your own joy and spiritual consolation were greater; and I desire this for you very particularly in the divine presence.

As to your staying where you are with our brother Master Simão [Rodrígues], while this may be considered a good idea sometime in the future, I do not think it is for now; you really should take upon yourself the little effort to look in here, for your consolation and mine, as well as for that of the lord ambassador, who has strongly charged me to write that you should set out for here immediately. And so, as a service to His Lordship, and because it is best for all concerned, I strongly request you in our Lord to come as quickly as you can to Rome—a journey which I am sure will be for the service of God our Lord and the consolation of your soul. And so I will keep other matters for us to discuss orally.

I shall say no more, except that I commend myself earnestly to your prayers, as we will commend you here in our prayers to God our Lord. May he by his infinite and sovereign goodness give to all of us his grace, so that we may always know his most holy will and entirely fulfill it.

Rome, September 22, 1554

✠

To Teotonio de Braganza

Rome, September 22, 1554

(4813: VII:563f.; in Spanish)

See the previous letter. Ignatius backs up his urging with a formal command under obedience.

May the sovereign grace and love, etc.

While I am confident in our Lord of the promptness of your obedience, and that upon learning that it is my desire and will for you to set out immediately so that we can meet, you will not delay to do so, nevertheless, because I consider it so important for the divine service that we meet soon, I decided that in addition to the other letter I would write you this one to command you in virtue of holy obedience that within four days of receiving it, you should set out for here and come to our house in Rome as quickly as you can without prejudice to your health; for I judge this to be best for the greater consolation and spiritual advantage of all concerned.

Rome, September 22, 1554

✠

To Teotonio de Braganza

Rome, September 22, 1554

(Letter 4814: VII:564; in Spanish)

Ignatius relieves a scruple which the foregoing command might have occasioned.

Although, in order to give you an excuse against the charity or importunity of anyone wanting to delay you, and to let you know my determined will and opinion in this matter of your coming to Rome, I command you in virtue of holy obedience to come, leaving within four days, etc., I declare herewith that it is not my intention to bind you under any sin in what I command you; thus, you should make use of obedience wherever it may be necessary, without a scruple about being bound under sin.

Rome, September 22, 1554

✠

To Giovan Francesco Araldo
from Juan de Polanco, by commission

Rome, September 23, 1554

(Letter 4821: VII:570f.; in Italian)

For the background on this letter, see letter 4788 above.

We have received a letter of Your Reverence on the same topic about which you wrote last week to Father Master Andrés [Oviedo], namely, Madonna Feliciana's girls. Though I was not written to specifically, I took care of it last Sunday. Now I will add that when I referred your letter to Our Father, he said that it contained no better words than where you said, "Woe to me if I do not mortify myself!" It is better to wait and find out from Father Master Salmerón what his reasons are, although Madonna Pellota, who interceded on behalf of that house, stated that a part of it adjoining our college is exposed. If this were so, it would certainly be most unfortunate, and it would be very good if the women would move to other rooms, or raise the wall up quite high. But in any case, it will be enough in similar situations for Your Reverence to represent your opinion and then leave it to the superior, not doubting that God will give you more light by which to see and order whatever is most pleasing to his Divine Majesty, and to handle the situation by this means. To try to bend the superior's will and conform it to your own is not—however good it may appear—in conformity with the rule of holy obedience.

I shall here say no more, except to pray Jesus Christ to give all of us perfect obedience and every other virtue.

Rome, September 23, 1554

✠

To Juan de Mendoza

Rome, October 14, 1554

(Letter 4870: VII:654f.; in Spanish)

Ascanio Colonna, whose matrimonial troubles had already occupied Ignatius (see letter 3014), was accused by the Pope [Paul IV(?)] of treasonable dealings with the French and imprisoned at Naples under the charge of Juan de Mendoza. Ignatius writes Mendoza, asking that his turbulent spiritual son be treated well. (Mendoza entered the Society in 1555. Colonna died in the Neapolitan prison in 1557.)

Ihs.

My Lord in our Lord:

May the sovereign grace and eternal love of Christ our Lord greet and visit you with his most holy gifts and spiritual graces.

Having learned of the gifts of God our Lord in your soul and of the desires he gives you of greatly serving him notwithstanding your noble rank and distinguished offices—for many persons so often an obstacle—I have for some time felt a special inclination in his Divine Majesty to serve you and make your acquaintance either personally or through letters. However, I have not done so until the present, when charity itself presents the occasion.

I have learned that an inmate of your castle is Signor Ascanio Colonna, whom God is visiting with trials in the final part of his life, as he so often does in the case of persons he loves and wishes to bring to a longing for their heavenly and eternal fatherland that is all the greater because of their afflictions from the pilgrimage of this earthly, temporal life. And though I am quite confident of Your Worship's humane and noble spirit, which, without prejudice to your duty, will have done and will continue doing all you can to give His Excellency the best possible treatment, nevertheless, confident that you take my doing so in good part, I cannot help commending to you most earnestly the good treatment of the person of one I have had spiritual dealings with and love deeply in our Lord. I also think it appropriate to mention that in private conversation with Don Ascanio, I once heard him say that he did not lack people urging him to go over to the French, but that he would never do what the prince of Salerno had done—that his house had always been for the Emperor and that he himself would be so as long as he lived. I heard this directly from him.

But there is no reason for my going further on this or any other matter, except to offer myself heartily to your greater service for the glory of God our Lord. May he in his divine and sovereign goodness advance in Your Worship the gifts of his grace, and may he give abundant grace to us all, so that we may always know his most holy will and perfectly fulfill it.

Rome, October 14, 1554

✠

To Giovan Francesco Araldo, by commission

Rome, October 28, 1554

(Letter 4909: VII:713f.; in Italian)

This is a gracious closing of the books on the incident of Araldo's untimely protest against his superior's handling of a delicate situation (see letters 4788 and 4821).

Jhus.

The peace of Christ.

Beloved Father Master Giovan Francesco:

I was much consoled by your letter of October 20, seeing the understanding on your part which it demonstrates, and your humble self-reprehension for the bygone little affair where your zeal and goodwill exceeded your circumspection. I do hope that from all this you will draw the spiritual gain of greater caution and less confidence in your own opinion and greater adherence to the infallible guidance of holy obedience, so that you will be able to verify that "for those who love God all things work together unto good" [Rom. 8:28]. So much for that.

The two young soldiers, Juan Rodríguez and Luis Campuzano, can be admitted [to the Jesuit novitiate] on the basis of your description. As for the other soldiers, about whom Father Mendoza asks whether they can be admitted for service, Our Father says to send information on each individual, and he will reply what he thinks ought to be done in each case.

The treatise on frequent Communion has not been gone through yet because of all there is to do now that school is beginning. When it has been looked over, either it will be printed, or a copy sent to Father Mendoza, or else the original sent so that it can be copied there.

Giacomo Calamazza and Mario [Berignuci] send greetings; they seem fine young men.

I commend myself to Your Reverence's prayers.

Rome, October 28, 1554

✠

How to Ask for Alms

November 1554

(Vol. XII: Appendix 6, no. 5, p. 656; in Italian)

Begging at the doors of prelates in Rome was a mortification performed by young Jesuits. Among them, for example, were members of important Spanish and Portuguese noble families, such as Diego de Guzman and Teotonio de Braganza. A specific itinerary was set for them through prominent streets of Rome, with stops at the residences and palaces of certain cardinals. Here they are given responses, sometimes humorous, to reproaches with which they might be greeted.

Jhus.

The formula for asking alms is, "Give alms to the Society of Jesus for the love of God."

1. When people scoff about the Society's name, the answer is, "This is the name that was given to our order by the supreme pontiffs."

2. When people reproach them for being fat, they should answer, "Even fat people need to eat; they have a human constitution."

3. When people say, "You are hale and hardy," answer, "I want to spend my strength and hardiness well in God's service."

4. When people say, "You are well clothed," answer: "If we were rich, we would not be begging aims."

5. When persons of importance ask, "Why do you go begging alms?" answer, "Because need obliges us to, and in order to imitate our fathers, who also did this."

The more usual response will be, "Brother, give us alms for the love of God."

[There follow detailed instructions on exactly which streets and houses each group of men should visit on their Saturday begging rounds through Rome.]

⊕

To Ercole Purino

Rome, November 3, 1554

(Letter 4921: VII:730–32; in Italian)

Purino was a great benefactor of the college of Modena, which he had helped to establish in 1551. He had just lost his only son, so Ignatius sends his customary consolation. Purino had earlier offered money to purchase a church that the Jesuits needed; hence the reference in the letter to the two possibilities. He had also politely but firmly protested the too frequent change of Jesuit confessors in Modena. Ignatius then assures him that a particularly beloved confessor who had to take up another work will be replaced.

Jhus.

Most Honored Sir in Our Lord:

May the sovereign grace and eternal love of Christ our Lord be always our protection and help.

Having yet to answer Your Lordship's letter of the nineteenth of last month, I received a second one yesterday, brought by our brother

Don Lorenzo;[18] I will reply to both briefly, since brief is the time allowed by my illnesses, through God's goodness.

I had already heard, before Your Lordship wrote me, of your son's illness and passage from this temporal life to the one that is eternal; and according to the debt of charity, strengthened by spiritual friendship in both this and the other life, I have striven to assist him with the prayers of this house and by several times offering to the eternal Father on his behalf the sacrifice of his son Jesus Christ our Lord at Mass. And although, moved by my love for both of you in our Lord, I could not but share the sorrow of Your Lordship, and of Her Ladyship your spouse, in parting from your only son, nevertheless, seeing that this was the will of God, our most wise and loving Father, I could not but thank him and be unshakably convinced that this is a good thing both for the son and for his father and mother. For as far as he is concerned, it is clearly to his good that he has been freed from the anxieties and dangers of the world and from its countless snares leading down to eternal misery, and that he has been so early admitted to enjoy, not an individual and earthly inheritance, but the kingdom, happiness, and felicity where he will be eternally blessed. As for Your Lordship and Your Ladyship, if you recall that we have here no abiding city, but seek the future city in the glory of God which is imparted to his faithful servants in the heavenly Jerusalem, our true fatherland, then the evil of the loss of temporal consolation is less than the good of having occasion to raise all your heart and love to the things above, since he is there who might have drawn your affections downward had he remained on earth. And it is certain, as Pope Gregory teaches us, that the infirmity of our nature, so turned towards earthly things, needs to be drawn upwards by the hope of eternal things, and also be impelled by temporal travails and afflictions which detach our love from the things of this life and elevate it to desire and strive towards the other life. And so I trust, in the divine clemency and in the most sweet disposition of his providence, that he will turn this affliction of Your Lordship and Ladyship to a great occasion for the highest good of both and also of consolation in this world if you strive, making yours the will of God, to give yourselves totally to loving and serving him, by adopting in your son's place some religious work where his name may be perpetually glorified and, in short, having Christ our Lord as your heir in his poor.

I shall say no more of this, except that we shall pray the divine and sovereign Goodness to possess both your hearts and to move them

---

[18] Father Juan Lorenzo de Patarinis.

always to things of greater perfection and of his greater service and glory.

As for the church of San Bartolomeo or San Bernardino, I shall write my opinion to our brother the rector, and he will confer with Your Lordship. However, I leave the choice between the two sites up to Your Lordship, together with the rectors of Ferrara and Modena.

Master Don Lorenzo has been called away to complete his studies and for several other considerations aimed at God's greater service. One day this week, I hope, another man will be sent, also Italian, and we will take care not to change him readily. Yet the love placed in the ministers or instruments of the divine Goodness is better placed solely in God; then one will make less of differences between one and the other.

May the eternal Wisdom daily grant all of us more light always to know his most holy will and perfectly to fulfill it.

Rome, November 3, 1554

✠

To Cristóbal de Mendoza

Rome, November 17, 1554

(Letter 4959: VIII:58f.; in Spanish)

A nephew of Cardinal de La Cueva who had brought a sum of money with him into the Society, Cristóbal had overloaded himself with books on his way to a new assignment, claiming the Society was apparently too poor to provide them for him there. Ignatius sets him straight about the Society's financial position and chides his pretensions to special treatment.

Ihus.

The peace of Christ.

I see from Your Reverence's letter that you are quite worried about taking some books to the house in Goletta should it be God's will that you go there.[19] Although some books are certainly needed, I think you can stop worrying; I shall worry about arranging with Cardinal de La Cueva for the purchase of any books that are necessary or useful, either at his own expense or at that of the one asking for Your Reverence. And

---

[19] A military post in Africa commanded by an uncle of Cristóbal's, who had requested him as a preacher.

if they should fail you, we will not fail you here in whatever is necessary. And we will not wait until we are rich to do this, as you state; for even with poverty present, we would do just as we would in abundance. Moreover, I want Your Reverence to know that this abundance is less than you apparently think. The money from you, together with that from Genoa, has arrived with the college [in Rome] in debt by more than five thousand scudi and the house by more than six hundred, with full-scale construction on the church getting underway and with over a hundred and forty mouths to feed—your own amount was needed just for grain and wine. Your Reverence has led me to mention this even though I am not fond of bewailing these woes, particularly since we receive them as comforts and visitations from God; and as effects of our mother poverty, they should not taste ill to us.

No more on this. On other matters, we are writing to Father Master Salmerón.

I commend myself very especially to Your Reverence's prayers.

Rome, November 17, 1554

Postscript: Father: I have been wondering whether to send back Your Reverence's letter for your closer reconsideration and to induce you to avoid henceforth letting your pen run loose on things which after consideration you would prefer not to have written.

I would draw something else to your attention, as one devoted to you in the Lord (as you know me to be). I would prefer that one not sense in your manner of speaking a note of personal assertion, seeming to imply that you should receive more privileged treatment because of having helped with your property, etc. Leave it to us to be aware of this, to speak to ourselves about it, and to take it into proper account. Do not give the impression that you claim a right to expect greater deference because of it. This would show a poor caliber of soul when a person makes much of what he ought to consider as nothing in terms of his own decision and of what is owed to God, for whose sake the thing is done. Consider this reminder as worth more than the ten scudi, which I would consider a quite paltry sum spent in satisfying Your Reverence's wishes.

No more for now.

✠

To Bartolomeo Romano, by commission

Rome, November 24, 1554

(Letter 4979: VIII:97; in Italian)

A wayward scholastic in Ferrara is called to order. But, even so, he is told that he can respond to whatever decision Ignatius comes to. See also letter 5130.

Jhus.

The peace of Christ.

Our Father has received bad news here about your behavior, though when you were sent out we thought you would do your duty and act with humility and obedience according to your profession. Our Father has not yet decided what he ought to do. Yet he says that if you have anything to say to him, you should write him. He will then commend the matter to God and make what he thinks is the best decision. You will, then, be able to reply and give an account of yourself—unless you are willing to reply with actions sooner than with words.

That is all for this letter.

Rome, November 24, 1554

✠

To Juan Ignacio Nieto

Rome, December 1, 1554

(Letter 4997: VIII:122f.; in Italian)

Juan Ignacio's efforts at preaching in Modena were troubled by his vacillating judgment about his own powers. Ignatius urges him to free himself from these concerns by submitting himself wholly to obedience in the matter.

The peace of Christ.

Dear Brother in Christ:

Since we are writing Father Rector what needs to be said in reply to the letters you wrote by his commission, I shall here be very brief. I have two things to say about your preaching. The first is that you should show to Father Rector what you have written; and if he occasionally tells you to preach somewhere, you should do so cheerfully, for God our Lord will aid you and make up with the virtue of obedience for any inadequacies. The second is that unless your superior asks you, you should not meddle or push your good desires beyond representing the matter to him—I refer to preaching. You will thereby be all the safer and more removed from the danger of any kind of presumption, which has no scope if you preach under obedience.

As for writing to your home place, we do not doubt that you do this out of spiritual love and not that of flesh and blood, and so your letters will be sent. Moreover, it will occasionally be not unseemly to write if you think it will be of help to their spirits without loss to your own.

Nothing else, except to commend ourselves earnestly to your prayers.

Rome, December 1, 1554

✠

To Ascanio Colonna

Rome, December 8, 1554

(Letter 5024: VIII:159f.; in Italian)

A letter of consolation to the duke of Palliani and Tagliacozzi, imprisoned for treason by Charles V.

Jhs.

My Illustrious Lord in our Lord:

May the sovereign grace and eternal love of Christ our Lord greet and visit Your Excellency with his most holy gifts and spiritual graces.

Although, because of my almost continuous illnesses, I have not replied in writing to Your Excellency's letter of October 26, I have done so many times by remembering Your Excellency in the presence of Christ our Lord and imploring his divine and supreme goodness to let Your Excellency's person and affairs be earnestly commended to him, and to let all these trials (his usual method of dealing with those he loves) cooperate towards Your Excellency's great spiritual good and advancement. I have no doubt that the more occasions Your Excellency's truly religious and Christian soul has for detaching itself from all love and affection for the earth, the more closely and fervently it will turn to the things of heaven, with a love for the supreme and eternal good which grows and is purchased in ever purer form by adhering to the Creator, to the extent that experience shows more clearly how ill placed is a love spent on the weak and fleeting good of created things.

The copy of the duke of Termoli's testimony which Your Excellency sent me had been read previously by Don Doimo [Nascio]; then and since then it has given us occasion to render many thanks to God our Lord, whose sweet providence will be pleased to make the truth known in due time as will be expedient for his glory and service, which I am sure Your Excellency desires above all else.

No more for now, except humbly to commend myself and this entire house to Your Excellency and to beg the supreme and divine clemency to grant all of us abundant grace always to know his most holy will and perfectly to fulfill it.

Rome, December 8, 1554

✠

To Violante Casali Gozzadini

Rome, December 22, 1554

(Letter 5041: VIII:183f.; in Italian)

Donna Violante, to whom Ignatius wrote this beautiful letter of condolence on the death of her son, Camillo, had been deeply impressed by Francis Xavier when he had preached in Bologna in 1537. In 1546 she asked Ignatius to send the Jesuits to Bologna to do pastoral work, and Ignatius complied. She also wanted to help found a Jesuit college there. After Camillo died, Donna Violante began talking about leaving her estate for such a college, because her other children were very well provided for. At that point, the situation became more complicated. Violante's relatives were not pleased at what she was proposing to do with her money. Already in Bologna a cartoon had been circulating, showing a Jesuit in biretta preaching to a group of women seated below his pulpit. The Jesuit had the face of a wolf and the women the faces of sheep. At that point, Ignatius wrote to the rector there, Benedetto Palmio, telling him that neither he nor any other Jesuit was to influence Donna Violante in any way as she made out her will. She died some time after Ignatius, in 1556, without having made a will, but as she was breathing her last, she whispered to her son Cesar, "I make you father and protector of the college at Bologna." Some time later Polanco noted dryly, "We have not had a single penny."

My Most Honored Lady in our Lord:

May the sovereign grace and eternal love of Christ our Lord greet and visit Your Ladyship with his most holy gifts and spiritual graces.

As we heard of the illness of your son, Master Camillo of happy memory, and then shortly after that of his passing from temporal to eternal life, at both pieces of news all of us here in the house and in the college turned to Christ our God and Lord with Masses and prayers of intercession on his behalf. We were prompted not merely by the charity which makes us everyone's debtors but particularly by the special charity we owe to Your Ladyship's numerous favors and your longstanding and persevering charitable intentions towards us. I am confident in him who is our true health and everlasting life that he did not hear our petition to grant him this present life—subject as it is to so many toils and dangers and finally to death—only so that he might grant him all the sooner that life which is everlasting and utterly secure and happy, for which he created and redeemed us at the price of his blood, and towards which every desire for our own and others' good ought to be ordered. I trust also that the same Father of mercies and God of all consolation, who through this visitation has demonstrated how much he loves Your Ladyship and how confidently he deals with you as a strong daughter and true servant of his, will have granted you light to see clearly what a great favor his divine and supreme Goodness does when he takes a person out of the wretchedness of earth—with that faith, hope, and charity which is his and aided by his holy sacraments—in order to transport him to the blessedness of heaven. I likewise trust that he will have granted Your Ladyship such conformity of your will to his that your grief at the loss of whatever human consolation you would have had from your son's presence will be less than your happiness over his having gone before you so well provided and assured of a place in our most happy fatherland, where we all hope to arrive and where we will rejoice together forever in the presence of our supreme and infinite Good. And may he deign to take daily more perfect possession of Your Ladyship's heart, turning it in all the greater union to himself and his holy kingdom in that you have less occasion for fastening it on anything less than him.

I will say no more, and will make no new offering of myself to Your Ladyship, since you know that we have long been wholly your own in our Lord. May he deign to make us always know his most holy will and perfectly fulfill it.

Rome, December 22, 1554

✳ 1555 ✳

For the Jesuit Superior in Ethiopia
Regarding Ethiopian Affairs

Rome, 1555

(VIII: 696–98: Appendix no. 5; in Spanish).

An instruction on maintaining the integrity of the Jesuit way of proceeding in the difficult circumstances expected in Ethiopia.

Jhus.

For Whoever Has Overall Charge of the Society in the Dominions of the Prester

He should take care to have the Constitutions and rules of the Society observed as far as this is possible; for unless this is done with prudence, the Society's spirit would be lost and many evils and scandals ensue; and he himself would have no one to make use of in a task as important as is the responsibility he holds.

There should be one provincial of the Society, to whom all shall have recourse.

As far as possible, wherever there are a number of men of the Society, there should be a rector or superior who will have the rules observed with entire obedience.

Wherever there are any members of the Society, even if only two, one should observe obedience towards the other.

The provincial should go and visit them and find out with great care how they are proceeding.

He should strive to have houses or colleges; and they should try to win members for the Society, devoting much effort to this, so that, as the Lord takes some of them, there will remain others with the spirit of the Society to enable whatever God may dispose to be perpetuated.

Those of the Society should not engage in judicial offices, so as not to incur enmities.

They should not engage in keeping account of the patriarch's incomes.

They should strive to have someone to teach Latin or Chaldean, as may be needed for the people of the country to make progress in doctrine; this should be strongly pursued.

Great care should be observed, as regards the persons not belonging to the Society whom the patriarch takes along, that it be known that they do not belong to it. Otherwise, they might give a bad example—by marrying, for instance—and scandalize the people of the country who thought they belonged to the Society. Hence, the people of the country must be clearly told, "These belong to the Society and those do not"; moreover, they should be obliged to wear different clothing.

✠

To Antonio Araoz

Rome, January 3, 1555

(Letter 5061: VIII:225; in Spanish)

A kindly letter urging the provincial to take in good part the comments about himself that members of his province send to Ignatius, and recommending that he follow the latter's example in making use of consultors.

Ihs

May the sovereign grace and eternal love of Christ our Lord be always our help and protection.

Since Master Polanco is writing of other matters on my commission, I will here say only that I have received the opinions of some members of your province regarding your own person. I enclose a copy of these and strongly urge you to take what they say in good part, for the writers' hearts have been good, and they were required to express their views by order of the commissary.[1] Still, I will mention one point to you: just as I regularly consult and confer with some persons in the house when I have to make some important decision, I would like you to do so as well, so that we may both alike follow the same way of proceeding, being mindful of the spirit of kindliness and charity commended to us by the vicar of Christ our Lord in the bulls of our Society's institution.

---

[1] The commissary was Jerónimo Nadal.

As for the rest, he who gives to all of us the desire to serve him will also graciously give us help to bear well the burden that has been laid upon us for his greater service and praise.

May he be pleased to give us his abundant grace, so that we may always know his most holy will and entirely fulfill it.

Rome, January 3, 1555

✠

To Princess Juana of Spain

Rome, January 3, 1555

(Letter 5066: VIII:235; in Spanish)

The full story of how the princess regent of Spain secretly became the only woman Jesuit in history is told by Hugo Rahner in St. Ignatius Loyola: Letters to Women *(New York: Herder and Herder, 1960), 52–67. The following is Ignatius's discreetly phrased letter accepting her into the Society.*

My Lady in our Lord:

May the sovereign grace and eternal love of Christ our Lord greet and visit Your Highness with his most holy gifts and spiritual graces.

From a letter of Father Francis Borgia I have understood what a great service it would be to Your Highness if we could find a way to comply with the religious and holy desires of a certain person. And although there was no small difficulty in this matter, it was all placed second to the will we all have of serving Your Highness in our Lord.

And since Father Francis will speak in detail about what Your Highness will want to know, I refer to what he will say on my part and say no more myself, except that I humbly beseech Your Highness to consider us as your own, for so we are in our Lord, and beg God's supreme goodness to grant all of us his abundant grace, so that we may always know his most holy will and entirely fulfill it.

Rome, January 3, 1553

✠

To Cardinal Reginald Pole

Rome, January 24, 1555

(Letter 5120: VIII:308–11; in Italian)

Almost two years earlier, in August 1553, Ignatius had written to Cardinal Pole when Pope Julius III had appointed the latter legate to England, hoping that he could arrange for the reestablishment of the Catholic faith there now that Mary Tudor had become queen. Ignatius assured the cardinal of prayers in all Jesuit houses for the success of his mission. In the present letter, Ignatius voices his joy at the success of Pole's mission and his hopes for the future. He also takes the occasion to tell the cardinal of the current works of the Society.

May the sovereign grace and eternal love of Christ our Lord greet and visit Your Most Reverend Lordship with his most holy gifts and spiritual graces.

From a letter of Your Most Reverend Lordship written from Brussels on November 11, at the time of your departure for England, I learned of the good hope which God our Lord was giving Your Most Reverend Lordship of the longed-for restoration of that kingdom to union with the Holy Catholic Church. Shortly thereafter the entire city here learned of the fulfillment of that hope, in so short a time that it was clearly the work of him who accomplishes without regard to time whatever pleases his divine and most perfect will. Your Most Reverend Lordship has doubtless been informed already of the universal joy and spiritual consolation inwardly communicated by the Father of mercies and the God of all consolation to this Holy See through this extraordinary boon. That which was and is felt by our own least Society in particular is beyond my powers of expression. May all creatures endlessly praise Jesus Christ our Lord, who has shown in this reconciliation of England how wide open is the treasury of his grace and charity, and how sweet and powerful the disposition of his providence. And since his works are perfect, may he be pleased to confirm and extend this singular favor shown to his whole Church, so that the knowledge and glory of his holy name may spread daily farther, and his most precious blood and life, offered to the eternal Father on behalf of souls, may be efficaciously applied to their salvation. I can also tell Your Most Reverend Lordship that upon us, deeply devoted and ever obliged as we are to Your Most Reverend Lordship's service, the divine Wisdom has bestowed a special additional consolation in vouchsafing to make particular use of your own ministry in this great work, by retaining Her Serene Majesty the Queen and His Majesty the King within the kingdom and Your Most Reverend Lordship outside of it, so as to render you effective fellow workers in the great grace of the restoration of your kingdom.[2]

---

[2] The queen and king are Mary Tudor and her consort, Prince Philip of Spain.

Knowing that even in the midst of such momentous affairs, Your Reverend Lordship's great charity towards us makes you mindful of us and interested in how we are, I would like to let you know that both in our own house and in the Roman College, as well as in the German College, God's service is on the increase. Besides the approximately sixty of us in our house, we have more than seventy of our men in the college. The disciplines (with the exception of law and medicine) are being taught with great success both to them and to extern students, who are themselves numerous—more than fifty. The students of the German College are likewise making good progress in learning and virtue, and we trust that the divine Goodness is preparing among them great ministers in his service for the spiritual help of their own nations. Among them we have an Englishman of excellent talent and character, and in our own college a rather promising Irishman. Moreover, if Your Most Reverend Lordship should find it appropriate to send some talented students with a capacity for study to either of these colleges, we are confident that before long they could be sent back considerably improved in their life and learning and strongly edified by the holy faith that is present here—for in these colleges care is taken that they derive benefit from what is good in this city and no harm from what is not. However, consideration of these things lies best with Your Reverend Lordship; we can only represent to you what comes to us from the special attachment which the divine and sovereign Charity has instilled in us towards the service of the souls in these kingdoms according to our least profession.

The consistory this week dealt with the thirteen priests of our Society who, as I had informed Your Reverend Lordship, were being sent to the kingdom of Prester John. At the urging of the King of Portugal, one was elected patriarch, with two coadjutors to be his successors, both bishops. The Sacred College approved unanimously, the Pope remarking that at least with these bishoprics no one could claim that avarice played a role. Indeed, there is more opportunity for martyrdom than for ambition in those regions, from which we received this year word of nine dead—may Jesus Christ be perfect life for them all.

His Holiness has appointed two of our men *motu proprio* to accompany Cardinal Morone to the diet in Germany, which will be held after all. Other men are being sent elsewhere on a project of reform. With these three missions occurring almost together within a few days, I thought it not inappropriate to inform Your Most Reverend Lordship of how his vicar on earth is deigning to make use of the ministry of this least Society.

Regarding England, I can also report that, once His Majesty the King had written to His Holiness and to a number of the cardinals as well as to me personally in support of our Roman College, His Holiness has demonstrated considerable eagerness to endow it, directing that funds for this be procured. The Reverend Cardinals here have accordingly sought them out, and it is to be hoped that His Holiness will soon put this excellent measure into effect. May Christ our Lord dispose of the whole project to his greater service and glory. And so with this—and humbly commending myself to Your Most Reverend Lordship's holy prayers—I will say no more except that I beg God our Lord that he will grant to all of us his grace always to know his most holy will and perfectly to fulfill it.

Rome, January 24, 1555

✠

To Bartolomeo Romano

Rome, January 26, 1555

(Letter 5130: VIII:328f.; in Italian)

A scholastic at the Jesuit college in Ferrara, Bartolomeo was dissatisfied with conditions there and wanted to be moved. The house at Ferrara was, as a matter of fact, having its troubles. The four Jesuits there were overworked and the citizens of the town were becoming disillusioned with the Jesuits. Ignatius had written to the superior, suggesting ways to improve the situation. In this letter to a scholastic who had been complaining strongly, Ignatius assured him that his difficulty was not the place but himself. See also letter 4979 for an earlier interaction between Ignatius and Romano.

Jesus

The peace of Christ.

Dear Brother Bartolomeo:

From your letters and also from those of others, but mostly from your own, we understand what your condition is, and we are all the sorrier about it since we so desire your spiritual good and eternal salvation. You are much mistaken in thinking that the cause of your unrest, or lack of progress in the Lord, is the place where you are or your superiors or your brethren. It comes from inside, not from without: from your lack of humility, lack of obedience, lack of prayer—in a word, from your lack of mortification and fervor in advancing along the way of perfection. You can change residence, superiors, and brethren; but unless you change your interior person, you will never do well; you will be the same wherever you are until you become humble, obedient, devout, and mortified in your self-love. And so this is the change you should seek, not the other; I mean, you should try to change the interior man and recall him to God's service. Give up the thought of any external change: you will either be good there in Ferrara or in none of the colleges. We are all the more certain of this because we know you will be able to be helped better in Ferrara than any place else. I give you one piece of advice: go to your superior in heartfelt humility, ask his help, open your heart to him in confession or however you like, and accept with devotion whatever remedies he may give you; busy yourself with examining and bewailing your own imperfections rather than with contemplating those of others. Try to give more edification in the future; do not try the patience of those who love you in Christ our Lord and would like to see you his good and perfect servant. Every month write a few lines on how you are doing in humility, obedience, prayer, and desire for your own perfection; and [write] also on how your studies are going. May Christ our Lord keep you.

Rome, January 26

✠

To Juan de Avila

Rome, February 7, 1555

(Letter 5154: VIII:362f.; in Spanish)

The saintly apostle of Andalucía was greatly devoted to the Society. He defended it publicly on several occasions and from among his own disciples sent to it several excellent men. Ignatius praises two such disciples, Guzman and Loarto, who became two excellent and important Jesuits in subsequent years. Ignatius also encourages the saint in his concerns over his health.

Very Reverend Father in Christ:

May the sovereign grace and eternal love of Christ our Lord be always our help and protection.

I am sure that between the great charity of Your Reverence and the news you have of my poor health, you will excuse my tardiness in answering your letter of July 27, which was brought by our brothers Don Diego de Guzmán and Doctor Loarte. As for Your Reverence's remembrance of me and this Society (more yours than ours) in your prayers and the special love from which this remembrance and so many other good deeds and favors proceed, I will not give Your Reverence thanks for them: no one expects thanks for what he does for what belongs to him—although there is abundant cause to give thanks to God our Lord, the author of all good, and to beg him to reward the great charity he has inspired in Your Reverence, by increasing it and perfecting it daily and drawing from it great fruit for the help of many souls and for his own glory, which is what Your Reverence pursues in all things. For myself and the rest of the Society here, I can assure you that we will be prevented from ever forgetting Your Reverence by the close union of the same spirit and desires which God our Lord gives to us for his service and praise.

As for your spiritual sons, Don Diego de Guzmán and Doctor Loarte, we have found by experience that the information given about them in your letter comes from someone who knows them well. Don Diego gives all of us great satisfaction and consolation with his goodness, and edifies everyone by the example of his humility and obedience. The Doctor is also progressing in every way; and although he has more work to do on himself, I trust that God our Lord will cause him to grow daily in all good, particularly with the help of your prayers for him and for us all. As to your ailments, we pray to him who is the true health and life of all to fulfill his will through them, and that both in sickness and in health he may be glorified through Your Reverence's person.

As for the attention Your Reverence is compelled to give to your own bodily treatment: since you take it solely for his service and as his business rather than your own, it is right to be patient and for us all to conform ourselves with what we see God our Creator and Lord wants of us. And may his divine and supreme goodness grant to all of us his abundant grace, so that we may always know his most holy will and entirely fulfill it.

Rome, February 7, 1555

✠

To Ponce Cogordan

Rome, February 12, 1555

(Letter 5174: VIII:395–97; in Spanish)

Ignatius had much at heart the apostolate of reform of houses of members of religious orders. He often accepted that apostolate and sent members of the Society to undertake a task of some difficulty. During his lifetime, Jesuits carried out this work in places as far apart as Sicily, France, Germany, Spain, and Italy. Cardinal Marcello Cervini (later to be Pope Marcellus II) charged Cogordan with the reform of a monastery of Benedictine nuns at Celle, in Provence. Ignatius wrote the following instruction; it stresses the patience and tact needed in this important ministry of the early Society. After a good deal of resistance from some of the nuns at this monastery, Cogordan had begun to see some few results before his ill health forced him to abandon the task.

Procedure To Be Followed There

1. Master Ponce should deliver the letters to those to whom they go and try to win the goodwill of those who govern the province and for whom he bears letters; he should try to get them to write to the governor of the country and some leading personages on his behalf, etc.

2. He should deliver the letters for the local personages and gain their friendship as far as he can, particularly that of the nuns' relatives.

3. He should make it understood by everyone, both in public and in private, that he has come for the common good and honor of the monastery and of the whole region; for this purpose he should deliver the [papal] bull of the [Blessed] Sacrament and have it solemnly published, etc.

4. He should set to winning credit both through spiritual conversations with the gentry and others persons and by visits to hospitals and other pious works if there are any.

5. With great love he should visit the nuns and make them understand that the cardinal has sent him for their spiritual consolation, and he should give them his letter. He should not talk at the beginning about reform until he has first gained credit both with them and with the region.

6. During this period he should deal with them in sermons and public exhortations and in private spiritual conversations, and he should try to find out who among them show greater recollection and goodness of life; he should try to win over some of these to the Lord, particularly the abbess and other important nuns.

7. When he has gained credit and come to know the nuns' souls, previous lives, and errors, he should tactfully begin the reform. For this he should find out who their confessor is; if the latter is a person who cannot help him, he should advise and get him not to visit the nuns for a time, but to leave them be until he himself tells him; and he should try to obtain his friendship.

8. He should learn what friar and other persons have contact with the monastery and with whom. He should advise and get them to stay away. As far as possible, he should ensure that no one visits them except those he knows will be helpful for the end desired. For this he should make use of whatever support he may have from the nuns' relatives.

9. He should persuade the nuns to remain enclosed during a certain period for their spiritual good, allowing no one into their monastery.

10. He should aim principally at getting them to go to confession and Communion, in particular doing his best to get a certain number to make a general confession and gain a plenary indulgence, so that these can give an example to the others.

11. He should help them with examinations of conscience and with spiritual exercises, particularly those of the First Week [of the Spiritual Exercises] at the beginning, and leave them some methods of prayer suited to each.

12. He should try with tact and charity to win their confidence, so that they will disclose their souls and their defects, which he should get them to see in such a way that they will realize that he is acting through charity and love and for their good.

13. If some are difficult and unwilling to be helped, he should not get discouraged or annoyed with them; rather, he should show them great charity and persistence in trying to help them.

14. He should employ no coercive measures with the nuns without further instructions from Rome.

15. Master Ponce must not eat at the nuns' expense or take anything from them by way of alms or anything else.

16. He should show no partiality, but use the same charity toward all of them.

Matters Needing Reform

1. If possible, the nuns should observe enclosure, even though their institute may not require it; they should only rarely let visitors into their monastery, and these should be women of noble birth and good life, never men.

2. They should lead a common life, and no one should have a servant or anything else of her own.

3. They should recite their office in choir, and have their mental prayers and spiritual exercises.

4. They should go to confession and Communion weekly or monthly, and their confessor should be a man of proven life and teaching, elderly in behavior as well as years; he should be named by the cardinal, or by the bishop with the cardinal's approval.

5. Each year the governors of the region should appoint two distinguished women, elderly and upright, to assume responsibility for helping the nuns in their needs, examining whether they are living correctly, whether they have any suspicious visitors, and anything else connected with the monastery.

What Should Be Brought from Rome

1. There should be a brief from the Pope commissioning Master Ponce and giving him full authority to reform and restore the monastery to the observance of its rule and to a full religious and upright life. It should also include authority to exercise coercion and impose censures on both the nuns and anyone else who directly or indirectly hinders the reformation and restoration, even exempt religious of any order whatsoever; it should also include faculties for absolving from heresy, excommunication, and any other censures and sins, etc.

2. In this or a different brief, he should carry a grant from His Holiness of a plenary indulgence for all the nuns who reform and make a general confession; also, for the convent and the village where it is located, a plenary indulgence for anyone who visits the convent after its restoration and says some prayer; also, on the anniversary of the reformation, or on the feast of the saint to whom the monastery is dedicated or the saint of the monastery's order, a plenary indulgence in memory of the restoration.

3. If possible, there should be letters from the King [of France] for the Parlement of Aix and the provincial viceroy, instructing them to write to the officers of justice in the region where the monastery is located. In the King's letters and in the others written from all other places, there should be mention of the Society's good reputation and of the fruits which it is producing wherever in Christendom it goes.

4. There should be edifying, loving letters of Cardinal Santa Croce [Cervini] for the nuns, as well as for the president of Aix, the provincial viceroy, and the governor of the monastery's region. If the cardinal is not the right person in some cases, he should have letters written by another cardinal, such as Farnese, Paris [Jean du Bellay], or [Georges d']Armagnac, vouching for the Society and for Master Ponce.

5. If there is any indication that letters from the local bishop or the general of the monastery's order would be useful, that would be good.

6. We should see if we could get letters for individuals in the region, relatives of the nuns, or other nobles.

7. Cardinal Santa Croce should invest Master Ponce with his complete authority for the reform, with a broad patent under his seal, as is customary.

8. Master Ponce should bring attestation that the Society is native to France, with testimony from some French cardinals.

9. Master Ponce should bring the bull of the Blessed Sacrament for the local region, in order to obtain credit and goodwill from all.

10. He should bring a rosary blessed by the Pope, or an indulgenced *Ave Maria* to be given to the monastery in common, and also some Agnus Deis.

Thought should be given to the appropriateness of taking this opportunity to get acceptance of the Society's bulls and faculties by the Parlement of Paris, and of bringing the Society to the notice of the French King.

✠

To Jerónimo Nadal and Diego Laínez

Rome, February 18, 1555

(Letter 5197: VIII:438–41; in Spanish)

Instructions for a visitation of Germany. This country and the Indies and Ethiopia as well were matters of great concern to Ignatius: in the two last-mentioned places he hoped to bring about the desired fruits; in the first-mentioned place he sought to preserve them. This letter is also typical of Ignatius's way of acting: he would give detailed instructions and then leave it to the recipients, the men on site, to judge their applicability and to act as they thought best.

1. Although Your Reverence together with Father Master Laínez will examine other measures and be better able to tell whether or not to implement the ones indicated here, I shall nevertheless mention a few, while leaving everything to the discerning charity of Your Reverences. I shall first mention some matters that might be of help for the German College, and then some others for the help of the Society.

2. First, you might approach the Most Reverend Cardinal of Augsburg [Otto Truchsess] to see if he will provide for the college what he

offered and subscribed to with his own hand, namely, 120 ducats a year. Although while he was here His Lordship was most lavish towards the college, since leaving he has provided nothing even though in letters he promised to do so.

3. The Most Reverend Legate [Cardinal Morone] and the Cardinal of Augsburg might induce some influential ecclesiastical prelates to send promising students of good character to the college, providing them with some temporary assistance even if not in perpetuity; after finishing their studies here these men could be returned to them improved in learning and virtues. Those particularly coming to mind are the bishops of Salzburg, Mainz, Trier, Cologne, Würzburg, and others whom you will better be able to determine there.

4. Also through the Reverend Legate and the Cardinal of Augsburg, you might try the duke of Bavaria [Albert V], whose secretary Master Heinrich [Schweiker] visited the college, was highly pleased with it, and was disposed to try to get his duke, while establishing a similar college in Ingolstadt, to send some good subjects to Rome with money for their support. If Your Reverences talk with this Master Heinrich, it would be good to show him the greatest goodwill, for he can be helpful in this and other regards.

5. See what can be done with the King of the Romans [Ferdinand I] in this matter, representing to him how important it would be to have able young men educated outside their countries who could then return, secure in the faith, with greater prudence, goodness, and learning, etc. You should know that the Most Reverend Legate has sent information to His Majesty the King, and I believe that they have requested the incomes of certain depopulated or abandoned monasteries whose substantial incomes are now being held and enjoyed by secular persons.

6. The Emperor [Charles V] also has been spoken to from the side of His Holiness—at least the nuncio was charged to do this—and furnished with information. It would be good to see if His Majesty can be approached—through his ambassador or however you think best—to assist with this holy work.

7. As for other princes and secular lords in Germany, you will be able to see if there is any readiness for successfully broaching this matter; for all of these the legate probably would be a good intermediary.

8 If not with money or incomes, they can at least help the college by sending some selected good and talented subjects; for obtaining this, besides the good reputation for progress in letters and virtues which the

Germans have here, a considerable help can be the prospect of benefices and dignities, etc., and the efforts of Brother Jonas, etc.[3]

For Assistance to the Society

1. Help can be given to the college at Vienna in the order and method of studies, as well as in spiritual matters, by explaining to them the Society's Constitutions and manner of proceeding.

2. You can also help in solidifying and expanding its financial basis.

3. Study the advisability or not of taking on responsibility for the university there and the attitude toward this.

4. Find out the situation of the college in Prague and whether its foundation should be held up more or less.

5. For they have requested twelve men for Prague, and this is a small number if there are to be classes; you should investigate whether a way can be found to support a large number of students, tactfully suggesting this to the King.

6. It would be good if the Society could receive a number of subjects in the college at Vienna, not to teach but to study, and even better if traveling money was sent for them.

7. The Cardinal of Augsburg had discussed a college of the Society for Augsburg, but the matter remained in the balance, no request being made one way or the other.

8. At Ingolstadt, according to what the duke wrote to Our Father and to the Pope, a college for our men has begun, and men have been offered to the duke over a period of time but not right away. Master Heinrich, his secretary, said that he would endow the college of the Society for ninety persons, and that alongside it there would be another college like the German college. All this by way of information.

9. The ambassador of the King of the Romans, Don Diego Lasso, wrote to His Majesty the King about starting a college here for Hungarians, Transylvanians, Bohemians, and others from his dominions; and I believe he received a favorable reply. This business would seem to have two points. One is that the King should have a concern for those peoples, seeing the need they have for good workers, etc., and [a concern as well] that they be educated by the Society outside their countries. The other is that he have a way of doing this without losing anything from his own pocket; and this could well be done by applying to this college

---

[3] Jonas Adler, Nadal's companion.

of the Society from among his vassals certain ecclesiastical incomes presently misused by secular persons, of which enormous quantities have been usurped.

10. For other helps that can be given to the Society when the occasion arises, Your Reverences require no advice; moreover, you can write if there is anything special to let us know about.

✠

To Claudius, negus of Ethiopia

Rome, February 23, 1555

(Letter 5205: VIII:460–67; in Spanish)

This is another letter on the famous expedition to Ethiopia, one of the missions most enthusiastically accepted from the Pope by St. Ignatius. Basically, it was to reconcile the Monophysite church of Ethiopia to the church of Rome. A group of Jesuits was sent, headed by the papally appointed patriarch, Andrés de Oviedo. In the following letter, Ignatius presents them to the negus, Claudius, and encourages him to full union with the pope. He expounds to Claudius the highly centralized and monarchical Roman ecclesiology of the day.

Jesus

My Lord in our Lord Jesus Christ:

May the sovereign grace and eternal love of Christ our Lord greet and visit Your Highness with his most holy gifts and spiritual graces.

His Serene Highness the King of Portugal, out of the great zeal given to him by God our Creator and Lord for the glory of his holy name and the salvation of souls redeemed with the precious blood and life of his only-begotten Son, has written me several times indicating his wish that twelve religious of our least Society, called by the name of Jesus, be appointed, one of them being chosen by His Highness as patriarch and two others to be his coadjutors and successors, in order to petition the supreme vicar of Christ our Lord to give them the appropriate authority, so that they, together with the other priests, could be sent to Your Highness's kingdom.

I, therefore, because among all Christian princes our entire Society has very special respect, devotion, and obligation to His Serene Highness the King of Portugal, did as he bade me; and as he wrote me again, I have appointed twelve priests besides the patriarch—out of devotion to the number of Christ our Lord and his twelve apostles which they represent—to go and place their persons amid all the hardships and dangers that may be required for the good of souls in the realms subject to Your Highness. I was all the more eager to do this because of the special desire which God our Lord has given to me and to all of our Society for serving Your Highness, since following in your predecessors' footsteps, Your Highness labors in the midst of so many infidels and enemies of our holy faith to preserve and advance the religion and the glory of Christ our God and Lord. There was even more reason to wish that Your Highness had the aid of spiritual fathers possessing the true authority and power of this holy Apostolic See and the unadulterated teaching of the Christian faith, which are the keys to the kingdom of heaven that Christ our Lord promised and subsequently granted to St. Peter and to those who would succeed in his chair. He promised these keys to him alone when he told him, as the evangelist St. Matthew relates: "I say to you that you are Peter, and upon this rock I will build my Church; and I will give you the keys of the kingdom of heaven, and whatever you shall bind upon earth will be bound also in heaven, and whatever you shall loose on earth shall be loosed also in heaven" [Matt. 16:18f.]. In fulfillment of his promise, he gave these keys to St. Peter after he arose and before he ascended into heaven. As St. John the evangelist relates, he asked him three times, "Simon, son of John, do you love me more than these? and upon receiving his answer told him, "Feed my sheep." He gave him charge not over some but of all his sheep, granting to him the fullness of power required to pasture all the faithful in Christian life and religion and to lead them at last to the pasture of everlasting happiness in the kingdom of heaven [John 21:15–17].

To his other apostles, Christ our Lord gave, as it were, delegated authority; to St. Peter and his successors, full and ordinary authority, to be communicated to all other pastors as they would need it. These are to receive and acknowledge the authority of this supreme shepherd. This was prefigured by the words of God our Lord in Isaiah, speaking of Eliakim the high priest: "And I will lay the key of the house of David upon his shoulder; and he shall open and none shall shut, and he shall shut and none shall open" [Isa. 22:22]. This prefigures St. Peter and his successors, who possess the fullness of power that is signified by the keys, which are customarily conferred in token of real and complete authority. Consequently, Your Highness should give thanks to God our Lord for the great mercy he bestows upon your realms in your days by sending to your kingdom true shepherds of your souls who are in union with the supreme shepherd and vicar whom Jesus Christ our Lord left on earth and from whom they have the very broad authority which they bear.

Not without reason, Your Highness's father and grandfather were unwilling to accept a patriarch from Alexandria. For just as a limb severed from the body does not receive vital influence, movement, or feeling from its head, so the patriarch in Alexandria or Cairo, being schismatic and separated from this Apostolic See and the supreme pontiff who is the head of the whole body of the Church, does not receive for himself the life of grace or any authority; nor can he lawfully impart it to another patriarch. The Catholic Church is but one throughout the whole world; there cannot be one church under the Roman pontiff and another under the Alexandrian. As Christ her bridegroom is one, so his spouse the Church is but one. Of her, Solomon says in the Canticle, speaking in the name of Christ our Lord, "One is my dove" [6:8]; and the prophet Hosea says, "The children of Judah and the children of Israel shall be gathered together, and they shall appoint themselves one head" [Hos. 1:11]. In the same sense St. John later said, "There shall be one fold and one shepherd" [John 10:16].

One was the ark of Noah, as we read in Genesis, and outside of it there was no way to be saved; one the tabernacle made by Moses; one the temple built in Jerusalem by Solomon for offering sacrifice and worship; one the synagogue by whose judgment all had to abide—all these prefiguring the Church, which is one and outside of which there is nothing that is good. For no one who is not united with the body of the Church will receive from its head, Christ our Lord, that influx of grace which will give life to the soul and prepare it for blessedness. To set forth this unity of the Church against certain heretics, the Church sings in the Creed, "I believe in one, holy, Catholic, and apostolic Church." It is an error condemned by the councils that there are particular churches—such as those of Alexandria, Constantinople, or the like—which are not subject to the universal head. This head is the pontiff of Rome, where—in continuous succession from St. Peter, who, as St. Marcellus the martyr tells us,[4] chose this see at the command of Christ our Lord and confirmed it with his death—the Roman pontiffs have continually abided, acknowledged as Christ's vicars by so many holy doctors, both Latin and Greek, and by all nations; revered by holy anchorites and pontiffs and other confessors; confirmed by so many mira-

---

[4] This refers to a pseudo-decretal which in Ignatius's time was considered a genuine letter of St. Marcellus.

cles and by the blood of such a host of martyrs who died in the faith and unity of this holy Roman Church.

Thus, the bishops assembled at the Council of Chalcedon unanimously acclaimed Pope Leo as "most holy, apostolic, universal."[5] The Council of Constance condemned the error of those who denied the primacy of the Roman pontiff over all the particular churches. The Council of Florence, held in the time of Pope Eugene IV and attended even by Greeks, Armenians, and Jacobites, decreed (in conformity with previous councils), that "the holy Apostolic See and the Roman Pontiff have the primacy over the whole world, and that he is the successor of St. Peter and the true vicar of Christ, the head of the whole Church, the father and teacher of all Christians; and that to him, in the person of blessed Peter, was given by the Lord Jesus Christ the full power of feeding, ruling, and governing the universal Church."[6]

Your Highness's father, the Most Serene King David of glorious memory, under the prompting of the Holy Spirit, sent his ambassador to acknowledge this Holy See and render obedience to the supreme pontiff at Rome. Among the many and praiseworthy deeds of your father and Your Highness himself, these will merit everlasting memory and perpetual celebration throughout your realms, with thanksgiving to God our Lord, the author of all good, for the high favor he has bestowed on you in return for Your Highnesses' diligence, concern, and great virtue—the father's in first of all rendering his obedience to the vicar of Christ our Lord, and the son's in bringing to his kingdom the first true patriarch and lawful son of this holy Apostolic See. For if it is a singular benefit to be united to the mystical body of the Catholic Church, which receives life and guidance from the Holy Spirit who, according to the evangelist, teaches her all truth [John 16:13]; and if it is a great gift to be illumined with the light of the Church's doctrine and to be grounded on the stability of the Church, which St. Paul tells Timothy is "the house of God, the pillar and ground of the truth" [1 Tim. 3:15] and to which Christ promised his assistance, according to the evangelist Matthew, in the words, "Behold, I am with you all days, even to the consummation of the world" [28:20], then it is right continually to render profound thanks throughout your realms to God our Creator and Lord, whose providence has bestowed so great a good upon them through Your High-

---

[5] This is not accurate. Neither in its acclamations nor it its official *Acta* or proceedings did Chalcedon use these terms.

[6] This definition can be found in Denziger-Schönmetzer, *Enchiridion Symbolorum*, no. 1307.

ness and your glorious father. And this all the more inasmuch as I trust in his infinite and supreme goodness that through this union and conformity to the holy Roman Catholic Church there must come to Your Highness's realms at one and the same time spiritual prosperity, an increase in temporal prosperity, and a great exaltation of your royal estate and the putting down of your enemies, so far as this will be for the greater service and glory of Christ our Lord.

All the priests being sent to Your Highness, particularly the patriarch and his two coadjutors and successors, are men very well known and tried in our Society, practiced in works of great charity. They have been chosen for this most important undertaking because of their high example of virtue and their wide and sound learning. They feel great enthusiasm and consolation at being sent, hoping to expend their toil and their lives in great service to God and to Your Highness by helping the souls of your subjects. They desire to imitate in some way the love of Christ our Lord, who gave his blood and life to redeem these souls from everlasting misery, declaring through the evangelist St. John, "I am the good shepherd; the good shepherd gives his life for his sheep" [John 10:11]. And so the patriarch and the others come ready not only to give their learning and counsel and spiritual help to souls but if necessary to lay down their lives for them. I trust that the more familiarly and intimately Your Highness deals with them, the more satisfaction and spiritual consolation you will receive in our Lord. Moreover, as regards their doctrine and the reliability of what they teach, they bear, as Your Highness knows—especially the patriarch—the very authority of the Supreme Pontiff: to believe what they say is to believe the Catholic Church, of whose mind they are to be the interpreters.

Inasmuch as it is necessary for all the faithful to believe and obey the Church in whatever it ordains and to have recourse to it in their difficulties, I have no doubt that in Your Highness's high Christianity and goodness, you will command the people in your realms to believe and obey and have recourse to the patriarch and those whom he may appoint in his place, since they hold the place and authority of the Supreme Pontiff which is that of Christ our Lord, communicated to his vicar on earth. In Deuteronomy [17:8–13] we see that those who had difficulties and doubts were referred to the synagogue as a figure of the Church; and thus Christ our Lord declares, "The scribes and the Pharisees have sat on the chair of Moses; whatever they tell you, observe and do" [Matt. 23:23]. Similarly, the wise Solomon was referring to the Church in Proverbs [1:8], when he said, "Do not dismiss the commands of your mother," that is, of the Church. Elsewhere he says [Prov.

22:28], "Do not pass beyond the boundaries set by your fathers," that is, the Church's prelates. So great is the credit Christ our Lord wants us to give to the Church that he says through the evangelist St. Luke, "He who hears you hears me, and he who despises you despises me" [10:16], and in St. Matthew, "If he will not hear the Church, let him be to you as the heathen and publican" [18:17]. No credit should be given to anything uttered against what is heard from those who interpret the mind of the Catholic Church—recalling what St. Paul said to the Galatians: "If an angel from heaven preaches to you another gospel than what we have preached to you, let him be anathema" [1:8]. This is what the holy doctors have taught us by word and example; this is what the councils have decreed; this is what has been approved by the common consent of all the faithful servants of Christ our Lord.

There is no doubt that both the patriarch and the others will always have the deepest respect and reverence for Your Highness and will strive to serve you and give you whatever satisfaction is possible for them to the glory of God our Lord.

May Your Highness consider that we of our least Society who remain behind here are deeply devoted to your entire service in our Lord, and that in our prayers and Sacrifices we will continue, as we have begun, to implore the Divine Majesty to preserve in his holy service Your Highness and your lofty royal estate, and to grant you prosperity here on earth in such wise that you may attain the true happiness of heaven.

May he give to all of us his abundant grace, so that we may always know his most holy will and entirely fulfill it.

Rome, February 23, 1555

✠

To Melchior Nunes Barreto

Rome, February 24, 1555

(Letter 5210: VIII:481–83; in Spanish)

It was over two years before the first unconfirmed word of Francis Xavier's death in 1552 reached Europe by way of a ship coming from the Far East. In case the report is true, Ignatius writes confirming the election of Nunes Barreto to replace Xavier as provincial in India.

May the sovereign grace and eternal love of Christ our Lord be always our help and protection.

This year, dearest brother, we have had no letters from India, although in Portugal, on the word of the captain of a single ship arriving there, they have heard and reported to us that our dearly beloved brother Master Francis has passed on from this life. If it is as they report, may he be with God; however, since we find certain inconsistencies in the story and have had no letters with eyewitness reports from our own men, we have not made up our minds to believe it. Whatever the truth may be, we are confident that the name of Christ our Lord will be glorified either in his life or in his death, and that from earth or from heaven his charity will continue to help us in the works of God's service.

We have also heard that our brothers Master Gaspar [Berze], his substitute in India, and Fathers [Manoel de] Morales and Urban [Fernandes], along with some others, have ended their pilgrimage on earth and passed to the heavenly and abiding fatherland. If so, and whatever the truth may be, may God our Lord, the true life and salvation of all, be praised. And may he graciously dispose of all of us who are or will be members of this least Society in whatever way will be to his greater service and glory. Amen.

From reports apart from letters, we hear that you have been elected provincial of India, as may be done, in accord with our bulls, until the superior general provides otherwise. Lacking any definite information on the situation, and relying on the good report I have of you personally, I will say only that I confirm our brothers' election and give you all the authority proper to your charge, just as it was enjoyed by your predecessor in it, until some other provision is made from here. And should our brother Master Francis still be alive among us in this mortal and passing life, it will be up to him to take whatever measures he judges best in our Lord, as is provided in our Institute and demanded by reason itself.

This year you will see a large number of our brothers there.

✠

To Melchior Carneiro

Rome, February 26, 1555
(Letter 5218: VIII:489f.; in Spanish)

Melchior Carneiro had been chosen as one of the two auxiliary bishops to accompany the patriarch, João Nunes Barreto, to Ethiopia. Ignatius urges him not to refuse the episcopal office and promises that the Society will remain close to him.

May the sovereign grace and eternal love of Christ our Lord be always our help and protection.

Although I know you will take as addressed to yourself what I write to Fathers João Nunes [Barreto] and Father Doctor Andrés de Oviedo, I did not want to miss writing this letter to you, since I do not know how long it will be before I can write you again. I want to beg you in our Lord not to make any difficulty about accepting the burden laid on your shoulders by the vicar of Christ our Lord on earth. Besides the hindrance this would bring to God's greater service, there would be a failure against what obedience to this holy Apostolic See requires. I will say no more on this point, since your letters give no grounds to fear that you fail to understand this, nor does your great store of virtue give any indication that you are unwilling to fulfill your obligation— particularly since those who dearly love you in our Lord are convinced of the rightness of this for his holy service through your person; and I know that your only desire is to glorify his holy name in your person by helping many souls.

It only remains for me to commend myself very earnestly to your prayers, and to ask God our Lord to give you his holy blessing and grace, so that you may devote all your labors to great and universal service of him and his holy Church.

And since I am convinced that on your part you will preserve complete unity with us so far as you can, I want to assure you that we on our part, whatever may be your state of life, will always keep you in our hearts, holding you in an interior union all the more tightly as you are further away from us physically.

May Christ our Lord give all of us his abundant grace, so that we may always know his most holy will and entirely fulfill it.

Rome, February 26, 1555

Remember me very especially to all the companions on the expedition to Ethiopia, and to all those whom we know personally from here; and with the same charity we also hold in our hearts those we have not yet met face to face, and we greet them warmly in our Lord.

✠

To Gaspar de Borja, bishop of Segorbe

Rome, March 12, 1555

(Letter 5248: VIII:535f.; in Spanish)

A letter of appreciation to the bishop, a relative of Francis Borgia, who had gener-
ously offered to endow a college of the Society in Zaragoza and another in Valencia.

Jhs.

My Most Reverend Lord in our Lord:

May the sovereign grace and eternal love of Christ our Lord greet
and visit Your Most Reverend Lordship with his most holy gifts and
spiritual graces.

After replying to other letters which Your Lordship did me the
favor of writing, I received your letter of October 15. From it as well
as from the letters of Master Estrada, we see growing day by day Your
Lordship's wish to grant your patronage and help to this least Society
(which is wholly yours) as a foremost instrument used by our Lord's
providence in the founding and furthering of the Society in those kingdoms. May he bring Your Lordship, by an increase of charity and the
gifts of his grace and by spiritual consolation, to perceive how important
for his divine service and the help of souls and how pleasing in his most
holy presence is the work on behalf of which Your Lordship is active for
his reverence and love. I trust that he will do so, and give Your Lordship even in this life a strong pledge and proof of the reward he is
keeping for you in life everlasting.

As to particular ways of helping, whether through a pension or
other means, Your Lordship will be able to see what is best; for he who
bestows the desire will also give understanding to see what is most
suitable for obtaining our aim of God's service.

I will say no more, except to beg Your Most Reverend Lordship
to consider as your own not merely the colleges in those three kingdoms,[7] along with the men living in them, but in the same way all of us
in every place who belong to this least Society; we are indeed yours
with a very special obligation and devotion in our Lord. May it please
him by his infinite and sovereign goodness to give all of us his abundant
grace always to know his most holy will and entirely to fulfill it.

Rome, March 12, 1555

---

[7] The kingdoms of Aragon, Catalonia, and Valencia.

To Robert Claysson

Rome, March 13, 1555

(Letter 5251: VIII:539f.; in Latin)

Claysson, a native of Bruges, had sent a report to Rome in a rather bombastic style, and Ignatius here reproves him for this. His comment that Claysson's letter could not be sent anywhere else without heavy editing refers to the fact that the reports of Jesuit activities regularly sent to Rome were often copied there and forwarded to other Jesuit houses and even made public as a way of making the Society better known. Claysson was a very learned, hard-working man, a good teacher and speaker, who later contributed to setting up at Billom in Auvergne the first college of the Society in France.

The peace of Christ.

Dearest Master Robert in Christ:

This first letter from me will let you know my attitude towards you, in that I feel so free, without further preliminaries, to admonish you about the style of your letter. Elegant and learned as your letter is in other respects, we find in this very elegance and learning a lack of τ ο πρέπον [what is appropriate]. Eloquence and charm in religious speech differs from that of secular speech. Just as in a mature woman one favors modest and unpretentious adornment, so in our men's speech or writing we like to see an eloquence redolent not of juvenile self-indulgence but of mature gravity, particularly in letters, which by their very nature demand a spare, concise style, with a greater abundance of matter than of words.

We hope Your Charity will receive in good part this advice, which our own charity did not allow us to forgo, for we do not dare send your letter anywhere without heavy editing.

Some selection of topics must also be made, and only those should be included in the quarterly letter which serve for edification. Moreover, while there are a good many passages in your letter which quite manfully display your happiness to share in the Lord's cross, there are some others which betray an occasionally somewhat petulant spirit that ill becomes a sturdy soldier of Christ.

Here then, dear brother, you have a censure of our own—so that you will not think that only the Sorbonne is entitled to issue censures! In repayment for my writing my mind to you with such frankness, confidence, and love, I beg your prayers and reciprocal admonition when it is needed.

Farewell in the Lord Jesus Christ.

Rome, March 13, 1555

✠

To Paschase Broët, by commission

Rome, March 14, 1555

(Letter 5252: VIII, 541–45; in Italian)

The first ten companions who founded the Society had all been students at the University of Paris, and Ignatius sought to adapt Parisian methods of instruction for the academic work of the Society. Already in 1540, the year in which Pope Paul IV officially approved the Society, Ignatius had sent a group of young Italian, Spanish, and French Jesuits to Paris to study at the university. In 1551 King Henri II gave legal status to the Society in France, and in 1552 Ignatius appointed Paschase Broët, one of the ten cofounders of the Society, as provincial of France. Meanwhile, a persistent opposition to the Society took form in Paris, led by a combination of the Parlement of Paris, the bishop and some of the diocesan clergy who were proponents of the "Gallican liberties" of the French church, and the University of Paris, which was unhappy at Jesuit educational activities. In 1553 the Parlement, with the support of the bishop and the university, refused legal registration of the King's recognition of the Society. The Theology Faculty of the university then issued a formal decree of censure against the Society's Institute and the bishop refused to ordain Robert Claysson and other young Jesuits there. Even though the Society gained support and worked with increasing ease in other parts of the country, originally under the sponsorship of Bishop du Prat of Clermont, the Parisian opposition endured long beyond this letter and beyond the death of Ignatius in 1556.

Jesus

The peace of Christ, etc.

We received Your Reverence's letters of December 3 and 8, of January 3, 11, and 15, and of February 2 and 13. I shall reply in the present letter to what you ask in all of them.

We have seen the Faculty of Theology's decree regarding our Institute. For now Our Father has been unwilling to resort to any means but our protector the Cardinal of Lorraine, to whom he has written the enclosed letter. Your Reverence will examine the copy of this and also the information. Then, when you speak with our protector the Cardinal of Lorraine, you will present him the letter from Our Father together with the information. If you think they should be put into Latin, have that done and let us know about the result. It is truly pitiful that so outstanding a university should give such scope to a single ill-informed and perhaps worse-intentioned person and put out decrees like this. Because of our veneration for the university and our esteem for the numerous good and learned men in it, we would be unwilling to credit such a censure to it, so very unbecoming do we find it to the authority and maturity of this assembly of theologians. However, as sons of this university, we have not given way to resentment, particularly seeing that they are quite evidently uninformed and ignorant of our Society, which is so sought after in numerous places that we have a hard time defending and excusing ourselves for our inability to satisfy them all. Even in Paris they give us a very different treatment than do these reverend doctors. But I trust that, just as in Rome, God our Lord will also have allowed this opposition in Paris the better to bring out the truth about our Institute, for his glory and for the augmentation of the Society. And God seems to be doing the college in Paris no small grace in letting it not only act for his honor and glory but also suffer for it.

Regarding the difficulties being raised for our brother Master Robert [Claysson], this does not seem to be the time to take on new conflicts, and so his unwillingness to go to law is commendable. The present seems to be a time for "bearing fruit in patience" [Luke 8:15] —not, however, failing on our part to do all that we can in the best way we can for the divine service according to our Institute.

As for his promotion to the priesthood, Your Reverence knows that we have authorization to have our men ordained by any bishop, even a titular one. Hence there is no need to turn to His Lordship the Bishop of Paris [Eustache du Bellay], since he is unwilling to do us this favor. The Reverend Bishop of Clermont [Guillaume du Prat] will suffice, or anyone else that can be found who is willing to do us this charity.

The thought came to us that the theologians' decree seems to imply that some member of our Society had incurred the stigma of criminality or infamy. While we are unable to think of anyone in the whole Society who might reasonably have afforded a basis for such a claim, it did occur to us that Cáceres may once have said he belonged to our Society;[8] but Your Reverence knows that he never did. Perhaps others may have cloaked themselves with our name, as happened in Flanders; but such persons do not seem to be worthy of consideration or

---

[8] Diego de Cáceres had been associated for a time with Ignatius in Spain.

of being relied upon by persons who ought to possess such maturity and circumspection.

From Ferrara, where they have heard something, I believe they will arrange for the duke and also for Madama to write to His Majesty the King; that is all for now, except that the testimonials mentioned in the information can be sought and obtained if necessary and will be quite favorable.

Our Father will write another time to the Reverend Bishop of Clermont and to Monsieur du Mont. Meanwhile, Your Reverence will transmit greetings and expressions of gratitude on Our Father's part as you deem appropriate; likewise [do so] to others who are friendly and devoted to us, etc.

If the men Your Reverence wrote would be going this Lent for the college of Billom are not sent, let us know if they would serve for the college which is supposed to start at Avignon this summer, according to the promise made to Cardinal Farnese, with whom Master Ponce [Cogordan] and another of our men embarked for Marseille. After he has delayed for a time near a monastery for whose reform Cardinal Santa Croce [Marcello Cervini] is sending him, he will leave for Avignon. I believe he will be writing frequently to Your Reverence; and if Cardinal Farnese is traveling there, he might be a good source of help in any matter; he might also help by letter even if he goes to court.

[There follow a number of other business items.]

✠

To Gerard Kalckbrenner (Hammontanus)

Rome, March 22, 1555

(Letter 5280: VIII:583–85; in Latin)

The zealous prior of the Cologne Carthusians was the intimate friend of Pierre Favre and Peter Canisius and through them close to Ignatius and the Society. Ignatius himself during his convalescence after Pamplona had read and prayed over the Life of Christ *and the Carthusian Ludolph of Saxony and for a brief time after his conversion had thought of becoming a Carthusian. The Cologne priory was a bastion of Catholicism against the Lutheranizing tendencies of some prominent churchmen in the city, and the prior sought every means of strengthening the Catholic faith there. Hence his desire for a Jesuit college in Cologne and his generous alms for the Society. Thanking him for the alms and for his desire to have a Jesuit college in that city, Ignatius describes the Society's educational efforts on behalf of Germany in Rome itself.*

May our Lord Jesus Christ preserve and increase his grace and peace in us unto its consummation in glory. Amen.

I have not yet answered Your Paternity's letter to me of September 27, even though the warmth of your great charity toward us and the depth of generosity which springs from it not only increased the debt of interior gratitude we feel but also prompted us to render thanks exteriorly to God the author of all good and to Your Paternity as a faithful minister of his providence. However, when I saw that Your Paternity (to use your own words) wanted neither a letter nor thanks but prayers and silence, since you had been moved to send us this substantial and timely assistance solely by the purest intention of charity, I thought that (at least for the time being) I ought to refrain from writing. But at the same time I have recorded the memory of this noble generosity in the book of the Society, and urged prayers and the cherishing of mutual charity with your holy order and monastery upon both our members living today and those who will follow us. Blessed be the name of our Lord Jesus Christ, who provides in so many ways for this least Society, not only granting it daily growth in numbers and spiritual fruit but also bestowing upon us, who seek the kingdom of God, all other things else as well.

As for starting a college of our Society in Cologne, we appreciate Your Paternity's interest and support, and pray that God will reward them abundantly. Indeed, I am sure that when it pleases the supreme Wisdom and Majesty, an opportunity will be opened for your active devotion and that of others who wish to provide the youth of Germany with teachers to train those of outstanding talent in letters and Christian virtue. But at the same time that God's providence has been moving persons to start colleges in Germany itself, he has inspired in us an intense desire to provide a formation here in Rome for young Germans who have been called to the ministry of the orthodox Catholic Church. He has also been inspiring many fine young men who flock to us here for education either in the German College, of which I am sure Your Paternity has heard, or in the college of our Society. Many arrive from upper as well as lower Germany, including some who, like roses from thorns, have come from association with heretic parents or friends. We have here more than seventy or eighty students from Germany.

Young men of excellent character from other nations too have been pouring in, as well as mature men of learning and distinguished reputation. There are today approximately a hundred and eighty of us here in Rome who follow the Institute of our Society, although some are always being sent off to different places. With about fifty students staying in the German College, our Lord Jesus Christ is evidently preparing soldiers for some noble campaign, intending this seedbed to produce abundant fruits in his Church. The worldly-wise think it strange, perhaps foolhardy, for us to take on so many dependents without any assured income, in disregard of the high cost of living and the shortage of money; but we have cast our anchor of hope in the goodness of God, who can feed large numbers as easily as small, in scarcity as easily as in abundance; consequently, we think we have no power or right to turn away men he calls to our Society through his holy inspirations.

And while, as Your Paternity writes, it seems that the Gospel is being transferred to unbelievers and taking leave of the Western nations because of their indifference, we still ought to hope and strive with all our might to do whatever we can by prayer, word, and example, and in every possible way, as worthless instruments of the divine Wisdom, to bring what help we can to both areas. But enough of this.

It remains for Your Paternity to vouchsafe to commend this whole Society of ours to God in your own holy prayers and those of your order. May his boundless charity bestow his grace and Holy Spirit upon us all, so that we may be able always to know and fulfill his divine will.

Rome, from the house of the Society of Jesus

March 22, 1555

✠

To Jerónimo Doménech, by commission

Rome, March 24, 1555

(Letter 5288: VIII:592f.; in Italian)

Pope Julius III had been very favorable to the Society of Jesus and in 1550 in the bull Exposcit debitum *had reaffirmed the original papal approval of the Society given by Pope Paul III in 1540. Ignatius here ordered prayers for the departed Pope and for the election of his successor. That successor was the devout and intelligent Cardinal Marcello Cervini, Pope Marcellus II, a choice acclaimed by those who saw the great need for Church reform. Unfortunately, he died after only twenty-three days in office and was succeeded by Paul IV.*

Jesus

The peace of Christ.

May the grace and peace of Christ our Lord be always our help and protection.

On the twenty third of this month, about midday, our Holy Father Julius III rendered his soul to his Creator. May he deign to number him among the saints in eternal blessedness. Because of the duty that all Christians owe to their shepherd, as well as our own Society's special duty towards whoever sits in this apostolic chair, and also because of the debt we owe to the goodwill and affection shown us by this vicar of Christ our Lord, we made continual prayers for him during the last days of his life; and after his passing Our Father has ordered that for nine days in the house and colleges of Rome the Holy Father's soul should be commended to Christ our Lord in our Masses and prayers. He has also ordered that the directions given for Rome be imitated throughout the Society. This is being written to the provincials and to some rectors who do not yet have a provincial, so that they may carry it out.

Likewise, given the importance of a good pope who is zealous for the honor of God and the reform of the Church—and if ever such a pope was needed, now seems to be the time—Our Father has ordered that all of us in Rome, totaling about two hundred and twenty in the residence and colleges, should offer urgent prayers for the election of a new pope who will be what is required for the universal welfare of Christendom. Each one is to offer special prayers to this effect at least three times each day, imploring the divine Clemency to provide his Church, not with such a shepherd as our sins deserve, but with one suited to the extremity of her spiritual need.

As for Masses, Our Father has ordered that of every two Masses said by each priest, one should be primarily to this effect and the other at least secondarily for the same intention. This is to be continued until the new pope is elected—although all our prayers and actions, and our sufferings as well, ought to be directed to this end during that period. Our Father desires that what has been ordered for Rome be observed by all members of the Society wherever they may be, so far as the circumstances of place and persons allow. Hence, Your Reverence should see that this directive is observed wherever your jurisdiction reaches, for we may hope that Christ our Lord will not forget or forsake this inheritance of his—bought back at the price of his life's blood—at a time of such dire need, unless our own tepidity and negligence prevent the working of his infinite and sovereign mercy.

Rome, March 24, 1555

To Juan Pérez de Calatayud

Rome, April 4, 1555

(Letter 5313: VIII:631–33; in Spanish)

Ignatius consoles him on his wife's death, mentions a business matter, and refers him to the Jesuits of Zaragoza.

My Most Honored Sir in Christ Jesus:

May the grace and peace of Christ our Lord be always present and grow in our souls.

I received two letters from Your Worship; and since I see from the second that you did not get my reply to the first, this will serve for both. I was most grateful to see your remembrance of me; were I wanting in the very special charity to respond to it, I would need to ask God our Lord to give it to me; but he knows that I have kept and still keep Your Worship deep within my soul and that I desire, within the limits of my poor powers and profession, to have occasion to employ myself in Your Worship's service, to his glory.

God our Lord's depriving you of so good a companion can only be considered as one of those visitations which divine Providence uses with its chosen ones to detach them all the more from the things of earth as they see that there is nothing stable or lasting upon it, and to raise their hearts with their hopes and desires heavenward in the measure that they have more pledges there, where each one will rejoice forever in those he loves in the divine presence.

If we had our fatherland and dwelling place and true peace in this world, it would be a great loss to us when persons or things which gave us so much happiness here are taken away. But being, as we are, pilgrims on this earth, with our lasting city in the kingdom of heaven, we should not consider it a great loss when those whom we love in our Lord depart a little before us, for the rest of us will soon follow them to where Christ our Lord and Redeemer has prepared for us the all-happy mansion of his blessedness. May he be pleased to comfort Your Worship's soul and direct all your affairs in the way he knows is best for bringing all your house to the last end for which we were created and redeemed by his blood and death.

Señor Gómez has spoken to me of a business affair of Your Worship's. I have given him my opinion and refer you to what he will write you. I am grieved at the embarrassment in which you find yourself for having done a kindness. May God our Lord direct the whole business to his greater service and to what is most for your own highest good.

Your Worship will doubtless have contact with those of our Society residing in Zaragoza and will endeavor to profit spiritually from their conversation, and so I need not enlarge on this matter.

They will also have information about anything you might wish to know regarding myself.

God our Lord does me a great mercy in employing me in the service of this holy Society, although on my side I do it quite negligently and imperfectly.

May he be pleased to increase his grace in all of us, so that the glory of his name may grow through our ministry. Amen.

Rome, April 4, 1555

✠

To Simão Rodrigues, by commission

Rome, April 6, 1555

(Letter 5329: VIII, 657f.; in Spanish)

Ignatius tried to treat Rodrigues with the greatest consideration after he had found it necessary to remove him from office in Portugal. He suggested, among other things, a pilgrimage to the Holy Land. Rodrigues at first reacted positively to the possibility, but then rejected it. He next proposed Rome, but Ignatius refused, proposing instead Ancona, Venice, Padua, or Bassano. Rodrigues replied with a querulous letter in December 1554. Ignatius sent Bobadilla to calm him down, but his mission was unsuccessful. Rodrigues sent two complaint-filled letters demanding money. In this reply, Ignatius agreed and had Polanco reply. On April 13 Rodriguez replied to this letter with an accounting of his expenses.

The peace of Christ.

I received Your Reverence's letter; for the most part, being a reply to my own, it needs no reply. As regards Your Reverence's mentioning that you will need to be provided with money for after Easter: since it may be presumed that you are mindful of our profession and yours—holy poverty being the mother of us all—I have no doubt that this is the case. And it is certainly true that despite our having about two hundred and twenty mouths here to feed, in a year of high prices and during a vacancy of the Holy See, with our debts running to thousands of scudi and with our being able to feed and clothe ourselves only with money borrowed at high interest, we would nevertheless in a way prefer to be deprived of what we need than have Your Reverence lack what is convenient. But so that Our Father can have more light on all this, it would be good if Your Reverence wrote, or got the rector, Master Cesare [Helmio],[9] to write, how he goes about drawing on the college what he supplies you with for your personal needs, and what has to be purchased for your bodily needs with funds obtained elsewhere. The fact is that Your Reverence has not yet been a whole year at the college, and what with the hundred and thirty scudi deposited for you in Venice, besides the travel money you drew in Rome, we would have a hard time explaining to anyone who asked how all that money could have been spent. For Our Father to be able to do this, he lacks information on how Your Reverence's needs ought to be provided for. It would be good for you to write us, or else inform the rector about this as well and we will write to him to see that Your Reverence lacks nothing that you need. If your necessary comfort is not suitably provided for where you are or in Padua, Our Father says that he will give directions for you to be provided for in some other college where you can reside more comfortably than perhaps in those colleges. In any case, and no matter where you are, from here we will always do everything possible—and even more than is reasonably possible—to see that Your Reverence has all that is necessary for your provision.

No more, except that we all commend ourselves heartily to your prayers.

Rome, April 6, 1555

[P.S.] Our Father has repeated to me that the rector is to supply you with twice whatever he spends on himself; and if they cannot afford it there, he will see that you get it in some other college.

✠

---

[9] He was rector of the Jesuit college in Venice and superintendent of the one in Padua.

To João Nunes Barreto, patriarch of Ethiopia
Appendix about Ethiopian Affairs

Rome, ca. April 7, 1555
(Vol. VIII, no. 2, 680–90; in Spanish)

The following instruction for the Jesuits going to Ethiopia is one of St. Ignatius's most important missionary documents, showing deep pastoral sensibility. The stress is entirely upon patiently winning the hearts of the Ethiopians, both rulers and people, so as to gradually and tactfully remove their ecclesiastical abuses and solidify their union with the Catholic Church.

Ihus.

Some Directives Sent to Father João Nunes as an Aid to Restoring the Kingdoms of Prester John to the Unity of the Catholic Church and Religion

Since the King of Ethiopia, Prester John, is humanly speaking the most important factor in this enterprise, and after him the people, some directives will be given which may help in winning over Prester John, and then some for dealing with the people and King together.

[For the King]

For winning over Prester John—besides the bulls addressed to him by the Pope—the letter written to him from here will be found helpful. It reminds him of the submission which his father David sent to this see, recommends and accredits the envoys sent to him, and contains other expressions of love. However, the chief and decisive help for winning him over (after that of God our Lord) must come from the King [of Portugal]. Not only will letters from His Highness be needed but, if he thinks fit, a special ambassador who will visit Prester John on his behalf and present to him the patriarch, the coadjutor bishops, and the other priests, explaining the procedure whereby it will no longer be necessary to receive their patriarchs from Moorish lands or from schismatic Christians. The more solemnly this presentation on the part of His Highness is made, the more authority it seems the patriarch will possess for God's service.

His Highness might also consider whether he thinks he ought to send some gifts of items that are prized in Ethiopia. He could also promise him that he will enjoy genuine union and friendship with Christian rulers when they all share an identical religion; also, that they would send him whatever kinds of artisans he desires; and that God will give him the grace to surmount and vanquish the Moors, so far as this will be for God's greater service.

It will also help to have letters from the King for persons who enjoy Prester John's special friendship and are consulted by him, notably the Portuguese, showing respect to them. If His Highness agrees, some unaddressed letters could also be sent, with the names of the addressees to be filled in as needed. Whether through letters or not, the friendship of such persons should be sought.

Likewise, the viceroy of the Indies could also do much to enhance the patriarch's authority with Prester John by sending a letter and a man of his own (should the King not send one).

The patriarch and those with him should try to get on familiar terms with Prester John and by every honorable means to gain his love. If he is receptive and if the opportunity presents itself, they should make him realize that there is no hope of salvation outside the Roman Catholic Church, and that to be saved one must believe all that she determines in faith or morals. If it is possible to get him to accept this general point, numerous particular points will have been gained which depend upon it and can progressively be deduced from it.

If you get some highly placed persons who have great influence with him, or even get Prester John himself, to make the Exercises and get a taste for prayer and meditation and spiritual things, this would be the most effective means of all to get them to lay less store by or even abandon their extreme corporal practices.

Remember that they have a prophecy that in these days a king from here in the West (apparently they are thinking of no other than the King of Portugal) is to destroy the Moors. A closer friendship with this sovereign will thus be another motive for accepting uniformity of religion, for without disagreement in religion there will be a closer union of love between them, etc.

Note also that Prester John has hitherto held ecclesiastical as well as civil jurisdiction. Consider informing him that in the Catholic Church kings and great princes usually have the presentation to certain important posts, but that the actual conferral of these and all offices is by the supreme pontiff and by the bishops, archbishops, and patriarchs in their dioceses. Conformity with the Roman Church and her princes in this matter could be of much help to him.

For the People and King Together

You should carry with you and be able to show the ample faculties you have. The bulls or briefs should be as impressive looking as possible, and if translated into Abyssinian, all the better.

So far as possible, you should have ready at hand proofs for the dogmas on which they are in error, with definitions of the Apostolic See or councils where such exist. For once they grasp the single proposition that the Apostolic See cannot err when making solemn definitions on faith and morals, they will more easily be convinced of the rest. Hence, you should be fully equipped to prove this proposition in a way accommodated to the intelligence of the people there or of anyone else.

Regarding their abuses, first try to instruct Prester John and a few more influential persons. Then, unobtrusively, once these are well disposed, see what can be done to hold an assembly of the persons most distinguished for learning in those realms. While not depriving them of anything they are particularly attached to or value highly, try to get them to accept the Catholic truths and what needs to be held in the Church, and urge them to try to help the people come into conformity with the Roman Catholic Church.

Once the substantial abuses are done away with to the extent that they prejudice genuine faith (such as the observance of the Old Law as obligatory), it would be best to begin, with Prester John's support, removing or lessening the remaining abuses if this can be done. If it cannot, do what you can to make clear that these practices are not obligatory and that even when tolerated, they are better not observed. In this way they will soon fall into disuse, especially if some of the leading men can be brought to give an example.

Their austerities in fasts and other corporal penances might be gently tempered and brought within the bounds of discretion by four means. The first would be, on the testimony of Holy Scripture, to praise spiritual exercises more highly than bodily ones, since the latter "are profitable but little" [1 Tim. 4:8]—although this does not mean disapproval of bodily exercises, which to some degree are indispensable. Thus, once they lose their esteem for the practices now so highly esteemed among them, these will of themselves fall into disuse, being in any case rather repugnant to the flesh. The second is to praise and prefer moderation over extremes. The third is to use arguments showing that it is against charity and the common good for them to weaken themselves for good works by fasting to such an extent that their enemies invade and kill them, committing a host of crimes against God our

Lord. This argument should be easily grasped by Prester John and other perceptive persons. The fourth means would be the example that might be given by persons they regard as holy: once these persons are convinced that they should act in this way for God's greater service, they would doubtless do so. Observe, too, that while God our Lord calls some individuals by the path of penance and corporal austerities (and in that case they should be much commended), in general the measure of discretion is required for such austerities to be praiseworthy.

Another help in getting rid of certain abuses might be to have celebrations that appeal to the senses, such as Corpus Christi processions or others practiced in the Catholic Church. These could replace their baptisms, etc. Even our own common people, who are less crude, derive help from this.

Be very careful to conduct public services like Mass and vespers in a way edifying to the people, slowly and distinctly, since they do the contrary and consider our way more perfect. If the King approves having a choir with organ, this might be a help in the beginning; being alien to our Institute, however, this should be handled by persons outside the Society.

Vestments of priest, deacon, and subdeacon, altar cloths, chalices, altar stones, and equipment for making hosts ought to be of the best. Try to get them into the habit of making hosts for the Blessed Sacrament the way it is done here. Direct that Communion should be received after confession and not daily by anybody who comes to church, and that the Sacrament is to be brought to the homes of the sick who cannot come.

It would be good to instruct them in the administration of baptism, along with its ceremonies; they should be told there ought to be a single, not a multiple, baptism, such as they practice with their annual baptism.

Since they have not practiced confirmation, the sacrament ought to be administered to all the people, after instruction about this sacrament. You should also introduce the practice of extreme unction, of which they are ignorant.

At first you might hear the confessions of those you can understand. For the others, you should make an effort to learn Abyssinian. Through interpreters, their own confessors could be instructed on the procedure they should follow. They should be told of the reservation of cases reserved to bishops and patriarchs, and of the very severe penalties on confessors who reveal matter of confession, something which they say is done there. In sum, see that the abuses regarding these sacraments are carefully corrected.

As to holy orders, reform is needed with regard to the age, integrity, competence, and other qualities of those ordained, to the extent that the situation there permits.

As to matrimony (and in general all the sacraments), they should be told of the essential forms which must be observed. The accompanying ceremonies can be introduced step by step, as will best contribute to their edification. These external ceremonies should not be few in number, since the people are much given to them.

Both initially and for the future, it would be a great help for the complete restoration of those realms to start numerous schools there in Ethiopia to teach reading, writing, and grammar, as well as colleges for the training of young men (and others who may need it) in the Latin language and in Christian faith and morals. This would be the salvation of that nation, for these youths would grow up attached to the things they had learned early and in which they saw they surpassed their elders, and thus the errors and abuses of the older persons would soon decay and disappear. And if it appears too difficult among the people of that kingdom, habituated as they are to their own ways, to instruct their children properly, consider the advisability of Prester John's sending a number of intelligent ones to study outside the kingdom. A college could be opened in Goa and, if advisable, also in Coimbra, in Rome, and on Cyprus at the other end of the sea. Furnished with sound Catholic teaching, these could return to their kingdom and help the people of their nation. By coming to love the practices of the Latin Church, they would be the more steadfast in her way of proceeding.

The patriarch could either himself, using an interpreter, or through others begin giving discourses and exhortations to the people according to their capacity; similarly the bishops and the others.

Having the catechism widely taught by good ministers would also be of great importance.

Persons among the people there who have greater capacity and a good reputation ought to be won over by showing them esteem and assigning them ecclesiastical revenues and dignities, but not unless they show promise of being faithful ministers. These persons could be commissioned to preach.

Portuguese familiar with the Abyssinian language would well serve as interpreters if any of our men preach, and as instructors regarding the Abyssinian manner of preaching. Others could be brought from

Goa or elsewhere in India; and if there were children in India instructed in catechism who could provide a beginning for children's schools in the kingdom of Prester John, they could be of help.

Thought should be given to eventually setting up universities or institutions of higher studies.

Concentrate on the abuses or disorders that can be corrected gently and in a way that makes the need for reform evident to the people there; begin with these, and you will gain authority for reforming other abuses.

Since our men need to reduce that people's esteem for corporal penances, which they esteem and practice to excess, you ought to set charity before them by word and example. For this it would be good to have hospitals available for pilgrims and for the sick, both curable and incurable; to give and get others to give private and public alms to the poor; to help marry orphan girls; and to start confraternities for redeeming captives and rearing abandoned boys and girls, etc. This would let the people see in a tangible way works that are superior to their fasts, etc. Prester John, so generous with his alms, should if possible be involved in all these pious works.

In the spiritual works of mercy, the people there should also see you concerned to give aid and consolation to souls, as by teaching them virtue and letters—altogether gratis and for the love of Christ. Such works should be praised in sermons and conversations with texts from Holy Scripture and the example and sayings of the saints, as we indicated above.

Although you should be on the lookout to bring them into conformity with the Catholic Church, this must be done gently and without violence to minds long accustomed to different ways of living. Try to be loved and looked up to by the local people, maintaining the esteem due to learning and virtue without forfeiting humility, so that they will be helped in proportion as they esteem the persons helping them.

Take along good books, especially pontificals and other works setting forth the Church's external rites, as well as decrees of the Apostolic See and the councils. You should be well informed about these and know the number of bishops assembled at the councils, since they attach much importance to this; these will be quite helpful for them. You should also take along and know well the lives of saints, especially the life and miracles of Christ our Lord, for the same reason, and also the calendars of feast days. In sum, you should be expert in even the smallest of these ecclesiastical topics, for this is the discipline they understand best and consider most important, more so than subtler matters of which they would understand nothing.

It will also help if you go well furnished with church ornaments for altars and for the priests, deacons, subdeacons, and acolytes; with chalices, crosses, holy-water vessels; and with other items used in external worship.

You might think over and propose to His Highness in Portugal the advisability of your being accompanied by capable persons who can instruct them on bridging rivers, construction, agriculture, and fisheries, as well as other artisans, together with a physician or surgeon, so that the people may see that their complete good—even bodily good—comes to them along with religion.

You should consider taking along a few well-chosen books on civil law and ordinances, to improve their governmental practice and administration of justice.

Also consider taking along some relics of the saints for the devotion of the people.

Remember that they have prophecies or traditions that after a hundred patriarchs from Alexandria they were to receive one from Rome. The former ended with Abuna Marqos, and so after him they accepted a pseudo patriarch who came claiming to be from the see of Rome.[10] Thus, it would seem they will be ready to welcome the patriarch and, as a consequence, his teaching. For many good reasons, be sure that you are informed on everything that is known about the history of those kingdoms; it is important to know this so as to avoid dangers and be able to give greater help to the people there.

Consider using as a reward for the good ministers among them abbacies and other revenues which become vacant and which might be at the patriarch's disposal.

The bishops should set aside all pomp and comforts and as far as possible personally do the work of pastors. They and their assistants should avoid all appearance of avarice.

The patriarch will have his council to consult with on important matters; after hearing them he will make his decisions. The council should consist of four men, including, for the present, the two coadju-

---

[10] Marqos died in 1530. At his death a Portuguese adventurer named João Bermudes, the pseudo-patriarch mentioned by Ignatius, tried to get himself recognized as metropolitan, both by the negus and by Pope Clement VII.

tors. Normally, especially at the beginning, they should stay with the patriarch; if they leave him for important business, they should return soon after. If one does happen to be absent for a short time, the other three and the patriarch should choose a substitute.

If one of the four designated in Portugal dies or is unavoidably absent, the patriarch and other members of the Society sent with him should choose another person by majority vote.

Once dioceses are set up, consider which local men would make good bishops and archbishops. If there are any such, they could be consecrated; otherwise, write to the King of Portugal and to Rome so that others can be sent from here.

It also seems that beneficed curacies ought to be established and given to persons of good lives and sound learning, as far as possible. Their revenues should be assigned to them and they should be conferred by the choice of the bishops with the approval of the patriarch.

Attempts should be made, tactfully, to discredit the book of *Abitilis*,[11] which they claim contains the canons of the apostles. It is the source of their abuses and excesses. It is because they consider it a canonical Scripture from which there can be no dispensation that it has so far been impossible to undo their errors.

Since the people are so given to fasting and usually do not eat before nightfall, you should consider eating apart, so that you will not give nor they receive bad example.

You should visit the churches of canons and the monasteries of religious of both sexes, examining what reform is needed and providing it so far as possible.

All these remarks will serve as guidelines. However, the patriarch should not feel obliged to act in conformity with them, but rather with whatever may be dictated to him by discerning charity in the light of existing circumstances and by the anointing of the Holy Spirit, who must chiefly direct him in everything. Thus, in your own prayers and those of the whole Society and of the faithful both here and there, we must urge our petitions before the clemency and goodness of God, so

---

[11] This is the name which St. Ignatius gives to an Arabic anthology, entitled in the original tongue *I'tiraf al-aba*, and in the Ethiopic version *Hajmanota Abau* (Faith of the Fathers). It contains passages from the fathers from St. Irenaeus to the Alexandrian patriarch Cristodulus (1047–1077).

that he will take pity on these nations and deign to restore them to the unity of his holy Church and to the true religion and path of salvation for their souls, for his own honor and glory.

✠

To Everard Mercurian

Rome, May 2, 1555

(Letter 5360: IX:30–31; in Italian)

A scholastic had committed a public and scandalous breach of some sort. As Ignatius often did, he left the choice of penance to the guilty person, who in this instance chose the pilgrimage and public discipline mentioned in the letter to the rector at Perugia.

The peace of Christ.

The bearer of this is Brother Tomasso Romano. The Lord has deigned to come to his aid by making him recognize his faults and giving him a desire to amend them. It was proposed to him that he should choose some penance in satisfaction for his past behavior, and so he has chosen to return to Perugia as a pilgrim without being given even a farthing, to take a public discipline in the refectory for eight days in the presence of all those in the college, and to cook and do whatever other services Your Reverence decides, so that he can edify all those whom he has scandalized in the past.

No more for now, except to pray the Lord God to deign to give all of us grace to be able to comport ourselves worthily in his holy service, as becomes true religious.

Rome, May 2, 1555

Whenever Your Reverence sees that all who had been disedified by Tomasso are edified by the satisfaction he has already made and by his readiness to fulfill the rest, you can let him off the discipline and not have him continue it for the full eight days, but only for as many as are needed for the edification of our men. When everyone is satisfied with him, Your Reverence can keep him in your community for three more days, during which time such positive signs of regard can be made to him as will be for his greater help. And when he is in good standing with everyone, he should be sent back to Rome, with some travel money to help him on the journey.

Procedure for Dealing with Superiors

May 29, 1555

(Letter 5400a: IX:90–92 in Spanish, and 93–96 in Italian)

Guidelines for representing proposals to superiors, and for repeating the representation where necessary. These guidelines, nos. 1–7, are followed by directives for sending regular reports to Rome. The full text in two versions, Spanish and Italian, has no date, but a partial text exists in a damaged manuscript that has the date given above. The Italian version of the guidelines was destined for the colleges and houses in Italy and Sicily. They were later sent in Spanish, on May 24, 1555, to other members of the Society.

Ihs

Procedure for Dealing with Any Superior

1. Anyone having to deal with a superior should bring the matter well organized, having thought it over himself or consulted with others, depending upon whether it is of greater or lesser importance. However, in small matters, or in urgent ones where there is no time for reflection or consultation, it is left to his own good discretion whether or not to represent a matter to the superior without having consulted or thought it through.

2. After having organized and thought out the matter, he should present it and say, "I thought over this point personally (or with others, as the case may be), and I wondered (or, we gave thought to) whether it might be good this way or that way." In dealing with a superior, he should never say, "It is, or will be, good this way." Instead, he should put it conditionally, asking "whether it is, or will be, good."

3. Once the matter has been presented, it will be up to the superior to decide, or to wait till he has time to study it, or to refer the proposals back to the person or persons who had thought them out, or to name other persons to examine them or decide—depending upon the greater or lesser importance or difficulty of the matter.

4. If the person makes some rejoinder to the superior's decision or remarks, and the superior reaffirms his decision, there should be no further rejoinder or argument for then.

5. If after the superior's decision the person dealing with him thinks that a different course would be better or seems to him to have solid grounds, even when he suspends his own judgment, he may make a representation to the superior three or four hours later or on the following day, asking whether this or that might not be good—always

being careful to use language that excludes any appearance of dissension or argument, and accepting with silence what is decided at that point.

6. However, even where a thing has been decided one or two times, the person may still represent his opinion or thoughts again a month or more later, in the manner already indicated. For with time experience uncovers many things, and things themselves change with time.

7. A person who has dealings with a superior should accommodate himself to the latter's character and natural abilities. He should speak distinctly, audibly, clearly, and whenever possible at a time suitable for the superior.

8. Regarding the guidelines for writing on Saturday (or, for places outside Italy, at other regular or exceptional times for the departure of the post), they should as far as possible not wait until the day itself or the day before and then write in haste. They should try to start organizing and writing the Saturday letter beginning on the previous Sunday and continuing through the whole of Wednesday, leaving as little as possible still to be answered regarding the letters received until then, so that on Thursday, Friday, and Saturday they will be able to handle and answer any important matters that may turn up and need immediate response.

9. Letters should ordinarily be written to the various parts of Italy only once a month (and rectors should be informed of this directive which has been given) except in cases where a shorter interval is required.

10. Letters should be written to more distant regions every three months, except in cases of importance or to take advantage of the post.

11. With regard to receiving persons for the Society in Italy, all the colleges are being sent the following points, which cover the qualities required in persons admitted to the Society; until they have supplied information on all these points, one by one, nobody should be received there or sent here.

12. Nevertheless, if there be persons able to enter who fulfill all the criteria listed, and that in an outstanding and completely indubitable way, they may be received or even sent to Rome if they are of such quality or if there would be such danger in delay (and it will be up to superiors to determine this) that this seems highly advisable. However, it would still be better to advise the general in Rome and await an answer, since it might be all right as regards the persons in question but not for the house in Rome.

13. We are sending everywhere the same points and decisions which have been made for Italy and Sicily (which should always be understood when we speak of Italy). In a general way, it will useful for those in other places to know the practice here, so as to make use of it as best they can. Of course, in places far from Rome, such as other kingdoms, the general need not be consulted before admitting someone or sending him to Rome. The charity and discretion of the commissary or provincial, with whom lower superiors or rectors will consult, will take the place of this consultation; for there could well be cases which would not allow the delay of consulting the general.

14. Provision should be made that copies of this be sent to every place where members of our Society sojourn or reside; and in the register at Rome a notation should be made at the bottom of the page to indicate that this document was sent to each place and was received there. Until word of receipt comes, every letter that is sent should contain a reminder about this mailing and a request for notification of receipt.

15. The same instructions will be sent to the Indies, where the provincial should send it on to the remote parts of his jurisdiction. It can also be sent from Portugal to Brazil and the Congo. However, in such distant regions, especially among infidels and new Christians, while what is written here ought to be implemented as far as possible, it is left to the discretion of those in charge to take into account the condition of the country and other circumstances and act as they think best for the greater glory of God and the greater spiritual benefit of souls.

✠

To Francis Borgia, by commission

Rome, June 13, 1555

(Letter 5427: IX:144; in Spanish)

Borgia took very little care of his health, and the same was true of Araoz. When Córdoba told Ignatius about this, he wrote the following letter to Borgia, appointing a monitor to ensure that he would take care of his health. Ignatius also wrote to Córdoba, telling that after consulting three doctors, he would have the power to give these Jesuits orders about food, sleep, and other bodily needs.

Your Reverence has been somewhat faulted by Father Don Antonio [de Córdoba] for your treatment of your own person; and from other quarters also we understand that you do not treat yourself—your body, I mean—with the same charity you show towards others. You eat badly, overwork, and you do not let others assist you. Consequently, in view of the special charity shown by Father Don Antonio in this regard, Our Father is placing him in charge of Your Reverence's treatment of your body. You will have to put up with this—and so will Father Doctor Araoz, who has also been accused of harshness towards himself. Our Father has given this directive because he wishes to do whatever he can to ensure the strength and health of persons who employ these gifts to render such important service to God our Lord, and because in his view this requires better treatment of the body. Your Reverence will give Father Don Antonio his letters, reading them first yourself if you think it advisable.

June 13, 1555

✠

To Manuel López, by commission

Rome, June 17, 1555

(Letter 5446: IX:180–83; in Spanish)

A newsletter to the rector at Alcalá, with reflections on the sudden death of the Society's friend, Marcellus II, and the election of Paul IV; included also is other news about activities in Rome and Germany. This is a good example of the kind of correspondence among members of the Society that Ignatius much favored, because it aided the members to be more closely bound to one another.

Yhs.

The peace of Christ.

Long before this letter arrives, Your Reverences will have heard how God has taken our Holy Father Marcellus II, of happy memory, to an eternal pontificate, having left him in the toil of his temporal one for only twenty-three days. A happy exchange for him, and for us a great help towards placing in God alone our trust for the fulfillment of our desires for the Church universal and for our Society. If we had to ground this hope on human means, the principal one would have seemed to be this pontiff, who from the moment of his election, by word and example, had no other concern than to reform the Church, and who was so devoted to the Society that the very first time Our Father went to kiss his foot, he requested two of our men to stay with him in the palace for consultation and advice. Masters Laínez and Nadal were assigned to him. He desired to endow our colleges not only in

Rome but far beyond, with all the love that a member of the Society could have had. But then God our Lord took him to himself. Blessed be he who is powerful to raise up as many others as he wishes who will be as good as he, or even better, and "from these stones," etc. [Matt. 3:9].

Four of us had asked Our Father for permission to make a pilgrimage to Our Lady of Loreto to pray for his health: Father Luis Gonçalves, Doctor Loarte, Don Diego de Guzmán, and myself. He granted the permission, but before we arrived there we heard of his death. Thus God gave us more than we asked for: in place of bodily health he gave him that of heaven—and taught us, as I said above, that we should place our trust in him alone.

A few days after our return to Rome, the present Pope was elected. May it please Jesus Christ, our Lord and God, to make him an effective minister and agent of his providence for the universal good of his Church. Your Reverence, together with the members of your community, should earnestly ask this of the divine and supreme Goodness.

There has been no little consolation in the obedience which three envoys of the King and Queen of England have rendered these days to the Holy See and the vicar of Christ our Lord.[12] His Holiness has been giving them high entertainment, as well he might.

The Pope has spoken with warmth about the reform of the Church, saying that he intends to put all the talk into action or die trying. May God our Lord grant that we may see something soon.

Here in Rome we are quite numerous. Even though a number have recently been sent off to various places, there are more than a hundred and twelve in the colleges and sixty to seventy in the house.

We carry on as usual the ministries of confession and preaching in our own church, and elsewhere of giving the Exercises, reconciling enemies, helping long-standing and obstinate sinners out of their condition, teaching catechism, and other corporal and spiritual works of mercy. It would take too long to give all the details.

Though there has been some letup in studies because of the heat, we take constant care to ensure that the exercises go on regularly; and for this country, the attendance is high. Before long we will be sending some young men from the house to the college, all excellent

---

[12] Mary Tudor and her consort, Philip of Spain. The envoys had been sent to Marcellus, but arrived in Rome on the very day of the coronation of the new pope, Paul IV.

subjects, from various nations, whom God has sent us in recent months with a strong desire to follow our Institute. The German College is also doing quite well. Father Nadal has made an agreement with the King of the Romans that forty-eight students will be sent here to the college with their expenses paid; he himself expects to bring others with him. With large numbers coming from the northern nations to our Society and the German College, God our Lord gives us hope that he intends to take pity on those poor nations, living in such great darkness of error. It is difficult to help them except by training laborers who speak their own language.

And while Father Nadal himself does not speak it, he is certainly not idle in that country. After the legate Morone's return for the papal election, he remained behind at the request of the Cardinal of Augsburg to visit the college at Dillingen and our own college in Vienna,[13] as you will see from the copy of his letter if we can get it to you. In Vienna a thing was accomplished through his instrumentality which gave us great consolation, even though we have not had a letter from him about it; however, the Cardinal of Augsburg has heard from two sources that King Maximilian had a preacher whom he much favored and who was a Lutheran and preached Lutheran doctrine in public. Not only was there scandal from the actual harm done, but people were also heartsick at the thought that the King might be pleased with this teaching. We now understand that Master Nadal behaved in such a way that the preacher took flight, in danger of his life for having deceived the king.[14] Not only was the city rid of this plague, but people's minds were left consoled and edified at learning that the King's patronage of this evil man was not because he adhered to his false doctrine, but because he believed him in possession of the true. Praised be God our Lord, who does not abandon his own in the end; and may he be pleased everywhere to increase the knowledge and glory of his holy name. Amen.

Rome, June 17, 1555

Your Reverence's servant in Christ,

Joán de Polanco

✠

---

[13] The cardinal was Otto Truchsess.

[14] Actually, the departure of the preacher, Sebastian Pfauser, had little or nothing to do with Nadal's arrival in Vienna. Rather, some of the preaching of Peter Canisius had contributed to the sudden departure of the Lutheran preacher.

To Diego Miró

Rome, June 20, 1555

(Letter 5471: IX:226f.; in Spanish)

John III of Portugal and his brother, the cardinal infante Enrique, archbishop of Braga, wanted to have the medieval Portuguese Inquisition endowed with greater privileges, similar to those enjoyed by the Spanish Inquisition. The Pope was reluctant to accede to this request. At that point, the King asked the Jesuits to administer the Portuguese Inquisition. The Society owed so much to John III that it could hardly refuse. But Ignatius wanted it made clear that the Pope was ordering them to take on so dangerous a task. (In the end, however, the office went to a Dominican.)

The peace of Christ.

The sovereign grace and love of Christ our Lord be always our help and protection.

From your letter of May 4, I learned of His Highness's inclination to have our Society take charge of the Holy Office of the Inquisition in Lisbon (owing to the death of the person who held the position under the cardinal infante) unless this should be incompatible with our Institute, and also of your reply to His Highness.[15] In truth, this is a matter calling for much consideration, with many weighty reasons on either side. Consequently, besides examining the matter myself and commending it to God our Lord, I asked six men—Master Laínez, Master Salmerón, Master Bobadilla, Doctor Olave, Doctor Madrid, and Master Polanco—to say Mass for three days and reflect and confer about this matter, obtaining information from Luis Gonçalves in addition to the information you sent from there and discussing the matter with him, and afterwards to give me their opinions in writing. The conclusion we finally came to in our Lord is that you should place yourself entirely in His Highness's hands and obey him in whatever he thinks we ought to do for the glory of God our Lord. For inasmuch as this responsibility is not incompatible with our Institute, our Society, which belongs entirely in our Lord to His Highness, cannot rightly refuse this labor in a matter so closely touching his service and the purity of religion in that kingdom.

We think, however, that for the avoidance of many difficulties, it would be good if His Highness were willing to write the Pope asking him to command us to accept this charge. In fact, when His Holiness

---

[15] The cardinal infante was Enrique, the king's brother, who succeeded to the crown after the untimely death of the king's heir, Sebastião.

was dean of the cardinal inquisitors he already wanted the Society to take on a similar responsibility here, and so it will not be something opposed to his thinking. It would also help if His Highness wrote to our protector, Cardinal Carpi, the present dean of the inquisitors, and also to his own ambassador, charging him to handle this matter. However, if he judges it better not to write, we will still do whatever His Highness commands for the glory of God. If he does order us to accept, a few things should be represented to His Highness which, without prejudice to the goal aimed at, will help the Society attend to this holy work better and with more edification. And if His Highness judges it better not to await the Pope's answer, a start might be made by having one or two men serve in this office pro tempore until it could be formally accepted with a commission from His Holiness. But with this representation made, I have written that whatever His Highness desires should be fully complied with.

Referring you for other matters to what Master Polanco writes by my commission, I will say no more, except that I much commend myself to your prayers.

Rome, June 20, 1555

✠

To Alberto Azzolini

Rome, June 29, 1555

(Letter 5500: IX:266f.; in Italian)

The feminine fashions of Venice brought on a case of conscience in the context of a question of jurisdiction. The local Inquisition in that city forbade any priests less than thirty-six years old to hear women's confessions. The Society of Jesus by papal authority had the right to hear anyone's confession. But Ignatius did not want to press the case publicly. So he arranged that the only Jesuit in Venice beyond that minimum age, the forty-five-year-old Father Alberto Azzolini, would be the one to serve as confessor to any women who might seek out the sacrament from the Jesuits.

Alberto was pious and guileless, and in dealing with certain types of questions that came up in confession he had no self-confidence. He had begged Ignatius to take him out of his previous job as rector because, as he said of himself, he was manifestly inept at it. In response to a request from Azzolini for advice, the rector at Venice had urged him in early June 1555 to proceed more courageously in the confessional. Two weeks later, Azzolini wrote to Ignatius, who replied in the following letter. If some of what Ignatius says sounds rigorous to present-day ears, his advice was less rigorous than the common opinions of theologians of his time. And

one need only regard contemporary portraits of women of the nobility to whom
Ignatius was friend and advisor to know that they felt no need in those circum-
stances to go about uncoiffed, dressed in plain muslin gowns, and bereft of jewels.

Jesus

The peace of Christ.

Dear Father Master Alberto:

From a letter of Father Rector we learn that Your Reverence is uneasy about the practice of the women in Venice in matters of dress and personal adornment—and rightly so, for they give occasion (which others frequently take) to offend God our Lord. However, where the practice is general and there neither appears to be nor is there any going beyond the usual custom in the matter itself, nor any intention of sinning or leading others to sin, it is not considered mortally sinful. Indeed, if done by a woman to please her husband, it is not venially sinful. We have written to other places on this matter as follows. Where there is no excessive singularity or going beyond the ordinary and no evil intention, although there might be a degree of vanity in wanting to make a beautiful appearance among other women, etc., they could be absolved the first time with an admonition and some advice. But if they confess this again, especially if they receive the sacraments regularly, they must be gotten to give up this vanity and cut back these bad practices as much as possible. If they refuse, you could say that you will absolve them this time but not in the future, and that they should look for another confessor if they do not want to withdraw from their vanity, since even though not condemned as a mortal sin, it still is a great imperfection, and the Society does not want to be involved with people who are unwilling to withdraw from imperfection. However, since Your Reverence may be letting your holy zeal lead you astray, you should follow the judgment of the rector in such matters, since he too is able to be informed about things known and seen outside of confession; and you should avoid being fearful or anxious in matters where he thinks you should not.

I will say no more, except that charity and the desire to help souls usually makes the members of the Society courageous, and so God helps them. I pray that he will impart himself to Your Reverence with an abundance of his gifts.

Rome, June 29, 1555

✠

To Francisco Jiménez de Miranda, by commission

Rome, July 11, 1555

(Letter 5525: IX:308–11; in Spanish)

The abbot of Salas in Spain lived at Rome in illicit wedlock, squandering his church incomes. His brother had gotten him to renege on his original promise to endow the Jesuit college in Burgos. The Jesuits were convinced that the main obstacle was his sinful life, and they long campaigned in vain for his reform. Finally Ignatius had Polanco write this letter.

Yhs.

My Very Reverend and Distinguished Lord in Jesus Christ:

Having failed to gain an audience with Your Worship, even despite my attempts by messenger, note, or personal calls, I might easily tire if it were my own interests I was pursuing. But since I am sincerely pursuing a matter of God's service and your own salvation, I may not—if there is aught of charity in me—tire or fail to attempt by letter what I was unable to do by word of mouth.

Sir, what concerns me is not starting the college in Burgos; since it is very much a work for God's service, he will bring it about one way or another in good time. And although I would like Your Worship to be the founder, and we have done all we could on our side in conformity with your wishes—Our Father even offering to let Your Lordship do what you wish with our present house—I have nothing to request in this regard. Rather, what concerns me is your continued delays in the matter of your soul, in which I see a great and present danger. Loving you as I do in Christ our Lord and longing for your salvation, for which I daily beseech God in my Masses and prayers, I cannot help being deeply afflicted until I see you traveling on the path that leads to it. I see Your Worship's age; I see your state of health; I see that your ailments are such that I fear death may overtake you when we least expect it; and I would be extremely distressed if it found you unprovided with the penance you must do for your sins and the good and holy works needed in order to obtain eternal happiness.

My lord, this is no time for dissimulation on the part of those who love you. You should consider, not as your friend or servant, but as the deadly enemy of your soul any person who comes to you with flattering words, particularly words that reassure you and get you to continue in your sins. What Your Worship needs is penance—and no slight amount of it. This entails not just giving up and repenting your sin but also making satisfaction for past sins and relieving your conscience regarding your maladministration of so many church properties. I am not talking about acts against justice in the external forum, but about the fact that any church properties beyond what are needed to maintain you in accord with your state actually belong to the poor and to pious works; to deprive them of it, say the holy doctors, is an act of serious injustice. Your having been given possession or enjoyment of these revenues by the Rota or the Pope's Signaturas will not suffice for you to give an adequate accounting of yourself when you stand before the tribunal of Christ our Lord, who will demand of you a strict accounting of all that you took from the Church.[16] Very soon you will have to appear in person before his infinite justice, to await an absolute and unappealable sentence either to a happy and blessed life full of joy and consolation and inestimable honor, or to a wretched death and eternal damnation full of all the miseries and torments which the rigor and severity of divine justice has ready for those who die without having repented and made satisfaction for their sins.

Your Worship does not know whether this particular judgment upon your person will take place in September, or this month, or tonight. Many people with better health and more regular personal habits than yourself have lain down at night without a worry and not reached morning alive. For the love of Jesus Christ and by the blood he shed to redeem your soul, do not place it in this peril. Prepare to give a good accounting of yourself and of what God our Lord has given you to administer. Since he has been so mercifully patient with you up till now, do not let the brief time of life you have left slip by unprofitably, or you may find yourself in a situation where you would trade all you have and the worth of the entire world for a single hour in which to repent and do good, and it will be denied you, should you fail to make use of the time which the wisdom of God had allotted you.

Your Worship must pardon my frankness. Love constrains me; I do not want my conscience to reproach me for failing in the duty of a person devoted to your service and anxious for your eternal salvation, for which I pray every day to God's supreme clemency, unworthy though I am. Moreover, I am convinced that you have no one to remind you of your obligations, and I know that you have people reminding and telling you of the opposite—besides what the flesh and the devil add on their own.

---

[16] The Rota was a church court of appeals that at the time had jurisdiction over all ecclesiastical cases.

So great is my wish to see Your Worship dispose yourself for the grace of God our Lord by doing good and pious works that if you thought our college ought to be put off, I would be of the opinion that you should undertake any other good work that would bring relief to your conscience and your own greater merit before God our Lord. But it would not be such a work to bestow wealth on relatives who already have more than enough in accord with their state, or to erect memorials of little spiritual value or help to the common good. You should give to poor and pious works; this is what builds eternal memorials in heaven that can be enjoyed by the one who erects them, whereas vain worldly memorials earn a person torment and severe suffering. Remember that you are the steward, not the master, of your possessions, and that you will have to give an account of them. These remarks will suffice for a person of your intelligence.

Here we do not cease praying to God's goodness for Your Worship, nor shall we cease doing so, whether you thank us or not; for God is our end, and I have been for many years Your Worship's chaplain, although I doubt you consider me such or believe that my intentions are what they are. I am satisfied to have God as witness, and my own conscience. May the Holy Spirit be with Your Worship.

From Your Worship's house here, July 11, 1555

✠

To Cristóbal de Mendoza

Rome, July 14, 1555

(Letter 5535: IX:322f.; in Italian)

Ignatius could be firm in deciding that someone was not an apt candidate for membership in the Society, and he dismissed a good number of such men. But he was equally firm in wanting it to be done with kindness, in such a way as to protect the reputation of the man in question and to leave the person dismissed well disposed toward the Society.

The peace of Christ.

The bearer of this is Giovanni Antonio di Mauro. He was admitted to the Society on probation as a student, but is unable to do the studies. He has been tried out in various colleges in Rome and elsewhere, and his head has suffered severely thereby. He was willing to stay on and serve in the house, but in view of the extreme youthfulness of his age and behavior (stemming more from other causes than from

any bad will) it has seemed preferable for God's service and the edification of the others that he not remain in the house; and so we are sending him home. When he has matured in years and behavior, he might
eventually be reaccepted, since he is not being sent away because of any
unhappiness on his part or for any notable sin; he is being sent home
because in his present state he is not suited for our Society's Institute,
even though numerous trials have been made to see if he could control
himself and calm down. We strongly commend him to Your Reverences,
asking you to give him any spiritual help you can, for we all truly love
him in Christ our Lord and wish for his welfare, even if we were unable
to keep him here at the cost of disedification to the house.

That is all, except that Your Reverence may inform his family of
the contents of this letter, or send it to them.

We earnestly commend ourselves to the prayers of Your Reverence and the other brethren.

Rome, July 14, 1555

✠

To Jerónimo Doménech, by commission

July 18, 1555

(Letter 5544: IX:336–38; in Spanish)

*This letter typically shows the variety of affairs that daily occupied Ignatius. Here,
in a letter to the provincial of Sicily, Ignatius dealt with a change of assignment for
Laínez that greatly displeased the viceroy, a great friend and benefactor of the
Society. However, Ignatius could not change this assignment because the Pope himself
had requested it. Here Ignatius dealt also with the attempt (ultimately unsuccessful)
to ransom Jean de La Goutte, a French Jesuit captured by the Turks, as well as
with the ongoing saga of the young Jesuit Ottaviano Cesari and his mother's repeated attempts to get him to leave the Society.*

Jesús

The peace of Christ.

We have received Your Reverence's letters of June 17 from Poliz-
zi and July 7 from Messina. As regards Master Laínez, you will see from
the answer to the magistrates, a copy of which is being sent, what Our
Father is able to do. Of course, for the reasons which you mention, and
especially for the pleasure you say it would give His Excellency, Our

Father wishes he were able to comply.[17] But, after all, we must obey His Holiness and will have to be patient with his inconveniencing particular works that are just getting established in order to provide for the universal good. The college at Naples will also suffer badly from the absence of Master Salmerón, who has been selected for the diet and for Poland. Although the founding of his college was dependent upon him, he too will trust that God our Lord will provide by some other means.

The letter of Master Jean de La Goutte written from Jerba on Ascension Day has reached us. We were consoled in the Lord to know he was alive and in a definite place where he can be ransomed, although we were grieved at the terrible and inhuman treatment he is receiving. May Christ our Lord be served in everything. Your Reverence does not write that you have made efforts to find the slave they are asking for in exchange for him. If this involves Don Juan Osorio, it will soon be known at his house.[18] Our opinion here regarding the matter is that the Turk Velli, or any other whose disposition gives reason to hope for his conversion to Christianity, should not be handed over, but that we should instead pay the required sum. If there is no hope of the Turk's becoming a Christian, then efforts should be made through Don Juan de Vega to exchange him for Master Jean de La Goutte, paying his owner whatever he asks and values him at. If the Turk cannot be found, it would seem proper that a compensation be sent in sequins or some other customary means to the one asking for him, and that a person be commissioned to effect the ransom in the best way possible—since the Turks had no right under the treaty to take him captive, since he is a Frenchman. It does not seem unreasonable to expect that he should be surrendered for what he cost. But if a hundred pieces are not enough, we should pay up to a hundred and fifty or, if need be, two or three hundred. In fine, Our Father says that he must not remain there for lack of money and must by all means be ransomed this summer. This matter must not be handled remissly. Whatever expenditure is made there we shall later see how to divide up, so that Sicily is not burdened. Now that Your Reverence understands Our Father's mind, make every effort to act accordingly.

I shall add no more, except that if you think Ottaviano [Cesari] is wasting his time there and ought to be continuing with his studies, you can send him to Rome once the Turkish fleet has returned home and the sea is safe. Here we have no fear of his being coerced by His

---

[17] Polanco refers to Juan de Vega, the Spanish viceroy of Sicily.

[18] Osorio was a counselor of the viceroy of Sicily.

Holiness or anyone else. There will be no need for him to visit his mother in Naples; he should come to Rome, and if His Holiness orders that his vocation be examined here, we will obey.

May God our Lord give all of us his grace to be steadfast in his holy service and always to know and do his holy will.

Rome, July 18, 1555

✠

To Alfonso Salmerón

Rome, July 27, 1555

(Letter 5564: IX:374–78; in Italian)

Salmerón was sent to the meeting of the Imperial Diet of 1555, which turned out to be of immense importance to the religious future of Germany. In the event, it clearly marked the inability of the emperor, Charles V, despite his best efforts, to bring to an end the religious disunity of the empire. His attempted military pacification of Germany was frustrated when the Protestant princes defeated the imperial forces. Charles appointed his brother, Ferdinand, who was king of the Romans and later would be Emperor Ferdinand I, to negotiate a political settlement to the religious conflict. The result was the Peace of Augsburg and the principle "Cujus regio ejus religio," meaning that the religion of a particular ruler was to be determinative of whether a state was to be exclusively Catholic or Protestant.

As to Poland, although King Sigismund II Augustus never broke with Rome, much of the country at this time was in danger of turning Protestant, with a good number of burghers opting for Lutheranism and a good number of the nobility for Calvinism. At the end of his visit there with the legate, Salmerón was strongly of the opinion that, as matters then stood, the country would only with great difficulty be saved for Catholicism. It was only in the 1560s that the reinvigoration of the Catholic Church in Poland began.

Ihs.

For Father Salmerón
Reminders for the Diet

First, write down and keep firmly in mind what His Holiness told you of his purpose and desire in this mission, and strive to carry it out.

Discuss with the Most Reverend Nuncio, the bishop of Verona [Aloisio Lippomani], and think over for yourself the best means for obtaining the Apostolic See's aims at the diet. Get information from the apostolic nuncio [Zacharía Delfini] to the King of the Romans [Ferdinand], and if he or the bishop of Verona thinks good, make attempts—conforming yourself to the latter—to speak with the King of the Romans and any other nobles and persons of quality.

If you have an opportunity to debate or confer with heretics, do so with all possible modesty, for this is no less necessary than learning.

If you have an opportunity to write something on a controverted point, with the approval of the bishop of Verona, you should do that as well. See if there is the possibility of preaching or giving Latin lectures on topics pertinent to what the Apostolic See is seeking at the diet.

Remember that the King of the Romans' confessor [Urban Weber, bishop of Laibach in Slovenia], who is deeply Catholic, a good person, and a friend to us, could be an excellent channel for anything related to the King. The same holds for the chancellor [Jacob] Jonas.

Besides the business of the diet, try to obtain implementation of the promise which the King of the Romans made to the nuncio to His Majesty's court and to Master Nadal, that he would send forty-eight or fifty young German students, having them provided for by the bishops of their states, with additional help from himself. His Majesty can be told what edification he has given on this score at the court here, where this resolve which he expressed to the nuncio and to Master Nadal has become publicly known, etc.

For purposes of holding discussions and showing written documents, it will be good to take a copy of the bull for the German College, which speaks quite well about the success they are having, etc.

Through the bishop of Verona, the bishop of Laibach, or whomever you prefer, it will be good to get letters of recommendation from His Majesty for the King and Queen of Poland, etc., in which His Majesty might mention how he finds himself served by our men in the college at Vienna in matters of the Catholic religion. For other matters, he could refer to the bishop; and His Reverend Lordship, if he finds an opportunity, might speak about starting a college.

If you come across Master Nadal en route, he can give information on many matters, etc.

Jhs.

For Poland

As was said above, remember what His Holiness told you orally and bend all your efforts to achieving it.

Try to be supplied with information from here and on the way regarding the affairs of that kingdom, so as the better to serve God our Lord there.

Try to obtain the goodwill of the King [Sigismund II Augustus], his mother the Queen [Bona Sforza], and his wife [Catherine, daughter of Ferdinand, king of the Romans] (the letters you bear will lay the groundwork for this), and similarly of the other great nobles of the realm, by all the best means available.

Reflect for yourself and confer with the Reverend Bishop on steps for aiding the Catholic religion; and try to implement them as far as you can, whether in private conversations and exhortations, in debates, in preaching or lecturing on matters pertinent to the end pursued, or in writing as well—conforming yourself in all matters to the opinion of the bishop, with whom you should have "one heart," etc.

By the example of your life and by attending to our Society's regular works of mercy, try to spread that good reputation, etc.

By interceding with the nuncio in legitimate matters, try to win the minds of persons who seek some favor which it is in His Lordship's power to grant.

Since the corruption of religion stems in large part from evil preachers and schoolmasters, strive to obtain a rule (as far as is possible) that only Catholics may receive these offices.

If there is such a lack of learned Catholics that provision cannot be made with people of the country, it would seem expedient to attempt to start a college like the one in Vienna, where not only would Catholic doctrine be preached and the sacraments duly administered, but there would also be classes in all the faculties, beginning with the lowest, in which numerous persons could be brought up and taught by our Society and then later perform the same office themselves in many territories.

And since we have no one in the Society who knows Polish, it would be good to try to recruit some good subjects for the Society, sending them to Vienna or here, so that they could then be sent back to their country to produce fruit in their mother tongue.

If there should be no prospect of starting a college of our Society in Poland, but if the King or the old Queen [Bona Sforza] (who is very rich) seems disposed to pay the expenses of some talented Poles and send them to Rome like the students at the German College, or to be by themselves under the care of the Society, it would be good to send some talented men with their provisions. This could also be pursued with the prelates, lords, and persons who might do this—but always proceeding in such a way as to make clear how simply and disinterestedly our Society proceeds.

For this and for other purposes it will be good to take along the bulls of our Society and of the German College, as indicated above.

It might be that certain vacant ecclesiastical holdings at the nuncio's disposal could be used for founding a college, or at least for funding some men to be sent for studies at the German College.

Write here what readiness you find for bearing fruit in that realm, particularly by means of our Society.

Take care that N. has a good opinion of N. and holds him in esteem, etc.[19]

Your Reverence should try by means of Master Canisius or whomever you prefer, if things in Prague are in order, to have His Royal Majesty write His Holiness a word asking him to send with his blessing the persons here who will be needed for the college; likewise [write] to Our Father.

☩

To Pedro Camps

Rome, August 29, 1555

(Letter 5653: IX:507f.; in Spanish)

The recipient of this letter and his brother Dimas, archdeacon of Barcelona, were close friends and supporters of the Society's presence and work there, especially the foundation of a college. As to the "opposition that we meet," it included the usual problems, such as misunderstandings of the nature of the Society, unhappiness on the part of other institutions living on alms, territorial rights of a parish in which the college might be located, and privileges of mendicant orders that had to be taken into account.

My Lord in our Lord:

---

[19] It is not certain to whom Ignatius is referring here, but it may, perhaps, be King Sigismund having a good opinion of Pope Paul IV.

May the sovereign grace and eternal love of Christ our Lord be always our help and support.

From Your Worship's letter of last May 13, I see your joy in Christ our Lord that the members of the Society have settled in Barcelona with a house and church of their own. It is evident that your joy stems from the great charity given you by God towards us in particular; he himself will be its reward. I too find no small consolation in the Lord in that our efforts for his service in your city are a source of satisfaction to persons to whom we must earnestly wish it, along with every service for God's glory. The opposition that we met and still meet with is nothing new to us; in fact, from our experience in other places we trust that the service rendered to Christ our Lord in Barcelona will be all the greater, the more are the obstacles thrown up by him who constantly strives to impede his service and who to this end urges on various people who—we must believe with good intentions but bad information—without understanding it, oppose what they think ought to be opposed. I am confident in our Lord that the college there will not be disappointed in the help and support they look for from yourself and the archdeacon, even if it were offered with no other words beyond those which always display your love and charity.

For the living and dead that you commend to us, we shall do part of what we owe through our prayers; may they be heard by the divine and sovereign Goodness. And may it please him to give all of us his abundant grace always to know his most holy will and entirely to fulfill it.

Rome, August 29, 1555

✠

To Juana de Valencia

Rome, September 5, 1555

(Letter 5683: IX:552f.; in Spanish)

A letter of appreciation (and a glowing report) to a Spanish lady who had generously supported her son's vocation to the Society. She was a member of the house of Manrique de Lara, the family of the duke of Najera, viceroy of Navarre, under whom Ignatius had served until he was wounded at Pamplona. The young man, very rich and a page at Philip II's court, had been drawn to the Society during a meeting with Laínez. He lived a happy and productive life as a Jesuit before dying in 1588.

Jesus

My Lady in our Lord:

May the sovereign grace, etc.

Your letter brought me great consolation in our Lord. It showed me that the same spirit that moved your son Don Fadrique to follow this Institute and way of life that he is following in our Society has also moved you to find contentment in his decision. This is a proof that your great love for him partakes less of the tenderness of flesh and blood than of the spirit and charity by which we desire for those we love genuine and eternal goods rather than the temporal and perishable ones of this life. I can tell you with assurance that as far as we have been able to judge by experience till now, there is good reason for anyone who loves Don Fadrique to be consoled at seeing him in his present state of life. For besides his peace and happiness, it seems that every day God our Lord gives him an increase of his grace and virtue, by which he gives all of us great edification, and a hope that his Divine Majesty will be greatly served and glorified in him. He is also getting into his studies very well and is making more than ordinary progress. We are consequently highly satisfied with him; God our Lord be praised.

I have written what we think about him, knowing that it would bring you consolation. If our Society can be of service to you in any way, we would be only too glad to have you command us with every confidence.

And so I will say no more, except that I beg the divine and supreme Goodness to deign to give all of us his abundant grace, so that we may always know his most holy will and perfectly fulfill it.

Rome, September 5, 1555

✠

To Francis Borgia

Rome, September 17, 1555

(Letter 5736: IX:626f.; in Spanish)

This is one of three letter to Francis Borgia about raising money for the Roman College. Founded in 1551, it was dear to Ignatius and increasingly in need of financial resources to sustain it in its rapid growth. The "principal men of the house" referred to in this letter were Laínez, Polanco, and Christóbal de Madrid. They, along with Ignatius, recommended that Borgia, at that time commissary in Spain and a man with many important contacts, be entrusted with the responsibility of enlisting rich and powerful people there on behalf of the college. Polanco wrote two letters for Borgia to use. The first described the academic, personal, and financial status of the college; the second suggested ways that Borgia might raise money, offered advice on how to solicit it and whom to approach, for example, people such as the Emperor, various nobles, and well-off citizens. Ignatius then wrote this third letter, a succinct example of his way of acting, simultaneously both completely confiding in God and fully employing every human means that God had provided.

Ihus.

May the sovereign grace and eternal love of Christ our Lord be always our protection and help.

Inasmuch as in all matters I look to God our Lord to see what it pleases him that I should do; and considering it a mistake to trust and hope in any means or human efforts by themselves; and also considering it an unsafe procedure to hand over the whole thing to God our Lord without being willing to avail myself of what he has given me, for I deem in our Lord that I ought to employ both parts, desiring nothing else in all things but his greater praise and glory—I therefore ordered that the principal men of the house should meet together to see better in the Lord what should be done regarding the college and its students, as you will see from what the persons there write. For my own part, I am convinced, with complete tranquility of my soul, that two things are for God's greater glory. The first is that you, with great care, should take very special charge of this work. The second is that whatever means you judge best in the Lord will be judged wholly such by myself, so that whatever you judge right in his Divine Majesty will be judged by me as altogether best and most expedient, inasmuch as your will is the same as mine and you will be more informed about affairs there and about the princes, regarding whom you will be informed by those who write, as we also send complete information about what is taking place here.

I conclude, praying God our Lord, by his infinite and supreme goodness, to grant us his very abundant grace, so that we may know his most holy will and entirely fulfill it.

Rome, September 17, 1555

✠

Points Dictated to Juan Felipe Vito

October 1555

(XII, Appendix 6, no. 6., 659–61; in Spanish)

These points exist in a manuscript in the Jesuit archives in Rome under the heading Collect. de Instit., I, and are found in Ribadeneira's Life of Ignatius. Another such manuscript exists in the Royal Library at Brussels, sign. n.2847. It begins thus: "In the year before our Father died, he called Father John Philipp Vito, who helped Father Polanco in the secretariat, and said to him, 'Write that I want to say to the Society what I think on the subject of obedience'; and he dictated the following points."

1. At the entrance into religion, or upon entering it, I ought to be resigned in and for all things in the presence of God our Lord and of my superior.

2. I ought to desire to be governed and guided by my superior, looking to the denial of my own judgment and understanding.

3. In all things where there is no sin I should do his will and not my own.

4. There are three ways of obeying. The first is when I am commanded in virtue of holy obedience; this is good. The second, when I am ordered to do this or that; this is better. The third, when I do this or that at a mere sign from the superior, even though he neither commands nor orders me; this is much more perfect.

5. I should take no notice of whether my superior is the highest, middle, or lowest, but find all my devotion in obedience because he is in the place of God, our Lord; for in making distinctions here the force of obedience is lost.

6. Should I think that what the superior commands me is against my conscience or sinful, and the superior thinks otherwise, I should believe him unless the matter is demonstrably wrong. If I cannot bring myself to this, I should at least suspend my own judgment and understanding and leave the matter to the judgment of one, two, or three persons. If I cannot attain this, I am far from perfection and the qualities requisite in a real religious.

7. In a word, I should not belong to myself but to him who created me and to the one holding his place, letting myself be led and governed as a ball of wax lets itself be drawn by a thread, both as to writing or receiving letters and to speaking with these or those persons, placing all my devotion in doing as I am bidden.

8. I should be like a dead body, which has neither will nor understanding; or like a little crucifix which allows itself to be moved from one side to another without difficulty; or finally, I should be like a staff in the hand of an old man, who may put me where he pleases and

where I can be of most help to him. Thus, I must be ready to help and serve my religious order in any way I am commanded.

9. I should not ask, request, or petition the superior to send me to this or that place or assign me to this or that work, but present my thoughts and desires to him, and having done so, drop them to the ground and leave to the superior the decision and command, ready to judge and hold as best whatever he judges and commands.

10. However, in matters that are good and of less moment, one may request permission; for example, to go to make the stations, or to ask spiritual favors and the like—ready to consider that whether the superior grants it or not, that will be best.

11. The same is true with regard to poverty. Considering nothing as my own, I should look upon myself, as regards whatever I have for my use, as if clothed and adorned like a statue, which makes no resistance when or because its coverings are taken away.

✠

To Simão Rodrigues

Rome, October 12, 1555

(Letter 5799: IX:707f.; in Spanish)

Rodrígues was living in a hermitage at Bassano, still in a rebellious and resentful mood at his removal as provincial of Portugal. Letters from Rome were answered rudely. In March 1555, Bobadilla was sent to tell him that Ignatius was unwilling to let him return to Portugal. More recriminations followed. In July Nadal visited him and urged him to accept those decisions. Rodrígues insisted on the justice of his cause and on the respect due to one of the founders of the Society. In early September Nadal returned for further talks. At that point Rodrígues had a change of heart. He wrote to Ignatius, admitted that he was at fault, spoke of Ignatius as his father and asked for a "plenary indulgence with remission of guilt and penalty [hence that phrase in Ignatius's reply] and a blessing powerful enough to get to these mountains of Bassano, where exactly eighteen years ago you came to see me when I was at death's door. You will remember. God gave me then through your prayers health of body. Ask now through your prayers that he give me health of soul." Ignatius replied with joy and warmth.

May the sovereign grace and eternal love, etc.

I received your letter of September 4 and heard also from Master Nadal by word of mouth what was best to be done with regard to your person. Loving you very much in the Lord as I do, I am greatly consoled in him by any news of your doing well. As for the acknowledgement and the prompt willingness to obey which you show, I give thanks to God our Lord. May he deign to grant you the plenary indulgence with remission of guilt and penalty which you ask of me, for I on my part have always been and am quite ready to forget bygones, especially with one whom I have always loved so much, to God's glory. Indeed, I think I shall go much beyond rather than fall short of what you ask in your letter. Your residence, since you are doing well at the hermitage there, will be in that region—or in Padua or Venice, wherever you think it best and will be most consoling to you. We are writing to those in charge of the colleges there and of our houses to provide properly for your personal needs, while from this end even more is being done than what our present great necessity here would seem to allow—but we must believe that God's sovereign wisdom will direct everything as he sees will best enable us all to serve and glorify him and thereby attain our ultimate and supreme good.

Wherever you are, I would like you to be mindful of helping the souls that have cost Christ our Lord so dear, in accord with our profession, even if only through private conversation and exhortation—in short, in whatever way you are conveniently able.

That is all for now, except to beg God our Lord to keep you in his holy grace and give to all of us the grace always to know and fulfill his most holy will.

Rome, October 12, 1555

✠

To the Relatives of Silvestro Landini

Rome, October 18, 1555

(Letter 5816: IX:727f.; in Spanish)

Landini was a priest when he entered the Society in 1544, and rapidly became known as an extraordinarily effective preacher. When he died in 1554 during his mission on Corsica, Ignatius made the mistake of ceding his property to his sisters, whose husbands began a bitter quarrel over the division. In a very blunt letter, Ignatius threatens to reclaim the money himself unless they come to an agreement.

Jhs.

May the sovereign grace, etc.

Last year I wrote to Your Excellencies out of the desire inspired in me by fraternal charity to see peace and harmony among you, for which I felt a special responsibility because the occasion of your quarreling was apparently the property of our departed Don Silvestro. While I could have taken this property away from you all, I preferred not to do so, but to be generous instead and to leave these temporal goods to be divided among yourselves—never imagining they could be for you an occasion of eternal evil. It is certainly most distressful to hear that the brothers of such a servant of God could be so unlike him, destroying charity and peace among yourselves for the sake of property which was ceded to you for the greater service of God and in aid of this very charity, peace, and union among yourselves. And when I heard of the scandals that have ensued, I decided to let you know by this letter that I propose to do all I can to remove the cause of this evil from you; and I think I am in a position to do more than what the present holder of the property will like unless I hear that you have come to an agreement and follow a course which is appropriate between brother and sister. For I do not believe that it would be pleasing to God our Lord for me, when able to remove the cause for the feud by removing the property, to leave you with the one by leaving you with the other. And so, my dear friends in our Lord Jesus Christ, by the blood and life of him who died on the cross to bring you unity and peace, and by the dear memory of your brother and ours, Don Silvestro, I urge that you find a way to be reconciled, dividing this property according to the judgment of some capable arbitrators chosen by the two sides, and that each of you place a higher value on harmony and peace than on the interest or utility sought from the property of this good servant of God. And if you do not agree on this quickly and if I hear of more scandals like the past ones, be quite sure that I will do all I can from my side not to betray the intention and final will of the departed, in the way I have indicated above.

And so that is all, except that I pray the divine and supreme Goodness to grant to all of us grace always to know his most holy will and perfectly to fulfill it.

Rome, October 18, 1555

✠

To Those Sent from Rome

Rome, October 18, 1555

(Letter 5817: IX:729–31; in Italian)

The extreme poverty of the Roman and German Colleges compelled Ignatius to disperse some of their students. There follow detailed travel instructions for men dispatched to northern Italy and for others sent to pass through Genoa on their way to Portugal.

Instruction for All Those Sent to Various Places

1. On the way from Rome to Florence, the superior of all the others will be Master Lorenzo Scorzini, who will be obeyed both by those of the Society and by those from the German College.

2. He should see that the weaker ones go first and are less burdened, riding in the panniers. He should have special care of Bernardo the Japanese and Augustinicho, for they are frail, and of Francesco Alessandro for the same reason, and of the others as he sees their need, such as himself and Mario [Beringucci]. He should be mindful of the Germans, particularly Mark [Weber]; and if in addition to the six places in the panniers it is necessary to get another or to hire a post horse for a few miles to relieve one or another of them, he may do so.

3. He should take care that they all give edification by their example and conversation; and he will decide if one or the other who so desires should be allowed to preach in the squares or in the inns. He may also allow begging on the road or in the towns, directing by whom and when this should be done for their greater spiritual help.

4. In the inns, if possible, he should see that all stay together in adjoining rooms and that he is where he can keep track of them all. And since Augustino is small, he should keep him further away from strangers than the others.

5. When they get to Florence and go to our college, the rector will see whom he can put up in the house, and arrange for the others as best he can during their stay in Florence, although not at his own expense.

6. The rector will also make efforts by himself or through friends to find a good way to send to Genoa the fourteen men destined there. These will include Giovanni Pioneo, to whom a thick cloak will be given like that worn by mules; and since he is ill equipped with what is necessary against the cold, he should be provided for from the expenses of those going to Genoa. If they find a way of going by water to Pisa and from there to Genoa, and the route is considered safe, they may do this, or else go by land to Pisa, or even to Lerici, whichever they are advised by friends familiar with the situation.

7. They should try to collect the money which will be given them for a bill of exchange right away, or which the rector of Florence, to

whom the bill will be sent ahead by courier, will have already collected for them—having also made arrangements for the rest of their trip so as to shorten their stay there.

8. Those who are to stay in Florence—Master Lorenzo [Scorzini], Andreas [Piessino] the Bohemian, and Mark the German—will be lodged immediately at the house. Kolman [Kheysther] and Sebastian [Molitor] the Germans, who are going to Bologna and Ferrara, will be given one gold scudo for travel money, and told that this is for their ordinary expenses and not for horses (if they want to hire a horse occasionally, they can do it out of their other money); and anything left over when they get to our college in Bologna will be for Kolman on his further journey to Ferrara. This travel money will also be taken from the bill of exchange which is cashed for those going to Genoa; and the two Germans should be told how they are to proceed.

9. When they leave Florence for Genoa, Gaspare de Urbino will be the head of the others, with Ruggiero from Modena and Girolamo Fontana as his companions and coadjutors. They will be given this same instruction so as to observe as far as possible the directives provided for Master Lorenzo. The rector at Florence may give them additional instructions for the trip to Genoa, and the others will be under the obedience of Gaspar and his two coadjutors, just as they were to obey Master Lorenzo on the way to Florence.

10. Arriving in Genoa, they will go straight to our college. Balthasar the Bohemian will stay there, and Giulio [Fazio] given to them as a companion in his place. They will be taken to the place assigned for them, where they will spend what they need from the money left over from the trip, or other money which they get in Genoa from another bill of exchange; and they will await the arrival of Father Master Nadal and Father Luis Gonçalves, and at that point follow the instructions they are given.

✠

To Isabel de Vega

Rome, October 20, 1555

(Letter 5825: X:5-7; in Spanish)

The Vega family, Juan, the former imperial ambassador to Rome and later viceroy of Sicily, as well as his wife, Leonor, and their daughter, Isabel, were among those most devoted to Ignatius and the Jesuits. As a matter of fact, more letters written by Ignatius to Isabel are extant than to any other of the many women who were his correspondents. This letter of 1555, written while Ignatius was ill, was the last of a series of fourteen that had begun in 1548. Here Ignatius consoles Isabel at the untimely death of a young cousin, Fernando de Silva. The duke and his affairs mentioned below refer to a lawsuit in which her husband, the Duke de Luna, was a party. Rumor had it that Philip II was about to replace Juan de Vega as viceroy; her uncle Hernando de Vega was probably going to go to the court of the Emperor at Brussels. As for the Jesuit college at Bivona in Sicily, which the family was helping to establish, Isabel was so looking forward to its opening and so devoted to it that she even took care to choose the dinnerware for the Jesuit community. Ignatius understandably assures her that he is doing his best for the school.

Jhs.

My Lady in our Lord:

May the sovereign grace and eternal love of Christ our Lord greet and visit Your Ladyship with his most holy gifts and spiritual graces.

I received Your Ladyship's letter of August 10 somewhat late, and poor health has further delayed my answer, although not the prayers and Masses which you requested for the soul of Señor Don Fernando de Silva; may God keep him in heavenly glory. Even though death allowed him no time to avail himself of the holy sacraments, we may trust that divine Providence supplied for this out of the abyss of its infinite mercy, where the sacraments and all the other means of our spiritual salvation derive all their power. Moreover, besides his having made, to my knowledge, a general confession to Master Laínez when passing through Genoa, that he so urgently desired and asked to go to confession is a sign of the inward contrition which God our Lord gives to those to whom he wishes to show mercy.

Likewise, the remembrance which Your Ladyship bids me have of His Lordship the Duke and his affairs is so much a duty that it would be a great fault on my part to neglect it. May it please him who is the Author of all good to communicate himself to Your Ladyship and your illustrious house with abundant grace, as is my desire and earnest prayer in his divine presence.

Our Society should have very much at heart Don Juan de Vega's health, not only because he has been such a father and lord to us all but very particularly because of its importance for the general good and the glory of God, in which he has employed himself so truly and so effectively these many years. If the rumor now circulating in Rome about his being moved proves true, we will with all the more reason offer earnest prayers for his health to the one who is the true health of all. And his infinite Wisdom will deign to guide Señor Hernando de Vega in the important decision of which Your Ladyship writes. Here in this house we will pray for this.

As to the college of Bivona, the information which Master Jeróni-mo Doménech gives us shows the devotion and charity which attended its foundation. Because of this, I am confident in God our Lord that he will make great use of it. As to the staff needed to make a beginning of the usual program in our colleges, Master Jerónimo knows that we have done what we could, although not all we would have wanted had our resources been greater. God will augment these for his service, and the results will show that we all have the regard which is owed to a work begun and maintained with such charity for God's service.

Referring you for other matters to Master Jerónimo, I will add no more except to pray that God may constantly increase in Your Ladyship, along with even greater purity and a richer communication of his light and love, both contempt of self and an esteem for the gifts of the divine goodness and liberality. May he grant to all of us his grace, so that we may always know his most holy will and perfectly fulfill it.

Rome, October 20, 1555

✠

To Jerónimo Nadal

Rome, October 21, 1555

(Letter 5834: X:16–18; in Spanish)

Chosen vicar general of the Society because Ignatius was ill, Nadal was sent as visitor to Spain, which already had Francis Borgia as commissary, or superprovin-cial, in addition to several provincials. On the same day as this letter, Ignatius wrote to Borgia and to Antonio Araoz, informing them of the visit by Nadal and of his responsibilities and powers. Nadal was to consult both Borgia and Araoz on certain matters, the former because he was commissary and the latter because he was already an influential presence among members of the Spanish court. This writ for his visitation deals with the delicate problems of authority this multiplicity raised.

Ihs.

Instruction for Father Master Nadal on His Trip to Spain

1. We shall first indicate the purpose of this trip, and then the authority which he will bear from Our Father for it.

2. One of the main purposes which he has entrusted to him is the decision about the professed to be admitted in the provinces there.

3. Another is to assist Father Francis in the explanation and observance of the Constitutions in his provinces.

4. Another is to help him also with the rules; since they cannot be observed in the same way in all the colleges and houses and need to be adapted to each by adding, removing, or altering them according to circumstances, Father Francis will need someone to help him with this.

5. Another purpose is to assist him with the location, financial foundation, and organization of the various colleges which are being started and are still not fully organized; similarly with any other matters in which Father Francis may want to be helped or [his burdens] alleviated by Master Nadal.

6. Another is to help him in providing for the college in Rome, the importance and needs of which he well knows.

His Authority for Best Achieving This

Although with the common consent of the priests and others in Rome, Father Master Nadal was elected vicar general of our father Master Ignatius and vested with his own authority to help in his responsibilities because of his constant illnesses, nevertheless, since there is a commissary in Spain to fulfill this function for the provinces there, the authority conferred at that moment upon him will be suspended in the provinces of Spain, while remaining in force outside them. Thus, generally speaking, while in Spain he will have neither superior nor subjects, although he will do all he can in the Lord to help Father Francis, the provincials, and everyone else.

For the specific purposes mentioned above, he will possess authority in the following manner. As for admission to profession, even though they studied the matter there and named certain men who it was judged in the Lord ought to be admitted, nevertheless, Father Master Nadal should consult with Father Francis (and, if they think fit, with Father Doctor Araoz) and the two should decide between themselves; and Our Father leaves it up to them to do as they think right. Thus, this authority will be shared by the two in common.

As to the second and third points, having to do with the Constitutions and rules, Father Nadal can ask from the rectors and provincials an accounting of how they are proceeding; and where he is certain of the mind of Father Francis, he can give any orders he thinks good in the Lord. If he is uncertain whether it would be line with Father Francis's judgment and will, he should change nothing without consulting him; and what is to be done should be done with his judgment and approval. If Father Francis orders something to be done on his own after consulting with Father Nadal, here too he should prevail, since Master Nadal is there to help him and only temporarily, whereas Father Francis will have to stay for the long haul. If they wish to consult Doctor Araoz on these matters, they may do so.

He will possess the same authority on the fourth point as on the third, keeping in mind that he is going there to assist Father Francis in whatever way he can; and for this he will be helped by the letter of authorization from Our Father by which anything he writes or says will be by commission vested in him here by Our Father himself.

On the fifth point, that of [financial] provision, he will have full authority to take along or send any persons from one place to another, except for Father Francis and Father Don Antonio de Córdoba, and likewise to make any arrangements he thinks suitable; and he may make use of the letter of authorization and the signed blanks as he judges best in the Lord.

As for the Society's privileges, he will possess in Spain all of those which can be granted to an individual person. As for granting them to others, it would be preferable for the commissary to be the one who grants them as he sees needed in the Lord.

✠

To Philip of Austria, king of England

Rome, October 23, 1555

(Letter 5846: X:32–34; in Spanish)

Charles V had blocked the Society's legal establishment in the Low Countries, where a number of men had entered the order. His abdication in 1555 gave Ignatius a chance to renew the petition to his son and successor, Philip (of the [Austrian] house of Habsburg, king of Spain, and then husband of Queen Mary Tudor of England), who had been favorable to the Society in Spain. This formal request was presented to Philip in February 1556 by Pedro Ribadeneira, Ignatius's thirty-year-old ambassador. Despite one favor of Philip, negotiations dragged on for some time. They came to a successful conclusion on the eve of Ignatius's death in July 1556.

Ihs.

To His Holy Catholic Royal Majesty

My Lord in our Lord:

May the sovereign grace and eternal love of Christ our Lord greet and visit Your Majesty with his most holy gifts and spiritual graces.

Upon receiving the news here that His Majesty the Emperor had abdicated to Your Majesty the German Low Countries and his other states here, all of us, your servants, received great consolation in our Lord, both because of the holy example given by His Imperial Majesty in this action and because of our confidence that the divine Goodness will be served by the above-mentioned states being in the hands of Your Majesty; and this we continually beg of him in our poor prayers and sacrifices. And because we desire not only in this but in whatever else our lowliness is capable of, as we are bound, to serve Your Majesty in our Lord with all our strength; and because we are convinced that it would be for the service of God and of Your Majesty that members of this least Society of ours belonging to that nation and language might employ in the Low Countries the abilities conferred on them by our Lord—which because of their proximity to Germany are more exposed to harm than others, to the offense of our Lord and to Your Majesty's disservice—I have decided in our Lord to send Master Ribadeneira, who will give this letter to Your Majesty and explain our reasons for thinking this way; so that, should Your Majesty then judge it would indeed be for the service of God our Lord and of Your Majesty, you might deign to take this least Society under your wing and protection in those lands, as you have been pleased to do elsewhere, and grant them authorization to possess colleges in those lands, so that just as it employs the slight ability given to it by our Lord for the benefit of souls in Your Majesty's other realms and states, it might offer to Your Majesty in these places of greater need the service which it owes you, for the glory of God our Creator and Lord and the benefit of the peoples which he has placed in Your Majesty's hands. The above-mentioned Ribadeneira will explain this more fully to Your Majesty; and I ask that he be given the same faith and credence as would be given to my own person.

With this I conclude, imploring God our Lord to give to all of us his abundant grace, so that we may know his most holy will and entirely fulfill it.

Rome, October 23, 1555

Your Majesty's most humble and perpetual servant in our Lord,
IGNATIO

To Pedro de Zárate

Rome, October 29, 1955
(Letter 5863: X:59f.; in Spanish)

A letter of friendship to a Basque nobleman at the imperial court in Flanders. Zárate was long a close collaborator and generous benefactor of the Society. He gave money to the Roman Jesuits when they were in great need of it; and, as a Knight of the Holy Sepulcher, he had obtained from Pope Julius III a bull permitting the Society to establish colleges in Jerusalem, Cyprus, and Constantinople, an ambitious project never to be fulfilled.

My Lord in our Lord:

May the sovereign grace, etc.

Despite Your Worship's saying that you do not want us to have to exchange letters, I shall write occasionally to you anyway, taking advantage of your permission to do so less frequently but not to give it up entirely—my poor health will easily excuse me with your kindness, which I know well. But I am sorry that a part is played in this by your stomach ailment, for the hardships of your constant travels demand health. May he who is the eternal health grant you as much of it as he sees is needed for his greater service and glory, and compensate for whatever is lacking to the body with most complete health of soul.

Although Your Worship does not mention keeping up your good practice of frequent confession and Communion, I take for granted that it is still continuing; otherwise, the stomach ailment could be the just punishment of carelessness.

Master Polanco will write you of other matters as needed. One thing I would ask Your Worship is that in case Master Bernard [Olivier] absents himself for a time from the court there, you would do us the favor of taking care of some business I have entrusted to him. Realizing that charity, apart from many words on my part, will readily persuade Your Worship, I shall say no more, except that I earnestly beg to be commended to your benevolence and pray that God our Lord will give us most abundantly of his own grace, so that we may always know his most holy will and entirely fulfill it.

Rome, October 29, 1555

Please pay my respects to the lord bishop, and do me the kindness of warmly greeting Martín Ruiz for me.

To Girolamo Vignes, by commission

Rome, November 17, 1555

(Letter 5919: X:154–56; in Italian)

Vignes was a prominent Neapolitan who had two Jesuit brothers, Michele and Fabrizio. He himself wanted to enter the Society, but instead had to take care of his aged parents. He became a close friend of the Jesuits at Naples and a faithful agent of the Society in financial and legal matters, and those dealing with property, even though he was of a somewhat anxious temperament. Ignatius and he corresponded frequently. This letter is a good example of both the business affairs that necessarily had to occupy Ignatius and the personal relationships and spiritual guidance characteristic of his correspondence. Here Polanco writes him a business letter containing some counsels on preserving peace of soul amid difficult and demanding work.

Jhus.

The peace of Christ.

Most honorable Sir in Christ Jesus:

We received your letter of the tenth of this month with the accounts of the disposition of the fifteen hundred ducats, of which I think I still owe more than fifty. If Master Jerónimo Doménech has not left by the time this arrives, you might tell him he should send the balance from Sicily. If he has left, we will write him; and if he does not respond promptly, we will remit the sum from here in Rome, since I am trying to arrange a mortgage of a thousand scudi on our houses here to pay some debts, and from that sum we will pay what we still owe on the account mentioned above, unless we collect some money from Master Tommaso[Passitano]'s sum or that of Giovan Cola [Petrolla].

Regarding our brother Master Michele [Vignes], unless his being sent to Naples on orders from the doctors had been reasonable, we would not have done it, so as not to distress his parents or Your Lordship, for whom we desire every spiritual consolation in Christ our Lord.

As for Fabrizio [Vignes], do not think that he is dead or ill, because he is cured and has recovered from his sickness, nor have they written that he has fallen into another one. And so to disabuse his father of that opinion, I have written instructions to Ferrara that they write a letter about his being well now.

Concerning the prayers which Your Lordship seeks, you certainly partake of them in many ways, both in general and in particular. Moreover, I think that Your Lordship ought to make up your mind and then do whatever you can, calmly and gently. Do not be anxious about the rest; leave it to God's providence to take care of what your own cannot provide. And while God is pleased with our care and moderate solicitude in attending to what we ought to take care of by way of service, he is not pleased with anxiety and mental affliction; for he wishes that our limitations and weakness should lean upon his strength and omnipotence, and that we should trust that he in his goodness will make up for what is lacking in our imperfection and infirmity. Even a person who has to handle a great deal of business, even though [he does so] with a holy and good intention, needs to make his resolution to do what he can, and not get upset if he is unable to do all that he wishes. Following the dictate of his conscience, he should do all that a person can and should do; and if other things are left undone, one must have patience and not think that God our Lord demands what man cannot accomplish or that he wants a person to be distressed. And if one satisfies God, which is more important than satisfying men, there is no need to overexert yourself; make an adequate effort to do what is needed and leave the rest to him who can do all that he pleases. May it please his divine goodness always to communicate the light of his wisdom, so that we may always see and fulfill his will in ourselves and in others. Amen.

The news from India is largely translated, but not yet printed; we will have it done this week so that we do not have to write out so many copies.

I hope that the coming of the Duke of Alva will mean more assistance to the college, as I understand he is very well disposed.[20] God our Lord will always be our true helper and will move the instruments which his goodness may choose.

Regarding the brevet sought by that gentleman for mortgaging his house, we find ourselves rather unprepared, because, though we lay on mortgages daily, so to speak, we have not had similar brevets asked of us. Your Lordship might tell him to decide on the form he wants and send us a memorandum, so that we can obtain the brevet as he wishes, although it is hardly necessary, for the Society intends to remove his mortgage promptly.

That is all, except that Our Father and all of us commend ourselves heartily to Your Lordship's prayers.

Rome, November 17, 1555

---

[20] Fernando Alvarez de Toledo, the new viceroy of Naples.

To Girolamo Vignes, by commission

Rome, November 24, 1555

(Letter 5945: X:206-8; in Italian)

Besides some business matters, Ignatius consoles Vignes (see letter 5919 above) over the illness of his two Jesuit brothers, Fabrizio and Michele, which would prove to be fatal in the case of the latter. He again recommends peace amid the press of business.

Jesù

The peace of Christ.

Most Honorable Sir in Jesus Christ:

We received Your Lordship's letter of the sixteenth. For the money I refer you to what I wrote last week to Madonna Pellotta [Spinola].[21] I hope to have a somewhat longer discussion one day this week, and will be able to let you know, if needed, of what happens with her.

We are sorry for our sea travelers, whom God has willed to try; may he have given them a good voyage afterwards.

With regard to the bodily illness of our dear brother Master Michele [Vignes], may Christ be his spiritual health. We are rightly envious of him, because he has double merit: that of patience in his trials and that of charity by which he accepts and recognizes the favor as coming from God's hands, in the certainty that our most wise and loving Father sends him only what is suitable for his ultimate and supreme good. Considering how he also visits our other brother, Fabrizio (although without danger of death), and Your Lordship as well, with no slight trials, and in addition your parents (who I believe must be such as we can gather from their sons), I am convinced that God has a very special love for your entire blessed family, since he treats them as true children to whom he wishes to give consolation in his eternal kingdom more than in this exile. And yet I hope that even in this present life he will give them great consolation, seeing their sons so dedicated to every virtue and good servants of Christ, and consequently heirs of supreme and everlasting happiness. Your Lordship should decide whether or not to give Fabrizio's letter to your esteemed parents, or whether it ought to be touched up to avoid distressing them with the knowledge that their son has been occasionally experiencing pains. Master Jean Pelletier writes us that because of the present cold he will perhaps be staying in

---

[21] Pellotta was a very generous benefactor of the Jesuit college in Naples. She gave her home there to the Society and went to live in Rome in great simplicity.

the room with a fire, since he is helped by warmth and harmed by cold, although he has already been cured of his break by the relics.

The concern shown by Your Lordship over the approaching time for the payment of a large sum of money ought, I think, to be tempered, so that it elicits diligence but not anxiety. God our Lord, whose service is our sole aim, is very rich in power and mercy, and though he may repeatedly exercise us with difficulties in temporal affairs—this being a consequence of poverty—he does not and will not abandon us. His will is that we not forget our profession and that we exercise confidence in him and not rely too much on the things of earth. Still, we shall not fail to cooperate with his grace, pursuing the means which according to the course of his providence, we ought to pursue.

From the court they write us that they need to get letters from His Royal Majesty in favor of the college; and Master Pedro Ribadeneira will also do his duty. If Your Lordship thinks we should take some steps from Rome, we will. I am writing to Father Cristóbal [de Mendoza] to perform again the office which Your Lordship will tell him regarding Don Juan [de Mendoza], unless he has withdrawn his opposition.

May the Holy Spirit grant you consolation and continual spiritual progress.

Rome, November 24, 1555

✠

To Juan Luis González de Villasimplez

Rome, November 26, 1555

(Letter 5947: X:210–213; in Spanish)

Gonzalez was an official of the Kingdom of Aragon and a trusted correspondent of Ignatius. This letter records Ignatius's reaction to the very difficult circumstances in which the Jesuits established themselves in Zaragoza. The successful preaching of Father François Estrada in late 1554 led to the first moves toward a house and college of the Society. When the Jesuits began to work in the city in early 1555, opposition began and continued to grow during the summer. The archbishop of Zaragoza was very unsympathetic to the Society; several of the religious orders were opposed to a Jesuit college. The diocesan clergy supported the archbishop and filed suit against the Jesuits. Public opinion was aroused against them by portraying them as devils; several times their house was even stoned.

On the other hand, the bishop of Huesca thundered condemnations against those who would not acknowledge the Jesuits' papal privileges. The archbishop refused to publish the bulls containing those privileges. The Jesuit rector and community finally decided, for the sake of peace, to leave the city in early August. Princess Juana, who had earlier entered the fray on the side of the Society and its papal privileges, had the viceroy and the city council intervene and rather quickly public opinion turned around in favor of the Jesuits. The church censures against them were annulled and, at the request of the city authorities, on September 8 the fathers returned and were publicly escorted back to their house.

My Lord in our Lord:

May the sovereign grace and eternal love of Christ our Lord greet and visit Your Worship with his most holy gifts and spiritual graces.

I have been informed—although not yet by letters from our own men—of what took place between the united religious orders (except for the Hieronymites) and our own college that had started there—how the Most Reverend Lord Archbishop and his vicar and some rectors took the side of the religious, and how our men, to avoid greater scandal, ended up surrendering the keys to the city and leaving it. All things considered, those of us here find much occasion for praising God our Lord and giving thanks to him for this visitation of his, trusting that his divine wisdom will draw from it fruitfulness for his service, which is the only thing we aim at in either staying in or leaving any particular place.

I am willing to believe that the intention of the archbishop and the religious was good; and as for our own men, they are so few for the many places which urgently ask workers of us that I do not think they can complain of being deprived of opportunities for God's service and the help of souls. I am therefore writing them that they should not push to return unless the archbishop and the city call them with common agreement and satisfaction, and that they should be content to assist that city with their desires and prayers, while they assist with their preaching and the administration of the sacraments in other parts of Christ our Lord's vineyard, which is so large and short of workers that it does not seem right to insist on working in a place where their ministry is unwelcome and leave aside others where it is very welcome and the need no less, perhaps even greater.

I wanted to inform Your Worship of this because I know that your charity doubtless makes you concerned to know how this affair has been taken here. Know also that we have chosen not to appeal to the Pope or to any of our cardinal friends, or to make use of their favor in this matter.

After the above was written, we had duplicate letters of August 13 from our men, recounting the story of their conflict with the religious fathers and rectors of some churches there, together with letters of September 17, from which we learn of their return to their college and how it took place. Certainly, just as the first letter gave us consolation at what our men gained in the presence of Christ our Lord by suffering something for his service and bearing some of his cross, so the second does the like because of the consolation given to our spiritual friends, the edification for the city, and the end of the offense being done to God our Lord by some, though others may have been excused because of their good intention. May God our Lord be blessed and praised always in all his creatures and in all their conditions. Amen.

I consider it a great benefit on your part that the Reverend Lord Archbishop, better informed about us, is willing to consider us his sons and his very own. I trust that as far as our poor profession allows, he will find himself served by our men in every way we can rather than in any way ill-served. The protection of this college would be vested in no one as well as in His Reverend Lordship, for various reasons, and so we beg him to assume it.

God has also placed us under great obligation to the Most Reverend Lord Bishop of Huesca not only for what his great charity prompted him to do but also because of what it brought him to suffer. He will have his great rewarder in him who did and suffered so much for us all, whom I pray to answer for us to His Lordship, to Your Worship, and to Señor Morrano, and all the gentlemen who in this time of so much difficulty and opposition, have demonstrated their great charity towards the college, indeed towards our whole Society, which will remain always obliged to Your Worship's heartfelt service, to the glory of God our Lord. May his abundant grace be always in our souls, to know always and fulfill his most holy will.

Rome, November 26, 1555

⌖

To Enrique de La Cueva

Rome, November 28, 1555

(Letter 5953: X:222–24; in Spanish)

Fearing he would not be treated with due respect as a Jesuit in Spain, Enrique (see letter 4485 above) wanted to come to Rome. His father, a member of the Spanish nobility who had been made a cardinal by Pope Paul III, forbade this move, but insisted that Ignatius not dispense him from his vow and fully receive him into the Society. Ignatius here complies, attempting to reconcile Enrique with these measures.

Jhus.

The peace of Christ.

May the sovereign grace and eternal love of Christ our Lord be always our continual help and protection.

From your letter of September 29 to the Most Reverend Cardinal, our common lord and father in our Lord, I learned, not without some surprise, that you had not received the decision taken here concerning your state of life and the place to which you are to go for a few years in study. [The reason for my surprise is that] I had received letters of September 10 from Father Francis [Borgia] and Doctor Araoz, saying that they had sent you my letter and that now for the second time he was writing to you, thus carrying out the directive that I had sent him from here in several letters of my own. While I assume that by this time you have not only been apprised of this decision but have already begun carrying it out, I shall nevertheless repeat here, regarding the first part of the decision, that after conferring, carefully reflecting, and praying to God our Lord over the matter, we came to the conclusion that you ought to follow the vocation and Institute towards which he has inspired and moved you and in which you have dedicated yourself by special vow, offering yourself totally to his Divine and Supreme Majesty. And so, raising no doubts on this score, I write you as to one of my brethren whom God has entrusted especially to my care.

As to the second part, regarding a place to which you can move, you can be sure that I very much desire in our Lord that the best place be found for you so that you might get, along with your greater spiritual consolation and advancement, a better grounding and strengthening in the studies required by our profession. There being no such place at present in Italy, it will be—for valid reasons that move the Most Reverend Lord Cardinal—in some other place that is deemed most appropriate. It seems to me in our Lord that it would be more perfect on your part to leave this choice quite freely to Father Francis, who, as our commissary, has, in the place of Christ our Lord, full authority over our Society in those kingdoms. For—in addition to your being able to believe that the divine Wisdom will be communicated to him more fully because of the office it has entrusted to him—it is fitting that you or any true religious once having made the sacrifice of himself by offering himself whole and entire as a holocaust to the divine and supreme

Goodness, should hold back nothing of himself, as is done by those who still preserve their own wills and want to follow their own judgments, thereby taking back the chief part of what they had surrendered to God our Lord through the hands of their superiors. And because I have a very special reason and obligation to desire for you all the perfection that I most wish in any of my brethren, I would be much pleased if in this matter of the place you would put yourself with all confidence into the hands of Father Francis, whom I again charge to take the greatest care of what is owing to your person. It seems to me that if you are to deal with him, it would be better if you went where he is, or nearby; for you will be able to discuss more adequately by word of mouth than by letter what is best to do. I enclose a letter for him which I would like you to hand to him personally if possible.

And since I cannot help opening my heart to you, my dearest brother, as to one whom I dearly love in our Lord, I want you to know of my desire that no one enter this Society who does not distinguish himself in humbling and abasing himself much more genuinely than you have; you should reckon that in all those kingdoms there is no one in the Society lower than you or whom you should esteem less and hold in lower repute than yourself. In this way, before God our Lord and those who think as he does, you will be esteemed and reputed more highly, whereas if you should behave otherwise, you would neither advance your own soul nor give satisfaction either in heaven or on earth regarding your procedure. But I trust in him who by word and example urged this virtue of humility so earnestly upon us and invited us in a special way to imitate him in it, that he will bestow it upon you, and upon this foundation raise up in your soul many very great spiritual gifts, by means of which you will mightily serve and glorify his divine and supreme Goodness. May he be pleased to give to all of us his abundant grace, so that we may always know his most holy will and entirely fulfill it.

I commend myself very especially to your prayers.

Rome, November 28, 1555

✠

To Francis Borgia

Rome, November 28, 1555
(Letter 5954: X:225; in Spanish)

Directions regarding Enrique de La Cueva, a cleric who was somewhat thrust upon the Society by his father, Cardinal Bartolome de La Cueva. After Ignatius tells Enrique, in the letter immediately preceding this one, that he wanted him fully to put himself in Francis Borgia's hands as to where he would go for studies, he tells Borgia here that for reasons good in themselves he ought to be sent to Portugal, and also because La Cueva himself desires it. But the decision should come from Borgia.

Jhus.

May the sovereign grace and eternal love of Christ our Lord be always our continual protection and help.

I am sending herewith the copy of a letter I am writing to Don Enrique de La Cueva, from which you will see that he had not received my letter by September 29—although I think he probably got it later—with the decision reached here in his regard. However, in case the other was lost, I am sending this. And although I urge him to the indifference a religious man ought to have to one place or another, nevertheless, even if he places himself freely in your hands, we think in our Lord that he should be sent to Portugal, for that is what he wishes, and not without good reasons. And while for his own greater spiritual progress I would not like him to go there by his own will, I would like him to go by yours.

As for other matters regarding him and his affairs, I commend them to you as earnestly as I can in our Lord, since you know the obligations we are all under to the Most Reverend Lord Cardinal, to say nothing of what charity in itself demands of us.

Master Polanco is writing about other matters.

I commend myself to your prayers, and I beg of God our Lord to give us all his abundant grace, so that we may always know his most holy will and entirely fulfill it.

✠

To Alejo Fontana, by commission

Rome, December 7, 1555

(Letter 5981: X:270f.; in Spanish)

Ignatius communicates to the imperial secretary his sentiments on receiving the news of Charles V's abdication as emperor and his departure for Spain. Fontana had known Pierre Favre in Speyer and from then on was a very good friend of the Jesuits, to whom he turned for counsel and spiritual direction. Ignatius wrote to him frequently.

Jhus.

My Most Honored Sir in Jesus Christ:

The peace of Christ.

After I had written the other letters and was waiting to send some of the letters from India which accompany this (and others will go with the next post), a packet from Your Worship arrived with your letter of the twentieth of last month and one of Master Bernard [Olivier] of the thirteenth. We all send you our deepest respects for your constant kindnesses to us.

We were extremely happy to hear about His Imperial Majesty's embarkation. May Christ be pleased to give him a prosperous voyage and the grace to employ what remains of his life for his great service, since he has so courageously stripped himself of such vast estates in order not to bear their burden, and refused to retain the dignity and command without it. A rare example, one that few will imitate, though many ought to.

No more, except that Our Father and all of us send Your Worship our deepest respects, and ask God our Lord to grant all of us his grace so as to know and always fulfill his most holy will.

Rome, December 7, 1555

✠

To Bernard Olivier

Rome, December 9, 1555

(Letter 5991: X:296f.; in Italian)

Lambert, a brother of Everard Mercurian (later to be the fourth superior general of the Society), several times had reported that their aged father was living in dire poverty. There was some doubt about this because the father had been well off when Everard had joined the Society. Hence the tone of these instructions to Flanders for giving assistance to the father of Mercurian.

Postscript: A brother of Father Master Everard, rector of the college in Perugia, has arrived in Rome. He has caused distress to both him and us by reporting that Master Everard's father is living in great, almost extreme, want. He says he is blind and elderly, and does not have the means to live. And while we are not bound to believe this young man, for he does not deserve too much credence; and while Master Everard, being professed and thus dead to the world, is under no obligation to go and help his father, nevertheless, for greater security of conscience and the consolation of Master Everard, we thought it good to offer to write to Your Reverences to find out from friends near where Master Everard's father lives if he is really in such dire need, and if he is, to ask our friends in Liège or elsewhere to give him assistance. For charity's sake, would Your Reverence please take care of this with Father Master Adrian [Adriaansens] or whomever you like, and send us a reply we can show Master Everard. Enclosed is a list with the names.

That friend of Señor Zárate has answered that he will provide out of the seventy scudi.

Rome, December 9, 1555

✠

To Juan Pérez

Rome, December 12, 1555

(Letter 5998: X:307–9; in Spanish)

Juan Pérez of Calatayud was another great friend of the Society and had shared in the Jesuits' struggles to get established in Zaragoza. (See the introduction to letter no. 5947.) Ignatius thanks him for his efforts, and gives him general counsels on his vocational situation. He had longings to enter the Society, although he was the father of five young children.

Jhus.

My Most Honored Sir in Jesus Christ:

May the grace and peace of Christ our Lord be always present and grow in our souls. Amen.

I received Your Worship's letter of September 12 from these gentlemen and friends of yours, who very charitably undertook to carry back the reply. I was greatly consoled in Christ our Lord to see that his holy spirit, and the desires and holy aims that come from it, shone through your letter. As one who loves you dearly in our Lord, I cannot but greatly rejoice and give him many thanks for his gifts which I see in you. I beg him to add to them and to carry you from virtue to virtue, until you reach the perfection which he is accustomed to bestow on his chosen servants both in this world and in the other.

As to the trials met by our men in Zaragoza and the restoration which has been made to them, there is occasion in both to recognize a great favor of our most kind Father and Lord, since in the first [instance] he gave them so great an opportunity to serve him in patience, and in the second, he gives them an opportunity to help others for his service, as they gather no little fruit for their own progress and merit and for the spiritual edification and consolation of their neighbors, to God's glory.

For the kindly service rendered us by Your Worship and those gentlemen, your friends, and for your part in sharing the trials brought on you all by your charity, you will have a generous rewarder in Christ our Lord, for whose love and reverence you have acted. May it please his divine and sovereign goodness to answer in our stead, as befits himself. Amen.

We are convinced that since the devil has so opposed this work in Zaragoza, it is because he fears the losses which it will cause him; and so we hope for all the greater service of God our Lord in helping of his much beloved souls, which is what we are trying to do everywhere.

I was very happy in the Lord about Your Worship's going to Valladolid and Simancas to draw consolation from Father Francis [Borgia] and consult with him. So much goodwill, I am confident, will not return empty-handed; for he who gives it and moves you so will surely also have provided some good fruit for your spiritual benefit with which you will have returned home, particularly in making the Exercises and in the desire you indicate of entering this Society, should the need to care for your five children allow it. I am very eager to get word of what God our Lord has given Your Worship to understand.

As for your asking me to give my own opinion, I can hardly comply except in general terms, since I have no information about many particulars out of which ought to arise any opinion I gave if it were to be solidly grounded. I can say in general that your desires are good and holy, since they regard a state in which God our Lord is served with greater security and perfection; however, the prudence and reflection which you must use to satisfy the obligation given you by God of educating your family for his service is also very holy and necessary. You doubtless have some one nearer at hand to advise you. This I would say with confidence and without fear of error: You should have a very upright intention, keeping in view only God's will and desiring entire conformity with it. Thus, if you remain in your present state, try to perfect yourself in it, and perhaps it will happen that your children, or one of them, may take the place which is not open to you. Raise them in the fear and love of God, and give them the best instruction and religious formation that you can. Should you ever change your state of life, you will not do so without leaving everything provided for in such a way that you will be able to give a good account of all that God has entrusted to you; and this you could not do if you forsook what is of obligation for what is not. The most I can say is that I will promise to ask God graciously to direct all Your Worship's affairs and every day to increase the knowledge and love of him in your soul.

News of the Society you will receive by way of our men in Zaragoza. And I should like to be informed of what steps have been taken towards having some of ours come to Calatayud for the spiritual consolation of Your Worship and of the city there.

May Christ our Lord give all of us his grace always to know and to fulfill his most holy will.

Rome, December 12, 1555

Our father Master Ignatius, God be praised, is in good health—as compared with his usual condition—as are the rest of us here in the house. There are usually about sixty persons here and about a hundred of our students in the college. There were a great many more, but since September we have sent out more than a hundred from here to various colleges, and have received a great many others in their place. May Christ our Lord make use of them all.

✠

To Girolamo Vignes

Rome, December 15, 1555

(Letter 6007: X:322f.; in Italian)

Ignatius consoles his friend on the death of his Jesuit brother Michele, on whom he heaps praises. (See also the earlier letters about the Vigneses, nos. 5919 and 5945.)

Jhus.

My most honored Sir in Jesus Christ:

The peace of Christ.

From Your Lordship's letter of the eighth of this month, we learned that our beloved brother Michele was on the point of making his journey to the heavenly fatherland. Thanks be to Christ Jesus, our life and everlasting happiness, whose wisdom and goodness has thought it best not to leave so good a servant any longer among us, but to free him from the travail and perils of this pilgrimage and to substitute for them endless repose, peace, and happiness. Yesterday also we received word of another of our young brethren, a Fleming [Gerard Cools or Gerard Brassica], a very learned youth and a great servant of God, whom we were sending on the doctors' advice from Rome to his native land. Having gotten past Cologne, he was just nearing his own country when he rendered his soul to his Creator. We only say that we envy rather than compassionate the two of them; both have lived in our Society with great purity, obedience, and self-abnegation, and with a desire of serving and glorifying God our Lord. We have no doubt that he has gathered them like ripe fruit, unwilling to postpone any longer the inexpressible and inestimable reward which he has prepared for his true and faithful servants. If we find ourselves deprived of the consolation which their physical presence gave us, we should not so much grieve over that as congratulate ourselves on the supreme blessing and happiness of our brothers, who will help us better from heaven than they could have on earth in what pertains to God's service. This I can assert of Master Michele, that in all the places and for all the time he has lived in our Society, he has left the sweet odor of his rare virtue, and we have never heard anything to the contrary. We look upon him as a holy creature, possessed of the spirit of Christ our Creator and Lord. And although we believe he has no need for it, yet as an act of charity we have recommended him and will continue to recommend him to the sovereign goodness of God. May it please him to console his parents and Your Worship with the complete conformity of your own wills to his. Amen.

We all commend ourselves earnestly to Your Worship's prayers.

Rome, December 15, 1555

✠

To Lorenzo Scorzino

Rome, December 15, 1555

(Letter 6009: X:325f.; in Italian)

Earlier in the year, Scorzino was going to make the definitive renunciation of his property required before his final profession of vows in the Society; he planned to leave his estate to the Society itself. An uncle who had been administering his property thought that something was due to him in gratitude, but he could not find the accounts proving what he had actually done. Ignatius gives advice but leaves it to Scorzino to decide what to write. Eventually the uncle received something and Scorzino's mother was granted a modest annual income.

Jhus.

The peace of Christ.

Dearest Master Lorenzo:

I have seen a letter which a friend or relative wrote you about forgiving a debt your uncle may owe you and not requiring an accounting of it. The letter seems to mention two or three points: first, that you are under great obligation to this uncle; second, that he has burdened his conscience in order to be of benefit to you; and third, that he cannot find the accounts and is grieved about this, etc.

As for the first point, Your Reverence may answer him however you think best, in a loving way.

As for the second, you will tell him that it was not your intention that any usury be exacted or any illicit or dishonorable profit made, and that, if he should have done so against your will, you will be happy for him to make restitution—indeed request him to do so and [promise that] the amount will be restored; also [indicate] that you will be happy for him to charge the amount to you—after careful investigation of whether restitution actually needs to be made.

As for the third point, you will best be able to judge what ought to be done.

In general, I will say that I do not think you should proceed rigorously with your uncle; but neither do I think it right that if the amount he owes you can be approximately determined, this should not be done. Even if you wish to forgive him part or all of the balance, it would be good to know how much he is being given. Hence, I think I would write him in this matter that if he cannot figure out the exact amounts, he should make a rough estimate and tell you in conscience more or less how much of your funds he has in hand; that you have no wish for anything acquired at the expense of conscience; and that if he needs more time to reflect, he should take it and not get upset about it, since you will certainly not act tyrannically or harshly towards him; but that to satisfy your own conscience, you ought to have some clarity in the matter, so far as this is conveniently possible. If Your Reverence has a different opinion, write as you feel best. And may Christ our Lord be always the help and protection of us all. Amen.

Rome, December 15, 1555

✳ 1556 ✳

To the Rectors of the Society, by commission

Rome, January 1, 1556

(Letter 6068: X:451f.; in Italian)

Ignatius orders that throughout the Society the local language should be the one used in Jesuit houses. He had ordered this previously and repeated it at the beginning of the year. In Rome classes in Italian originally took place every other day; eventually they took place every day. In the present-day Society, such knowledge of the language of the country in which one resides is still the rule, as is the requirement that everyone learn at least one major language in addition to his own native tongue.

The peace of Christ.

It seems to be required for the benefit and edification of the peoples among whom our Society is living, and for unity and growth of charity and goodwill among its members themselves that wherever there is a college or house of the Society, all those who do not know the language which is in common use there should learn it and as a rule converse in it. If each one spoke his mother tongue, there would be much confusion and lack of union, since we are of different nations. For this reason Our Father has given orders that in all places where the Society exists, everyone should speak the language of that country: in Spain, Spanish; in France, French; in Germany, German; in Italy, Italian; etc. Here in Rome he has ordered that everyone should speak Italian. There are daily classes in Italian grammar to help those learn it who do not already know it; and they may not talk to the others, nor others to them, in any language other than Italian (except of course to translate the meaning of an occasional word and thus be better understood). He has also ordered that once a week someone preach an Italian sermon in the refectory, at either dinner or supper (in addition to the regular declamation exercises). The preacher is given help by a person who knows Italian well, to make composing the sermon easier; and anyone failing in this is given a good penance.

Our Father has also given orders that this same rule be sent out and observed as carefully as possible everywhere in the Society, due consideration being had for differences of places and persons. For this reason, we are writing to Your Reverence to see that it is observed. Please acknowledge receipt of this.

May Jesus Christ be with us all.

✠

To Juana de Valencia

Rome, January 7, 1556

(Letter 6087: X:483f.; in Spanish)

Another letter of spiritual appreciation to a Spanish lady who had willingly given her son to the Society (see letter 5683 above).

Jhus.

May the sovereign grace, etc.

After having replied to a letter received several months ago from Your Worship, I have been given another of April 10. The more your letters show your motherly love toward Don Fadrique, the more we are edified at the conformity of your own will with God's. Evidently the same spirit that brought Don Fadrique from the world into religious life has taught you to find peace and happiness in his decision, supplying with the power of his grace the frailty of nature. May he be pleased to increase his light and charity in your soul, so that you may experience more consolation every day at seeing one you love so much devote himself to the service of him who must be loved above all things, in whom and for whose glory all things are to be loved. For the rest, Don Fadrique is now your own as much as and even more than ever in our Lord, whose love will perfect the natural love he owes you as a son. When he has made more progress in his studies (which with the ability he shows will not take long), he will one day be able to come and visit Your Worship with his bodily presence. Meanwhile, he himself, as his virtue and religious life and excellent example deserve, will certainly be very much in our prayers and much loved in Christ our Lord by all who deal with him, with more care being taken of his person because of Your Worship's so strongly commending him to us.

May the divine and sovereign Goodness preserve that of Your Worship in his holy service; and may he give all of us his abundant grace, so that we may always know his most holy will and perfectly fulfill it.

Rome, January 8, 1556

To Luis Gonçalves da Câmara, by commission

Rome, January 15, 1556
(Letter 6099: X:505–11; in Spanish)

To Gonçalves da Câmara Ignatius dictated what came to be known as his autobiography. Remaining in Rome for seven months in 1555, da Câmara was able to record in detail what went on in the Jesuit house there and Ignatius's reactions to these occurrences. Some twenty years later, at the request of the general at that time, Everard Mercurian, he supplemented the entries in that journal by writing a commentary on his own entries. Together they are known as the Memoriale, *translated into English under the title* Remembering Inigo. *At the request of the provincial of Portugal, Miguel de Torres, he was sent there in late 1555 to visit the houses and colleges and to help Torres in governing the province as his "collateral" associate. The "collateral" was an office established by Ignatius (see* Constitutions, *nos. 659 and 661). The person holding that office was to serve as a support to the superior, his close advisor. Neither subject to the jurisdiction of the superior nor superior himself, the collateral was asked to be intimately concerned with the superior's governance without himself being authorized to govern, a very delicate task. The office in practice did not last long in the Society of Jesus.*

Da Câmara, a member of the Portuguese nobility, entered the Society of Jesus in 1545. Ordained a priest a year later, he was rector at Coimbra in 1547 and did pastoral work between 1548 and 1553. Next he went to Rome until 1555. He returned to Rome briefly in 1558–59 and then went back to Portugal, where he was tutor and confessor to the young king Sebastian and served at the court. He died in 1575.

Jhus.

MEMORANDUM FOR FATHER LUIS GONÇALVES

For our end of God's service and glory and the common good, and for helping the Society in the pursuit of that end, specifically in Portugal and in the Indies and Brazil, it would seem to be useful for Your Reverence to divide your considerations and efforts under four headings: the King and the nobility, the people, the Society, and yourself.

1. First, as regards the King and the nobility: by your prayers and your counsels, you should work for whatever will help the King's person both in understanding and in effectively willing to fulfill the obligations imposed on him by his office, as well as in executing it in the way and by the means most suitable for the good governance of his states.

2. You also should try to maintain the King's love and good opinion of the Society, both its head and its entire body, and particularly for the part in his own realms.

3. You should likewise urge His Highness to put this goodwill into effect both by temporal assistance to our men where this is appropriate and by using his authority and patronage to expedite matters of God's service by means of the Society in his realms.

4. If occasion arises to suggest ways His Highness can advance God's service by other means outside the Society, this should be done also, even though it would be more appropriate to deal with matters that can be accomplished by our own ministry.

5. With the Queen, the infantes, and other nobles and influential persons, you should observe proportionately what has been said of the King. That is, you should strive both to help them personally and also to help the Society and the common good through them. If you have any influence with such persons, whose spiritual advancement redounds so much to the good of many others, it would seem that you should not fail to put this talent [see Matt. 25:14–30] to use, although nothing definite can be said from here on how to go about it. Your starting point would seem to be conversation: God our Lord will teach you with whom and by what means to proceed further, augmenting the light of discernment with his grace.

AS REGARDS THE PEOPLE

1. Generally speaking, the way to help the people, apart from your prayers and Masses and the example of your life, will be through conversation and the administration of the sacraments, especially confession, and also by giving the Spiritual Exercises to some. The Exercises should be given to those whose own spiritual progress can be extended to larger numbers; for example, those in high position or public office, or certain persons suitable for becoming apostolic workers themselves, etc. With these persons you should be more willing to spend time or have others do so.

2. You will be able to extend your help to larger numbers through sermons and Bible lectures in a style adapted to the people. However, discernment will show you whether you yourself ought to make use of these means, for which there are others who may be able to do the same, or perhaps different means for which not so many are qualified.

3. You should earnestly strive to obtain other workers who can help the people: your efforts here will be more productive for the universal good than perhaps a lot of exhausting toil on your own part. You should extend this concern not only to people in Portugal but also to the new plantings in the Indies and Brazil and to the Portuguese there. For

these persons, as well as for everything connected with the preservation and growth of religion in those territories, you ought to have a special concern as the angel of those lands, giving thought to the best measures to help souls there, discussing them with the provincial and the commissary (and with Our Father if necessary), and doing all you can to see them carried out.[1]

AS REGARDS THE SOCIETY

1. As regards the Society, whose welfare redounds to the common good mentioned above, Your Reverence could assist by securing the financial stability of our present foundations and any others which in the course of time may seem advisable for God's service, especially in the Indies. [Something similar can be said about] other financial assistance, to the extent that temporal means are judged helpful for the greater promotion of the Lord's work. This would be a matter to be discussed especially with Their Highnesses and with other powerful personages.

2. Throughout the body of the Society in those realms, you should work for the unity and conformity of the members with each other and—especially in the case of those who are more important—with the Society's head, that is, the General, for whom you should try to get them to have appropriate esteem, love, and reverence. Here conversation would seem to be a helpful means, as well as others which Your Reverence will better know how to employ than I to write.

3. Likewise, you will be able to benefit the entire body by bringing them to understand and observe the Constitutions and rules according to what you know to be Our Father's mind, and by getting all to proceed with the same spirit, so that we may "all think the same" [Phil. 3:16], all say the same, etc. Try to put a halt to any making of national distinctions that may exist or other behaviors that are more human than spiritual.

4. Being the provincial's collateral as you are, even though you are not obliged to reside where he does, you still ought to be especially concerned to assist him, particularly in the more important aspects of his office. You should advise him wherever you feel he needs counsel or admonition regarding his person or his government. This you should do with the charity and prudence which Your Reverence will know how to employ. You should try to ensure that the provincial receives your admo-

---

[1] The commissary was the "superprovincial," Francis Borgia, whose jurisdiction in that office included both Spain and Portugal.

nitions with love and is pleased with the help you afford him by giving them, indeed seeks it out and has no cause for keeping things to himself or avoiding communication with Your Reverence, as is often the case towards disagreeable censors. For this it will help if you hold him in great respect and show yourself quite eager to obey him even in matters where you are not obliged to do so. In sum, you should try to get the provincial to love you and have great confidence in you.

5. The better to help him, put yourself in his person and responsibilities as if it all lay upon you except for the power of commanding. Thus, you will devote your attention to every area—both in Portugal and in the Indies—that he is responsible for.

6. You can help both the provincial and the other local superiors by explaining, when you are asked, your views on questions that might arise regarding our Constitutions, rules, and mode of proceeding. Even without being asked, you could give your advice if you see them diverging from the mind of Our Father Master Ignatius.

7. Just as with the provincial, you can put yourself in the person of any superior of a house or college where you happen to be, as if you had his entire responsibility with the exception of the power of commanding. In this way you can strive to achieve proportionately for them what we said above you should aim at with the provincial. However, matters may arise which you think it better not to take up with them but with their superiors, whether the provincial, the commissary, or the General.

8. It seems that wherever you are it would be good for you to converse familiarly with the individual men, trying to get to know them all, especially those of greater quality, talent, or promise. Thus you might have occasion to assist many of them in their spiritual difficulties or bodily needs (both of which you should give attention to), and also to learn from them much that will be of use in helping the superiors and the common good. You should take special care to be an angel of peace and unity between individuals and their immediate superiors, between rectors or local superiors and the provincial, and also between the provincial and the commissary.

9. You should also be in communication with Our Father in Rome and with the commissary of Spain, providing them with whatever information and advice you think pertinent regarding the persons and affairs of those provinces.

10. You should devote special attention to the conduct of the classes, especially at Coimbra, so that the common good can be promoted through proper instruction of the young in letters and good behavior.

Take care to produce from among our members persons suitable for teaching the languages and arts [philosophy], and to detain workers no longer than is necessary when they are already mature for bearing fruit among souls.

AS REGARDS YOUR PERSON

1. As for your own person, to be the better able to attend to the above-mentioned tasks, you should take care to keep hale and strong, and for this purpose to eat and dress however you know to be best for your bodily well-being.

2. If for the sake of the result to be obtained and to give example, you judge it proper on occasion to go off to different places for short periods of preaching, it would seem that you ought to return promptly to one of the Society's colleges or houses or to the court. Since your presence will be to the benefit of the places where you stay and this is the reason for residing there, you should have no scruple about staying for long periods in any of the colleges. Moreover, you might stay there as superintendent (like Master André des Freux or Doctor Olave), as visitor (if the provincial wishes), or in some other official capacity— although it would suffice for you to act as confessor, preach, teach, or help them in understanding the Society's rules and manner of proceeding, or in other matters directed to their general good.

3. As for how to go about all this, you would do well to divide up your considerations. For a given period of days you should reflect in greater detail upon the needs of one area, such as India; then for another period on those of Brazil; for another on studies in Portugal; for another on the public activities of preaching, teaching Christian doctrine, hearing confessions; for another on internal concerns of the Society regarding its members; for another on material things, such as the endowment of the foundations, etc.—and so forth on other important issues.

4. You should seek out some persons you consider to have particularly solid judgment, whether among the superiors, their consultors, or others. You should then use three touchstones in testing out your ideas and plans. The first will be to sleep on them and recommend them to God, examining them at least two or three times, especially in the case of important or difficult matters. The second will be to talk them over with one of the above-mentioned persons, listening to their opinions and refining the matter. The third will be to propose your ideas, along

with the reasons behind them, to the local superiors there, or to the provincial, or, if need be, to the commissary or General.

5. You should ask or charge some person, either your companion or someone with whom you have more frequent dealings, to admonish you if he detects anything in your person or behavior that requires being called to your attention. You should receive this admonition in such a way as to ensure that having done it once for you, the person will be encouraged to do it again if needed.

6. You ought to reside for a certain amount of time at São Roque [the Lisbon professed house], another at São Antonio [the Lisbon college], another at Coimbra, and another at Évora. At each place you should find out what is going on, note it down, and then communicate it to the appropriate person, as said above.

7. Should there be time, it would be good if you could listen to the lectures of the teachers with a bit of critical spirit, in order to help them if they need assistance in their method of teaching, for the greater advancement in letters and good behavior of those both inside and outside the Society.

☧

To Girolamo Vignes, by commission

Rome, January 18, 1556

(Letter 6110: X:528–30; in Italian)

Here Ignatius writes to the Society's great friend and agent in Naples. It is not clear to whom Master Tommaso refers, but Vignes acted for the Society in many of its dealings and this was surely one of them. The marriage proposal mentioned here referred to Vignes himself. Someone had suggested that he marry. He could not because he had earlier vowed to serve God in the Society when his duties to his elderly parents allowed. The urging that he not work so hard and not worry so much about business matters was appropriate; Vignes was prone to both.

Jhus.

The peace of Christ.

We received Your Lordship's of the eleventh. I have seen the earlier one of Master Giovanni Tomaso; it does not indicate that the two or three scudi were given to him, although he did request them. Neither is its clear that even if given, they were not repaid. And it is most unlikely that Master Giovanni Tomaso, when giving his property to religious works, would have failed to do his duty by paying the debt. We can clear this up quickly by writing to Master Giovanni Tomaso in Portugal. However, Your Lordship should freely do what you think best: the sum is small and perhaps the person showing the note is worthy of belief.

Regarding the gentleman who wished to propose a marriage to the other, I think Your Lordship should try to dissuade him; under a promise of secrecy you might even tell him the reason. I myself have no doubt whatever about this, although Our Father, for good reasons, has declined to give an opinion either way.

As to Your Lordship's being somewhat unwell, I am not surprised, since we understand that you work too hard and seemingly allow things that can annoy you to make too great an impression on you. We would like moderation on both points; for in performing tasks, even religious ones, moderation is needed to ensure that one's efforts can last, which is impossible when they become excessive. As for the outcome, one should have his soul ready to welcome either alternative—success or failure—with a good will as from the hand of God. It is enough for us to do what we can according to our weakness; the rest we should leave to divine Providence, whose responsibility it is and whose course men do not understand, so that they sometimes become distressed when they really should be glad.

As for Your Lordship, I am convinced that God our Lord wishes to make use of you here below for a good while yet before he brings you to eternal happiness—to help many people in many ways through your ministry on earth and so to have so much more to reward you for in heaven. Consequently, do away with your imaginings. Be ready for whatever hour God may be pleased to call you, and let his divine wisdom take care of things, not giving too much thought to what you mention in your letter. I would even add this: You ought to take a bit more recreation than you do; and I would not give in to any melancholy thoughts, which are usually encouraged by the devil in order to prevent at least the greater good.

We had a letter dated November 3 from Master Salmerón in Vilna, a city of Lithuania near Moscow and Lesser Tartary. We have since heard that he arrived at Vienna in Austria, which is rather close to Italy. We have not had a letter from him; when we do, we will let Your Lordship know.

Master Pedro de Ribadeneira reached Louvain and the imperial court, and has begun preaching, to the great edification and admiration of all, as Your Lordship will see from a copy of a letter which I enclose from our Master Bernard Olivier, himself a fine preacher.

Nothing more, except that we all commend ourselves to the prayers of Your Lordship.

Since the ninth Our Father's health has been rather bad, but he is at present improving.

Please show to our men what is said about Ribadeneira and Salmerón.

Rome, February 18, 1556

✠

To Albert V, duke of Bavaria

Rome, January 20, 1556

(Letter 6116: X:538–40; in Latin)

In the midst of the Reformation, the rulers of Bavaria were ardent champions of Catholicism. As early as 1549, Jesuits had come to Ingolstadt at the request of Duke William IV to work at the almost defunct university, with the hope of eventually starting a college there. The duke's death brought an end to the project until 1555, when his son and successor, Duke Albert V, began negotiations and quickly concluded a draft agreement with Peter Canisius for a college. Canisius was careful about details, for example, carefully specifying the amount of the annual income for the college and the provision of a garden for the Jesuit community (on which he strongly insisted). The duke wanted the endowment of the college to be contingent on teaching theology and preaching under a binding contractual obligation. Ignatius politely refused that obligation; he wanted neither to tie down the faculty to such requirements nor to undertake them except gratuitously. In May 1556 the duke agreed to the foundation terms and within a year there were five priests and thirteen scholastics from Germany, the Netherlands, Spain, Austria, Italy, and France who had arrived and set to work in the college. But they never got the garden.

Ihus.

Most Illustrious Prince and Most Honored Lord in Christ:

May the sovereign grace and eternal love of our God and Lord Jesus Christ adorn Your Excellency with a continual increase of his spiritual gifts.

Through Your Excellency's letter to me on December 12 and one from Doctor Canisius on the eighteenth, with the accompanying articles

signed by both parties, I have been apprised of Your Excellency's decision—holy and befitting the dignity of so Catholic and excellent a
prince—to found a college at Ingolstadt and provide a seminary there
for good and faithful ministers of the Catholic religion. This entire
proposal, together with Your Excellency's eagerness to provide what
pertains to yourself in the articles, and your insistence in requiring from
us the ministry which the demands of charity had impelled us to offer
and in urging us to send the men for the college as soon as possible,
constitute for us a proof of Your Excellency's noble mind and determination to champion the true religion in your lands. Zealous as we already were to labor strenuously for the cause of the faith in Germany,
particularly in Bavaria, Your Excellency's zeal has inflamed our desire
even more. And our resolve is therefore not just eventually to fulfill
what we have promised but truly to surpass it, and to make whatever
effort lies in our slight power to carry out the terms of the articles sent
to us, all of which tend to the general good of religion. However, the
character of our Institute requires that we give altogether freely what
we have freely received; neither our custom nor our Constitutions permit us to accept the endowment of a college contingently upon obligation to preach or to teach theology. We are ready to provide these services, but we cannot be bound to do so by contract or obligation—nor,
conversely, do we wish Your Excellency under any such obligation. On
our side, the heartfelt debt we owe to Your Excellency and to your
illustrious house, as the strong pillar of the Catholic faith in Germany,
together with our own impulse of charity to come to the aid of orthodox
religion in its deep distress, will be the equivalent of any articles or
contracts in moving us to endeavor not just to maintain but to increase
every day the services we shall have begun to furnish. And as for Your
Excellency and your illustrious successors, we trust that you too, spontaneously and prompted by charity towards your own domains and towards
our Society (which is deeply devoted to you), will foster this college of
ours (or rather, yours) and deem that the income assigned it should be
increased, not diminished, as its numbers increase, for as long a time as
our men prove themselves of value to the commonwealth. Should they
ever cease to be so (God forbid), then we ourselves would prefer to
forgo the income and see it turned to more useful religious purposes.

I am nevertheless sending Your Excellency what our Society's
Institute binds us to furnish, even unbidden, to founders of the Society's colleges; this is not a contractual obligation but one binding us on
the basis of our own Constitutions, which were drafted and enacted by

us prior to the establishment of any of our numerous colleges in Christian and infidel lands.

Your Excellency's request that we send the college staff without delay will, so far as in us lies, by all means be met. Within twenty days of the arrival of Your Excellency's reply to this letter, the men will be dispatched from Rome.

However, the men destined for the college are not all in one place, and there will doubtless be difficulty in getting them free from their present locations. Hence, it would greatly expedite things if Your Excellency wrote to the Sovereign Pontiff of your intention, requesting him to order me to effect the immediate transfer of the men destined for Your Excellency, and also asking him to bestow his blessing upon the men as they depart. In this way His Holiness's influence will make it easier for me to withdraw the men destined for you from wherever they will have to be taken. However, if Your Excellency would rather not write to the Sovereign Pontiff, I will still deliver on my promise, and with God's guidance the men will be able to reach Ingolstadt before the onset of summer.

The honorable Lord Heinrich, to whom I shall write more fully, will be able to inform Your Excellency about the number of men to be sent and other details.[2]

Meanwhile, I beseech the divine Goodness to have pity at long last on the suffering church of Germany, and to pour out lavishly upon Your Illustrious Excellency, as its strongest and most faithful defender, the gifts of his grace.

Rome, January 20, 1556

> Your Excellency's most humble servant in the Lord,
>
> [Ignatius]

☩

To Nicoló-Pietro Cesari

Rome, February 2, 1556

(Letter 6155: X:612–6f.; in Italian)

---

[2] Heinrich Schweicker, Albert V's secretary.

Ignatius had brought Ottaviano Cesari from Sicily to Rome in 1555. Then when Paul IV became pope, Ottaviano's father again renewed his campaign there that Ottaviano be allowed to visit his mother in Naples (see earlier letters nos. 4115, 4116, and 5544). Meanwhile, when the young man fell ill in Rome, Ignatius gave in, hoping the visit would not harm his vocation. The young man started out firm therein; but by early May of 1556 he wrote to Ignatius from his parent's home, saying that he was useless to the Society and requesting his dismissal. This was then granted.

Jhus.

My Most Honored Lord in Jesus Christ:

May the sovereign grace and eternal love of Christ our Lord be always our help and protection.

Having promised to send our brother Ottaviano to Naples for a period of vacation once the worst of the winter was over, in order to give satisfaction to his lady mother, we have decided to do so as soon as possible, so that he could be there during the vacation before Lent and console his mother in our Lord with frequent visits, though he will stay at the college—where, however, any special regime he may need in order to gain strength will be provided. For the rest, I am confident both Your Lordship and his mother and your whole household will encourage him in his vocation rather than the contrary; otherwise, I do not think he would be willing to stay in Naples, nor could I expose him to a danger he could perhaps not withstand.

Since he himself will bear this letter, there is no need to add anything except that I earnestly recommend and offer myself to Your Lordships, and pray to God our Lord that he may give to all of us grace always to know his most holy will and perfectly to fulfill it.

Rome, February 2, 1556

✠

To Juan de Mendoza

Rome, February 7, 1556

(Letter 6177: X:650f.; in Spanish)

Mendoza is urged to await the arrival from Flanders of King Philip's approval for his entering the Society before he comes from Naples to Rome.

Jhus.

My Lord in our Lord:

We have been informed by special letter from the rector of our college in Naples of Your Worship's strong wish to come to Rome, since it seems to you that permission from the court is too long in arriving and would never be gotten otherwise. While your ardor for placing yourself in a state of greater perfection and your impatience over the delay to these good and holy desires is highly edifying to us all, I nevertheless believe in our Lord that in consideration of what is best both for yourself and for the Society, you ought to wait a bit longer. It is possible that the King's permission may have been obtained by now, and that you would soon be able to do with His Majesty's gracious approval what you would now do without it. For love of Christ our Lord and of myself, I beg Your Worship to do me the favor of waiting at least until we get word back from our men, meanwhile thinking that your body is already where your heart is, and taking this [period of] waiting as one of the greatest probations Your Worship would have to undergo.

I shall add no more, except to ask God our Lord to direct all Your Worship's affairs with a very special providence as will be for his greater service and glory, and to grant all of us the grace of always knowing his most holy will and entirely fulfilling it.

Rome, February 7, 1556

✠

For Those Going to Begin the College in Prague
by Commission

Rome, February 12, 1556

(Letter 6205: X:689–97; in Italian)

The situation of the Catholic faith in Bohemia in the mid-sixteenth century gave every reason to doubt whether it would long survive. The Hussite heritage and the Utraquist controversy of the previous decades about Communion under the forms of both bread and wine; the resistance of much of the Czech nobility, already in part Protestant, to the new King Ferdinand I, who was both Catholic and German; the attraction of Lutheranism to a large portion of the middle class; and the general falling away of the peasantry all contributed to that doubt.

In 1554 King Ferdinand asked the Jesuits to come to help turn the tide. He entered into negotiations with Canisius for the foundation of a college. In June

1556 four priests, five scholastics, and three brothers began the enterprise in a former Dominican convent, St. Clement, which had been given to them. The institution had a very difficult time at its beginning. There were few students, most were ill prepared, some of the citizens were openly hostile and, despite great promises of support, money was in very short supply. In the long run, however, Ignatius's willingness to take on a difficult mission was fully vindicated. The Clementinum, as the college came to be known, turned out to be one of the great success stories of the Jesuit educational apostolate.

This letter is typical of the orderly and detailed instructions that Ignatius often produced for important new ventures.

INSTRUCTION FOR THE COLLEGE AT PRAGUE

Three aims should be pursued in Prague. The first is the edification of the city and realm. The second is the preservation and growth of our own men in spirit, learning, and numbers. The third is working toward the permanent material foundation of the college, for the better service of God our Lord in the first and second aims.

THE EDIFICATION OF THE CITY AND REALM

We ought to have due care and solicitude not only to preserve and further the spiritual progress of those who are Catholics there, but also to win over the heretics and schismatics, who are numerous, so that they may be brought back to the bosom of holy Church and the way of salvation.

The ordinary means for assisting these two classes of persons are the following:

1. A holy desire and zeal for the salvation of those souls and for the honor of God: this will give rise to prayer, which should be offered daily for this intention. Also, among the intentions in our sacrifices of the Mass we should always have this one, offering Christ crucified to the eternal Father for the salvation of the souls in that city and kingdom; even if there are other intentions, this one should never be missing.

2. The men's example of every Christian virtue: this more than anything else will move the spirits of those who know them to imitate their faith and way of living.

3. Familiar and loving conversation, especially by those of our men who have a gift for this. Since this requires the expenditure of time, it is best invested in persons suited to helping others, such as those who

are influential because of their authority or learning, or who one thinks might be won to the divine service in religious life. The superior should carefully consider who ought to converse with externs and who not, and who with which persons.

4. The Spiritual Exercises. However, those of the First Week can be extended to many persons, the others to fewer—those mentioned in the preceding paragraph with whom one would best invest time in conversation.

5. Preaching in German, Latin, or both (until this can be done in Bohemian). Here the aim should be to establish and confirm Catholic dogma rather than to refute the opposing sects, so as not to alienate people's minds right from the beginning; [this should] also [be our aim] because the strengthening of Catholics does much to confute the adversaries. In all this one should convey to the hearers charity and desire for the heretics' and schismatics' salvation, avoiding all rabble-rousing contentiousness. However, if there should be a sect with few followers and little influence, it would not be unsuitable to preach against them.

6. Lectures on Scholastic theology (if there is a likely audience). Thought should be given to which books to teach, and to whether it would be good to lecture on Doctor Canisius's or some other theological compendium (consultations on this can be done in Vienna and also in Prague), or on the Master of the Sentences [Peter Lombard] or some other doctor suited to the place and time. Moreover, in refuting dogmas opposed to Catholic teaching, what was said above about preaching should be observed: all appearance of contentiousness ought to be avoided and heartfelt charity displayed towards all.

7. Scripture lectures: here too passages should be selected which advice from experts indicates as most appropriate. As for the manner, see whether it should be adapted to theology students or to the people, and whether part of the lecture ought to be devoted to exhortation or preaching—keeping in mind what was said above about discussing contrary dogmas.

8. Consider whether it would be useful, in addition to preaching, also to teach Christian doctrine to schoolboys and uneducated persons, in German or in Latin, in one or more classes, or in the church on feast days or also weekdays. Care should be taken to have a form of catechism which children and simple persons can purchase, adequately grasp, and learn by heart. This should be done for the students as well. I believe Dr. Canisius has put out such a catechism.

9. Consider the advisability of holding lectures on cases of conscience; in any case, there should be lectures on mathematics.

10. For the present three classes of languages and humane letters will suffice: one for intermediate students who can understand a teacher in Latin; one for the more advanced, with instruction in rhetoric and the more important books; and one for Greek and Hebrew. The latter could be attended by students from the first two classes if it is taught at a time when they can come. At present it would be best not to assign teachers or classes for little boys, partly since we have no one who knows Bohemian to do it, partly so as to win for the college greater prestige, and partly to create a desire for classes and instruction for young boys. Then at a later time we can render the city a more pleasing service by providing persons to take care of the lowest level.

11. Consider whether to have exercises in disputation, with modesty and discretion as regards the contrary dogmas, as indicated above; and also whether to have the students write compositions, taking care that they make progress in letters and spirit.

12. Consider whether on Sundays, following the Roman practice, it would be good to have one of the house or an extern student give a public oration on a theme proposed by the teacher and corrected by him; these could treat topics of edification regarding Christian religion and morals.

13. There might be occasional presentations of dialogues, poetry, or declamations, as at Rome, to aid and encourage the students and their families and to gain authority for the classes.

14. While accepting into the classes persons of every sort who are willing to observe due decorum and discipline, efforts should be made to get them to give up indecent language, oaths, blasphemies, and other evil habits.

15. Charitable works should be attended to, such as visiting and helping in prisons and hospitals in spiritual and, if possible, corporal matters; in general, care should be taken to practice the works of mercy according to the Society's Institute.

16. As for heretics and schismatics, special care should be taken to be armed against their teaching and to have ready to mind the grounds opposed to their errors, so as to employ them at the proper time and place with that dexterity and kindliness suited to draw them to Catholic thinking.

17. Those who claim that they communicate under both species by permission of the Church, and it is clear that they are telling the truth and are otherwise Catholic, should not be denied absolution. If they are students, it would be good to have them observe the practice of monthly confession and daily Mass, and the other regulations of our colleges appropriate for them; but they should not be given Communion in our church unless they agree to receive it under one species, as do our men. If they are in some error against the Catholic religion or if it is not clear that they have a permission to communicate under both species which excuses them from sin, they should not be given absolution, nor should they be allowed to make their confession in our house or attend our Masses. Otherwise, however, they should be treated with all charity, and every possible effort should be made to win them over. Even if they are excommunicated, we can converse with them in order to help them. In the case of innocent younger boys, we may more readily believe they will let themselves be restored and guided.

18. With Catholics, we should strive that they do not fail to go to confession and Communion regularly every month (if they have the requisite age) according to the practice of the Roman church; through exhortations they might also be brought to receive these sacraments more often than once a month.

19. We should attempt to get Catholics to observe as far as possible the precepts of the Church regarding foods and fasting (if they are of the appropriate age); similarly with the other precepts—but exercising leniency in matters where this is allowable, as with children in Christ.

20. For all these matters it will help to learn the mind of His Royal Majesty and his counselors and to confer with our men at Vienna and with Dr. Canisius, who in any case ought to go and stay at Prague during this initial period. What course to take on the above matters should be left up to him and to the rector with his consultors; in addition, advice might be obtained on other matter from friends in the country there.

THE PRESERVATION AND GROWTH OF OUR MEN IN SPIRIT, LEARNING, AND NUMBERS

1. The better our men are in themselves, the better instruments they will be for the edification of others. Hence, every man should strive for a right intention, so that he seeks not his own interests but those of Christ Jesus. They should strive to acquire great resolves and desires to be true and faithful servants of God and to render a good

account of themselves in whatever is entrusted to them, with genuine abnegation of their own will and judgment, submitting themselves to God's governance through obedience, whether they are employed in high things or lowly. They should strive in their prayers to obtain this grace from the Giver of every good thing. And their head should give them these reminders and others which will be for their spiritual benefit.

2. They will observe the practice and procedure for confessing every week, examining their conscience, and hearing Mass, according to the custom at Rome; similarly with the time of prayer and other rules observed here which can be adapted to the college in Prague. However, this will have to be done selectively and after hearing the opinion of our men there who have more experience of Germany. They should send us a copy of whichever rules they select for use in the college at Prague.

3. They should practice preaching in the house at meals, one each time, with no more than an hour to think out the sermon; and sometimes [they should preach] extempore, on a topic assigned them. This should be sometimes in German, sometimes in Latin, or even in Bohemian when they learn it. They should endeavor to adopt the style deemed suitable for satisfying and moving the people who are to hear their sermons. Regarding this style, Dr. Canisius and our men in Vienna can give them whatever indications they think good.

4. The scholastics should strive to make progress in letters, as directed by their teachers or superiors, with exercises in composition and debate. Efforts should be made to free them from household duties by obtaining coadjutors in Prague for the kitchen, dispensary, and so forth, so that our men are not kept busy with these things—even though they may have exercises of humility during the hours when they cannot study, as is the practice here in Rome.

5. The teachers will be the two doctors, [James] Tilia in Scholastic theology and Heinrich [Blyssem] in Scripture and Hebrew; and Master William [Droghens] in Greek and rhetoric; and Peter Silvius [van der Bossche] in humanities unless at the beginning or later on it appears another should teach for him. Whoever the teachers are, they should have special concern for our scholastics; and Dr. Heinrich can be the syndic or prefect of studies.

6. Care should be taken to keep our men healthy and strong enough for the labors of God's service. Hence, the rector should not let them exhaust themselves in studies or other devotions, but see that everything is moderated in accord with the qualities of individual persons.

7. They should strive for the Society's good reputation and [attempt] to give edification by their example and conversation, rendering themselves amiable to everyone and worthy of being esteemed and reputed servants of God.

8. They should be on the lookout to gain or win for Christ new members in Prague and Bohemia who possess or show promise of acquiring ability for the service of God and the help of souls. Nevertheless, no one attending the classes may be accepted without the consent of those who have responsibility for him. However, they can be urged to persevere in their good desires and in frequenting the sacraments, and in trying to get their families' consent. If they are somewhat older, they might indicate to their families that they wish to go elsewhere to study, either to Rome at the German College, or to Ingolstadt when there is a college there, or to Vienna, without revealing any wish to become religious if their families are not aware of it. There is less difficulty about accepting persons wishing to enter the Society who are not from our classes. If any uproar or disturbance is feared, they can be sent somewhere else, as indicated above. But it would be good to forewarn the other place and await reply, except in the case of such excellent candidates that there can be no doubt about their suitability for admission; these could be sent right away when it would be inconvenient to wait for a reply.

9. The rector will have two or three consultors; these should probably be the two doctors and Peter Silvius [van der Bossche].

THE PERMANENT MATERIAL FOUNDATION AND EXPANSION OF THE COLLEGE

1. The observance of the above-mentioned points will be calculated to render the college's permanent foundation more likely, the more useful it proves for the common good.

2. They should treat with the King to ensure that the Dominican friars who are leaving their monastery be given sufficient sureties and guarantees that they will continue receiving their income in the monastery where they are going. The one to take care of this will be Dr. Canisius or whomever he designates.

3. Steps should be taken to ensure that the income to be applied to the new college be firmly set, and that the amount be increased as much as possible to furnish support for a good number of men who will be recruited there or sent there from other places.

4. Each one should have his own bed, books, and other necessaries, either in common or individually, so that there is no want of what is needed for maintenance, health, and study.

5. For all these purposes they should strive to preserve and increase the goodwill of His Royal Majesty, the city, and persons who can be of greater help, bending to their wishes and serving them in charitable works and in whatever else they can, for the greater glory of God.

6. They should strive to preserve and increase their good reputation with these persons; and the latter should be given to know that the Society can be expected to go forward and increase, for such is its practice, and not fall short from its side.

7. Consider the advisability of their carrying on these temporal matters through others rather than themselves; or, if they do it themselves, it should be in such a way as to make clear that they are motivated by desire for the common good, as indeed they are, and not by any greed for temporal goods.

8. They should write at least every month to Rome, and to the colleges in Germany as often as they shall have mutually agreed to do.

February 12, 1556

9. Each week the rector should take an hour to read through this instruction.

By commission of Our Father Master Ignatius,
JOAN DE POLANCO

✠

To Alejo Fontana, from Juan de Polanco
by commission

Rome, February 16, 1556

(Letter 6216: XI:5f.; in Spanish)

Fontana had long been an official of the imperial chancellery of Charles V in the Netherlands and in Germany. At Speyer, in that latter country, he had come to know Pierre Favre and ever after became a lasting friend of the Society, always ready to help it. In Brussels he had given good advice to Pedro Ribadeneira, who had come there to present to Charles V a petition for the establishment of the Society in the Netherlands. Printing the letter from the Indies was a way of expanding knowledge of the Society and of awakening a missionary spirit. The com-

*ment on Zaragoza refers to the problems that the Jesuits encountered in establishing
a house there.*

My Most Excellent Sir in Jesus Christ:

The peace of Christ.

After writing the letters in this post (which we were unable to
send by way of Milan), we received Your Worship's of January 18 with
others from Señor Pedro de Zárate; but those from Master Pedro Ribadeneira which, as you wrote, were accompanying yours did not arrive.
However, we received great comfort and consolation from the content of
your letter (and Our Father sends you his deepest respects) informing
us of His Imperial Majesty's renunciation of his estates and departure
for Spain. The world surely has plentiful reason to give thanks to God
our Lord at the sight of an example like this, one which would hardly
be believed if not seen, so tightly do men cling to far-lesser things of
the earth. May God, the infinite and supreme good, fill the father
[Charles V]'s heart with the things of heaven; and may he increase his
gifts in the son [Philip II], so that he will not let himself be overwhelmed by governing such vast and important dominions, and will
administer them for the great glory of him who bestowed them, for the
universal good, and for his own merit and crown of eternal happiness. It
is only right that all good men should implore the divine and supreme
Goodness for very special graces for His Majesty to enable him to admi-
rably carry this burden upon his shoulders, however great it is.

Your Worship will do us a great favor by letting us know the
address of Señor Vargas, and consequently your own.

What you say of Master Pedro Ribadeneira's way of handling
affairs and preaching carries great weight, as one might expect, with Our
Father and all of us; we have therefore rejoiced not a little in our Lord,
although we hope to hear more details upon arrival of the letters that
must have been left there.

After the copybooks with the letters from the Indies, Your Worship will have received the letters that were printed out in full, for they
were sent shortly afterwards. Regarding whether to print them in the
vernacular or not, Your Worships will better be able to tell what will be
more edifying, to the glory of God our Lord, which alone is what we
aim at. My own view is that a good disposition of mind, or the lack of
it, has a lot to do with whether these things are taken well or not.

On the matter of Zaragoza we have no more recent news than
what we sent you. If God grants that the news be true that they sent

here yesterday about the five-year peace, this will entail, among many other goods, that we will be able to communicate with each other more frequently. In any case, we trust that God our Lord will draw some good from the disorders in that city, as is the wont of his omnipotence and goodness. May he be pleased to preserve always and increase in Your Worship the gifts of his grace, and give to all of us grace to know always and fulfill his most holy will.

Rome, February 16, 1556.

☩

To Olivier Mannaerts

Rome, February 22, 1556

(Letter 6230 XI:37f.; in Italian)

Diomede, a scholastic under Mannaerts's jurisdiction at Loreto,[3] about whom there is no further information, had been corresponding secretly with his family, who showed dislike of religious life and of the Society of Jesus in particular, especially its name. The letter directly addressed to Diomede no longer exists. As for the name of this new group, the Society of Jesus, it had often been strongly attacked. Was not the whole Church the society of Jesus, as they charged, and was it not pretentious for a single group to arrogate the name to itself? Ignatius adamantly insisted upon retaining the name, not least of all because the pope had approved it. The reference to "the inquisitors" is understandable in the heightened concern for orthodoxy at the time and in Ignatius's own experience of false accusations about the orthodoxy of his own teachings.

Enclosed is a letter for Diomede. Your Reverence will decide whether to give it to him or not. I do not know what he wrote, and here we do not have time to read all the letters like his which the men write to their families. But Your Reverence should give an order for no one to write from his college without his letters being seen. In our view, it would be good for Diomede to write his family a letter saying that the previous one had been written without his superiors' knowledge, that is, without their having corrected it. But since you see that this would be neither agreeable nor helpful to him, he shall stop writing to them, especially in view of the little affection they show for religious orders, and in particular for the one to which Diomede has been called by God and whose name they find so offensive. To help him see that he is wrong, you could send him the enclosed copy of the reasons for this

---

[3] Mannaerts's name was variously spelled Manaerts or Manare or Manareus.

name, and write to him on the part of his superiors that Catholics are accustomed and obliged to speak more respectfully about things which have been approved by the Apostolic See. For should anyone wish to show this letter of his to the inquisitors, it might suffice to bring the writer under suspicion of thinking ill of the religious state and of the supreme Vicar of Christ our Lord—the usual errors of the heretics of our time. Tell him that for his own greater good we urge him to think about such matters with more humility and purity. If you think it preferable to give him no answer, then do so. Silence and ignoring him will be an answer of sorts. In that case, please return the letter to us.

✠

To Andrés de Oviedo

Rome, February 27, 1556

(Letter 6243: XI:57f.; in Spanish)

Oviedo, named coadjutor bishop to the patriarch João Nunes Barreto for the mission to Ethiopia that the King of Portugal was sponsoring, wrote to Ignatius describing the canonical scruples that made him reluctant to accept the episcopacy, and his worry about his responsibility to his titular see of Hierapolis, a defunct ancient diocese in Phrygia in Turkey. How could he minister to its people if he was in Ethiopia? As a matter of fact, Oviedo heroically spent about twenty years in Ethiopia, expending all his efforts almost for naught, and dying there in great poverty.

Jesus

May the sovereign grace and love of Christ our Lord be always our continual protection and help.

Since I am writing at length to the patriarch and the letter is to a great extent for both of you, this one will be shorter. I commend myself in a special way to your prayers and Sacrifices. I wish to have a share in all the good and holy works of your ministry of working in those kingdoms; and I offer you a share in all the merits of the Society, which considers you her own no less than before, but in a certain sense even more—as you also will consider us as your own in our Lord. May it please the divine and sovereign Wisdom and Goodness to enlighten you always and to make of you a very important and universal instrument of his divine service and help for the common good.

I am writing to the patriarch that he already has *in petto* the dispensations from going to Rome, the relaxation of the oath to observe the canons, and many others, such as for using the Society's faculties and the rest. There will be no need for scruples on this score.

We do not know where the Diocese of Hierapolis is, and there is no reason for going to the trouble of finding out, since His Holiness's intention was that it should merely serve you as a title, and that all your efforts and ministry should be devoted to the great and ample vineyard of Christ our Lord in Ethiopia. You are to assist the patriarch and then succeed in his place if you outlive him. If, while there, you should desire to resign, you will be able to do so, or send a document from there renouncing the Bishopric of Hierapolis into His Holiness's hands.

It has consoled us in our Lord to hear of the edification which they write us you have given by your example and teaching and numerous holy labors in the Archbishopric of Évora and elsewhere. May God our Lord keep and increase you always in his holy spirit and grace, for he knows it is much needed for an enterprise of such great moment for his service; may he give all of us his grace always to know his sovereign will and perfectly to fulfill it.

Rome, February 27, 1556

Entirely yours in our Lord,
IGNACIO

✠

To Nicolás Bobadilla

Rome, March 8, 1556

(Letter 6281: XI:116f.; in Italian)

Nicolás Bobadilla had been sent as papal visitor several times to reform convents and monasteries. This time it was to the Silvestrine monks that he was sent to reform some twenty of their houses in Umbria, Tuscany, and the Marches of Ancona, a task that necessitated a good deal of hard travel. In one instance, he had a recalcitrant monk imprisoned, only to have him calling on influential friends for help. The friends then complained to Ignatius. This letter walks a fine line between not interfering with Bobadilla while still responding to the requests of an influential and important benefactor.

Jhus.

May the sovereign grace and everlasting love of Christ our Lord be always our continual help and protection.

Yesterday the Most Reverend Cardinal d'Armagnac sent me one of his gentlemen with a letter written to him on behalf of Don Girardo di Sassoferrato, who on your order has been in prison for some months, not without danger to his life. What is asked is that this religious be treated less rigorously and his case be settled justly. I am confident in the Lord that your behavior has been in accord with religion and charity, and that without any other urging than that of your own conscience you will do what is asked. Nevertheless, with the intervention of the respect we owe to the Most Reverend Cardinal, in whom the whole Society has had from the beginning such a loving patron and benefactor and to whom we are so indebted and anxious to render every service for the glory of God our Lord, I cannot help strongly urging you, so far as justice and regard for the general good of the Silvestrine Order allow, to show consideration for this religious upon the recommendation of the Most Reverend Cardinal. The latter has no desire that justice and the common good should suffer, but only that so far as can be done in God's sight, all possible clemency and kindness should be used. To me as well it will bring great satisfaction and consolation in our Lord. May his grace bring us always to know and carry out his most holy will.

Rome, March 8, 1556

✠

To Francis Borgia

Rome, March 9, 1556
(Letter 6282: XI:117f.; in Spanish)

Enrique de La Cueva had made a vow to enter the Society (see letters 4485 and 5953) and had renewed it later in the presence of Nadal. Now he sought a dispensation from his vow. Borgia thought he should be allowed to depart; Nadal and Araoz thought the same. They awaited a decision from Ignatius, who was reluctant to let La Cueva leave, but was willing to let him postpone a departure, because he was engaged in fruitful apostolic works. In the end, however, he left the decision to Borgia. In response to a lengthy plea from Enrique, Ignatius eventually dissolved his vow. (The "added comment" seems to have been written by Polanco.)

To write what I think: I would not dare to loose his vows, by which he offered and dedicated himself entirely to the service and glory of God, perpetual chastity, poverty, and obedience. For it is more reasonable to help him go forward rather than turn back, so far as we can. On the other hand, if he has at present no devotion for entering the Society in the same form as its other members, I would have no difficulty with his staying for a time in his present state of life, for we understand that he devotes himself to preaching and bearing fruit among his neighbors, and we believe that he will give good example with his life. Hence, if you judge there that he ought to be loosed from his vow, this should not be done without informing us first. As for the other matter of putting off for a year, more or less, his coming to live among our men and as they do, depending upon the devotion he displays or what you think best in the Lord, I leave that up to you. *[Added comment:]* I am not sure Our Father refers to the vow this man made before entering upon probation and repented of a year later, etc., but this is likely.

✠

To Miguel de Torres

Rome, March 15, 1556

(Letter 6295: XI:134; in Spanish)

Scholastics who have not yet pronounced final vows have renounced use or management of their property but not ownership of it until their last vows. Could they accept a benefice if so ordered by superiors? Ignatius answers Torres, the provincial of Portugal, in the affirmative, as long as they are ready to relinquish it when so commanded. Sometimes it would be proper to accept a benefice under that condition. One reason for this provision was that if someone left the Society in the probationary period, he would not be without resources. But if such a benefice involved the care of souls as an obligation, its occupant had to make provision for another to undertake that care. Writing the Portuguese provincial, Ignatius combines a caution against premature renunciation of goods with cultivation of an attitude of complete inner detachment from them.

The students who have the three vows of poverty, chastity, and obedience, not unconditionally but as prescribed in the Constitutions, which state that the poverty they promise is not actual poverty until they make profession or the vows of a formed coadjutor, do not violate their vow when they accept a benefice at the command of the superior and remain ready to relinquish it at any moment and whenever so commanded after the first year of probation. The advisability of this is another matter. In some cases, barring disedification, retaining the benefices could be proper, and numerous men here have been permitted this for a long time, especially where they are not curates. Even in the latter case, it may be allowed for some just cause ordained to God's greater service, provided the occupants attend to the care of the souls.

To Alfonso Ramírez de Vergara

Rome, March 30, 1556

(Letter 6327: XI:184–86; in Spanish)

Ramírez, an eminent ecclesiastic, a good friend of the Society, and a special benefactor of the Jesuit colleges of Alcalá and Cuenca, had made the Exercises under Francisco Villanueva and later under Francis Borgia. He had also defended the Exercises against the attacks of the Dominicans Melchior Cano and Tomás Pedroche. In his reason he saw clearly that he should enter the Society, but in his affections he felt moved to remain outside as its benefactor. He put off a decision for so long that he was growing old. In his dilemma, he wrote to Ignatius several times about the choice to be made. Ignatius refers him to the Holy Spirit, but assures him that one can well follow reason in such a case, without requiring a new interior movement of the will.

Ihs.

My dear Sir in our Lord:

May the sovereign grace and eternal love of Christ our Lord always be our continual help and protection.

Through your own letter of February 4 and another from Father Francisco Villanueva, I have learned about your personal situation and your decision. As for commending you to God our Lord and having others do the same, I most willingly accept the charge; for I wish for you—as I ought—not only every perfection but every consolation as well.

The means for relishing with the affection and carrying out with sweetness a course which reason dictates to be for God's greater service and glory is something that will be taught you by the Holy Spirit better than by anyone else. Of course, it is true that in pursuing what is better and more perfect, it suffices to be moved by reason, and the other movement, that of the will, even if it did not precede the decision and execution, can easily follow it, as God our Lord repays our trust in his providence, our complete self-abandonment, and our giving up of our own consolation by giving us a deep contentment and relish, and a spiritual consolation that is all the richer the less we aim at it and the more purely we seek his glory and will. May his infinite and supreme goodness deign to guide all your affairs as he sees will best lead to this end.

The business matters you have entrusted to me will be taken care of. Master Polanco will write more fully about this, and I refer you to him.

As for the other matters you discussed with Father Francis [Borgia] in Alcalá and about which Master Nadal brought a memorandum, I commend them to him, confident that he will not fail to do whatever he can for your service and consolation.

May Christ our Lord give to all of us his grace always to know his most holy will and entirely to fulfill it.

Rome, March 30, 1556

I am writing to Father Francis that if it can be done without prejudice to God's greater service, it would console me to satisfy you by having Father Villanueva come to Alcalá. I hope that he will, although he may be delayed somewhat by getting the work launched at Plasencia —a work which will be no less your own than the one at Alcalá.

Date as above.

Entirely yours in our Lord,

IGNAÇIO

✠

To Alejo Fontana

Rome, March 31, 1556

(Letter 6330: XI:189f.; in Spanish)

This letter principally takes up two matters. Juan de Mendoza, the governor of Castel Nuovo in Naples, had left his position there, without receiving the permission of his parents or of King Philip II, in order to enter the Society. He betook himself to the Jesuit college in Naples, but Ignatius did not want to receive him until he had been pardoned for his disobedience to the King and allowed to enter. The first part of the letter expresses satisfaction that the case has been settled.

This letter next deals with the situation that arose when Philip II took over as King of Spain after the abdication of his father, Charles, and proceeded to relieve Fontana, the longtime friend and benefactor of the Society, of his long-held position in the chancellery. Fontana was understandably disappointed at being replaced but, as Polanco remarked, saw the hand of God in the situation and accepted it as a help to his spiritual life. He was later named treasurer of the island of Sardinia and in 1557 founded a college of the Society there.

Jhus.

My Lord in our Lord:

May the sovereign grace, etc.

A few days after receiving Your Worship's letter of the tenth of this month, I received the much longer one of the ninth as a great favor, since it gave details on matters we were eager to know about. The procedure observed in handling the two packets dealing with Don Juan de Mendoza was excellent. We received word from Señor Ruy Gómez a few days ago that we would be able to accept Don Juan, and he has consequently come from Naples to the house here in Rome, where he is applying himself to his probations to the great satisfaction of all; and we trust that God our Lord will give him the grace to be a true servant of his. At the same time we got news of the favor granted by His Royal Majesty to Don Alvaro [de Mendoza] regarding the castle. May God's will be done in all of them.

Regarding the distribution of secretarial offices, it seems to me that you are quite right in taking this event as from the hand of God, whose greater service and glory, in all conditions and states of life, ought to be purely what we seek. When a person with that end in view tries one means and then another, he should be convinced that the one that did not work out was not the right one for the end he had in view, and he should therefore give no less heartfelt thanks to God's supreme goodness for putting what he sought out of reach than he would for his obtaining it. The contentment and peace which you experience in this regard is a strong sign of the sincere concern and desire for God our Lord's greater service which he gives to you. May he be pleased, in the deliberation which you mention, to give you his light and spirit so that you may make the correct choice of what will be for his greater glory and praise and for your own greater perfection. As is only right, we shall pray here for this intention. I will merely add that I think it quite reasonable for you to take your health into account, and not to tire yourself beyond what your forces and person can endure, but preserve your health for God's greater service.

Regarding Master Pedro de Ribadeneira and Master Bernard [Olivier] and the business they have in hand, I will add nothing except that I pray that God our Lord will guide them according as he wills; and I do not doubt that Your Worship will do so for them and for all in whatever arises.

Enclosed are some letters for them, which I beg Your Worship to have delivered. If you have the time, you might read the unsealed ones, or any part that you might wish.

May Christ our Lord grant to all of us his grace so that we may always know his most holy will and entirely fulfill it.

Rome, the last of March, 1556

Besides the usual persons, the abbot Jiménez sends his deepest respects.

To Pedro de Ribadeneira, by commission

Rome, April 14, 1556

(Letter 6371: XI:252f.; in Spanish)

The Society of Jesus did not easily gain legal recognition in the Netherlands. After Charles V had abdicated, it was up to his son and successor, Philip II, to grant that formal entry into the country. Ribadeneira, acting on behalf of Ignatius, had presented the petition for such recognition. It was sent to two of the most important court officials referred to in the letter. Vigilius van Zwichem was the head of the Privy Council. He was later made archbishop of Malines, a cardinal, and viceroy of Naples. Granvelle was intransigent at anything that would infringe on Spanish power in the Netherlands and reluctant to recognize the Society of Jesus with its papal privileges. In this letter, Ignatius authorizes Ribadeneira to accept restrictions on the use of the spiritual faculties granted to the Society by the Holy See. Negotiations took a very long time.

Jhus.

The peace of Christ.

We have learned of the difficulties being raised by the Most Reverend Bishop of Arras and the Lord President Vigilius [van Zwichem], who are of the opinion that nothing should be done to the prejudice of the reverend bishops or pastors.[4] This is our view also. But we do prejudice to neither by using the faculties granted us by the Apostolic See for the help of souls. Both their authority and ours flows from the same source, and the supreme Vicar of Christ on earth was as able to give it to us as to them. It appears surprising that amid such a lack of faithful and learned workers in the vineyard entrusted to them by Christ our Lord, they are not delighted to have our men serving them without remuneration. Our men ask their permission and offer themselves as ministers with entire submission, carrying as much as they can of the burden which lies on their souls. Hence, it is difficult to come up with a good argument from the side of the churchmen; and they have

---

[4] The bishop was Antoine Perrenot Granvelle. He had been secretary of state under Charles V; later he was prime minister to Margaret of Parma in the Netherlands, cardinal, and viceroy of Naples. Ribadeneira relied greatly on his advice for the affairs of the Netherlands. Margaret of Parma was Philip II's stepsister when she was regent in the Netherlands.

no need to concern themselves with restricting or limiting the faculties which the Holy See has granted us. Nevertheless, if His Royal Majesty thinks that the Society ought to temper the exercise of its faculties for reasons that are just and ordered to the common good, our Society is willing to employ the faculties in those states only insofar as His Majesty and his successors see fit. If necessary, Our Father Master Ignatius will issue a patent under the seal of the Society and his own signature binding all those under the obedience of the Society in those states to make use of our faculties as His Majesty shall determine to be more for God's service and the help of souls; for that is our only aim.

Other matters are being written in a separate letter.

May Christ our Lord direct us all how best to serve him. Amen.

Rome, April 14, 1556

✠

To Antonio Soldevila

Rome, April 19, 1556

(Letter 6386: XI:275–77; in Spanish)

This is one of the most direct and blunt letters that Ignatius ever wrote. Its recipient, Antonio Soldevila, a Catalan, gave more than occasion for it. He entered the Society of Jesus in 1551 in Valencia and came to Rome in 1553. At first he had a reputation for devotion and spirituality, but he soon showed how eccentric and hardheaded he was. Depending on the circumstances, he was energetic or lazy; and he regularly proposed to others in the Society strange theories and interpretations of obedience.

At one point, when Soldevila was giving far-too-severe spiritual direction to a young theologian and had resisted any advice to mitigate his rigor, Ignatius finally gave him the equally severe penance of disciplining himself in the community dining room while wearing what seem to be a pair of cardboard wings and repeating, "No flying without wings." Ignatius then dismissed Soldevila from the Society, but readmitted him six months later and made him minister of the Curia community in Rome, where he again proved himself rigorist and lax by turn with the members of the community. After a few months in that position, he was named rector at Genoa, a post at which he was completely unsatisfactory; at the end of the year he had to be removed. He was ordered back to Rome, where he wanted to study. Nadal advised that in the future he never be given any responsibility involving the governing of others.

He was then sent to Naples to take charge of the cases in moral theology proposed for solution in the community. He did well at that despite continuing to be very eccentric. He became something of a hypochondriac, spending "half of his time attending to his health and the other half on theories and interpretations of obedience" that put limits upon whatever orders he was given because, he said, "obedience was a slow suicide." Finally, Ignatius wrote this letter, severely reprimanding him.

Apparently it had a good effect; Soldevila reformed and, instead of sending him to Sicily or dismissing him, Ignatius made him a community consultor in Naples. The reform did not last long. In less than three months, the rector in Naples was told to inform Soldevila that if he did not amend his ways, the Society could no longer put up with him and his conduct, and he would be dismissed. Slowly he settled down and changed for the better, devoted himself to studies, and continued to live as a Jesuit in Naples, where he worked for almost half a century until his death in 1601.

Jhus.

The peace of Christ.

I wish that my first letter to you could deal with matters of greater spiritual relish than this one will, for both its writer's and its reader's sake. However, it would be wrong not to swallow this annoyance, to see if it may not profit you more than it appears likely that it will in view of our past experience. For God our Lord is almighty, his grace is great, and it is he who guides hearts; moreover, my desire for Your Reverence's good makes me have some hope, even where there is little grounds for it from a human point of view.

We have been informed that you have not kept the promise you made to Father Madrid (not to mention others) that you would obey like a dead thing and signalize yourself in this respect, after having failed so badly in the past, as your memory together with your conscience, if you are willing to recall, will bear you abundant witness. For one who has found himself so often mistaken in his own judgment, it would be reasonable to accept and put into practice that saying of the wise Solomon, "Lean not upon your own prudence" [Prov. 3:5]. For beyond our obligation to believe Scripture, as well as the dictate of reason that no one is a good judge in his own cause, experience has taught you this to your own heavy cost. It seems to me that with your study of the logicians' teachings on obedience, you have made so much progress that both yourself and those who associate with you are apparently making yourselves out to be great interpreters and circumscribers of obedience, saying at every step that you will not be your own murderers, etc. This is the worst and most pernicious teaching that could be employed for the unity we aim at in the Society and the perfection of obedience informed by charity. It suffices, like a pestilence, to infect a whole college in short order. This is properly the spirit of pride; it undermines all the simplicity and magnanimity of obedience, and its end is voluntary apostasy or else dismissal to prevent others from being infected. Nevertheless, in this matter the Society will have regard for whatever charity it can exercise toward an individual without prejudice to the general good.

We are writing the rector [Cristobal de Mendoza], urging him to do his duty and see that obedience is observed and to give to those who need such curbing a list of the persons with whom they may talk. You will have yours. And with those to whom you do speak, take care not to teach the doctrine mentioned above; it will by no means be tolerated in the Society. Overall, see that you repent and amend, and that you do not fall back into the old difficulties you had at Rome and at Genoa. Unless you can acquire the Society's spirit and way of proceeding, you would be much better off outside it.

For the rest, I refer you to the rector, to whom we are writing.

May it please Christ our Lord to grant us true humility and abnegation of our wills and judgments, so that we may deserve to begin to be his disciples. Amen.

Rome, April 19, 1556

☩

To Gaspar Loarte

Rome, May 7, 1556

(Letter 6434: XI:340; in Spanish)

This letter prepares the rector at Genoa to tell a delinquent Jesuit, when he arrived there, of his dismissal from the Society. Whatever the fault he had committed on this occasion, he had previously been a problem, showing himself stubbornly attached to his own will, and had enjoyed little success with the students he had been teaching. Then the "escapade" became known at the court of the duke, Cosimo de Medici, and this made dismissing him desirable.

Jhus.

On Saturday we will write a letter to Florence instructing them to send Lázaro de Olmedo to Genoa. He is presently in Florence for a certain escapade he committed. As Your Reverence will see from the copies of two letters of his—one before he left and the other from outside the house—he subsequently returned and is asking for pardon. It is being given—but not so as to stay in the Society. Your Reverence ought not receive him in the house, but tell him from Our Father that his vows are dissolved and that he remains free; let him go with God. If it is possible to give him some help for taking ship for Spain, it would be good, so that he will not remain in these parts. He could also be given one or two scudi, or else directed to a hostel—as a poor man and not as a member of the Society, from which he is dismissed.

Rome, May 7, 1556

✠

To Ottaviano Cesari

Rome, May 10, 1556

(Letter 6443: XI:351; in Italian)

Transferred from Rome to Naples, Ottaviano continued to be ill. Ignatius writes to encourage him. See letters 3640, 3706, 3920, 4115, 4116, 4222, 5544, and 6155 on Cesari and his family problems.

Jhus.

The peace of Christ.

Even though you do not write us, dear brother Ottaviano, we get news every week about how you are, since we had so instructed the rector. We long to hear that you are doing better both in body and in soul, should the former be God's will—for we have no doubt of his will as regards the latter. We particularly desire that you show yourself in this illness more observant than ever of those of our rules which can and should be observed in your situation, such as the rule that the sick should try to edify those about them by their patience, and that they should be obedient to the doctor and the infirmarian. And so we urge you, dearest brother, to show your good spirit to everyone in this regard, and you will then recover your health more quickly if you are to render greater service to God our Lord thereby. We also urge upon you the respect and reverence that are owed to your parents according to the flesh in whatever is not opposed to your spiritual welfare.

You will have other news from the letter which we are writing to our men today. And so nothing more except that we all recommend ourselves to your prayers, short though they may be, and urge you to keep up your goodwill and accept your illness cheerfully from the hand of God our Lord, at the same time as you do all you can for your health.

May Christ our Lord give us life and perfect well-being. Amen.
Rome, May 10, 1556

✠

To the Jesuits Going to Clermont

Rome, May 11, 1556

(Letter 6452: XI:366–72; in Italian)

The bishop of Clermont, Guillaume du Prat, was one of the early and very generous benefactors of the Society in France. Despite the hostility of the Paris theological faculty and its decree against the Society in 1554, du Prat gave part of his Paris property for a Jesuit residence and for the foundation of a college there. When the school was founded, it became known, first, as the Collège de Clermont and afterwards as the Collège Louis-le-Grand. It was to become one of the most famous of the schools of the pre-suppression Society. Du Prat invited the Society to establish a college at Billom in his diocese of Clermont; it was the first educational establishment of the Society of Jesus in France. The school was enthusiastically received by the town of Billom, so much so that its citizens called its presence a "rebirth of the infant church."

Ignatius's instructions here for those going to Billom are similar to the ones he proposed for other groups of Jesuits sent off to inaugurate new educational and other apostolic ventures in various cities in Europe.

Jhus.

INSTRUCTION FOR THOSE OF THE SOCIETY SENT

TO CLERMONT MAY 11, 1556

Three things should be aimed at in Billom and in the Diocese of Clermont. The first regards the college of our men; the second the classes; and the third the city and diocese of His Reverence [Guillaume du Prat], the bishop of Clermont.

REGARDING THE COLLEGE

Care should be taken for our own men's preservation and increase in spirit, learning, and numbers; and also that they be supplied with lodging and other necessities according to the Institute of the Society.

1. The better our men are in themselves, the more they will be suitable instruments of divine grace in helping others. Therefore, all should strive to have a right intention, seeking exclusively "not the things that are their own but the things that are Jesus Christ's" [Phil. 2:21]. They should endeavor to have and frequently renew their resolves and desires to be true and faithful servants of God and to render a good account of themselves in whatever responsibilities they are given, with a genuine abnegation of their own will and judgment and a submission of themselves to God's governance of them by means of holy obedience, whether they are employed in high or lowly tasks. They should strive in their daily prayers to obtain this grace from the Giver of every good. Moreover, the one in charge should give them these reminders and others which will be helpful for their spiritual advancement.

2. Our men should observe the practice and method of weekly confession and Communion (with the priests celebrating more frequently), examinations of conscience, prayers, and other regulations observed in Rome. However, if the superior thinks that some of these cannot be observed, after consulting with those more versed in the matter, he should send notification to Rome of any changes made in the rules.

3. They should practice speaking the French language and preaching in French in the house during meals, now one and then another, adapting themselves to the manner best suited for making an impression on the minds of listeners from those territories. On this our own men who have experience and judicious friends will be able to give advice.

4. Our own students and the masters should follow the superior's directions in the matter of the subjects, method, and times of their studies. He will have to see to it that everyone is properly occupied, taking as his goal their own and others' aid in learning. And so that they will be less encumbered by domestic duties, the superior should try to have some coadjutors for the kitchen, the dispensary, and similar matters—although until such can be found, each one must be ready to do any service which he is commanded, especially those who are not teaching. Even if there are coadjutors, they can practice humility by helping

in some lowly service during hours when they are unable to study, as is done here in Rome.

5. The superior for the whole Diocese of Clermont will be Don Battista Viola; having been commissary of the Society in Italy, he will be the same in this diocese, although under obedience to the provincial of the kingdom, Father Don Paschase [Broët].

6. The rector will be the one appointed by Father Don Paschase; he should consider whether Master Pietro Canale might be suitable, since he will be less able than the others to attend to studies and the spiritual help of others in sermons and confessions, etc.; for he is not healthy, but should perhaps for that very reason be employed in governing.

7. Three or four consultors will be appointed as their superior, namely, the commissary, thinks best, with the provincial's approval. And should two suffice for the time being, the number of four can be reached later when we have more men in the college.

8. The superior should take care that everyone stays healthy and strong enough in body to sustain the toil of God's service. Hence, he should not let them get overtired in their studies or other devotions or spiritual exercises in the aid of souls; everything must be moderated according to the quality of persons, places, and times. A prefect of health should be appointed to watch over its preservation, in addition to the infirmarian for the sick. Even more special care must be taken of the latter, so that they do not lack a physician or whatever the physician orders in aid of their health.

9. To enable the rules and Constitutions to be kept and the task assumed at Billom to be better carried out, and also so that it can become a seedbed for increasing the workers and reaping greater fruit in the Diocese of Clermont and elsewhere, they should strive to increase the number of scholastics in the college as much as possible—even though for the present we are not sending many, in accord with the wishes of the Reverend Bishop, who asks to have only teachers and other workers and not scholastics, although in the Society's colleges it is better and usual to have many more scholastics than teachers, besides the coadjutors.

10. For this purpose they should be sure that in the building to be constructed or the house to be given for our college, there is plenty of room for a substantial number of members of the Society, besides the different classrooms for the various grades of students who will be studying under different teachers.

11. They should also attend to obtaining a solid and stable endowment for maintaining the largest possible number, in the matter of food, clothing, furniture, books, etc.

12. For these purposes they should strive always to keep the great goodwill of the Reverend Bishop, with due tact and diligence, so that if possible during his lifetime, or at least after his death, the college will be solidly endowed and established.

13. The chapter, even ecclesiastical, and the city and secular community will be able to assist, along with some particularly wealthy individuals, although the principal founder ought to be the Reverend Bishop, who should be shown the gratitude customary to other founders. Until the endowment has been made final, the Reverend Bishop will presumably make full provision; however, if discretion dictates that something be accepted from other friends and His Reverend Lordship does not take it amiss, this would not be inappropriate. In any case, the superior should make sure everyone has his own bed, clothes, and the books he needs according to the Society's practice. In all these temporal matters, ordered to spiritual good, a help will be the good reputation which proceeds from true and genuine virtues, as well as retaining as much as possible the goodwill of those who are able to help them.

THE CLASSES

1. They should examine the Society's Constitutions on universities and try their best to follow them; and it would seem that the more simply they can proceed, making use of the fewest ceremonies and the least showy insignia, all the while still attending to matters of substance as regards studies, the better it would be.

2. They should also study the rules and counsels for teachers and students at Rome so that each one can carry out his own office better; and they should make use of them as persons, places, and times allow.

3. For now, while there are no students with a grounding in theology, not much stress should be laid on teaching it. In the same way, if there are not enough students sufficiently advanced in humane letters, they should not at present try to teach the arts [philosophy] course, but instead stress humane letters, Latin and Greek, along with rhetoric; then when a suitable body of students has been prepared for the arts, they can begin that course; and when the arts students have finished their course, it will be possible to give a course of Scholastic theology with good grounding, and from that point on to continue these courses

with students being sent onward from the humanities into philosophy and from philosophy into theology.

4. Master Robert Claysson will be able to give lectures on Sacred Scripture or cases of conscience for the clergy; or if there is need and he can handle both, our men, or some of them, might attend if the superior thinks good.

5. Master Leonardo [Massero] could teach Greek and also help out with rhetoric, if needed.

6. Master Nicholas Paredense will be able to teach rhetoric or other humanistic subjects, and also Greek if necessary.

7. Master Louis [Gierardino] will be able to teach humanities and grammar; and Lambert will be his assistant or help in one of the lower classes.

8. Should more teachers be needed for the lower classes, some of our men should be provided from Paris, or else whomever they can recruit where they are; or they should manage the best they can.

9. If there is a call for Hebrew, it will be taught by whoever knows it; I think this would Master Robert.

10. The time spent in the classes should be moderate, taking into account the strength of the teachers who have poor health, and also the school practice of Billom and the readiness of the persons.

11. If they are requested for other duties, these should not be accepted without previously consulting Rome, even though they can be performed temporarily at the superior's discretion after consulting the deputies of the house and if he thinks good, some trustworthy friend outside.

12. A class in mathematics, especially on the spheres or on cosmography, could be useful, should any of our men be competent or able to give it.

13. They should try to keep alive the exercise of holding disputations, delivering public orations about edifying topics on Sundays, and writing compositions during the week, if they have suitably capable students.

14. A few times a year they could stage dialogues and have orations or verses declaimed to encourage both the students and their families, carefully rehearsing the boys or young students for this.

15. At the beginning of the studies, our men should deliver public speeches, and occasionally exercise their style in composition, aided by whomever the superior judges most capable among them for this.

REGARDING THE CITY AND THE DIOCESE

1. For the edification of others, the first help will be the example of all Christian virtues, as well as zeal and longing for the salvation of the souls in that place and for God's honor in them. This will give rise to prayers and holy sacrifices, which they will frequently offer to the eternal Father for this effect, having at least this intention—I mean spiritual good—among the others.

2. Another help will be familiar and loving conversations at due times and places and with persons who the superior judges will profit from such conversation, for example, those who are suitable for helping others. This would include persons influential either through authority or learning, or who it is thought might be won for God's service in religious life. The superior should take care to decide who should converse with outsiders and who not, or who with these persons and who with those.

3. The Spiritual Exercises of the First Week can be given to numerous persons, the remaining Weeks to fewer; however, they may be given to those mentioned in the previous paragraph who could be suitable for helping others.

4. A more universal means for helping every sort of person will be preaching in French in and outside Billom. Master Robert Claysson will be able to preach on feast days and Sundays; or Master Nicholas Paredense or Master Jérôme Le Bas, or as the superior decides. If it appears that they should visit other parts of the diocese during vacation time, or when so urged by the devotion of the people or by the Reverend Bishop, the superior will see how long they should stay out of Billom, and whatever he directs should be done; however, he should not be too liberal in this regard.

5. If the territory is free of heresy, one need not bring it up, but instead adapt to the needs of the hearers.

6. The teaching and explanation of Christian doctrine will be very useful both for the people and for the students, who should be made to learn the main points of it by heart; and if this requires translating it into vernacular French, this may be done.

7. They should see about having a church where, besides preaching and Christian doctrine, they can say their own Masses, hear confessions,

and administer the most holy sacrament of the Eucharist. [By promoting] the frequent reception of these sacraments, they will be able to draw many persons to the service of God our Lord and to a spiritual life.

8. It would also be good for them to attend to works of charity, occasionally visiting the hospitals and prisons and practicing the other works of mercy in aid of souls and of the universal good, according to our Institute and the Society's manner of proceeding.

9. These rules should be read at least once every two weeks at the beginning until they are known well. If the superior judges it good to dispense from any of them, he may do so, informing the superior in Rome of any such dispensations.

✠

To Adrian Adriaenssens

Rome, May 12, 1556

(Letter 6454: XI:374f.; in Latin)

The rector at Louvain frequently consulted Ignatius on a variety of questions. In this letter Ignatius treats Adriaenssens' problem of providing the proper food for his scholastics of different nationalities and physical constitutions. While Ignatius recommends having all get used to the ordinary local diet, he is clear about providing generous exceptions for those in poor health. It was often the case, that after giving general guidelines, Ignatius would observe that particular cases are to be left to a discerning judgement.

Jhus.

The peace of Christ.

We received Your Reverence's letter of March 31, and our brief response to its main contents is as follows: We are all for frugality, for economy, and for giving a good example to others in matters of food, to the extent that this is possible; but we do not think it good to cut back from what the physician prescribes as necessary for the recovery or preservation of health (although he needs to be mindful of our profession of poverty). This much in general. That it is good, moreover, for a person who has health and a good constitution to get used to more ordinary and more easily obtained foods and drink accords with both reason and our own Institute, which prescribes that our members have an ordinary diet. Therefore, if health permits someone to habituate himself even to water, beer, or cider where these are the usual beverages, he should drink these and not—with more expense and less edification—imported wines. Nevertheless, there may be some whose health is frail, such as your Master Adrian Candidus [Whitte], Master Bernard [Olivier], or Master Pedro de Ribadeneira. As long as these men treat their frail bodies well, they will have enough strength for works of piety and charity in the help of souls and edification of their neighbor; if they do not, they fall sick and prove of little benefit to their neighbor. Indeed, they can become a burden, as happened with Masters Bernard and Adrian in Italy. I certainly do not think these men should be required to get used to cheaper food or drink except insofar as it can be done without prejudice to their health. Indeed, I would rather see the servants of God—persons ready to bear the heaviest burdens for Christ—enjoying these comforts supplied by God rather than other people who contribute less to the common good. However, we must make sure that the superfluous does not slip in under the guise of the necessary, or the pleasurable under that of the healthful, and that a praiseworthy use does not become an abuse. And if disedification should be caused by the public eating or drinking of things prescribed as necessary by the physicians, then they should be taken in private. Thus, avoiding scandal, we should do what is needed for health. So much can be said in general. Prudence will descend to particular cases, discerning them after weighing all the circumstances.

May the Lord give us the light of holy discernment to make use of creatures in the light of the Creator. Amen.

Rome, May 12, 1556

Spiritual men do not think it strange or reprehensible to have different foods and drinks taken at the same table, as good or poor health require. However, where weaker persons are present who might take scandal, these necessary foods can be taken in a separate place. We should keep in mind Paul's words about not scandalizing the weak [1 Cor. 8:13; Rom. 14:21].

✠

To Francis Borgia

Rome, May 14, 1556

(Letter 6463: XI:387; in Spanish)

Often founders of Jesuit colleges wanted as a condition of such foundations to impose contractual obligations on the Society that went beyond the activities directly connected with the schools. Ignatius was consistently opposed to such conditions.

You have already been advised how Our Father does not want us to be obliged to teach theology and, even less, to preach or to hear confessions as a condition to the foundation of a college, since this goes contrary to the way in which the Society quite strictly seeks to carry out its ideal of giving freely what one has freely received. And if the founders have confidence in the Society, there would be need to oblige it when this kind of thing became an issue. If the Society were to be permitted to yield in such a matter, it would be for classes in the humanities and rhetoric in one language or other. And when it is a question of taking on universities, it is a different case, which consequently would oblige the Society to teach the usual courses there.

✠

To Gaspar Loarte

Rome, May 14, 1556

(Letter 6465 XI:389; in Italian)

The rector of the college in Genoa is urged to take strong measures against one of the priests there, Joán Blet, who was lacking in obedience. He was Professor of Greek there and also a preacher, but not a very capable one. The thinking was that he could possibly become a good confessor, but he apparently refused to accept the decision that he take on that task. Sending him on pilgrimage, a common penance at the time, was the next step to be taken.

Jhus.

Regarding Joán the Catalonian: Your Reverence should make him understand obedience, and tell him that you have been ordered from Rome not to keep anyone in the house who does not obey. Meanwhile, we will think about what ought to be done. And if Your Reverence has some other suitable priest there, it would not be a bad idea, in case he does not do his duty, to send him on pilgrimage to Loreto and Rome. That is all.

To Lorenzo Bresciani

Rome, May 16, 1556

(Letter 6481: XI:408f.; in Italian)

The Society "regards the mingling of human attachments with charity as imperfect."

Jhs.

The peace of Christ.

Dear Father and Brother in Christ, Don Lorenzo of Modena:

We have been informed that you sent rosaries and a certain dialogue full of errors to an undetermined number of ladies who are attached to you. If this was done without your superiors' permission, it was ill done on many counts. In any case, Your Reverence should know that as our Society practices a universal charity toward all nations and types of persons, it does not approve having particular affections toward individual peoples or persons, except as demanded by well-ordered charity. It regards the mingling of human attachment with charity as imperfect; and unnecessary gifts and letters seem to indicate this kind of attachment. Moreover, it is also a part of the Society's special spirit not to want others to have such mixed feelings towards us; wherever we find they do, we should do all we can to purify them, or else remove the occasion from such men or women by having little to do with them.

Let this reminder suffice; and I commend myself from the heart to your prayers.

Rome, May 16, 1556

✠

To Bernardino Taro

Rome, May 17, 1556

(Letter 6483: XI:410f.; in Italian)

This is one of the letters that were exchanged between the Society and Taro during protracted discussions with the Society about the sale price and terms of purchase of a house he owned in Naples. Taro came to believe he was being toyed with. He is assured that this is not true either of the Society or of the agent arranging the deal and that the Society values his friendship more than having or not having the house.

Jhus.

The peace of Christ.

My Honored and Reverend Sir in our Lord:

We have received a letter from your Lordship expressing your displeasure with our handling of the negotiations for the house destined for pious purposes. You say that having first offered twenty-six hundred ducats, we then offered twenty-five hundred, and then a reckoning as if it were eighteen hundred and no more. We are people who behave with such simplicity that it may at times seem excessive; it is not our way to ridicule or make fun of anybody as you suggest—and certainly not your Lordship, who has always shown such great readiness to help us out and do us favors. If the first offer of twenty-six hundred ducats suits your Lordship better than the second of twenty-five hundred, please take it, and we will be just as content as with the second offer—indeed more so. Since Your Reverence has the letters, please reread them; and if you have lost them we will send the copy from our register. If neither the first nor the second offer pleases Your Lordship, then you may dispose of your house as you like; but our wish is always to keep our friendship and our desire to render every service to Your Lordship for the glory of God our Lord, as holy charity requires.

No more for the present, except to beseech the divine Goodness to give to all the grace always to know and fulfill his most holy will.

Rome, May 17, 1556

One thing I will add: Your Lordship must not think Master Onofrio guilty of any improper dealings in this affair. We know for a truth that the opposite is the case. The truth is that he mentioned to us twenty-five hundred ducats, which he was authorized for, and encouraged us to make the purchase in the form which was more difficult for us than the first, although perhaps not more advantageous for Your Lordship. However, matters like this are difficult to handle by letter and never get fully understood.

⊕

To Girolamo Vignes, by commission

Rome, May 17, 1556

(Letter 6486: XI:413–15; in Italian)

Polanco congratulates Vignes on his recovered health, and urges moderation and detachment in his work. He enlists his help with the financial arrangements of an ecclesiastic who had come to Rome and planned to give some of his property to the Society. The opportunity to acquire places of recreation for the Jesuit communities was a regular concern for Ignatius.

Jhus.

The peace of Christ.

This letter is to thank God our Lord along with Your Lordship for the recovery of your health; and to beseech His Majesty to turn it to his daily greater service and glory, for it is the time granted for our pilgrimage and for the purpose or end to which is conjoined our supreme good and happiness.

In the future, please try to devote yourself to works of brotherly charity in a way that does not bring too much effort or anxiety; instead, work with moderation and be satisfied with having done what was right on your part; whatever the result or outcome, accept it peacefully in the confidence that God our Lord will supply whatever is lacking on our side.

We have taken care of Don Giovanni Antonio [Rosso] as charity required and Your Lordship recommended, and it looks as if he will live consoled in God's service with the step he has taken. Apparently he would like to have his furnishings brought to Rome, and he is writing a letter to a certain woman who has them. Would Your Lordship be so kind as to have someone get them? Once you have them, you can do one of two things: either have them sold and send the money here, or send them here by boat—or else take a middle way and sell part of them there and send part to Rome, whatever will be best. He says that some of his mattresses are valuable; I leave it to you. I know that he has not brought four or five scudi to pay his expenses at the German College; but I promised him I would pay them until he can collect certain of his moneys from a house and rents that he has; and with these furnishings he will be better able to maintain himself. I learn from him that he is part owner of a villa or vacation house with a garden and excellent air, two miles from Naples, the whole bringing in income of about thirty scudi. On the other hand, he has shares with his brothers in a farm worth about two thousand scudi, with a quarter at least coming to Don Giovanni Antonio; he also has two hundred scudi besides this farm of his brothers. Assuming that Don Giovanni Antonio wants to get rid of his temporal property and will do whatever is told him, I thought that it would be good for him to make an agreement with his brothers: in exchange for his share in the farm, they would leave him the garden and the vacation house, which could then serve the college at Naples for a change of air and recreation. Write me what Your Lordship thinks.

As for his benefice that carries with it pastoral responsibilities, I am thinking of having him renounce it simply into the hands of the patron, since it is de jure a patronage of the Marquis of Vasto or of the presently living Marchioness; and that he should inform his brothers before any one else finds out, so that they will not complain against him. If Your Lordship thinks otherwise, let us know. For Don Giovanni Antonio must not keep a benefice and those responsibilities and cannot renounce it in favor of someone he does not know deserves it; hence, it seems best to leave this responsibility to the patron.

Master Bernardino Villa here is sending Your Lordship a little book. Our Father and all of us recommend ourselves to you, and we pray Jesus Christ our Lord that he will grant to all of us the grace to know always and to fulfill his most holy will.

Rome, May 17, 1556.

☩

To Eleanor Mascarenhas

Rome, May 19, 1556

(Letter 6487: XI:415f.; in Spanish)

Eleanor Marcarenhas was one of the oldest and closest friends of Ignatius and among the very generous benefactors of the Society of Jesus. When she first came to know Ignatius, she was a lady-in-waiting to Empress Isabella, wife of Charles V and governess of their son, the future King Philip II of Spain. When Ignatius was a prisoner of the Inquisition at Alcalá, she visited him and offered to use her influence to have him freed. Ignatius declined this help, wanting to be vindicated on his own account. From that time on, she had a deep respect for and attachment to him. She frankly stated at one time that she would have joined the Society of Jesus if she could have; but, failing that, she helped it in many ways. Ignatius referred to her as a "true mother of the Society of Jesus."

As the years went by, Ignatius, burdened by the governance of the Society, wrote less often than Eleanor would have wanted, and through Jesuits in Spain she let

Ignatius know of her hopes for more frequent letters. More recently, after she had relinquished the governance of Don Carlos, the ill-fated son of Philip II, and before the present letter of reply, she had written to Ignatius especially about her hope to leave the service of the court and retire to a convent. The King wanted her to stay at the court. She asked Ignatius's advice on the matter. Ignatius, already ill and with only a few weeks more to live, in this letter responded to her request.

Most often reserved in any display of affection, Ignatius in this letter makes clear that depth of his attachment when early in the letter he refers to the intense love and charity that he sees in her as it was also "written in my own soul since the first time we met in our Lord," something that he trusts in God's goodness "on both your side and mine . . . will always remain and go on increasing forever." And toward the end of the letter, Ignatius is "mindful, as I said above, how much I have held you and still hold you in my inmost soul, and even more intensely if that were possible." By the time Eleanor received this letter, Ignatius had gone on to God.

JHS.

May the sovereign grace and eternal love of Christ our Lord be always our protection and help.

I received two letters from you, dated in November and December, on the very same day at the end of April; and I see in them the very thing that has been written in my own soul since the first time we met in our Lord: your intense love and charity towards me in his Divine Majesty. And I trust in his divine goodness that on both your side and mine this will always remain and go on increasing forever. As for the difficulties of your position and your corporal ailments, I have done what you so earnestly urged upon me in your letters, namely, to have recourse to God our Lord in prayer so that he will show you the best way to serve him. You add that I should write you what I think and tell you what to do. Speaking in the presence of God and thinking in his Divine Majesty as I think I would if I were Your Worship, remain firm and steady in the condition and state where His Highness put me until I was directed by him to do otherwise. For this purpose, and to ensure that everything is managed for God's greater glory, I would write the whole matter to him—my wishes, my ailments, and whatever else might occur to me on the subject. Having done this, I cannot doubt that whatever His Highness decides, having fully examined the situation, will be for God's greater glory; and with this Your Worship should be consoled and at peace in our Lord.

As for Your Worship's urging me so strongly to commend the prince, who is now by God's grace king over numerous realms, earnestly to God our Lord in my prayers: I certainly do so daily, and I trust in his Divine Majesty that throughout the few days still left to me, I shall do so even more, since he is our own sovereign and we are under great obligations to him, and also because of Your Worship's desire and devotion in reminding me of a matter so binding upon myself and this entire least Society.

Some twelve or fifteen days before I received your letters, a woman devoted to me in the Lord sent me a spiritual present, from which I chose two decorated Agnus Deis to send to Your Worship along with a letter, mindful, as I said above, how much I have held you and still hold you in my inmost soul, and even more intensely if that were possible.

Since the receipt of your letters, other Agnus Deis were sent from the Pope's palace, and I have decided to add eight more to the two, so that Your Grace can have them decorated according to your own preference and devotion, or employ them however you may think more to God's glory.

May it please his infinite and sovereign Goodness to give us his abundant grace, so that we may know his most holy will and perfectly fulfill it.

Rome, May 19, 1556

Entirely Your Worship's in our Lord,
IGNATIO

✠

To Giovanni Battista Guidini

Rome, May 23, 1556

(Letter 6502: XI:437f.; in Italian)

A reproof to a discontented coadjutor brother, the buyer at the college of Padua, who was agitating to study for the priesthood. There had been several letters between the rector at Padua and Ignatius about the matter. He wrote to the rector on the same day as the present letter, saying that "the temptation of Brother Giovanni Battista is all the clearer in that he is very incapable of studies."

Jhus.

The peace of Christ.

Dear Brother Giovanni Battista:

While we are not surprised at your temptation regarding studies, for we know that it is the devil's usual practice to unsettle and perturb God's servants, you ought to be surprised at yourself for having admitted this temptation and forgotten that a religious should have no will of his own, and that in order to do God's will, he ought to do that of his superiors. And you should have welcomed the devil's insinuations in this matter all the less, in that right from the beginning you were expressly told that you should not think of studies, but exercise yourself in the offices of charity and humility, since in view of your age and aptitudes, it was judged that you would waste your time in studies and could make better use of it in other employments in God's service.

In the body not all the members are eyes, or ears, or hands, or feet. Each member has its own function and is content with it. Similarly, in the body of the Society, not all can be learned, not all can be priests; rather, each one must be content with the employment which falls to him according to the will and judgment of the superior, who must give an account to God of all his subjects.

Finally, Giovanni Battista, if you have given all to God, allow yourself to be guided by God; act not in your own way but in God's way. And this way you are to learn by obedience to your superior.

If anyone tells you differently, even if he transfigures himself into an angel of light, you can be sure that it is the devil trying to draw you out of the Society, which will not tolerate this self-will of yours if you do not truly amend; for though you may have the name of a religious, if you lack obedience you are not one. Now, for the good we desire for you, we want you to examine yourself and alter the way you have been proceeding for some time now.

May God our Lord give you the grace for this.

Rome, May 23, 1556

✠

To Emerio de Bonis, by commission

Rome, May 23, 1556

(Letter 6503: XI:439f.; in Italian)

Emerio de Bonis was a twenty-five-year-old scholastic strongly troubled by temptations against chastity. He had been in the Society for five years and felt overly uncertain about himself. He had revealed his state of soul to Ignatius. This reply came from Ignatius, who commissioned Polanco to write it for him. De Bonis later became a renowned spiritual director and writer.

Jhus.

The peace of Christ.

My dear Master Emerio in Christ:

Our Father has understood what you wrote. And while you show a good spirit in overcoming by God's grace the enemy that up to the present has harassed but not vanquished you, nevertheless, judging that it would be to your greater consolation, he leaves it up to you to decide whether to come to Rome next September, stay in Padua, or move to some other college where you would have charge of the first class, as you do there.

In the meantime, with God's help, defend yourself. Besides prayer, make it a point not to look anyone fixedly in the face who might cause you uneasiness of spirit. In general, when you deal with the neighbor, let your eyes be lowered and try not to think of this person or that as being good-looking or ugly, but rather as the image of the Most Holy Trinity, as a member of Christ and bathed in his blood. Moreover, do not become familiar with anyone. It will be enough in the colleges if you fulfill the teacher's duties out of pure charity and obedience. Always deal with them in public and not in private or secluded places—extern students should not be walking through the house except with the rector's dispensation in particular cases. If you do this, and attend to your growth in God's service and the way of perfection, God will help you as he has in the past, and even more.

Be on your guard also in those times and situations where you are usually assailed, raising your mind somewhat towards God. Above all, make an effort to keep him present, recalling frequently that your whole heart and outward man is in the sight of his infinite wisdom.

There will be no need to multiply remedies if these are properly used and if you do not forget the first one, about the eyes, so that you will never lament with him who says, "My eye has wasted my soul" [Lam. 3:51].

Our Father and all of us commend ourselves to your prayers.

Rome, May 23, 1556

✠

To Girolamo Rubiola

Rome, May 21, 1556

(Letter 6510: XI:446; in Italian)

Giovanni Battista, a young candidate for the Society, and Cosmo, another such candidate, earlier had been sent to Florence. For some reason here unknown, there was no single bed available there for the former.

We wrote on May 23 to the rector of the college that, because there were no accommodations for Giovanni Battista, the Florentine, to sleep in his own bed, but instead had to share a bed with another person, he is to be be sent to Rome with Cosmo. He should also write to them, commanding them to carefully observe the rule that each of them is to sleep in his own bed, etc.

✠

To Charles, Cardinal of Lorraine

Rome, May 23, 1556

(Letter 6512: XI:448–51; in Italian)

This is a refutation of unfounded charges in the decree of the theological faculty of the University of Paris that condemned the Society of Jesus. Charles of Guise, known as the Cardinal of Lorraine, was archbishop of Reims. He headed his family after the assassination of his brother, the Duke de Guise, in 1563 and continued the family policy of strongly supporting the Catholic cause against the Huguenots. He was as favorable toward the Society of Jesus as the theological faculty of Paris was hostile to it.

Ihs.

Information to Be Shown to the Illustrious and Most Reverend Cardinal of Lorraine regarding the Decree or Censure by the Faculty of Theology of the University of Paris

First, it would be good to show His Most Reverend Lordship that faculty's decree or censure—which, however, we have been unwilling to show here in Rome to the Pope or any other ministers of the Apostolic See, or to the cardinals, out of the respect and love we bear this celebrated university, of which our first members are sons.

With regard to the points which the censure touches upon in its condemnation of our Institute, it would be improper for us to employ arguments in support of what is already of itself supported by the apostolic authority, which subsequent to several examinations and the opposition of some, approved our Institute in 1540, confirmed it in 1543, and reconfirmed it in 1550—so that the censure is more against the Apostolic See than against the Society.

We have refrained from showing the decree out of respect for the authority and good reputation of that faculty of theology; for it would truly be harmful to their reputation to wish to pass a censure in a matter of such importance, involving, as has been said, the Apostolic See, without correct information or a true understanding of the Society and its affairs. Thus, they say that the Society "accepts indiscriminately all true of the Society: such men are absolutely excluded by its Constitutions; indeed it may not receive persons who are homicides or have incurred infamy through heresy, schism, or any other grave sin, even if their status has been restored.

They are also obviously ill-informed when they claim that this occasion is an opportunity for members of other orders to apostatize, as if the Society were an asylum for fugitives from other orders, whereas in truth its Constitutions prohibit admitting such persons; to this day it has never admitted a religious from another order—indeed, it may not admit anyone who has worn a religious habit for even a day. The Society has a very high regard for every approved order and has led many an apostate friar back to his congregation. This can be seen especially in the orders of SS. Francis and Dominic, in the Carmelites, and in others as well, where there are numbers who through our instrumentality have entered for the first time or returned from their apostasy.

It is also astonishing that they claim we have no laws, whereas— if they had wished to be informed in the matter—the apostolic letters themselves speak of the Constitutions.

Their claim that the Society works to the prejudice of the bishops, parish priests, secular rulers, people, and universities is quite contrary to the truth. Our purpose is to help them and serve them with all our strength in spiritual matters and even in the corporal works of mercy. If our Most Illustrious and Reverend Protector wishes to see the public testimonials of princes and Christian lords, nations, the universities, and peoples, and likewise of bishops wherever our men reside throughout Christendom and even among infidels, these can be requested and sent, so that anyone who is willing can come to see that God our Lord is employing this new growth for the help of souls everywhere, and that by his grace there neither seems to be nor is anything to the contrary; for our Society walks in the light and before the eyes of men. Both here in the Apostolic See and in other important lands to which it has been able to spread, it will not be difficult to have such testimonials.

We understand that there are only a few persons, and they perhaps from outside the faculty, who by means of this misinformation have procured the aforementioned censure, and that they are attempting, by themselves or through other means, to misinform His Most Reverend Lordship, and even His Most Christian Majesty [Henry III]. But the truth is mighty; we trust that it will, as is its wont, overcome the falsehoods accruing either from error or deliberate ill will, so far as this shall be to the greater service and glory of God.

Our aim, therefore, in the present document is that our Most Illustrious and Reverend Protector might be informed and, should it be opportune, inform His Majesty the King as well, and also that he might deign to intervene with the Faculty of Theology to emend its decree and not wait for the Apostolic See to repeal it, which would be little to its honor. When His Most Christian Majesty is informed, he could hardly help condemning and being ill-pleased with the decree. However, whatever is deemed best by the most reverend and illustrious prelate of Lorraine, our protector, is what ought to be done.

✠

To Juan de Vega, viceroy of Sicily

Rome, June 5, 1556

(Letter 6545: XI:496–98; in Spanish)

A letter of consolation to this great friend of the Society on the death of his brother Hernando.

My Lord in our Lord:

May the sovereign grace and eternal love of Christ our Lord greet and visit Your Most Illustrious Lordship with his most holy gifts and spiritual graces.

From several letters of Master Pedro Ribadeneira, a priest of our Society, we have learned of the course and conclusion of Señor Hernando de Vega's illness; he is now in glory, and the sorrow left in us by his departure from this world, with all the love and attachment we had for him in the Lord, can never be so great as to take away the awareness and consolation we ought to have regarding his greater good, seeing how he left this mortal and miserable life in such a way that we cannot doubt that it was to enter early into the eternal and most blessed life through the mercy of God our Lord, who both in his life and in his death so clearly showed that he held him in the number of his chosen servants and treated him as such. In the same way, I trust that the divine and supreme Goodness which has endowed Your Lordship with so great a spirit and imprinted on it such a lively faith and hope in his unchanging and eternal blessings will not allow you to grieve over the brief absence of so good a brother to the extent of failing to recognize and delight in the rare favor shown him; [I trust] as well that Your

Lordship will bear with patience the loss of the consolation you might have had from his presence here below, inasmuch as he has gone ahead to the blessedness and happiness to which our Lord has raised him, bestowing upon him in the midpoint of his years what is the goal of all our years: to prepare for the final and blessed end for which he created and redeemed us through the blood and death of his only-begotten Son. We took great care here to commend him to God our Lord during his illness and later to pray for the eternal salvation and happiness of his soul, although we trust that there will be little need of our prayers, as we may judge from a letter of Master Pedro to Master Jerónimo Doménech which I am herewith sending you open, since I think Your Illustrious Lordship will take satisfaction in seeing it and will give thanks to him who is our life and all our good. May it please him in this and in all his visitations to give Your Lordship an abundant anointing of his grace so as to accept them with full conformity to his divine will, and to grow through all of them in merit and the love of our most kind and wise Father, who with exceeding charity sends them for our greater good. I close, begging the same God our Lord by his infinite and supreme goodness to grant us his abundant grace, so that we may know his most holy will and entirely fulfill it.

Rome, June 5, 1556

> Your Illustrious Lordship's most humble servant in our Lord,
>
> IGNATIO

✠

To Giovanni Battista di Fermo

Rome, June 6, 1556

(Letter 6547: XI:501–2; in Italian)

Fermo was a brilliant preacher whom Ignatius had sent to Siena several months earlier with the hope that the "great spiritual and material needs of the city will move you in your work there." He was very successful in his preaching and, among other works there, in reconciling enemies with one another. At the same time, he was equally set in his own ways and often at odds with the superior in Siena. In a discouraged mood he wrote to Ignatius about his burdens and asked to be relieved of his responsibilities there. Ignatius replies that the obedient draw on God's own strength.

Jhus.

The peace of Christ.

From several letters of Your Reverence, we learn that you complain of the burden of preaching that weighs on your shoulders. I believe you have all too much cause to consider it heavy if you look to yourself; but if you look to how powerful God our Lord is to bring about great things, even through the weakest instruments provided they are moved by holy obedience, you will not be in the least dismayed; rather, the more you abase yourself interiorly by consideration of your own infirmity, the more you will be lifted up by considering God's power and goodness, which he deploys on behalf of the weakest members of the Society. Consequently, as long as Your Reverence is called upon to perform this office, do so with good courage and with trust in the power of obedience, that is, of Christ our Lord, in whose place you obey the superior.

That the church is out of the way does not agree with the report we first had that it was in the middle of the city; should this be true, even if the spot is not very populated, it would not seem unsuited for a college. However, if with time it is judged otherwise, we can do something about it.

Cosimo [Romei] and Giovanni Battista [Monte] are well as they do their probations. May God make them his servants, and give to all of us the grace always to know and fulfill his most holy will.

Rome, June 6, 1556

All of us here commend ourselves to Your Reverence's holy sacrifices and prayers.

✠

To Ottaviano Cesari, by commission

Rome, June 7, 1556

(Letter 6558: XI:516; in Italian)

Still in bad health and now living in his parents' house, Ottaviano had written that he wanted to leave the Society. Polanco writes to encourage Ottaviano in his attempts to regain his health and urges him to keep up his sense of belonging to the Society.

Jhus.

The peace of Christ.

Dearest Brother in Christ:

From the rector's letter we had understood that your health was better. From your own letter of May 30, it appears that you are not well in every respect. May God our Lord give you health in both the inward and the outward man, for his greater service, for your own eternal happiness, and for the common good. However, you must make efforts to recover your strength. Make whatever arrangements you think most satisfactory in our college or at your parents' home. Wherever you stay, you will still enjoy the merit of obedience, because it is obedience that commands you to devote yourself to the recovery of your health, suspending your spiritual or bodily exercises and any other rules which might hinder your convalescence. Just be sure to preserve yourself in fear and love of God. Thus, you should not fail to go to weekly confession to one of our men. In other matters, even if you are unable to do more yourself, you will have a share in what is being practiced by your other brothers in Christ, as a member of the same Society. And from here, since we all have a special love for you in Christ our Lord, we will not fail to commend you to his Divine Majesty. May he be pleased to preserve and keep you always in his grace, and increase in you the gifts of his grace as he has begun them.

Our Father and all of us commend ourselves to your prayers.

Rome, June 7, 1556

✠

To Those Going to the College of Ingolstadt

Rome, June 9, 1556

(Letter 6565: XI:530–44; in Italian)

This letter had been immediately preceded by a half dozen other to Peter Canisius, appointing him provincial of the newly created German Province, to Heinrich Schweicher, a friend of the Society and the agent of the Duke of Bavaria in setting up the Jesuit college at Ingolstadt, and to Duke Alert himself along with a list of names and backgrounds of the Jesuits being sent to the new foundation. The present letter sets out a detailed program of action for this large contingent of Jesuits sent there. At the same time, the letter makes it clear that, if advisable, they can disregard the details, especially relying on the experience and advice of Canisius. Given the heatedly polemical religious atmosphere in Germany at the time, Ignatius's insistence at several places in this instruction on an irenic approach in teaching and preaching is especially noteworthy. (The paragraphs in italics are found almost verbatim in other such instructions, such as that for the college of Billom, no. 6452 above.)

Ihus.

INSTRUCTION FOR THE COLLEGE TO BE SET UP IN INGOLSTADT

Four aims should be chiefly pursued in the college of Ingolstadt; one for the members of the college being sent there; one for the classes; one for the city and state of the duke; and one for the financial foundation of the college, ordered to the foregoing aims.

REGARDING THE MEMBERS OF THE COLLEGE

1. The rector will be Master Thomas [van Lenth], his collateral Master Hurtado [Pérez]. The superintendent will be Doctor [Jean] Couvillon, who, however, will not be concerned with governance so that he can better attend to the matters appropriate to his profession. Nevertheless, if he thinks something important ought to be done that the rector is not doing, or that something ought not to be done that the rector is doing, he should talk with the rector; and if they are in agreement, what Doctor Couvillon says should be done. If they are not in agreement, the matter should be held in suspension until their provincial, Doctor Canisius, is consulted, or else the General in Rome. The three above-named will not be under one another's obedience. But as Master Hurtado may perform the office of collateral towards the rector, he may do the same towards the superintendent.

2. The rector should have four consultors: besides the superintendent and the collateral, the other two will be Doctor Hermann Dorkens and Master Theodor van Pelt. While the rector is to consult these men, the power of decision will still be his.

3. The three named will choose a syndic, who can be one of themselves; his office will be to inform the rector about anything regarding his subjects which he does not find good. Moreover, he can report or write to the provincial, Canisius, or to the General in Rome about the rector, collateral, or superintendent.

4. The rector should choose a minister to assist him. This should be someone not excessively occupied with studies or spiritual responsibilities and who has some gift for assisting him in governance of the house.

5. Those leaving Italy for Ingolstadt will be eighteen. They will pick up four in Loreto: Francesco de Saloneta, Biagio de Augubio, Giacomo de Tilla, and Marsilio de Ulloa, or anyone with whom the rector may choose to replace one of these. In Germany they will pick up another two, three, or four if needed for service in the house, kitchen, dispensary, and other services, so that the scholastics will not have to be

occupied in these. If they find persons suitable for the Society who will perform these services, that would be more desirable; if not, they should hire some persons through a friend who knows them.

6. In Loreto, leaving Giovanni and Pietro behind, they will make their way by water or by land, according as they are advised. If they travel by water, they will arrive at Chiozza, within sight of Venice. If they wish to bypass Venice, they can take the river up to Padua and there, or in Bassano, buy a couple of horses, or however the rector decides, with the help of our men in Padua at the Ponte Pedocchioso or in Bassano, where Master Gaspare [Gropillo] is staying a little outside of town. If they take the land route from Loreto, they should buy the horses there; and they need not pass through Venice or Padua but can take the straight route to Trent through Bologna, Mantua, Verona, or however they are instructed.

7. From Trent, passing through Innsbruck, they will take the road to Munich, where His Excellency the duke usually resides. They will salute His Excellency with a Latin speech showing how they come minded to render his Excellency obedient service in the aid of his subjects, not only with their efforts and skill but even with their lives if necessary for God's glory. They will also give the duke the letter from Our Father, either before or after the speech. They will give another letter to the Honorable Master Heinrich [Schweicker], His Excellency's secretary and counselor, telling him that they have been enjoined by Our Father to have recourse to His Lordship and to be guided by his advice as the principal promoter of this college and its friend and special patron. Master Heinrich will instruct them and introduce them to the duke. If this Heinrich is not in Munich, they will have to manage as best they can.

8. When they get to Ingolstadt, if they have an escort from the duke, they will go where they are escorted; otherwise, they will find Doctor Canisius and follow his instructions. If they get no other directions, some of them should go to the superintendent of the university and find out where they should stay.

9. If they find Master Heinrich there, they will offer what is left of the travel money to him or to whoever seems to be the chief minister of the duke in their regard, although they will have to use this or some other money for clothes and lodging, so that each man has his own bed and whatever is necessary; and if this is impossible at first, it should be done as quickly as possible.

10. They should attend to preparing their living quarters, and obtain a church in which to exercise our profession apart from the classes.

11. The better our men are in themselves, the more they will be suitable instruments of God's grace in helping others. Therefore, each one should strive to have a right intention, seeking exclusively "not the things that are their own but the things that are Jesus Christ's" [Phil. 2:21]. They should endeavor to have and frequently renew their resolves and desires to be true and faithful servants of God and to render a good account of themselves in whatever responsibilities they are given, with a genuine abnegation of their own will and judgment and a submission of themselves to God's governance of them by means of holy obedience, whether they are employed in high or lowly tasks. They should strive in their daily prayers to obtain this grace from the Giver of every good. Moreover, the one in charge should give them these reminders and others which will be helpful for their spiritual advancement.

12. They should observe the practice and method of weekly confession and Communion (with the priests celebrating more frequently), examinations of conscience, prayers, and other regulations observed in Rome. However, if the superior thinks that some of these cannot be observed, after consulting with those more versed in the matter, he should omit them, informing Rome of any changes being made in the rules.

13. Those able to do so should practice speaking the German language and preaching in German in the house during meals, now one and now another, adapting themselves to the manner best suited for making an impression on the minds of listeners from those territories. On this our own men who have experience and judicious friends will be able to give advice.

14. Our own students and the masters should follow the superior's directions in the matter of the subjects, method, and times of their studies. He will have to see to it that everyone is properly occupied, taking as his goal their own and others' aid in learning—although until coadjutors can be found to do the service, each one must be ready to do any service which he is commanded, especially those who are not teaching. Even if there are coadjutors, they can practice humility by helping in some lowly service during hours when they are unable to study, as is done here in Rome.

15. If the income or provision from the duke suffices to support more than eighteen persons, with the coadjutors who will be needed, and they are able to get some good subjects to enter the Society and cannot easily await replies from Rome or from their provincial, they may accept them as guests until they receive word from the provincial or from here. If the provision does not suffice, they will have to talk to Master Heinrich or to some friend of ours close to the duke; and no one should be accepted into the house without His Excellency's approval. However, if

they have provisions of their own and the duke does not need to be burdened on their account, they may be accepted. When there is no way to accept them, they can be sent to Prague or Vienna if the rectors or the provincial approves, or to Rome, advising us ahead of time, however, unless they are extraordinarily qualified.

16. The superior should take care that everyone stays healthy and strong enough in body to sustain the toil of God's service. Hence, he should not let them get overtired in their studies or other devotions or spiritual exercises in the aid of souls; everything must be moderated according to the quality of persons, places, and times. A prefect of health should be appointed—this could be Master Hurtado —*to watch over its preservation, in addition to the infirmarian for the sick. Even more special care must be taken of the latter, so that they do not lack a physician or whatever the physician orders in aid of their health.* And since Master Hurtado is unwell and going specifically to see if the change of air will do him some good, he should not be given or accept more work than he can easily bear, even though with the change of air and food, we trust he will be better able to labor in God's service.

17. They should write regularly at least once a week to Rome so that they can be aided from here by suitable advice, which will be more useful the better information is had.

18. They should see who can and who cannot drink beer. The diet (with the advice of a friendly physician) should be sober and exemplary, and yet adequate for health and physical strength.

19. They should not accept alms or gifts from the students, nor readily accept them from anyone except the duke. However, should a friend offer a chalice or the like for the church, it could be accepted, and similarly with other matters, as Doctor Canisius will direct.

20. No one should suggest that the duke or anyone else write to Our Father requesting more men or that they should have to sing [in liturgical services]. If they think something like this is needed, they should write Our Father, and with his permission they can then make the suggestion or not as seems expedient. They should also send a memorandum of this to their provincial.

REGARDING THE CLASSES

1. If, as said above, Doctor Canisius is there, because of his experience and his office they will proceed in the classes as he directs; it is taken for granted that anything in the following directives can be disre-

garded or changed as he thinks best. See if it would be good to have one of our men give a public address in Latin at the beginning (after showing it to Doctor Canisius) to explain to the university the reason for their coming; and also [to give] a sermon in German to the people, likewise indicating the purpose of their coming, and how they will provide not only for theological lectures but also for the education of youth in humane letters, Latin, Greek, and Hebrew, and in good morals and Christian doctrine. This Latin address could be given by Doctor Couvillon, Doctor Hermann, Master Theodor, or Master Gerard, or whoever seems best. The one in German would best be given by Doctor Canisius or, in his absence, by Doctor Hermann.

2. During the summer heat, when there is usually a vacation, they should not begin their classes or regular school exercises; instead, they should get ready and gather materials, so that when school recommences they will better be able to perform their functions.

3. Meantime, however, if experienced friends think it advisable, they could give some sample classes of Scripture, humane letters, or cosmography or of several such subjects; they could also teach Christian doctrine. The teachers could also draft and practice the speeches at home which they will give at the inauguration of the studies and classes.

4. They should also study the rules and counsels for teachers and students at Rome to help them perform their office; and they should make use of them as persons, places, and times require.

5. The two professors of Scholastic theology and Scripture will for the present be Doctor Couvillon and Doctor Hermann. They will work on polishing their Latin (as will the rector also) and demonstrate that they are not ignorant of Greek and Hebrew, showing this in a way that brings them authority and credit and not a suspicion of vanity. Masters Hurtado and Gerard could attend their lectures, unless something else appears preferable on the spot.

6. Care should be taken to provide help in the theology and other classes for the scholars being supported by His Excellency the Duke and all the others who attend the classes, having them observe as far as possible the constitutions used in the Society's colleges as regards monthly confession and Communion for those who are able, and the other usual rules. If it proves impossible to get one or the other of these observed, they should not expel the scholars from the classes, but show special esteem towards those who do observe them.

7. They should not accept governance over the college of those not belonging to the Society without informing us first.

8. Master Theodor will teach rhetoric and Greek for the more difficult books (grammar and the easier authors can be taught by someone else); he could also alternate Hebrew classes, or have a half hour of Greek and a half hour of Hebrew. If this is too tiring, he could divide the work with Master Gerard. Doctor Hermann could perhaps also help with Hebrew and Doctor Couvillon with Greek. If there are no students ready for such advanced classes, the Greek could be deferred until there are some ready to follow the classes, and easier ones could be given; however, this should be discussed with Master Heinrich or some other friend who is close to the duke.

9. Master Georg will teach the second class and Masters Jodocus and Dionysius the third and fourth. These classes should probably suffice at the beginning, if there is someone to help with the last. It would be good for Jodocus not to have a large class, so that he can easily hand it over to someone else when he has to preach outside Ingolstadt. Master Gerard could substitute in the upper classes and Stefan and Zimmer in the lower, in place of the assigned teachers.

10. There is no need to assign an arts [philosophy] professor for now, although Master Hurtado might give some classes on cosmography or the like, and this would probably be edifying.

11. Thought should be given to the advisability of teaching Doctor Canisius's *Christian Doctrine* in lieu of Scholastic theology, or some classes on cases of conscience; Doctor Canisius and Master Heinrich should be consulted on this.

12. Great care must be taken to present orthodox truth in such a way that even if heretics are present, they will sense Christian charity and modesty; they should in no way be insulted, nor should any animus against them be visible, but rather compassion. Nor should their errors be openly attacked; instead the Catholic teachings should be established, and this will make clear the falsity of their contraries. If the duke judges that errors should be openly attacked in classes and from the pulpit, this should nevertheless be done in a way that is modest and manifests love for their salvation.

13. Care should be given to the practice of disputation among the theologians, following as far as possible the Roman model; the humanists too should have their disputations and colloquies and composition, care being given to their progress in letters.

14. On Sundays it will be good for one of the house or an extern student to give a public discourse, as in Rome, on a topic proposed by the master and corrected by him; these could treat edifying matters

regarding Christian religion and morals. If this cannot be done every Sunday, then every two weeks or once a month.

15. Our men should take care when the opportunity presents itself, through examples or otherwise, to inculcate Catholic teachings in the minds of their hearers, even the small ones, without criticizing or even mentioning evil ones. They should be concerned to be teachers of good morals and virtues no less than of letters.

16. There should be a brief *Christian Doctrine* in the vernacular which the boys could be made to learn and which could be explained a few days a week in class; I believe Doctor Canisius has written one.

17. Persons of every kind will be accepted into the classes who are willing to behave properly and observe appropriate discipline. For their own and their families' encouragement and consolation, a few times during the year orations, verses, and dialogues should be declaimed as [is done] at Rome; this will also increase the prestige of the classes.

18. At the inauguration of the term our men should give discourses in good Latin, both the theologians and the others, although the humanists might do more in this regard; these discourses should all be seen by the consultors.

19. Their labors should be tempered with discretion, and with the necessary interruptions for preserving health and obtaining what is needed for the body.

20. The time spent in the classes should be moderate, so that the teachers can sustain the pace and the students keep up their concentration. It would be good to have a day or a half day off each week (if Doctor Canisius agrees) for taking some recreation.

21. The classes for boys should have a corrector to punish them as directed by the teachers, who should themselves never lay hands on anyone.

REGARDING THE DUKE'S CITY AND STATE

1. Thought should be given to the advisability of going outside Ingolstadt to preach or teach Christian doctrine, with the least distraction possible, during vacations or on feast days in places close by, or in Lent.

2. *For the edification of others, the first help will be the example of all Christian virtues, as well as zeal and longing for the salvation of the souls in that place and for God's honor in them. This will give rise to prayers and holy sacrifices,*

which they will frequently offer to the eternal Father for this effect, having at least this intention—I mean the spiritual good of the Bavarian state—among the others.

3. *Another help will be familiar and loving conversations at due times and places and with persons on whom the superior judges conversation will be profitably spent, such as those who are suitable for helping others. This would include persons influential either through authority or learning, or who it is thought might be won for God's service in religious life. The superior should take care to decide who should converse with outsiders and who not, or who with these persons and who with those.*

4. Preaching and teaching Christian doctrine in German will be a universal means for helping every kind of person; and although at the beginning Doctor Canisius (if he is there) will preach on feast days and Sundays, Doctor Hermann will need to get used to preaching, either in less frequented places or inside the college, concentrating on the German language and the style of preaching that is most effective in that country; here Doctor Canisius will be a help. Jodocus and any others deemed capable can try preaching, either in Ingolstadt or in nearby places outside town, although their doctrine should first be examined by the theologians or by one of them.

6. Preachers should keep in mind what was said about the teachers; namely, that they ought to expound solid Catholic doctrine and not be concerned with debating against the heretics or their errors. Nevertheless, they, like our men in general, should make a special study of controversial matters, so that in private conversations they can confute the errors in more detail, with a manifestation of charity and zeal for truth; for truth, when established on good and solid foundations, of itself dispels contrary errors. In this way even the heretics will be better disposed towards them and will listen to the preaching of the truth, whereas if they were openly persecuted, they might become more obstinate and so never hear Catholic doctrine and "return to the heart" [Isa. 46:8]. However, if the duke thinks it would be good to refute heretical errors from the pulpit, this should be done with zeal for the salvation of souls and a manifestation of compassion, as indicated above.

7. Latin sermons might be given by Doctor Couvillon, Doctor Hermann, Master Gerard, and Master Theodor, as the rector judges appropriate; this might arouse admiration and edification, as it has elsewhere.

8. It is recommended that they attend to works of charity as far as conveniently possible, such as visiting the hospitals and prisons in spiritual matters and, if possible, also corporal ones; and in general [they are

urged] to practice the works of mercy according to the Society's Institute.

9. They should not administer Communion under the second form to anyone or absolve anyone who insists on communicating under both forms. To remove persons from these errors, they should be armed (as mentioned above) with learning and deploy it with due tact and evident love, so as to bring such persons to a Catholic mind.

10. They should make efforts to have Catholics observe the precepts of the Church as far as possible—but being lenient with them as with children in Christ to the extent that this is allowable.

11. They should take care to visit and keep up friendship with the principal figures of the university and those who can be helpful in matters of God's service. They should make particular efforts to maintain and increase the favor of the duke, complying with His Excellency's wishes as far as possible according to God; and if they can render any spiritual service to the duke, or at least to those who are closest to him, this would be very important. They should take along a copy of the terms of agreement with the duke; while Our Father did not accept it as a contract, he wants what is set down in it—and even more—to be carried out, but freely.

12. Persons not inclined to religious life but evidently suitable for serving God in it could be urged to come to the German College in Rome if they have a way to pay the expenses; it would also be good if the duke could support some men in the German College or in ours, who would later be sent back more advanced in learning and good morals.

13. It is recommended that they promote frequent reception of the sacraments, drawing persons to confession and Communion and attending to these.

REGARDING THE MATERIAL AND TEMPORAL FOUNDATION

1. The observance of the above points will be the most effective means for getting the college established, particularly to the extent that it proves itself to be of value for the common good.

2. Efforts should be made to obtain immediate destination of the money and items which His Excellency promised—as can be seen in the copy of the terms of agreement which in his last letter he stated he intended to observe, so that what His Excellency destines can be collected by his own authority conveniently at the proper times, thus

making his provisions advantageous to himself and sparing our men any distraction.

3. The more firmly and perpetually the incomes are destined the better, but not subject to conditions, even though without a compact our Society will do what it is able to do and what the duke commands. As soon as the destination has been made, we will begin to observe with the duke what our Constitutions prescribe for founders, both the Masses and the [symbolic gift of a] candle; they should let us know here, so that the Masses can be said throughout the Society, and His Excellency should be informed of this, so that he will be further encouraged to do what he ought from his side.

4. At the beginning, they will not have a stable and permanent location; but they should try to make the best of what is given them. They should keep in mind that we should one day have a location of our own. If the duke were to construct it in our style, he would become more attached to the work. Our friends will work on this, or seek some other way for us to remain comfortably in a location of our own.

5. The friendship of the secretary, Master Heinrich, and of others who have influence with the duke will be of value for the material foundation, both for solidifying it and for increasing it; attention should be given to the latter when the duke begins to become more attached, so that it will become a larger seedbed for manpower that will then spread throughout his state. Perhaps through the assignment of ecclesiastical incomes, such as canonries or other benefices, the work could be expanded without burdening the duke's exchequer.

6. If there is question of the Society's being given responsibility for the arts [philosophy], it would seem consistent that it be given responsibility for those university faculties being handled by the Society. However, this responsibility should not be accepted without informing Rome, since accepting it would entail a corresponding increase in the number of our men to provide a stable body of hearers for the lectures.

7. As indicated above, the goodwill and love of the important persons should be preserved; and while small gifts should not be accepted, if anyone is of a mind to increase the endowment from either secular or ecclesiastical incomes, such could be accepted provided it would not displease the duke, as we are sure it would not.

8. They should preserve the good reputation and esteem of the college and their authority in letters and virtues, and be on the lookout

to increase and not diminish what is done for the service of God and the common good.

9. If they themselves handle temporal matters, they should do so in a way that is clearly prompted by a desire for the common good and not by greed, for this is the case. But, where possible, it is better to have such matters handled by our friends.

✠

To Valentín Marín, by commission

Rome, June 24, 1556

(Letter 6615: XII:30f.; in Spanish)

This young Spanish Jesuit, working in Sicily, was known as an excellent preacher despite a disagreeable voice, and was greatly praised by his superior for his learning and his holiness. But Marín was constantly beset by scruples. Ignatius, who took a personal interest in his troubles, had earlier instructed his provincial and rector to help him. In this letter Ignatius writes again about those scruples, arising in great part from Marín's excessive attachment to his own judgment.

Jhus.

Through letters from Father Master Jerónimo [Doménech] and also from Father Eleuthère [Dupont], Our Father has been informed how God our Lord is making use of the ministry of our men in the town where you are. And we have no doubt that he would do so even more if it were not for the hindrance of Your Reverence's unwarranted scruples, abetted by your lack of humble resignation. Scrupulosity, up to a certain point, is usually not harmful as long as it makes a person be more vigilant and careful about avoiding offenses against God while at the same time refraining from any judgment that this or that is a sin (even though he suspects or fears it might be), and so long as he relies on the judgment of some person whom he ought to trust, setting aside his own judgment and accepting this person's opinion. Without these two aids, a scrupulous person runs the gravest risk of offending God by not avoiding what he thinks is sinful (though it is not), as well as of losing occasions and ability to serve him—or even his natural good judgment.

And so, Master Marín, determine to keep fixed in your mind these two resolutions: first, not to form a judgment or personal determination that something is sinful when it is not clearly such and is ordinarily not considered such by others; second, even when you are very fearful that something is a sin, to submit to the judgment of your superior, Father Eleuthère, and rely upon what he says—not as Father Eleuthère (although even as such he is a highly spiritual and prudent man whose judgment deserves confidence), but as the superior who holds the place of Christ our Lord. You should behave in this way with any other superior you may have, humbling yourself and trusting that God's providence will rule and guide you through him. Believe me, if you had real humility and submission, your scruples would not trouble you so much. They are nourished by a certain pride and tendency to trust more in your own judgment and less in that of others, as you should. You should also ask God our Lord in your Masses and prayers to free you from this passion or infirmity sufficiently for you not to offend him or hinder his greater service; and you should ask others to pray for this also. I commend myself to your own prayers, promising you mine.

May Christ our Lord grant all of us his grace, so that we may always know and fulfill his most holy will.

Rome, June 24, 1556

✠

To Josef Strakonicky

Rome, July 4, 1556

(Letter 6647: XII:71f.; in Latin)

This young man from Prague seems to have entered the Society with little or no intention of really living as a Jesuit, and had managed to waste a good deal of the Society's money. Ignatius frees him from his vows and from any indebtedness, but also urges him to repent of his unworthy behavior.

Yhs.

The peace of Christ.

Dear Brother Josef:

Because of the goodwill and charity with which we embrace you and the rest of your companions on the way, indeed to your entire nation in Christ Jesus, we have put up for a long time with the unsteadiness of spirit—to give it no worse a name—by which you have either abandoned the holy aim of our Institute that you had taken up, or else pretended to have taken up while in fact your mind was foreign to what your words and other outward actions professed. But although we have left no stone unturned to assist you spiritually, we see at last that all our efforts are in vain and have finally decided that we must act for the general good of our Society. We are therefore writing to the father rector, Master Olivier [Manaerts], that if you persist in your intention of not pursuing our way of life, he should dismiss you in peace to go where you like. On our part, we willingly write off any offenses or monetary damage arising from what you have cost the Society. But you have a responsibility to repent before God and to compensate for these ill deeds by other good works worthy of a pious and religious man. You should not think it a slight or inconsequential matter that we so lovingly extended our hospitality to you, admitting you to our Society at your own repeated request and treating you just as we do all our beloved brothers, only to be so unjustly duped by you; or that, both here in our house, where you did the probations customary for our brothers, and in the college of Loreto you have taken up the place and resources belonging to servants of God who have totally consecrated themselves in our Society to God's service and the help of their neighbor. I say this not to berate you but to move you to repentance.

I commend you to God. If you are quite determined to follow some other way of life, go where you like; if our own, you may stay on at Loreto, or come to Rome after the worst of the heat. But if you are still wavering, come to a decision outside our colleges on how you are going to live. Wherever you go we will commend you to God and hope and pray for your eternal salvation.

Farewell in our Lord Jesus Christ.

Rome, July 4, 1556

✠

To Giovanni Battista de Bianchi, by commission

Rome, July 5, 1556

(Letter 6657: XII:89; in Italian)

The young Bianchi had already earlier exhibited in his letters to Rome a worldly spirit more preoccupied with literary style than with religious substance. When asked to amend his ways, he had only replied in elegant turns of phrase. Attempts by his superior to help him change his style had produced little result and thus given rise to this rather scolding letter.

Jhus.

The peace of Christ.

Dearest Brother in Jesus Christ:

We have received your latest letter, dated the twenty-ninth of last month. It was filled with irrelevant words, though you may think otherwise. I tell you this: our fathers here were so disgusted with it that they refused to hear it to the end, and have commissioned me to write you that what is wanted from you is to hear that you are moving forward from good to better in holy virtues and religious practices; we are not concerned with the style of your letters. Good behavior is shown by deeds, not fancy words. The time you spend in quest of elegant words can be put to more profitable use. And so you are hereby expressly commanded to keep to a maximum of two pages the weekly report on your behavior that you have been ordered to write, as you have already been instructed.

May the Lord in his mercy be pleased to give all of us the grace to walk in his holy path with that simplicity in which his true servants have walked and do walk.

I heartily commend myself to your prayers, etc.

Rome, July 5, 1556

✠

To Alfonso Román

Rome, July 14, 1556

(Letter 6677: XII:119; in Spanish)

The difficulties that the Society experienced in Zaragoza weighed heavily on the Jesuits there and its rector. (See letters 5947 and 5998.) For example, the archbishop was firmly opposed to their being in his archdiocese and had excommunicated them and anyone who frequented their church or heard their sermons. The populace had been encouraged to throw stones at their windows and parade through the streets bearing obscene caricatures of them. In these circumstances Ignatius sends the rector this note of encouragement.

Jesus

Going by what we regularly experience—that where there is much opposition much fruit follows, and the Society is even more solidly founded—it appears that there will be a great and outstanding spiritual edifice there where you are, since such deep foundations of opposition

have been laid; and so we must trust in God our Lord that he will
do this.

✠

To Luis Gonçalves da Câmara
Rome, July 17, 1556
(Letter 6683: xii:129; in Spanish)

This letter is interesting for its description of the length of time those entering the
Society of Jesus were to spend in probation and the occupations in which those
admitted to probation might engage. Gonçalves da Câmara was the recipient of the
recollections of Ignatius commonly known as his autobiography. Da Câmara's own
notes and a later commentary on them describing Ignatius's life and activities at the
Curia in 1555 became known as his Memoriale. *By the time this letter was writ-*
ten, he had returned to Portugal.

To keep in probation for two years those who enter the Society
cannot be regarded as contrary to the Constitutions but neither is it
thus contrary that they study during this period, especially those among
them who are progressing satisfactorily. And I say the same about
preaching and teaching Christian doctrine and attending classes; and we
do that here, as Your Reverence knows, in part because of the needs of
the men involved and in part because it is advisable for them; and they
no less prove themselves in such activities that they do in the houses of
probation themselves.

Rome July 17, 1556

✠

To Diego Guzman
July 18, 1556
Letter 6690; xii:138f.; in Italian

Guzman, member of a very distinguished Spanish noble family, was already a priest
when he entered the Society in 1552. He was highly esteemed by Ignatius for his
character and his apostolic activities. As to the young men in question in the letter,
Polanco also refers in his Chronicon *to two students in Florence named Zenobio*
who had very successfully recited Christian doctrine from memory in the presence of
a large audience, "one or both of whose admittance to the Society was strongly

supported by the Jesuits in Florence but who, at not more than fourteen years of
age, were too young."

Jesus

The peace of Christ.

We rejoice in the Lord that Your Reverence is in better health
and that you are free of your former illness.

As for the two Zenobio boys, their good desires are to be praised
and they are to be encouraged to continue in them and to persevere [in
their desire]; give them reason to hope that they will be accepted in
due time. It is true that it is not appropriate to accept them almost
immediately; moreover, Giovanni Baptista being so small, even though
he is placid and good, it seems better that they stay at home for some
time. You can, however, tell them that they will be accepted into the
Society in good time. As for the money owed to [Didaco] de Carvajal,
Your Reverence will reach an agreement with him and then later inform
us of the sum involved, so that we can provide him with what you have
agreed upon. As soon as we have some information about Father Master
[John of] Avila, we will send it to Your Reverence.

Perhaps the letters sent by way of Perugia will already have
arrived.

We all earnestly commend ourselves to the prayers of Your Reverence.

From Rome, July 18, 1556

✠

To Fulvio Androzzi, by commission

Rome, July 18, 1556

(Letter 6692: XII:141–43; in Italian)

Androzzi was already a priest when he made the Spiritual Exercises under the
direction of Laínez in 1555 and entered the Society. Almost immediately he em-
barked upon a life of successful ministries. He was one of the early spiritual writers
in the Society, and his works, published posthumously, went through many editions
and translations. In this letter Ignatius advises him to trust in Christ, organize
himself better, concentrate on giving the Exercises, establish priorities and delegate,
and counter his personal limitations by growing spiritually. His accomplishments
testify to his having taken to heart the advice given here.

Jesus

The peace of Christ.

We received two letters from Your Reverence dated the twentieth of last month and the fourth of this, and we rejoice in our Lord over the opportunities that his goodness furnishes you for serving him in the help and spiritual consolation of the patrons, their household, and the people of the land;[5] also [we rejoice] over the good health and spiritual contentment he bestows on you. And even if you have little time left to prepare your sermons, Christ our Lord will supply for it. Moreover, you might arrange your day's activities so that more time is left over in case more is needed for one thing than for another. Their Lordships' goodwill and devotion will be a great help to you in making any needed arrangements. Let us know when you think you will have satisfied Signor Leonello's purposes, so that you and your companion can leave there in his good graces—or [remain there] if there are circumstances that will require you to stay longer.

Among the means that are of great and interior assistance to people, Your Reverence is aware of one that is outstanding: the Exercises. I remind you, therefore, to make use of this weapon, so familiar to our Society—although it is the First Week that could be given to large numbers, together with some methods of prayer. To give them in full form, one needs to find subjects who are capable and suitable for helping others after being helped themselves; otherwise, one should not go beyond the First Week. Your Reverence should look around a bit to see if you can find some good prospects for the Lord's service; for them this method would be excellent. Frequentation of the sacraments also tends to be strongly motivating.

When you are very busy, you need to make a choice and devote your efforts to the more important occupations, that is, those in which there is greater service of God, greater spiritual advantage for the neighbor, more universal or perfect good, etc. Reserving a little time to organize yourself and your own activities will also be a considerable help for this. If there are people from the area who could take your place in some matters, it would be good to share some of the labor with them so as to be free for more important matters. Thus, it would be good for someone else to take charge of the processions you mention; they are not all that appropriate to our way of proceeding, although it is a fine thing that in order to get this holy practice launched, you started it off and gave the example to the others.

---

[5] The patrons were the family of Cardinal Carpi.

Some persons who have passed through Meldola and others who have informed us by letter have remarked how edified they were by you and your companion. We commend to both of you Our Father and all those you know.

As for the matters regarding your own person which you say sometimes cause you distress or sorrow, I hope that you will be daily freer of them through God's grace; its greater enlightenment and increasing charity heals all these and other even worse infirmities of our nature. And I trust that Your Reverence has such a master in the Holy Spirit that there is no need for excessively multiplying advice on our part.

I enclose a letter from Ortenzio, and if you wish I will send other letters from our men who have been sent out from Loreto.[6] I understand that our Curzio is moving ahead with great purity and edification.

Master Gian Filippo [Vito] will also write about some other matters.

May God our Lord grant all of us grace always to know and fulfill his will.

Rome, July 18, 1556

✠

To Cristóbal de Mendoza

Rome, July 19, 1556

(Letter 6693: XII:143; in Italian)

According to this letter, the rector of Naples is to comply with Paul IV's edict of excommunication levied against the Colonnas. Pope Paul IV and the Colonnas had been at political odds for some time and the Pope did not hesitate to use the weapon of excommunication. He deeply resented the independence of the Roman nobles, of whom the Colonnas were among the most prominent, and the family's support of Spain in his long quarrels with that country. In some ways Paul IV's actions put Ignatius in a delicate position, for he was on friendly terms with the Colonnas. The papal excommunication was later lifted, and under Pope Pius V Marcantonio Colonna became a hero of the battle of Lepanto in 1571.

The peace of Christ.

We and all the other religious orders have been given a command that when either Signor Ascanio or Signor Marcantonio, his son, at-

---

[6] Ortenzio and the Curzio mentioned just below were Fulvio's brothers.

tempts to enter our churches, divine service should be halted until they leave, since they have been excommunicated by His Holiness, from whose side this command has been issued. Your Reverence will see that it is observed, so that we will not fail in the duty of obedience, even though we ought to embrace all in our charity and pray the divine and supreme Goodness graciously to pacify and calm things down and to give to all the grace always to know and fulfill his most holy will.

Rome, July 19, 1556

✠

To Stefano Casanova

Rome, July 20, 1556

(Letter 6699: XII:151f.; in Italian)

Ignatius writes to an ailing young Jesuit who was teaching in the college at Tivoli, instructing him to systematically repress only his sinful sensual cravings, adding, however, that for health's sake it can sometimes be more meritorious to indulge harmless ones than to mortify them. Whether the young man followed Ignatius's advice is not known, but his health continued to fail and he died in earlier 1559. At the time Ignatius wrote this letter, he himself was seriously ill and in great pain, and had only eleven days to live.

Jesus

The peace of Christ.

Dear Master Stefano:

I received your letter, in which you assert as a certainty that it is the repressing of your sensuality which takes away your strength, and that you are therefore determined to concentrate on the main business of your soul. First, although it could well be that this weakness of yours comes partly from such repression, I do not think it is the whole cause; on the contrary, mental exercises, particularly immoderate and unseasonable ones, must also play a part. So continue following my previous directions until you write again and permission is given you to change that regimen.

Moreover, this repressing can be of two sorts. One is when through reason and light from God you become aware of a movement of sensuality or of the sensitive faculty which is against God's will and would be sinful, and you repress this out of the fear and love of God. This is the right thing to do even if weakness or any other bodily ill ensues, since we may never commit any sin for this or any other consideration. But there is another kind of repressing one's sensuality, when you feel a desire for some recreation or anything else that is lawful and entirely without sin, but out of a desire for mortification or love of the cross you deny yourself what you long for. This second sort of repression is not appropriate for everyone, nor at all times. In fact, there are times when in order to sustain one's strength over the long haul in God's service, it is more meritorious to take some honest recreation for the senses than to repress them. And so you can see that the first sort of repression is good for you, but not the second—even when you aim at proceeding by the way that is most perfect and pleasing to God.

For further particulars I refer you to your confessor, to whom you will show this letter, and I commend myself to your prayers.

Rome, July 20, 1556

✠

To Father Nicolás Bobadilla, by commission

Rome, July 20, 2556

(Letter 6700: XII:152f.; in Spanish)

Even though by this time Ignatius was gravely ill and in great pain and at "the vineyard," the country house or villa of Santa Balbina, he asked Polanco to write to Bobadilla, who himself was not feeling well. This, it seems is the last letter from Ignatius to anyone of the first companions/founders of the Society of Jesus.

The Peace of Christ.

Our Father is staying in the house at the vineyard and has been suffering some stomach pains during these days, but he recovered more easily than usual; he has been there since I left Tivoli and his stay there is restful. Let us pray God that it is beneficial.

We learn from Your Reverence that you continue to suffer some indisposition; and I believe that with proper care rather than with medicine you will be helped in your work of preaching and teaching. Even if you put aside heavy toil, it is a lot of work; my experience tells me so.

What was on Antonio[de Robore]'s list will be attended to; I mean what has not already been taken care of.

All of us here in the three houses ask that you pray for us, and we rejoice in the Lord that you are doing thus and we hope for the fruit thereof. May Christ be at work in our souls and in the souls of those near to us.

✠

To Pietro, a priest in Bologna, by commission

Rome, July 23, 1556

(Letter 6718: XII:173f.; in Italian)

These are words of encouragement to a priest thinking of entering the Society but deterred by fears about his health. The Don Pantaleone to whom the letter refers was a close friend of Pietro. He had become a Jesuit in 1551 and was at the time of this letter the director of novices in Sicily. Polanco's Chronicon notes that Pietro finally did make up his mind and entered the Society in Genoa. But he stayed not even twenty-four hours, returning to Bologna the same day he had joined the Jesuits.

Jesus

The peace of Christ.

Dear Don Pietro in Christ Jesus:

Since Our Father is unwell, I will reply in his place to your letter of the fifteenth of this month, in which you manifest that you are unwell physically but not as regards your spirits, which is ready to serve God in the Institute of our Society. The truth is, our only wish is that each person wait upon the Divine Majesty in the way that will best please him; and if you could find another way better suited to your attaining the same end, that would please us even more. And yet we may rightly wonder whether this spirit that makes you so fearful about going forward is a spirit from God. It seems rather to be some frail human affection of feelings for relatives and country, or a desire to live freely and in your own way. For, after all, the labors which we understand you bore earlier in your care of souls were no less than those that await you in our Society, although they were less meritorious; nor was the treatment of your person, diet, etc., any better. And so, as far as health is concerned, you will enjoy as much or more in the Society than out of it. To get clarity on this spirit, therefore, it would be good for you to try to resign yourself once more into God's hands, and to consider your case in the way a man of judgment and a servant of God ought to; and if you find that God gives you the confidence to serve him in the state of religious perfection, let us know. But if you think that you ought to return to the world, we will be your friends as before, because we are interested in nothing else than your good and the greater service of God. May his grace remain and ever grow in your heart.

Your friend Don Pantaleone [Rodino] sends greetings; it appears he would like to have you with him in Messina, obedience allowing. However, his wish could not be realized until after more lengthy trials of your constancy.

We commend ourselves to your prayers.

Rome, July 23, 1556

✠

To Stefano Baroello

Rome, July 25, 1556

(Letter 6725: XII:186–87; in Italian)

A Jesuit studying alone is advised to concentrate on compendiums of the moral and sacramental parts of Aquinas's Summa, *on the Fathers for preaching, and above all on Scripture. The office of syndic mentioned in the letter was one of the usual officials of medieval universities. As described in the* Constitutions *[271], he was to watch over the external conduct of members of the community and to inform the superior of it; or, if he had received the right to do so, he was to admonish the person whom he had observed at fault in his conduct. The office did not last long in the life of the Society.*

The peace of Christ.

We received your letters of the twentieth of last month and the eighteenth of this; most of what was contained in them, not being reports, requires no reply.

Regarding the study of scholastic theology, it does not appear good to take Dionysius the Carthusian on the *Sentences* [of Peter Lombard]; it is a thicket or catena of various authors. It is better to take St. Thomas, and not all of him since not all of it is necessary, to say nothing of the considerable difficulty, especially for anyone studying alone and without much foundation in philosophy and metaphysics. It would be good to concentrate on the "Secunda Secundæ" and also the "Pars Tertia" on the sacraments and subsequent topics. And so as not to read these works at their full length, it would be good to use a compendium of the *Parts* of St. Thomas by Dionysius the Carthusian. This is easily available in Modena or Bologna, or at least in Padua. This summary embraces the whole of Scholastic theology. However it would also be good to read a few of the doctors, such as Chrysostom, Bernard, and

Jerome, who are useful for preaching and conversing. Finally, you should devote more study to Scripture than to anything else.

As for being freed of the office of syndic, we will examine what is appropriate and try to get it done. For now you may have to keep it only for a bit longer. But whichever happens, a decision from Ferrara will accompany this letter.

We all commend ourselves to your prayers.

Rome, July 25, 1556

☒

To the Rectors of Italy

Rome July 31, 1556

(Letter 6740: XII:200f.; in Italian)

A letter of recommendation, dated the day of St. Ignatius's death, for a young man traveling to the Carthusian house in Cologne. At the bottom of this letter is this notation: "Thus far by order of our blessed father Ignatius, whom God our Lord took to heaven on the last day of July, and it will go out by order of our father, Master Laínez, the vicar."

The peace of Christ.

The bearer of the present letter is an excellent young Frenchman, learned in humanities and law, who was unable to be received into our Society because of a congenital infirmity of the eyes and is traveling on our advice to the Carthusian house in Cologne. Your Reverences will be pleased to show him the charity of lodging him in the house for a day or two as a guest should he wish. There will be no need to give him traveling money as God our Lord will assist him from elsewhere.

Other matters will be written about in the regular letter.

We all earnestly commend ourselves to your Reverences' prayers.

Rome, July 31, 1556

INDEX

Inclusive page numbers of letters addressed to individuals or groups are printed in boldface in this index.